A Guide and Reference with Readings

P9-DID-471

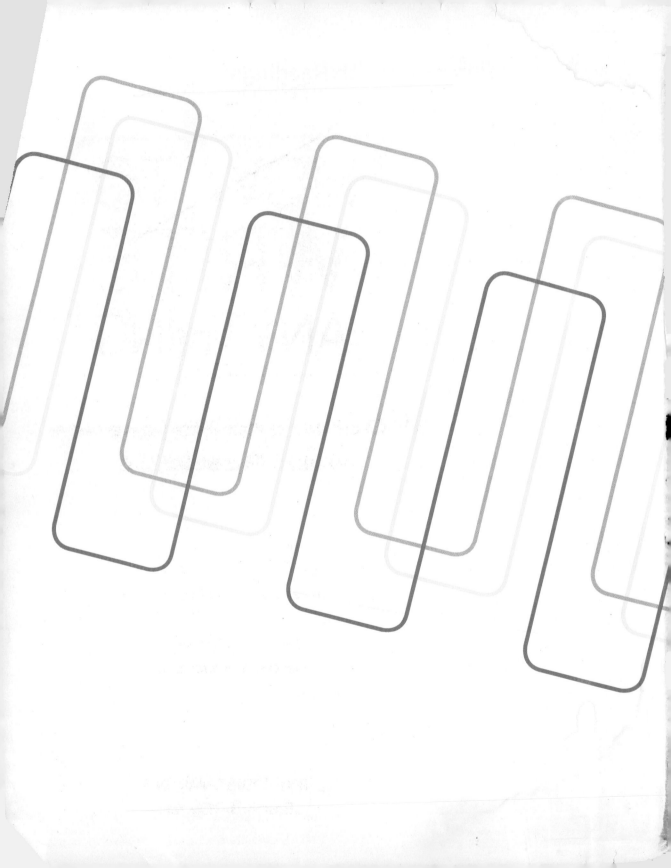

THIRD EDITION

HOW TO WRITE ANYTHING

A Guide and Reference with Readings

John J. Ruszkiewicz
UNIVERSITY OF TEXAS AT AUSTIN

Jay T. Dolmage
UNIVERSITY OF WATERLOO

BEDFORD/ST. MARTIN'S
Boston ◆ New York

For Bedford/St. Martin's

Vice President, Editorial, Macmillan Higher Education Humanities:
Edwin Hill
Editorial Director for English and Music: Karen Henry
Publisher for Composition and Business and Technical Writing:
Leasa Burton
Executive Editor: Molly Parke
Developmental Editor: Sarah Macomber
Senior Production Editor: Deborah Baker
Assistant Production Manager: Joe Ford
Marketing Manager: Emily Rowin
Editorial Assistant: Rachel Childs
Copyeditor: Jennifer Greenstein
Indexer: Steve Csipke
Director of Rights and Permissions: Hilary Newman
Senior Art Director: Anna Palchik
Text Design: Anna Palchik
Cover Design: Billy Boardman
Composition: Cenveo Publisher Services
Printing and Binding: RR Donnelley and Sons

Manufactured in the United States of America.

9 8 7 6 5
f   e   d   c   b

For information, write: Bedford/St. Martin's, 75 Arlington Street, Boston, MA 02116
(617-399-4000)

ISBN: 978-1-4576-6703-9

Acknowledgments

Preface

Through its first two editions, readers of *How to Write Anything: A Guide and Reference* have been intrigued—and perhaps attracted—by its title, admittedly not a humble one. Should any book, especially one designed expressly as a guide for college writers, promise so much? The simple answer is *no*; the more intriguing one is *maybe*.

What, after all, do experienced writers do when they face an assignment? As the new Introduction to this edition explains in detail, they size up a project to figure out what *genre* of writing best meets their needs and those of readers. They locate and examine specific examples of that genre, imitating some features and modifying or rejecting others. Then they shape a work within that genre themselves, bringing appropriate rhetorical, organizational, research, and language skills to bear on their writing. It is the goal of *How to Write Anything* to guide college writers through these complex choices for their most common academic and professional assignments. In doing so, it lays out key strategies to follow in any situation that requires purposeful writing.

But rarely do different writers work in the same order, and the same writer is likely to follow different paths for different projects. So *How to Write Anything* doesn't define a single process of writing or imagine that all students using it will have the same skills and interests. Instead, a modular chapter organization and an innovative system of cross-references enables writers to find exactly the information they want at the level of specificity they need—which pretty much sums up the rationale for the book. *How to Write Anything* is both focused and flexible, marrying the resources of a full rhetoric to the efficiency of a compact handbook. That commitment to clarity and efficiency is even more evident in this latest edition.

A Guide, Reference, and Reader

Parts 1 and 2 of *How to Write Anything* make up the Guide, which covers genres of writing that instructors assign in composition classes or that students encounter in other college courses. For each genre, writers are offered a framework presented as a flexible series of rhetorical choices—Exploring purpose and topic; Understanding your audience; Finding and developing materials; Creating a structure; and Choosing a style and design. The explanations here are direct, practical, and economical, encouraging students to explore a range of options within genres. If writers do need more help with a particular topic, targeted cross-references make it easy to find in the Reference section.

The Reference section (Parts 3 through 9) covers key aspects of the writing process—with separate parts devoted to Ideas; Shaping & Drafting; Style; Revising & Editing; Research & Sources; Media & Design; and Common Errors. Points mentioned in the Guide section get expanded treatment here for students who need it. For instance, writers might turn to these sections to find techniques for generating arguments, improving their sentences, or overcoming writer's block. The organization of *How to Write Anything* lets students find precisely what they need without getting bogged down in other material.

Part 10, the Reader, is an anthology of forty additional contemporary selections organized by genres covered in the Guide. Drawn from a variety of sources such as print and online journals, books, scholarly and popular magazines, blogs, and graphic novels, the readings offer both solid models for writing as well as compelling topics for students to respond to. Some examples include Jane McGonigal on how an hour a day of video games can enrich our lives, Neil deGrasse Tyson on the "cosmic perspective," and evaluations of everything from cooking shows to Jay-Z to Domino's pizza. The Reader includes fresh content from established authors such as Zadie Smith, Patton Oswalt, and Sasha Frere-Jones, as well as from newer voices such as Kamakshi Ayyar and Ross Perlin. Headnotes provide context for all readings in the text, and selections in the Reader are followed by analysis questions and writing assignments, which feature cross-references from the questions back to the Guide and Reference sections of the book. These readings, and the questions that follow them, are intended to help students more deeply consider and use the major genres in *How to Write Anything*.

Key Features

A Flexible Writing Process and Design that Works

How to Write Anything works hard to make its materials accessible and attractive to writers accustomed to intuitive design. For instance, "How to Start" questions at the opening of each chapter in the Guide anticipate where writers get stuck and direct them to exactly what they need: One writer might seek advice about finding a topic for a report, while another with a topic already in hand wants prompts for developing that idea.

Similarly, frequent cross-references between the Guide and Reference sections target the topics that students are likely to want to know more about. The simple language and unobtrusive design of the cross-references make it easy for students to stay focused on their own writing while finding related material—no explanations necessary and minimal clutter on the page. Readings and images throughout the book are similarly highlighted and variously annotated so that readers, once again, find information they need precisely when and where they require it.

Media-savvy students know that learning occurs in more than just words, so this edition preserves one of the favorite design features of *How To Write Anything:* its context-rich "How To" Visual Tutorials. Through drawings, photographs, and screenshots, these items offer step-by-step instructions for topics, ranging from how to use a writing center productively to how to cite selected materials in both MLA and APA formats.

Writing Worth Reading—From Professionals and Students

How to Write Anything: A Guide and Reference contains an ample selection of readings, more than thirty in the Guide chapters alone, representing a wide range of genres. Selections illustrate key principles and show how genres change in response to different contexts, audiences, and—increasingly important—media. Every chapter in the Guide includes many complete examples of the genres under discussion, most of these texts annotated to show how they meet criteria set down in *How to Write Anything*. The assignments at the end of the Part 1 chapters are closely tied to the chapter readings, so students can use the sample texts both as models and as springboards for discussion and exploration.

Just as important, the models in *How to Write Anything* are approachable. The readings—some by published professionals and others by student writers—reveal the diversity of contemporary writing being done in these genres. The student samples are especially inventive—chosen to motivate undergraduates to take comparable risks with their own writing. Together, the readings and exercises suggest to writers the many creative possibilities of working in these genres.

New to This Edition

How to Write Anything was designed from the outset to be a practical, highly readable guide to writing for a generation not fond of long books. The third edition doubles down on that commitment. It's smarter, more efficient, and shorter.

- **Vibrant new Introduction.** Designed as a starting point for a course, a new Introduction explains the structure and rationale of *How to Write Anything* in practical terms students will appreciate. Concepts that play a key role in the book such as *genre, subgenres, writing processes,* and even *audiences* are defined and discussed.

- **New chapter on writing portfolios.** Because more and more courses and college programs ask students to assemble writing portfolios, *How to Write Anything* introduces a new chapter (Chapter 17) explaining exactly how to compose, select, edit, and present materials for this assignment. The chapter gives special attention to composing student reflections on their coursework.

- **New "Reading the Genre" prompts.** All major readings in Part 1 are now preceded by a brief exercise or query designed to make readers think about the reading's genre or genre strategies.

- **Improved chapter organization.** Each chapter in the Guide sections has been reviewed to enhance the clarity of its presentations. Chapter 8, Rhetorical Analyses, for example, now offers a chart to summarize key questions for such a paper. And every chapter in Part 2, Special Assignments, has a new structure that makes the discussion of the genre clearer and, in most cases, simpler.

- **Focused writing throughout the book.** *How to Write Anything* has been fine-tuned to acknowledge students' preference for brevity and clarity. Chapters get to the point quicker, examples have been tightened, and some chapters have been combined to eliminate overlap.

- **Fresh readings and images.** New readings and images throughout the book keep *How to Write Anything* topical and challenging. New materials include a literacy narrative by Allegra Goodman, a movie review of *The Hunger Games*, a student's research report on women running marathons, a Jen Sorensen editorial cartoon on student debt, and Bert and Ernie on the cover of *The New Yorker*.

- **New "Genre Moves" prompts in the Reader section.** All chapters in the Reader section now begin with a brief excerpt by a well-known writer, followed by a prompt designed to get readers thinking about the genre presented.

Get the Most Out of Your Course with *How to Write Anything*

Bedford/St. Martin's offers resources and format choices that help you and your students get even more out of your book and course. To learn more about or to order any of the following products, contact your Bedford/St. Martin's sales representative, e-mail sales support (**sales_support@bfwpub.com**), or visit the Web site at **macmillanhighered.com/howtowrite3e/catalog**.

LaunchPad for *How to Write Anything with Readings:* Where Students Learn

LaunchPad provides engaging content and new ways to get the most out of your course. Get an **interactive e-book** combined with **unique, book-specific materials** in a fully customizable course space; then assign and mix our resources with yours.

- Multimedia selections that make the most of what the Web can do with carefully selected video and multimodal readings for each chapter in Part 1.

- **Pre-built units**—including readings, videos, quizzes, discussion groups, and more—are **easy to adapt and assign** by adding your own materials and mixing them with our high-quality multimedia content and ready-made assessment options, such as **LearningCurve** adaptive quizzing.

- LaunchPad also provides access to a **gradebook** that provides a clear window on the performance of your whole class, individual students, and even individual assignments.

- A **streamlined interface** helps students focus on what's due, and social commenting tools let them **engage**, make connections, and learn from each other. Use LaunchPad on its own or integrate it with your school's learning management system so that your class is always on the same page.

To get the most out of your course, order LaunchPad for *How to Write Anything with Readings* packaged with the print book **free** for a limited time. (LaunchPad for *How to Write Anything with Readings* can also be purchased on its own.) An activation code is required.

To order LaunchPad for *How to Write Anything with Readings* with the print book, use **ISBN 978-1-319-02421-5.**

Choose from Alternative Formats of *How to Write Anything*

Bedford/St. Martin's offers a range of affordable formats, allowing students to choose the one that works best for them. For details, visit **macmillanhighered .com/howtowrite3e/formats.**

- **Spiral-bound.** To order the spiral-bound edition of *How to Write Anything* (the brief version of this book), use **ISBN 978-1-4576-9368-7.**

- *Bedford e-Book to Go.* A portable, downloadable e-book is available at about half the price of the print book. To order the *Bedford e-Book to Go for How to Write Anything,* use **ISBN 978-1-4576-9373-1.** To order the *Bedford e-Book to Go for How to Write Anything with Readings,* use **ISBN 978-1-4576-9388-5.**

- **Other popular e-book formats.** For details, visit **macmillanhighered .com/ebooks.**

Select Value Packages

Add value to your text by packaging one of the following resources with *How to Write Anything.* To learn more about package options for any of the following products, contact your Bedford/St. Martin's sales representative or visit **macmillanhighered.com/howtowrite3e/catalog.**

LearningCurve for Readers and Writers, Bedford/St. Martin's adaptive quizzing program, quickly learns what students already know and helps them practice what they don't yet understand. Game-like quizzing motivates students to engage with their course, and reporting tools help teachers discern their students' needs. *LearningCurve for Readers and Writers* can be packaged with *How to Write Anything* at a significant discount. An activation code is required. To order LearningCurve packaged with the print book, use ISBN 978-1-319-03135-1. For details, visit **learningcurveworks.com.**

i-series This popular series presents multimedia tutorials in a flexible format—because there are things you can't do in a book.

- *ix visualizing composition 2.0* helps students put into practice key rhetorical and visual concepts. To order *ix visualizing composition* packaged with the print book, contact your sales representative for a package ISBN.

- *i-claim: visualizing argument* offers a new way to see argument—with 6 multimedia tutorials, an illustrated glossary, and a wide array of multimedia arguments. To order *i-claim: visualizing argument* packaged with the print book, contact your sales representative for a package ISBN.

Portfolio Keeping, **Third Edition, by Nedra Reynolds and Elizabeth Davis** provides all the information students need to use the portfolio method successfully in a writing course. *Portfolio Teaching*, a companion guide for writing instructors, provides the practical information instructors and writing program administrators need to teach using the portfolio method. To order *Portfolio Keeping* packaged with the print book, contact your sales representative for a package ISBN.

Make Learning Fun with *Re:Writing 3*

macmillanhighered.com/rewriting

New open online resources with videos and interactive elements engage students in new ways of writing. You'll find tutorials about using common digital writing tools, an interactive peer review game, Extreme Paragraph Makeover, and more—all for free and for fun. Visit **macmillanhighered.com/rewriting.**

Instructor Resources

macmillanhighered.com/howtowrite3e

You have a lot to do in your course. Bedford/St. Martin's wants to make it easy for you to find the support you need—and to get it quickly.

Teaching with How to Write Anything: A Guide and Reference with Readings is available in print and as a PDF that can be downloaded from the Bedford/St. Martin's online catalog at the URL above. In addition to chapter overviews and teaching tips, the instructor's manual includes sample syllabi, classroom activities, and teaching goals.

Teaching Central offers the entire list of Bedford/St. Martin's print and online professional resources in one place. You'll find landmark reference works, sourcebooks on pedagogical issues, award-winning collections, and practical advice for the classroom—all free for instructors. Visit **macmillanhighered .com/teachingcentral**.

Bits collects creative ideas for teaching a range of composition topics in an easily searchable blog format. A community of teachers—leading scholars, authors, and editors—discuss revision, research, grammar and style, technology, peer review, and much more. Take, use, adapt, and pass the ideas around. Then, come back to the site to comment or share your own suggestion. Visit **bedfordbits.com**.

Acknowledgments

The following reviewers were very helpful through several drafts of this book: Patricia Baines, Middle Tennessee State University; Patricia Bonner, North Carolina A&T State University; Jonathan Bradley, Middle Tennessee State University; Bob Brown, Chippewa Valley Technical College; Diana Kaye Campbell, Forsyth Technical Community College; Tricia Capansky, University of Tennessee at Martin; Susan Chism, Greenville College; Cheri Crenshaw, Dixie State University; Linsey Cuti, Kankakee Community College; Jason DePolo, North Carolina A&T State University; Amy Eggert, Bradley University; Bart Ganzert, Forsyth Technical Community College; Carl Gerriets, Century College; Anissa Graham, University of North Alabama; Gary Hafer, Lycoming College; Elizabeth Hope, Delgado Community College; Pamela Kincheloe, Rochester Institute of

Technology; Michael Leggs, Saint Paul College; Lila MacLellan, Pace University; Nicholas Mauriello, University of North Alabama; Chanomi Maxwell-Parish, Northern Michigan University; Linda Miller, Middlesex Community College; Gayle Murchison, College of William and Mary; Sein Oh, University of Illinois at Chicago; Sayanti Ganguly Puckett, Johnson County Community College; Christa Raney, University of North Alabama; Jeremy Reed, Central Methodist University; Theodore Rollins, Johnson County Community College; James Sprouse, Piedmont International University; Janette Thompson, University of Nebraska at Kearney; Patrick Tompkins, John Tyler Community College; Jonathan Torres, Front Range Community College; and Justin Williamson, Pearl River Community College.

All textbooks are collaborations, but we have never before worked on a project that more creatively drew upon the resources of an editorial team and publisher. *How to Write Anything* began with the confidence of Joan Feinberg, Director of Digital Composition, that we could develop a groundbreaking brief rhetoric. She had the patience to allow the idea to develop at its own pace and then assembled an incredible team to support it. We are grateful for the contributions of Edwin Hill, Vice President; Karen Henry, Editorial Director; and Leasa Burton, Publisher. We are also indebted to Anna Palchik, Senior Art Director and designer of the text, and Deb Baker, Senior Production Editor. Special thanks to Peter Arkle and Anna Veltfort for their drawings, Christian Wise for his photographs, and to Kate Mayhew for her help with art research. They all deserve credit for the distinctive and accessible visual style of *How to Write Anything*.

For her marketing efforts, we are grateful to the guidance offered by Emily Rowin and, of course, to the efforts of the incomparable Bedford/St. Martin's sales team. And for all manner of tasks, including coordinating permissions and manuscript preparation, we thank Rachel Childs.

Our greatest debt is to Ellen Darion, who was our original editor on this lengthy project and saw this edition through to the completion of its first draft: always confident about what we could accomplish, patient when chapters went off-track, and perpetually good-humored. If *How to Write Anything* works, it is because Ellen never wavered from our high aspirations for the book. Her hand is in every chapter, every choice of reading, and every assignment.

Succeeding Ellen as editor on this latest version, Sarah Macomber joined a project she was well familiar with—having conceived *How to Write Anything*'s much admired visual tutorials. Sarah has given thoughtful attention to every corner of the book, helping to assure that this edition is tight, lively, and imaginative. It has been a pleasure to work with her.

Finally, we are extraordinarily grateful to our former students whose papers or paragraphs appear in *How to Write Anything*. Their writing speaks for itself, but we have been inspired, too, by their personal dedication and character. These are the sort of students who motivate teachers, and so we are very proud to see their work published in *How to Write Anything*: Alysha Behn, Jordyn Brown, Stefan Casso, Marissa Dahlstrom, Manasi Deshpande, Micah T. Eades, Wade Lamb, Desiree Lopez, Cheryl Lovelady, Shane McNamee, Matthew Nance, Lily Parish, Miles Pequeno, Heidi Rogers, Kanaka Sathasivan, J. Reagan Tankersley, Katelyn Vincent, and Susan Wilcox.

John J. Ruszkiewicz

Jay T. Dolmage

Correlation to the Council of Writing Program Administrators' (WPA) Outcomes Statement

How to Write Anything helps students build proficiency in the five categories of learning that writing programs across the country use to assess their work: rhetorical knowledge; critical thinking, reading, and writing; writing processes; knowledge of conventions; and composing in electronic environments. A detailed correlation follows.

Features of *How to Write Anything: A Guide and Reference with Readings,* Third Edition, Correlated to the WPA Outcomes Statement

Note: This chart aligns with the latest WPA Outcomes Statement, ratified in July 2014.

WPA Outcomes	Relevant Features of *How to Write Anything*
Rhetorical Knowledge	
Learn and use key rhetorical concepts through analyzing and composing a variety of texts.	Each assignment chapter in the Guide includes three texts in a wide variety of genres. Questions, headnotes, and "Reading the Genre" prompts encourage students to examine and understand the key rhetorical concepts behind each genre of writing. Writing activities and prompts guide students through composing a range of texts. In addition, the Reader includes more than 40 more texts for student analysis.
Gain experience reading and composing in several genres to understand how genre conventions shape and are shaped by readers' and writers' practices and purposes.	The Introduction provides a foundation for thinking about genre, while each assignment chapter in the Guide offers a thorough look at each genre's conventions and how those conventions have developed and changed, as well as how to apply them to students' own writing situations. Each chapter in the Reader includes a "Genre Moves" feature, which analyzes a classic model to highlight a specific genre convention and suggest ways students might make use of it.
Develop facility in responding to a variety of situations and contexts, calling for purposeful shifts in voice, tone, level of formality, design, medium, and/or structure.	Each assignment chapter in the Guide offers detailed advice on responding to a particular rhetorical situation, from arguing a claim and proposing a solution to writing an e-mail or a résumé. See "Choosing a Style and Design" sections in Part 1 chapters, and the "Getting the Details Right" sections in Part 2 chapters for advice on situation-specific style and design. Part 5 features chapters on "High, Middle, and Low Style" (32); "Inclusive and Culturally Sensitive Style" (33); and "Vigorous, Clear, Economical Style" (34).
Understand and use a variety of technologies to address a range of audiences.	Chapter 48 covers digital media, including blogs, social networks, Web sites, wikis, podcasts, maps, and videos. Chapter 49 covers creating and using visuals to present data and ideas. Each assignment chapter includes at least one visual example of the genre that the chapter focuses on, and several of the reference chapters include Visual Tutorials featuring photographs and illustrations that provide students with step-by-step instructions for challenging topics, such as using the Web to browse for ideas. This emphasis on visuals, media, and design helps students develop visual and technological literacy they can use in their own work. Chapter 13 covers e-mail; Chapters 17 and 18 address portfolio and presentation software; and Chapters 38 and 40 cover finding, evaluating, and using print and electronic resources for research.

WPA Outcomes	Relevant Features of *How to Write Anything*
Rhetorical Knowledge (*continued*)	
Match the capacities of different environments (e.g., print and electronic) to varying rhetorical situations.	The text and LaunchPad include a wide range of print and multimodal genres from essays and scholarly articles to photographs, infographics, Web sites, and audio and video presentations. Rhetorical choices that students make in each genre are covered in the Guide chapters and appear in discussions of the writing context and in abundant models in the book.
Critical Thinking, Reading, and Composing	
Use composing and reading for inquiry, learning, thinking, and communicating in various rhetorical contexts.	The assignment chapters in the Guide emphasize the connection between reading and writing a particular genre: Each chapter includes model readings with annotations that address the key features of the genre. Each Part 1 chapter shows students the rhetorical choices they need to consider when writing their own papers in these genres and offers assignments to actively engage them in these choices.
	Chapter 21, "Critical Thinking," explains rhetorical appeals and logical fallacies.
	Reference chapters in Parts 3 through 8 cover invention, reading, writing, research, and design strategies that work across all genres.
Read a diverse range of texts, attending especially to relationships between assertion and evidence, to patterns of organization, to interplay between verbal and nonverbal elements, and how these features function for different audiences and situations.	Each assignment chapter in the Guide includes three texts in a wide variety of genres. In addition, the Reader includes more than 40 more texts for student analysis.
	Each of the Guide chapters also includes sections on understanding audience, creating a structure, finding and developing material (including evidence), and choosing a style and design that best reflect the genre of writing.
	Chapter 20, "Smart Reading," helps students read deeply and "against the grain," while in Chapter 21, "Critical Thinking," students learn about claims, assumptions, and evidence. Chapter 26, "Organization," gives advice on devising a structure for a piece of writing.
Locate and evaluate primary and secondary research materials, including journal articles, essays, books, databases, and informal Internet sources.	Part 7 covers research and sources in depth, with chapters on beginning your research, finding print and online sources, doing field research, evaluating and annotating sources, and documenting sources.

WPA Outcomes	Relevant Features of *How to Write Anything*
Critical Thinking, Reading, and Composing (*continued*)	
Use strategies — such as interpretation, synthesis, response, critique, and design/redesign — to compose texts that integrate the writer's ideas with those from appropriate sources.	Chapters 41 ("Annotating Sources"), 42 ("Paraphrasing Sources"), and 44 ("Incorporating Sources into Your Work") explore a variety of strategies for integrating the writer's ideas with ideas and information from sources. Chapter 12, "Synthesis Papers," shows students how to summarize, compare, and assess the views offered by different sources.
Processes	
Develop a writing project through multiple drafts.	Chapter 35, "Revising Your Own Work," discusses the importance of revising and gives detailed advice on how to approach different types of revision. Targeted cross-references throughout the text help students get the revision help they need when they need it.
Develop flexible strategies for reading, drafting, reviewing, collaboration, revising, rewriting, rereading, and editing.	The Reference's brief, targeted chapters and cross-references lend themselves to a flexible approach to writing process, with an array of strategies for students to choose from whether they're crafting an introduction or preparing to revise a first draft. Genre-specific advice in the Guide chapters helps students tailor each step of the writing process to their writing situation, while process-based chapters in the Reference offer guidance that can be applied to any type of writing.
Use composing processes and tools as a means to discover and reconsider ideas.	Each Part 1 chapter includes two sections that encourage students to use the composing process as a means of discovery. "Deciding to write . . . " covers the reasons a writer might choose a specific form of writing, while "Exploring purpose and topic" prompts students to challenge their own ideas about a subject and write to discover what they think when they look more deeply at it.
Experience the collaborative and social aspects of writing processes.	Several chapters in the Reference send students out into their worlds for advice, information, and feedback. Chapter 22, "Experts," talks about the kinds of experts — such as librarians, instructors, peers, and writing center tutors — that students can call on for help. Chapter 39, "Doing Field Research," discusses the whys and hows of interviewing and observing people as part of the research process. Chapter 36, "Peer Editing," offers advice for helping peers improve their work.
Learn to give and act on productive feedback to works in progress.	Chapter 36, "Peer Editing," encourages students to give specific, helpful advice to peers and think about peer editing in the same way they revise their own work.

WPA Outcomes	Relevant Features of *How to Write Anything*
Processes (*continued*)	
Adapt composing processes for a variety of technologies and modalities.	Chapter 48 focuses on digital media, including blogs, Web sites, wikis, podcasts, maps, and videos.
	Chapter 13 covers e-mail; Chapters 17 and 18 address portfolio and presentation software; and Chapters 38 and 40 cover finding, evaluating, and using print and electronic resources for research.
Reflect on the development of composing practices and how those practices influence their work.	The new Introduction invites students to consider their writing practices and how the choices they make during invention, drafting, research, and revision shape their process and their work.
Knowledge of Conventions	
Develop knowledge of linguistic structures, including grammar, punctuation, and spelling, through practice in composing and revising.	Part 9 (Common Errors) includes chapters on grammar, punctuation, and mechanics, while Chapters 35 and 36 provide editing and proofreading advice. Targeted cross-references throughout the text send students to these chapters as needed.
Understand why genre conventions for structure, paragraphing, tone, and mechanics vary.	Each Part 1 chapter includes a section on choosing style and design to help students understand how their choice of style, structure, tone, and mechanics is shaped by the genre in which they're writing.
Gain experience negotiating variations in genre conventions.	Models of work from several subgenres within the book's main genres show students the variations that exist within the confines of a given genre. In addition, "Reading the Genre" prompts help students identify and understand the genre conventions at work in each selection.
Learn common formats and/or design features for different kinds of texts.	Each assignment chapter in the Guide covers a format specific to the genre covered there; see "Choosing a Style and Design" in the Part 1 chapters and "Getting the Details Right" in the Part 2 chapters.
Explore the concepts of intellectual property (such as fair use and copyright) that motivate documentation conventions.	Chapter 45, "Documenting Sources," helps students understand why documentation is important and what's at stake in properly identifying and citing material used from sources.
Practice applying citation conventions systematically in their own work.	Chapters 46, "MLA Documentation and Format," and 47, "APA Documentation and Format," include detailed guidance for citing sources according to each style's conventions. Visual Tutorials in each chapter help students identify and find the information they need in order to create accurate citations.

Introduction

If a blank page or empty screen scares you, join the club. Even professional writers freeze up when facing new and unfamiliar assignments or intimidating audiences. It's only natural for you to wonder how you'll handle all the tasks you face in school or on the job—the reports, evaluations, personal statements, opinion pieces, reviews, and more. Much more. Even writing you do for pleasure has a learning curve.

So how do you get rolling? Exactly the way experienced authors do, by examining the strategies other writers have used to achieve similar goals for demanding audiences. That's not very creative, you might object. But in fact, it's the way inventive people in many fields operate. They get a feel for the shape and features, structures and strategies, materials and styles of whatever they hope to construct themselves, and then they work from that knowledge to fashion new ideas. They become masters of their *genre*. This book will introduce you to writing by taking exactly the same approach.

Understand Genres of Writing

So what is a *genre*? An old-school definition might describe it as a variety of writing we recognize by its distinctive purpose and features. For instance, a work that fits into the genre of *narrative* usually tells a story and emphasizes characterization, dialogue, and descriptions; a *report* presents reliable facts and information and relies on research and documentation; an *argument* defends a claim with reasons and evidence and uses lots of powerful language and even, sometimes, pulls at your heartstrings. *How To Write Anything* introduces you to these three familiar genres, along with five others you'll run up against throughout your academic and professional life: *evaluations*, *causal analyses*, *proposals*, *literary analyses*, and *rhetorical analyses*.

But if you are expecting simple formulas, templates, and step-by-step instructions for each category, guess again. No one learns to write by filling in blanks because the processes are too complicated. So this book treats genres far more dynamically—as real-life responses to ever-changing writing situations. You'll find that genres aren't arbitrary, inflexible, predictable, or dull. Instead, they change constantly—maybe the better term is *evolve*—to serve the needs of writers *and* readers. (Consider how just in the past few years personal and professional letters have metamorphosed into e-mails, text messages, and tweets.)

Though it still makes sense to draw upon patterns and models that work reliably, that's only half the process of learning to write. First you study what existing genres can teach you (and that's a lot). Then you bend the genres to fit actual assignments you get and, just as important, the kind of work you'd like to do on your own. You figure out what to say within a genre, tailor those concepts to the people you hope to influence, organize your ideas strategically, and state them powerfully in appropriate media—including visual, oral, and online formats. That's what Part 1 of *How to Write Anything* is about. It walks you through the full range of choices you face in making genres work for you—and not the other way around.

It might help to think of genres as shortcuts to success. When you learn a new genre, you don't necessarily acquire a hard-and-fast set of rules for writing; instead, you gain control over that genre's *possibilities*. Who knows where those insights might take you?

Connect Purpose to Subgenres

But let's step back a moment and think about the "specific assignments" you'll be facing, especially in school. One of the first matters to settle is always the aim or purpose of a given paper, and it is rarely just *to write* or even to compose open-ended narratives, reports, or arguments. Instead, you'll be asked or required to compose projects so narrowly focused that they actually turn broad *genres* into *subgenres*. A subgenre is simply a specialized version of a genre, one that adapts its general principles to immediate purposes: For example, you need to tell a good story to talk yourself out of an expensive parking ticket or into an honors program.

To put it more formally, you won't ordinarily compose a nonspecific report; you'll write a history term paper detailing some aspect of the Cuban Missile Crisis or a newspaper column explaining NCAA recruitment policies. You won't do a causal analysis for the exercise; you'll write a topic proposal to determine the feasibility of a thesis idea. You won't argue just for the fun of it; you'll dash off an editorial to persuade student government to fix its election code. In effect, you are encouraged to modify a genre to fit your more immediate needs. And that's a good thing.

Why? Because you can base your work in subgenres on very specific models readily available in print and online—they're materials you read and work with every day. In *How to Write Anything*, for instance, the chapter on "Evaluations" presents basic strategies for making smart judgments about people and things, explaining in detail how to establish and apply criteria of evaluation and how to present the evidence you collect. Fair enough.

But your purpose in preparing (or even reading) evaluations will often be much more focused. You'll want to know whether a restaurant is worth your dollar, a book is smart and challenging, a school program up-to-snuff academically. So you'll likely consult book, restaurant, or program reviews you've come to regard as trustworthy, probably because of how well they handle criteria of evaluation and evidence. Once you know how a genre works, you'll appreciate how its subgenres refine those moves. Suddenly, your task as a writer is easier because knowing a genre gives you a method and vocabulary for dealing with all its subgenres—and appreciating how they operate.

Subgenres, then, work the same way as genres, presenting an array of specific features and strategies for you to emulate and modify. You'll find connections between genre and subgenres throughout *How to Write Anything*. Each of the major readings in Part 1 is identified by a subgenre, and all the major writing assignments suggest that you take one of the items as a pattern to help you with a project of your own. Part 2 "Special Assignments" is entirely about subgenres crucial to people in school or entering the job market—items such as essay examinations, résumés, personal statements, and oral reports. In this section, you'll clearly see how practical and action-oriented subgenres can be. At the end of this introduction, you'll find a list of the genres and subgenres covered in *How to Write Anything*.

Choose Audiences

Remember the claim that genres serve the needs of writers *and* demanding audiences? It's very important. As an analogy, just consider how much you rely on genres to select what movies you will see: *sci-fi films, westerns, action/adventure films, romances* (a.k.a. "chick flicks"), *horror movies,* and so on. You bring expectations to films in these categories based upon your past experiences. You may be satisfied when a movie meets or exceeds your expectations, angry when a work fails to live up to genre standards, and *really* excited when a flick manages to do something new—stretches a genre the way *The Dark Knight* or *Marvel's The Avengers* did.

Readers of *your* work will react the same way, which is why you'll find sections on "Understanding Your Audience" in each of the genre chapters of *How to Write Anything.* Audiences you target with a particular genre will bring specific expectations to your work, based on their understanding of your project. For example, a highly academic genre such as a "literary analysis" usually has a narrower and more demanding readership than, let's say, a movie review you post on a blog. You've got to learn how to make genres work for their typical readers—which means understanding them or at least being aware of what they bring to the table when they read.

But as a writer working in genres, you'll also discover you have the power sometimes to define or summon audiences for your work. You might, for example, decide to write a report on bullying aimed at middle-school students; it would differ significantly from a report on the same topic aimed at parents, wouldn't it? Or you might consider how academic readers might be convinced to take a topic such as zombies in films seriously: What features in your text would signal your serious intentions to them? Your analysis of such choices is exactly what makes writing within genres exciting and challenging.

Manage Structure and Style

How to Write Anything gives as much attention to structure and style as to audience in each of the genre chapters—and for good reason. Like the treatment of audience, these elements can make genres seem familiar and comfortable, or they can stretch their boundaries to breaking, depending entirely on choices you make.

Many subgenres, for example, are rigid in their organization: You wouldn't want to experiment with the structure of a lab report or grant application. Nor would you take chances with the formal style expected in these documents. Get a little funky and you've flunked chemistry or lost your funding. Common sense, you say, and you'd be right.

But other genres have lots of give, and so chapters on these genres suggest how that flexibility creates opportunities for innovation and experimentation. For instance, not all narratives have to move in lockstep from beginning to middle to end, but if you are going to tell a story out of sequence or via flash-backs, there are consequences: You might befuddle some readers and push them away. Or think about the range of style you have in narratives—from descriptions that are elegant and formal to dialogue that tells it like it is. You might even use these choices of style to attract readers you want—that is, people who share your values or taste. Even a genre as sober as evaluation has room for enormous range in structure and style—which we signal in this edition by featuring a satire as one of the models.

Develop Writing Processes

For more than a generation now, writing has been taught in schools as a sequential process. You probably learned it that way, working steadily from finding ideas, developing them, writing a first draft, and proofreading a final one. There's nothing wrong with the model, especially the parts that encourage revision. But in working with genres, you'll discover that writing behaviors grow more complicated. Simply put, there are many processes and pathways to successful composing.

Each chapter in Part 1 of *How to Write Anything* outlines a process for creating a particular genre. Some kinds of writing require intense personal reflection, others send reporters into the field for interviews or into libraries for research, and still others may push you deep inside texts for experiences in close reading. Some genres will develop your skills with media or make you examine the clarity of charts and graphs. Others will have you playing with and repeatedly refining your choice of words.

Because of these individual demands, you'll discover that all the genre chapters in the Guide section of *How to Write Anything* (Parts 1–2) are strategically cross-referenced to supplemental materials in what's called the "Reference" section (Parts 3–9). The reference chapters are designed to support your specific needs as a writer, whatever the genre you might be exploring. If you have a problem with writer's block, you will find detailed advice to get you moving. If a genre assignment pushes you to a library catalog, a reference chapter will explain the tools and resources you'll find there and offer sensible strategies. If you have to document a paper or you've forgotten how to get pronouns to agree with fussy antecedents, you have a place to go. It's worth noting that the reference chapters are, for the most part, written in the same informal style as the rest of the book. So don't ignore them. You might even find stuff there to write about.

Invitation to Write

How to Write Anything was designed and edited to be compact and efficient. But you'll find that it has a personal voice, frank and occasionally humorous. Why? Because yet another textbook lacking style or character probably won't convince you that your own prose should speak to real audiences. And if some chapters operate like reference materials, they still aren't written coldly or dispassionately—not even the section on Common Errors.

If *How to Write Anything* seems like an oddly ambitious title, maybe it's because learning to write should be a heady enterprise, undertaken with confidence and optimism. Give it a try.

Genres and Subgenres in *How to Write Anything*

Narratives

- Literacy narrative
- Memoir/reflection
- Graphic narrative
- Personal statement

Reports

- Research report
- Feature story
- Infographic
- Essay examination
- Annotated bibliography
- Synthesis paper
- E-mail
- Business letter
- Résumé
- Oral report

Arguments

- Support of a thesis
- Refutation
- Visual argument
- Position paper

Evaluations

- Arts review
- Satire
- Product review
- Parody
- Portfolio review
- Peer review

Causal Analyses

- Causal argument
- Research analysis
- Cultural analysis

Proposals

- Trial balloon
- Manifesto
- Visual proposal
- Topic proposal

Literary Analysis

- Thematic analysis
- Close reading
- Photographs as literary texts

Rhetorical Analysis

- Rhetorical analysis
- Close analysis of an argument
- Film analysis

Contents

guide

Part 1 Genres 2

2   **Reports   36**

3 Arguments 66

8   Rhetorical Analyses   218

11 Annotated Bibliographies 266

12 Synthesis Papers 272

reference

reader

65 Evaluations: Readings 720

66 Causal Analyses: Readings 759

67 Proposals: Readings 809

guide

Genres

Need a form you don't see here? Try "Special Assignments," p. 250.

How to start
- Need a **topic**? See page 10.
- Need to choose the right **details**? See page 13.
- Need to **organize the events** in your story? See page 15.

1 Narratives

chronicle
events in
people's lives

Chances are you've shared bits and pieces of your life story in writing many times. In doing so, you've written personal narratives. *Personal* does not mean that writers of personal narratives are always baring their souls. Instead, it suggests that they are telling stories from an individual perspective, providing details only they could know and insights only they could have.

LITERACY NARRATIVE
To work at the campus writing center, you need to submit a *literacy narrative* detailing your own experiences with writing and language.

MEMOIR/ REFLECTION
You direct your grandparents to a community group that is collecting *memoirs* from local citizens who entered the United States as immigrants.

GRAPHIC NARRATIVE
You want more people to think about bicycling to work, so you create a *visual narrative* about your experiences as an urban cyclist, posting both photographs and videos on a blog.

DECIDING TO WRITE A NARRATIVE.   Narratives describe events that people want to share with readers in words or through other media, including photographs, film, songs, cartoons, and more (see the Introduction for more on choosing a genre). These stories may be about family or work experiences, growing up, personal tragedies, relationships, and so on. Expect a narrative you compose to do the following.

Tell a story.   In a narrative, something usually happens. Maybe all you do is reflect on a moment when something peculiar caught your attention. Or your story could recount a series of events — the classic road-trip script. Or you might spin a tale complicated enough to resemble a movie plot, with a connected beginning, middle, and end. But your job is always to focus on some action. Otherwise you are rambling.

Introduce characters.   They may be people or animals or animate objects, but a story usually needs someone or something for readers to care about. You

Telling stories — sometimes competitively — in clubs and restaurants has become a form of entertainment in cities across the United States. Marvin Joseph/ The Washington Post via Getty Images.

needn't pile on physical descriptions or build elaborate backstories. But you ordinarily need characters with names and interesting relationships who speak believable dialogue. Sometimes that fascinating person is you.

Make a point — usually.   There's usually a reason for writing a narrative. When an insurance agent asks about your recent fender bender, she expects you to explain what happened and how you are involved. Most narratives, however, will be less clinical and more reflective, enabling you to connect with readers creatively — to amuse, enlighten, and, perhaps, even to change them. ○ Some narratives are therapeutic too, helping you confront personal issues or get a weight off your chest.

Report details.   What brings a narrative to life are its details — the colors, shapes, sounds, textures, and other physical impressions that convince people a story is credible and authentic. They prove that you were close enough to an experience to have an insider's perspective and that the story really belongs to you. Don't fall back on clichés.

develop a statement
p. 362

A noteworthy subgenre of narratives explores the processes by which people learn to read or write or acquire other life-changing intellectual skills. In the following selection from a slightly longer piece originally published in the *New York Times* "Writers on Writing" series, contemporary novelist Allegra Goodman reflects on how she learned to overcome the doubts that plague many writers. Her most recent work is *The Cookbook Collector* (2010).

Reading the Genre   As you read the selection, pay attention to the way Goodman uses pronouns, especially *I/me* and *you/your*. To whom is the essay directed? Are there places where Goodman seems to be talking as much to herself as to readers? How does that move add interest to the story?

O.K., You're Not Shakespeare. Now Get Back to Work

ALLEGRA GOODMAN

They say writing is lonely work. But that's an exaggeration. Even alone at their desks, writers entertain visitors: characters of a novel, famous and not so famous figures from the past. On good days, all these come to the table. On bad days, however, only unwelcome visitors appear: The specter of the third-grade teacher who despaired of your penmanship. The ghost of the first person who told you that spelling counts. The voice of reason pointing out that what you are about to attempt has already been done — and done far better than you might even hope.

So why bother? Why even begin? It is, after all, abundantly clear that you are not Henry James. Your themes are hackneyed, your style imitative. As for your emotions, memories, insights, and invented characters, what makes you think anyone will care? These are the perfectly logical questions of the famous, petty, and implacable inner critic.

What should a writer do when the inner critic comes to call? How to silence these disparaging whispers? I have no magic cure, but here, from my own experience, is a modest proposal to combat the fiend.

> Details in the opening paragraphs introduce the general theme of the narrative: a writer's self-doubts.

Forget the past. Nothing stops the creative juices like thoughts of the literary tradition. "You'll never be John Donne!" your inner critic shrieks. Or: "*Middlemarch*! Now that was a book!" These thoughts used to fill me with gloom. Then I went to graduate school at Stanford, and I steeped myself in Shakespeare, Wordsworth, and Defoe. The experience set me free.

It happened like this. I was sitting in Green Library trying to write a story, and I looked at all the shelves of books around me, and suddenly the obvious occurred to me. All the great Romantic poets and Elizabethan playwrights and Victorian novelists that tower over me — they're dead! Oh, they still cast their shadow, but I'm alive, and they are irrefutably dead. Their language is exquisite, their scenes divine, but what have these writers done lately? Not a damn thing. Think about it. The idea should give you hope. Past masters are done. Their achievements are finite, known, measurable. Present writers, on the other hand, live in possibility. Your masterpiece could be just around the corner. Genius could befall you at any moment.

"Well," your inner critic counters gloomily, "just remember that when you're gone, your books will suffer the same fate as all the rest. They'll be relics at best. More likely, they'll just languish in obscurity." To which I have to say: So what? I won't be around to care.

Carpe diem. Know your literary tradition, savor it, steal from it, but when you sit down to write, forget about worshiping greatness and fetishizing masterpieces. If your inner critic continues to plague you with invidious comparisons, scream, "Ancestor worship!" and leave the building.

Treat writing as a sacred act. Just as the inner critic loves to dwell on the past, she delights in worrying about the future. "Who would want to read this?" she demands. "Nobody is going to publish a book like that!" Such nagging can incapacitate unpublished writers. Published writers, on the other hand, know that terrible books come out all the time. They anguish: "The reviewers are going to crucify me, and nobody will want to publish me after that."

But take a step back. What are you really afraid of here? When you come down to it, this is just a case of the inner critic masquerading as public opinion, and playing on your vanity.

I know only one way out of this trap, which is to concentrate on your writing itself, for itself. Figuring out what the public wants, or even what

The story turns personal and its setting is specific.

Goodman offers glimpses into her thinking as a writer.

the public is: That's the job of pollsters and publicists and advertisers. All those people study the marketplace. But the creative artist can change the world. A true writer opens people's ears and eyes, not merely playing to the public, but changing minds and lives. This is sacred work. . . .

Ultimately every writer must choose between safety and invention; between life as a literary couch potato and imaginative exercise. You must decide which you like better, the perfectionist within or the flawed pages at hand.

Perhaps you'd rather hold yourself to the impossibly high standards of writers long dead. Or perhaps you'd rather not waste time writing something that will go unpublished, unnoticed, and unread. You have received no encouragement from anyone else, and so you would never think of encouraging yourself. Or you choose to be a realist. You're smart enough to see your talent is limited, your gift too small to pursue. You can convince yourself of all this, or you can listen to your imagination instead. You can fire yourself up with words and voices. You can look out into the world teeming with stories and cast your net.

Goodman's personal reflections lead to advice for would-be writers.

Exploring purpose and topic

▶ topic

You don't need to search for a topic when writing a narrative on your own. You know what aspects of your life you want to share on Facebook or in a journal. You also understand your audiences well enough to fit your stories to people likely to read them.

But you face tougher choices when asked to write a narrative for school. Typically, such an assignment invites you to describe an event that has shaped or changed you. Or perhaps an instructor wants a story that explores a dimension of your personality or reveals something about the communities you belong to. When no topic ideas suggest themselves, consider the following strategies.

Brainstorm, freewrite, build lists, and use memory prompts. To find a story worth recounting, pick up a yearbook, scroll through photographs, or browse your social media sites. Talk with others about their choices of subjects and share ideas on a class Web site.

Choose a manageable subject. You might be tempted to focus on life-changing events so dramatic that they can seem clichéd: deaths, graduations, car wrecks, winning hits, or first love. But for such topics to work, you have to make them fresh for readers who've probably undergone similar experiences — or seen the movie. If you can find that novel perspective (maybe a satiric or ironic one), take the risk. O

Alternatively, try narrating a slice of life rather than the whole side of beef — your toast at a wedding rather than the three-hour reception, a single encounter on a road trip rather than the entire cross-country adventure, or just the scariest part of your encounter with Superstorm Sandy. Most big adventures contain within them dozens of more manageable tales.

A photograph can jog your memory. For example, this picture of Niki de Saint Phalle's sculpture *Sun God* got one student writing about her colorful trip to San Diego, California. *Sun God*, 1983. Concrete structure, paint, 413.4 x 177.2 x 118 inches. Stuart Collection, University of California La Jolla Campus San Diego, California, U.S.A.

get an idea
p. 331

Understanding your audience

People like to read stories, so the audiences for narratives are large, diverse, and receptive. Most of these eager readers probably expect narratives to make some point or reveal an insight. They hope to be moved by what they read, learn something from it, or perhaps be amused by it.

You can capitalize on such expectations, using stories to introduce ideas that readers might be less eager to entertain if presented more formally. As Zadie Smith puts it, "A writer hopes to make connections where the lazy eye sees only a chasm of difference." Women and members of outsider groups have long used narratives to document the adversities they face and to affirm their solidarity. But good stories also cross boundaries and win sympathetic readers from well outside the original target audience.

Of course, you might sometimes decide that the target audience of a narrative is really yourself: You can write about personal experiences to get a handle on them. Even then, be demanding. Think about how your story might sound ten or twenty years from now. Whatever the audience, you have choices to make.

Focus on people.   They are what readers care about, so give them names and define their relationships. But don't slow the action to characterize or describe them. Let your readers figure out the people you are presenting through what they do and say.

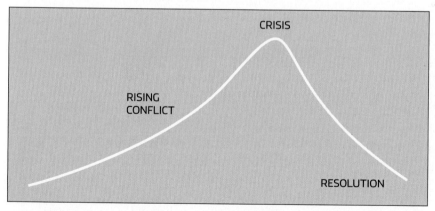

A Classic Narrative Arc   You'll need to decide where to start your story and where to stop. The plan shown in this illustration is effective because the action unfolds in a way that meets audience expectations.

Select events that will keep readers engaged.   Which events represent high points in the action or moments that could not logically be omitted? Which are the most intriguing and entertaining? Focus on these and consider cutting the others. Build toward a few major events in the story that support one or two key themes.

Pace the story.   After a brisk start, slow the narrative to fill in necessary details about characters and set up expectations for what will follow. If a person plays a role later in the story, introduce him or her briefly in the early paragraphs. If a cat matters, mention the cat. But don't dwell on incidentals: Keep the story moving.

Adjust your writing to appeal to the intended readers.   Here, for example, is a serious anecdote offered in an application to graduate school.

> During my third year of Russian, I auditioned for the role of the evil stepsister Anna in a stage production of *Zolushka*. Although I welcomed the chance to act, I was terrified because I could not pronounce a Russian *r*. I had tried but was only able to produce an embarrassing sputter. Leading up to the play, I practiced daily with my professor, repeating "ryba" with a pencil in my mouth. When the play opened, I was able to say "*Kakoe urodstvo!*" with confidence. I had discovered the power to isolate a problem, seek the necessary help, and ultimately solve it. Now I want to pass this power along to others by becoming a Russian language instructor.
>
> — Melissa Miller

But can you imagine Melissa describing her problems with the Russian *r* differently to her peers, maybe even comically? Such an adjustment would only be natural. And it's the kind of shift you have to learn to make as well.

A narrative you write for academic readers might need to be as sober and deliberate as Melissa's statement, and when writing it you might have to keep a tight rein on how you present your life. ○ But don't be too cautious. Any story has to have enough grit to make your experiences seem authentic. So pay close attention to how your instructor defines the audience you are supposed to address in a narrative assignment. If need be, ask questions.

refine your tone
p. 400

Finding and developing materials

When you write about an event soon after it occurs — for instance, in an accident report for an insurance claim — you have the facts fresh in your mind. Yet even in such cases, evidence helps back up your recollections. That's why insurance companies encourage drivers to carry a camera in their cars in case they have a collision. The photo freezes details that human memory, especially under pressure, could ignore or forget. Needless to say, when writing about events in the more distant past, other aids to memory help.

Consult documents.   A journal, if you keep one, will be full of narrative possibilities. But even a daily planner or electronic calendar might hold the facts needed to reconstruct a sequence of events: Just knowing when important meetings occurred may refresh your memory.

Consult images.   Not only do photographs and videos document people and places, but they may also generate ideas for personal narratives. Such prompts may revive past events and the feelings they stir up too. Visual images also remind you of physical details — locales, clothing, hairstyles — that can add authenticity to a narrative.

Talk to the people involved.   A phone call home or a posting on social media might bring a wealth of information. Family and friends might remember details of a story you've forgotten (or suppressed.) They might also see events from a perspective you haven't considered.

Trust your experiences.   Assigned a narrative, lots of people wonder, "What have I done worth writing about"? ○ They underestimate the quality of their own experiences. College students, for example, are incredibly knowledgeable

◀ develop
details

Photographs such as this one taken at a Fourth of July parade may help you recall not only the scene but also the moment the photo was taken, who was there, and so on. © The Orange County Register/ZUMAPress.com.

find a topic
p. 331

about high school or the local music scene or working minimum-wage jobs or dealing with narrow-minded parents. You don't have to be a salaried professional to observe life or have something to say about it.

Here's humorist David Sedaris — who has made a career writing about his very middle-class life from his unique personal perspective — describing the insecurity of many writers:

> When I was teaching — I taught for a while — my students would write as if they were raised by wolves. Or raised on the streets. They were middle-class kids and they were ashamed of their background. They felt like unless they grew up in poverty, they had nothing to write about. Which was interesting because I had always thought that poor people were the ones who were ashamed. But it's not. It's middle-class people who are ashamed of their lives. And it doesn't really matter what your life was like, you can write about anything. It's just the writing of it that is the challenge. I felt sorry for these kids, that they thought that their whole past was absolutely worthless because it was less than remarkable.
>
> — David Sedaris, interviewed in *January Magazine*, June 2000

If every picture tells a story, what narrative does this image suggest? Consider the missing windmill blade, the worker's posture, the quiet sky, and any other details that seem important.
John J. Ruszkiewicz.

Creating a structure

Don't be intimidated by the prospect of organizing a narrative. ◯ You know a lot about narrative structure from reading books or watching films or TV. Many of the plot devices there — from foreshadowing to flashback — can be adapted to stories you write. But you need to plan ahead, know how much space you have to tell a story, and then connect the incidents in your narrative with transitional devices.

organize ◄ events

Consider a simple sequence. It's a natural choice when one event follows another chronologically. Journals and diaries may have the most bare-bones sequential structures, with writers connecting one event to another by little more than a date.

First event
Next event
Next event
Final event

Build toward a climax. Narratives become more complicated when you present a series of incidents that lead to a *climax* or an *epiphany*. Readers usually expect one or the other in a personal narrative. A climax is the moment when the action of a story peaks, takes an important turn, or is resolved: The criminal gets caught. An epiphany is a moment of revelation or insight when a writer or character suddenly sees events in a new way: The detective realizes that he's not much different from the felon.

First event
Next event
Next event
Climax and/or epiphany
Final event

Narratives often have both a climax and an epiphany — it's only logical for major events in life to trigger heightened awareness or illumination. To organize a story this way, decide what the pivotal event of the story will be and then figure out what elements lead up to or explain it. Delete all actions, characters, descriptions, or passages of dialogue that don't contribute to that point, however much you love them. ◯ Or refocus your narrative on a moment that you do love.

connect ideas
p. 387

revise and edit
p. 422

Choosing a style and design

Narratives are usually written in approachable middle or low styles because they nicely mimic the human voice through devices such as contractions and dialogue. Both styles are also comfortable with *I*, the point of view of many stories. A middle style may be perfect for reaching academic or professional audiences. But a low style, dipping into slang and unconventional speech, may sometimes feel more authentic to more general readers. It's your choice.

Style is important because narratives get their energy and textures from sentence structures and vocabulary choices. Narratives require tight but expressive language — *tight* to keep the action moving, *expressive* to capture the gist of events. In a first draft, run with your ideas and don't do much editing. Flesh out the story as you have designed it and then go back to see if it works technically: Characters should be introduced, locations identified and colored, events clearly explained and sequenced, key points made memorably and emphatically. You'll need several drafts to get these key elements into shape.

Then look to your language and allow plenty of time to revise it. Begin with Chapter 34, "Vigorous, Clear, Economical Style." Here are some options for your narrative.

Don't hesitate to use first person — *I*.   Most personal narratives are about the writer, so first-person pronouns are used without apology. ○ A narrative often must take readers where the *I* has been, and using the first-person pronoun helps make writing authentic. Consider online journalist Michael Yon's explanation of why he reported on the Iraq War using *I* rather than a more objective third-person perspective:

> I write in first person because I am actually there at the events I write about. When I write about the bombs exploding, or the smell of blood, or the bullets snapping by, and I say *I*, it's because I was there. Yesterday a sniper shot at us, and seven of my neighbors were injured by a large bomb. These are my neighbors. These are soldiers. . . . I feel the fire from the explosions, and am lucky, very lucky, still to be alive. Everything here is first person.
>
> — From Glenn Reynolds, *An Army of Davids*

And yet don't count out telling a story from a third-person point of view, even when you are writing about yourself. You may find it bracing to present yourself as someone else might see you.

define your style
p. 400

Use figures of speech such as similes, metaphors, and analogies to make memorable comparisons.   *Similes* make comparisons by using *like* or as: *He used his camera* like *a rifle*. *Metaphors* drop the *like* or *as* to gain even more power: *His camera was a rifle aimed at enemies*. An *analogy* extends the comparison: *His camera became a rifle aimed at his imaginary enemies, their private lives in his crosshairs*.

People make comparisons habitually. Some are so common they've been reduced to invisible clichés: *hit me like a ton of bricks; dumb as an ox; clear as a bell*. In your own narratives, you want similes and metaphors fresher than these and yet not contrived or strained. Here's science writer Michael Chorost effortlessly deploying both a metaphor (*spins up*) and a simile (*like riding a roller coaster*) to describe what he experiences as he awaits surgery.

> I can feel the bustle and clatter around me as the surgical team spins up to take-off speed. It is like riding a roller coaster upward to the first great plunge, strapped in and committed.
>
> — *Rebuilt: How Becoming Part Computer Made Me More Human*

In choosing verbs, favor active rather than passive voice.   Active verbs propel the action (*Estela signed the petition*), while passive verbs slow it down by an unneeded word or two (*The petition was signed by Estela*). ○

Since narratives are all about movement, build sentences around strong verbs that do things. Edit until you get down to the nub of the action. You will produce sentences as effortless as these from Joseph Epstein, describing the pleasures of catching plagiarists. ○ Verbs are highlighted in this passage; only one (*is followed*) is passive.

> In thirty years of teaching university students I never encountered a case of plagiarism, or even one that I suspected. Teachers I've known who have caught students in this sad act report that the capture gives one an odd sense of power. The power derives from the authority that resides behind the word *gotcha*. This is followed by that awful moment — a veritable sadist's Mardi Gras — when one calls the student into one's office and points out the odd coincidence that he seems to have written about existentialism in precisely the same words Jean-Paul Sartre used fifty-two years earlier.
>
> — "Plagiary, It's Crawling All Over Me," *Weekly Standard*, March 6, 2006

> Need help seeing the big picture? See "How to Revise Your Work" on pp. 426–27.

improve your
sentences p. 412

avoid plagiarism
p. 466

> The difference between the almost right word and the right word is really a large matter — it's the difference between the lightning bug and the lightning.

—Mark Twain

Library of Congress, Prints and Photographs Division, LC-USZ62-5513.

Keep the language simple.　Your language need not be elaborate when it is fresh and authentic. Look for concrete expressions that help readers visualize a scene. And when it comes to modifiers, one strong word is usually better than several weaker ones (*freezing* rather than *very cold*; *doltish* rather than *not very bright*). In the paragraph below from a narrative about telling ghost stories, notice how simple items clearly detailed (oil lamp, soft blankets, *pan dulce*) draw you into the scene.

> When we tell scary stories, we're usually in the half-light of an old oil lamp that my Tío Fernando brings out from the storage room in back. Its flame flickers on the walls — creating dancing shadows — and the smell of oil permeates the room. We pass soft blankets around to cuddle beneath and keep terrors at bay. Snacks are set on the kitchen table for us to munch on: chips with spicy hot sauce, *pan dulce*, leftover *burritos de chile colorado* from earlier in the day. We make ourselves comfortable and settle in for a long night — one full of chills that will likely give us nightmares.
>
> — Alexandra Rayo, "The Thrill of Terror"

Develop major characters through action and dialogue.　It's usually better to portray people via their words and actions than through static descriptions: The mantra is, *show, don't tell*. Remember it! If a character is conceited or cheap, let readers see him glancing in mirrors or heading to the restroom as the lunch bill arrives.

You can also bring people to life in a story by what they say — and without much commentary from you. Just be sure your characters' lines sound natural, following the advice of author John Steinbeck: "If you are using dialogue — say it aloud as you write it. Only then will it have the sound of speech." Avoid using dialogue to explain complicated plot points. No one believes it when characters plunge into detailed (and perfectly grammatical) passages of exposition: "Oh look, the house is in flames and here comes the first of several emergency vehicles!" *No* dialogue is better than awkward dialogue.

The following is a selection from a personal narrative about a student's trip to South Africa that artfully melds precise observation, deft characterization, and believable dialogue. Note, too, how the use of the present tense makes the moment seem immediate and dramatic.

At last we arrive at the Ikageng Itereleng AIDS Ministry center, a sanctuary that emerges from a cloud of dust. It is an organization run by Carol Dyanti. She is everyone's mama, a hero to her community. From her modest building she passes out food, clothing, and school supplies to families in need. But all the families are in need. I watch as Carol embraces two bashful young women with their gazes fixed downward. She sends them away with a gallon of cooking oil and a sack of corn meal for *mieliepap*.

Carol turns to us and offers the same loving hugs.

"Those two," she tells me, "they're sisters, twelve and fourteen. They live alone now because their parents abandoned them. They can't even go to school because they must work now."

I watch them walk away. They have no smiles, no girlish giggles, or sisterly quarrels. They walk slowly, bent against a crisp winter wind.

Carol runs her organization from donations of both supplies and money from outreach groups. Some groups are local, but most are from Western countries. Oprah Winfrey, for example, has given money and vans to help Ikageng Itereleng.

"But see, she just comes in and gives money — there is no thought behind it," Carol tells me. "Sometimes we don't see any of it because of how poorly everything is managed. She is a wonderful lady, but . . ." Carol pauses. "She only sees what she wants to see. And that doesn't help us much."

— Lily Parish, "Sala Kahle, South Africa," 2013

For the record, dialogue ordinarily requires quotation marks and new paragraphs for each change of speaker. And keep the tags simple: You don't have to vary much from *he said* or *she said.*

Your Turn Good dialogue is hard to write. So practice. Write a one-page story mostly in dialogue. Tell readers what you must about your characters, but let most of the action occur within their words. Then read your story aloud over and over and revise it until the dialogue sounds authentic. Get feedback from your classmates and give them suggestions on their stories as well.

Develop the setting to set the context and mood.   Show readers where and when events are occurring if the setting makes a difference — and most of the time it will. Location (Times Square; dusty street in Gallup, New Mexico; your bedroom), as well as climate and time of day (cool dawn, exotic dusk, broiling afternoon), will help readers get a fix on the story. But don't churn out paragraphs of description just for their own sake; readers will skate right over them. ○

Use images to tell a story.   Consider the ways photos attached to a narrative might help readers grasp the setting and situation. More complex stories about your life or community can be told by combining your words and pictures in photo-essays or other media environments. ○ Or use images simply to illustrate a sequence of events. An illustrated timeline is a simple form of this sort of narrative, as are scrapbooks or high school yearbooks.

Fisherman with His Catch, a 32-Inch, 18-Pound Striped Bass Note how the photograph conveys far more than the statistics alone would. Courtesy of Sid Darion.

develop a draft
p. 367

think visually
p. 557

Examining models

MEMOIR/REFLECTION   In the following essay, Miles Pequeno uses a narrative about a chess match to describe a changing relationship with his father and preserve an important memory. He wrote this paper in response to an assignment in an upper-division college writing class.

Reading the Genre   An epiphany is a sudden moment of insight that may occur at some moment in a personal narrative, often in the conclusion. Would you describe Pequeno's final paragraph as an epiphany? Does it seem like an appropriate ending for the piece?

Pequeno 1

Miles Pequeno

Professor Mitchell

English 102

May 12, 20--

Check. Mate?

"Checkmate! Right? You can't move him anywhere, right? I got you again!" I couldn't control my glee. For good measure, I even grabbed my rook, which stood next to his king, and gave him a posthumous beating. The deposed king tumbled from the round table and onto the hardwood floor with a thud. The sound of sure victory. Being eight, it was easy to get excited about chess. It gave me not only at least a few minutes of Dad's attention and approval, but the comfort of knowing I'd taste victory every time. Either Dad was letting me always win, or I was the prodigy he wanted me to be. I always liked to believe it was the latter.

The relationship I had with my father was always complicated. I loved him and he loved me; that much was

> Narrative opens with dialogue and action.

For an additional reading, see **macmillanhighered.com/howtowrite3e**.
e-readings › Katerina Cizek, *Out My Window* [MULTIMEDIA DOCUMENTARY]

21

Pequeno 2

Uses particular details to explain relationship with father.

understood. But his idea of fatherhood was a little unorthodox (or maybe too orthodox, I'm not sure which). We didn't play catch in the yard, but he did make flash cards to teach me my multiplication tables when I was still in kindergarten. He didn't take me to Astros games, but he made sure I knew lots of big words from the newspaper. We were close, but only on his terms.

Using first person, Pequeno draws on personal experience to describe and characterize his father.

Save for the ever-graying hair near his temples, he looks much the same now as he did when I was little: round belly, round face, and big brown eyes that pierced while they silently observed and inwardly critiqued. His black hair, coarse and thick, and day-or-two-old beard usually gave away his heritage. He came to our suburb of Houston from Mexico when he was a toddler, learned English watching Spider-Man cartoons, and has since spent his life catching up, constantly working at moving up in the world. Even more was expected of me, the extension of his hard work and dreams for the future. I had no idea at the time, but back when I was beating him at chess as a kid, I myself was a pawn. He was planning something.

Then a funny thing happened. After winning every game since age eight, the five-year winning streak ended. I lost. This time, Dad had decided to take off the training wheels. Just as he was thrust into the real world unceremoniously with my birth when he was but eighteen years old, I was forced to grow up a little early too. The message was clear: Nothing is being handed to you anymore, Son.

Notice how a metaphor here (training wheels) blossoms into an analogy about growing up.

Pequeno 3

This abrupt lesson changed my outlook. I no longer wanted to make Dad proud; I wanted to equal or better him. I'd been conditioned to seek his attention and approval, and then the rug was pulled from beneath my feet. I awoke to the realization that it was now my job to prove that the student could become the teacher.

I spent time after school every day playing chess against the artificial intelligence of my little Windows 95 computer. I knew what problems I had to correct because Dad was sure to point them out in the days after forcing that first loss. I had trouble using my queen. Dad always either knocked her out early or made me too afraid to put her in play. The result was my king slaughtered time and time again as his bride, the queen, sat idle on the far side of the board.

Our chess set was made of marble, with green and white hand-carved pieces sitting atop the thick, round board. Dad kept the set next to the TV and, most nights, we'd take it down from the entertainment center and put it on the coffee table in front of the sofa, where we sat side by side and played chess while halfway paying attention to the television. One night after Mom's spaghetti dinner, I casually walked into the living room to find Dad sitting sipping a Corona and watching the Rockets game. Hakeem Olajuwon was having a great night. Usually, if Dad was really into something on TV, we'd go our separate ways and maybe play later. This night, I picked up the remote control from the coffee table. Off.

> Provides background information that is important later in story.

> Paragraph sets the physical scene for climactic chess match.

Pequeno 4

"Let's play," I said resolutely. I grabbed the marble chess set, with all the pieces exactly where I had put them in anticipation of this game. The board seemed heavier than usual as I carried it to the coffee table. I sat down next to him on the sofa and stared at the pieces, suddenly going blank. The bishops might as well have been knights. I froze as Dad asked me what color I wanted. Traditionally, this had been merely a formality. I'd always picked white before because I wanted to have the first move. That was the rule: *White moves first, green next.*

"Green."

Then it all came back to me. The certainty of my declaration surprised him. He furrowed his brows slightly and leaned back just enough to show good-natured condescension.

"You sure? That means I go first."

"I'm sure. Take white."

So he began his attack. He started off controlling one side of the board, slowly advancing. The knights led the charge, with the pawns waiting in the wings to form an impenetrable wall around the royal family, who remained in their little castle of two adjacent spaces.

Every move was made with painful precision. Now and then after my moves, he'd sigh and sink a little into the sofa. He'd furrow those big black brows, his eyes darting quickly from one side of the board to the other, thinking two or three moves ahead. Some of his mannerisms this time were completely new, like the hesitation of his hand as he'd reach for a piece and then

---

First dialogue since opening signals rising action.

"Combat" metaphor in next few paragraphs moves story forward.

Pequeno 5

jerk it back quickly, realizing that my strategy had shut more than a few doors for him.

Eventually I worked up the courage to thrust the queen into action. She moved with great trepidation at first, never attacking, merely sneaking down the board. In the meantime, Dad's advancing rooks and knights were taking out my line of pawns, which I'd foolishly put too far into play. Every risk either of us took was clearly calculated. Sometimes he'd mutter to himself, slowly realizing this game wasn't as usual.

Things were looking good. Even if I didn't win, I'd already won a victory by challenging him. But that wasn't what I had practiced for. It wasn't why I'd turned off the television, and it certainly wasn't why I was concentrating so hard on these white and green figurines.

I was locked in. This was more than father and son. This was an epic battle between generals who knew each other well enough to keep the other at bay. But I was advancing. Sure, there were losses, but that was the cost of war. I had a mission.

My queen finally reached his king unharmed.

"Check."

I uttered the word silently. As the game had progressed, gaining intensity and meaning, there was no conversation. In its place were sporadic comments, muttered with deference. So when I said "check," I made sure not to make a big deal of it. I said it quietly, softly. I didn't want to jinx myself with bragging, and I certainly didn't want to get too excited and break my own

Another extended analogy.

Pequeno 6

concentration. As his king scrambled for a safe hiding place, my knights continued their advance. I had planned for this stage of the game several moves before, which was apparently at least one move more than Dad was thinking ahead. Check again. More scrambling, and another check. It seemed I had him cornered. Then . . .

"Check." It wasn't the first time I had him in check, and I didn't expect it to be the last in this game.

"Mate," he whispered, faint hints of a smile beginning to show on the corners of his mouth, pushing his cheeks up slightly. I hadn't realized that I had won until he conceded defeat with that word. Raising his eyebrows, he leaned back into the cushion of the sofa. He looked a little tired.

"Mate?" I wasn't sure he was right. I didn't let myself believe it until I stared at these little marble men. Sure enough, his desperate king was cornered.

"Good game, Son."

And that was it. There was his approval right there, manifesting itself in that smile that said "I love you" and "you sneaky son of a bitch" at the same time. But I didn't feel like any more of a man than I had an hour before. In fact, I felt a little hollow. So I just kept my seat next to him, picked up the remote control again, and watched the Rockets finish off the Mavericks. Business as usual after that. I went back to my room and did some homework, but kept the chess game at the forefront of my mind.

> Note that story climax occurs mostly through dialogue.

> Father's smile signals change in father-son relationship.

Pequeno 7

Wait a second. Had he let me win? Damn it, I'd worked so hard just for him to toy with me again, even worse than when he'd let me beat him before. No, there's no way he let me win. Or maybe he did. I don't know.

I walked back into the living room.

"Rematch?"

So we played again, and I lost. It didn't hurt, though. It didn't feel nearly as bad as when he first took off the training wheels. This was a different kind of defeat, and it didn't bother me one bit. I had nothing left to prove. If I'd lost, so what? I'd already shown what I could do.

But what if he'd let me win?

Again, so what? I had made myself a better player than I was before. I didn't need him to pass me a torch. I'd taken the flame myself, like a thirteen-year-old Prometheus. After that night, I was my own man, ready for everything: high school, my first girlfriend, my parents' divorce, my first job, moving away to college, starting a career. I never lost the feeling that I could make everything work if I just chose the right moves. I still live by that principle.

GRAPHIC NARRATIVE (EXCERPT)   In *Persepolis* (2003), Marjane Satrapi uses the medium of the graphic novel to narrate the story of her girlhood in Iran. As she grew up, she witnessed the overthrow of the shah and the Islamic Revolution, and the subsequent war with Iraq. The selection on the following pages describes life under the shah.

Reading the Genre   Describe the specific devices Satrapi uses to tell her story and portray characters. What features does *Persepolis* share with prose narratives? With movies or documentaries?

HE EVEN WENT TO THE GRAVE OF CYRUS THE GREAT, WHO RULED OVER THE ANCIENT WORLD.

CYRUS, REST IN PEACE, WE ARE LOOKING AFTER PERSIA.

ALL THE COUNTRY'S MONEY WENT INTO RIDICULOUS CELEBRA-TIONS OF THE 2500 YEARS OF DYNASTY AND OTHER FRIVOLITIES... ALL OF THIS TO IMPRESS HEADS OF STATE; THE POPULATION COULDN'T HAVE CARED LESS.

I AM SO HAPPY THAT THERE IS FINALLY A REVOLUTION BECAUSE THE SHAH...

I'M HUNGRY!

I BOUGHT YOU SOME BOOKS. YOU WILL SEE WHY THE PEOPLE ARE REVOLTING.

SHE WON'T TELL ME ABOUT GRANDPA.

HE TOOK PHOTOS EVERY DAY. IT WAS STRICTLY FORBIDDEN. HE HAD EVEN BEEN ARRESTED ONCE BUT ESCAPED AT THE LAST MINUTE.

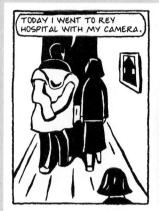

TODAY I WENT TO REY HOSPITAL WITH MY CAMERA.

PEOPLE CAME OUT CARRYING THE BODY OF A YOUNG MAN KILLED BY THE ARMY. HE WAS HONORED LIKE A MARTYR. A CROWD GATHERED TO TAKE HIM TO THE BAHESHTE ZAHRA CEMETERY.

THEN THERE WAS ANOTHER CADAVER, AN OLD MAN CARRIED OUT ON A STRETCHER. THOSE WHO DIDN'T FOLLOW THE FIRST ONE WENT OVER TO THE OLD MAN, SHOUTING REVOLUTIONARY SLOGANS AND CALLING HIM A HERO.

HERE IS ANOTHER MARTYR.

WELL, I WAS TAKING MY PHOTOS WHEN I NOTICED AN OLD WOMAN NEXT TO ME. I UNDERSTOOD THAT SHE WAS THE WIDOW OF THE VICTIM. I HAD SEEN HER LEAVE THE HOSPITAL WITH THE BODY.

PLEASE! STOP IT! STOP IT!

WHAT? WHAT IS IT?

STOP IT!

WHO ARE YOU?

HIS WIDOW!

ARE YOU A ROYALIST?

NO, BUT MY HUSBAND DIED OF CANCER...

1. **Literacy Narrative:** After reading Allegra Goodman's "O.K., You're Not Shakespeare. Now Get Back to Work" (p. 7), write a literacy narrative of your own, perhaps recalling how you learned to read or write. Describe books that changed you or any ambitions you might now have to pursue a writing or media career. However, you don't have to be an aspiring writer to make sense of this assignment. Remember that there are many kinds of literacy. The narrative you compose may be about your encounters with paintings, films, music, fashion, architecture, or maybe even video games. Or it may explore any intellectual passion — from mathematics to foreign policy.

2. **Memoir/Reflection:** Using Miles Pequeno's "Check. Mate?" (p. 21) as a model, compose a short narrative describing how an individual (like Pequeno's father) changed your life or made you see the world differently. Give readers a strong sense both of this person and of your relationship to him or her. Make this a paper you might want to keep.

3. **Graphic Narrative:** *Persepolis* (p. 28) demonstrates that a story can be told in various media: This graphic novel even became an animated film in 2007. Using a medium other than words alone, tell a story from your own life or from your community. Draw it, use photographs, craft a collage, create a video, record interviews, or combine other media suited to your nonfiction tale.

4. **Your Choice:** Compose a personal narrative about a subject and for an audience of your choosing. Perhaps you have to prepare a personal statement for a scholarship application or you'd like to turn some blog entries you wrote while traveling in South America into a more coherent tale. You may experiment with media too, combining prose and images in a Web project or trying your hand at creating a photo narrative.

How to start ▶ ● Need a **topic**? See page 47.

● Need to **find information**? See page 50.

● Need to **organize that information**?
See page 52.

2 Reports

provide readers with reliable information

You've been preparing reports since the second grade, when you probably used an encyclopedia to explain why volcanoes erupt or who Franklin Roosevelt was. Today, the reports you write may be more ambitious.

RESEARCH REPORT
You write a *research report* drawing from a music archive on campus to document the influence of two important blues pioneers.

FEATURE STORY
You do a *feature story* on countries that are competing for international attention by building skyscrapers or other signature buildings.

INFOGRAPHIC
You design an *infographic* to present recent data on the gender and ethnic makeup of students graduating from local high schools.

DECIDING TO WRITE A REPORT.   As you might guess, reports make up one of the broadest genres of writing. If you use Google to search the term online, you will turn up an unwieldy 4.6 billion items, opening with dictionary entries and the *Drudge Report* and moving on to sites that cover everything from financial news to morbidity studies. Such sites may not resemble the term papers, presentations, and lab reports you'll prepare for school. But they'll share at least some of the same goals (for more on choosing a genre, see the Introduction).

U.S. ENVIRONMENTAL PROTECTION AGENCY

OFFICE OF INSPECTOR GENERAL

This report was issued by the EPA's Office of Inspector General, in response to a Congressional inquiry about an EPA emergency order against a gas drilling company. The report includes an "At a Glance" page describing the report's background and results, before the detailed full report, which includes visual aids such as a map and a chemical analysis chart. U.S. Environmental Protection Agency and the Office of the Inspector General/Cover photo: Outside the Range Resources' Butler and Teal hydraulic fracturing well sites. EPA OIG photo.

Response to Congressional Inquiry Regarding the EPA's Emergency Order to the Range Resources Gas Drilling Company

Report No. 14-P-0044   December 20, 2013

Present information.   People read reports to discover what they don't already know or to confirm what they do. So they'll expect what you offer to be timely and accurate. Sometimes, information you present *will*, in fact, be new (as in *news*), built upon recent events or fresh data. But just as often, your academic reports will repackage research from existing sources. *Are dogs really color-blind?* The answer to such a question is already out there for you to find — if you know where to look.

Find reliable sources.   The heart and soul of any report will be reliable sources that provide or confirm information—whether they are "high government officials" quoted anonymously in news stories or scholarly articles listed in the bibliographies of college term papers. If asked to write a report about a topic new to you, immediately plan to do library and online research. O

The information in reports may also come from careful experiments and observations—as would be the case when you prepare a lab report for a biology or chemistry course. Even personal experience may provide material for reports, though observations and anecdotes of this kind usually need corroboration to be convincing.

Aim for objectivity.   Writers and institutions (such as newspapers or government agencies) know that they lose credibility when their factual presentations seem incomplete or biased. Of course, smart readers understand that reports on contentious subjects—climate change, energy policy, or health-care reform, for example—may lean one way or another. In fact, you may develop strong opinions based on the research you've done and be inclined to favor certain ideas. But most readers of reports prefer to draw their own conclusions.

Present information clearly.   Readers expect material in reports and reference material to be arranged (and perhaps illustrated) for their benefit. O So when you put forward information, state your claims quickly and support them with data. You'll gain no points for surprises, twists, or suspense in a report. In fact, you'll usually give away the game on the first page of most reports by announcing not only your thesis but also perhaps your conclusions.

find a topic
p. 331

think visually
p. 557

When Susan Wilcox received an open-ended assignment to write a report, she responded with a traditionally researched academic essay on a subject important to her, one that she wanted her classmates to learn more about. The essay is formally documented in MLA style.

Reading the Genre   Wilcox's report prepared for an academic course draws on a wide range of sources, from personal interviews to books. What impact might this list of sources have on a reader's reception of the report?

Wilcox 1

Susan Wilcox

Professor Longmire

Rhetoric 325M

March 7, 20--

Marathons for Women

Today in America, five women are running. Two of them

live in Minnesota, one in Virginia, and two in Texas. Their

careers are different, their political views are divergent, and

their other hobbies are irrelevant, for it is running that draws

these women together. They are marathoners. Between them,

they are eighteen-time veterans of the 26.2-mile march of

exhaustion and exhilaration.

These five women are not alone; over 205,000 women in the

United States alone ran a marathon in 2010 (RunningUSA). They

sacrifice sleeping late, watching TV, and sometimes even

toenails (lost toenails are a common malady among marathon

runners) for the sake of their sport. Why do these women do this

Opening paragraphs establish a context for a report on women marathon runners, engaging readers.

to themselves? Karin Warren explains, ("It)started out being about losing weight and getting fit again. But I enjoyed running so much—not just how physically fit I felt afterward, but the actual act of running and how it cleared my mind and made me feel better about myself in all aspects of my life—that it became a part of who I am." The other women agree, using words like "conquer," "powerful," and "confident" to describe how running makes them feel.

However these women know that only a generation ago, marathons weren't considered suitable for women. Tammy Moriearty and Wendy Anderson remember hearing that running could make a woman's uterus fall out; Tammy adds, "It floors me that medical professionals used to believe that." Michelle Gibson says that her friends cautioned her against running when she was pregnant (she ran anyway; it's safe). Naomi Olson has never heard a specific caution, but "lots of people think I am crazy," she says. Female runners, like their male counterparts, do have to maintain adequate nutrition during training (Third Age), but "there are no inherent health risks involved with marathon preparation and participation" (Dilworth). Unfortunately, scientists were not researching running health for women when the marathon was born, and most people thought women were too fragile to run that far. The myth that marathoning is dangerous for women was allowed to fester in the minds of race organizers around the world.

Author uses interviews with runners to define myths about women and marathoning.

Wilcox 3

Legend holds that the original marathon runner, Pheidippides, ran from the Battle of Marathon to Athens to bring news of the Athenian victory over Persia. Pheidippides died of exhaustion after giving the news, and the marathon race today is held in honor of his final journey (Lovett x). Historians doubt all the details of this legend, including that a professional runner in Greece would die after what would have been a relatively short distance for him (x-xi). Nevertheless, the myth remains. When the Olympic Games were revived in Athens in 1896, a race covering Pheidippides's route from Marathon to Athens was scheduled as the final Olympic event (xii). Even though no women were permitted to compete, a Greek woman known as Melpomene arrived on the day of the race, ready to run. Race officials denied her access to the course, so she ran alongside it, eventually finishing an hour and a half after the winner. However, the first woman known to have run the marathon distance was a different Greek woman, Stamatis Rovithi, who ran the course from Marathon to Athens in March of 1896, a few months before the Olympic Games (Lovett 126). Even without proper medical research, these two women were proof that the marathon was not too far for a woman to run.

The occasional woman would run a marathon throughout the first half of the twentieth century (Lovett 126), but never with sufficient fanfare to attract attention to her accomplishment. That changed in 1966, when Roberta Gibb

The report is organized by time and sequence.

Wilcox 4

decided to enter the Boston Marathon. At the time, Gibb would sometimes cover 40 miles on a training run, so she was shocked when her entry was returned with a note informing her that "women [are] not physiologically capable of running 26 miles" (Gibb). Gibb was not put off by such assertions; she hid in the bushes at the starting line and wore her brother's clothes to hide her gender. It was obvious to the men running around her that she was a woman, though, and buoyed by their support, Gibb took off the bulky sweatshirt she was wearing, delighting the crowd who hadn't expected to see a woman running Boston.

By the time Gibb reached the finish, the governor of Massachusetts was there to greet her. *Sports Illustrated* reported of Gibb's achievement, "[The] performance should do much to phase out the old-fashioned notion that a female is too frail for distance running" (Brown). Race officials were less pleased, insisting that Gibb "merely covered the same route as the official race while it was in progress. No girl has ever run in the Boston Marathon" (Brown). The fight was on.

The following year, another woman took on Boston, this time as an official entrant. Kathrine Switzer's coach, like so many others, thought that women couldn't handle the marathon distance (Switzer 49). He had insisted that she prove her ability before he would allow her to enter the race, and once she did so, he also insisted that she be an official registrant to avoid being suspended from collegiate athletics (70). Switzer

Wilcox 5

Officials attempt to remove Kathrine Switzer from the 1967 Boston Marathon. *Source:* Associated Press.

AP photo in the report provides visual evidence.

registered using her initials, not revealing her gender. On the day of the race, once word spread that a woman was running with a race number, officials tried to remove Switzer from the course. Her teammates protected her from the attack in full view of the press truck; once again, a woman running Boston was front-page news (Lovett 127).

Women continued to run Boston unofficially for the next four years, but it was the New York City Marathon that first moved toward equality, allowing women runners for the first time in 1971. In the face of this inclusion by the neighbor race, Boston officials relented and allowed women to enter in 1972 (Run Like a Girl). The Boston Marathon is popular enough to require qualifying times for competitors, so it holds a mystique in the

Wilcox 6

minds of many runners. On any given marathon day, many runners cross the start line hoping to finish in a Boston qualifying time.

Even after the prestigious New York and Boston races accepted women, the fight raged on for a women's Olympic marathon. Other race distances for women were also on the Olympic wish list, and Lovett notes, "Some lobbyists felt that the addition of women's races should be made gradually" (128), a notion that did not sit well with many women who were longing to compete on the world's largest stage. Marathoner Jacqueline Hansen pointed out, "They didn't ask [two-time Olympic marathon gold medalist] Frank Shorter to wait another four years" (Run Like a Girl). After years of lobbying from supporters, including Nike and the now-famous Switzer, the International Olympic Committee agreed. Joan Benoit from Maine launched herself into stardom and gained iconic status when she finished first at the inaugural Olympic marathon in 1984 (Lovett 136).

The evolution of women's running is not over. In September 2011, the governing body of running (the International Association of Athletics Federations, or IAAF) announced that beginning in 2012, women's finishing times can only be considered for world records if they are set in women-only races. The rule is in the interest of fairness: Women running with men have faster competitors to pace themselves with, while men have no such pacers (Associated Press). Runners worldwide reacted with shock, since current women's marathon world record holder

The report champions women runners, though its style generally avoids connotative language.

Paula Radcliffe would lose her time of 2:15.25, set at the 2003 London Marathon. That record would now be called a "world best," and the new official record would be shifted to 2:17.42, Radcliffe's time in the 2005 women-only London Marathon (Longman). However, under "the vehemence of protests," the IAAF has insisted that Radcliffe's faster time will be allowed to stand as the world record (Associated Press) and that this rule only applies to future races. The controversy is ongoing, and IAAF has been known to change policy before.

Thousands of women run today, competitively and recreationally, at distances ranging from across the front lawn to 100-mile ultramarathons. Our five women all agree that running makes their lives better, no matter what the distance. And they agree on one more thing: No one has ever told any of them that they shouldn't run just because they are women. The fight for running equality was a generation before these women, but they do not fail to be grateful for the benefits. Women run marathons because they can.

Works Cited

Anderson, Wendy. Facebook interview. 25 Feb. 2012.

Associated Press. "Paula Radcliffe to Keep Marathon Record." *ESPN Olympic Sports*. ESPN, 9 Nov. 2011. Web. 19 Feb. 2012.

Wilcox 9

Brown, Gwilym S. "A Game Girl in a Man's Game." *Sports
    Illustrated*. SI Vault, 2 May 1966. Web. 19 Feb. 2012.

Dilworth, Mark. "Women Running Marathons: Health Risks."
    EmpowHER. EmpowHER Media, 23 Apr. 2010. Web. 19 Feb.
    2012.

Gibb, Roberta. "A Run of One's Own." *Running Past*. Running
    Past, 2011. Web. 19 Feb. 2014.

Gibson, Michelle. Facebook interview. 20 Feb. 2012.

Longman, Jeré. "Still Playing Catch-Up." *New York Times*. New
    York Times, 5 Nov. 2011. Web. 19 Feb. 2012.

Lovett, Charles C. *Olympic Marathon: A Centennial History of the
    Games' Most Storied Race*. Westport: Praeger-Greenwood, 1997.
    Print.

Moriearty, Tammy. Facebook interview. 21 Feb. 2012.

Olson, Naomi. Facebook interview. 21 Feb. 2012.

Run Like a Girl. "History of Women's Distance Running." *Run
    Like a Girl Film*. Run Like a Girl, n.d. Web. 20 Feb. 2012.

RunningUSA. "RunningUSA's Annual Marathon Report."
    RunningUSA. RunningUSA, 16 Mar. 2011. Web. 19 Feb. 2012.

Switzer, Kathrine. *Marathon Woman: Running the Race to
    Revolutionize Women's Sports*. New York: Avalon, 2007. Print.

Third Age. "Women Running Marathons: Do Benefits Outweigh
    Risks?" *Third Age*. Third Age Media, 1 July 2008. Web. 19
    Feb. 2012.

Warren, Karin. Facebook interview. 21 Feb. 2012.

Exploring purpose and topic

When you are assigned a report, carefully identify the subgenre (psychology term paper, physics lab report, article for an arts journal) and the kinds of information your report will require. Will your report merely answer a factual question about a topic and deliver basic information? Or are you expected to do a more in-depth study or compare different points of view, as you would in an investigative report? Or might the report deliver information based on your own research or experiments? Consider your various options as you select a topic.

topic ◀

Answer questions.   For this kind of report, include basic facts and, perhaps, an overview of key features, issues, or problems. Think of an encyclopedia entry as a model: Facts are laid out cleanly, usually under a series of headings. The discussions are generally efficient and basic, not exhaustive.

Assigned an informative piece like this, you can choose topics that might otherwise seem overly ambitious. When readers expect an overview, not expertise, you can easily write two or three fact-filled pages on "Atonal Music" or "The Battle of Salamis" by focusing on just a few key figures, events, or concepts. Given a prompt of this sort, consider a topic that introduces you to new ideas or perspectives—providing you this opportunity could, in fact, be an instructor's rationale for such an assignment.

Review what is already known about a subject.   Instructors who ask you to write five- or ten-page reports on specific subjects within a field—for example, to compare banking practices in Japan and the European Union or to describe current trends in museum architecture—doubtless know plenty about those subjects already. They want you to look at the topic in some depth to increase what *you* know. But the subject may also be one evolving rapidly because of current events, technological changes, or ongoing research.

So consider updating an idea introduced in a lecture or textbook: You might be surprised by how much you can add to what an instructor has presented. If workers are striking in Greece again, make that a focal point of your general report on European Union economic policies; if your course covers globalism, consider how a world community made smaller by jet travel compli-cates the response to epidemic diseases. In considering topics for in-depth reports, you'll find "research guides" especially helpful. ⓞ You may also want to consult librarians or experts in the field you're writing about. ⓞ

Field research is one way to acquire new information. © The Natural History Museum/The Image Works.

Report new knowledge.   Many schools encourage undergraduates to conduct original research in college. In most cases, this work is done under the supervision of an instructor in your major field, and you'll probably choose a topic only after developing expertise in some area. For a sampling of research topics students from different schools have explored, search "undergraduate research journal" on the Web.

If you have trouble finding a subject for a report, try the brainstorming techniques suggested in Chapter 19, both to identify topic ideas and to narrow them to manageable size.

> **Your Turn**   Having trouble finding a fresh topic for a report? Let your curiosity guide you. Make a list of things you'd simply like to know more about within the general area of your topic. If you need prompts, check out HowStuffWorks.com, especially its blogs and podcasts, such as "Stuff You Missed in History Class." You'll see that almost any subject or topic area is filled with interesting nooks and crannies.

Understanding your audience

You know that you should attune any report to its potential readers. Well-informed audiences expect detailed reports that use technical language, but if your potential audience includes a range of readers, from experts to amateurs, design your work to engage them all. Perhaps you can use headings to ease novices through your report while simultaneously signaling to more knowledgeable readers what sections they might skip. ○ Make audience-sensitive moves like this routinely, whenever you are composing.

However, sometimes it's not the content that you must modify for potential readers but their perceptions of you. They'll look at you differently according to the expertise you bring to the project. What are the options?

Suppose you are the expert. This may be the typical stance of most writers of professional reports, who smoothly present material they know well enough to teach. But knowledgeable people often make two common mistakes in presenting information. Either they assume an audience is as informed as they are, and so omit the very details and helpful transitions that many readers need, or they underestimate the intelligence of their readers and consequently bore them with trivial and unnecessary explanations. ○ Readers want a confident guide but also one who knows when—*and when not*—to define a term, provide a graph, or supply some context.

Suppose you are the novice. In a typical report for school, you're probably dealing with material relatively new to you. Your expertise on language acquisition in childhood may be only a book chapter and two journal articles thick, but you may still have to write ten pages on the topic to pass a psychology course. Moreover, not only do you have to provide information in a report, but you also have to convince an expert reader—your instructor—that you have earned the credentials to write about this subject.

Suppose you are the peer. For some reports, your peers may be your primary audience. That's especially true of oral presentations in class. You know that an instructor is watching your presentation and is probably grading the content—including your topic, organization, and sources. But that instructor may also be watching how well you adapt that material to the interests and capabilities of your classmates. ○

> Tips for Writing
> Credible Reports
>
> - Choose a serious subject you know you can research.
> - Model the project on professional reports in that area.
> - Select sources recognized in the field.
> - Document those sources correctly.
> - Use the discipline's technical vocabulary and conventions.

think visually
p. 557

respect your
readers p. 408

understand oral
reports p. 322

Finding and developing materials

▶ find
information

Once you have settled on a research topic and thesis, plan to spend time gathering data. You can start with reference works such as dictionaries and encyclopedias, but you need to move quickly to resources created or used by experts in the field, including scholarly books published by university presses, articles in academic journals, government reports (also known as white papers), oral histories, and so on. Look for materials that push you well beyond what you knew at the outset of the project. Such works may intimidate you at first, but that's a signal that you are learning something new—an outcome your instructor probably intended.

To get reports right, follow these basic principles.

Base reports on the best available sources.   You will embarrass yourself quickly if you don't develop procedures and instincts for evaluating sources. Look for materials—including data such as statistics and photographic reproductions—presented by reliable authors and experts and supported by major institutions in government, business, and the media. For academic papers, take your information whenever possible from journals and books published by university presses and professional organizations. ○

Need help finding relevant sources? See "How to Browse for Ideas" on pp. 338–39.

With Web materials, track them back to their original sources and then assess them. Use the Google search engine for "Korean War," for instance, and you might find an item that seems generic—except that its URL indicates a military location (.mil). Opening the URL, you discover that a government institution—the Naval Historical Center—supports the site. So its information is likely to be credible but will reflect the perspectives of the Department of the Navy. That's information you need to know as you read material from the site.

Base reports on multiple sources.   Don't rely on a limited or biased selection of material. You need not give equal weight to all ideas or points of view, but neither should you ignore important perspectives you disagree with. Above all, avoid the temptation to base a report on a single source, even one that is genuinely excellent. You may find yourself merely paraphrasing the material, not writing a report of your own. ○

find reliable
sources p. 451

restate ideas
p. 463

Fact-check your report.   It's a shame to get the big picture in focus in a report and then lose credibility because you slip up on a few easily verifiable facts. In a lengthy project, these errors might seem inevitable or just a nuisance. But misstatements can take on a life of their own and become lore—like the initial and exaggerated reports of crime and mayhem during Hurricane Katrina. So take the extra few minutes required to get the details right.

Some Online Sites for Locating Facts and Information

- **Bartleby.com: Great Books Online** Includes online versions of key reference and literary works, from *Gray's Anatomy* to the *Oxford Shakespeare*.
- **Biography.com** A collection of twenty-five thousand brief biographies, from Julius Caesar to Miley Cyrus.
- **FedStats** *The* site for finding information gathered by the federal government. Also check out USA.gov.
- **Internet Public Library** Provides links to material on most major academic fields and subjects. Includes reference collections as well.
- **The World Factbook** Check here for data about any country—compiled by the CIA.

Creating a structure

▶ organize
  information

How does a report work? Not like a shopping mall—where the escalators and aisles are designed to keep you wandering and buying, deliberately confused. Not like a mystery novel that leads up to an unexpected climax, or even like an argument, which steadily builds in power to a memorable conclusion. Instead, reports lay all their cards on the table right at the start and harbor no secrets. They announce what they intend to do and then do it, providing clear markers all along the way.

Clarity doesn't come easily; it only seems that way when a writer has been successful. You have to know a topic in depth to explain it to others. Then you need to choose a structure that supports what you want to say. Among patterns you might choose for drafting a report are the following, some of which overlap. ○

Organize by date, time, or sequence. Drafting a history report, you may not think twice about arranging your material chronologically: In 1958, the Soviet Union launched *Sputnik*, the first Earth satellite; in 1961, the Soviets launched a cosmonaut into Earth's orbit; in 1969, the United States put two men on the moon. This structure puts information into a relationship readers understand immediately as a competition. You'd still have blanks to fill in with facts and details to tell the story of the race to the moon, but a chronological structure helps readers keep complicated events in perspective.

By presenting a simple sequence of events, you can use time to organize reports involving many kinds of information, from the scores in football games to the movement of stock markets to the flow of blood through the human heart. ○

Organize by magnitude or order of importance. Many reports present their subjects in sequence, ranked from biggest to smallest (or vice versa), most important to least important, most common/frequent to least, and so on. Such structures assume, naturally, that you have already done the research to position the items you expect to present. At first glance, reports of this kind might seem tailored to the popular media: "Ten Best Restaurants in Seattle," "One Hundred Fattest American Cities." But you might also use such a framework to report on the disputed causes of a war, the multiple effects of a stock market crash, or even the factors responsible for a disease.

develop a
draft p. 367

shape your
work p. 374

Organize by division.   It's natural to arrange some reports by simply breaking a subject into its major parts. A report on the federal government, for example, might be organized by treating each of its three branches in turn: executive, legislative, and judicial. A report on the Elizabethan stage might examine the individual parts of a typical theater: the "heavens," the balcony, the stage wall, the stage, the pit, and so on. Of course, you'd then have to decide in what order to present the items, perhaps spatially or in order of importance. For example, you might use an illustration to clarify your report, working from top to bottom. Simple but effective.

Organize by classification.   Classification is the division of a group of concepts or items according to specified and consistent principles. Reports organized by classification are easy to set up when you borrow a structure that is already well established—such as those that follow.

- **Psychology** (by type of study): abnormal, clinical, comparative, developmental, educational, industrial, social
- **Plays** (by type): tragedy, comedy, tragicomedy, epic, pastoral, musical
- **Nations** (by form of government): monarchy, oligarchy, democracy, dictatorship
- **Passenger cars** (by engine placement): front engine, mid-engine, rear engine
- **Dogs** (by breed group): sporting, hound, working, terrier, toy, nonsporting, herding

A project becomes more challenging when you try to create a new system — perhaps to classify the various political groups on your campus or to describe the behavior of participants in a psychology experiment. But such inventiveness can be worth the effort.

Organize by position, location, or space.   Organizing a report spatially is a powerful strategy for arranging ideas—even more so today, given the ease with which material can be illustrated. **O** A map, for example, is a report organized by position and location. But it is only one type of spatial structure.

think visually
p. 557

You use spatial organization in describing a painting from left to right, a building from top to bottom, a cell from nucleus to membrane. A report on medical conditions might be presented most effectively via cutaways that expose different layers of tissues and organs. Or a report on an art exhibition might follow a viewer through a virtual 3-D gallery.

The Swan Theatre
The architectural layout of this Elizabethan theater, shown in this 1596 sketch by Johannes de Witt, might suggest the structure of a report describing the theater.

Organize by definition.   Typically, definitions begin by identifying an object by its "genus" and "species" and then listing its distinguishing features, functions, or variations. This useful structure is the pattern behind most entries in dictionaries, encyclopedias, and other reference works. Once the genus and species have been established, you can expand a definition through explanatory details: *Ontario* is a *province of Canada* between Hudson Bay and the Great Lakes. That's a good start, but what are its geographical features, history, products, and major cities—all the things that distinguish it from other provinces? You could write a book, let alone a report, based on this simple structure.

Organize by comparison/contrast.   You probably learned this pattern in the fourth grade, but that doesn't make comparison/contrast any less potent for college-level reports. ○ You compare and contrast to highlight distinctions that might otherwise not be readily apparent. Items are often compared one at a time or feature by feature.

The images here compare two important "technologies" for reading, the scroll (below) and the codex (right). For a report contrasting these devices with the electronic screens readers use today, see page 59. *Below:* Museo Archeologico Nazionale, Naples, Italy/De Agostini Picture Library/The Bridgeman Art Library. *Right:* Museo Lazaro Galdiano, Madrid, Spain/The Bridgeman Art Library.

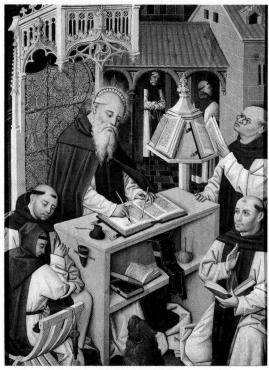

understand
evaluation p. 100

Organize by thesis statement.   Obviously, you have many options for organizing a report; moreover, a single report might use several structural patterns. So it helps if you explain early in a report what its method of organization will be. That idea may be announced in a single thesis sentence, a full paragraph (or section), or even a PowerPoint slide. ○

SENTENCE ANNOUNCES STRUCTURE

In the late thirteenth century, Native Puebloans may have abandoned their cliff dwellings for several related reasons, including an exhaustion of natural resources, political disintegration, and, most likely, a prolonged drought.

— Kendrick Frazier, *People of Chaco: A Canyon and Its Culture*

PARAGRAPH EXPLAINS STRUCTURE

In order to detect a problem in the beginning of life, medical professionals and caregivers must be knowledgeable about normal development and potential warning signs. Research provides this knowledge. In most cases, research also allows for accurate diagnosis and effective intervention. Such is the case with cri du chat syndrome (CDCS), also commonly known as cat cry syndrome.

— Marissa Dahlstrom, "Developmental Disorders: Cri du Chat Syndrome"

develop a
statement p. 362

Choosing a style and design

Reports are typically written in a formal or *high* style—free of contentious language that might make them sound like arguments. ○ To separate fact from opinion, scientific and professional reports usually avoid personal reflections as well as devices such as contractions and dialogue. Reports in newspapers, magazines, and even encyclopedias may be less formal: You might detect a person behind the prose. But the style will still strive for impartiality, signaling that the writer's opinions are (or, at least, *should* be) less important than the facts reported.

Why tone down the emotional, personal, or argumentative temper of the language in reports? It's a matter of audience. The moment readers suspect that you are twisting language to advocate an agenda or moving away from a sober presentation of facts, they will question the accuracy of your report. So review your drafts to see if a word or phrase might be sending the wrong signals to readers. Give your language the appearance of neutrality, balance, and thoughtfulness.

Present the facts cleanly.   Get right to the point and answer key questions directly: *Who? What? Where? When? How? Why?* Organize paragraphs around topic sentences so readers know what will follow. Don't go off on tangents. Keep the exposition controlled and focus on data. When you do, the prose will seem coolly efficient and trustworthy.

Keep out of it.   Write from a neutral, third-person perspective, avoiding the pronouns *I* and *you*. When perusing a report, readers usually don't care about the writer's personal opinion unless that writer's individual experiences are part of the story. But like all guidelines, this one has exceptions, and it certainly doesn't apply across the board to other genres of writing. Increasingly, even scientific and scholarly reports in some fields allow researchers to explain them-selves directly to readers—as you'll see in a model report on page 59.

Avoid connotative language.   Maintaining objectivity is not easy because language is rife with *connotations*—the powerful cultural associations that may surround words, enlarging their meanings and sometimes imposing value judgments. Connotations make *shadowy* and *gloomy* differ from *dark*; *porcine* and *tubby*, from *overweight*. What's more, the connotations of individual words are not the same for every reader. One person may have no problem

define your
style p. 400

with a term like *slums*, but another person living in *low-income housing* may beg to differ.

Given the hotbed of protest that writing can be, don't use loaded words when more neutral terms are available and just as accurate. Choose *confident*, not *overweening* or *pompous*; try *corporate official* rather than *robber baron*—unless, of course, the more colorful term fits the context. ○

Pay attention to elements of design.   Clear and effective design is particularly important in reports. ○ If your paper runs more than a few pages and can be divided into coherent parts, consider inserting headings to help readers appreciate its structure or locate information they need. Documents such as term papers and lab reports may even follow patterns and templates you need to use.

Many types of factual information are best presented graphically. This is especially the case with numbers and statistics. So don't hesitate to use charts, graphs, photos, illustrations, and also captions in your work. Software such as Microsoft Word allows you to create modest tables and simple graphics; you can generate more complex tables and graphs with software such as Excel, OmniGraffle or VectorDesigner. And remember that any visual items should be purposeful, not ornamental.

Many reports these days are, in fact, oral presentations that rely on presentation software such as PowerPoint, Keynote, or Prezi. You'll want to learn how to use these tools effectively.

improve your
sentences p. 412

think visually
p. 557

Examining models

FEATURE STORY In a lively feature item published in the *New York Times*, Lev Grossman outlines core differences between the three major forms the book has had over the past several millennia. Though an advocate for the familiar paper book — or codex — Grossman does a fascinating job explaining what's been gained and lost with each shift in technology. Arguably, the thesis of this piece is not stated until the final paragraph.

Reading the Genre Reports work especially well when they have "surprise value" — that is, they teach you something new. Take note of any new information you learn from Grossman's feature story. Do these details keep you reading?

From Scroll to Screen

Lev Grossman

> In a playful middle style, Grossman quickly identifies the topic.

Something very important and very weird is happening to the book right now: It's shedding its papery corpus and transmigrating into a bodiless digital form, right before our eyes. We're witnessing the bibliographical equivalent of the rapture. If anything we may be lowballing the weirdness of it all.

The last time a change of this magnitude occurred was circa 1450, when Johannes Gutenberg invented movable type. But if you go back further there's a more helpful precedent for what's going on. Starting in the first century AD, Western readers discarded the scroll in favor of the codex — the bound book as we know it today.

> Analogies here and throughout help readers understand key ideas.

In the classical world, the scroll was the book format of choice and the state of the art in information technology. Essentially it was a long, rolled-up piece of paper or parchment. To read a scroll you gradually unrolled it, exposing a bit of the text at a time; when you were done you had to roll it back up the right way, not unlike that other obsolete medium, the VHS tape. English is still littered with words left over from the scroll age. The first page of a scroll, which listed information about

---

e For an additional reading, see **macmillanhighered.com/howtowrite3e.**
e-readings > UNICEF, *Innovations for Child Health in Uganda* [VIDEO REPORT]

59

where it was made, was called the "protocol." The reason books are sometimes called volumes is that the root of "volume" is *volvere*, to roll: To read a scroll, you revolved it.

Scrolls were the prestige format, used for important works only: sacred texts, legal documents, history, literature. To compile a shopping list or do their algebra, citizens of the ancient world wrote on wax-covered wooden tablets using the pointy end of a stick called a stylus. Tablets were for disposable text — the stylus also had a flat end, which you used to squash and scrape the wax flat when you were done. At some point someone had the very clever idea of stringing a few tablets together in a bundle. Eventually the bundled tablets were replaced with leaves of parchment and thus, probably, was born the codex. But nobody realized what a good idea it was until a very interesting group of people with some very radical ideas adopted it for their own purposes. Nowadays those people are known as Christians, and they used the codex as a way of distributing the Bible.

One reason the early Christians liked the codex was that it helped differentiate them from the Jews, who kept (and still keep) their sacred text in the form of a scroll. But some very alert early Christian must also have recognized that the codex was a powerful form of information technology — compact, highly portable, and easily concealable. It was also cheap — you could write on both sides of the pages, which saved paper — and it could hold more words than a scroll. The Bible was a long book.

The codex also came with a fringe benefit: It created a very different reading experience. With a codex, for the first time, you could jump to any point in a text instantly, nonlinearly. You could flip back and forth between two pages and even study them both at once. You could cross-check passages and compare them and bookmark them. You could skim if you were bored, and jump back to reread your favorite parts. It was the paper equivalent of random-access memory, and it must have been almost supernaturally empowering. With a scroll you could only trudge through texts the long way, linearly. (Some ancients found temporary fixes for this bug — Suetonius apparently suggested that Julius Caesar created a proto-notebook by stacking sheets of papyrus one on top of another.)

Structure is chronological, augmented by comparisons.

Piece is thick with information.

Over the next few centuries the codex rendered the scroll all but obsolete. In his "Confessions," which dates from the end of the fourth century, St. Augustine famously hears a voice telling him to "pick up and read." He interprets this as a command from God to pick up the Bible, open it at random, and read the first passage he sees. He does so, the scales fall from his eyes, and he becomes a Christian. Then he book-marks the page. You could never do that with a scroll.

Right now we're avidly road-testing a new format for the book, just as the early Christians did. Over the first quarter of this year e-book sales were up 160 percent. Print sales — codex sales — were down 9 percent. Those are big numbers. But unlike last time it's not a clear-cut case of a superior technology displacing an inferior one. It's more complex than that. It's more about trade-offs.

On the one hand, the e-book is far more compact and portable than the codex, almost absurdly so. E-books are also searchable, and they're green, or greenish anyway (if you want to give yourself nightmares, look up the ecological cost of building a single Kindle). On the other hand the codex requires no batteries, and no electronic display has yet matched the elegance, clarity, and cool matte comfort of a printed page.

But so far the great e-book debate has barely touched on the most important feature that the codex introduced: the nonlinear reading that so impressed St. Augustine. If the fable of the scroll and codex has a moral, this is it. We usually associate digital technology with nonlinear-ity, the forking paths that Web surfers beat through the Internet's underbrush as they click from link to link. But e-books and nonlinearity don't turn out to be very compatible. Trying to jump from place to place in a long document like a novel is painfully awkward on an e-reader, like trying to play the piano with numb fingers. You either creep through the book incrementally, page by page, or leap wildly from point to point and search term to search term. It's no wonder that the rise of e-reading has revived two words for classical-era reading technologies: scroll and tablet. That's the kind of reading you do in an e-book.

The codex is built for nonlinear reading — not the way a Web surfer does it, aimlessly questing from document to document, but the way a deep reader does it, navigating the network of internal connections that

Transitions carefully mark passage of time.

Note how the paragraph structures an important comparison.

The novel *Cloud Atlas* connects six related stories.

exists within a single rich document like a novel. Indeed, the codex isn't just another format, it's the one for which the novel is optimized. The contemporary novel's dense, layered language took root and grew in the codex, and it demands the kind of navigation that only the codex provides. Imagine trying to negotiate the nested, echoing labyrinth of David Mitchell's *Cloud Atlas* if it were transcribed onto a scroll. It couldn't be done.

Final paragraph reveals the thesis of the report.

God knows, there was great literature before there was the codex, and should it pass away, there will be great literature after it. But if we stop reading on paper, we should keep in mind what we're sacrificing: that nonlinear experience, which is unique to the codex. You don't get it from any other medium — not movies, or TV, or music, or video games. The codex won out over the scroll because it did what good technologies are supposed to do: It gave readers a power they never had before, power over the flow of their own reading experience. And until I hear God personally say to me, "Boot up and read," I won't be giving it up.

INFOGRAPHIC   Infographics are visual reports designed to present data memorably and powerfully. If they do their job well, they can also make convincing arguments. So it should be no surprise that most of the infographics available on the official White House site carry partisan messages (see http://www.whitehouse.gov/share/infographics). Nonetheless, a government-sponsored item such as "Wind Technologies Market Report 2012," reproduced on the following page, can still be rich in basic facts and information—in this case helping readers to appreciate the accomplishments of a rapidly growing industry.

Reading the Genre   Study the infographic that follows, paying attention to the way it presents data about growth in the energy sector. Aside from presenting numbers and information, what messages do the designers of the relatively modest chart try to convey? What visual devices do its creators use to emphasize key points about wind energy? Why is it important that "Share on Facebook" and "Share on Twitter" buttons accompany this item when viewed online?

Wind Technologies Market Report 2012

America is home to one of the largest and fastest growing wind markets in the world. Here are a few of the major milestones achieved by the U.S. wind industry in 2012.

THE BIG PICTURE

Total U.S. wind power capacity surpassed 60 gigawatts (GW) -- enough to power more than 15 million homes every year.

RECORD BREAKING GROWTH

U.S. Wind power installations were more than **90% higher** than in 2011. With 13.1 GW of new capacity added, **the U.S. installed more wind capacity than any other country last year.**

BUILT TO LAST

72%

72% of turbine equipment installed at U.S. wind farms -- including blades, gears and generators -- was **made in America.**

WIND ALL-STARS

TX

IA   KS   SD

Texas added more new wind power capacity than any other state. In **South Dakota, Iowa and Kansas,** wind power contributes **more than 20%** of electricity generation.

VIABLE ENERGY

Wind power was the leading source of U.S. electric generating capacity additions in 2012 -- overtaking natural gas.

EVOLVING TECH

Since 1998, **average turbine capacity has increased by 170%.** Average nameplate capacity of wind turbines installed in 2012 stands at 1.94 megawatts.

JOB CREATOR

The wind sector employs more than 80,000 American workers -- from engineers to construction workers.

PRICING TRENDS

The price of wind sold under new contracts averaged **4 cents per kilowatt-hour** -- that's **50% lower than in 2009.**

© ENERGY.GOV

Infographic by Sarah Gerrity, Courtesy of the U.S. Department of Energy.

Assignments

1. **Research Report:** Susan Wilcox, author of "Marathons for Women" (p. 39), is a runner who turned a subject personally important to her into a fully documented academic paper of general interest. Write a similar factual report based on a serious topic from your major or on a subject you would like more people to know about. Narrow your subject to a specific claim you can explore in several pages. Use trustworthy sources and document them correctly.

2. **Feature Story:** As a novelist and book critic for *Time* magazine, Lev Grossman, the author of "From Scroll to Screen" (p. 59), obviously has an enthusiast's interest in writing about technologies that affect his livelihood. Identify a topic that has a comparable impact on you and write a fact-filled story of interest to general readers modeled upon Grossman's report. It can be from any area of interest, academic or not. Perhaps you wonder how developments in biomedical engineering might alter the sports you love. Or maybe you wonder what exactly a college campus might look like in the age of MOOCs. Do the necessary research and present what you learn to a general audience. Like Grossman, you may use first person in this report and, if you are adventurous, you might try holding off on your thesis or point until the final section or paragraph. Present any sources you use responsibly, mentioning them in the body of the paper or (if your instructor prefers) citing them in traditional academic form — see Susan Wilcox's research report on page 39.

3. **Infographic:** "Wind Technologies Market Report 2012" (p. 64) not only conveys information but also offers a perspective on a new technology. Using a data source such as FedStats, The World Factbook (see p. 51), or SportsStats.com, create a factual report based upon interesting or surprising statistics or information. Be creative, perhaps using statistics pertinent to your local environment or community. You can write a paper, create a slide presentation, or even try your hand at designing an infographic.

4. **Your Choice:** Identify a *controversial* topic you would love to know more about, choosing one that has at least two clearly defined and disputed sides. Do the necessary research to find out much more about the controversy, narrowing the matter down to manageable size for a paper or oral presentation. Then either prepare a written version of the report to submit to your instructor or an oral version to share with a wider audience, perhaps your classmates if you have the opportunity. In your report, explain the controversy *without taking sides*.

How to start

- Need a **topic**? See page 77.
- Need **support for your argument**? See page 83.
- Need to **organize your ideas**? See page 86.

3

Arguments

ask readers to consider debatable ideas

It doesn't take much to spark an argument these days—a casual remark, a political observation, a dumb joke that hurts someone's feelings. Loud voices and angry gestures may follow, leaving observers upset and frustrated. But arguments aren't polarizing or hostile by nature, not when people are more interested in generating light than heat offers them. Arguments should make us smarter and better able to deal with problems in the world. In fact, you probably make such constructive arguments all the time without raising blood pressures, at least not too much.

ARGUMENT TO ADVANCE A THESIS	In an op-ed for the local paper, you *argue for the thesis* that people who talk on cell phones while driving are a greater hazard than drunk drivers because they are more numerous and more callous.
REFUTATION ARGUMENT	In a term paper, you use facts and logic to *refute the argument* that students with college degrees will probably earn more in their lifetimes than students with only high school diplomas.
VISUAL ARGUMENT	Rather than write a letter to the editor about out-of-control salaries for NCAA football coaches, you create a *visual argument*—an editorial cartoon—suggesting that a local coach is paid more than the entire faculty.

DECIDING TO WRITE AN ARGUMENT.   Arguments come in many shapes to serve different purposes. Subsequent chapters in this section cover specialized genres of argument often assigned in the classroom, including *evaluations*, *proposals*, and *literary analyses* (for more on choosing a genre, see the Introduction). But even less formal arguments have distinctive features. In your projects, you'll aim to do the following.

Offer levelheaded and disputable claims.   You won't influence audiences by making points no one cares about. Something consequential should be at stake in an argument you offer for public consumption. Maybe you want to change reader's minds about an issue that everyone else thinks has been settled. Or maybe you want to shore up what people already believe. In either case, you need a well-defined point, either stated or implied, if you hope to influence the kind of readers worth impressing: thoughtful, levelheaded people. O

What claim does this ad from the Utah Department of Public Safety actually make? Might anyone dispute it? Do you find the ad effective visually? Utah Department of Highway Safety. Creative Director/Art Director: Ryan Anderson, Creative Director/Copywriter: Gary Sume, Account Supervisor: Peggy Lander, Agency Richter7.

develop a
statement p. 362

Offer good reasons to support a claim.   Without evidence and supporting reasons, a claim is just an assertion—and little better than a shout or a slogan. Slogans do have their appeal in advertising and politics. But they don't become arguments until they are backed by solid reasoning and a paper trail of evidence. No one said writing arguments is easy. Allow time for finding the facts.

Understand opposing claims and points of view.   You won't make a strong case of your own until you can *honestly* paraphrase ○ the logic of those who see matters differently. Many people find that tough to do because it forces them to consider alternative points of view. But you will seem more credible when you acknowledge these other *reasonable* opinions even as you refute them. When you face less than rational claims, rebut them calmly but firmly. Avoid the impulse to respond with an insult or a petty comment of your own.

Frame arguments powerfully—and not in words only.   Sensible opinions still have to dress for the occasion: You need the right words and images to move a case forward. ○ Fortunately, strategies for making effective arguments also cue you in to appeals that are less legitimate. We've all been seduced by claims just because they are stylish, hip, or repeated so often that they begin to seem true. But if such persuasion doesn't seem fair or sensible, that's all the more reason to reach for a higher standard in your own appeals.

restate ideas
p. 463

think visually
p. 557

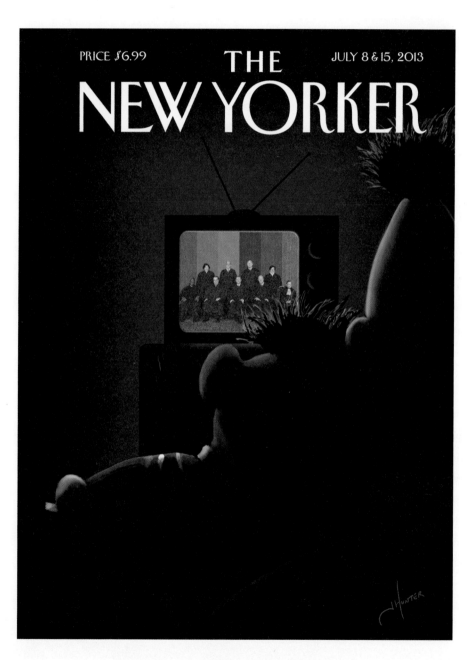

Immediately following a U.S. Supreme Court decision striking down federal prohibitions against same-sex marriage, the *New Yorker* — famous for its memorable covers — added another to its collection. Without a word, the magazine expressed its opinion of the ruling. What elements in the cover make it an argument? How might you phrase the claim it makes visually? © New Yorker Magazine/Jack Hunter/Condé Nast.

Here's an ingenious argument that Stefan Casso, a student in a college writing class, took on as a deliberate challenge: Could he defend a thesis that—to many of his colleagues—seemed indefensible? Aristotle defined rhetoric as the art of discovering all the available means of persuasion in a given case. That's exactly what Casso has to do here. You can decide—or maybe argue—how well he did his job.

Reading the Genre   As you read Casso's essay, try to identify those places where you are most aware of being moved by the author to consider claims that you hadn't considered before or had perhaps already rejected. Can you think of other arguments that Casso might have used to defend Lance Armstrong?

Casso 1

Stefan Casso

Rhetoric 325M

April 30, 2013

Worth the Lie

At age sixty-four, Barbara Grossman was diagnosed with
bone marrow cancer. With no family to help her face her
upcoming struggles, Barbara was scared. She would presumably
spend the remainder of her life alone in a hospital bed without
any emotional support. Then, just as she began giving up hope,
a ray of light pierced the abyss. In an adjacent hospital room,
Barbara had caught a glimpse of a poster depicting Lance
Armstrong—a cancer survivor—on his bicycle. She immediately
asked for pictures of the athlete to be displayed in her room as
well. After months of treatment and countless rounds of
chemotherapy, Barbara's cancer went into remission. In a letter

Casso 2

to Armstrong, as reported by ESPN's Brian Triplett, Barbara wrote, "I spent minutes, hours, weeks, and months getting inspiration from your pictures. . . . I was wondering if it would be possible to shake your hand and say thank you personally for the inspiration you gave me in fighting this dreaded disease called cancer!"

An emotional anecdote sets a context for the argument.

Browsing through a wide range of Lance Armstrong–related articles from early in this century, I discovered Barbara's account is not atypical. I found countless stories of cancer victims expressing gratitude toward Armstrong. Some attribute their recovery entirely to the inspiration they got from his uplifting story. Armstrong, diagnosed with testicular cancer at twenty-five, overcame all odds not only to beat the disease but also to become the greatest cyclist of all time. He soared to the top of his profession, winning seven straight Tours de France — a grueling race spanning twenty-one days and covering two thousand miles. As a result of his amazing performances, Lance Armstrong stole the hearts of millions, including my own, and became a living hero. But as is the case with many people placed high upon a pedestal, he fell back to earth. Hard.

The author makes a personal connection to the Lance Armstrong story, establishing his credibility or *ethos*.

After a decade of fervently denying the use of performance-enhancing drugs, Armstrong finally admitted on January 17, 2013, that he had used them. Human growth hormone, testosterone, cortisone, and blood transfusions were part of his doping regimen, a common practice for the vast majority of cyclists in

Casso 3

the years Armstrong was competing in the Tour de France. His

defamation suits against former friends like Frankie Andreu, who

testified to hearing Armstrong speak of using banned substances,

and hostile attacks against the U.S. Anti-Doping Agency for its

public suspicions were all just an elaborate charade. One big fat lie.

I'm not here to defend Armstrong's inexplicable cheating. Rules are

rules. But do I believe his lie was worth the subsequent backlash?

In this rare case, does the end justify the means? Absolutely.

Today on lancesupport.org, people are leaving comments of

encouragement for Lance Armstrong. There are pages and

pages of commentaries dated after his admission on January 17.

And many of them had me on the verge of tears. For these

people, Lance Armstrong is not a fraud, he's a hero:

> "Your story gave me hope and gave me confidence that
> cancer can be beat." —Kim
> "Reading your book gave us courage to carry on . . .
> discussing the Tour everyday with Dad kept him going."
> —Sonia
> "I am a cancer survivor and you were giving me
> courage when I needed it most . . . my hero forever."
> — Celou

Comment upon comment tells stories of how Armstrong

delivered hope when all seemed lost. His inspiring example

provided cancer patients with the courage to undergo painful

Casso uses a series of short sentences to make a controversial and bold claim.

Casso 4

treatments and the confidence to stay optimistic. It brought comfort to victims' families, who could dream of a day when their loved ones, too, could return to strength. His story even illustrated to people with no connection to cancer how perseverance and hard work could culminate in dreams. Armstrong had touched these people's lives, and nothing could now take that away.

In 2007, *USA Today* ranked Lance Armstrong as the eighth most influential person in the world over the past twenty-five years—beating the likes of Michael Jordan, Nelson Mandela, and Pope John Paul II. After he was struck by testicular cancer, his merely riding a bike around a park would have been inspirational, so it's clear why winning the Tour de France seven consecutive times raised him to a rock-star level. If he had confessed to taking performance-enhancing drugs after his first win, however, his influence would have been exponentially smaller. He would have given false hope to his fans and further diminished cancer victims' dreams of making full recoveries. People would have been left to look for a hero elsewhere. Maybe they never would have found him or her. Though it evolved from his lie, without Armstrong's inspiration, we might have lost people like Kim, Celou, and Sonia's dad from the disease.

Despite his lies (or maybe because of them), Lance Armstrong saved lives through his work with the Livestrong Foundation, launched in 2003. That year marked the fourth Tour

First means of persuasion is to cite evidence that Armstrong gave hope to cancer survivors.

Second line of argument is to consider the possible consequences of truth telling early on.

Casso 5

de France win for Lance Armstrong. This same year he was
given the Outstanding Male Athlete Award by the ESPYs, an
annual award show hosted by ESPN. Armstrong's fame and
influence had reached an all-time high. It marked the perfect
time to launch his foundation, which hit the ground running.
Millions of dollars poured in, and the Livestrong Foundation
quickly became a nationwide institution for cancer information
and support.

The Livestrong Foundation "unites, inspires, and empowers
people affected by cancer." The foundation provides support to
families dealing with the consequences of cancer. Foundation
members provide one-on-one dialogue with victims to ensure
their attitudes remain strong and positive. Unity, they believe, is
the key to fighting the disease. Additionally, the Livestrong
Foundation aims at enhancing knowledge about cancer. It hosts
numerous awareness-spreading events across the country,
resulting in plentiful donations that go directly to cancer
research. With total revenue of close to $36 million in 2011, the
Livestrong Foundation has established itself as one of the
leading cancer-support foundations in the world.

As would have been the case with the inspiration
Armstrong offered cancer victims, had he confessed to using
banned substances early on in his career, all of this charitable
work would have been erased. He simply would not have had
the money, prominence, or backing to create Livestrong.

Most fully developed line of argument focuses on legacy of Armstrong's Livestrong Foundation.

Moreover, it is important to note how Armstrong chose to spend his money. He could have easily kept it all, bought himself five beach houses, and tried his luck at becoming a movie star. Instead, Armstrong used his fame and fortune to give back to the community, much as John D. Rockefeller did—a perceived villain in his own time.

In the early 1900s, Rockefeller, owner of Standard Oil, was among the most hated entrepreneurs in America because of his monopolistic business methods. He eventually became the richest man America had ever produced. Like Armstrong, Rockefeller chose to use his riches not only for himself but also for noble purposes. He created the Rockefeller Foundation to promote public heath and the General Education Board to support education in impoverished areas. According to the Rockefeller Archive Center, his charitable donations reached over $540 million. Rockefeller is now remembered as much as a philanthropist as a businessman—and as one of the most respected men in American history. And soon Lance Armstrong may be reconsidered, too, as a man who, despite his faults, made a real difference in the world.

Lance Armstrong will have his critics. The way in which he deceived his sport, his fans, and his country is tough for anyone to defend. But ultimately, one should look at the results of it all. Armstrong's lies led to lives being saved, whether it was through his inspiration or his foundation. Armstrong will forever

A final line of argument involves an extended analogy.

Casso 7

be remembered for his contributions to society—if not by the
masses, then at least by the cancer survivors and victims'
families whom he touched. Armstrong's lie was undoubtedly
worth it. The end did justify the means.

Casso 8

Works Consulted

"John D. Rockefeller, 1839–1937." *Rockefeller Archive Center*.
    Rockefeller Archive Center, n.d. Web. 10 Apr. 2013.

Livestrong Foundation. *Livestrong Foundation*. Livestrong
    Foundation, n.d. Web. 17 Mar. 2013.

"Messages of Support." *Support for Lance*. Real Estate
    Webmasters, n.d. Web. 17 Mar. 2013.

Page, Susan. "Most Influential People." *USA Today*. USA Today,
    9 Sept. 2007. Web. 17 Mar. 2013.

Triplett, Brian. "Inspirations of Lance." *ESPN.com*. ESPN, 25 July
    2004. Web. 17 Mar. 2013.

Exploring purpose and topic

topic ◀

In a college assignment, you could be asked to write arguments about general topics related to courses, but you probably won't be told what your claims should be. That's your responsibility, based on your knowledge, experiences, and leanings. So choose subjects you genuinely care about—not issues the media or someone else defines as controversial. You'll do a more credible job defending your questionable choice *not* to wear a helmet when motorcycling than explaining, one more time, why the environment should concern us all. And if environmental matters do roil you, stake your claim on a well-defined ecological problem—perhaps from within your community—that you might actually influence by the power of your rhetoric. ○

If you really are stumped, the Yahoo! Directory's list of "Issues and Causes"—with topics from *abortion* to *zoos*—offers problems enough to keep pundits from MSNBC and Fox News buzzing to the end of the century. To find it, search "Society and Culture" or "Issues and Causes" on the site's main Web directory. ("Society and Culture" itself offers a menu of intriguing topic areas.) Once you have an issue or even a specific claim, your real work begins.

Learn much more about your subject. Your first task is to do basic library and online research to get a better handle on your topic—*especially* when you think you already have all the answers. Chances are, you don't.

State a preliminary claim, if only for yourself. Some arguments fail because writers never focus their thinking. They wander around vague topics, throwing out ideas or making contradictory assertions and leaving it to readers to assemble the random parts. To avoid this blunder, begin with a claim — a *complete* sentence that states a position you hope to defend. Such a statement will keep you on track as you explore a topic. Even a simple sentence helps:

> The college rankings published annually by *U.S. News & World Report* do more harm than good.

> People who oppose gay marriage don't know what they are talking about.

get an idea
p. 331

Arguments take many different forms, but finger-pointing is rarely a good persuasive tool. *Top:* Ghislain and Marie David de Lessy/The Image Bank/ Getty Images. *Bottom:* Courtesy of Dr. Susan Farrell.

Qualify your claim to make it reasonable.
As you learn more about a subject, revise your topic idea to reflect the complications you encounter. ◯ Your thesis will probably grow longer or take several sentences to explain, but the topic itself will actually narrow because of the specific issues you've identified. You'll also have less work to do, thanks to qualifying expressions such as *some, most, a few, often, under certain conditions, occasionally, when necessary,* and so on. Other qualifying expressions are highlighted below.

> The statistically unreliable college ratings published by *U.S. News & World Report* usually do more harm than good to students because some claim that they lead admissions officers to award scholarships on the basis of merit rather than need.

> Many conservative critics who oppose gay marriage unwittingly undermine their own core principles, especially monogamy and honesty.

Examine your core assumptions.   Claims may be supported by reasons and evidence, but they are based on assumptions. *Assumptions* are the principles and values upon which we base our beliefs and actions. Sometimes these assumptions are controversial and stand right out. At other times, they're so close to us, they seem invisible—they are part of the air we breathe. Expect to spend a paragraph defending any assumptions your readers might find questionable or controversial. ◯

think critically
p. 343

develop ideas
p. 383

CLAIM

The statistically unreliable college ratings published by *U.S. News & World Report* usually do more harm than good to students because some claim that they lead admissions officers to award scholarships on the basis of merit rather than need.

ASSUMPTION

Alleviating need in our society is more important than rewarding merit.
[Probably controversial]

CLAIM

Westerners should be more willing to defend their cultural values and intellectual achievements if they hope to defend freedom against its enemies.

ASSUMPTION

Freedom needs to be defended at all costs.
[Possibly controversial for some audiences]

CLAIM

Many conservative critics who oppose gay marriage unwittingly undermine their own core principles, especially monogamy and honesty.

ASSUMPTION

People should be consistent about their principles.
[Probably not controversial]

Your Turn Many writers have a tough time expressing their topic in a complete sentence. They will offer a tentative word or phrase or sentence fragment instead of making the commitment that a full sentence demands, especially one with subordinators and qualifiers that begin to tie their ideas together. So give it a try. Take a topic you might write about and turn it into a full-bore sentence that tells readers what your claim is and how you intend to support it.

Understanding your audience

Retailers know audiences. In fact, they go to great lengths to pinpoint the groups most likely to buy their fried chicken or hybrid cars. They then tailor their brand images and Web advertising to precisely those customers. You'll play to audiences the same way when you write arguments—if maybe a little less cynically.

Understand that you won't ever please everyone in a general audience, even if you write bland, colorless mush—because some readers will then regard you as craven and spineless. In fact, how readers imagine you, *as the person presenting an argument*, may determine their willingness to consider your claims at all.

Consider and control your ethos.   People who study persuasion describe the identity that writers create for themselves within an argument as their *ethos*—the voice and attitude they fashion to enhance their appeal. It is a powerful concept, worth remembering. Surely you notice when writers are coming across as, let's say, ingratiatingly confident or stupidly obnoxious. And don't you respond in kind, giving ear to the likable voice and dismissing the malicious one? A few audiences—like those for political blogs—may actually prefer a writer with a snarky ethos. But most readers respond better when writers seem reasonable, knowledgeable, and fair—neither insulting those who disagree with them nor making those who share their views embarrassed to have them on their side.

You can shape your ethos by adjusting the style, tone, and vocabulary of your argument: For instance, contractions can make you seem friendly (or too casual); an impressive vocabulary suggests that you are smart (or maybe just pompous); lots of name-dropping makes you seem hip (or perhaps pretentious). You may have to write several drafts to find a suitable ethos for a particular argument. ○ And, yes, your ethos may change from paper to paper, audience to audience.

revise and edit
p. 422

Your Turn   Chances are you have some favorite Web sites or blogs you consult daily. Choose one of those sites, find an entry in it that expresses the ethos of the contributor(s) or the site itself, and then analyze that ethos. Is the character of the site friendly and down-to-earth? Arrogant and authoritative? Serious and politically concerned? Point to specific features of the site that help create its ethos. If you don't consult blogs or Web sites, apply your analysis to a printed or oral text, perhaps an op-ed by a favorite columnist or a political speech by a public figure.

Consider self-imposed limits.   If you read newspapers and magazines that mostly confirm your own political views, you might be in for a wake-up call when you venture an opinion beyond your small circle of friends. Tread softly. There are good reasons why people don't talk politics at parties. When you do argue about social, political, or religious issues, be respectful of those who work from premises different from your own.

Consider the worlds of your readers.   When arguing about topics such as education, politics, art, economics, ethics, or even athletics, you'll quickly realize that people bring their entire lives into the discussion of such issues. Their views are shaped, in part, by their gender, race, ethnicity, sexual orientation, income, age, and upbringing—and more, and in ever-varying combinations. Dealing with such considerations, you should be sensitive but not gutless. ○

Men and women, for instance, whether straight or gay, may not inhabit quite the same worlds. But, even so, you shouldn't argue, either, as if all men and all women think the same way—or should.

People's lives are similarly defined by their economic situations—and the assumptions that follow from privilege, poverty, or something in between. Think it would be cool to have an outdoor pool on campus or a convenient

> Need help supporting your argument? See "How to Use the Writing Center" on pp. 354–55.

respect your
readers p. 408

new parking garage? You may find other students less willing than you to absorb the impact such proposals might have on their tuition. And if you intend to complain about fat cats, ridicule soccer moms, or poke fun at rednecks, is it because you can't imagine people different from you among your readers?

Obviously, age matters too: You'd write differently for children than for their parents on almost any subject, changing your style, vocabulary, and allusions. But consider that people of different ages really have lived different lives. Each generation grows up with shared attitudes, values, heroes, and villains. As a writer, you have to factor such considerations into the arguments you write.

Gender attitudes develop early, along with some argument strategies. Courtesy of Dr. Susan Farrell.

Finding and developing materials

You could write a book from the materials you'll collect researching some arguments. Since arguments often deal with current events and topics, start with a resource such as the Yahoo! Directory's "Issues and Causes" list mentioned earlier. Explore your subject, too, in *LexisNexis*, if your library gives you access to this huge database of newspaper articles. ○

develop support ◀

As you gather materials, though, consider how much space you have to make your argument. Sometimes a claim has to fit within the confines of a letter to the editor, an op-ed column in a local paper, or a fifteen-minute PowerPoint talk. Aristotle, still one of the best theorists on persuasion, thought arguments *should* be brief, with speakers limiting examples to the *minimum* necessary to make a case—no extra points for piling on. So gather big, and then select only the best stuff for your argument.

List your reasons. You'll come up with reasons to support your claim almost as soon as you choose a subject. Write those down. Then start reading and continue to list new reasons as they arise, not being too fussy at this point. Be careful to paraphrase these ideas so that you don't inadvertently plagiarize them later.

Then, when your reading and research are complete, review your notes and try to group the arguments that support your position. It's likely you'll detect patterns and relationships among these reasons, and an unwieldy initial list of potential arguments may be streamlined into just three or four—which could become the key reasons behind your claim. Study these points and look for logical connections or sequences. Readers will expect your ideas to converge on a claim or lead logically toward it. ○

Assemble your hard evidence. Gather examples, illustrations, quotations, and numbers to support each main point. Record these items as you read in some reliable way, keeping track of all bibliographical information (author, title, publication info, URL) just as you would when preparing a term paper—even if you aren't required to document your argument. You want that data on hand in case your credibility is challenged later.

If you borrow facts from a Web site, do your best to trace the information to its actual source. For example, if a blogger quotes statistics from the U.S. Department of Agriculture, find that table or graph on the USDA Web site itself and make sure the numbers reported are accurate. ○

> The whole is greater than the sum of its parts.

–Aristotle

Popperfoto/Getty Images.

refine your
search p. 442

shape your
work p. 374

analyze claims
and evidence p. 456

Cull the best quotations.   You've done your homework for an assignment, reading the best available sources. So prove it in your argument by quoting from them intelligently. Choose quotations that do one or more of the following:

- Put your issue in focus or context.
- Make a point with special power and economy.
- Support a claim or piece of evidence that readers might doubt.
- State an opposing point well.

Copy passages that appeal to you, but don't figure on using all of them. An argument that is a patchwork of quotations reads like a patchwork of quotations—which is to say, *boring.* Be sure to copy the quotations accurately and be certain you can document them. ○

Find counterarguments.   If you study a subject thoroughly, you'll come across plenty of honest disagreement. List all reasonable objections you can find to your claim, either to your basic argument or to any controversial evidence you expect to cite. When possible, cluster these objections to reduce them to a manageable few. Decide which you must refute in detail, which you might handle briefly, and which you can afford to dismiss. ○

Watch, for example, how in an editorial, the *New York Times* anticipates objections to its defense of a *Rolling Stone* magazine cover (August 2013) featuring accused Boston Marathon bomber Dzhokhar Tsarnaev. The *Times* concedes that merchants and consumers alike might resist the cover, but then it counterpunches:

> Stores have a right to refuse to sell products because, say, they are unhealthy, like cigarettes. . . . Consumers have every right to avoid buying a magazine that offends them, like *Guns & Ammo* or *Rolling Stone.*
>
> But singling out one magazine issue for shunning is over the top, especially since the photo has already appeared in a lot of prominent places, including the front page of this newspaper, without an outcry. As any seasoned reader should know, magazine covers are not endorsements.
>
> — The Editorial Board, "Judging Rolling Stone by Its Cover," *New York Times*, July 18, 2013

understand citation
styles p. 470

develop ideas
p. 383

Consider emotional appeals. Feelings play a powerful role in many arguments, a fact you cannot afford to ignore when a claim you make stirs people up. Questions to answer about possible emotional appeals include the following:

- What emotions might be effectively raised to support my point?

- How might I responsibly introduce such feelings: through words, images,
- color, sound?

- How might any feelings my subject arouses work contrary to my claims or reasons?

Well-chosen visuals add power to an argument. A writer trying to persuade readers not to buy fur might include this photo in an article. How would this image influence you, as a reader? Jeff Foott/Discovery Channel Images/Getty Images.

Creating a structure

▶ organize ideas

It's easy to sketch a standard structure for arguments: one that leads from claim to supporting reasons to evidence and even accommodates a counterargument or two.

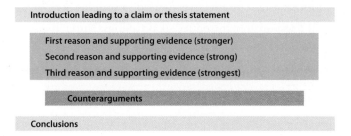

The problem is that you won't read many effective arguments, either in or out of school, that follow this template. The structure isn't defective, just too simple to describe the way arguments really move when ideas matter. You won't write a horrible paper if you use the traditional model because all the parts will be in place. Thesis? Check. Three supporting reasons? Check. Counterarguments? Check. But you will sound exactly like what you are: A writer going through the motions instead of engaging with ideas. Here's how to get your ideas to breathe in an argument—while still hitting all the marks.

Make a point or build toward one.   Arguments can unfurl just as reports do, with unmistakable claims followed by reams of supporting evidence. But they can also work like crime dramas, in which the evidence in a case builds toward a compelling conclusion—your thesis perhaps. This is your call. ○ But don't just jump into a claim: Take a few sentences or paragraphs to set up the situation. Quote a nasty politician or tell an eye-popping story or two. Get readers invested in what's to come.

Spell out what's at stake.   When you write an argument, you initiate a controversy, so you'd better explain it clearly—as Stefan Casso does in "Worth the Lie" earlier in this chapter. Do you hope to fix a looming problem? Then describe your concern and make readers share it. Do you intend to correct a false notion or bad reporting? Then tell readers why setting the record straight matters. Appalled by the apathy of voters, the dangers of global warming, the infringements of free speech on campus? Explain why readers should care. ○

order ideas
p. 377

develop a statement
p. 362

Address counterpoints when necessary, not in a separate section.
Necessary is when your readers start thinking to themselves, "Yeah, but what
about . . . ?" Such doubts will probably surface approximately where your own
do—and, admit it, you have some misgivings about your argument. So take them
on. Strategically, it rarely makes sense to consign all objections to a lengthy section near the end of a paper. That's asking for trouble. Do you really want to offer
a case for the opposition just when your readers are finishing up? On the plus
side, dealing with opposing arguments (or writing a refutation itself—see p. 92)
can be like caffeine for your prose, sharpening your attention and reflexes.

Save your best arguments for the end.   Of course, you want strong
points throughout the paper. But you need a high note early on to get readers interested and then another choral moment as you finish to send them
out the door humming. If you must summarize an argument, don't let a dull
recap of your main points squander an important opportunity to influence
readers. End with a rhetorical flourish that reminds readers how compelling
your arguments are. ○

A pithy phrase, an ironic twist, and a question to contemplate can also lock
down your case. Here's Maureen Dowd, bleakly—and memorably—concluding
an argument defending the job journalists had done covering the Iraq War:

> Journalists die and we know who they are. We know they liked to cook and play
> Scrabble. But we don't know who killed them, and their killers will never be
> brought to justice. The enemy has no face, just a finger on a detonator.

—"Live from Baghdad: More Dying," *New York Times*, May 31, 2006

shape an
ending p. 391

Choosing a style and design

Arguments vary widely in style. An unsigned editorial you write to represent the opinion of a student newspaper might sound formal and serious. Composing an op-ed under your own name, you'd probably ease up on the dramatic metaphors and allow yourself more personal pronouns. Arguing a point in an alternative magazine, you might even slip into the lingo of its vegan or survivalist subscribers. Routine adjustments like these really matter when you need to attract and hold readers.

You should also write with sensitivity since some people reading arguments may well be wavering, defensive, or eager to be offended. There's no reason to distract them with fighting words if you want to offer a serious argument. Here's how political commentator Ann Coulter described a politically active group of 9/11 widows who she believed were using their status to shield their anti–Iraq War opinions from criticism:

> These broads are millionaires, lionized on TV and in articles about them, reveling in their status as celebrities and stalked by grief-arazzis. I have never seen people enjoying their husbands' deaths so much.
>
> — *Godless: The Church of Liberalism* (2006)

Any point Coulter might make simply gets lost in the viciousness of the attack.

There are many powerful and aggressive ways to frame an argument without resorting to provocative language or fallacies of argument. ○ Some of these strategies follow.

Invite readers with a strong opening.   Arguments—like advertisements—are usually discretionary reading. People can turn away the moment they grow irritated or bored. So you may need to open with a little surprise or drama. Try a blunt statement, an anecdote, or a striking example if it helps—maybe an image too. Or consider personalizing the lead-in, giving readers a stake in the claim you are about to make. The following is a remarkable opening paragraph from an argument by Malcolm Gladwell on the wisdom of banning dogs by breed. When you finish, ask yourself whether Gladwell has earned your attention. Would you read the rest of the piece?

> One afternoon last February, Guy Clairoux picked up his two-and-a-half-year-old son, Jayden, from day care and walked him back to their house in the west end of Ottawa, Ontario. They were almost home. Jayden was straggling behind, and, as his father's back was turned, a pit bull jumped over a backyard fence

avoid fallacies
p. 343

and lunged at Jayden. "The dog had his head in its mouth and started to do this shake," Clairoux's wife, JoAnn Hartley, said later. As she watched in horror, two more pit bulls jumped over the fence, joining in the assault. She and Clairoux came running, and he punched the first of the dogs in the head, until it dropped Jayden, and then he threw the boy toward his mother. Hartley fell on her son, protecting him with her body. "JoAnn!" Clairoux cried out, as all three dogs descended on his wife. "Cover your neck, cover your neck." A neighbor, sitting by her window, screamed for help. Her partner and a friend, Mario Gauthier, ran outside. A neighborhood boy grabbed his hockey stick and threw it to Gauthier. He began hitting one of the dogs over the head, until the stick broke. "They wouldn't stop," Gauthier said. "As soon as you'd stop, they'd attack again. I've never seen a dog go so crazy. They were like Tasmanian devils." The police came. The dogs were pulled away, and the Clairouxes and one of the rescuers were taken to the hospital. Five days later, the Ontario legislature banned the ownership of pit bulls. "Just as we wouldn't let a great white shark in a swimming pool," the province's attorney general, Michael Bryant, had said, "maybe we shouldn't have these animals on the civilized streets."

— "Troublemakers," *New Yorker*, February 6, 2006

Write vibrant sentences.   You can write arguments full throttle, using a complete range of rhetorical devices, from deliberate repetition and parallelism to dialogue and quotation. Metaphors, similes, and analogies fit right in too. The trick is to create sentences rich enough to keep readers hooked, yet lean enough to advance an argument. In the following three paragraphs, follow the highlighting to see how Thomas L. Friedman uses parallelism and one intriguing metaphor after another to argue in favor of immigration legislation after witnessing the diversity in a high school graduation class in Maryland. ○

There is a lot to be worried about in America today: a war in Iraq that is getting worse not better, an administration whose fiscal irresponsibility we will be paying for for a long time, an education system that is not producing enough young Americans skilled in math and science, and inner cities where way too many black males are failing. We must work harder and get smarter if we want to maintain our standard of living.

But if there is one reason to still be optimistic about America it is represented by the stunning diversity of the Montgomery Blair class of 2006. America is still the world's greatest human magnet. We are not the only country that

improve your sentences p. 412

embraces diversity, but there is something about our free society and free
market that still attracts people like no other. Our greatest asset is our ability to
still cream off not only the first-round intellectual draft choices from around
the world but the low-skilled, high-aspiring ones as well, and that is the main
reason that I am not yet ready to cede the twenty-first century to China. Our
Chinese will still beat their Chinese.

This influx of brainy and brawny immigrants is our oil well — one that
never runs dry. It is an endless source of renewable human energy and
creativity. Congress ought to stop debating gay marriage and finally give us a
framework to maintain a free flow of legal immigration.

— "A Well of Smiths and Xias," *New York Times*, June 7, 2006

Ask rhetorical questions.   The danger of rhetorical questions is that they
can seem stagy and readers might not answer them the way you want. But
the device can be very powerful in hammering a point home. Good questions
also invite readers to think about an issue in exactly the terms that a writer
prefers. Here's George Will using rhetorical questions to conclude a piece on
global warming:

In fact, the earth is always experiencing either warming or cooling. But suppose
the scientists and their journalistic conduits, who today say they were so
spectacularly wrong so recently, are now correct. Suppose the earth is warming
and suppose the warming is caused by human activity. Are we sure there will
be proportionate benefits from whatever climate change can be purchased at
the cost of slowing economic growth and spending trillions? Are we sure the
consequences of climate change — remember, a thick sheet of ice once
covered the Midwest — must be bad? Or has the science-journalism complex
decided that debate about these questions, too, is "over"?

— "Let Cooler Heads Prevail," *Washington Post*, April 2, 2006

Use images and design to make a point.   If we didn't know it already
(and we did), the video and photographic images from 9/11, the *Deepwater
Horizon* oil spill in the Gulf of Mexico, or the 2012–13 political protests in
Egypt clearly prove that persuasion doesn't occur by words only. We react
powerfully to what we see with our own eyes. Consider this image from the
Associated Press of gay rights activists at a rally in St. Petersburg, Russia. The

Associated Press/Dmitry Lovetsky.

accompanying caption pointed out that police both guarded and detained activists, who were outnumbered by anti-gay protesters at the authorized gay rights rally. This image and others like it sparked debate on Russia's legislation targeting gay people and the personal safety of gay Russians.

And yet words still play a part because most images become *focused* arguments only when accompanied by commentary—as commentators routinely prove when they put a spin on news photographs or video. And because digital technology now makes it so easy to incorporate nonverbal media into texts, whether on a page, screen, or Prezi whiteboard, you should always consider how just the right image might enhance the case you want to make. **O**

think visually
p. 557

Examining models

REFUTATION ARGUMENT   An important subgenre of arguments is the refutation, a piece that takes apart someone else's claims and sometimes seeks to correct them. In the following example of this engaging but prickly form, Bjørn Lomborg, author of *The Skeptical Environmentalist* (2001), explains where and how an influential environmental study went awry and the consequences of what he perceives as its errors. Needless to say, a refutation is, itself, an argument that deserves careful scrutiny.

Reading the Genre   How did readers on *Slate.com* (where this argument was posted) react to Lomborg's refutation of *The Limits of Growth*? Spend some time checking those responses at www.slate.com/authors.bjrn_lomborg.html or, on your own, speculate how and where critics might take issue with Lomborg.

The Limits of Panic

BJØRN LOMBORG

We often hear how the world as we know it will end, usually through ecological collapse. Indeed, more than forty years after the Club of Rome released the mother of all apocalyptic forecasts, *The Limits to Growth*, its basic ideas are still with us. But time has not been kind.

The Limits to Growth warned humanity in 1972 that devastating collapse was just around the corner. But, while we have seen financial panics since then, there have been no real shortages or productive breakdowns. Instead, the resources generated by human ingenuity remain far ahead of human consumption.

But the report's fundamental legacy remains: We have inherited a tendency to obsess over misguided remedies for largely trivial problems, while often ignoring big problems and sensible remedies.

In the early 1970s, the flush of technological optimism was over, the Vietnam War was a disaster, societies were in turmoil, and economies were stagnating. Rachel Carson's 1962 book *Silent Spring* had raised fears about pollution and launched the modern environmental movement; Paul Ehrlich's 1968 title *The Population Bomb* said it all. The first Earth Day, in 1970, was deeply pessimistic.

Opening paragraphs outline Lomborg's intention to critique the legacy of *The Limits of Growth*.

92

For an additional reading, see **macmillanhighered.com/howtowrite3e.**
e-readings > 5 Gyres, *Understanding Plastic Pollution through Exploration, Education, and Action*
[INTERACTIVE WEB SITE]

The author summarizes his take on *The Limits of Growth*.

The genius of *The Limits to Growth* was to fuse these worries with fears of running out of stuff. We were doomed, because too many people would consume too much. Even if our ingenuity bought us some time, we would end up killing the planet and ourselves with pollution. The only hope was to stop economic growth itself, cut consumption, recycle, and force people to have fewer children, stabilizing society at a significantly poorer level.

That message still resonates today, though it was spectacularly wrong. For example, the authors of *The Limits to Growth* predicted that before 2013, the world would have run out of aluminum, copper, gold, lead, mercury, molybdenum, natural gas, oil, silver, tin, tungsten, and zinc.

Instead, despite recent increases, commodity prices have generally fallen to about a third of their level 150 years ago. Technological innovations have replaced mercury in batteries, dental fillings, and thermometers: Mercury consumption is down 98 percent and, by 2000, the price was down 90 percent. More broadly, since 1946, supplies of copper, aluminum, iron, and zinc have outstripped consumption, owing to the discovery of additional reserves and new technologies to extract them economically.

Throughout the refutation, statistics play a major role.

Similarly, oil and natural gas were to run out in 1990 and 1992, respectively; today, reserves of both are larger than they were in 1970, although we consume dramatically more. Within the past six years, shale gas alone has doubled potential gas resources in the United States and halved the price.

As for economic collapse, the Intergovernmental Panel on Climate Change estimates that global GDP per capita will increase 14-fold over this century and 24-fold in the developing world.

Lomborg speculates on why predictions in *The Limits of Growth* went awry.

The Limits of Growth got it so wrong because its authors overlooked the greatest resource of all: our own resourcefulness. Population growth has been slowing since the late 1960s. Food supply has not collapsed (1.5 billion hectares of arable land are being used, but another 2.7 billion hectares are in reserve). Malnourishment has dropped by more than half, from 35 percent of the world's population to under 16 percent.

Nor are we choking on pollution. Whereas the Club of Rome imagined an idyllic past with no particulate air pollution and happy farmers, and a future strangled by belching smokestacks, reality is entirely the reverse.

In 1900, when the global human population was 1.5 billion, almost 3 million people—roughly one in 500—died each year from air pollution, mostly from wretched indoor air. Today, the risk has receded to one death per 2,000 people. While pollution still kills more people than malaria does, the mortality rate is falling, not rising.

Nonetheless, the mind-set nurtured by *The Limits to Growth* continues to shape popular and elite thinking.

Consider recycling, which is often just a feel-good gesture with little environmental benefit and significant cost. Paper, for example, typically comes from sustainable forests, not rain forests. The processing and government subsidies associated with recycling yield lower-quality paper to save a resource that is not threatened.

Likewise, fears of overpopulation framed self-destructive policies, such as China's one-child policy and forced sterilization in India. And, while pesticides and other pollutants were seen to kill off perhaps half of humanity, well-regulated pesticides cause about 20 deaths each year in the United States, whereas they have significant upsides in creating cheaper and more plentiful food.

Indeed, reliance solely on organic farming—a movement inspired by the pesticide fear—would cost more than $100 billion annually in the United States. At 16 percent lower efficiency, current output would require another 65 million acres of farmland—an area more than half the size of California. Higher prices would reduce consumption of fruits and vegetables, causing myriad adverse health effects (including tens of thousands of additional cancer deaths per year).

Obsession with doom-and-gloom scenarios distracts us from the real global threats. Poverty is one of the greatest killers of all, while easily curable diseases still claim 15 million lives every year—25 percent of all deaths.

The solution is economic growth. When lifted out of poverty, most people can afford to avoid infectious diseases. China has pulled more than 680 million people out of poverty in the last three decades, leading a worldwide poverty decline of almost 1 billion people. This has created massive improvements in health, longevity, and quality of life.

> *The author blames questionable policies on assumptions The Limits of Growth fostered.*

> *Readers are pounded with numbers and statistics.*

> *Lomborg ends the refutation with recommendations of his own.*

The four decades since *The Limits of Growth* have shown that we need more of it, not less. An expansion of trade, with estimated benefits exceeding $100 trillion annually toward the end of the century, would do thousands of times more good than timid feel-good policies that result from fearmongering. But that requires abandoning an antigrowth mentality and using our enormous potential to create a brighter future.

VISUAL ARGUMENT   Matt Bors is angry and he's not going to take it anymore, or at least that's the tenor of his "Can We Stop Worrying about Millennials Yet?"—a multipanel visual argument that appeared under the "Opinion" tab of CNN's Web site on July 9, 2013. Bors, a thirtyish, Pulitzer Prize–nominated editorial cartoonist, mocks complaints made about his generation—one that reached adulthood around the turn of the century and then ran smack into the Great Recession. Who can blame him for being ticked off?

Reading the Genre   Compare the aggressive and detailed (almost "busy") arguments Matt Bors makes in his multiple cartoon panels to the calm and wordless argument made by the *New Yorker* cover on page 69. Could you turn Bors's multipanel argument into a single image? How might it differ in aim and impact? Or would it be more interesting to translate the visual argument into a conventional essay or editorial? Consider, for example, how a written text might recreate the sarcasm in Bors's drawings. ▶

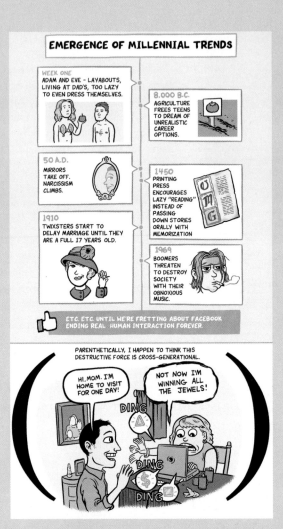

All images pages 96–98: Matt Bors.

PEAK MILLENNIAL SLANDER OCCURRED WITH **TIME**'S JUNE 2013 COVER STORY "THE ME ME ME GENERATION." THEY WERE LATE TO THE GEN Y-BASHING PARTY, BUT THEIR TROLLING STANDS OUT AS EXEMPLARY.

CHOICE QUOTE:

"Not only do millennials lack the kind of empathy that allows them to feel concerned for others, but they even have trouble even intellectually understanding others' points of view."

TRACKING THESE STORIES IS MADDENING. I WAS RECOVERING FROM THE TIME STORY WHEN I CAME ACROSS A WASHINGTON POST TREND PIECE THAT SEEMED TO BE A PARODY OF SOMETHING YOU WRITE WHEN YOU HAVE A DEADLINE IN THREE HOURS AND NOTHING TO SAY.

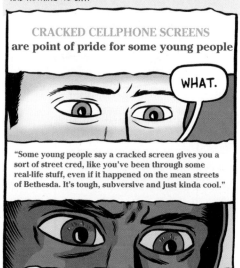

CRACKED CELLPHONE SCREENS
are point of pride for some young people

WHAT.

"Some young people say a cracked screen gives you a sort of street cred, like you've been through some real-life stuff, even if it happened on the mean streets of Bethesda. It's tough, subversive and just kinda cool."

SUDDENLY, I WAS RAGE-READING MILLENNIAL TREND PIECES EVERY DAY. PERHAPS A NEW TREND DESERVING OF ITS OWN PROFILE?

Rage Read

The new, hip thing for Gen Me? Fuming over trend pieces about themselves. "I hate you. Please stop," cartoonist Matt Bors demanded. "Stop writing this story immediately."

Enough.

IT'S TIME TO STOP WRITING GARBAGE ARTICLES ABOUT TWEETING AND TIGHT T-SHIRTS. EDITORS WHO STOP ASSIGNING TREND PIECES ON MILLENNIALS SHOULD ALL GET TROPHIES. (TO HELP DEVELOP THEIR POOR SELF-ESTEEM.)

THE STORY ABOUT YOUNG PEOPLE ISN'T WHICH COMPANY'S MARKETING PLATFORM WE'RE POSTING UPDATES ON.

THE STATUS UPDATE IS:

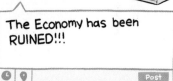

The Economy has been RUINED!!!

Post

MILLENNIALS AREN'T MARRYING, BUYING HOUSES, AND HAVING KIDS LATER THAN PREVIOUS GENERATIONS BECAUSE THEY'RE SITTING AROUND TRYING TO BEAT A VIDEO GAME. THEY'RE "DELAYING ADULTHOOD" BECAUSE THE JOB MARKET IS THE WORST IT'S BEEN SINCE THE GREAT DEPRESSION.

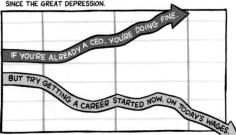

IF YOU'RE ALREADY A CEO, YOU'RE DOING FINE.

BUT TRY GETTING A CAREER STARTED NOW. ON TODAY'S WAGES.

WE ARE SAID TO BE ENTITLED. WE THINK WE DESERVE SOMETHING, THAT THE WORLD SHOULD HAND US SOMETHING FOR BEING HERE. WE DO. LIKE JOBS. (ARE THERE THOSE YET?) WE'RE CERTAINLY ENTITLED TO UNPAID JOBS – "INTERNSHIPS" AS THE SCAM IS KNOWN. BUT SOME OF US NEED MONEY BECAUSE STUDENT LOANS CAN'T BE PAID OFF WITH AIR.

AND THE PRICE OF EDUCATION IS A BIT HIGH THESE DAYS. SO IF YOU SAY:

IN MY DAY, WE WORKED A SUMMER JOB TO PAY FOR COLLEGE!

YOU SHOULD GET A PALLET OF $1 TRILLION IN STUDENT LOAN DEBT DROPPED ON YOUR HEAD.

IT'S PROBABLY NOT YOUR FAULT. YOU'RE PROBABLY STRUGGLING TOO. (IF YOU'RE A POLITICIAN OR INVESTMENT BANKER READING THIS, IGNORE WHAT I JUST SAID.)

MOST ECONOMIC GAINS SINCE THE RECOVERY WERE VACUUMED UP BY THE 1 PERCENT– NOT THE KIDS.

SO INSTEAD OF CONDESCENDING TO THE PEOPLE WHO WILL CARE FOR YOU WHEN YOU'RE DYING, MAYBE YOU CAN HELP NOT SHRED OUR SOCIAL SECURITY BENEFITS?

UNITED STATES TREASURY

STOP HATING ON MILLENNIALS. WE DIDN'T CREATE THIS MESS. WE CAME LATE TO THE BANQUET AND WERE SERVED UP CRUMBS.

WHICH WE WILL INSTAGRAM BEFORE WE EAT.

#YUM

1. **Argument to Advance a Thesis:** Review the way Stefan Casso supports a clearly stated and controversial thesis in "Worth the Lie" (p. 70). Then write an argument that similarly provides direct support for a controversial claim in the public sphere — one that has implications for other people. Like Casso, take the time to explain the issue you are addressing and then try to offer multiple reasons to support your thesis.

2. **Refutation Argument:** Find a text with which you strongly disagree and then systematically refute it, as Bjørn Lomborg does in "The Limits of Panic" (p. 92). The text can be a position or policy promoted by a politician or public or corporate official, or it can be an argument in itself — a column, an editorial, or even a section in a textbook. Make your opposition clear, but also be fair to the position you are attempting to refute. It is especially important that your readers be able to understand whatever you are analyzing, even if they aren't familiar with it. That's a real challenge, so don't hesitate to summarize, paraphrase, or quote from the material.

3. **Visual Argument:** Study the way Matt Bors incorporates a wide range of persuasive devices in his visual argument (p. 95); he uses everything from direct quotations to stereotypes. Like many visual arguments, his piece combines images and words to make a point. Create a visual argument of your own using whatever medium you believe will convey your message most powerfully. Start with a clear point in mind ("Stop hating on Millennials!"). Then figure out how to present your claim memorably.

4. **Your Choice:** These days, most serious arguments explode across interactive online environments, where they often take on a life of their own. Working with a group, design a media project (blog, Web site, mash-up, video, etc.) to focus on an issue that members of your group believe deserves more attention. Pool your talents to develop the site technically, rhetorically, and visually. Be sure your project introduces the subject, explains its purpose, encourages interaction, and includes relevant images and, if possible, links.

How to start
- Need a **topic**? See page 106.
- Need **criteria for your evaluation**? See page 109.
- Need to **organize your criteria and evidence**? See page 112.

4 Evaluations

make a claim about the merit of something

Evaluations and reviews are so much a part of our lives that you might notice them only when they are specifically assigned. Commentary and criticism of all sorts just happen.

ARTS REVIEW
You're never shy about sharing your opinions of movies, films, and restaurants, but you find it painful when you have to write an *arts review* of *Götterdämmerung* for a music appreciation course. The opera lasts longer than a football game!

SOCIAL SATIRE
Tired of self-righteous cyclists who preach eco-fundamentalism and then clog traffic with monthly Critical Mass rides, you do what any irate citizen would—you mock them in a *social satire*.

PRODUCT REVIEW
Given your work experience at a camera store, you are invited to write a *product review* for a co-op newsletter about cell phone cameras.

DECIDING TO WRITE AN EVALUATION.   It's one thing to offer an opinion, yet it's an entirely different matter to back up a claim with reasons and evidence. Only when you do will readers (or listeners) take you seriously. But you'll also have to convince them that you know *how* to evaluate a book, a social policy, a cultural trend, or even a cup of coffee by reasonable criteria. It helps if you can use objective standards to make judgments, counting or measuring varying degrees of excellence. But perhaps more often, evaluations involve people debating matters of taste—an act that draws good sense and wit into the mix. Here's how to frame this kind of argument (for more on choosing a genre, see the Introduction).

Explain your mission.   Just what do you intend to evaluate and for whom? Maybe you'll assess or rank particular products, productions, or performances or challenge opinions others have offered about them. Or maybe you want to turn social critic, making people aware of their failures or foibles. Or perhaps you see yourself as a sports pundit or fashion guru. You need to share your intentions and credentials with readers.

Every four years at the Summer Olympics, judges decide who gets a medal in gymnastics. Associated Press/Gregory Bull.

Establish and defend criteria.   *Criteria* are the standards by which objects are measured: *A good furnace should heat a home quickly and efficiently. Successful presidents leave office with the country in better shape than when they entered.* When readers are likely to share your criteria, you need to explain little about them. But when readers might object, prepare to defend your principles. ○ And sometimes you'll break new ground—as happened when critics first asked, *What is good Web design?* or *Which are the most significant social networks?* In such cases, criteria of evaluation had to be invented, explained, and defended.

Offer convincing evidence.   Evidence makes the connection between an opinion and the criteria of evaluation that support it. It comes in many forms: facts, statistics, testimony, photographs, and even good sense and keen observations. If good furnaces heat homes quickly and efficiently, then you'd have to supply data to show that a product you judged faulty didn't meet those minimal standards. (It might be noisy and unreliable to boot.)

Offer worthwhile advice.   Some evaluations are just for fun: Consider all the hoopla that arguments about sports rankings generate. But done right, most evaluations and reviews provide usable information, beneficial criticism, or even ranked choices—think restaurant or entertainment reviews on Yelp.

develop ideas
p. 383

People rely on critics of every kind of entertainment to help them decide what to read, watch, see, or hear. For many years, readers of *Entertainment Weekly* turned to Lisa Schwarzbaum for film reviews. Appraising the first of the *Hunger Games* movies, she has to accommodate avid fans of Suzanne Collins's books, as well as moviegoers entirely new to the dystopian trilogy. Both are tough audiences.

Reading the Genre   At the end of her review, you'll see that Schwarzbaum gives the movie a letter grade. Is it consistent with the full review? What role do symbols such as grades, stars, or even thumbs play in this genre?

Entertainment Weekly

Posted: April 3, 2012
Reviewed by: Lisa Schwarzbaum

The Hunger Games

Young people, selected by lottery, slaughter one another with kill-or-be-killed desperation in *The Hunger Games*. The savagery is a yearly ritual mandated by the tyrannical regime of Panem, a broken nation built, after a terrible war, on the futuristic ruins of North America. It's also broadcast on live TV, a national media event. This horrific vision of a near future in which teenagers are in peril is sickening, but the individual heroism of some who fight is also thrilling, as millions of readers can attest: Suzanne Collins's *Hunger Games* trilogy is a literary sensation. The good news now coming out of Panem, both for those who already know just how brutal the Games become and those who are new to the dystopian tale, is that the movie adaptation knows how to play too.

This *Hunger Games* is a muscular, honorable, unflinching translation of Collins's vision. It's brutal where it needs to be, particularly when children fight and bleed. It conveys both the miseries of the oppressed, represented by the poorly fed and clothed citizens of

Schwarzbaum acknowledges her mission and dual audiences.

To succeed, the film must *translate* the vision of the original book.

Panem's twelve suffering districts, and the rotted values of the oppressors, evident in the gaudy decadence of those who live in the Capitol. Best of all, the movie effectively showcases the allure of the story's remarkable, kick-ass sixteen-year-old heroine, Katniss Everdeen.

Katniss — who volunteers to fight in place of her sister as one of District 12's two unfortunate "tributes" when the little girl is chosen — is the heart and soul of the story, one of those feisty female protagonists pitched to the YA [young adult] market but appealing to adults as well. Katniss is happiest when she's hunting food for her family with the bow-and-arrow precision that is her specialty. She's a tomboy with a trademark brunet braid down her back, and she's a graceful young woman — strong, self-possessed, and unaware of her own beauty, whether dressed like a backwoods scout or dolled up for pageant display in gorgeous gowns. And Jennifer Lawrence, previously dressed as a backwoods scout in her galvanizing breakout, *Winter's Bone*, is, in her gravity, her intensity, and her own unmannered beauty, about as impressive a Hollywood incarnation of Katniss as one could ever imagine. Much of Katniss's experience throughout

A lengthy paragraph explains the film's heroine and why Jennifer Lawrence works in the role.

THE HUNGER GAMES, Jennifer Lawrence, 2012/ photo: Murray Close/© Lionsgate/Courtesy Everett Collection.

the Games — as she improvises with an ingenuity far beyond the scope of any TV *Survivor* contestant — is interior, silent. Lawrence is expressive in her stillness, and moves with athletic confidence.

Fans of the book and moviegoers coming to the story fresh may reach different conclusions about the effectiveness of Josh Hutcherson as Peeta, the baker's son from District 12 who is at once Katniss's competitor and the boy who loves her. In the book, interesting edges rough up his niceness; he's not quite so easy to peg. But to these eyes, on screen he's been sanded down to a generic sensitive good guy, so much so that it's difficult to understand why Katniss is prickly around him. Meanwhile, so little is seen of Liam Hemsworth as Gale, Katniss's soul mate / fellow hunter, in this first episode that the uninitiated might not pay attention to the third angle of the story's romantic triangle — about the only element this high-quality pop culture phenomenon has in common with the swoons of *Twilight*.

Director Gary Ross does a tight job of establishing the future-meets-*1984* vibe in Panem: the slog of daily life, the hopelessness that dulls the citizens, the fear that returns each year at the Hunger Games lottery known as the Reaping. Aided by outré costumes from designer Judianna Makovsky, he also goes to town in the Capitol sequences. Elizabeth Banks as Effie the PR handler, Woody Harrelson as Haymitch the mentor, Lenny Kravitz as Cinna the stylist, Stanley Tucci as Caesar the unctuous TV interviewer — they're all reasonable facsimiles of what's on the page, and fabulous oddities for those who are just meeting them. And if the depiction of the death-by-death progress of the Games themselves, as Katniss struggles mightily to save her own life on behalf of her sister, doesn't match the psychological tension on the page, well, thems may be the rules of the adaptation game. The movie shows how, but the book shows why. **A–**

Sidebar notes:

Schwarzbaum explains potential differences in audience reactions to the film.

Final line comments on differences between movies and books.

Exploring purpose and topic

▶ topic

Most evaluations you're required to prepare for school or work come with assigned topics. But here are strategies to follow when you have a choice. ○

Evaluate a subject you know well. This is the safest option, built on the assumption that everyone is an expert on something. Years of reading *Cook's Illustrated* magazine or playing tennis might make it natural for you to review restaurants or tennis rackets. You've accumulated not only basic facts but also lots of hands-on knowledge—the sort that gives you the confidence to offer an opinion. So go ahead and demonstrate your expertise.

Evaluate a subject you need to investigate. Perhaps you are applying to law schools, looking for family-friendly companies to work for, or thinking about purchasing an HDTV. To make such choices, you'll need information. So kill two birds with a single assignment: Use the school project to explore personal or professional choices you face, find the necessary facts and data, and make a case for (or against) Arizona State, Whole Foods, or Sony.

Evaluate a subject you'd like to know more about. How do wine connoisseurs tell one cabernet from another and rank them so confidently? How would a college football championship team from the 1950s match up against more recent winning teams? Use an assignment to settle questions like these that you and friends may have debated late into the evening.

Evaluate a subject that's been on your mind. Not all evaluations are driven by decisions of the moment. Instead, you may want to make a point about social, cultural, and political matters: You believe a particular piece of health-care or immigration legislation is bad policy or find yourself disturbed by changes in society. An evaluation is often the appropriate genre for giving voice to such thoughts, whether you compose a conventional piece or venture into the realms of satire or parody.

find a topic
p. 331

Understanding your audience

Your job as a reviewer is easier when readers care about your opinions. Fortunately, most people consult evaluations and reviews routinely, often hoping to find specific information: *Is the latest Stephen L. Carter novel up to snuff? Who's the most important American architect working today? Phillies or Braves in the National League East this year?* But you'll still have to make accommodations for differing audiences—as Lisa Schwarzbaum does in her review of *The Hunger Games* (p. 103).

Write for experts.   Knowledgeable readers can be a tough group because they may bring strong, maybe inflexible, opinions to a topic. But if you know your stuff, you can take on the experts because they know their stuff too: You don't have to repeat tedious background information or discuss criteria of evaluation in detail. You can use the technical vocabulary experts share and make allusions to people and concepts they'd recognize. ○ Here are a few in-crowd sentences from a review of the football video game *Backbreaker* from an online gaming site:

> *Backbreaker* joins the sports design trend of placing emphasis on the right analog stick. It's everything from your swim/rip move on defense, to your bonecrunching hit or tackle, to juking, spinning, selecting receivers and passing. You use the right trigger as an action modifier ("aggressive mode") to go into other areas of your player's toolset. Everything is contextual to the type of player you control and it's pick-up-and-play intuitive after one trip through the tutorial.
>
> — Kotaku, "*Backbreaker* Review: The Challenger Crashes"

Write for a general audience.   General audiences need more hand-holding than specialists. You may have to spell out criteria of evaluation, provide lots of background information, and define key terms. But general readers usually are willing to learn more about a topic. Here's noted film critic Roger Ebert explaining how to watch time-travel films:

> *The Lake House* tells the story of a romance that spans years but involves only a few kisses. It succeeds despite being based on two paradoxes: time travel and the ability of two people to have conversations that are, under the terms

> Need help thinking about your audience? See "How to Revise Your Work" on pp. 426–27.

established by the film, impossible. Neither one of these problems bothered me in the slightest. Take time travel: I used to get distracted by its logical flaws and contradictory timelines. Now in my wisdom I have decided to simply accept it as a premise, no questions asked. A time-travel story works on emotional, not temporal, logic.

— rogerebert.com, June 16, 2006

Write for novices.   You have a lot of explaining to do when readers are absolutely fresh to a subject. Prepare to give them context and background information. For example, Digital Photography Review, a Web site that examines photographic equipment in great detail, attaches the following note to all its camera reviews: "If you're new to digital photography you may wish to read the Digital Photography Glossary before diving into this article (it may help you understand some of the terms used)." Smart reviewers anticipate the needs of their audiences.

Are buffalo dangerous?
For some audiences, you have to explain everything. John J. Ruszkiewicz.

Finding and developing materials

When you are assigned a review, investigate your subject thoroughly. Online research is easy: To figure out what others are thinking, just type the name of whatever you are evaluating into a browser, followed by the word *review* or *critic*. ○ Read what you find critically and carefully, giving close attention to reviews from reputable sources. But don't just repeat the opinions you turn up. Feel free to challenge prevailing views whenever you can make a better argument or offer a fresh perspective. To do that, focus on criteria and evidence.

develop criteria ◀

Decide on your criteria.   Clarify your standards, even if you're just evaluating pizza. Should the crust be hard or soft? Should the sauce be red and spicy, or white and creamy? How thick should the pizza be? How salty? And, for all these opinions—*why*?

Didn't expect the *why*? You really don't have a criterion until you attach a plausible reason to it. ○ The rationale should be clear in your own mind even if you don't expect to explain it in the review or evaluation itself: *Great pizza comes with a soft crust that wraps each bite and topping in a floury texture that merges the contrasting flavors.* More important, any criterion you use will have to make sense to readers either on its own (*Public art should be beautiful*) or after you've explained and defended it (*Public art should be scandalous because people need to be jolted out of conformist thinking*).

Look for hard criteria.   You'll seem objective when your criteria at least seem grounded in numbers or corroborated observations. Think, for example, of how instructors set measurable standards for your performance in their courses, translating all sorts of activities, from papers to class participation, into numbers. Teachers aren't alone in deferring to numbers. CNET Reviews, for instance, relies heavily on precise measurements in evaluating televisions and explains those criteria in excruciating detail on its Web site. The following is how CNET assesses just one aspect of an HDTV's performance:

> **Black luminance (0%)** *Example result: 0.0140*
> This is the measure of the luminance of "black" in fL (footlamberts), and a lower number is better. It's often referred to as MLL, for minimum luminance level, but since this measurement is taken post-calibration it may be higher than the TV's minimum. We consider the post-calibration black level most important because the calibration process aims to prevent crushing of shadow detail and "tricks"

refine your search p. 442

develop a statement p. 362

like dynamic contrast that can affect this measurement. The measurement is taken of a completely black screen (except for a 5% stripe on near the bottom), created by using the Quantum Data's 0% window pattern.

Good: +/– less than 0.009
Average: +/– 0.009 to 0.019
Poor: +/– 0.02 or higher

Got that? Probably not, but aren't you now inclined to take a CNET product review seriously?

Argue for criteria that can't be measured.   How do you measure the success or failure of something that can't be objectively calculated—a student dance recital, Bruno Mars's latest track, or the new abstract sculpture just hauled onto campus? Look into how such topics are evaluated and discussed in public media. Get familiar with what sensible critics have to say about whatever you're evaluating and how they say it—whether it's contemporary art, fine saddles, good teaching, or successful foreign policy. If you read carefully, you'll find values and criteria embedded in all your sources. O

In the following excerpt, for example, James Morris explains why he believes American television is often better than Hollywood films. Morris's implied criteria are highlighted.

Stated directly, Morris's criteria might sound like this: Good entertainment is intelligent; it is tailored to its medium; it does not require special effects to keep people interested; it is disciplined.

What I admire most about these shows, and most deplore about contemporary movies, is the quality of the scripts. The TV series are devised and written by smart people who seem to be allowed to let their intelligence show. Yes, the individual and ensemble performances on several of the series are superb, but would the actors be as good as they are if they were miming the action? TV shows are designed for the small screen and cannot rely, as movies do, on visual and aural effects to distract audiences. If what's being said on TV isn't interesting, why bother to watch? Television is rigorous, right down to the confinement of hour or half-hour time slots, further reduced by commercials. There's no room for the narrative bloat that inflates so many Hollywood movies from their natural party-balloon size to Thanksgiving-parade dimensions.

— "My Favorite Wasteland," *Wilson Quarterly*, Autumn 2005

read closely
p. 340

Stand by your values.   Make sure you define criteria that apply to more than just the case you are examining at the moment. Think about what makes socially conscious rap music, world-class sculpture, or a great politician. For instance, you might admire artists or actors who overcome great personal tragedies on their paths to stardom. But to make such heroics a necessary criterion for artistic achievement might look like special pleading.

Gather your evidence.   Some materials for a review will necessarily come from secondary sources. Before judging the merits of Obamacare or Truman's decision to drop atomic bombs to end World War II, expect to do a lot of critical reading in a range of sources. Then weigh the evidence before offering your opinion—being sure to credit those sources in your review. O

Other evidence will come from shrewd observation. Sometimes you just need to be attuned to the world around you—as Jordyn Brown is in cataloging the rudeness of cell phone users (see p. 118). When reviewing a book, a movie, a restaurant, or a similar item, take notes. If appropriate, measure, weigh, photograph, or interview your subjects. (Does that gut-buster or quarter pounder measure up?) When it matters, survey what others think about an issue (a campus political flap, for example) and record such opinions. Finally, keep an open mind. Be willing to change an opinion when evidence points in directions you hadn't expected.

Andy Singer.

Creating a structure

▶ organize
criteria

Like other arguments, evaluations have distinct parts that can be arranged into patterns or structures.

Choose a simple structure when your criteria and categories are predictable. A straightforward review might announce its subject and claim, list criteria of evaluation, present evidence to show whether the subject meets those standards, and draw conclusions. Here's one version of that pattern with the criteria discussed all at once, at the opening of the piece:

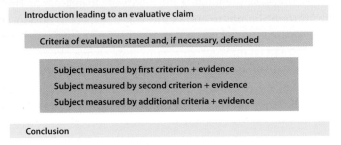

> Introduction leading to an evaluative claim
>
> Criteria of evaluation stated and, if necessary, defended
>
> Subject measured by first criterion + evidence
> Subject measured by second criterion + evidence
> Subject measured by additional criteria + evidence
>
> Conclusion

And here's a template with the criteria of evaluation introduced one at a time:

> Introduction leading to an evaluative claim
>
> First criterion of evaluation stated and, if necessary, defended
>
> Subject measured by first criterion + evidence
>
> Second criterion stated/defended
>
> Subject measured by second criterion + evidence
>
> Additional criteria stated/defended
>
> Subject measured by additional criteria + evidence
>
> Conclusion

You might find structures this formulaic in job-performance reviews at work or in consumer magazines. Once a pattern is established for assessing computers, paint sprayers, video games, or even teachers (consider those forms you fill in at the end of the term), it can be repeated for each new subject and results can be compared.

Yet what works for hardware and tech products is less convincing when applied to music, books, political policies, or societal behaviors that are more than the sum of their parts. Imagine a film critic whose *every* review marched through the same predictable set of criteria: acting, directing, writing, cinematography, and special effects. When a subject can't (or shouldn't) be reviewed via simple categories, you decide which of its aspects and elements deserve attention. ○

Choose a focal point.   You could, in fact, organize an entire review around one or more shrewd insights, and many reviewers do. The trick is to support any stellar perception with clear and specific evidence. Consider, for example, how Lisa Schwarzbaum ties her claim that the first *Hunger Games* movie is a "muscular, honorable, unflinching translation" of the book to her portrait of Jennifer Lawrence as Katniss. Or look carefully at Jordyn Brown's scathing portrait of cell phone users (p. 118): You'll discover that what holds her satire together is a fear that too many people are missing important aspects of their lives. Brown dramatizes that problem by beginning and ending the paper at a birthday party that she and a dozen friends are just barely attending:

> This dinner was supposed to be a festive gathering to celebrate our good friend Stacey's birthday. But no one mingled or celebrated, not even Stacey. Everyone seemed to be somewhere else. They had all wandered off to Google-town, Twitter-ville, and Texting-My-Boyfriend City, and I was left there alone at the Cheesecake Factory.... Twelve people preferred phone activities to talking to each other and me over three-tiered red velvet cheesecake. Seriously, people. Put those phones down. You're not thinking clearly.

Compare and contrast.   Another obvious way to organize an evaluation is to examine differences. ○ Strengths and weaknesses stand out especially well when similar subjects are examined critically. When *Automobile* columnist Jamie Kitman, for example, wants to make a tongue-in-cheek case that the best American police car is one that looks most intimidating, he first has to explain his odd criterion of evaluation:

> Here [in the United States], police cars aren't meant to make us feel all fuzzy but to instill powerful sensations of fear.... At their best, police cars look strong, stout, capable, and most of all, mean. To the extent that they make bad people feel scared, they make those of us who ought to feel safe (because we have done nothing wrong) feel safer, while still feeling scared.

shape your
work p. 374

use comparison and
contrast p. 367

After that, it's a simple matter of comparing candidates. He dismisses Ford Tauruses and Explorers because they "don't scare enough, even with light bars on top and armed with police-academy graduates inside." GM police cruisers are even less able to terrify the citizenry: They have "the scare factor of un-spoiled rice pudding." Fortunately, he has found a winner, a model already described in the column as "malevolent" and looking "pissed off, angry, and unreasonable":

> That leaves the Dodge Charger, America's indisputable reigning champion cop car, to reign longer. It's the distilled automotive essence of every TV cop who ever drove a car, from Broderick Crawford on, all rolled into one angry, authori-tarian appliance. No wonder countless agencies across the country favor Chargers. They're not kidding around, and you might as well know it.

Kitman's comparison is fun, but it makes sense—scary sense—especially when visual evidence is attached.

Courtesy of the Chrysler Foundation.

Choosing a style and design

Evaluations can be composed in any style, from high to low—depending, as always, on aim and audience. ○ Look for opportunities to present evaluations visually too. They can simplify your task.

Use a high or formal style.   Technical reviews tend to be formal and impersonal: They may be almost indistinguishable from reports, describing their findings in plain, unemotional language. Such a style gives the impression of scientific objectivity, even though the work may reflect someone's agenda. For instance, here's a paragraph in formal style from the National Assessment of Educational Progress summarizing the performance of American students in science:

> Of all the racial/ethnic groups reported, Asian/Pacific Islander students had the highest percentage of fourth- and eighth-graders performing at or above the *Proficient* level in mathematics and reading in 2013. Results by gender show higher percentages of male students than female students at or above *Proficient* in mathematics at both grades in 2013. In reading, female students had higher percentages at or above the *Proficient* level than male students at both grades.
>
> — *Nation's Report Card*, 2013 Mathematics and Reading Assessment (http://nationsreportcard.gov/reading_math_2013/#/student-groups)

Use a middle style.   When a writer has a more direct stake in the work—as is typical in book or movie reviews, for example—the style moves more decisively toward the middle. You sense a person behind the writing, making judgments and offering opinions. That's certainly the case in these two paragraphs by Clive Crook, written shortly after the death of noted economist John Kenneth Galbraith: Words, phrases, and even sentence fragments that humanize the assessment are highlighted, while a contrast to economist Milton Friedman also sharpens the portrait.

> Galbraith, despite the Harvard professorship, was never really an economist in the ordinary sense in the first place. In one of countless well-turned pronouncements, he said, "Economics is extremely useful as a form of employment for economists." He disdained the scientific pretensions and formal apparatus of modern economics — all that math and number crunching — believing that it

define your
style p. 400

missed the point. This view did not spring from mastery of the techniques: Galbraith disdained them from the outset, which saved time.

Friedman, in contrast, devoted his career to grinding out top-quality scholarly work, while publishing the occasional best seller as a sideline. He too was no math whiz, but he was painstakingly scientific in his methods (when engaged in scholarly research) and devoted to data. All that was rather beneath Galbraith. Brilliant, yes; productive, certainly. But he was a bureaucrat, a diplomat, a political pundit, and a popular economics writer of commanding presence more than a serious economic thinker, let alone a great one.

— "John Kenneth Galbraith, Revisited," *National Journal*, May 15, 2006

Use a low style.   Many reviewers get personal with readers, some so direct that they verge on rudeness. Consider the product reviews on Amazon.com or almost any comment section online. In contrast, the evaluations you write for academic or work assignments should be (relatively) polite and low-key in style. But you do have an enormous range of options—especially when offering social and political commentary. Then, if your evaluations turn into satire or parody, all the gloves come off. In such situations, humor or sarcasm can become powerful tools, full of insider humor, colloquial turns of phrase, bizarre allusions, and grammar on the edge. But no style is more difficult to manage. So look for models of the kinds of evaluation you want to compose. Study the ones you admire for lessons in style using language effectively.

Present evaluations visually.   Evaluations work especially well when their claims can be supported by tables, charts, graphs, or other visual elements. These allow readers to see relationships that could not be conveyed quite as efficiently in words alone. ○ And sometimes the images simply have more impact. Consider your response to images of real fast-food items posted on an offbeat Web site called the West Virginia Surf Report. Here's the description of the feature that appeared on the site:

> **Fast Food: Ads vs. Reality** Each item was purchased, taken home, and photographed immediately. Nothing was tampered with, run over by a car, or anything of the sort. It is an accurate representation in every case. Shiny, neon-orange, liquefied pump-cheese, and all.

display data
p. 550

Here are several of the images the site presented of products purchased from well-known national chains:

  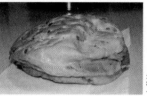

Jeff Kay.

All you need to do is recall the carefully crafted professional photographs of these items you've seen posted in the fast-food restaurants and you can draw your own conclusion: *Caveat emptor!*

Your Turn   Almost everyone reads at least one critic or type of review regularly — of restaurants, movies, TV shows, sports teams, gizmos, video games, and so on. Pick a review by your favorite critic or, alternatively, a review you have read recently and noted. Then examine its style closely. Is it formal, informal, or casual? Technical or general? Serious or humorous? Full of allusions to stuff regular readers would get? What features of the style do you like? Do you have any reservations about its style? In a detailed paragraph, evaluate only the style of the reviewer or review (not the substance of the review), organizing your work to support a clear thesis.

Examining models

SOCIAL SATIRE   Satires, which poke fun at the foibles of society in order to correct them, often require writers to draw exaggerated but recognizable portraits of people and situations. That's what Jordyn Brown attempts to do in a paper aimed at getting her friends to shut off their cell phones and pay more attention to life. If readers laugh too, that's all to the good.

Reading the Genre   To keep readers interested, satires have to be perceptive, entertaining, and funny. Can you point to specific moments in Jordyn Brown's "A Word from My Anti-Phone Soapbox" when these qualities come together? What images or ideas are you most likely to remember after reading the piece?

Brown 1

Jordyn Brown

Professor Ruszkiewicz

Rhetoric 325M

May 5, 20--

A Word from My Anti-Phone Soapbox

I sat for at least five minutes staring at the tops of the other dinner guests' heads. All twenty-four eyes (that's twelve pairs) were unwaveringly fixed on their respective laps. I didn't understand why my friends held their phones under the table. We weren't in class. Perhaps it was a subconscious admittance of shame for their inattentiveness. I sat at the dinner table confused. This dinner was supposed to be a festive gathering to celebrate our good friend Stacey's birthday. But no one mingled or celebrated, not even Stacey. Everyone seemed to be somewhere else. They had all wandered off to Google-town,

> Opening paragraph, especially its final sentence, sets the scene and the tone.

:e   For an additional reading, see **macmillanhighered.com/howtowrite3e**.
e-readings › Ivan Penn and the *Tampa Bay Times*, *Mandarin Chinese, Rosetta Stone Style* [PRODUCT TEST]

Brown 4

And I don't care what you had for lunch. Don't TwitPic a picture of your meal, because it makes no sense. What if you'd done that ten years ago? If you had skipped into school with a picture you had gotten developed at the drugstore and gone around showing it to people, saying, "Hey guys, look what I had for dinner!" the whole fifth-grade class would have looked at you like you were insane. Twitter has made nonsense commonplace. No thought is too base to fill a tweet's 140 characters. Pitiful.

Sad to say, these handheld devices have turned you into technologically overindulged brats. You break into temper tantrums, stomping around, pouting, throwing your Blackberries at soft surfaces, and crossing your arms in agitation whenever you hit a dead zone and can't access your precious Internet. And you have even less patience for your friends when you text or call them. After all, everything you have to say—spoken or in text—is infinitely more important than anything else in their lives. The meaning of the word urgent has evolved since the earliest days of portable and instant communication devices. Once only physicians routinely received urgent messages: "Hurry, we need you, Dr. Cardiologist, to fix this man's horrible heart." But now *urgent* can mean, "911! What do you feel like eating for dinner? I'm at the grocery store now. Hurry and call me back!!!" And I wouldn't dare let a text message from you sit in my in-box for more than an hour or I'd be in for a scolding the next time I see you.

The examples throughout work if readers recognize some truth under the exaggerations.

The paragraph shows how smartphones are leading to breakdowns in social relations.

Brown 5

So, Earth to you, the people who never part from their cell phones. I'm sure you've taken several breaks while reading this rant to check your e-mail and respond to a few texts. You probably missed most of the points of my argument too, much like you're missing what's going on in the world around you. Cell phones were initially meant to connect us, broadening the time frame during which people could communicate with one another. But with all the new apps being incorporated into these devices, isolation only grows, shrinking your world and perspective. You're all constantly talking and thinking about how *you* feel and what *you* think. You don't talk to Rachel or Stephen but to the "Twitter-verse" or to Facebook at large. You communicate without any idea of who's really listening.

Twelve people preferred phone activities to talking to each other and *me* over three-tiered red velvet cheesecake. Seriously, people. Put those phones down. You're not thinking clearly.

> Like most satires, this one turns serious and offers a simple solution: Turn off the phone.

PRODUCT REVIEW   Shortly after the debut of the 2013 summer film *Monsters University*, Eric Brown spent some time reviewing a promotional Web site Disney/Pixar posted for the imaginary school, a dead-ringer for real college and university home pages. (You can find it online by searching "Monsters University.") We reproduce Brown's essay from *The Chronicle of Higher Education* here. In it, Brown argues that there's a lot to admire about Disney/Pixar's make-believe college site, which itself functions as a special subgenre of evaluation.

Reading the Genre   After reading Eric Hoover's "Monsters U.'s Site Just Might Give You 'Web-Site Envy'" and perusing the MU Web site itself online, examine the home page of your current school or employer and discuss its strengths and weaknesses with colleagues.

▶

The Chronicle of Higher Education

Posted: July 2, 2013
From: Eric Hoover

Monsters U.'s Site Just Might Give You "Web-Site Envy"

Thesis is simple and direct.

Okay, I'll admit that I've yet to see *Monsters University*, the No. 1 movie in the nation. But I've spent a good hour tooling around the promotional Web site for the fictional institution. It's scary good.

Fascinated by how this portal both mimics and mocks real-life college Web sites, I asked Ashley Hennigan, assistant director of social media strategy at Cornell University, to share her thoughts on the MU site — and what admissions officers might learn from it.

For one thing, the design is clean and consistent, a far cry from the hodgepodge, thrown-together look of some college sites. This one captures higher-education convention so well, Ms. Hennigan writes in an e-mail, that "I'm sure some universities have Web-site envy."

MU's Web site mostly measures up to a whole series of criteria.

The first things Ms. Hennigan looks for on college Web sites are a modern design, brand continuity, and simple navigation. On those counts, she says, the Monsters U. site is a success. The home page includes a carousel of images, with news and events featured prominently, and that design is carried through the secondary pages. This, folks, is a triumph of branding.

When visiting college sites, Ms. Hennigan also looks for connections to students. Do applicants have a way of communicating with the people — er, monsters — who know the campus best? "While these monsters aren't blogging," she writes, "they are making YouTube videos and providing their own testimonials."

Evidence is cited for the Web site's effectiveness.

MU's site conveys warmth, a sense of the folks students will meet on the campus (yeah, yeah, I realize these are cartoon creatures). Take the faculty profile of the inspiring Dean Hardscrabble, dean of the School of Scaring. "If you can survive a class taught by her, then the human world is a breeze," says a former MU student. Note the emphasis on teaching here; there's no mention of the dean's publishing prowess.

Ms. Hennigan says she was struck by the welcome video. "Swap out the campus and the university name, and this would be a great promo," she writes. "Hitting all of the great branding key-words — legacy, tradition, diversity, and integrity. They get bonus points for using YouTube throughout the site for recruitment." I like the array of hilarious slogans that are no more hilarious than some colleges' actual slogans ("Your future is knocking. Open the door.").

The review is playful, poking fun at genuine college Web sites.

On the admission page, there's some advice for applicants from admission counselors. The applications that stand out, one coun-selor writes, "tell a great story" about how MU will affect the life of a student: "Great students can go lots of places. We want to know that MU and the student is a great match."

Of course, like real sites, that for Monsters U omits some scary details.

Ms. Hennigan applauds that message. "I'm happy to see the scary counselor asking how attending MU will change the monster's life," she writes, "acknowledging that there are plenty of places to go and that being a great match is more important than just being a great student."

What's lacking? Oh, information about paying for all this. The financial-aid page doesn't mention the cost of attendance, and there are only vague references to meeting financial need. The par-ents' page is also thin on details about finances. "Our human par-ents would demand much more," Ms. Hennigan writes. "They want to see real numbers, financial costs, and outcome statistics."

And how much hunting should a visitor have to do? "It should take only one click off the admissions home page to find location, academic programs, and cost," Ms. Hennigan writes. "MU could up their content with these quick facts and figures." As she notes, though, there's a campus-safety page, complete with reports of specific incidents (Thursday at 12:08 AM: "Four female students report prank phone calls from an unknown male caller pretending to be a lost human.").

I laughed at the following line before realizing that it's more or less what many colleges tell families, with a straight face: "Don't let a little debt scare you and your child away from the best educational opportunity money can buy."

Perhaps no college Web site is complete without a little bragging. This factoid caught my eye: "Each year, over 26,000 high school and transfer monsters apply to MU, but only a fraction get admitted." You see, Monsters University is awesome, and it touts its acceptance rate as evidence. Can you imagine a real college doing that?

VISUAL COMPARISON   How might the Insurance Institute for Highway Safety memorably celebrate its fiftieth anniversary? By crashing two cars fifty years apart in age to show how much crash safety has improved, thanks in part to the efforts of the group. The visual evidence represents a startling and memorable evaluation of their work.

Reading the Genre   The pre- and post-test images in "Crash Test" leave little doubt about progress in vehicle safety. What similar image pairings might you use to evaluate either progress or decline in some other area of human life—technology, education, lifestyles, or culture? Look for images that provide specific, convincing, and maybe even measurable evidence.

▶

of research & communications

Crash Test

Insurance Institute for Highway Safety

Top photo testifies to the violence of the 40-mph crash.

In the 50 years since U.S. insurers organized the Insurance Institute for Highway Safety, car crashworthiness has improved. Demonstrating this was a crash test conducted on Sept. 9 between a 1959 Chevrolet Bel Air and a 2009 Chevrolet Malibu. In a real-world collision similar to this test, occupants of the new model would fare much better than in the vintage Chevy.

"It was night and day, the difference in occupant protection," says Institute president Adrian Lund. "What this test shows is that automakers don't build cars like they used to. They build them better."

The crash test was conducted at an event to celebrate the contributions of auto insurers to highway safety progress over 50 years. Beginning with the Institute's 1959 founding, insurers have maintained the resolve, articulated in the 1950s, to "conduct, sponsor, and encourage programs designed to aid in the conservation and preservation of life and property from the hazards of highway accidents."

Test compares crashworthiness then and now: 1959 Chevrolet Bel Air and 2009 Chevrolet Malibu in 40 mph frontal offset test (click on photos to see larger images).

Watch a video of the crash test

2009 Chevrolet Malibu   1959 Chevrolet Bel Air

Malibu post-crash   Bel Air post-crash

The collision demolishes the front ends of both vehicles.

In the crash test involving the two Chevrolets, the 2009 Malibu's occupant compartment remained intact (above left) while the one in the 1959 Bel Air (right) collapsed.

But the passenger compartments tell a different story, providing clear evidence of fifty years of progress in structural design and safety.

Assignments

1. **Arts Review:** Drawing on your expertise as a consumer of popular culture — the way Lisa Schwarzbaum does in her *Entertainment Weekly* review of *The Hunger Games* (p. 103) — review a movie, book, television series, musical piece, artist, or work of art for a publication that you specify. It might be the equivalent of *Entertainment Weekly* or you might aim your work at a local or student publication. Consider, too, writing a substantive piece for an online site that takes reviews — such as Amazon.com or IMDb. Write a review strong enough to change someone's mind.

2. **Social Satire:** Using the techniques of social satire modeled in "A Word from My Anti-Phone Soapbox" (p. 118), assess a public policy, social movement, or cultural trend you believe deserves serious and detailed criticism. But don't write a paper simply describing your target as dangerous, pathetic, or unsuccessful. Instead, make people laugh at your target while also offering a plausible alternative.

3. **Product Review:** Choose an item that you own, buy, or use regularly, anything from a Coleman lantern to Dunkin' Donuts coffee to a Web site, app, or social network you couldn't live without. Then write a fully developed review, making sure to name your criteria of evaluation as clearly as Ashley Hennigan does in Eric Hoover's essay on the Monsters University site (p. 123). Be attentive to your specific audience and generous with the supporting details. Use graphics if appropriate.

4. **Visual Comparison or Review:** Construct an evaluation in which a visual comparison or some other media evidence plays a major role. You might use photographs the way the West Virginia Surf Report (pp. 116–17) does. Or perhaps you can work in another medium to show, for example, how good or bad the instructions in a technical manual are, how much the brownies you baked differ from the ones pictured on the box, or how images on your school's or an employer's Web site stereotype the people who attend or work there. Be creative.

5. **Your Choice:** Evaluate a program or facility in some institution you know well (school, business, church, recreation center) that you believe works efficiently or poorly. Prepare a presentation in the medium of your choice and imagine that your audience is an administrator with the power to reward or shut down the operation.

How to start
- Need a **topic**? See page 135.
- Need to identify **possible causes**? See page 140.
- Need to **organize your analysis**? See page 142.

5 Causal Analyses

explain how, why, or what if something happens

We all analyze and explain things daily. Someone asks, "Why?" We reply, "Because . . ." and then offer reasons and rationales. Such a response comes naturally.

CAUSAL ANALYSIS An instructor asks for a ten-page *causal analysis* of the political or economic forces responsible for a major armed conflict during the twentieth century. You choose to write about the Korean War because you know almost nothing about it.

RESEARCH STUDY You notice that most students now walk across campus chatting on cell phones or listening to music. You develop a *research study* to examine whether this phenomenon has any relationship to a recent drop in the numbers of students joining campus clubs and activities across the country.

CULTURAL ANALYSIS Why, you wonder, in a fully illustrated *cultural analysis*, did blue jeans become a fashion phenomenon the world over? What explains their enduring popularity?

DECIDING TO WRITE A CAUSAL ANALYSIS. From climate change to childhood obesity to high school students' poor performance on standardized tests, the daily news is full of problems framed by *how*, *why*, and *what if* questions. These are often described as issues of *cause and effect*, terms we'll use frequently in this chapter. Take childhood obesity. The public wants to know why we have a generation of overweight kids. Too many cheeseburgers? Not enough dodgeball? People worry, too, about the consequences of the trend. Will overweight children grow into obese adults? Will they develop medical problems?

We're interested in such questions because they really do matter, and we're often curious to find answers. But successful analyses of this sort call for more than a passing interest. They demand persistence, precision, and research (for more on choosing a genre, see the Introduction). Even then, you'll have to deal with a world that seems complicated or contradictory. Not every problem or issue can—or should—be explained simply. ○

Don't jump to conclusions. Think you know why attitudes toward gay marriage changed so quickly or why people have started to resist Hollywood's summer blockbusters? Guess again. Nothing's as simple as it seems and trying to argue causes and effects to other people will quickly teach you humility—even if you *don't* jump to hasty conclusions. It's just plain hard to identify which factors, separately or working together, account for a particular event, activity, or behavior. It is tougher still to predict how what's happening today might affect the future. So approach causal arguments cautiously and prepare to use qualifiers (*sometimes, perhaps, possibly*)—lots of them. ○

Appreciate your limits. There are rarely easy answers when investigating why things happen the way they do. The space shuttle *Columbia* burned up on reentry in 2003 because a 1.67-pound piece of foam hit the wing of the 240,000-pound craft on liftoff. Who could have imagined so unlikely a sequence of events? Yet investigators had to follow the evidence relentlessly to its conclusion, in this case working backwards—from effect to cause.

analyze claims and
evidence p. 456

develop a
statement p. 362

The Funnel Effect

We've all ground to a halt on freeways without obstacles in sight — no weather issues, no collisions, no ducks crossing the pavement. What gives? Highway engineers know. The Plain Dealer/Landov.

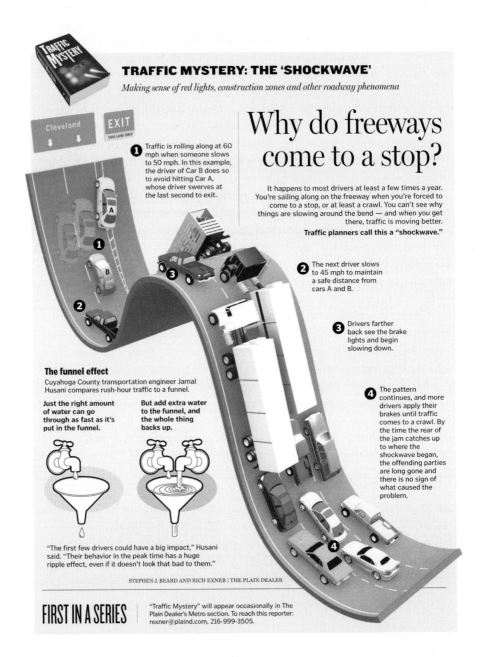

TRAFFIC MYSTERY: THE 'SHOCKWAVE'

Making sense of red lights, construction zones and other roadway phenomena

Why do freeways come to a stop?

It happens to most drivers at least a few times a year. You're sailing along on the freeway when you're forced to come to a stop, or at least a crawl. You can't see why things are slowing around the bend — and when you get there, traffic is moving better.

Traffic planners call this a "shockwave."

① Traffic is rolling along at 60 mph when someone slows to 50 mph. In this example, the driver of Car B does so to avoid hitting Car A, whose driver swerves at the last second to exit.

② The next driver slows to 45 mph to maintain a safe distance from cars A and B.

③ Drivers farther back see the brake lights and begin slowing down.

④ The pattern continues, and more drivers apply their brakes until traffic comes to a crawl. By the time the rear of the jam catches up to where the shockwave began, the offending parties are long gone and there is no sign of what caused the problem.

The funnel effect

Cuyahoga County transportation engineer Jamal Husani compares rush-hour traffic to a funnel.

Just the right amount of water can go through as fast as it's put in the funnel.

But add extra water to the funnel, and the whole thing backs up.

"The first few drivers could have a big impact," Husani said. "Their behavior in the peak time has a huge ripple effect, even if it doesn't look that bad to them."

STEPHEN J. BEARD AND RICH EXNER | THE PLAIN DEALER

FIRST IN A SERIES   "Traffic Mystery" will appear occasionally in The Plain Dealer's Metro section. To reach this reporter: rexner@plaind.com, 216-999-3505.

The fact is that you'll often have to settle for causal explanations that are merely plausible or probable because—outside of the hard sciences—you are often dealing with imprecise and unpredictable forces (especially *people*).

Offer sufficient evidence for claims.   Your academic and professional analyses of cause and effect will be held to high standards of proof—particularly in the sciences. The evidence you provide may be a little looser when you write for popular media, where some readers will tolerate anecdotal and personal examples. But even then, give readers ample reasons to believe you. Avoid hearsay, qualify your claims, and admit when you are merely speculating.

From presidents to pundits, public figures writing about current events find themselves relying on "expert opinion" that is itself open to interpretation. So do individual citizens. This short piece by Jonah Goldberg, a political commentator and global warming skeptic, typifies the dilemma. Not a scientist himself, Goldberg is in no position to make authoritative claims about the causes of climate change. But he can — and does — raise questions about how the studies are being reported to the public.

Reading the Genre   Goldberg is expressing a decidedly minority opinion in this cause-and-effect argument: The scientific consensus favoring human influence on climate change is overwhelming. If you find Goldberg credible, point to strategies in the piece he uses to establish his ethos. If you are unimpressed by his analysis, explain why he is unable to win you over.

National Review Online

Posted: September 2, 2009
From: Jonah Goldberg

Global Warming and the Sun

The style of the analysis is colloquial, as might be expected in a blog.

On the last day of August, scientists spotted a teeny-weeny sunspot, breaking a 51-day streak of blemish-free days for the sun. If it had gone just a bit longer, it would have broken a 96-year record of 53 days without any of the magnetic disruptions that cause solar flares. That record was nearly broken last year as well.

Wait, it gets even more exciting.

During what scientists call the Maunder Minimum — a period of solar inactivity from 1645 to 1715 — the world experienced the worst of the cold streak dubbed the Little Ice Age. At Christmastime, Londoners ice-skated on the Thames, and New Yorkers (then New Amsterdamers) sometimes walked over the Hudson from Manhattan to Staten Island.

Identifies the "Maunder Minimum" and acknowledges that its relationship to the "Little Ice Age" is controversial.

Of course, it could have been a coincidence. The Little Ice Age began before the onset of the Maunder Minimum. Many scientists think volcanic activity was a more likely, or at least a more significant, culprit. Or perhaps the big chill was, in the words of scientist Alan Cutler, writing in the *Washington Post* in 1997, a "one-two punch from a dimmer sun and a dustier atmosphere."

Well, we just might find out. A new study in the American Geophysical Union's journal, *Eos*, suggests that we may be heading into another quiet phase similar to the Maunder Minimum.

Meanwhile, the journal *Science* reports that a study led by the National Center for Atmospheric Research, or NCAR, has finally figured out why increased sunspots have a dramatic effect on the weather, increasing temperatures more than the increase in solar energy should explain. Apparently, sunspots heat the stratosphere, which in turn amplifies the warming of the climate.

Scientists have known for centuries that sunspots affect the climate; they just never understood how. Now, allegedly, the mystery has been solved.

Last month, in another study, also released in *Science*, Oregon State University researchers claimed to settle the debate over what caused and ended the last Ice Age. Increased solar radiation coming from slight changes in the Earth's rotation, not greenhouse-gas levels, were to blame.

What is the significance of all this? To say I have no idea is quite an understatement, but it will have to do.

Nonetheless, what I find interesting is the eagerness of the authors and the media to make it clear that this doesn't have any particular significance for the debate over climate change. "For those wondering how the (NCAR) study bears on global warming, Gerald Meehl, lead author on the study, says that it doesn't — at least not directly," writes Moises Velasquez-Manoff of the *Christian Science Monitor*. "Global warming is a long-term trend, Dr. Meehl says. . . . This study attempts to explain the processes behind a periodic occurrence."

> Goldberg is careful to cite what will look like credible sources: *Eos, Science*.

> Though not competent to critique the science itself, Goldberg is willing to comment on how scientific results are reported.

This overlooks the fact that solar cycles are permanent "periodic occurrences," a.k.a. a very long-term trend. Yet Meehl insists the only significance for the debate is that his study proves climate modeling is steadily improving.

I applaud Meehl's reluctance to go beyond where the science takes him. For all I know, he's right. But such humility and skepticism seem to manifest themselves only when the data point to something other than the mainstream narrative about global warming. For instance, when we have terribly hot weather, or bad hurricanes, the media see portentous proof of climate change. When we don't, it's a moment to teach the masses how weather and climate are very different things.

No, I'm not denying that man-made pollution and other activity have played a role in planetary warming since the Industrial Revolution.

But we live in a moment when we are told, nay lectured and harangued, that if we use the wrong toilet paper or eat the wrong cereal, we are frying the planet. But the sun? Well, that's a distraction. Don't you dare forget your reusable shopping bags, but pay no attention to that burning ball of gas in the sky — it's just the only thing that prevents the planet from being a lifeless ball of ice engulfed in darkness. Never mind that sunspot activity doubled during the twentieth century, when the bulk of global warming has taken place.

What does it say that the modeling that guaranteed disastrous increases in global temperatures never predicted the halt in planetary warming since the late 1990s? (MIT's Richard Lindzen says that "there has been no warming since 1997 and no statistically significant warming since 1995.") What does it say that the modelers have only just now discovered how sunspots make the Earth warmer?

I don't know what it tells you, but it tells me that maybe we should study a bit more before we spend billions to "solve" a problem we don't understand so well.

Goldberg complains that causal claims about climate are reported inconsistently.

Note that this analysis ends up with more questions than answers.

The analysis grows highly rhetorical here to underscore what Goldberg sees as hypocrisy in climate change explanations.

Exploring purpose and topic

To find a topic for an explanatory paper or causal analysis, begin a sentence with *why*, *how*, or *what if* and then finish it, drawing on what you may already know about an issue, trend, or problem. ⭕

topic ◄

> Why are fewer young Americans marrying?
>
> Why is the occurrence of juvenile asthma spiking?
>
> Why do so few men study nursing or so few women study petroleum engineering?

There are, of course, many other ways to phrase questions about cause and effect in order to attach important conditions and qualifications.

> What if scientists figure out how to stop the human aging process—as now seems plausible within twenty years? What are the consequences for society?
>
> How likely is it that a successful third political party might develop in the United States to end the deadlock between Republicans and Democrats?

A satirical infographic suggests that Twitter is destroying the environment. Courtesy CableTV.com.

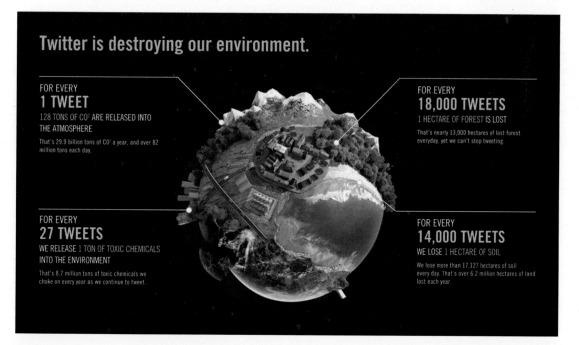

Twitter is destroying our environment.

FOR EVERY
1 TWEET
128 TONS OF CO² ARE RELEASED INTO THE ATMOSPHERE

That's 29.9 billion tons of CO² a year, and over 82 million tons each day.

FOR EVERY
18,000 TWEETS
1 HECTARE OF FOREST IS LOST

That's nearly 13,000 hectares of lost forest everyday, yet we can't stop tweeting.

FOR EVERY
27 TWEETS
WE RELEASE 1 TON OF TOXIC CHEMICALS INTO THE ENVIRONMENT

That's 8.7 million tons of toxic chemicals we choke on every year as we continue to tweet.

FOR EVERY
14,000 TWEETS
WE LOSE 1 HECTARE OF SOIL

We lose more than 17,127 hectares of soil every day. That's over 6.2 million hectares of land lost each year.

find a topic
p. 331

As you can see, none of these topics would just drop from a tree. They require cultural or technical knowledge and a willingness to speculate. Look for such cause-and-effect issues in your academic courses or professional life. Or search for them in the media—though you should shy away from worn-out subjects, such as plagiarism, credit card debt, and celebrity scandals, unless you can offer fresh insights.

To find a subject, try the following approaches.

Look again at a subject you know well.   It may be one that has affected you personally or might in the future. For instance, you may have experienced firsthand the effects of high-stakes testing in high school or you may have theories about why people your age still smoke despite the risks. Offer a hypothesis.

Look for an issue new to you.   Choose a subject you've always wanted to know more about (for example, the long-term cultural effects of the 9/11 attacks). You probably won't be able to venture a thesis or hypothesis until you've done some research, but that's the appeal of this strategy. The material is novel and you are energized. O

Examine a local issue.   Look for recent changes on campus or in the community and examine why they happened or what their consequences may be. Talk to the people responsible or affected. O Tuition raised? Admissions standards lowered? Speech code modified? Why, or what if?

Choose a challenging subject.   An issue that is complicated or vexed will push you to think harder. Don't rush to judgment; remain open-minded about contrary evidence, conflicting motives, and different points of view.

find a topic
p. 331

interview and
observe p. 447

Tackle an issue that seems settled.   If you have guts, look for a phenomenon that most people assume has been adequately explained. Tired of the way Republicans, Wall Street economists, vegans, fundamentalists, or those women on *The View* smugly explain the way things are? Pick one sore point and offer a different—and better—analysis.

> **Your Turn**   After Richard Nixon won forty-nine states in the 1972 presidential election, the distinguished film critic Pauline Kael is reported to have said, "How can he have won? I don't know anyone who voted for him." Can you think of any times when you have similarly misread a situation because you did not have a perspective broad enough to understand all the forces in play? Identify such a situation and consider whether it might provide you with a topic for an explanatory paper. Alternatively, consider some of the times—maybe even beginning in childhood—when you have heard explanations for phenomena that you recognized as wildly implausible because they were superstitions, stereotypes, or simply errors. Consider whether you might turn one of these misconceptions into a topic for an explanatory paper.

Understanding your audience

Readers for cause-and-effect analyses and explanations are diverse, but you might notice a difference between audiences you create yourself by drawing attention to a neglected subject and readers who come to your work because your topic already interests them.

Create an audience. In some situations, you must convince readers to pay attention to the phenomenon you intend to explore. ○ Assume they are smart enough to care about subjects that might affect their lives. But make the case for your subject aggressively. That's exactly what the editors of the *Wall Street Journal* do in an editorial noting the steady *decrease* in traffic deaths that followed a congressional decision ten years earlier to do away with a national 55-mph speed limit.

Anticipates readers who might ask, "Why does this issue matter?"

This may seem noncontroversial now, but at the time the debate was shrill and filled with predictions of doom. Ralph Nader claimed that "history will never forgive Congress for this assault on the sanctity of human life." Judith Stone, president of the Advocates for Highway and Auto Safety, predicted to Katie Couric on NBC's *Today Show* that there would be "6,400 added highway fatalities a year and millions of more injuries." Federico Peña, the Clinton administration's secretary of transportation, declared: "Allowing speed limits to rise above 55 simply means that more Americans will die and be injured on our highways."

— "Safe at Any Speed," July 7, 2006

Write to an existing audience. In most cases, you'll enter cause-and-effect debates already in progress. Whether you intend to uphold what most people already believe or, more controversially, ask them to rethink their positions, you'll probably face readers as knowledgeable (and opinionated) as you are. In the following opening paragraphs, for example, from an article exploring the decline of fine art in America, notice how cultural critic Camille Paglia presumes an intelligent audience already engaged by her topic but possibly offended by her title: "How Capitalism Can Save Art."

Paglia wants readers who care about art to consider what the future holds.

Does art have a future? Performance genres like opera, theater, music, and dance are thriving all over the world, but the visual arts have been in slow decline for nearly forty years. No major figure of profound influence has emerged in painting or sculpture since the waning of Pop Art and the birth of Minimalism in the early 1970s.

develop a
statement p. 362

Yet work of bold originality and stunning beauty continues to be done in architecture, a frankly commercial field. Outstanding examples are Frank Gehry's Guggenheim Museum Bilbao in Spain, Rem Koolhaas's CCTV headquarters in Beijing, and Zaha Hadid's London Aquatic Center for the 2012 Summer Olympics.

Points out that architecture is now more inventive than painting.

What has sapped artistic creativity and innovation in the arts? Two major causes can be identified, one relating to an expansion of form and the other to a contraction of ideology.

Poses causal questions knowledgeable readers will appreciate.

Painting was the prestige genre in the fine arts from the Renaissance on. But painting was dethroned by the brash multimedia revolution of the 1960s and '70s. Permanence faded as a goal of art-making.

But there is a larger question: What do contemporary artists have to say, and to whom are they saying it? Unfortunately, too many artists have lost touch with the general audience and have retreated to an airless echo chamber. The art world, like humanities faculties, suffers from a monolithic political orthodoxy — an upper-middle-class liberalism far from the fiery antiestablishment leftism of the 1960s. (I am speaking as a libertarian Democrat who voted for Barack Obama in 2008.)

Diagnoses the artistic problem: political orthodoxy.

Paglia asserts her credentials.

— "How Capitalism Can Save Art," *Wall Street Journal*, October 5, 2012

Finding and developing materials

▶ consider
causes

Expect to do as much research for a causal analysis as for any fact-based report or argument. You need to be careful to show that you have thoughtfully considered what others have written on a subject. ○

Equally important is learning how exactly causal relationships work so that any claims you make about them are accurate. Causality is intriguing because it demands precision and subtlety—as the categories explained in this section demonstrate. But once you grasp them, you'll also be better able to identify faulty causal claims when you come across them. (Exposing faulty causality makes for notably powerful and winning arguments.) ○

Understand necessary causes. A *necessary cause* is any factor that must be in place for something to occur. For example, sunlight, chlorophyll, and water are all necessary for photosynthesis to happen. Remove one of these elements from the equation and the natural process simply doesn't take place. But since none of them could cause photosynthesis on their own, they are necessary causes, yet not sufficient (see *sufficient causes* below).

On a less scientific level, necessary causes are those that seem so crucial that we can't imagine something happening without them. For example, you might argue that a team could not win a World Series without a specific pitcher on the roster: Remove him and the team doesn't even get to the playoffs. Or you might claim that, while fanaticism doesn't itself cause terrorism, terrorism doesn't exist without fanaticism. In any such analysis, it helps to separate necessary causes from those that may be merely contributing factors.

Understand sufficient causes. A *sufficient cause*, by itself, is enough to bring on a particular effect. Driving drunk or shoplifting are two sufficient causes for being arrested in the United States. In a causal argument, you might need to figure out which of several plausible sufficient causes is responsible for a specific phenomenon—assuming that a single explanation exists. A plane might have crashed because it was overloaded, ran out of fuel, had a structural failure, encountered severe wind shear, and so on.

Understand precipitating causes. Think of a *precipitating cause* as the proverbial straw that breaks a camel's back. In itself, the factor may seem trivial. But it becomes the spark that sets a field gone dry for months ablaze.

refine your
search p. 442

read closely
p. 340

By refusing to give up her bus seat to a white passenger in Montgomery, Alabama, Rosa Parks triggered a civil rights movement in 1955, but she didn't actually cause it: The necessary conditions had been accumulating for generations.

Understand proximate causes.   A *proximate cause* is nearby and often easy to spot. A corporation declares bankruptcy when it can no longer meet its massive debt obligations; a minivan crashes because a front tire explodes; a student fails a course because she plagiarizes a paper. But in a causal analysis, getting the facts right about such proximate causes may just be your starting point. You need to work toward a deeper understanding of a situation. As you might guess, proximate causes may sometimes also be sufficient causes.

Understand remote causes.   A *remote cause*, as the term suggests, may act at some distance from an event but be closely tied to it. That bankrupt corporation may have defaulted on its loans because of a full decade of bad management decisions; the tire exploded because it was underinflated and its tread was worn; the student resorted to plagiarism *because* she ran out of time *because* she was working two jobs to pay for a Hawaiian vacation *because* she wanted a memorable spring break to impress her friends—a string of remote causes. Remote causes make many causal analyses challenging and interesting: Figuring them out is like detective work.

Need help assessing your own work? See "How to Use the Writing Center" on pp. 354–55.

Understand reciprocal causes.   You have a *reciprocal* situation when a cause leads to an effect that, in turn, strengthens the cause. Consider how creating science internships for college women might encourage more women to become scientists, who then sponsor more internships, creating yet more female scientists. Many analyses of global warming describe reciprocal relationships, with CO_2 emissions supposedly leading to warming, which increases plant growth or alters ocean currents, which in turn releases more CO_2 or heat, and so on.

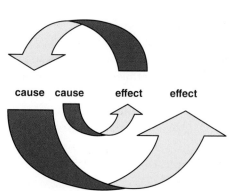

cause cause   effect   effect

Creating a structure

▶ organize
ideas

The introduction to a cause-and-effect argument should provide enough details for readers to see the point of your project. Spend as many paragraphs as you need to offer background information. The following brief paragraph might seem like an adequate opening for an essay on the failures of dog training. ○

> For thousands of years, humans have been training dogs to be hunters, herders, searchers, guards, and companions. Why are we doing so badly? The problem may lie more with our methods than with us.
>
> — Jon Katz, "Train in Vain," *Slate.com*, January 14, 2005

In fact, *seven* paragraphs precede this one to set up the causal claim. Those additional paragraphs help readers (especially dog owners) fully appreciate a problem many will find familiar. The actual first paragraph has author Jon Katz narrating a dog owner's dilemma.

> Sam was distressed. His West Highland terrier, aptly named Lightning, was constantly darting out of doors and dashing into busy suburban Connecticut streets. Sam owned three acres behind his house, and he was afraid to let the dog roam any of it.

By paragraph seven, Katz has offered enough corroborating evidence to describe a crisis in dogdom, a problem that leaves readers hoping for an explanation.

> The results of this failure are everywhere: Neurotic and compulsive dog behaviors like barking, biting, chasing cars, and chewing furniture — sometimes severe enough to warrant antidepressants — are growing. Lesser training problems — an inability to sit, stop begging, come, or stay — are epidemic.

Like Katz, you'll want to take the time necessary to introduce your subject and get readers invested in the issue. Then you have a number of options for developing your explanation or causal analysis.

Explain why something happened.   When simply suggesting causes to explain a phenomenon, you can move quickly from an introduction that explains the phenomenon to a thesis or hypothesis. Then work through your list of factors toward a conclusion. Build toward the most convincing explanation.

shape a
beginning p. 391

> **Introduction leading to an explanatory or causal claim**
>
> > First cause explored + reasons/evidence
> > Next cause explored + reasons/evidence . . .
> > Best cause explored + reasons/evidence
>
> **Conclusion**

Explain the consequences of a phenomenon.   When exploring effects that follow from some cause, event, policy, or change in the status quo, open by describing the situation you believe will have serious consequences. Then work through those effects, connecting them as you need to. Draw out the implications of your analysis in the conclusion.

> **Introduction describing a significant cause**
>
> > First effect likely to follow + reasons
> > Other effect(s) likely to follow + reasons . . .
>
> **Conclusion and discussion of implications**

Suggest an alternative view of cause and effect.   A natural strategy is to open a causal analysis by refuting someone else's faulty claim and then offering a better one of your own. After all, we often think about causality when someone makes a claim we disagree with.

> **Introduction questioning a causal claim**
>
> > Reasons to doubt claim offered + evidence
> > Alternative cause(s) explored . . .
> > Best cause examined + reasons/evidence
>
> **Conclusion**

Explain a chain of causes.   Sometimes you'll describe causes that operate in order, one by one: A causes B, B leads to C, C trips D, and so on. In such cases, use a sequential or narrative pattern of organization, giving special attention to the links (or transitions) within the chain. ○

Introduction suggesting a chain of causes/consequences

First link presented + reasons/evidence
Next link(s) presented + reasons/evidence . . .
Final link presented + reasons/evidence

Conclusion

People have been writing causal analysis for centuries. Here is the title page of Edward Jenner's 1798 publication, *An Inquiry into the Causes and Effects of the Variolae Vaccinae*. Jenner's research led to a vaccine that protected human beings from smallpox. © Mary Evans Picture Library/Everett Collection.

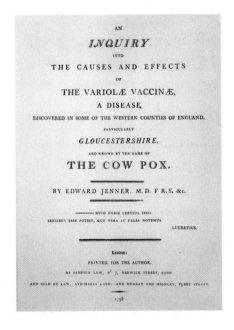

AN
INQUIRY
INTO
THE CAUSES AND EFFECTS
OF
THE VARIOLÆ VACCINÆ,
A DISEASE,
DISCOVERED IN SOME OF THE WESTERN COUNTIES OF ENGLAND,
PARTICULARLY
GLOUCESTERSHIRE,
AND KNOWN BY THE NAME OF
THE COW POX.

BY EDWARD JENNER, M. D. F. R. S. &c.

——— QUID NOBIS CERTIUS IPSIS
SENSIBUS ESSE POTEST, QUO VERA AC FALSA NOTEMUS
                                                    LUCRETIUS.

London:
PRINTED, FOR THE AUTHOR,
BY SAMPSON LOW, N° 7, BERWICK STREET, SOHO
AND SOLD BY LAW, AVE-MARIA LANE; AND MURRAY AND HIGHLEY, FLEET STREET.

1798

shape your
work p. 374

Choosing a style and design

When you analyze cause and effect, you'll often be offering an argument or exploring an idea for an audience you need to interest. You can do that through both style and design.

Consider a middle style.   Even causal analyses written for fairly academic audiences incline toward the middle style because of its flexibility: It can be both familiar and serious. ○ Here Robert Bruegmann, discussing the causes of urban sprawl, uses language that is simple, clear, and colloquial—and almost entirely free of technical jargon.

> When asked, most Americans declare themselves to be against sprawl, just as they say they are against pollution or the destruction of historic buildings. But the very development that one individual targets as sprawl is often another family's much-loved community. Very few people believe that they themselves live in sprawl or contribute to sprawl. Sprawl is where other people live, particularly people with less good taste. Much antisprawl activism is based on a desire to reform these other people's lives.
>
> — "How Sprawl Got a Bad Name," *American Enterprise*, June 2006

Adapt the style to the subject matter.   Friendly as it is, a middle style can still make demands of readers, as the following passage from an essay by Professor Paula Marantz Cohen of Drexel University demonstrates. In it she explains how our culture is training us to expect clear and accessible explanations for subtle and complex matters, pointing to her own experience with a DVD that tries to be too helpful. Though the language is sophisticated—see the items highlighted—this is middle style at its best, making complex claims and proving them in a way that keeps knowledgeable readers interested. (You can read the entire essay on p. 221.)

> Consider some other ways we have been conditioned to expect hard explanations for soft things (e.g., works of the imagination, and moral and philosophical questions). DVDs give us "special features," that often seem to diminish our understanding of the film or our appreciation of it. The idea applies to television

define your
style p. 400

as well. After watching the last episode of [HBO's] *Girls*, I happened to let the show run on to the after-show sequence, in which creator and star Lena Dunham explained what we had just seen. Not only did her banal exegesis lessen the power of the episode, it made me less interested in her quirky persona. What had looked smart and funny, creative and irreverent, was forced into an explanatory mold and both became uninteresting and co-opted into the very sort of neatly packaged form that the show seems to oppose. I didn't want to see a counterculture icon giving me a lecture on relationship stability.

—"Too Much Information," *The American Scholar*, June 18, 2013

Use appropriate supporting media.   Causal analyses have no special design features. But, like reports and arguments, they can employ charts that summarize information and graphics that illustrate ideas. *USA Today*, for instance, uses its daily "snapshots" to present causal data culled from surveys. Because causal analyses usually have distinct sections or parts (see "Creating a structure," p. 142), they do fit nicely into PowerPoint presentations. O

think visually
p. 557

Examining models

In a college research paper, Alysha Behn explores the reasons that women, despite talent and interest, so rarely pursue careers in technology and, more specifically, computer programming. Drawing heavily on research studies, Behn's causal analysis is detailed, complicated, and challenging.

Reading the Genre You may be surprised that Behn's causal argument ends on a pessimistic note, pointing out that no one-size-fits-all solution will resolve the complex issues keeping women out of technical careers. Does so tentative a conclusion weaken or add authority to the author's ethos? Does it affect how credibly she comes across to readers? (Notice that *I* does not occur in this academic paper.)

Behn 1

Alysha Behn

Professor Ruszkiewicz

Rhetoric 325M

February 20, 20--

Where Have All the Women Gone?

In 1984, 37.1 percent of computer science graduates were women. In 2009, around 11 percent of computer science graduates were women. What happened?

It's important to make clear what hasn't gone wrong. Experts dismiss the idea that men are more capable than women of succeeding at computer science, and there are no institutional barriers preventing women from pursuing a computer science degree or a tech career. In fact, rather than discriminating against women, colleges and corporations are competing desperately for female applicants. They just can't

> Opening uses statistics to identify the point of the paper.

For an additional reading, see **macmillanhighered.com/howtowrite3e**.
e-readings › *TheAtlantic.com, Think Again* [MULTIMODAL PROJECT]

147

Behn 2

find any. Women aren't pursuing careers in computer science anymore, and two decades of research hasn't found a way to stop the exodus.

Behn quickly dismisses some conventional explanations.

The root of the problem may be the flawed way sociologists and computer scientists are researching the problem, according to Katrina Markwick, a former researcher at the Monash University Department of Education. If researchers are asking the wrong questions, it follows that the solutions they suggest are going to be ineffective.

Much of the research Markwick criticizes focused on increasing women's access to technological education through equal opportunity (EO) strategies, which try to increase women's participation in a male-dominated field without questioning the culture that made that field male dominated (Markwick 258). Equal opportunity programs focus on removing institutional barriers or encouraging a group to participate more—for example, you could instruct math teachers on how to avoid treating girls differently from boys in class, or you could organize a math- and science-oriented summer camp just for girls in order to generate interest in those fields. The problem with the EO approach is that "[these] policies were predicated on the assumption of ontological equality, a belief in the fundamental sameness of individuals, and the EO mind-set produced an acceptance that white, nondisabled, heterosexual men's experiences and interpretations of organizational life were universally applicable" (Moss and Gunn 448). In other

Behn 3

words, EO programs and strategies implicitly ask women to conform—to be more like men—in order to have a career in computer science.

A research-based paragraph explains why EO-based strategies don't attract women to tech fields.

There's a fascinating body of research that suggests that the equal opportunity paradigm can't address all the factors turning women away from pursuing technology careers. For example, a 2008 study demonstrated that men prefer the aesthetics of Web sites designed by men, and women prefer the aesthetics of Web sites designed by women (Moss and Gunn 457-58)—and, as a result, people tend to spend more time browsing Web sites designed by a member of their own gender. Given that most computer games are made by men, it similarly follows that "young men are more attracted to playing computer games and . . . young women tend to prefer more passive purposeful games and game playing is not a major part of their leisure activities (Lang, 1999)" (Lang 221).

Although this paper is documented in MLA style, the quotes include APA citations.

What's problematic about all this is that both playing with video games and tooling around on the Internet indirectly teach computer literacy. What's more, kids who don't enjoy playing with computers aren't likely to pursue careers devoted to tinkering with them. All this points to a positive feedback loop that's responsible for turning men on to technology careers and pushing women away: As more men and fewer women are responsible for designing software and hardware, fewer technological products (even products intended to look gender

Behn 4

neutral, like the Apple iPad) will be designed with women's interests and aesthetic preferences in mind. Thus, fewer women will be interested in using these products, so fewer women will become skilled at using these technologies or drawn toward a career in making them.

Equal opportunity programs also don't take into account the process of socialization of gender—that is, learning from others what our gender role is—and aren't always well equipped to combat the negative lessons most women learn about themselves:

> The role socialization plays . . . cannot be underempha-
> sized in explaining the continued presence of the gender
> gap. . . . By the end of middle school, students develop
> the notion that mathematics, sciences, and computing
> fields are for white males (Clewell & Braddock, 2000).
> Furthermore, these perceptions are found to exist more
> often for girls than for boys (Trauth, 2002). (Varma 302)

Often the process of socialization is so subtle and pervasive that many women do not even notice it themselves (Varma 308). The perception that "boys are good at math" often leads counselors, parents, and teachers to subtly steer boys toward challenging math and science and away from liberal arts courses in high school, while for women the reverse holds true (Varma 306; Cheryan and Plaut). The result is that many women enter college less prepared for a computer science program than

Academic socialization steers students toward and away from tech careers.

Behn 5

their male peers. Even when male and female students are equally prepared, male students generally express more confidence in their skills, while women take as long as two years to feel that they are competent. In study after study, women have cited anxiety about performance and loss of self-confidence as a primary reason for leaving the field; in fact, some have suggested that professors have a lower opinion of female students' ability to do well than they do of their male students' (Varma 303). Thus, "Irani (2004) has argued that the act of establishing an 'identity of competence' is necessary for women to situate themselves in CS culture and verify legitimacy" (Varma 303).

In some cases the gendered socialization is a little less subtle. The anonymity afforded by online gaming and the Internet has made unapologetic misogyny disturbingly common in gaming and Internet culture. "The Rules of the Internet," a popular document created by an anonymous poster on the online forum 4chan, include the following: "28. Always question a person's gender—just in case it's really a man. 29. In the Internet all girls are men and all kids are undercover FBI agents" (Lolrus). Such rules establish that it is the norm to be male on the Internet, and to be a woman is to be the exception to the rule. Online gaming and participation in popular Web sites like 4chan and Reddit are frequently cited as factors that attract men to computing careers, so an online culture in which

Behn uses research studies to clarify and support her causal argument.

Behn 6

women are explicitly made to feel unwelcome is undoubtedly part of the problem.

Let's describe the last gendered assumption this way: Close your eyes and picture a programmer.

Behn offers a cultural reason that women avoid tech careers and suggests a way around the problem.

You probably pictured a nerdy-looking guy, perhaps with glasses, alone at his computer in a dark basement. Right? Here's the thing: The basement might be passé but the "alone" bit definitely isn't. And women show a marked aversion to programming alone (Lang 220-21). Fortunately, this is a problem we do have a solution for, and it's one that's catching on fast. Pair programming— a programming style where one partner types at the keyboard and the other partner watches closely, making suggestions and watching for errors—is an attractive solution not only because women prefer it but because the resulting code is consistently better than code written alone (Simon and Hanks 73-82). While younger companies have been eager to adopt pair programming practices, older giants like Microsoft and IBM have shown more reluctance. Furthermore, the success of pair programming will remain irrelevant until tech companies and colleges do a little PR to combat the isolated-nerd-in-a-basement image. Until then, the pair programming shift is more likely to aid retention of women in tech majors than to attract more of them to computing careers.

Behn resists any simple solution, noting a flaw in assumptions about women's participation in tech careers.

Markwick also criticized a second paradigm for increasing women's interest in technical fields, one emphasizing the values of femininity and suggesting solutions like a "girl friendly"

Behn 7

curriculum (Markwick 258-59): "This entailed 'celebrating the female side' of the gender binary and revaluing 'women's ways of knowing' (Belenky, Clinchy, Goldberger, & Tarule, 1986) . . . but it treated girls as an essentialized category, neglecting differences between girls" (Markwick 260). While this is without question a step forward from asking women to conform to the masculine norms of the computing industry, it also substitutes one false assumption—that men and women are basically the same—for another: in this case, that all women are fundamentally the same.

Few studies take into account the fact that women are not a homogeneous group (Varma 306). A solution that tries to attract women to technology careers by designing machines that appeal to women will not have much impact on minority women who can't afford that technology in the first place. Nor would a solution oriented around changing the culture of computer science classrooms do much to attract women who want a career that is known to be compatible with raising a family. A solution that tries to combat the "math is for boys" perception isn't going to make it easier for a woman to go to college if she needs to care for a young child. The list goes on. Too frequently, researchers have tried to pinpoint a single issue and define a one-size-fits-all solution, but moving women into tech careers is much more complicated than that.

Behn 8

Works Cited

Cheryan, Sapna, and Victoria C. Plaut. "Explaining

    Underrepresentation: A Theory of Precluded Interest." *Sex*

    Roles 63.7-8 (2010): 475-88. Print.

Lang, Catherine. "Twenty-First Century Australian Women and

    IT: Exercising the Power of Choice." *Computer Science*

    Education 17.3 (2007): 215-26. Web. 15 Feb. 2012.

Lolrus. "Rules of the Internet." *Internet Meme Database: Know*

    Your Meme. Know Your Meme, 2010. Web. 19 Feb. 2012.

Markwick, Katrina. "Under the Feminist Post-structuralist Lens:

    Women in Computing Education." *Journal of Educational*

    Computing Research 34.3 (2006): 257-79. Web. 15 Feb. 2012.

Moss, G. A., and R. W. Gunn. "Gender Differences in Website

    Production and Preference Aesthetics: Preliminary

    Implications for ICT in Education and Beyond." *Behaviour &*

    Information Technology 28.5 (2009): 447-60. *Computer*

    Source. Web. 15 Feb. 2012.

Simon, Beth, and Brian Hanks. "First Year Students'

    Impressions of Pair Programming in CS1." *ICER '07:*

    Proceedings of the Third International Workshop on

    Computing Education Research (2007): 73-85. *ACM Digital*

    Library. Web. 20 Feb. 2012.

Varma, Roli. "Why So Few Women Enroll in Computing? Gender

    and Ethnic Differences in Students' Perception." *Computer*

    Science Education 20.4 (2010): 301-16. Web. 15 Feb. 2012.

Documentation style used is MLA.

CULTURAL ANALYSIS   Ambitiously accounting for why people act as they do is one of the pleasures of writing causal arguments—providing that the answers offered are not too pat or predictable. (See Paula Marantz Cohen's comments on resisting "hard explanations for soft things" on p. 145.) Lance Hosey aims big in this short and entertaining cultural analysis that originally appeared in the *New York Times*.

Reading the Genre   Much of this analysis functions like a report: Hosey reviews what scientists have learned about human reactions to aesthetic stimuli. But what do you take from his conclusion—that great design could really be a matter of "diligent and informed study"? Does science trump art, now that technicians know the formulas for aesthetic pleasure? Or are scientists mere stragglers here, trailing after artists and architects who centuries ago learned how to make beautiful objects?

Why We Love Beautiful Things

Lance Hosey

February 15, 2013

The causal question is raised and, surprisingly, Hosey suggests answers may be on the horizon.

German scientists explain why we respond positively to natural shades and shapes.

Great design, the management expert Gary Hamel once said, is like Justice Potter Stewart's famous definition of pornography—you know it when you see it. You want it, too: brain scan studies reveal that the sight of an attractive product can trigger the part of the motor cerebellum that governs hand movement. Instinctively, we reach out for attractive things; beauty literally moves us.

Yet, while we are drawn to good design, as Mr. Hamel points out, we're not quite sure why.

This is starting to change. A revolution in the science of design is already under way, and most people, including designers, aren't even aware of it.

Take color. Last year, German researchers found that just glancing at shades of green can boost creativity and motivation. It's not hard to guess why: We associate verdant colors with food-bearing vegetation—hues that promise nourishment.

This could partly explain why window views of landscapes, research shows, can speed patient recovery in hospitals, aid learning in classrooms, and spur productivity in the workplace. In studies of call centers, for example, workers who could see the outdoors completed tasks 6 to 7 percent more efficiently than those who couldn't, generating an annual savings of nearly $3,000 per employee.

In some cases the same effect can happen with a photographic or even painted mural, whether or not it looks like an actual view of the outdoors. Corporations invest heavily to understand what incentivizes employees, and it turns out that a little color and a mural could do the trick.

Simple geometry is leading to similar revelations. For more than two thousand years, philosophers, mathematicians, and artists have marveled at the unique properties of the "golden rectangle": subtract a square from a golden rectangle, and what remains is another golden rectangle, and so on and so on — an infinite spiral. These so-called magical proportions (about 5 by 8) are common in the shapes of books, television sets, and credit cards, and they provide the underlying structure for some of the most beloved designs in history: the façades of the Parthenon and Notre Dame, the face of the *Mona Lisa*, the Stradivarius violin, and the original iPod.

Experiments going back to the nineteenth century repeatedly show that people invariably prefer images in these proportions, but no one has known why.

Then, in 2009, a Duke University professor demonstrated that our eyes can scan an image fastest when its shape is a golden rectangle. For instance, it's the ideal layout of a paragraph of text, the one most conducive to reading and retention. This simple shape speeds up our ability to perceive the world, and without realizing it, we employ it wherever we can.

Certain patterns also have universal appeal. Natural fractals — irregular, self-similar geometry — occur virtually everywhere in nature: in coastlines and riverways, in snowflakes and leaf veins, even in our own lungs. In recent years, physicists have found that people invariably prefer a certain mathematical density of fractals — not too thick, not too sparse. The theory is that this particular pattern echoes the shapes of trees, specifically the acacia, on the African savanna, the place stored in our genetic memory from the cradle of the human race. To paraphrase one biologist, beauty is in the genes of the beholder — home is where the genome is.

Proportions matter too — for deeply imbedded reasons.

Beauty seems built in.

Parthenon.
Funkystock/age footstock.

Pollock. *No. 1A*, 1948 (oil on canvas), Jackson Pollock (1912–1956)/Museum of Modern Art, New York, NY, USA/Photo © Boltin Picture Library/The Bridgeman Art Library; © 2014 The Pollock-Krasner Foundation/Artists Rights Society (ARS), New York.

Life magazine named Jackson Pollock "the greatest living painter in the United States" in 1949, when he was creating canvases now known to conform to the optimal fractal density (about 1.3 on a scale of 1 to 2 from void to solid). Could Pollock's late paintings result from his lifelong effort to excavate an image buried in all of our brains?

We respond so dramatically to this pattern that it can reduce stress levels by as much as 60 percent — just by being in our field of vision. One researcher has calculated that since Americans spend $300 billion a year dealing with stress-related illness, the economic benefits of these shapes, widely applied, could be in the billions.

It should come as no surprise that good design, often in very subtle ways, can have such dramatic effects. After all, bad design works the other way: Poorly designed computers can injure your wrists, awkward chairs can strain your back, and over-bright lighting and computer screens can fatigue your eyes.

Conclusion suggests that beauty is as much science as art.

We think of great design as art, not science, a mysterious gift from the gods, not something that results just from diligent and informed study. But if every designer understood more about the mathematics of attraction, the mechanics of affection, all design — from houses to cell phones to offices and cars — could both look good and be good for you.

Assignments

1. **Causal Analysis:** Like Jonah Goldberg in "Global Warming and the Sun" (p. 132), you've probably been curious about or even skeptical of some causal claims made routinely. It might just be college faculty complaining about why students browse the Web during classes. Or, more seriously, maybe you belong to a group that has been the subject of causal analyses verging on prejudicial. If so, refute what you regard as some faulty analysis of cause and effect by offering a more plausible explanation.

2. **Research Study:** Using Alysha Behn's research essay "Where Have All the Women Gone?" (p. 147) as a model, write a paper based on sources that examines an issue or problem in your major or in some area of special concern to you. The issue should be one that involves questions of how, why, or what if. Base your analysis on a variety of academic or public sources, fully documented. Draw on interviews if appropriate to your subject.

3. **Cultural Analysis:** In "Why We Love Beautiful Things" (p. 155), Lance Hosey answers a daunting causal question with research-based studies. Be ambitious yourself and pose a similar open-ended question, perhaps one that is somewhat narrower, about an aspect of culture or society you might be in a position to address. Pick a subject that genuinely puzzles you. Why, for example, have commercials become as important a part of the Super Bowl as the game itself? Why do women like shoes? What exactly makes a video go viral? As much as possible, try to find serious evidence to support your causal argument.

4. **Your Choice:** Politicians and pundits alike are fond of offering predictions, some hopeful, but many dire. The economy, they might suggest, is about to boom or slide into depression; sports dynasties are destined to blossom or collapse; printed books will disappear; American teens will grow even fonder of vinyl records and old audio equipment. Identify one such prediction about which you have some doubts and develop a cause-and-effect analysis to suggest why it is likely to go awry. Be sure to explain in detail what factors you expect will make the prediction go wrong. If you are brave, offer an alternative vision of the future.

How to start

- Need a **topic**? See page 166.
- Need to come up with a **solution**? See page 170.
- Need to **organize your ideas**? See page 172.

6 Proposals

define a problem and suggest a solution

Proposals are written to solve problems. Typically, you'll make a proposal to initiate an action or change. At a minimum, you hope to alter someone's thinking—even if only to recommend leaving things as they are.

TRIAL BALLOON
Degree programs at your school have so many complicated requirements that most students take far more time to graduate than they expect—adding thousands of dollars to their loans. As a *trial balloon*, you suggest that the catalog include accurate "time-to-degree" estimates for all degree programs and certificates.

MANIFESTO
Packaging is getting out of hand and you've had enough. People can barely open the products they buy because everything is zipped up, shrink-wrapped, blister-packed, containerized, or child-protected. So you write a *manifesto* calling for saner and more eco-friendly approaches to product protection.

VISUAL PROPOSAL
You create a PowerPoint so members of your co-op can visualize how much better your building's study area would look with a few inexpensive tweaks in furniture, paint, and lighting. Your *visual proposal* gets you the job of implementing the changes.

DECIDING TO WRITE A PROPOSAL. *Got an issue or a problem? Good—let's deal with it.* That's the logic driving most proposals, both the professional types that pursue grant money and the less formal propositions that are part of everyday life, academic or otherwise. Like evaluations and some explanations, proposals are another form of argument (for more on choosing a genre, see the Introduction).

Although grant writing shares some elements of informal proposals, it is driven by rigid formulas set by foundations and government agencies, usually covering things like budgets, personnel, evaluation, outcomes, and so on. Informal proposals are much easier. Though they may not funnel large sums of cash your way, they're still important tools for addressing problems. A sensible proposal can make a difference in any situation—be it academic, personal, or political.

In offering a proposal, you'll need to make many of the moves outlined below. In a first-round pitch, for example, you might launch a trial balloon to test whether an idea will work at all, roughing out a scheme with the details to

Use Only What You Need How do you persuade people in a community to save water? Denver Water created an innovative multimedia ad campaign to sell its proposal cleverly to its community. Courtesy of Denver Water.

follow. A more serious plan headed for public debate and scrutiny would have to punch the ticket on more of the items.

Define a problem.   Set the stage for a proposal by describing the specific situation, problem, or opportunity in enough detail that readers *get it*: They see a compelling need for action. In many cases, a proposal needs to explain what's wrong with the status quo.

Make specific recommendations.   This is the trial balloon. Don't just complain that someone else has botched a situation or opportunity: Explain what you propose to do about the problem. The more concrete your solution is, the better.

Target the proposal.   To make a difference, you have to reach people with the power to change a situation. That means first identifying such individuals (or groups) and then tailoring your proposal to their expectations. Use the Web or library, for example, to get the names and contact information of government or corporate officials. ○ When the people in power *are* the problem, go over their heads to more general audiences with clout of their own: voters, consumers, women, fellow citizens, the elderly, and so on.

Consider reasonable alternatives.   Your proposal won't be taken seriously unless you have weighed all the workable possibilities, explaining their advantages and downsides. Only then will you be prepared to make a case for your own ideas.

Make realistic recommendations.   You need to address two related issues: *feasibility* and *implementation*. A proposal is feasible if it can be achieved with available resources and is acceptable to the parties involved. And, of course, a feasible plan still needs a plausible pathway to completion: *First we do this; then we do this.*

plan a
project p. 436

The following proposal originally appeared in *Time* (August 21, 2005). Its author, Barrett Seaman, doesn't have the space to do much more than alert the general public (or, more likely, parents of college students) to the need for action to end alcohol abuse on campuses. Still, he does offer a surprising suggestion — a trial balloon for dealing with bingeing. Although many readers might reject his idea initially, the proposal does what it must: It makes a plausible case and gets people thinking.

Reading the Genre One of the major tasks in writing a proposal argument is defining the problem. How much of Seaman's essay is concerned with explaining the problem of binge drinking on campus? To whom is this information addressed?

How Bingeing Became the New College Sport

BARRETT SEAMAN

In the coming weeks, millions of students will begin their fall semester of college, with all the attendant rituals of campus life: freshman orientation, registering for classes, rushing by fraternities and sororities, and, in a more recent nocturnal college tradition, "pregaming" in their rooms.

> Defines problem he intends to address: bingeing known as "pregaming."

Pregaming is probably unfamiliar to people who went to college before the 1990s. But it is now a common practice among eighteen-, nineteen-, and twenty-year-old students who cannot legally buy or consume alcohol. It usually involves sitting in a dorm room or an off-campus apartment and drinking as much hard liquor as possible before heading out for the evening's parties. While reporting for my book *Binge*, I witnessed the hospitalization of several students for acute alcohol poisoning. Among them was a Hamilton College freshman who had consumed twenty-two shots of vodka while sitting in a dorm room with her friends. Such hospitalizations are routine on campuses across the nation. By the Thanksgiving break of the year I visited Harvard, the university's health center had admitted nearly seventy students for alcohol poisoning.

> Proposal draws on research the author has done.

When students are hospitalized — or worse yet, die from alcohol poisoning, which happens about three hundred times each year — college

Points out that current solutions to college drinking don't work.

Explains factors responsible for the spike in alcohol abuse.

presidents tend to react by declaring their campuses dry or shutting down fraternity houses. But tighter enforcement of the minimum drinking age of twenty-one is not the solution. It's part of the problem.

Over the past forty years, the United States has taken a confusing approach to the age-appropriateness of various rights, privileges, and behaviors. It used to be that twenty-one was the age that legally defined adulthood. On the heels of the student revolution of the late '60s, however, came sweeping changes: The voting age was reduced to eighteen; privacy laws were enacted that protected college students' academic, health, and disciplinary records from outsiders, including parents; and the drinking age, which had varied from state to state, was lowered to eighteen.

Then, thanks in large measure to intense lobbying by Mothers Against Drunk Driving, Congress in 1984 effectively blackmailed states into hiking the minimum drinking age to twenty-one by passing a law that tied

Do current strict drinking laws in the United States actually encourage students to abuse alcohol? In 2008, a coalition of presidents from one hundred colleges recommended lowering the drinking age to eighteen.
AP Photo/Israel Leal.

compliance to the distribution of federal-aid highway funds—an amount that will average $690 million per state this year. There is no doubt that the law, which achieved full fifty-state compliance in 1988, saved lives, but it had the unintended consequence of creating a covert culture around alcohol as the young adult's forbidden fruit.

Drinking has been an aspect of college life since the first Western universities in the fourteenth century. My friends and I drank in college in the 1960s—sometimes a lot but not so much that we had to be hospitalized. Veteran college administrators cite a sea change in campus culture that began, not without coincidence, in the 1990s. It was marked by a shift from beer to hard liquor, consumed not in large social settings, since that is now illegal, but furtively and dangerously in students' residences.

In my reporting at colleges around the country, I did not meet any presidents or deans who felt that the twenty-one-year age minimum helps their efforts to curb the abuse of alcohol on their campuses. Quite the opposite. They thought the law impeded their efforts since it takes away the ability to monitor and supervise drinking activity.

What would happen if the drinking age was rolled back to eighteen or nineteen? Initially, there would be a surge in binge drinking as young adults savored their newfound freedom. But over time, I predict, U.S. college students would settle into the saner approach to alcohol I saw on the one campus I visited where the legal drinking age is eighteen: Montreal's McGill University, which enrolls about two thousand American undergraduates a year. Many, when they first arrive, go overboard, exploiting their ability to drink legally. But by midterms, when McGill's demanding academic standards must be met, the vast majority have put drinking into its practical place among their priorities.

A culture like that is achievable at U.S. colleges if Congress can muster the fortitude to reverse a bad policy. If lawmakers want to reduce drunk driving, they should do what the Norwegians do: Throw the book at offenders no matter what their age. Meanwhile, we should let the pregamers come out of their dorm rooms so that they can learn to handle alcohol like the adults we hope and expect them to be.

Margin notes:

Points out that current law makes it harder to deal with bingeing.

Proposal stands up to tests of feasibility, acceptability, and practicality.

Offers specific proposal tentatively, posed as question.

States his thesis and then offers precedents for students behaving more responsibly with lower drinking age.

Exploring purpose and topic

▶ topic

Most people will agree to a reasonable proposal—as long as it doesn't cost them anything. But moving audiences from *I agree* to *I'll actually do something about it* takes a powerful act of persuasion. And for that reason, proposals are typically structured as arguments, requiring all the strategies used in that genre. ○

Occasionally, you'll be asked to solve a particular problem in school or on the job. Having an assigned topic makes your task a little easier, but you can bet that any such problem will be complex and open to multiple solutions. Otherwise, there would be no challenge to it.

When choosing a proposal topic on your own, keep in mind the following concerns. ○

Look for a genuine issue. Spend the first part of your project defining a problem readers will care about. You may think it's a shame no one retails Prada close to campus, but your classmates probably care more about out-of-control student fees or the high price of housing. Go beyond your own concerns in settling on a problem.

Look for a challenging problem. It helps if others have tried to fix it in the past but failed—and you are able to figure out why. Times change, attitudes shift, technology improves: Factors like these might make what once seemed like an intractable problem more manageable now. Choose a serious topic to which you can bring fresh perspectives.

Look for a soluble problem. Challenges *are* good, but impossible dreams are for Broadway musicals. Parking on campus is the classic impasse—always present, always frustrating. Steer clear of problems no one has ever solved, unless you have a *really* good idea.

Look for a local issue. It's best to leave "world peace" to beauty pageant contestants. Instead, investigate a problem in your community, where you can interview affected people or search local archives. ○ Doing so also makes it easier to find an audience you can influence, including people potentially able to improve the situation. You're far more likely to get the attention of your dean of students than the secretary of state.

> Need help deciding what to write about? See "How to Browse for Ideas" on pp. 338–39.

166

understand argument p. 66

find a topic p. 331

interview and observe p. 447

FISCAL CLIFF FIX

Columbus Dispatch editorial cartoonist Nate Beeler offers a proposal for solving the country's budget woes. Nate Beeler, courtesy of Cagle Cartoons.

Your Turn   In 46 BCE, Julius Caesar used his authority as dictator to impose a new calendar on Rome because the old one had fallen five months out of sync with the seasons. Play Caesar today by imagining what problems you would fix if you could simply impose your will. Make a list. Narrow your more grandiose schemes (free pizza for all) to more plausible ones (less rowdiness in the student section at football games), and then consider which items on your roster could be argued rationally and compellingly in a short paper. Compare your list with those of other students and discuss workable proposal topics.

Understanding your audience

While preparing a proposal, keep two audiences in mind—one fairly narrow and the other more broad. The first group includes people who could possibly do something about a problem; the second consists of general readers who could influence those in the first group by bringing the weight of public opinion down on them. And public opinion makes a difference.

Writers calibrate proposals for specific readers all the time. Grant writers, especially, make it a point to learn what agencies and institutions expect in applications. Quite often, it takes two or three tries to figure out how to present a winning grant submission. You won't have that luxury with most academic or political pieces, but you can look for examples of successful proposals and study them.

Appeal to people who can make a difference.   For example, a personal letter you prepare for the dean of students to protest her policies against displaying political posters in university buildings (including dormitories) should have a respectful and perhaps legalistic tone, pointing to case law on the subject and university policies on freedom of speech. You'd also want to assure the dean of your goodwill and provide her with sound reasons for loosening the restrictions.

Rally people who represent public opinion.   No response from the dean of students on the political poster proposal you made? Then take the issue to the public, perhaps via an op-ed or letter in the student paper. Keeping the dean still firmly in mind, you'd now also write to stir up student and community opinion. Your new piece could be more emotional than your letter and less burdened by legal points—though still citing facts and presenting solid reasons for giving students more leeway in expressing political beliefs on campus. ○

The fact is that people often need a spur to move them—that is, a persuasive strategy that helps them imagine their role in solving a problem. Again, you'd be in good company in leading an audience to your position. As shown on page 169, when President John F. Kennedy proposed a mission to the moon in 1962, he did it in language that stirred a public skeptical about the cost and challenges of such an implausible undertaking.

refine your
tone p. 400

JFK Aims High In 1962, the president challenged Americans to go to the moon; today American astronauts ride to the International Space Station on a Russian Soyuz. © Corbis.

There is no strife, no prejudice, no national conflict in outer space as yet. Its hazards are hostile to us all. Its conquest deserves the best of all mankind, and its opportunity for peaceful cooperation may never come again. But why, some say, the moon? Why choose this as our goal? And they may well ask why climb the highest mountain? Why, thirty-five years ago, fly the Atlantic? Why does Rice play Texas?

We choose to go to the moon. We choose to go to the moon in this decade and do the other things, not because they are easy, but because they are hard, because that goal will serve to organize and measure the best of our energies and skills, because that challenge is one that we are willing to accept, one we are unwilling to postpone, and one which we intend to win, and the others, too.

— Rice Stadium "Moon Speech," September 12, 1962

Finding and developing materials

▶ consider
solutions

Proposals might begin with whining and complaining (*I want easier parking!*), but they can't stay in that mode long. They require sober thought and research. What makes proposals distinctive, however, is the sheer variety of strategies a single document might employ. To write a convincing proposal, you may need to narrate, report, argue, evaluate, and analyze. Here's how to develop those various parts.

Define the problem.   Research the existing situation thoroughly enough to explain it concisely to readers. To be sure you've got the basics of your topic down cold, run through the traditional journalist's questions—*Who? What? Where? When? Why? How?* When appropriate, interview experts or people involved with an issue; for instance, in college communities, the best repositories of institutional memory will usually be staff. ○ Search for any documents with hard facts on the matter that might convince skeptical readers. For instance, if you propose to change a long-standing policy, find out when it was created, by whom, and for what reasons.

The Journalist's Questions

Who?	What?
Where?	When?
Why?	How?

Examine prior solutions.   If a problem is persistent, other people have tried to solve it—or maybe they even caused it. In either case, do the research necessary to figure out, as best you can, what happened in these previous efforts. But expect controversy. You may have to sort through contentious and contradictory narratives. Once you know the history of an issue, shift into an evaluative mode to figure out why earlier strategies faltered. ○ Then explain them to readers so that they can later compare these failed approaches to your own proposal and appreciate its ingenuity.

Outline a proposal.   Coming up with a sensible proposal may take more creativity than you can muster. So consider working collaboratively, when that's an option. ○ Brainstorm aggressively with classmates and be sure to write down ideas as they emerge. Be specific about details, especially numbers and costs.

interview and
observe p. 447

understand
evaluation p. 100

collaborate
p. 428

Defend the proposal.   Any ideas that threaten the status quo will surely raise hackles. That's half the fun of proposing change. So advance your position by using all the tools of argument available to you—logical, factual, and, yes, emotional. Present yourself as smart and competent. Anticipate objections, because readers invested in the status quo will offer them in spades. Above all, show that your idea will work and that it is *feasible*—that it can be achieved with existing or new resources. For example, you might actually solve your school's traffic problems by proposing a monorail linking the central campus to huge new parking garages. But who would pay for the multimillion-dollar system?

And yet, you shouldn't be put off too easily by the objection that *we can't possibly do that*. A little chutzpah is not out of line—it's part of the problem-solving process.

Figure out how to implement the proposal.   Readers will need assurances that your ideas can be put into action: Show them how. ○ Figure out exactly what will happen: where new resources will come from, how personnel can be recruited and hired, where brochures or manuals will be printed, and so on. Provide a timetable if you can.

think critically
p. 343

Creating a structure

► organize
ideas

Proposals follow the thought processes most people go through in dealing with issues, and some of these problems raise more complications than others. ○ Generally, the less formal the proposal, the fewer structural elements it will have. So adapt the following template to your needs, using it as a checklist of *possible* issues to consider in framing a proposal.

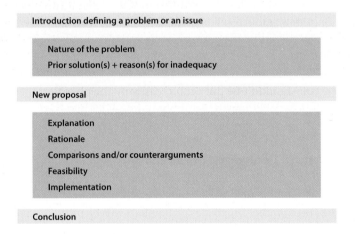

Introduction defining a problem or an issue

> Nature of the problem
> Prior solution(s) + reason(s) for inadequacy

New proposal

> Explanation
> Rationale
> Comparisons and/or counterarguments
> Feasibility
> Implementation

Conclusion

You might use a similar structure whenever you need to examine what effects—good or bad—might follow some action, event, policy, or change in the status quo. Once again, you'd begin with an introduction that fully describes the action you believe will have significant consequences; then you explain those consequences to readers, showing how they are connected. Finally, a conclusion could draw out the implications of your analysis.

shape your
work p. 374

Choosing a style and design

Proposals do come in many forms and, occasionally, they may be frivolous or comic. But whenever you suggest changing people's lives or spending someone else's money, show a little respect and humility.

Use a formal style. Professional proposals—especially those seeking grant money—are typically written in a high style, formal and impersonal, almost as if the project would be jeopardized by reviewers detecting the slightest hint of enthusiasm or personality. ○ Academic audiences are often just as poker-faced. So use a formal style in proposals you write for school when your intended readers are formidable and "official"— professors, deans and provosts, or administrators (and pay attention to their titles!).

Observe the no-nonsense tone Thao Tran adopts early in an academic essay whose title alone suggests its sober intentions: "Coping with Population Aging in the Industrialized World."

Leaders of industrialized nations and children of baby boomers must understand the consequences of population aging and minimize its economic effects. This report will recommend steps for coping with aging in the industrialized world and will assess counterarguments to those steps. With a dwindling workforce and rising elderly population, industrialized countries must take a multistep approach to expand the workforce and support the elderly. Governments should attempt to attract immigrants, women, and elderly people into the workforce. Supporting an increasing elderly population will require reforming pension systems and raising indirect taxes. It will also require developing pronatalist policies, in which governments subsidize child-rearing costs to encourage births. Many of these strategies will challenge traditional cultural notions and require a change in cultural attitudes. While change will not be easy, industrialized nations must recognize and address this trend quickly in order to reduce its effects.

Point of view is impersonal: *This report* rather than *I.*

Purpose of proposal is clearly explained.

Premises and assumptions of proposal are offered in abstract language.

Use a middle style, when appropriate. Shift to a middle style when you need to persuade a general audience or whenever establishing a personal relationship with readers might help your proposal.

It is possible, too, for styles to vary within a document. Your language might be coldly efficient as you scrutinize previous failures or tick off the advantages of your specific proposal. But as you near the end of the piece, you might decide another style would better reflect your vision for the future or

define your
style p. 400

your enthusiasm for an idea. Environmentalist David R. Brower offered many technical arguments to explain why his radical proposal for draining Lake Powell would make commercial sense. But he concluded his appeal on a more emotional note:

> The sooner we begin, the sooner lost paradises will begin to recover — Cathedral in the Desert, Music Temple, Hidden Passage, Dove Canyon, Little Arch, Dungeon, and a hundred others. Glen Canyon itself can probably lose its ugly white sidewalls in two or three decades. The tapestries can reemerge, along with the desert varnish, the exiled species of plants and animals, the pictographs, and other mementos of people long gone. The canyon's music will be known again, and "the sudden poetry of springs," Wallace Stegner's beautiful phrase, will be revealed again below the sculptured walls of Navajo sandstone. The phrase, "as long as the rivers shall run and the grasses grow," will regain its meaning.

Place names listed have poetic effect.

Lush details add to emotional appeal of proposal.

Final quotation summarizes mission of proposal.

Pay attention to elements of design. Writers often incorporate images, charts, tables, graphs, and flowcharts to illustrate what is at stake in a proposal or to make comparisons easy. Images also help readers imagine solutions or proposals and make those ideas attractive. The SmartArt Graphics icon in the Microsoft Word Gallery opens up a range of templates you might use to help readers visualize a project. **O**

Your Turn   The style of proposals varies dramatically, depending on audience and purpose. Review the proposals in this chapter offered as models — including the visual items. Then explain in some detail exactly how the language of one of those items works to make its case. You can focus on a whole piece, but you may find it more interesting just to explicate a few sentences or paragraphs or one or two visual details. For example, when does Barrett Seaman (p. 163), Nate Beeler (p. 167), Katelyn Vincent (p. 175), or Jen Sorensen (p. 182) score style points with you? Be ready to explain your observation orally.

think visually
p. 557

Examining models

Proposals often arise from a critical look at contemporary culture. Here, Katelyn Vincent draws upon her own experiences to argue, finally, that technology is taking up too much of our lives. She dramatizes the issue by describing her own struggle to survive for twelve hours without the Internet.

Reading the Genre The narrative structure Vincent uses in "Technology Time-Out" is not typical of more formal proposals, especially those that follow the pattern outlined on p. 172. But as she tells the story of her twelve hours without the Internet, which elements of a typical proposal do you find in the essay? How well does Vincent's proposal make a case for taking a break from technology?

Vincent 1

Katelyn Vincent

Professor Ruszkiewicz

Composition 2

November 11, 20--

Technology Time-Out

"Are you sure you want to shut down?" A gray box has popped up and is waiting for my answer. No, I think to myself, I'm really not—and it's true. I have become so reliant on my computer that the thought of willingly turning it off during the day feels strange, almost wrong. And these days, it seems that everyone else shares the same addiction. The other day, when my roommate's Internet was down for a few hours, she had a mild panic attack. I thought it was silly—until I realized I would have had the same reaction if something similar had happened to me. Now, I consider myself to be a reasonably independent

For an additional reading, see **macmillanhighered.com/howtowrite3e.**
e-readings › Michael Pollan, *Celebrate School Lunch* [VIDEO]

175

Vincent 2

person, and the thought of being so dependent on something—
especially a *machine*—horrified me. So I made a resolution—
to avoid the Internet for twelve hours.

The gray box still waits. A blue button flashes on the
screen in front of me, and the words "Shut Down" pulsate
before my eyes, daring me to make my decision. Giving in to my
curiosity, I click and watch as the luminous rectangle in front of
me fades slowly to black. That was easy enough, I think to
myself. Maybe I can handle this after all.

Looking for something to do now that my primary source
of entertainment (and procrastination) has dissolved into
nothingness, I realize that it is eight o'clock and I have not eaten
anything since breakfast. In the kitchen, I reach for the Fruity
Cheerios on the top shelf of the pantry—a food staple since I
started college—and am this close to pouring when I realize
that *making* dinner might actually be fun. Heck, I haven't made
myself a real dinner in several weeks, and since I usually spend
this time Facebook-stalking casual acquaintances from third
grade and reading random health articles on a too-familiar 9 × 13
glowing screen, today I have the time to spare. Eagerly, I pull
out the pasta box that has been sleeping on my shelf for the
past four months and get to work. You know what would be
great with this, I think—some chicken. Mmm, I know, they have
an amazing chicken pasta recipe on Allrecipes.com, I'll just go
and . . . dammit. Never mind, I'll improvise. Surprisingly, the

The problem of
Web addiction
is identified,
connecting the
essay to a wide
audience.

Vincent shifts
to present
tense to inten-
sify the action.

The details are
homey and
believable.

Vincent 3

chicken doesn't turn out horribly. My dinner is no "Nicole's Tailgate Party Chicken Salad," but an alarmingly strong lemon taste gives me a zesty kick in the mouth. And to be honest, the fact that dinner is warm and homemade makes it infinitely better than Fruity Cheerios.

After dinner I again find myself bored—and wondering how many people have commented on my Facebook status. Wait a minute—why am I so concerned about this? Am I really so lame that my happiness depends on what people comment on my Facebook posts? God, I hope not. Trying to distract myself from this disturbing thought, I pull out my textbook to study—and once again, something doesn't feel right. I realize it has been over an hour since I checked Hotmail, Facebook, or MSN. My hand itches to press the power button and start clicking and clacking away—my prestudy ritual. Who knows how many e-mails, Facebook notifications, and important articles are popping up without my knowledge? What if I am missing something hugely important? Still, determined to stick it out, I dig in my backpack and stare into *Corporate Finance*, Second Edition. After three minutes, all I can think about is how much I would love to put in my headphones and crank up Pandora.com and my Michael Bublé playlist. This is going to be a long night.

I guess, not surprisingly, I am more focused on *Corporate Finance* than I have ever been, which isn't saying much, but

The strategy is to describe symptoms of Internet addiction that readers will recognize.

Vincent 4

Without getting technical, a full paragraph examines the limits of multitasking and the potential consequences for college students.

still—I'm impressed. I have turned off my cell phone and iPod as well, and before I know it I have read two whole sections of the book and done a chapter's worth of questions. Not bad for two hours of studying. Afterwards, I delve into marketing and manage to read an entire chapter from that book as well. I have to say, it feels good to accomplish something and not have to stress about it. And I actually think I learned something—a feeling I don't always get from studying, which for me is usually marked more by frantic memorization than any real retention of information. I guess part of the reason for my inability to recall is that studying for me usually means multitasking between chapter skimming, shopping for new boots on Amazon.com, and watching online clips from an old episode of *Glee*. I usually switch back and forth between book and computer, spending about five minutes (max) on the book before some arbitrary whim or want enters my head and I have to go online and check it out before I can resume studying. It's gratifying to do something well for a change.

The paragraph ends with a clever but important insight, driving home a key theme of the paper.

It's also kind of nice not to be in continuous contact with the rest of the world, I think to myself. What with e-mail, Facebook, calling, and texting, I feel as if I am constantly communicating with everyone I know. I can text my mom, talk on the phone with my sister, Facebook-chat with my friend, and e-mail my professor—all at the same time! While establishing relationships with other people is fine, it is also enjoyable to

Vincent 5

spend some time alone once in a while: I feel as though I haven't been truly alone in ages. Even while studying finance, I realize I am calmer than I have been in weeks. For a change, I get the chance to recharge *my* batteries instead of just my Mac's.

The next morning I am back to Fruity Cheerios and instinctively reach for the power button on my Mac as soon as I wake up. Still moving around in the foggy space of sleepiness, it takes me a moment to realize that my self-imposed sentence is not up. So much for checking my e-mail and Weather.com before I head out. Then again, I realize, I go to bed so late that it doesn't really make sense that I would have gotten any new e-mails since the last time I checked—most normal people are in bed between the hours of 2 and 6 AM, after all. Why do I have to check everything in the morning again? I have done it for so long that I guess it's just habit by now. I could be using those twenty minutes to spend more time getting ready or, even better, sleeping. I guess the only Web site it really makes sense to check in the morning is Weather.com, and even that's not a complete necessity.

The extra moments give me more time to get ready, and those seemingly insignificant twenty minutes turn my usually hectic morning routine into a much calmer transition between sleep and class. For the first time this semester, I am *not* lathering myself into a frenzy, *not* frantically applying lip gloss on my way out, and *not* running to catch the bus that's about to

Vincent realizes that technology has complicated her life and, by implication, the lives of her readers.

Vincent 6

leave (there goes my exercise). In fact, my entire morning is pretty mellow, and I don't even think about getting online again until lunchtime. By then, the twelve hours is up—but the only reason I get online is to register for classes. Why mess with a good thing?

As it turns out, the "hugely important" somethings I was missing during my online off-time consisted of one offer for a free colon cleanse, two "Take this quiz!" pop-ups on Facebook, a new MSN article on the latest *Dancing with the Stars* results, and only one actual, legitimate e-mail—from my mother. Granted, I do get some important e-mails from time to time, but when I think about it, how many of them actually require that I respond immediately? Most likely, none.

So what did I learn from all this? That I *am* addicted to technology and our online world—and I have a feeling I am not too different from the rest of society. I couldn't go twelve hours Internet free without driving myself a little crazy. But at the same time, this addiction of ours is one that we, to some degree, have been forced into. While Amazon and Pandora are, admittedly, somewhat superfluous, the use of e-mail as the primary means of communication and Facebook as the major place of social interaction nowadays means that those who ignore them are left behind. We can't just decide to ignore technology completely; it has become a part of our world and something that we have to deal with daily, whether we want to or not.

> The humor here is yet another gesture to win over readers, who have probably received similar e-mails.

> The essay concedes that most of us can't ignore technology: Turning off the Web entirely is not feasible.

Vincent 7

But at the same time, it shouldn't be our *whole* world.
After all, if our online world becomes our entire universe — what
happens when the computer crashes? We crash with it. The
only way to ensure that doesn't happen is to distance ourselves,
when possible, from that which is slowly sucking us into
dependency. We need to take some time to learn how to do
things on our own, take time to do things well again, take time
for ourselves, and, ultimately, just take time to learn that easier
doesn't always mean better.

In highly
rhetorical lan-
guage, Vincent
makes a call for
independence
and change.

VISUAL PROPOSAL   Jen Sorensen is an editorial cartoonist fond of four-panel spreads with political messages. The medium requires that messages be expressed economically, so Sorensen uses broad strokes to criticize a proposal affecting student loans.

Reading the Genre   Only one character in Sorensen's cartoon "Loan Bone" speaks. What do her words suggest about possible real solutions to the problem of student debt? You may want to compare the brief proposal here to the more extended visual argument by Matt Bors on page 95.

Loan Bone

First panel identifies a specific problem.

Victims and villains are clearly identified.

Solutions offered are deliberately implausible.

Twitter: @JenSorensen   www.jensorensen.com   © 2013 Jen Sorensen

1. **Trial Balloon:** In calling for reducing the drinking age, Barrett Seaman's "How Bingeing Became the New College Sport" (p. 163) offers a solution to alcohol abuse that some might call "politically incorrect" — lowering the drinking age. Indeed, many politicians or school officials would probably be reluctant to support such a proposal — even if it might make people more responsible. Choose an issue that you think needs as radical a rethinking as college-age drinking and write a research-based proposal of your own. Like Seaman, be sure to offer your ideas in language calm and persuasive enough to make responsible adults at least consider them.

2. **Manifesto:** You probably identify with at least some of the issues Katelyn Vincent presents in "Technology Time-Out" (p. 175) and with the manifesto she enunciates in her final paragraphs. Look for a problem that others might similarly recognize, describe the issue in enough detail to explain why adjustments may be necessary or desirable, and then make a compelling call for change.

3. **Visual Proposal:** Both editorial cartoonists in this chapter — Nate Beeler and Jen Sorensen — offer enough "data" in their drawings (pp. 167 and 182) to lead readers to perceive problems and draw their own conclusions. But it's not as easy as it looks. Try your hand at creating a visual proposal of your own that accomplishes the same.

4. **Your Choice:** Proposals are usually practical documents, serving a specific need. Identify such a need in your life and address it through a clear, fact-based proposal. For example, you might write to your academic adviser or dean suggesting that a service-learning experience would be a better senior project for you than a traditional written thesis — given your talents and interests. Or perhaps you might write to a banker (or wealthy relative) explaining why loaning you money to open a barbecue restaurant would make sound fiscal sense, especially since no one else in town serves decent brisket and ribs. In other words, write a paper to make your life better.

How to start

- Need to **find a text to analyze**? See page 190.
- Need to come up with **ideas**? See page 194.
- Need to **organize your ideas**? See page 200.

7 Literary Analyses

respond critically to cultural works

Unless you're an English major, the papers you write for Literature 101 may seem as mechanical as chemistry lab reports—something done just to get a degree. But hardly a day goes by when you don't respond strongly to some literary or cultural experience, sharing your insights and opinions about the books, music, and entertainment you love. It's worth learning to do this well.

THEMATIC INTERPRETATION

After discussing Rudolfo Anaya's novel *Bless Me, Ultima* with classmates in a contemporary novels course, you write a *thematic interpretation* of the work, arguing that it fits into the category of mythic coming-of-age story.

CLOSE READING

Unconvinced by a teacher's casual suggestion that the Anglo-Saxon author of "The Wanderer" (c. tenth century CE) was experiencing what we now call "alienation," you write a *close reading* of the poem to show why the modern concept doesn't fit the poem.

ANALYSIS OF A VISUAL TEXT

Rather than roll your eyes like your companions, you take abstract art seriously. So you study El Anatsui's sculpture (on p. 185) and then write a *visual analysis* to explain what you see in the work to someone who "doesn't get it."

DECIDING TO WRITE A LITERARY ANALYSIS. In a traditional literary analysis, you respond to a poem, novel, play, or short story. That response can be interpretive, looking at theme, plot, structure, characters, genre, style, and so on. Or it can be critical, theoretical, or evaluative—locating works within their social, political, historic, and even philosophic neighborhoods. Or you might approach a literary work expressively, describing how you connect with it intellectually and emotionally. Or you can combine these approaches or imagine alternatives—reflecting new attitudes and assumptions about media.

Other potential media for analysis include films, TV shows, popular music, comic books, and games (for more on choosing a genre, see the Introduction). Distinctions between high and popular culture have not so much dissolved as ceased to be interesting. After all, you can say dumb things about *Hamlet* and smart things about *Game of Thrones*. Moreover, every genre of artistic expression—from sonnets to opera to graphic novels—at some point struggled for respectability.

Duvor Cloth (Communal Cloth)
The Ghanaian artist El Anatsui builds his remarkable abstract sculptures from street materials, including metal fragments and bottle caps. He explains, "I believe that artists are better off working with whatever their environment throws up." El Anatsui (Ghanaian, born 1944), *Duvor Cloth (Communal Cloth)*, 2007, aluminum and copper wire, 13 × 17 ft. Indianapolis Museum of Art, Ann M. Stack Fund for Contemporary Art, 2007.25. © El Anatsui/The Bridgeman Art Library.

What matters is the quality of a literary analysis and whether you help readers appreciate the novel *Pride and Prejudice* or, maybe, the video game *Red Dead Redemption*. Expect your literary or cultural analyses to do *some* of the following.

Begin with a close reading. In an analysis, you slow the pace at which people in a 24/7 world typically operate to examine a text or object meticulously. You study the way individual words and images connect in a poem, or how plot evolves in a novel, or how complex editing shapes the character of a movie. In short, you study the *calculated* choices writers and artists make in creating their works. ○

Make a claim or an observation. The point you want to make about a work won't always be argumentative or controversial: You may be amazed at the simplicity of Wordsworth's Lucy poems or blown away by Jimi Hendrix's take on "All Along the Watchtower." But more typically, you'll make an observation that you believe is worth proving either by research or by evidence you discover within the work itself.

Use texts for evidence. An analysis helps readers appreciate the complexities in creative works: You direct them to the neat stuff in a poem, novel, drama, or song. For that reason, you have to pay attention to the details—words, images, textures, techniques—that support your claims about a literary or cultural experience.

Present works in context. Works of art respond to the world; that's what we like about them and why they sometimes change our lives. Your analysis can explore these relationships among texts, people, and society.

Draw on previous research. Your response to a work need not match what others have felt. But you should be willing to learn from previous scholarship and criticism—readily available in libraries or online. ○

read closely
p. 340

plan a
project p. 436

In "Great Expectations: What Gatsby's Really Looking For," literary critic William Deresiewicz tries once again to explain the enduring appeal of a book almost everyone reads either in high school or college, F. Scott Fitzgerald's *The Great Gatsby* (1925). His essay appeared in *The American Scholar* just shortly after yet another film version premiered in spring 2013, with Leonardo DiCaprio in the title role.

Reading the Genre   Chances are you have written literary papers in school, analyzing poems or books. Does Deresiewicz's essay feel like the papers you have prepared? In what ways is it similar and, perhaps more important, how is it different? How do you account for the differences?

Great Expectations

What Gatsby's Really Looking For

WILLIAM DERESIEWICZ

Opening teases readers to discover what *Gatsby* is really about.

I recently reread *The Great Gatsby*, for obvious reasons. (And no, I haven't worked up the stomach to see the movie yet.) Here's what I discovered: It's about the American Dream. I know, I know, but the real question is, what is the American Dream about? What is Gatsby really after? It isn't money, and it isn't Daisy, and it isn't money as a way of getting Daisy. Don't believe that Tin Pan Alley sentimentality—all the crap that Gatsby spouts about "the secret place above the trees" and "the tuning fork that had been struck upon a star"—which even Nick refers to as "appalling." Money is a way of getting Daisy, but Daisy is a way of getting something else.

Gatsby wants to arrive. He wants admission to the inner circle. He wants acceptance into what we'd later call—in the twilight of their power, once we could afford to laugh at them—the WASPs, our homegrown aristocracy. He wants what Tom and Nick, who graduated from "New Haven," represent. He's from the West; he wants to make it to the East—a dichotomy Fitzgerald maps onto the local spaces of his two Long Island towns, the famous Eggs. Money's not the point; it's only a prerequisite. Gatsby is already

Argues Gatsby wants entry to elite society.

fabulously wealthy by the time the novel starts. But he can't cross over any-way, and not because Daisy is married. That would be an incidental ob-stacle, as everyone makes clear, if only she were willing.

The problem is he can't pull off the act. Wolfsheim buys it — "I saw right away he was a fine-appearing, gentlemanly young man, and when he told me he was an Oggsford I knew I could use him good" — but people like the Buchanans can tell the difference. Gatsby's downfall comes when Daisy fi-nally goes to one of his parties and sees how vulgar they are. Since he doesn't have access to the aristocracy, he substitutes the world of celebrity, that simulacrum of it that emerged around this time (and that's replaced it altogether now). "She was appalled by West Egg, this unprecedented 'place' that Broadway had begotten upon a Long Island fishing village." (West Egg, as everybody would have understood, was a thinly veiled version of Great Neck, which was being colonized by showbiz types like Sid Caesar and the Marx Brothers. Gatsby's association with Jews, the ultimate crass arrivistes, goes deeper than his gangster friend.) It's not that Gatsby's money's dirty; it's that he hasn't had a chance to wash the newness off it yet. The process takes at least a generation. Daddy gets rich; Junior goes to "New Haven," to learn how to act like the rich.

> Explains in detail the East/West divides in the novel.

We talk about money, in America, but we're thinking about status (which we never talk about). For all of our well-known materialism, I believe we love money as much as we do just because, in the absence of a real aristoc-racy, it's always been our route to status. There's only so much you can buy. I sometimes wonder if the drive for endless accumulation is nothing but an evolutionary anachronism, a vestige of the time when resources had to be stockpiled, because you never knew when they might become scarce. But then I remember about status, of which it's never possible to have enough. That is the secret American hunger: a legacy, no doubt, of our colonial past, the long centuries during which we looked across the ocean — east — for af-firmation. We want to get from nowhere, which is where we are (Gatsby is from North Dakota, more or less synonymous with nowhere), to that ever-elusive somewhere, full of orchids and ease and gold and girls.

> Argues that status matters more than money to Americans.

Five pages from the end of the book, Fitzgerald delivers his sociological punch line: "I see now that this has been a story of the West, after

Cites the text to clinch the argument.

all—Tom and Gatsby, Daisy and Jordan and I, were all Westerners, and perhaps we possessed some deficiency in common which made us subtly unadaptable to Eastern life." Even the novel fails to make it East. Even Tom and Daisy feel like frauds. There is no arrival, it seems—or not, at least, for such as us.

A Different Kind of Criticism Lisa Brown has done a series of cartoon-style book reviews for the *San Francisco Chronicle.* This is her take on *The Great Gatsby.* © 2013 Lisa M. Brown.

Exploring purpose and topic

▶ find a
text

In most cases, you write a literary analysis to meet a course requirement, a paper usually designed to improve your skills as a reader of literature and art. Such a lofty goal, however, doesn't mean you can't enjoy the project or put your own spin on it.

Your first priority is to read any assignment sheet closely to find out exactly what you are asked to do. Underline any key words in the project description and take them seriously. Typically, you will see terms such as *compare and contrast*, *classify*, *analyze*, or *interpret*. They mean different things, and each entails a different strategy.

Once you know your goal in writing an analysis, you may have to choose a subject. ○ It's not unusual to have your instructor assign a work (*Three pages on* The House on Mango Street *by Friday*). But just as often, you'll select a work to study from within a range defined by the title of the course: Mexican American Literature; Major Works of Dostoyevsky; Banned Books. Which should you choose?

Choose a text you connect with.   It makes sense to spend time writing about works that move you, perhaps because they touch on an aspect of your life or identity. You may feel more confident studying them because of who you are and what you've experienced.

Choose a text you want to learn more about.   In the backs of their minds, most people have lists of works and artists they've always wanted to explore. So turn an assignment into an opportunity to sample one of them: *Beowulf*; *The Chronicles of Narnia*; or the work of William Gibson, Leslie Marmon Silko, or the Clash. Or use an assignment to push beyond the works that are from within your comfort zone, or familiar to your own experience: Examine writers and artists from cultures different from your own and with challenging points of view.

Choose a text you don't understand.   Most students write about accessible works that are relatively new: Why struggle with a hoary epic poem when you can just watch *The Lord of the Rings* on DVD? One obvious reason may be

get an
idea p. 331

to figure out how works from unfamiliar times still powerfully connect to our own; the very strangeness of older and more mysterious texts may even rouse you to ask better questions. You'll pay more attention to literary texts that puzzle you.

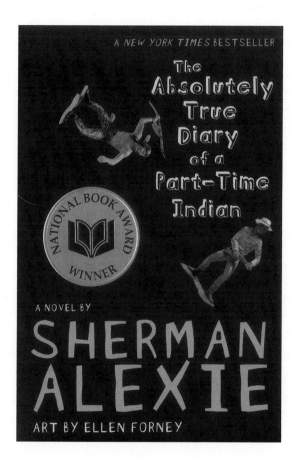

Cover of Sherman Alexie's Award-Winning Novel *The Absolutely True Diary of a Part-Time Indian* How much do you know about Native American fiction or film? Use an assignment as an opportunity to learn more. *The Absolutely True Diary of a Part-Time Indian*, by Sherman Alexie, art by Ellen Forney, published by Little Brown and Company, Books for Your Readers, Hachette Book Group, Inc. Used with permission.

Understanding your audience

Unless you write book reviews or essays for a campus literary magazine, the people reading your analyses of works of art and culture are most likely a professor and other students in your course. But in either situation, assume a degree of expertise among your readers. Understand, too, that people who read literary and cultural analyses on their own expect to learn something. So make good use of their time.

Clearly identify the author and works you are analyzing. It seems like common sense, but this courtesy is neglected in many academic papers because students assume that *the teacher must know what I'm doing*. Don't make this mistake. Also briefly recap what happens in the works you are analyzing—especially with texts not everyone has read recently. ○ Follow the model of good reviewers, who typically review key story elements before commenting on them. Such summaries give readers their bearings at the beginning of a paper. Here's James Wood introducing a novel by Marilynne Robinson that he will be reviewing for the *New York Times*.

> *Gilead* is set in 1956 in the small town of Gilead, Iowa, and is narrated by a seventy-six-year-old pastor named John Ames, who has recently been told he has angina pectoris and believes he is facing imminent death. In this terminal spirit, he decides to write a long letter to his seven-year-old son, the fruit of a recent marriage to a much younger woman. This novel is that letter, set down in the easy, discontinuous form of a diary, mixing long and short entries, reminiscences, moral advice, and so on.

Define key terms. Literary analyses use many specialized and technical expressions. Your instructor will doubtless know what an *epithet, peripeteia*, or *rondel* might be, but you need to define terms like these for wider audiences—your classmates, for instance. Alternatively, you can look for more familiar synonyms.

sum up
ideas p. 460

Don't aim to please professional critics.   Are you tempted to imitate the style of serious academic theorists you've encountered while researching your paper? No need—your instructor probably won't expect you to write in that way, at least not until graduate school.

> **Your Turn**   In "Great Expectations: What Gatsby's Really Looking For" (p. 187), William Deresiewicz summarizes the familiar novel only minimally for his audience—the readers of a journal titled *The American Scholar*. What adjustments might he have to make for a more general—or, let's say, a less academic—audience? Did you find yourself lost or confused when reading the essay and, if so, where?

Finding and developing materials

► develop
ideas

With an assignment in hand and works to analyze, the next step—and it's a necessary one—is to establish that you have a reliable "text" of whatever you'll be studying. In a course, a professor may assign a particular edition or literary anthology for you to use, making your job easier.

This Bedford/St. Martin's edition of *Frankenstein* provides important textual information and background. Look for texts with such material when studying classic novels, poems, and plays. © Bedford/St. Martin's.

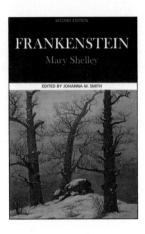

Be aware that many texts are available in multiple editions. (For instance, the novel *Frankenstein* first appeared in 1818, but the revised third edition of 1831 is the one most widely read today.) For classical works, such as the plays of Shakespeare, choose an edition from a major publisher, preferably one that includes thorough notes and perhaps some critical essays. When in doubt, ask your professor which texts to use. Don't just browse the library shelves.

Other kinds of media pose interesting problems as well. For instance, you may have to decide which version of a movie to study—the one seen by audiences in theaters or the "director's cut" on a DVD. Similarly, you might find multiple recordings of classical music: Look for widely respected performances. Even popular music may come in several versions: studio (*American Idiot*), live (*Bullet in a Bible*), alternative recording (*American Idiot: The Original Broadway Cast Recording*). Then there is the question of drama: Do you read a play on the page, watch a video when one is available, or see it in a theater? Perhaps you do all three. But whatever versions of a text you choose for study, be sure to identify them in your project, either in the text itself or on the works cited page. O

Establishing a text is the easy part. Once that's done, how do you find an angle on the subject? O Try the following strategies and approaches.

understand citation
styles p. 470

find a topic
p. 331

Examine the text closely.   Guided by your assignment, carefully read, watch, or examine the selected work(s) and take notes. Obviously, you'll treat some works differently from others. You can read a Seamus Heaney sonnet a dozen times to absorb its nuances, but it's unlikely you'd push through Rudolfo Anaya's novel *Bless Me, Ultima* more than once or twice for a paper. But, in either case, you'll need an effective way to keep notes or to annotate what you're studying.

Honestly, you should count on a minimum of two readings or viewings of any text, the first one to get familiar with the work and find a potential approach, the second and subsequent ones to confirm your thesis and to find evidence for it. And do read the actual novel or play, not some "no fear" version.

Focus on the text itself.   Your earliest literature papers probably tackled basic questions about plot, character, setting, theme, and language. But these are exactly the kinds of issues that fascinate many readers. So look for moments when the plot of the novel you're analyzing establishes its themes or study how characters develop in response to specific events. Even the setting of a short story or film might be worth writing about when it becomes a factor in the story: Can you imagine the film *Casablanca* taking place in any other location?

Questions about language always loom large in literary analyses. How does word choice shape the mood of a poem? How does a writer create irony through diction or dialogue? Indeed, any technical feature of a work might be studied and researched, from the narrators in novels to the rhyme schemes in poetry.

Focus on meanings, themes, and interpretations.   Although tracing themes in literary works seems like an occupation mostly for English majors, the impulse to find meanings is irresistible. If you take any work seriously, you'll discover angles and ideas worth sharing with readers. Maybe *Seinfeld* is a modern version of *Everyman*, or *O Brother, Where Art Thou?* is a retelling of the *Odyssey* by Homer, or maybe not. Open your mind to possible connections: What have you seen like this before? What structural patterns do you detect? What ideas are supported or undercut?

Focus on authorship and history.   Some artists stand apart from their creations, while others cannot be separated from them. So you might explore closely how a work mirrors the life, education, and attitudes of its author. Is the author writing to represent his or her gender, race, ethnicity, or class? Or does the work repudiate its author's identity, class, or religion? What psychological forces or religious perspectives drive the work's characters or themes?

Similarly, consider how a text embodies the assumptions, attitudes, politics, fashions, and even technology of the times during which it was composed. A work as familiar as Jonathan Swift's "A Modest Proposal" still requires readers to know at least a *little* about Irish and English politics in the eighteenth century. How does Swift's satire expand in scope when you learn a little more about its environment?

Focus on genre.   Literary genres are formulas. Take a noble hero, give him a catastrophic flaw, have him make bad choices, and then kill him off: That's tragedy—or, in the wrong hands, melodrama. With a little brainstorming, you could identify dozens of other genres and subcategories: epics, sonnets, historical novels, superhero comics, grand opera, soap opera, and so on. Artists often create works that fall between genres, sometimes producing new ones. Readers, too, bring clear-cut expectations to a text: Try to turn a 007 action-spy thriller into a three-hankie chick flick, and you've got trouble in River City.

You can analyze genre in various ways. For instance, track a text backward to discover its literary forebears—the works an author used for models. Even works that revolt against older genres bear traces of what their authors have rejected. It's also possible to study the way artists combine different genres or play with or against the expectations of audiences. Needless to say, you can also explore the relationships of works within a genre. For example, what do twentieth-century coming-of-age stories such as *A Separate Peace*, *The Catcher in the Rye*, and *Lord of the Flies* have in common?

Focus on influences.   Some works have an obvious impact on life or society, changing how people think or behave: *Uncle Tom's Cabin, To Kill a Mockingbird, Roots, Schindler's List*. TV shows have broadened people's notions of family; musical genres such as jazz and gospel have created and sustained entire communities.

But impact doesn't always occur on such a grand scale or express itself through social movements. Books influence other books, films other films, and so on—with not a few texts crossing genres. For better or worse, books, movies, and other cultural productions influence styles, fashions, and even the way people speak. Consider *Breaking Bad*, *Glee*, or *Game of Thrones*. You may have to think outside the box, but projects that trace and study influence can shake things up.

Focus on social connections. In recent decades, many texts have been studied for what they reveal about relationships between genders, races, ethnicities, and social classes. Works by newer writers are now more widely read in schools, and hard questions are asked about texts traditionally taught: What do they reveal about the treatment of women or minorities? Whose lives have been ignored in "canonical" texts? What responsibility do such texts have for maintaining repressive political or social arrangements? Critical analyses of this sort have changed how many people view literature and art, and you can follow up on such studies and extend them to texts you believe deserve more attention.

Find good sources. Developing a literary paper provides you with many opportunities and choices. Fortunately, you needn't make all your decisions on your own. Ample commentary and research are available on almost any literary subject or method, both in print and online. ○ Your instructor and local librarians can help you focus on the best resources for your project, but the following boxes list some possibilities.

refine your
search p. 442

Literary Resources in Print

Abrams, M. H., and Geoffrey Harpham. *A Glossary of Literary Terms*. 11th ed. Boston: Wadsworth Cengage, 2014.

Beacham, Walton, ed. *Research Guide to Biography and Criticism*. Washington: Beacham, 1990.

Birch, Dinah, ed. *The Oxford Companion to English Literature*. 7th ed. Oxford: Oxford UP, 2009.

Crystal, David. *The Cambridge Encyclopedia of Language*. 3rd ed. New York: Cambridge UP, 2010.

Encyclopedia of World Literature in the 20th Century. 3rd ed. Farmington Hills: St. James, 1999.

Gates, Henry Louis, Jr., et al. *The Norton Anthology of African American Literature*. 3rd ed. New York: Norton, 2014.

Gilbert, Sandra M., and Susan Gubar. *The Norton Anthology of Literature by Women: The Traditions in English*. 3rd ed. New York: Norton, 2007.

Greene, Roland, et al. *The Princeton Encyclopedia of Poetry and Poetics*. 4th ed. Princeton: Princeton UP, 2012.

Harmon, William, and Hugh Holman. *A Handbook to Literature*. 12th ed. New York: Prentice, 2012.

Harner, James L. *Literary Research Guide: A Guide to Reference Sources for the Study of Literature in English and Related Topics*. 5th ed. New York: MLA, 2008.

Hart, James D., and Phillip W. Leininger. *The Oxford Companion to American Literature*. 6th ed. New York: Oxford UP, 1995.

Howatson, M. C. *The Oxford Companion to Classical Literature*. 3rd ed. New York: Oxford UP, 2011.

Leitch, Vincent, et al. *The Norton Anthology of Theory and Criticism*. 2nd ed. New York: Norton, 2010.

Sage, Lorna. *The Cambridge Guide to Women's Writing in English*. Cambridge: Cambridge UP, 1999.

Literary Resources Online

Annual Bibliography of English Language and Literature (ABELL) (subscription)

The Atlantic (http://www.theatlantic.com) (for culture and reviews)

Browne Popular Culture Library (http://www.bgsu.edu/colleges/library/pcl)

The Complete Works of William Shakespeare (http://shakespeare.mit.edu)

Eserver.org: Accessible Writing (http://eserver.org)

A Handbook of Rhetorical Devices (http://www.virtualsalt.com/rhetoric.htm)

Internet Public Library: Literary Criticism (http://www.ipl.org/div/litcrit/)

Literary Resources on the Net (http://andromeda.rutgers.edu/~jlynch/Lit)

Literature Resource Center (Gale Group — subscription)

MLA on the Web (http://www.mla.org)

New York Review of Books (http://www.nybooks.com/)

New York Times Book Review (http://www.nytimes.com/pages/books)

The Online Books Page (http://onlinebooks.library.upenn.edu)

Yahoo! Arts: Humanities: Literature (http://dir.yahoo.com/arts/humanities/literature/)

Creating a structure

▶ organize ideas

Build the structure for your literary analysis around the particular observation, claim, or point you hope to make. Your project will be organized like a report if you're interested in sharing information and explaining what is already known. Or it will develop like an argument if your thesis offers fresh claims or veers toward controversy. ○ What matters most, however, is that you organize your work in ways that make sense to readers.

Imagine a structure. Analyses of literature and culture can head in various directions. One analysis might present a string of evidence to support a thematic claim; another might examine similarities and differences between two or more works; yet another might explore an open-ended question, with ideas emerging expressively, rather than demonstrating a single point. Consider how the following claims might lead to very different structures:

STUDY OF THEME
In *Bless Me, Ultima*, the youngster Antonio has to reconcile his mystical beliefs with Ultima's prediction that he will become a "man of learning."

CONTRAST OF GENRES
The movie version of Annie Proulx's short story "Brokeback Mountain" actually improves on the original work, making the narrative more appealing, moving, and believable.

CULTURAL ANALYSIS
One likely impact of digital technology will be to eliminate traditional barriers between art, entertainment, and business — with books becoming films that morph into games that inspire commercial art and even music.

Here are three simple forms a literary analysis might take, the first developing from a thesis stated early on, the second comparing two works to make a point, and the third building toward a conclusion rather than opening with a traditional thesis. ○

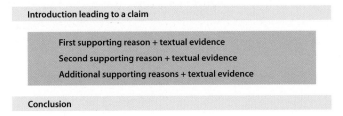

Introduction leading to a claim

First supporting reason + textual evidence
Second supporting reason + textual evidence
Additional supporting reasons + textual evidence

Conclusion

understand
argument p. 66

develop a
statement p. 362

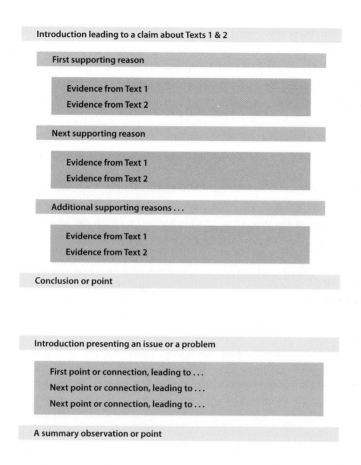

Work on your opening.   Be sure that the introductory paragraphs of your literary or cultural analyses identify the works you are examining, explain what you hope to accomplish, and provide necessary background information (including brief plot summaries, for example). ○ Always provide enough context so that the project stands on its own and would make sense to someone other than the instructor who assigned it.

Choosing a style and design

Literary analyses are traditional assignments still typically done in an academic style and following specific conventions of language and MLA documentation. ○ But such analyses also lend themselves surprisingly well to new media, especially when their topics focus on video or aural texts. So style and media can be important issues in literary and cultural projects.

Use a formal style for most assignments.   As the student example in this chapter suggests, literary analyses you write for courses will be serious in tone, formal in vocabulary, and, for the most part, impersonal—all markers of a formal or high style. ○ Elements of that style can be identified in this paragraph from an academic paper in which Manasi Deshpande analyzes Emily Brontë's *Wuthering Heights*. Here she explores the character of its Byronic hero, Heathcliff:

Examines Heathcliff from the perspective of a potential reader, not from her own.

Complex sentences smoothly incorporate quotations and documentation.

Related points are expressed in parallel clauses.

Vocabulary throughout is accessible but formal. No contractions are used.

In witnessing Heathcliff's blatantly violent behavior, the reader is caught between sympathy for the tormented Heathcliff and shock at the intensity of his cruelty and mistreatment of others. Intent on avenging Hindley's treatment of him, Heathcliff turns his wrath toward Hareton by keeping him in such an uneducated and dependent state that young Cathy becomes "upset at the bare notion of relationship with such a clown" (193). Living first under Hindley's neglect and later under Heathcliff's wrath, Hareton escapes his situation only when Catherine befriends him and Heathcliff dies. In addition, Heathcliff marries Isabella only because Catherine wants to "'torture [him] to death for [her] amusement'" and must "'allow [him] to amuse [himself] a little in the same style'" (111). Heathcliff's sole objective in seducing and running away with Isabella is to take revenge on Catherine for abandoning him. Heathcliff's sadism is so strong that he is willing to harm innocent third parties in order to punish those who have caused his misery. He even forces young Cathy and Linton to marry by locking them in Wuthering Heights and keeping Cathy from her dying father until she has married Linton, further illustrating his willingness to torture others out of spite and vengeance.

cite in
MLA p. 472

define your
style p. 400

Use a middle style for informal or personal papers.   Occasionally, for example, you may have to write brief essays called *response* or *position papers*, in which you record your immediate reactions to poems, short stories, or other readings. In these assignments, an instructor may want to hear your voice and may even encourage exploratory reactions. Here is Cheryl Lovelady responding somewhat personally to a proposal to revive the Broadway musical *Fiddler on the Roof*:

> How can a play set in a small, tradition-bound Jewish village during the Russian Revolution be modernized? I would argue that *Fiddler on the Roof* is actually an apt portrayal of our own time. Throughout the show, the conflicted main character, Tevye, is on the brink of pivotal decisions. Perplexed by his daughters' increasingly modern choices, Tevye prays aloud, "Where do they think they are, America?" Tevye identifies America as a symbol of personal freedom — the antithesis of the tradition that keeps his life from being "as shaky as a fiddler on the roof." Forty years after the play's debut, America has become startlingly more like the Anatevka Tevye knows than the America he envisions. Post-9/11 America parallels Anatevka in a multitude of ways: Political agendas ideologically separate the United States from most of the world; public safety and conventional wisdom are valued over individual freedoms; Americans have felt the shock of violence brought onto their own soil; minority groups are isolated or isolate themselves in closed communities; and societal taboos dictate whom people may marry.

Question focuses paragraph. Reply suggests strong personal opinion.

Basic style remains serious and quite formal: Note series of roughly parallel clauses that follow colon.

Follow the conventions of literary analysis.   One of those norms is to set the action in a novel, poem, or movie in the present tense when you describe or summarize it: "Hamlet kills his uncle just moments before he himself dies."

Another convention is to furnish the dates of birth and death for any major authors or artists you mention in an analysis. Similarly, give a year of publication or release date for any major works of art you mention. The dates usually appear in parentheses.

> Joan Didion (b. 1934) is the author of *Play It as It Lays* (1970), *Slouching Towards Bethlehem* (1968), and *The Year of Magical Thinking* (2005).

Finally, since you'll be frequently citing passages from literary works as well as quoting critics and reviewers, thoroughly review the rules for handling quotations. ○ All quoted materials need to be appropriately introduced and, if necessary, modified to fit smoothly into your sentences and paragraphs.

use quotations
p. 466

A 1964 production of the musical *Fiddler on the Roof*. United Artists/Photofest.

Cite plays correctly.   Plays are cited by act, scene, and line number. In the past, passages from Shakespeare were routinely identified using a combination of Roman and Arabic numerals. But currently, MLA recommends Arabic numerals only for such references.

FORMER STYLE

Hamlet's final words are "The rest is silence" (*Ham.* V.ii.358).

CURRENT STYLE

Hamlet's final words are "The rest is silence" (*Ham.* 5.2.358).

Explore alternative media.   You can be creative with literary and cultural projects, depending on the tools and media available to you. ○ For example, an oral presentation on a literary text can be handled impressively using presentation software such as PowerPoint or Prezi. Or Google Maps might be used to trace the physical locations or journeys in literary works. Naturally, if your project is to be submitted in electronic form, you can incorporate photographs, images, or the spoken word into your project, as appropriate. "Appropriate" means that the media elements genuinely enrich your analysis.

go multimodal
p. 542

Examining models

CLOSE READING   In "Insanity: Two Women," Kanaka Sathasivan examines a poem (Emily Dickinson's "I felt a Funeral, in my Brain") and a short story (Charlotte Perkins Gilman's "The Yellow Wallpaper") to discover a disturbing common theme in the work of these two American women writers. The essay, written in a formal academic style, uses a structure that examines the works individually, drawing comparisons in a final paragraph. Note, in particular, how Sathasivan manages the close reading of the poem by Emily Dickinson, moving through it almost line by line to draw out its themes and meanings. Here's the text of "I felt a Funeral, in my Brain."

I felt a Funeral, in my Brain,
And Mourners to and fro
Kept treading — treading — till it seemed
That Sense was breaking through —

And when they all were seated,
A Service, like a Drum —
Kept beating — beating — till I thought
My Mind was going numb —

And then I heard them lift a Box
And creak across my Soul
With those same Boots of Lead, again,
Then Space — began to toll,

As all the Heavens were a Bell,
And Being, but an Ear,
And I, and Silence, some strange Race
Wrecked, solitary, here —

And then a Plank in Reason, broke,
And I dropped down, and down —
And hit a World, at every plunge,
And Finished knowing — then —

For an additional reading, see **macmillanhighered.com/howtowrite3e.**
e-readings › Erik Didriksen, *Pop Sonnet: Royals* [PARODY]

205

You can find the full text of "The Yellow Wallpaper" by searching online by the title. One such text is available at the University of Virginia Library Electronic Text Center: http://etext.virginia.edu/toc/modeng/public/GilYell.html.

Reading the Genre   Like any skillful academic paper, Sathasivan's "Insanity: Two Women" follows a great many conventions in structure, style, and mechanics. Go through the essay paragraph by paragraph and list as many of these moves as you can identify — right through the works cited page. Compare your list with those produced by several classmates.

Sathasivan 1

Kanaka Sathasivan

Professor Glotzer

English 102

March 3, 20--

Insanity: Two Women

The societal expectations of women in the late nineteenth century served to keep women demure, submissive, and dumb. Although women's rights had begun to improve as more people rejected these stereotypes, many women remained trapped in their roles because of the pressures placed on them by men. Their suppression had deep impacts not only on their lives but also on their art. At a time when women writers often published under male aliases to gain respect, two of America's well-known authors, Emily Dickinson (1830-1886) and Charlotte Perkins

> Works to be analyzed are set in context: late nineteenth century.

Sathasivan 2

Identifies authors and sets works in thematic relationship.

Gilman (1860-1935), both wrote disturbing pieces describing the spiritual and mental imprisonment of women. In verse, Dickinson uses a funeral as a metaphor for the silencing of women and the insanity it subsequently causes. Gilman's prose piece "The Yellow Wallpaper" (1899) gives us a firsthand look into the mental degradation of a suppressed woman. These two works use vivid sensory images and rhythmic narration to describe sequential declines into madness.

States thesis for the comparison.

In "I felt a Funeral, in my Brain" (first published in 1896), Dickinson outlines the stages of a burial ceremony, using them as metaphors for a silenced woman's departure from sanity. The first verse, the arrival of Mourners, symbolizes the imposition of men and society on her mind. They are "treading" "to and fro," breaking down her thoughts and principles, until even she is convinced of their ideas (Dickinson 3, 2). The Service comes next, representing the closure—the acceptance of fate. Her "Mind was going numb" as the sounds of the service force her to stop thinking and begin accepting her doomed life. These first two verses use repetition at parallel points as they describe the Mourners as "treading—treading" and the service as a drum "beating— beating" (Dickinson 3, 7). The repetition emphasizes the incessant insistence of men; they try to control threatening women with such vigor and persistence that eventually even the women themselves begin to believe men's ideas and allow their minds to be silenced.

Offers close reading of Dickinson's poem.

Sathasivan 3

As the funeral progresses, the Mourners carry her casket from the service. Here Dickinson describes how they scar her very Soul using the "same Boots of Lead" which destroyed her mind (Dickinson 11). From the rest of the poem, one can infer that the service took place inside a church, and the act of parting from a house of God places another level of finality on the loss of her spirituality. While the figures in the poem transport her, the church's chimes begin to ring, and, as if "all the Heavens were a Bell / And Being, but an Ear," the noise consumes her (Dickinson 13-14). In this tremendous sound, her voice finally dissolves forever; her race with Silence has ended, "Wrecked," and Silence has won (Dickinson 16). Finally, after the loss of her mind, her soul, and her voice, she loses her sanity as they lower her casket into the grave and bury her. She "hit a World, at every plunge, / And Finished knowing" (Dickinson 19-20). The worlds she hits represent further stages of psychosis, and she plunges deeper until she hits the bottom, completely broken.

Like Dickinson, Gilman in "The Yellow Wallpaper" also segments her character's descent into madness. The narrator of the story expresses her thoughts in a diary written while she takes a vacation for her health. Each journal entry represents another step toward insanity, and Gilman reveals the woman's psychosis with subtle hints and clues placed discreetly within

With simple transition, turns to Gilman's short story.

Sathasivan 4

the entries. These often take the form of new information about the yellow room the woman has been confined to, such as the peeled wallpaper or bite marks on the bedpost. The inconspicuous presentation of such details leads the reader to think that these artifacts have long existed, created by someone else, and only now does the narrator share them with us. "I wonder how it was done and who did it, and what they did it for," she says, speaking of a groove that follows the perimeter of the walls (Gilman 400). Here, Gilman reuses specific words at crucial points in the narration to allude to the state of her character's mental health. In this particular example, both the narrator and the maid use the word "smooch" to describe, respectively, the groove in the wall and yellow smudges on the narrator's clothes (Gilman 400). This repetition indicates that she created the groove in the room, a fact affirmed at the end of the story.

Gilman's narrator not only seems to believe other people have caused the damage she sees but also imagines a woman lives trapped within the paper, shaking the pattern in her attempts to escape. "I think that woman gets out in the daytime!" the narrator exclaims, recounting her memories of a woman "creeping" about the garden (Gilman 400, 401). Again, Gilman uses repetition to make associations for the reader as the narrator uses "creeping" to describe her own exploits. As in the previous example, the end of the story reveals that the

Uses present tense to describe action in "The Yellow Wallpaper."

Sathasivan 5

woman in the paper is none other than the narrator, tricked by her insanity. This connection also symbolizes the narrator's oppression. The design of the wallpaper trapping the woman represents the spiritual bars placed on the narrator by her husband and doctor, who prescribes mental rest, forbidding her from working or thinking. Even the description of the room lends itself to the image of a dungeon or cell, with "barred" windows and "rings and things in the walls" (Gilman 392). Just as the woman escapes during the daytime, so, too, does the narrator, giving in to her sickness and disobeying her husband by writing. Finally, like the woman in the paper breaking free, the narrator succumbs to her insanity.

Both Dickinson's and Gilman's works explore society's influence on a woman's mental health. Like Dickinson's character, Gilman's narrator has also been compelled into silence by a man. Although she knows she is sick, her husband insists it isn't so and that she, a fragile woman, simply needs to avoid intellectual stimulation. Like a Mourner, "treading—treading," he continually assures her he knows best and that she shouldn't socialize or work. This advice, however, only leads to further degradation as her solitude allows her to indulge her mental delusions. When the narrator attempts to argue with her husband, she is silenced, losing the same race as Dickinson's character.

Draws attention to common themes and strategies in the two works.

Sathasivan 6

In both these pieces, the characters remain mildly aware of their declining mental health, but neither tries to fight it. In Dickinson's poem, the woman passively observes her funeral, commenting objectively on her suppression and burial. Dickinson uses sound to describe every step, creating the feel of secondary sensory images—images that cannot create a picture alone and require interpretation to do so. Gilman's narrator also talks of her sickness passively, showing her decline only by describing mental fatigue. In these moments she often comments that her husband "loves [her] very dearly" and she usually accepts the advice he offers (Gilman 396). Even on those rare occasions when she disagrees, she remains submissive and allows her suppression to continue. In contrast to Dickinson, Gilman uses visual images to create this portrait, describing most of all how the narrator sees the yellow wallpaper, an approach that allows insight into the narrator's mental state.

Both Dickinson and Gilman used their writing to make profound statements about the painful lives led by many women in the nineteenth century. Through repetition, metaphor, symbolism, and sensory images, both "I felt a Funeral, in my Brain" and "The Yellow Wallpaper" describe a woman's mental breakdown, as caused by societal expectations and oppression. The poetry and prose parallel one another and together give insight into a horrific picture of insanity.

Notes difference in technique between authors.

Concludes that writers use similar techniques to explore a common theme in two very different works.

Sathasivan 7

Works Cited

Dickinson, Emily. "I felt a Funeral, in my Brain." *Concise*
        Anthology of American Literature. 7th ed. Ed. George
        McMichael. Boston: Longman, 2011. 1139. Print.

Gilman, Charlotte Perkins. "The Yellow Wallpaper." *The*
        American Short Story and Its Writer, An Anthology. Ed. Ann
        Charters. Boston: Bedford, 2000. 391-403. Print.

MLA
documentation
style used for
in-text notes
and works
cited.

PHOTOGRAPHS AS LITERARY TEXTS Photography attained its status as art in the twentieth century. Even documentary photographs not originally conceived as works of art became prized for their striking depictions of the human condition. Three artists recognized for such work are Dorothea Lange (1895–1965), Walker Evans (1903–1975), and Gordon Parks (1912–2006). During the Great Depression and subsequent years, they produced photographs for the Farm Security Administration (FSA) intended to record all aspects of American life. But their best portraits of people and places often reach beyond the immediate historical context, as the following three images demonstrate. Note how these photographs present and frame their subjects, encouraging viewers to expand and interpret their meanings.

Reading the Genre If you have a smartphone, chances are you take "documentary" photographs all the time to record what you do and see and whom you meet. How do these photographs differ from those by Lange, Evans, and Parks? How would you define serious "documentary photography," and have you taken any shots that fall into that category?

Dorothea Lange, *Jobless on Edge of Pea Field, Imperial Valley, California* (1937). Library of Congress, Prints and Photographs Division/FSA/OWI Collection.

Walker Evans, *Burroughs Family Cabin, Hale County, Alabama* (1936).
Library of Congress, Prints and Photographs Division/FSA/OWI Collection, LC-USF342-
T01-008133.

Gordon Parks, *American Gothic* (1942). Library of Congress, Prints and Photographs Division/ FSA/OWI Collection.

1. **Thematic Interpretation:** Review William Deresiewicz's "Great Expectations: What Gatsby's Really Looking For" (p. 187). Then try your hand at similarly describing a theme or issue explored in a literary or cultural work you particularly admire. Perhaps you have a take on Neil Gaiman's *Sandman* series that you want to share or you view a more conventional work (*Tom Sawyer*; *The Scarlet Letter*) in ways that other readers typically do not. Because of its magazine audience, Deresiewicz's essay is relatively short and has no documentation. Your essay might follow the same format, but be respectful in acknowledging sources informally.

2. **Close Reading:** In "Insanity: Two Women" (p. 205), Kanaka Sathasivan does a close, almost line-by-line analysis of Emily Dickinson's "I felt a Funeral, in my Brain"; then she compares the themes and strategies of the poem to those she finds in Charlotte Perkins Gilman's "The Yellow Wallpaper." For a project of your own, do *either* a close reading of a favorite short poem or song *or* a comparison of two works from different genres or media.

For the close reading, tease out all the meanings and strategies you can uncover and show readers how the text works. For the comparison, be sure to begin with works that interest you because of some important similarity: They may share a theme or plot, or even be the *same* work in two different media—*Game of Thrones* in novel and television forms, for instance.

3. **Analysis of a Visual Text:** Photographers Dorothea Lange, Walker Evans, and Gordon Parks (pp. 213–16) recorded images documenting the long-term effects of the Great Depression. In a short paper, describe the specific scenes you would photograph today if you hoped to leave as important a documentary legacy as Lange, Evans, and Parks. To make the project manageable, focus on your local community. Showcase your own images in a photo-essay.

4. **Your Choice:** Write a paper about any work of poetry or fiction that you wish more people would read. Use your essay to explain (or, if necessary, defend) the qualities of the work that make it worth someone's serious attention.

How to start ● Need to **find a text to analyze**? See page 224.

● Need to come up with **ideas**? See page 227.

● Need to **organize your ideas**? See page 230.

Rhetorical Analyses

examine in
detail the
way texts
work

Rhetorical analyses foster the kind of careful reading that makes writers better thinkers. Moreover, they're everywhere in daily life, especially in politics and law. In fact, they're hard to avoid, especially if you spend much time reading new media.

RHETORICAL ANALYSIS
You've seen too many slick TV spots touting smartphones that do everything but wash dishes. Your own new phone doesn't work quite so well. You decide to write a *rhetorical analysis* of the ads to explain why consumers (like you) fall so easily for questionable claims.

CLOSE READING OF AN ARGUMENT
For an assignment in a writing class, you do a *close reading of an argument* a politician makes in an important campaign speech. You want to discover exactly how and why he manages to sound so much more persuasive than most Washington pols.

CULTURAL ANALYSIS
Management has heard that the mostly blue-collar customers of a clothing store where you work don't like its Web site. You understand the problem: The models online all frolic at expensive resorts while looking ridiculously thin, young, and upper class. You write a brief *cultural analysis* of the situation, suggesting changes to align the store's online presence to the diversity of its actual customers.

DECIDING TO WRITE A RHETORICAL ANALYSIS.   You react to what others say or write all the time. Sometimes an advertisement, a speech, or maybe a cultural image grabs you so hard that you want to take it apart to see how it works. Put those discoveries into words and you've composed a *rhetorical analysis* (for more on choosing a genre, see the Introduction).

"Twinkies"   At first glance, this editorial cartoon by Nate Beeler of the *Columbus Dispatch* might seem just a riff on the return of Hostess Twinkies to the marketplace in 2013. But how exactly do the images in the panel mesh with the remark made by one of its characters: "There is something seriously wrong with America"? What exactly is going on here — rhetorically? Nate Beeler, courtesy of Cagle Cartoons.

Rhetoric is the art of using language and media to achieve particular ends. In rhetorical analyses, you identify the specific techniques that writers, speakers, artists, or advertisers use to be persuasive and then assess their effectiveness objectively. ○ You take a rhetorical analysis one step further when you cast neutrality aside and offer good reasons for endorsing or disagreeing with a particular argument—in effect making a case of your own. Such a detailed inspection of a text is sometimes called a *critical analysis*.

When you write a rhetorical analysis, you'll make the following moves.

Take words and images seriously.   When you compose rhetorical analyses, hold writers to high standards because their choices have consequences. Fair and effective techniques of persuasion deserve to be identified and applauded. And crooked ones should be ferreted out, exposed, and sent packing. It takes practice to distinguish one from the other—which is what rhetorical analyses provide.

Spend time with texts.   You cannot evaluate the techniques of a writer, speaker, or artist until you know them inside out. But we blow through most of what we read (and see) without much thought. Serious rhetorical analysis does just the opposite: It makes texts move like bullets in *The Matrix*, their motion slowed and their trajectories magnified for careful study. ○

Pay attention to audience.   When you do a rhetorical analysis, understanding for *whom* a text is written can be as important as *what* it says. In fact, audiences determine the content, shape, and language of most arguments.

Mine texts for evidence.   Find and cite any rhetorical moves that casual readers of a text are likely to miss. Point to subtle or ironic language, overblown emotional appeals, intricate logic, or covert bigotry. Moves such as these will be the best support for your claims in a rhetorical analysis. Expect to quote often. ○

understand
argument p. 66

read closely
p. 340

use quotations
p. 466

In "Too Much Information," an essay originally published in *The American Scholar* (June 18, 2013), Professor Paula Marantz Cohen of Drexel University examines what happens to us as a result of living in a society that insists on answering, indeed *anticipating*, all the questions we might have in our daily lives. Her article is a rhetorical analysis because it demonstrates how modes of communication shape — and then sometimes diminish — our capacity to think. But Cohen also explores why we now demand immediate answers to complex questions — which is why you will find a selection from this piece quoted in the chapter on causal analyses (see p. 145).

Reading the Genre The title and subtitle of Cohen's essay likely start you thinking about the problem she identifies. Is information overload an issue you have encountered yourself? After reading the piece, consider whether you find Cohen's discussion convincing. Do your own experiences tend to confirm her thesis, or might you be inclined to challenge it — perhaps from a generational point of view?

Too Much Information

The Pleasure of Figuring Things Out for Yourself

PAULA MARANTZ COHEN

Cohen identifies a question that puzzles her.

When did we start wanting everything explained to us? Why can't we be content with indeterminate meaning and subjective interpretation?

Part of the explanatory drive comes, I believe, from the nature of higher education. The cost of college is so great that students and their parents feel they should get their money's worth — which is to say, get answers to all the difficult questions.

She looks to media habits for an answer.

Another reason is the Internet. The other day, a colleague came into my office disgusted. He had asked his students to write a paragraph about the symbolism of the flower pot in Raymond Carver's story "Popular Mechanics." The answers that came back were similar, he said, not because students had copied from each other, but because they had all Googled "Popular Mechanics," "Carver," "flower pot," and "symbolism," scanned what came up,

221

She finds more examples of media hustling to serve our curiosity — inadequately.

and found the "answer." They had no idea that this wasn't the way to proceed. They figured that the question had a singular answer, much in the way a math problem has an answer.

Consider some other ways we have been conditioned to expect hard explanations for soft things (e.g., works of the imagination, and moral and philosophical questions). DVDs give us "special features" that often seem to diminish our understanding of the film or our appreciation of it. The idea applies to television as well. After watching the last episode of [HBO's] *Girls*, I happened to let the show run on to the after-show sequence, in which creator and star Lena Dunham explained what we had just seen. Not only did her banal exegesis lessen the power of the episode, it made me less interested in her quirky persona. What had looked smart and funny, creative and irreverent, was forced into an explanatory mold and both became uninteresting and co-opted into the very sort of neatly packaged form that the show seems to oppose. I didn't want to see a counterculture icon giving me a lecture on relationship stability.

Museums are another example. I usually bypass the audiotapes that accompany a special exhibit. I don't like the didactic tone — being told what to feel about this or that picture, or the development of this or that artist. Biographical information about the artist, some gossip about his or her circle, what other artists have been influenced by this one — yes. But to be told that this is X's most accomplished work, or that Y shows particular genius here, or that the depiction of the young girl in the corner is especially moving in what it says about isolation and alienation — no thanks. Such commentary also frequently appears on the cards used to identify paintings on the wall. Along with the date and a few details as to where the work was painted, we are now likely to get a mini-dissertation on how the green background is a statement about the artist's wish to return to the bucolic farm of his boyhood. Driving the trend is the assumption that people want more information — they want to get their money's worth.

Cohen exposes how habitual the move to provide information has become, a key insight.

I recently received an e-mail from a student asking if she could use No Fear Shakespeare for my Shakespeare class. I had no idea what No Fear Shakespeare was, though the phrase made me shudder in anticipation. I soon learned that it gives you Shakespeare's play on one side and "regular" English on the other.

I don't think there's a genuine pedagogical impulse behind our explanatory culture. It's more about selling more product—in this case, cultural product. And it's about control. I'm not a conspiracy theorist, believing that some Big Brother is trying to control my every move, but I do think the tendency of a capitalist economy is to know where consumers are (which includes how we think) all the time in order to sell us stuff. This is why movie theaters bombard us with commercials and movie-related tidbits even before the endless previews begin. It's also why the TV now runs continually in doctors' offices. And why, as a friend of mine pointed out, we need to have signs on the highway telling us that a "Scenic Overlook" is coming up, as though prescribing in advance what is photoworthy—and also to have a kiosk available to sell us throwaway cameras, Kleenex, and bags of chips.

All this chattery explanation seems designed to refuse us a moment of peace in which to think for ourselves. Despite my jab at capitalism, the problem is more existential than economic. It's like the sort of chanting that goes on in a house of worship. The effect is soothing but also distracting. It keeps us from focusing on the difficult, unanswerable questions associated with the human condition—from gazing into the abyss and learning about the best use of our lives and the best way to face our eventual deaths. We may be getting explanations a mile a minute but we're not getting wisdom.

She then analyzes the motives for selling "cultural product."

The analysis argues that "chattery explanation" preempts deeper thinking.

Exploring purpose and topic

▶ find a text

Make a difference.   Done right, rhetorical analyses can be as important as the texts they examine. They may change readers' opinions, open their eyes to new ideas, or keep an important argument going. They may also draw attention to rhetorical strategies and techniques worth imitating or avoiding.

When you write an angry letter to the editor complaining about bias in news coverage, you won't fret much about defining your purpose and topic— they are given. But when responding to a course assignment, particularly when you can choose a text on your own to analyze rhetorically, you've got to establish the boundaries. Given a choice, select a text to analyze with the following characteristics.

Choose a text you can work with.   Find a gutsy piece that makes a claim you or someone else might actually disagree with. It helps if you have a stake in the issue and already know something about it. The text should also be of a manageable length so that you can explore it coherently within the limits of the assignment.

Choose a text you can learn more about.   Some items won't make much sense out of context. So choose a text or series of texts that you can study and research. ○ It will obviously help to know who created it; where it first appeared; and when it was written, presented, or produced. This information is just as important for visual texts, such as advertisements, posters, and films, as for traditional speeches or articles.

Choose a text with handles.   Investigate arguments that do interesting things. Maybe a speech uses lots of anecdotes or repetition to generate emotional appeals; perhaps a photo-essay's commentary is more provocative than the images; a print ad may arrest attention by its simplicity but still be full of cultural significance. You've got to write about the piece. Make sure it offers you adventurous things to say.

Need help deciding what to write about? See "How to Browse for Ideas" on pp. 338–39.

plan your
research p. 436

Choose a text you know how to analyze.   Stick to printed texts if you aren't sure how to write about ads or films or even speeches. But don't sell yourself short. You can pick up the necessary vocabulary by reading models of rhetorical and critical analysis. Moreover, you don't always need highly technical terms to describe poor logic, inept design, or offensive strategies, wherever they appear. Nor do you need special expertise to describe cultural trends or detect political motives.

Your Turn   You don't need a highbrow or sophisticated topic for a successful rhetorical analysis, as Professor Cohen's look at Google, DVDs, and No Fear Shakespeare suggests (p. 221). It's a much better strategy to dissect a text that genuinely interests you and then make an audience as intrigued by it as you are. If you take something seriously (zombies, for example; see p. 238), chances are that your readers will too. So begin an open-ended assignment by listing the sorts of texts you work with regularly. Even text messages and tweets can be studied rhetorically if you approach them from a new angle.

Understanding your audience

Some published rhetorical analyses are written for ready-made audiences already inclined to agree with the authors. Riled up by an offensive editorial or a political campaign, people these days may even seek out and enjoy mean-spirited, over-the-top criticism, especially on the Web. But the rhetorical and critical analyses you write for class should be relatively restrained because you can't predict how your readers might feel about the arguments you are critiquing. So assume that you are writing for a diverse and thoughtful audience, full of readers who prefer reflective analysis to clever put-downs. You don't have to be dull or passionless. Just avoid the easy slide into rudeness. ○

The Shelter Pet Project Advertisements featuring animals appeal to audiences, especially when they involve animal care or welfare. Here's a pitch to adopt shelter pets that may be — like humans — a little less than perfect. The Humane Society of the United States, Maddie's Fund ®, and the Ad Council.

respect your
readers p. 408

Finding and developing materials

Before you analyze a text of any kind, do some background research. Discover all you can about its author, creator, publisher, sponsor, and so on. For example, you would need to know if a TV commercial you intend to examine has aired only on sports networks or lifestyle programs on cable. Figure out, too, the contexts in which an argument occurs. If you reply to a *Wall Street Journal* editorial, know what events sparked that item and investigate the paper's editorial slant.

ideas ◄

Read the piece carefully just for information first, highlighting names or allusions you need to look up; there's very little you can't uncover these days via a Web search. When you think you understand the basics, you are prepared to approach the text rhetorically. Persuasive texts are often analyzed according to how they use three types of rhetorical appeal. Typically, a text may establish the character and credibility of its author (*ethos*), generate emotions in order to move audiences (*pathos*), and use evidence and logic to make its case (*logos*).

Consider the ethos of the author.   Ethos—the appeal to character—may be the toughest argumentative strategy to understand. Every text and argument is presented by someone, whether an individual, a group, or an institution. Audiences, whether they realize it or not, are influenced by that self-presentation: They are swayed by writers or speakers who come across as knowledgeable, honest, fair-minded, and believable. They are less friendly to people or institutions that seem to be deceptive, untrustworthy, or incompetent.

Here Michael Ruse describes a witness whose frank words established his ethos in a 1981 court case dealing with requiring creation science in Arkansas schools.

> The assistant attorney general was trying to tie him into knots over some technical point in evolutionary biology. Finally, the man blurted out, "Mr. Williams, I'm not a scientist. . . . I am an educator, and I have my pride and professional responsibilities. And I just can't teach that stuff [meaning creationism] to my kids."
>
> — "Science for Science Teachers," *Chronicle of Higher Education*, January 13, 2010

Look for such moments in texts—though such frank testimony will be rare. Instead, you may find indications of writers' authority and competence (or lack thereof) in how they describe their credentials, how they use sources, how they address readers, or how they use language. Even the absence of a "self" in a piece, as is typically the case in a scientific paper or academic article, can suggest a persuasive objectivity and rigor. Writers also bring their careers and reputations to a piece, and that stature may be enhanced (or diminished) by where they publish, yet another aspect of ethos.

Consider how a writer plays to emotions.   *Pathos*—the emotional appeal—is usually easy to detect but sometimes difficult to assess. Look for places where a text generates strong feelings to support its points, win over readers, or influence them in other ways. Then consider how appropriate the tactic is for advancing a particular argument. The strategy is legitimate so long as raising emotions such as pity, fear, pride, outrage, and the like fits the moment and doesn't move audiences to make choices based upon distorted perceptions of the facts. Columnist Peggy Noonan, for example, routinely uses emotions to make her political points.

> We fought a war to free slaves. We sent millions of white men to battle and destroyed a portion of our nation to free millions of black men. What kind of nation does this? We went to Europe, fought, died, and won, and then taxed ourselves to save our enemies with the Marshall Plan. What kind of nation does this? Soviet communism stalked the world and we were the ones who steeled ourselves and taxed ourselves to stop it. Again: What kind of nation does this?
>   Only a very great one.
>
> —"Patriots, Then and Now," *Wall Street Journal*, March 30, 2006

Obviously, patriotic sentiments like these can be a smoke screen in some political debates. Your challenge in a rhetorical analysis is to point out emotional appeals and to determine whether they move audiences to act humanely or manipulate them into making bad or even stupid choices.

Consider how well reasoned a piece is.   *Logos*—the appeal to reason and evidence—is most favored in academic texts. In a rhetorical analysis, you look carefully at the claims a text offers and whether they are supported by facts, data, testimony, and good reasons. What assumptions lie beneath the argument? That's a crucial query.

Ask questions about evidence too. Does it come from reliable sources or valid research? Is it up-to-date? Has it been reported accurately and fully? Has due attention been given to alternative points of view and explanations? Has enough evidence been offered to make a valid point? You might pose such objections, for example, when Peter Bregman, an expert on leadership training in business, makes an especially controversial argument.

A *study* of 829 companies over thirty-one years showed that diversity training had "no positive effects in the average *workplace*." Millions of dollars a year were spent on the training resulting in, well, nothing. Attitudes — and the diversity of the organizations — remained the same.

It gets worse. The researchers — Frank Dobbin of Harvard, Alexandra Kalev of Berkeley, and Erin Kelly of the University of Minnesota — concluded that "In firms where training is mandatory or emphasizes the threat of lawsuits, training actually has negative effects on management diversity."

— "Diversity Training Doesn't Work," *Harvard Business Review Blog Network*, March 12, 2012

Clearly, you have your work cut out for you: Suddenly you are dealing not solely with Bregman but also with the study he cites (and a link in his blog posting takes you right to it). The bottom line is that the logic of every major claim in a text may need such scrutiny in a rhetorical analysis. You are simultaneously fact-checker and skeptic.

Questions for a Rhetorical Analysis

Consider the topic.	What is **fresh** or striking about the topic? How well defined is it? **Does the piece make a point?** Could it be clearer? Is **the topic** important? Relevant? Controversial? Is the subject covered comprehensively or selectively **and with obvious biases**? What is the level of detail?
Consider the audiences of the text.	To whom is the piece addressed? How **well** is the text **adapted** to its audience? Who is **excluded** from the audience and how can you tell? What does the text offer its audience: information, controversy, entertainment? What does it **expect** from its audience?
Consider the author.	What is the author's relationship to the material? Is the writer or creator personally **invested** or **distant**? Is the author an expert, a knowledgeable amateur, or something else? What does the author **aim** to accomplish?
Consider the medium and design.	What is the medium or **genre** of the text: essay, article, editorial, advertisement, book excerpt, poster, video, podcast, or other format? How well does the medium **fit** the subject? How might the material look different in another medium? How do the various **elements** of design — such as arrangement, color, fonts, images, white space, audio, video, and so on — support the medium or genre?
Examine the language.	What is the **level** of the language: formal, informal, colloquial? What is the **tone** of the text — logical, sarcastic, humorous, angry, condescending?
Consider the occasion.	Why was the text created? To what circumstances or situations does it respond, and what might **public reaction** to it be? What problems does it solve or create? What pleasure might it give? Who benefits from the text?

Creating a structure

► organize
  ideas

In a rhetorical analysis, you'll make a statement about how well the argumenta-tive strategy of a piece works. Don't expect to come up with a thesis immedi-ately or easily: You need to study a text closely to figure out how it works and then ponder its strengths and weaknesses. Draft a tentative thesis and then refine it throughout the process of writing until you have a thought-provoking claim you can prove. ○

Your thesis should do more than just list rhetorical features: *This ad has good logical arguments and uses emotions and rhetorical questions.* Why would someone want to read (or write) a paper with such an empty claim? The following thesis promises a far more interesting rhetorical analysis:

> The latest government antidrug posters offer good reasons for avoiding
> steroids but do it in a visual style so bland that most students will ignore them.

Once you have a thesis or hypothesis, try sketching a design based on a thesis / supporting reason / evidence plan. Focus on those features of the text that illustrate the points you wish to make. You don't have to discuss every facet of the text.

Introduction leading to a claim
First supporting reason + textual evidence
Second supporting reason + textual evidence
Additional supporting reasons + textual evidence
Conclusion

In some cases, you might perform a line-by-line or paragraph-by-paragraph deconstruction of a text. This structure shows up frequently online. Such analyses practically organize themselves, but your commentary must be smart, accurate, and stylish to keep readers on board.

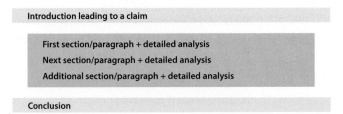

Introduction leading to a claim
First section/paragraph + detailed analysis
Next section/paragraph + detailed analysis
Additional section/paragraph + detailed analysis
Conclusion

develop a
statement p. 362

Choosing a style and design

The style of your rhetorical analyses will vary depending on audience, but you always face one problem that can sometimes be overcome by clever design: sharing the work you are analyzing with readers. They have to know what you are talking about.

Consider a high style.   Rhetorical and critical analyses for school usually need a formal or high style. ○ Keep the tone respectful, the vocabulary technical, and the perspective impersonal—avoiding *I* and *you*. Such a style gives the impression of objectivity and seriousness and enhances your ethos as a critic.

Consider a middle style.   Rhetorical and critical analyses appearing in the public arena—rather than in the classroom—are often less formal. To win over readers not compelled to read their stuff, writers turn to the middle style, which gives them ample options for expressing strong opinions and feelings (sometimes including anger, outrage, and contempt). Public writing is full of distinctive personal voices—from Stephen Carter and Paul Krugman to Naomi Klein and Peggy Noonan—offering opinions, making judgments, and advancing agendas. The ethos of middle style is often more cordial and sympathetic than that of high style, if somewhat less authoritative and commanding. You win the assent of readers by making them like and trust you.

Make the text accessible to readers.   Your rhetorical analysis should be written *as if readers do not have the text you are analyzing in hand or in front of them.* One way to achieve that clarity is to summarize and quote selectively from the text as you examine it, or to provide visual images that are captioned or annotated. You can see examples of this technique in Matthew James Nance's essay on pages 232–38 and in J. Reagan Tankersley's analysis on pages 239–48. Of course, you can always also attach photocopies or images of any short items you are analyzing or provide Web links to them. With other types of subjects—such as movies, advertising campaigns, and so on—simply describe or summarize the content of the work. Whatever you examine, always be sure to identify authors (or creators), titles, places/modes of publication, and dates in your paper.

define your
style p. 400

Examining models

ANALYSIS OF AN ARGUMENT For a class assignment on rhetorical analysis, Matthew James Nance chose as his subject the award-winning feature article "Can't Die for Trying" by journalist Laura Miller — who later would serve as mayor of Dallas. In the essay, Nance explains in detail how Miller manages to present the story of a convicted killer who wants to be executed to readers who might have contrary views about capital punishment. Nance's analysis is both technical and objective. He does an especially good job of helping readers follow the argument of "Can't Die for Trying," a fairly long and complicated article.

Reading the Genre Nance skillfully handles an important technical feature of many rhetorical analyses: quotations. Read this piece with a focus on the ways he introduces material from Laura Miller's "Can't Die for Trying." Note how smoothly he merges her words with his and how strategically he introduces quotations to make or confirm his analyses.

Nance 1

Matthew James Nance

Professor Norcia

English 2

June 14, 20--

A Mockery of Justice

    In 1987, David Martin Long was convicted of double homicide and sentenced to death. He made no attempt to appeal this sentence and, surprisingly, did everything he could to expedite his execution. Nonetheless, due to an automatic appeals process, Long remained on Texas's Death Row for twelve years before he was finally executed. For various

Sets scene carefully and provides necessary background information.

ⓔ For an additional reading, see **macmillanhighered.com/howtowrite3e.**
e-readings › Nickolay Lamm, *The History of Music* [INFOGRAPHIC]

Nance 2

reasons, including investigations into whether he was mentally ill, the state of Texas had continued to postpone his execution date. In 1994, when David Long was still in the middle of his appeals process, *Dallas Observer* columnist Laura Miller took up his case in the award-winning article "Can't Die for Trying." In this article, Miller explores the enigma of a legal system in which a sociopath willing to die continues to be mired in the legal process. The article is no typical plea on behalf of a death-row inmate, and Miller manages to avoid a facile political stance on capital punishment. Instead, Miller uses an effective combination of logical reasoning and emotional appeal to evoke from readers a sense of frustration at the system's absurdity.

> Miller defies expectations and Nance explains why in his thesis.

To show that David Martin Long's execution should be carried out as soon as possible, Miller offers a reasoned argument based on two premises: that he wants death and that he deserves it. Miller cites Long's statement from the day he was arrested: "I realize what I did was wrong. I don't belong in this society. I never have. . . . I'd just wish they'd hurry up and get this over with" (5). She emphasizes that this desire has not changed, by quoting Long's correspondence from 1988, 1991, and 1992. In this way, Miller makes Long's argument seem reasoned and well thought out, not simply a temporary gesture of desperation. "'Yes, there are innocent men here, retarded men, insane men, and men who just plain deserve another

> Long paragraph furnishes detailed evidence for Miller's two premises.

Nance 3

chance,' Long wrote [State District Judge Larry] Baraka in April 1992, 'But I am none of these!'" (5). Miller also points out his guilty plea, and the jury's remarkably short deliberation: "The jury took only an hour to find Long guilty of capital murder—and forty-five minutes to give him the death penalty" (5). Miller does not stop there, however. She gives a grisly description of the murders themselves, followed by Long's calculated behavior in the aftermath:

> He hacked away at Laura twenty-one times before going back inside where he gave Donna fourteen chops. The blind woman, who lay in bed screaming while he savaged Donna, got five chops. Long washed the hatchet, stuck it in the kitchen sink, and headed out of town in Donna's brown station wagon. (5)

Miller's juxtaposition of reasoned deliberation with the bloody narrative of the murders allows her to show that Long, in refusing to appeal, is reacting justly to his own sociopathy. Not only is it right that he die; it is also right that he does not object to his death.

In the midst of this reasoned argument, Miller expresses frustration at the bureaucratic inefficiency that is at odds with her logic. She offers a pragmatic, resource-based view of the situation:

> Of course, in the handful of instances where a person is wrongly accused . . . this [death-penalty activism] is noble, important work. But I would argue that in others—David Martin Long in particular—it is a sheer waste of taxpayer dollars. And a mockery of justice. (6)

Provides both summaries and quotations from article so that readers can follow Miller's argument.

To clarify Miller's point, Nance adds a phrase in brackets to the quotation.

Nance 4

Miller portrays the system as being practically incompatible with her brand of pragmatism. The figures involved in Long's case are painted as invisible, equivocal, or both. For instance, in spite of Long's plea, Judge Baraka was forced to appoint one of Long's attorneys to start the appeals process. "The judge didn't have a choice. Texas law requires that a death-penalty verdict be automatically appealed. . . . [This] is supposed to expedite the process. But the court sat on Long's case for four long years" (5). Miller also mentions Danny Burn, a Fort Worth lawyer in association with the Texas Resource Center, one of the "do-good . . . organizations whose sole feverish purpose is to get people off Death Row. . . . No matter how airtight the cases" (6). Burn filed on Long's behalf, though he never met Long in person. This fact underscores Miller's notion of the death-row bureaucracy as being inaccessible and, by extension, incomprehensible.

This parade of equivocal incompetence culminates in Miller's interview with John Blume, another activist who argued on Long's behalf. Miller paints Blume as so equivocal that he comes across as a straw man. "As a general rule," says Blume, "I tend to think most people who are telling you that are telling you something else, and that's their way of expressing it. There's something else they're depressed or upset about" (6). The article ends with Miller's rejoinder: "Well, I'd wager, Mr. Blume, that something is a lawyer like you" (6). Whereas the article up to this point has maintained a balance between

> Notice how smoothly quotations merge into Nance's sentences.

Nance 5

Nance makes a clear judgment about Miller's objectivity — then offers evidence for his claim.

reason and frustration, here Miller seems to let gradually building frustration get the best of her. She does not adequately address whether Blume might be correct in implying that Long is insane, mentally ill, or otherwise misguided. She attempts to dismiss this idea by repeatedly pointing out Long's consistency in his stance and his own statements that he is not retarded, but her fallacy is obvious: Consistency does not imply sanity. Clearly, Miller would have benefited from citing Long's medical history and comparing his case with those of other death-row inmates, both mentally ill and well. Then her frustrated attack on Blume would seem more justified.

Nance examines the way Miller deals with the problem she has portraying a cold-blooded killer to readers.

Miller also evokes frustration through her empathetic portrayal of Long. Although the article is essentially a plea for Long to get what he wants, this fact itself prevents Miller from portraying Long sympathetically. Miller is stuck in a rhetorical bind; if her readers become sympathetic toward Long, they won't want him to die. However, the audience needs an emotional connection with Long to accept the argument on his behalf. Miller gets around this problem by abandoning sympathy altogether, portraying Long as a cold-blooded killer. The quotation "I've never seen a more cold-blooded, steel-eyed sociopath ever" (5) is set apart from the text in a large font, and Miller notes, "This is a case of a really bad dude, plain and simple. . . . Use any cliché you want. It fits" (5). Miller here opts for a weak appeal, evoking from the audience the same negative emotion that

Nance 6

Long feels. She gives voice to Long's frustration over his interminable appeals: "Long stewed. . . . Long steamed. . . . Long fumes . . ." (6). She also points out Long's fear of himself: "I fear I'll kill again" (6). Clearly, the audience is meant to echo these feelings of frustration and fear. This may seem like a weak emotional connection with Long, but perhaps it is the best Miller could do, given that a primary goal of hers was to show that Long deserves death.

Laura Miller won the H. L. Mencken Award for this article, which raises important questions about the legal process. Part of its appeal is that it approaches capital punishment without taking a simplistic position. It can appeal to people on both sides of the capital punishment debate. The argument is logically valid, and for the most part, the emotional appeal is effective. Its deficiencies, including the weak emotional appeal for Long, are ultimately outweighed by Miller's overarching rationale, which calls for pragmatism in the face of absurdity.

Nance 7

Work Cited

Miller, Laura. "Can't Die for Trying." *Dallas Observer* 12 Jan.
1994: 5-6. Print.

CULTURAL ANALYSIS   Rhetorical analyses can illuminate cultural trends. In "Humankind's Ouroboros," J. Reagan Tankersley explores the phenomenon of zombies from a historical and cultural perspective. He argues that these disembodied creatures increasingly popular in movies and, more recently, television series, have come to represent what the public in general fears most in any given era. Hence, zombies embody our anxieties. The paper includes shots from *Dracula*, *Night of the Living Dead*, *28 Days Later*, and *The Walking Dead*.

Reading the Genre   Arguably, what makes Tankersley's essay a rhetorical analysis is the way it connects zombie films and television series to the changing, culturally shared fears of audiences who watch them. How plausible do you find his argument? Does it explain how these films work rhetorically to you?

Tankersley 1

J. Reagan Tankersley

Professor Wilkes

Composition 1

November 24, 20--

Humankind's Ouroboros

Arguably, what we fear is perhaps the greatest indicator of how we behave as human animals. Fear is the emotion with the greatest impact on our fight or flight instincts; our animal brain is exposed when we decide to cover our eyes or keep on watching. It is why both lanes of traffic slow when there's been an accident: One lane brakes due to the obstruction; drivers in the other lane linger because they all want to see what happened, knowing it could've been them.

Horror films act in the same way. The monster movie of the Golden Age of Hollywood was the first sign that people can't always look away from what scares them. And it was lucrative. The horror genre remains one of the most prolific and profitable of the eleven classic genres of film, beginning with such titles as *Frankenstein* and *Dracula*. Within this body of works, none seems more prevalent today than the zombie movie, with the possible exception of highly sexualized vampire and werewolf dramas. Yet, despite a singular ability to scare audiences, the zombie movie has never been a solid form in itself. The zombies

Tankersley 2

of Classical Hollywood are strikingly different from those seen in the summer blockbusters of the past few years. More than any other monster, the zombie is able to evolve according to what will scare us the most, depending on where we stand in our own history. So the ever-evolving design of the zombie is an arguably strong tether to our fears, to how we react as humans.

The first film considered to be a zombie movie was released in 1932, in the heart of the Classical Hollywood era, and starred the master of the monster film, Bela Lugosi. While *White Zombie* is a long stretch from the zombie films of today, it broke ground on the very concept of "zombification." The plot involves a plantation owner from Haiti who, using witchcraft to win his love interest, accidentally turns her into a zombie obeying his every command.

A scene from *Dracula*. Everett Collection.

> Tankersley introduces his thesis: that zombies in films embody the current fears of our society.

Tankersley 3

This plot hints at the roots of the zombie concept, which lie in voodoo legends, the word *zombie* originating in West Africa. The film was also the first to present on screen something akin to our modern image of the zombie: After she becomes a zombie, the love interest of the film is pale white, with the look of a corpse.

The film of that era that best predicted the future of the zombie film was the aptly named *Things to Come*, released in 1936. This adaptation of H. G. Wells's novel of the same name does not directly focus on zombies; however, its epic storyline includes a viral plague, which causes the infected to wander aimlessly, spreading the contagion on contact—an essential plot point in the large-scale zombie films of today. Both of these films reflect the concerns of the horror audience of the 1930s: fear of the mystical and fear of the future. *White Zombie* played to an uneasiness with voodoo magic, which some people associated with postslavery African American culture. *Things to Come* captured the signature pessimism of H. G. Wells during an era of economic recession in the troubled period between two great wars.

Zombies took a backseat in the horror genre following the fall of Classical Hollywood. Moreover, the new medium of television did not allow for such sensational and scary subject matter. Things changed, however, with the rise of the New American Cinema in the 1960s, a school of filmmaking that promoted noncontinuous editing and deliberately explicit images. George A. Romero, considered the father of the modern

The analysis explores the historical roots of today's zombie films.

Tankersley 4

zombie, released *Night of the Living Dead* to horrify audiences in 1968. Romero is given this lofty title simply because he introduced what is considered the paradigmatic zombie, that is, the walking corpse who exists only to eat the flesh of the living. The film broke many cinematic taboos of the time, especially with a sequence involving a zombified child eating her parents. The shocking imagery from this scene sent tremors through the film community. This reimagining of the zombie played to an audience perhaps changed by the televised violence of the Vietnam War era; certainly, the explicit images of cannibalistic corpses brought the horror genre to a much higher level than the monster films of the previous age.

Romero's cult masterpiece was followed by a slew of mediocre-to-downright-horrible zombie films, all produced in the wake of *Night*'s success. These cheap imitations were quelled only briefly by Romero's next project, *Dawn of the Dead*, which debuted in 1978. Although it was released just ten years after the original, the film altered the nature of the zombie to again depict the current fears of the audience. With the demoralizing end of the Vietnam War, Americans adopted a more critical view of their national values. Romero's film, which takes place primarily in a shopping mall, became a direct commentary on growing levels of consumerism in America. Romero heightened his societal critique by increasing the scale of the zombie outbreak, presenting images of zombies — once people

Tankersley focuses on the visual imagery of modern zombie films.

Tankersley 5

A scene from *Night of the Living Dead*. Everett Collection.

themselves—mindlessly consuming other people in a shopping mall, of all places. This level of rebuke represents a paradigm shift in the zombie film: It shows that the fear we experience from zombies comes not just from the gore and frightening images. Rather, it is from the fact that zombies *are* society, without its rules or adornments. Zombies became mindless consumers, a description increasingly given to society itself.

    Romero's cinematic shift to a larger-scale zombie drama with social commentary failed to have much impact until recently. Between the original *Dawn of the Dead* and Zack Snyder's remake in 2004, there was again a very long train of awful zombie films. It wasn't until 2002, with the release of *28 Days Later*, that the zombie film again became a genre to be reckoned with. Danny Boyle's foray into the zombie film is most

Presents the post–Vietnam War zombie as a metaphor for consumerism.

Tankersley 6

notable for its sweeping views of an abandoned London, providing a postmortem view of society destroyed by an infection. Not only did Boyle manage to make the catastrophe seem brutally real through such heart-wrenching images as a notice board plastered with missing persons reports, but he also revolutionized the zombie as a species. His ghouls—the result of animal testing gone horribly wrong—were more realistic and more frightening, leaving their infected victims with something similar to rabies. The defining differences between Boyle's zombies and those of the past, however, were their ability to run and their virus's aggressive capacity to infect on contact, transforming a victim into the undead in a matter of seconds. This gave the zombie genre a much-needed boost, especially since previous films were often criticized for featuring antagonists who could barely walk. Boyle's new zombies could sprint for longer periods than normal humans, due to a lack of physical pain, leaving the protagonists with no safe place to hide for long.

Boyle's film made another point: that zombie films can be constructed around more than just spooky lighting, token characters, cheap scares, and nauseating images. He achieved this goal by focusing on the living characters: Their personal fears and their realization that all the people they loved were gone raised the question of what there was to survive for. This approach made the fear of zombies as much internal as external; the fear becomes personal to each individual audience member.

Tankersley analyzes the physical details of 28 *Days Later*.

Tankersley 7

A scene from *28 Days Later*. Mary Evans Picture Library/© 20th Century Fox/
Everett Collection.

A scene in which the protagonist finds his parents—who
committed suicide before the infection spread to them—is
all one needs to understand the real terror that an event
as widespread as a zombie infection would create.

   Numerous films after *28 Days Later* have approached
the human dimension of the zombie film similarly, ensuring
that audiences would effectively place themselves in dire

Tankersley 8

A scene from *The Walking Dead*. *The Walking Dead*, foreground, left to right, Norman Reedus, Andrew Lincoln in "Seed" (Season 3, Episode 1, aired October 14, 2012), 2010–, photo: Gene Page/© AMC/courtesy Everett Collection.

emotional situations. Of course, there remain the blood-filled blockbusters, such as the *Resident Evil* franchise, but Boyle's film, and some that followed, gave a film buff something to appreciate in a zombie movie. This greater sophistication is evident in what is currently the zombie production to see, *The Walking Dead*, a television series on AMC. The story has its origin in a popular comic book series, but the television show, directed by Frank Darabont (*The Shawshank Redemption*), follows in Boyle's footsteps, exploring the internal dramas of the characters as much as the physical threat of the zombies. The series, still in release, has so far been lauded by zombie enthusiasts, primarily because it pulls back

Tankersley 9

to the traditional zombies of Romero's age, the aimlessly
hobbling, sunken-eyed corpses. Thus far, the show appears to
have found a place in the zombie canon.

The zombie began as a mysterious creature of mystical
origin, with no will of its own. It quickly evolved into the
flesh-eating monster that many associate with the term today.
And, although it has recently become the product of viral
testing and chemical warfare, the textbook zombie remains
unwavering in its basic mission—to scare people. At the
beginning of the twentieth century, audiences feared the
unknown, whether that was mysticism or troubling political
events. In the post-Vietnam War era, people began to question
themselves, doubting their values and wondering if they were
still the good guys that American leaders made them out to be.
And finally, with the increasing threat of terrorism, people have
returned to fearing the possibilities the future might bring. Now,
The Walking Dead has moved beyond even this horror, with the
source of its zombie infection completely unnamed. In the
zombie films of the past ten years, it is clear that what we fear
most is ourselves. We fear what people next to us may be
capable of if their reason is taken from them by some man-made
virus, unknown pathogen, or something else entirely. We all
know that deep down, people are capable of heinous acts, and it
is only reason that can stop them. But when reason is lost,
human society has every faculty to consume itself.

Tankersley
explains how
zombie films
are currently
evolving.

The conclusion
finally explains
the visual
image offered
in the title of
the paper: the
serpent that
devours itself.

Tankersley 10

Works Consulted

Dirks, Tim. "Main Film Genres." *The Greatest Films: The "Greatest" and the "Best" in Cinematic History.* AMC, 2010. Web. 15 Nov. 2011.

The Internet Movie Database (IMDb). Amazon, n.d. Web. 15 Nov. 2011.

"List of Zombie Films." *Wikipedia.* Wikimedia Foundation, 13 Nov. 2010. Web. 15 Nov. 2011.

1. **Rhetorical Analysis:** Using Paula Marantz Cohen's "Too Much Information" (p. 221) as a model, write an essay in which you examine how some modes of communication, media platforms, or habits of thought are shaping the way you encounter the world. If that sounds awfully abstract, consider what Cohen discusses in her essay — everything from students' use of Google to the star's comments following an episode of HBO's *Girls*. You might find a subject in your addiction to apps, your reliance on tweeting, or your grandparents' inability to translate emojis.

2. **Close Reading of an Argument:** Browse recent news or popular-interest magazines or Web sites (such as *Time*, *The Atlantic*, *GQ*, the *New Yorker*, and so on) to locate a serious article you find especially well argued and persuasive. As Matthew James Nance does in "A Mockery of Justice" (p. 232), study the piece carefully enough to understand the techniques it uses to influence readers. Then write a rhetorical analysis in which you make and support a specific claim about the rhetorical strategies of the piece.

3. **Cultural Analysis:** Identify a cultural phenomenon (TV talent shows), theme (men who won't grow up), trend (divorce parties), or type of image (disaster photos) and examine the way it either influences society or reflects the way that people are thinking or behaving. Make the analysis rhetorical by focusing on questions related to audience, social context, techniques of persuasion, or language. Help readers see your subject in a new light or from a fresh perspective. Use J. Reagan Tankersley's "Humankind's Ouroboros" (p. 238) as a starting point.

4. **Your Choice:** Fed up by the blustering of a talk-show host, political figure, op-ed columnist, local editorialist, or stupid advertiser? Try an item-by-item or paragraph-by-paragraph refutation of such a target, taking on his or her poorly reasoned claims, inadequate evidence, emotional excesses, or lack of credibility. If possible, locate a transcript or reproduction of the text you want to refute so that you can work from the facts just as they have been offered. If you are examining a visual text you can reproduce electronically, experiment with using callouts to annotate the problems as you find them.

Special Assignments

2

Need a form you don't see here? Try "Genres," p. 2.

How to start

● **Got a test tomorrow?**
Read exam questions carefully. See page 253.

9 Essay Examinations

**require
answers
written
within a
time limit**

Essay examinations test not only your knowledge of a subject but also your ability to write about it coherently and professionally.

- For a class in nursing, you must write a short essay about the role health-care providers play in dealing with patients who have been victims of domestic abuse.

- For an examination in a literature course, you must do a close reading of a sonnet, explicating its argument and poetic images line by line.

- For a standardized test, you must read a passage by a critic of globalization and respond to the claim made and evidence presented.

- For a psychology exam, you must explore the ethical issues raised by two research articles on brain research and the nature of consciousness.

UNDERSTANDING ESSAY EXAMS.   You've probably taken enough essay exams to know that there are no magic bullets to slay this dragon and that the best approach is to know the material well enough to make credible points within the time limit. You must also write—*under pressure*—coherent sentences and paragraphs. ○ Here are some strategies to increase your odds of success.

got a test ◄
tomorrow?

Anticipate the types of questions to be asked.   What occurs in class— the concepts presented, issues raised, assignments given—is like a coming-attractions trailer for an exam. Attend class regularly and do the required readings, and you'll figure out many of an instructor's habitual moves and learn something to boot. Read over your notes, attend any review sessions, and look over sample essay exams—they may even be available on a course Web site.

Read exam questions carefully.   Underscore key words such as *divide, classify, evaluate, compare, compare* and *contrast*, and *analyze* and then respect the differences between these strategies. ○ Exam questions may be like short essays themselves, furnishing contextual information or offering materials to read be-fore the actual query appears. Respond to that specific question and not to your own take on the introductory materials.

Sketch out a plan for your essay(s).   The first part of the plan should deal with *time*. Read all the exam questions carefully and then estimate how many minutes to spend on each— understanding that some will need more work than others. (Pay attention to point totals too: Focus on essay questions that count more, but don't ignore any. Five points is five points.) Allow time for planning, writing, and briefly editing each answer. Then stick to your time limits.

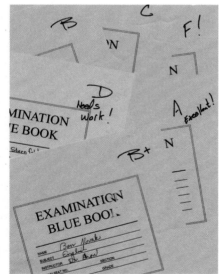

© Bill Aron/PhotoEdit.

Organize your answers strategically.   As quickly as pos-sible, create a scratch outline and thesis for longer answers. ○ In the first paragraph, state this main point and then preview the structure of the whole essay. That way, even if you cannot finish, a reader will know where you were heading and possibly give you partial credit for incomplete work.

improve your
sentences p. 412

develop a
draft p. 367

develop a
statement p. 362

Offer strong evidence for your claims.   The overall pattern of your responses to exam questions should convey your grasp of ideas—your ability to see the big picture. Within that structure, provide details and evidence to prove your command of the subject. Use memorable examples culled from class reading to make key points: Mention important names, concepts, and dates; touch on all critical issues and terms; rattle off the accurate titles of books and articles.

Come to a conclusion.   Even if you run short on time, find a moment to write a paragraph (or even a sentence) that brings your ideas together. Don't just repeat the topic sentences of your paragraphs. A reader will already have those ideas firmly in mind. So add something new at the end—an implication or extrapolation. ○

Keep the tone serious.   Write essay examinations in a high or middle style. ○ Avoid a personal point of view unless the question invites your opinions. Given the time constraints, you can probably get away with contractions and standard abbreviations. But make sure the essay reads like prose, not a text message.

Keep your eye on the clock.   But *don't panic*. Everyone is working under the same constraints and will produce only so much prose in an hour or two. If you have prepared for the exam and start with a plan, ideas will come. Even if they don't, keep writing. You'll get no credit for blank pages.

> **Your Turn**   Preparing for an examination now? Take a moment to list *from memory* as many as you can of the key names, titles, and concepts likely to appear on that exam—terms you are certain to need when you compose your essays. Then check these terms as you have written them down against the way they appear in your notes or textbooks, or on the course Web site. Have you gotten the names and titles right? Have you phrased the concepts correctly, and can you explain what they mean? Just as important, as you review your course materials, do you notice any important ideas that should have made your list but didn't?

shape an
ending p. 391

refine your
tone p. 400

Getting the details right

Save a few minutes near the end of the exam period to reread your essays and insert corrections and emendations. You won't have time to fix large-scale problems: If you've confused the Spanish Armada with Torquemada, you're toast. But a quick edit may catch embarrassing gaffes or omissions. When you write quickly, you may leave out or transpose some words or simply use the wrong expressions (*it's* for *its* or *there* for *their*). Edit these fixable errors. In the process, you may also amplify or repair an idea or two. Here are some other useful strategies.

Use transitional words and phrases.   Essay examinations are the perfect place to deploy conspicuous transitions such as *first, second,* and *third,* or *next, nonetheless, even more important, in contrast, in conclusion,* and so on. Don't be subtle: Transitions keep you on track as you compose and they help your instructor follow what you have to say. ○ You will seem in charge of the material.

Do a quick check of grammar, mechanics, and spelling.   Some instructors take great offense at mechanical slips, even minor ones. At a minimum, avoid the common errors covered in Part 9 of this book. ○ Also be sure to spell correctly any names and concepts you've been reviewing in preparation for the examination. It's Macbeth, not McBeth.

Write legibly or print.   Few people do much writing by hand anymore. But paper or blue books are still used sometimes for essay examinations. If your handwriting is flat-out illegible, then print and use a pen, as pencil can be faint and hard to read. Printing takes more time, but instructors appreciate the clarity. Also consider double-spacing your essays to allow room for corrections and additions. But don't spread your words too far apart. A blue book with just a few sentences per page undermines your ethos: It looks juvenile.

transitions
p. 416

help with common
errors p. 566

Examining a model

Wade Lamb offered the following response to this essay question on a midterm essay examination in a course titled Classical to Modern Rhetoric:

> The structure of Plato's *Phaedrus* is dominated by three speeches about the lover and non-lover—one by Lysias and two by Socrates. How do these speeches differ in their themes and strategies, and what point do they make about rhetoric and truth?

Lamb 1

Wade Lamb

Professor Karishky

Rhetoric 101

September 19, 20--

Plato's *Phaedrus* is unique among Platonic dialogues because it takes place in a rural setting between only two characters—Socrates and the youth Phaedrus. It is, however, like Plato's *Gorgias* in that it is "based on a distinction between knowledge and belief" and focuses on some of the ways we can use rhetoric to seek the truth.

The first speech presented in *Phaedrus*, written by Lysias and read aloud by Phaedrus, is the simplest of the three. Composed by Lysias to demonstrate the power of rhetoric to persuade an audience, it claims perversely that it is better to have a sexual relationship with someone who doesn't love you than someone who does.

Socrates responds with a speech of his own making the same point, which he composes on the spot, but which he describes as

Opening focuses directly on issues posed in question.

Short quotation functions as piece of evidence.

Sensibly organized around three speeches to be examined: one paragraph per speech.

Lamb 2

"a greater lie than Lysias's." Unlike Lysias, however, Socrates begins by carefully defining his terms and organizes his speech more effectively. He does so to teach Phaedrus that in order to persuade an audience, an orator must first understand the subject and divide it into its appropriate parts. However, Socrates delivers this speech with a veil over his head because he knows that what he and Lysias have claimed about love is false.

The third speech—again composed by Socrates—is the most important. In it, Socrates demonstrates that persuasion that leads merely to belief (not truth) damages both the orator and the audience. He compares rhetoric such as that used by Lysias to the unconcerned and harmful lust of a non-lover. Good rhetoric, on the other hand—which Socrates says is persuasion that leads to knowledge—is like the true lover who seeks to lead his beloved to transcendent truth. Socrates shows that he believes good rhetoric should ultimately be concerned with finding and teaching truth, not just with making a clever argument someone might falsely believe, as Lysias's speech does.

By comparing the three speeches in *Phaedrus*, Plato shows that he gives some value to rhetoric, but not in the form practiced by orators such as Lysias. Plato emphasizes the importance of the distinction between belief and knowledge and argues that rhetoric should search for and communicate the truth.

> Most important speech gets lengthiest and most detailed treatment.

> Conclusion states Lamb's thesis, describing the point he believes Plato wished to make about rhetoric in *Phaedrus*.

How to start ▶ **Confused?**
Read the assignment carefully. See page 260.

10

**require a
brief critical
response**

Position Papers

A course instructor may ask you to respond to an assigned reading, lecture, film, or other activity with a position paper in which you record your reactions to the material, such as your impressions or observations. Such a paper is usually brief—often not much longer than a page or two—and due the next class session. Typically, you won't have time for more than a draft and quick revision.

- You summarize and assess the findings of a journal article studying the relationship between a full night's sleep and student success on college exams.

- You speculate about how a feminist philosopher of science, whose work you have read for a class, might react to recent developments in genetics.

- You respond to ideas raised by a panel of your classmates discussing a proposition to restore the military draft or require an alternative form of national service.

- You offer a gut reaction to your first-ever viewing of *Triumph of the Will*, a notorious propaganda film made by director Leni Riefenstahl for Germany's National Socialist (Nazi) Party in 1935.

UNDERSTANDING POSITION PAPERS. Instructors have various reasons for assigning position or response papers: to focus attention on particular readings or class presentations; to measure how well you've understood course materials; to push you to connect course concepts or readings. Instructors may mark position papers less completely than full essays and grade them by different standards because they want to encourage you to take risks.

But don't blow off these quick, low-stakes assignments. Position papers give you practice in writing about a subject and thus prepare you for other papers and exams. These assignments *may* even preview the style of essay questions an instructor favors. Just as important, position papers establish your ethos in a course, marking you as a conscientious reader and thinker or, alternatively, someone just along for the ride.

Use a few simple strategies to write a strong position paper.

Protesters Taking a Position While some feel that security cameras ensure safety, others believe them to be an invasion of privacy. © George Steinmetz/Corbis.

▶ confused?

Read the assignment carefully.   Understand exactly what your instructor wants: Look for key words such as *summarize, describe, classify, evaluate, compare, compare and contrast,* and *analyze* and then respect the differences between them. ○

Review the assigned material.   Consider printing or photocopying readings so that you can annotate their margins or underscore key claims and evidence. Look for conflicts, points of difference, or issues raised in class or in the public arena—what some writers call *hooks.* Then use the most provocative material to jump-start your thinking, using whatever brainstorming techniques work best for you. ○

Mine the texts for evidence.   Look for key sentences worth quoting or ideas worth describing in detail. ○ Anchor your position paper around such strong materials. Quote a brief passage you admire for how well it explains a key concept or highlight a paragraph full of claims that you resist. Then talk about these passages. Be sure you merge any quoted materials smoothly with your own writing.

Organize the paper sensibly.   Unless the assignment specifically states otherwise, don't write the position paper off the top of your head. Take the time to offer a thesis or to set up a comparison, an evaluation, or another pattern of organization. Give a position paper the same structural integrity you would a longer and more consequential assignment.

develop a
draft p. 367

get an
idea p. 331

use quotations
p. 466

Getting the details right

Though the assignment may seem minor, edit and proofread a position paper carefully. ○ Think of a position paper as a trial run for a longer paper. As such, it should follow the conventions of any given field or major.

Identify key terms and concepts and use them correctly and often.
The instructor may be checking to see how carefully you read. So, in your paper, make a point of referring to the new concepts or terms you've found in your reading, as Heidi Rogers does with *ethos*, *pathos*, and *logos* in the model essay on page 262.

Treat your sources appropriately. Either identify them by author and title within the paper or list them at the end in the correct documentation form (e.g., MLA or APA). Make sure quotations are set up accurately, properly introduced, and documented. Offer page numbers for any direct quotations. ○

Spell names and concepts correctly. You lose credibility *very* quickly if you misspell technical terms or proper nouns that appear throughout the course readings. In literary papers especially, get characters' names and book titles right.

Respond to your classmates' work. Position papers are often posted to electronic discussion boards to jump-start conversations. So take the opportunity to reply substantively to what your classmates have written. Don't just say "I agree" or "You're kidding!" Add good reasons and evidence to your remarks. Remember, too, that your instructor might review these comments, looking for evidence of engagement with the course material. ○

revise and edit
p. 422

understand citation
styles p. 470

comment
p. 428

Examining a model

Here's a position paper written by Heidi Rogers as an early assignment in a lower-level course on visual rhetoric. Rogers's assignment was to offer an honest response to director Leni Riefenstahl's infamous documentary, *Triumph of the Will*, which showcases the National Socialist Party rallies in Munich in 1934. In the film, we see the German people embracing Hitler and his Nazi regime as they consolidate their power.

Rogers 1

Heidi Rogers

Professor Wachtel

Writing 203

September 22, 20--

Triumph of the Lens

> **Offers a thesis to explain how the film makes Hitler attractive.**

The 1935 film *Triumph of the Will*, directed by Leni Riefenstahl, masterfully shows how visuals can be a powerful form of rhetoric. In the documentary we see Adolf Hitler, one of the greatest mass murderers in history, portrayed as an inspirational leader who could be the savior of Germany. Watching the film, I was taken aback. I am supposed to detest Hitler for his brutal crimes against humanity, and yet I found myself liking him, even smiling as he greets his fellow Germans on the streets of Munich. How did Riefenstahl accomplish this, drawing viewers into her film and giving Germans such pride in their leader?

Riefenstahl's technique is to layer selected visuals so as to evoke the emotions she wants her audience to feel toward Hitler and his regime. Her first step is to introduce images of nature and locations that are peaceful and soothing. Next, she

> **Rogers describes pattern she sees in Riefenstahl's editing technique.**

Rogers 2

inserts images of the German people themselves: children playing, women blowing kisses to Hitler, men in uniform proudly united under the Nazi flag. The next step is to weave images of Hitler himself among these German people, so that even when he isn't smiling or showing any emotions, it seems as if he is conveying the happiness, pride, or strength evoked by the images edited around him. The final piece of the puzzle is always to put Hitler front and center, usually giving a rousing speech, which makes him seem larger than life.

Provides extended example to support claim about how *Triumph of the Will* was edited.

A good example of this technique comes during the youth rally sequence. First, Riefenstahl presents peaceful images of the area around the Munich stadium, including beautiful trees with the sun streaming between the branches. We then see the vastness of the city stadium, designed by Hitler himself. Then we watch thousands of young boys and girls smiling and cheering in the stands. These masses erupt when Hitler enters the arena and Riefenstahl artfully juxtaposes images of him, usually with a cold, emotionless face, with enthusiastic youth looking up to him as if he were a god. Hitler then delivers an intoxicating speech about the future of Germany and the greatness that the people will achieve under his leadership. The crowd goes wild as he leaves the stage and we see an audience filled with awe and purpose.

Rogers 3

Explores implications of claim — that clever editing enabled Riefenstahl to reach many audiences.

What Riefenstahl did in *Triumph of the Will* is a common technique in film editing. When you have to reach a massive audience, you want to cover all of your bases and appeal to all of them at once. Therefore, the more kinds of *ethos*, *pathos*, and *logos* you can layer onto a piece of film, the better your chances will be of convincing the greatest number of people of your cause. As hard as this is to admit, if I had lived in a devastated 1935 Germany and I had seen this film, I might have wanted this guy to lead my country too.

Triumph of the Will features numerous imposing shots of crowds cheering for Hitler. NSDAP/The Kobal Collection at Art Resource, NY.

Your Turn   Many blogs and online publications (such as *Slate.com*, *Salon .com*, or national newspapers) encourage readers to comment on their postings. Use such sites to practice your skill at responding to what you read. On a news blog or another serious blog you scan regularly, locate a thought-provoking article to which some readers have already offered substantive responses (more than a line or two). First, read the article, thinking about what you might post in response. Then read through the actual postings. How does your brief response compare with what others have said? What strategies have they used that you admire? How did the best responders establish their credibility? And which responders did you take less seriously, *and why?*

Chances are you'll be disappointed in much of what you read in online commentary. People may respond from prejudiced positions, focus on irrelevant points, or take personal potshots at the original author. But from such respondents, you may learn what *not* to do in a serious academic paper.

● **Need to write a summary?**
Check Chapter 42 for more details. See page 460.

Annotated Bibliographies

**summarize
and assess
sources**

When you are preparing a term paper, senior thesis, or other lengthy research project, an instructor may expect you to submit an annotated bibliography. The bibliography may be due weeks before you turn in the paper, or it may be turned in with the finished project.

● A sociology instructor asks that your topic proposal for a midterm paper on rural poverty include an annotated bibliography that demonstrates a range of perspectives in your reading.

● Your senior history thesis is based upon letters and archival materials found only in a local museum. So you attach an annotated bibliography to your completed project to give readers a clearer sense of what some of the handwritten documents cover.

● In writing a term paper on the cultural roots and connections of gangsta/reality rap, you decide to annotate your works cited items to let readers know what sources you found most authoritative and useful for future research.

UNDERSTANDING ANNOTATED BIBLIOGRAPHIES.   An annotated bibliography is an alphabetical list of the sources and documents you have used in developing a research project, with each item in the list summarized and, very often, evaluated.

Instructors usually ask you to attach an annotated bibliography to the final version of a project so that they can determine at a glance how well you've researched your subject. But some may ask you to submit an annotated bibliography earlier in the writing process—sometimes even as part of the topic proposal—to be sure you're staying on track, poring over good materials, and getting the most out of them. ○

Begin with an accurate record of research materials.   Items recorded in the alphabetical list should follow the guidelines of some documentation system, typically MLA or APA. In a paper using MLA documentation, the list is labeled "Works Cited" and includes only books, articles, and other source materials actually mentioned in the project; it is labeled "Works Consulted" if you also want to include works you've read but not actually cited. In a project using APA style, the list is called "References." ○

need to write a ◀
summary?

Describe or summarize the content of each item in the bibliography.   These summaries should be *very* brief, often just one or two sentences. Begin with a concise description of the work if it isn't self-evident (*a review of; an interview with; a CIA report on*). Then, in your own words, describe its contents, scope, audience, perspective, or other features relevant to your project. Your language should be descriptive and impartial. Be sure to follow any special guidelines offered by your instructor. For more about summarizing, see Chapter 42, "Summarizing Sources." ○

Lauren Nicole/Getty Images.

plan a project
p. 436

cite in APA
p. 512

understand citation
styles p. 470

Assess the significance or quality of the work.   Immediately following the summary, offer a brief appraisal of the item, responding to its authority, thoroughness, length, relevance, usefulness, age (e.g., *up-to-date/dated*), reputation in field (if known), and so on. Your remarks should be professional and academic: You aren't writing a movie review.

Explain the role the work plays in your research.   When an annotated bibliography is part of a topic proposal, size up the materials you have found so far and describe how you expect to use them in your project. Highlight the works that provide creative or fresh ideas, authoritative coverage, up-to-date research, diverse perspectives, or ample bibliographies.

Getting the details right

You will grasp the value of annotated bibliographies the moment you find a trustworthy one covering a subject you are researching. As you prepare such a list of your own, think how your work might help other readers and researchers.

Record the information on your sources accurately.   As you format the items in your list, be sure that the titles, authors, page numbers, and dates are error-free so that users can quickly locate the materials you have used.

Follow a single documentation style.   Documentation systems like MLA and APA can seem fussy, but they make life easier for researchers by standardizing the way all the identifying features of a source are treated. So when you get an entry right in your annotated bibliography, you make life easier for the next person who needs to cite that source. ○

Keep summaries and assessments brief.   Don't get carried away. In most cases, instructors and other readers will want an annotated bibliography that they can scan. They'll appreciate writing that is both precise and succinct.

Follow directions carefully.   Some instructors may provide specific directions for annotated bibliographies, depending on the field or subject of your research. For example, they may ask you to supply the volume numbers, locations, and physical dimensions of books; describe illustrations; provide URLs; and so on.

understand citation
styles p. 470

Examining a model

The following three items are from an annotated bibliography offered as part of a topic proposal on the cultural impact of the iPod.

Stephenson, Seth. "You and Your Shadow." *Slate.com*. Slate Group, 2 Mar. 2004. Web. 3 Mar. 2014. This article from *Slate.com*'s "Ad Report Card" series argues that the original iPod ads featuring silhouetted dancers may alienate viewers by suggesting that the product is cooler than the people who buy it. Stephenson explains why some people may resent the advertisements. The piece may be useful for explaining early reactions to the iPod as a cultural phenomenon.

Sullivan, Andrew. "Society Is Dead: We Have Retreated into the iWorld." *Sunday Times*. Times Newspapers, 20 Feb. 2005. Web. 27 Feb. 2014. In this opinion piece, Sullivan examines how people in cities use iPods to isolate themselves from their surroundings. The author makes a highly personal but plausible case for turning off the machines. The column demonstrates how quickly the iPod has changed society and culture.

Walker, Rob. "The Guts of a New Machine." *New York Times Magazine*, 30 Nov. 2003. *Academic OneFile*. Web. 1 Mar. 2014. This lengthy report describes in detail how Apple developed the concept and technology of the iPod. Walker not only provides a detailed early look at the product but also shows how badly Apple's competitors underestimated its market strength. May help explain Apple's later dominance in smartphones as well.

Full bibliographical citation in MLA style.

Summary of Stephenson's argument.

Potential role source might play in paper.

Evaluation of Sullivan's opinion piece.

Citation demonstrates how to cite an article from a database — in this case, *Academic OneFile*.

Your Turn   For a quick exercise in preparing an annotated bibliography, choose a film that has opened very recently, locate five or six reviews or news articles about it, and then prepare an annotated bibliography using these items. Imagine that you'll be writing a research paper about the public and critical reception the film received when it debuted. (Public and critical reaction may be quite different.) Be sure to choose a documentation system for your bibliography and to use it appropriately.

How to start ● **Need to write a synthesis paper?**
Summarize and paraphrase what you have read.
See page 273.

12 Synthesis Papers

require a response to multiple sources

In some classes, you may be asked to write a synthesis paper, in which you summarize, compare, or assess the views of a variety of authors on a specific topic. The assignment might also require you to come up with a thesis of your own on that subject, based on your research. A synthesis paper (also sometimes described as a "review of literature") gives you practice in using sources in academic papers.

● For a first-year writing course, you write a detailed synthesis examining the positions of authors who both support and challenge your view that we have no choice but to adapt to new media and technology.

● For an engineering course, you prepare a literature review covering the most recently published research on lithium-ion polymer batteries.

● In preparing a prospectus for an end-of-semester research paper, you include a section in which you summarize the sources you expect to use and explain the different positions they represent.

UNDERSTANDING SYNTHESIS PAPERS.   In a synthesis, you typically survey a range of opinions on a topic, often a controversial one, summarizing and assessing a selection of reputable authorities. But pay close attention to the actual assignment: Note what types of sources you must review, whether you may quote from them, how to document them, ○ and whether you are, in fact, expected to develop a thesis of your own after reviewing all the material.

need to write ◀
a synthesis
paper?

If your assignment is to prepare a review of literature, you will identify and report on the most important books and articles on a subject, usually over a specified period of time: *currently, from the last five years, over the past three decades*. The topic of the review may be assigned to you or it may be one you must prepare as part of a thesis, term paper, or capstone project. In either case, check whether your summary must follow a specific pattern of organization: Most literature reviews are chronological, though some are thematic, and still others are arranged by comparison and contrast. ○

Identify reputable sources on your subject.   Expect to find multiple articles, books, and research studies on any significant topic. You can locate relevant material using library catalogs, research guides, or online tools (see Chapter 38). Work with your instructor or a research librarian to separate mainstream and essential works from outliers, which may or may not deserve a closer look.

In 1993, artists Tibor Kalman and Scott Stowell erected this yellow billboard in New York City's heavily trafficked Times Square perhaps to suggest a world of limitless choices. Exploring a new topic, you face similar possibilities and need to sort them out. © 1993, Maggie Hopp, photographer, Courtesy of Maira Kalman.

Summarize and paraphrase the works you have identified.   Take these notes carefully. Summaries capture the gist of every source you read, even those that don't pan out. Paraphrases are lengthier notes you take when you expect to refer to sources extensively or quote from them directly. (Review these skills, as necessary, in Chapters 42–43.)

understand
citation styles p. 470

develop a
draft p. 367

Look for connections between your sources.   Once you have summarized and paraphrased a range of sources, examine them *in relationship to each other* to determine where they come down on your issue. Think about categories to describe their stances: *similarity/difference, congruence/divergence, consistency/inconsistency, conventional/radical*, and so on. Look for sources, too, that explain how a controversy has evolved and where it stands now. Introduce such materials with verbs of attribution such as *describes, reports, points out, asserts, argues, claims, agrees, concurs.*

Acknowledge disagreements and rebuttals.   Describe all the opinions you encounter accurately, introducing them with verbs of attribution such as *questions, denies, disagrees, contradicts, undermines, disputes, calls into question, takes issue with.* Your synthesis should represent a full range of opinions; be sure to present reputable sources that challenge any thesis you intend to develop.

Don't rush to judgment.   In synthesizing, writers sometimes divide their sources too conveniently between those that merely support a claim and those that oppose it, ignoring complications and subtleties. Quite often, the most interesting relationships are to be found in places where belligerent authors unexpectedly agree or orthodox research generates unexpected results. Don't precook the results or try to fit your materials into an existing framework.

Cite materials that both support and challenge your own thesis.   Any thesis you develop yourself as a result of your synthesis (as seen in the sample essay on p. 279) should reflect the inclusiveness of your research. Of course, you will draw on, quote from, and amplify the materials that help define you position. But be sure to acknowledge materials that run counter to your thesis too. In academic and professional writing, you must not only acknowledge these dissenters but also outline their ideas objectively and introduce any quotations from them fairly (Rosen *says*, not Rosen *whines*). ○

use quotations
p. 466

Getting the details right

Although synthesis assignments vary enormously, certain organizational strategies and conventions are worth noting.

Provide a context for your topic.   Open a synthesis paper by identifying your subject and placing it in historical or cultural context. Identify writers or sources that have defined the topic, and explain the rationale for your project. Help readers appreciate why an issue is important.

Tell a story.   Whether your synthesis merely summarizes varying points of view or defends a thesis statement, it's often a good strategy to create a narrative readers can follow. ○ Help them understand the issues as you have come to appreciate them yourself. Separate major issues from minor ones, and use transitions as necessary to establish connections (*consequently*), highlight contrasts (*on the other hand*), show parallels (*similarly*), and so on.

Pay attention to language.   Keep the style of your synthesis objective, neutral, and fairly formal. In most cases, avoid *I* when summarizing and paraphrasing. ○ Remember that the summaries of materials you cite should be in your own words; some synthesis assignments may even prohibit direct quotations. If you do quote from sources, choose statements that cogently represent the positions of your sources.

Be sure to document your sources.   Record full bibliographic information for all the materials you read. You'll need it for the works cited or references page required at the end of most synthesis papers.

> **Your Turn**   On pages 276–78, you'll find paragraphs from sources used in the model synthesis paper on page 279. All these articles are available online. Choose two or three, find and read them, and then write a detailed synthesis of their authors' full positions, being sure to highlight the similarities and/or differences. Keep your analysis as neutral and objective as you can, *especially* if you find yourself taking sides. When you are done, a reader should have some sense of the overall media controversy that these pieces address, but have no idea where you might stand.

understand narratives p. 4   refine your tone p. 400

Examining a model

To give you an idea of how to bring sources together, we'll build a brief synthesis paper from selections drawn from essays that focus on one topic: whether new media technologies like the Web pose a threat to literacy and culture. Ideas that play a role in the synthesis essay are highlighted. Here are the sources, presented alphabetically by author:

I ask my students about their reading habits, and though I'm not surprised to find that few read newspapers or print magazines, many check in with online news sources, aggregate sites, incessantly. They are seldom away from their screens for long, but that's true of us, their parents, as well.

— Sven Birkerts, "Reading in a Digital Age"

The picture emerging from the research is deeply troubling, at least to anyone who values the depth, rather than just the velocity, of human thought. People who read text studded with links, the studies show, comprehend less than those who read traditional linear text. People who watch busy multimedia presentations remember less than those who take in information in a more sedate and focused manner. People who are continually distracted by e-mails, alerts, and other messages understand less than those who are able to concentrate. And people who juggle many tasks are less creative and less productive than those who do one thing at a time.

Top: Jackie Ricciardi/*The Augusta Chronicle*/ZUMA PRESS. *Bottom:* Will Vragovis/*St. Petersburg Times*/ZUMA PRESS.

It is this control, this mental discipline, that we are at risk of losing as we spend ever more time scanning and skimming online. If the slow progression of words across printed pages damped our craving to be inundated by mental stimulation, the Internet indulges it. It returns us to our native state of distractedness, while presenting us with far more distractions than our ancestors ever had to contend with.

— Nicholas Carr, "Does the Internet Make You Dumber?"

Today some 4.5 billion digital screens illuminate our lives. Words have migrated from wood pulp to pixels on computers, phones, laptops, game consoles, televisions, billboards, and tablets. Letters are no longer fixed in black ink on paper, but flitter on a glass surface in a rainbow of colors as fast as our eyes can blink. Screens fill our pockets, briefcases, dashboards, living room walls, and the sides of buildings. They sit in front of us when we work — regardless of what we do. We are now people of the screen. And of course, these newly ubiquitous screens have changed how we read and write.

— Kevin Kelly, "Reading in a Whole New Way"

I have been reading a lot on my iPad recently, and I have some complaints — not about the iPad but about the state of digital reading generally. Reading is a subtle thing, and its subtleties are artifacts of a venerable medium: words printed in ink on paper. Glass and pixels aren't the same.

— Verlyn Klinkenborg, "Further Thoughts of a Novice E-reader"

Top: ZUMA PRESS. *Bottom:* Lannis Waters/ *The Palm Beach Post*/ZUMA PRESS.

The new media have caught on for a reason. Knowledge is increasing exponentially; human brain-power and waking hours are not. Fortunately, the Internet and information technologies are helping us manage, search, and retrieve our collective intellectual output at different scales, from Twitter and previews to e-books and online encyclopedias. Far from making us stupid, these technologies are the only things that will keep us smart.

— Steven Pinker, "Mind over Mass Media"

No teenager that I know of regularly reads a newspaper, as most do not have the time and cannot be bothered to read pages and pages of text while they could watch the news summarized on the Internet or on TV.

— Matthew Robson, "How Teenagers Consume Media"

Then again, perhaps we will simply adjust and come to accept what James called "acquired inattention." E-mails pouring in, cell phones ringing, televisions blaring, podcasts streaming — all this may become background noise, like the "din of a foundry or factory" that James observed workers could scarcely avoid at first, but which eventually became just another part of their daily routine. For the younger generation of multitaskers, the great electronic din is an expected part of everyday life. And given what neuroscience and anecdotal evidence have shown us, this state of constant intentional self-distraction could well be of profound detriment to individual and cultural well-being. When people do their work only in the "interstices of their mind-wandering," with crumbs of attention rationed out among many competing tasks, their culture may gain in information, but it will surely weaken in wisdom.

— Christine Rosen, "The Myth of Multitasking"

The past was not as golden, nor is the present as tawdry, as the pessimists suggest, but the only thing really worth arguing about is the future. It is our misfortune, as a historical generation, to live through the largest expansion in expressive capability in human history, a misfortune because abundance breaks more things than scarcity. We are now witnessing the rapid stress of older institutions accompanied by the slow and fitful development of cultural alternatives. Just as required education was a response to print, using the Internet well will require new cultural institutions as well, not just new technologies.

— Clay Shirky, "Does the Internet Make You Smarter?"

Both Carr and Rosen are right about one thing: The changeover to digital reading brings challenges and changes, requiring a reconsideration of what books are and what they're supposed to do. That doesn't mean the shift won't be worth it. The change will also bring innovations impossible on Gutenberg's printed page, from text mixed with multimedia to components that allow readers to interact with the author and fellow consumers.

— Peter Suderman, "Don't Fear the E-reader"

Here is a brief paper that synthesizes the positions represented in the preceding materials, quoting extensively from them and leading up to a thesis. We have boldfaced the authors' names the first time they appear, to emphasize the number of sources used in this short example.

Chiu 1

Lauren Chiu

Professor Larondo

Writing 203

September 19, 2012

Time to Adapt?

There is considerable agreement that the Internet and other electronic media are changing the way people read, write, think, and behave. Scholars such as **Sven Birkerts** report that their students do not seem to read printed materials anymore, a fact confirmed by fifteen-year-old intern **Matthew Robson**, when asked by his employer Morgan Stanley to describe the media habits of teenagers in England: "No teenager that I know of regularly reads a newspaper, as most do not have the time and cannot be bothered to read pages and pages of text."

But the changes we are experiencing may be more significant than just students abandoning the printed word. Working with an iPad, for instance, makes **Verlyn Klinkenborg** wonder whether reading on a screen may actually be a different and less perceptive experience than reading on paper. More worrisome, **Nicholas Carr** points to a growing body of research suggesting that the cognitive abilities of those who use media frequently may actually be degraded, weakening their comprehension and concentration. Yet, according to **Clay Shirky**, the Internet is increasing our ability to communicate immeasurably,

> Two sources are cited to support a general claim about the media.

> Other authorities amplify and complicate the issue.

> Carr and Shirky are well-known authors with opposing views of the Web.

Chiu 2

and so we simply have to deal with whatever consequences follow from such a major shift in technology. Thinkers like Shirky argue that we do not, in fact, have any choice but to adapt to such changes.

Even **Christine Rosen**, a critic of technology, acknowledges that people will probably have to adjust to their diminished attention spans (110). After all, are there really any alternatives to the speed, convenience, and power of the new technologies when we have become what **Kevin Kelly** describes as "people of the screen" and are no more likely to return to paper for reading than we are to vinyl for music recordings? Fears of the Internet may be overblown too. **Peter Suderman** observes that changes in media allow us to do vastly more than we can with print alone. Moreover, because the sheer amount of knowledge is increasing so quickly, **Steven Pinker** argues that we absolutely need the new ways of communicating: "[T]hese technologies are the only things that will keep us smart."

We cannot, however, ignore voices of caution. The differences Carr describes between habits of deep reading and skimming are especially troubling because so many users of the Web have experienced them. And who can doubt the loss of seriousness in our public and political discussions these days? Maybe Rosen *is* right when she worries that our culture is trading wisdom for a glut of information. But it seems more likely that society will be better off trying to fix the problems electronic media are causing than imagining that we can return to simpler technologies that have already just about vanished.

In a full-length essay, this section would be much longer and quote more sources.

Concerns about the Web are portrayed as reasonable.

The writer states a thesis that might guide a longer analysis.

Chiu 3

Works Cited

Birkerts, Sven. "Reading in a Digital Age." *The American Scholar*. Phi Beta Kappa, Spring 2010. Web. 10 Sept. 2012.

Carr, Nicholas. "Does the Internet Make You Dumber?" *Wall Street Journal*. Wall Street Journal, 5 June 2010. Web. 9 Sept. 2012.

Kelly, Kevin. "Reading in a Whole New Way." *Smithsonian.com*. Smithsonian, Aug. 2010. Web. 13 Sept. 2012.

Klinkenborg, Verlyn. "Further Thoughts of a Novice E-reader." *New York Times*. New York Times, 28 May 2010. Web. 12 Sept. 2012.

Pinker, Steven. "Mind over Mass Media." *New York Times*. New York Times, 10 June 2010. Web. 12 Sept. 2012.

Robson, Matthew. "How Teenagers Consume Media." *Guardian*. Guardian News and Media, 13 July 2009. Web. 14 Sept. 2012.

Rosen, Christine. "The Myth of Multitasking." *The New Atlantis* 20 (Spring 2008): 105-10. Print.

Shirky, Clay. "Does the Internet Make You Smarter?" *Wall Street Journal*. Wall Street Journal, 4 June 2010. Web. 9 Sept. 2012.

Suderman, Peter. "Don't Fear the E-reader." *Reason.com*. Reason Magazine, 23 Mar. 2010. Web. 11 Sept. 2012.

How to start

Want to get the reader's attention?
Choose a sensible subject line. See page 285.

13 E-mails

**communicate
electronically**

E-mail is the preferred method for most business (and personal) communication because it is quick, efficient, easy to archive, and easy to search.

- You write to the coordinator of the writing center to apply for a job as a tutor, courtesy copying the message to a professor who has agreed to serve as a reference.

- You send an e-mail to classmates in a writing class, looking for someone to collaborate on a Web project.

- You e-mail the entire College of Liberal Arts faculty to invite them to attend a student production of Chekhov's *Uncle Vanya*.

- You e-mail a complaint to your cable supplier because a premium sports channel you subscribe to has been unavailable for a week.

UNDERSTANDING E-MAIL.   E-mail is so common and informal that writers sometimes forget its professional side. Though usually composed quickly, e-mails have a long shelf life once they're archived. They can also spread well beyond their original audiences. So you need to take care with messages sent to organizations, businesses, professors, groups of classmates, and so on. The following strategies will help.

Explain your purpose clearly and logically.   Use both the subject line and first paragraph of an e-mail to explain your reason for writing. Be specific about names, titles, dates, places, expectations, requirements, and so on, especially when your message announces an event, explains a policy, invites a discussion, or makes an inquiry. Write your message so that it will still make sense a year or more later.

Tell readers what you want them to do.   In a professional e-mail, lay out a clear agenda for accomplishing one major task: Ask for a document, a response, or a reply by a specific date. If you have multiple requests to make of a single person or group, consider writing separate e-mails. It's easier to track short, single-purpose e-mails than to deal with complex documents requiring several different actions.

Write for intended and unintended audiences.   The specific audience in the "To" line is usually the only audience for your message. But e-mail is more public than traditional surface mail, easily duplicated and sent to whole networks of recipients with just a click. So compose your business e-mails as if they *might* be read by everyone in a unit or even published in a local paper. Assume that nothing in business e-mail is private.

Keep your messages brief.   Lengthy blocks of e-mail prose without paragraph breaks irritate readers. Indeed, meandering or chatty e-mails in business situations can make a writer seem disorganized and out of control. Try to limit your e-mail messages to what fits on a single screen. Remember that people routinely view e-mail on mobile devices. Keep messages simple. **O**

think visually
p. 557

Distribute your messages sensibly.   Send a copy of an e-mail to anyone directly involved in the message, as well as to those who might need to be informed. For example, if you were filing a grade complaint with an instructor, you might also copy the chair of his or her academic department or the dean of students. But don't let the copy (CC) and blind copy (BCC) lines in the e-mail header tempt you to send messages beyond the essential audience.

"You invented a time machine to come back and hit Reply instead of Reply All?"
© Tom Toro/New Yorker Magazine/Condé Nast.

Getting the details right

Because most people receive e-mail messages frequently, make any you send easy to follow.

want to get ◀ the reader's attention?

Choose a sensible subject line.   The subject line should clearly identify the topic and include helpful keywords that might later be searched. If your e-mail is specifically about a grading policy, your student loan, or mold in your gym locker, make sure a word you'll recall afterward—like *policy*, *loan*, or *mold*—gets in the subject line. In professional e-mails, subjects such as *A question, Hi!* or *Meeting* are useless.

Arrange your text sensibly.   You can do almost as much visually in e-mail as you can in a word-processing program, including choosing fonts, inserting lines, and adding color, images, and videos. But because so many people read messages on mobile devices, a simple block style with spaces between single-spaced paragraphs works best. Keep the paragraphs brief.

Check the recipient list before you hit send.   Routinely double-check all the recipient fields—especially when you're replying to a message. The original writer may have copied the message widely: Do you want to send your reply to that entire group or just to the original writer?

Include an appropriate signature.   Professional e-mail of any kind should include a signature that identifies you and provides contact information readers need. Your e-mail address alone may not be clear enough to identify who you are, especially when you are writing to an instructor. Be sure to set up a signature for your laptop, desktop, or mobile device.

But be careful: Don't provide readers with a *home* phone number or address since you won't know who might see your e-mail message. When you send e-mail, the recipient can reach you simply by replying.

Consider, too, that a list of incoming e-mails on a cell phone typically previews just the first few lines of a message. If you want a reader's attention, make your point quickly.

Use standard grammar.   Professional e-mails should be almost as polished as business letters: At least give readers the courtesy of a quick review to catch humiliating gaffes or misspellings. ○ Emoticons and smiley faces have also disappeared from most professional communications.

Have a sensible e-mail address.   You might enjoy communicating with friends as HorribleHagar or DaisyGirl, but an e-mail signature like that will undermine your credibility with a professor or potential employer. Save the oddball name for a private e-mail account.

Don't be a pain.   You just add to the daily clutter if you send unnecessary replies to e-mails—a pointless *thanks* or *Yes!* or *WooHoo!* Just as bad is CCing everyone on a list when you've received a query that needs to go to one person only.

> **Your Turn**   Take a quick look at the formatting of the e-mails that appear on a mobile device. Most phones now display images, complex page formats, or other textual features within e-mail. But note the limitations too. Images can clutter a message on a small screen, so place them after your text. And you might not want to put links you include too close together because they can be hard to select.

revise and edit p. 422

Examining a model

Here's a fairly typical e-mail from a student to a professor. The e-mail provides clear and direct informa-tion (note that the student's majors are identified in the signature) and poses one clear question. It gets to the point quickly and politely asks for a response.

To: John Ruszkiewicz

From: Kori Strickland
Sent: October 3, 2015 11:56 AM

Specific subject line

Re: Writing Center Course Eligibility
CC: Davida Charney

Dear Professor Ruszkiewicz,

Opening paragraph explains point of e-mail.

I'm currently a junior at the University of Texas at Austin applying for your Rheto-ric 368C Writing Center Internship course in spring 2016. I have a question about my eligibility.

Business letters use a colon after greeting, but e-mails are often less formal.

The course description online says preference is given to students who can work two or more semesters in the writing center after they take the class. Do I still stand a reasonable chance at being admitted to RHE 368C if I will be able to work only one semester because of a study-abroad opportunity my senior year?

Second paragraph poses one specific question.

Tone is professional and correct.

Please let me know. In any case, I am attaching the required writing sample and have asked Professor Charney to write the brief recommendation requested for RHE 368C candidates.

Sincerely,
Kori Strickland

Final paragraph asks for a reply and spells out other actions the writer has taken.

Signature is simple, informative, and professional.

University of Texas | Political Communication and Rhetoric
Fine Arts Council | Co-president

RHE 368C W...ple (22 KB)

Attachment included as indicated in the letter.

How to start ➤ ● **Want to get a response?**
Explain your purpose clearly and logically.
See page 289.

14 Business Letters

communicate formally

The formal business letter remains an important instrument for sending information in professional situations. Though business letters can be transmitted electronically these days, legal letters or decisions about admissions to schools or programs often still arrive on paper, complete with a real signature.

- Responding to a summer internship opportunity, you outline your credentials for the position in a cover letter and attach your résumé.

- You send a brief letter to the director of admissions of a law school, graciously declining your acceptance into the program.

- You send a letter of complaint to an auto company, documenting the list of problems you've had with your SUV and indicating your intention to seek redress under your state's "lemon law."

- You write to a management company to accept the terms of a lease, enclosing a check for the security deposit on your future apartment.

UNDERSTANDING BUSINESS LETTERS.   Business letters are generally formal in tone and follow conventions designed to make the document a suitable record and to support additional communication. The principles for composing a business or job letter do not differ much from those for business e-mails. ○

want to get a ◀ response?

Explain your purpose clearly and logically.   Use the first paragraph to explain your purpose and announce any specific concerns. Anticipate familiar *who*, *what*, *where*, *when*, *how*, and *why* questions; be specific about names, titles, dates, and places. If you're applying for a job, scholarship, or admission to a program, name the exact position or program and mention that your résumé is attached. Remember that your letter may have a long life in a file cabinet: Write a document that will make sense months or years later.

Tell readers what you want them to do.   Don't leave them guessing about how to respond to your message. Lay out a clear agenda for accomplishing one task: Apply for a job, request information, or make an inquiry or complaint. Don't hesitate to ask for a reply, even by a specific date when that is necessary.

Write for your audience.   Quite often, you won't know the people to whom you are sending a business letter. So you have to construct a letter imagining how an executive, employer, admissions officer, or complaints manager might be most effectively persuaded. Courtesy and goodwill go a

Left: Tim Graham/Tim Graham Photo Library/Getty Images. *Right:* © Brigette M. Sullivan/PhotoEdit.

understand
e-mail p. 282

long way—though you may have to be firm and impersonal in many situations. Avoid phony emotions or tributes.

A job application or cover letter (with your résumé attached) poses special challenges. You want to present your credentials in the best possible light without seeming full of yourself. Be succinct and specific, letting achievements speak mostly for themselves—though you can fill in details that a reader might not appreciate. Focus on recent credentials and accomplishments and underscore the skills and strengths you bring to the job. Speak in your own voice, clipped slightly by a formal style. O

Keep the letter focused and brief.   Like e-mails, business letters become hard to read when they extend much beyond one page. A busy administrator or employee prefers a concise message, handsomely laid out on good stationery. Even a job-application letter should be relatively short, highlighting just your strongest credentials: Leave it to the accompanying résumé or dossier to flesh out the details.

Follow a conventional form.   All business letters should include your address (called the *return address*), the date of the message, the address of the person to whom you are writing (called the *inside address*), a formal salutation or greeting, a closing, a signature in ink (when possible), and information about copies or enclosures.

Both block format and *modified-block format* are acceptable in business communication. In block forms, all elements are aligned against the left-hand margin (with the exception of the letterhead address at the top). In modified-block form, the return address, date, closing, and signature are aligned with the center of the page. In both cases, paragraphs in the body of the letter are set as single-spaced blocks of type, their first lines not indented, and with an extra line space between paragraphs.

In indented form (not shown), the elements of the letter are arranged as in modified-block form, but the first lines of body paragraphs are indented five spaces, with no line spaces between the single-spaced paragraphs.

define your
style p. 400

Getting the details right

Perhaps the most important detail in a business letter is keeping the format you use consistent and correct. Be sure to print your letter on good-quality paper or letterhead and to send it in a proper business envelope, one large enough to accommodate a page 8½ inches wide.

Use consistent margins and spacing. Generally, 1-inch margins all around work well, but you can use larger margins (up to 1½ inches) when your message is short. The top margin can also be adjusted if you want to balance the letter on the page, though the body need not be centered.

Finesse the greeting. Write to a particular person at a firm or institution. Address him or her as *Mr.* or *Ms.*—unless you actually know that a woman prefers *Mrs.* You may also address people by their full names: *Dear Margaret Hitchens.* When you don't have a name, you might use a person's title: *Dear Admissions Director* or *Dear Hiring Manager.* Or you can fall back on *Dear Sir or Madam* or *To Whom It May Concern,* though these forms of address (especially *madam*) are increasingly dated. When it doesn't sound absurd, you can even address the institution or entity: *Dear Exxon* or *Dear IRS*—again, this is not a preferred form.

Distribute copies of your letter sensibly. Copy anyone involved in a message, as well as anyone who might have a legitimate interest in your action. For example, in filing a product complaint with a company, you may also want to send your letter to the state office of consumer affairs. Copies are noted and listed at the bottom of the letter, introduced by the abbreviation *CC* (for *courtesy copy*).

Spell everything right. Be scrupulous about the grammar and mechanics too—especially in a job-application letter. Until you get an interview, that piece of paper represents you to a potential client or employer. Would you hire someone who misspelled your company's name or made noticeable errors? O

© Gero Greloer/dpa/Corbis.

help with common errors p. 566

Photocopy the letter as a record.   An important business letter needs a paper copy, even when you have an electronic version archived: The photocopied signature may mean something.

Don't forget the promised enclosures.   A résumé should routinely accompany a job-application letter. ○

Fold the letter correctly and send it in a suitable envelope.   Business letters always go on $8\frac{1}{2} \times 11$-inch paper and are sent in standard business envelopes, generally $4\frac{1}{8} \times 9\frac{1}{2}$ inches. Fold the letter in three sections, trying to put the creases through white space in the letter so that the body of the message remains readable.

John Humbert
95 Primrose Lane
Columbus, OH 43209

September 23, 2014

Home Design Magazine
3652 Delmar Drive
Prince, NY 10012

Dear *Home Design* Magazine:

I am a subscriber to your magazine, but I never received my July 2014 or August 2014 issues. When my subscription expires at the end of this year, please extend it two more months at no charge to make up for this error. Originally, my last issue would have been the December 2014 magazine. Since I have missed two issues and since my subscription was paid in full almost a year ago, please send me the January and February 2015 issues of *Home Design* at no additional charge.

Thank you for your attention.

Sincerely,
J. Humbert
John Humbert

understand
résumés p. 296

Examining models

The following are two business letters: The first is a concise letter of complaint; the second is a cover letter written by a student sending a résumé in a quest for a summer internship.

John Humbert
95 Primrose Lane
Columbus, OH 43209

September 23, 2014

Home Design Magazine
3652 Delmar Drive
Prince, NY 10012

Dear *Home Design* Magazine:

I am a subscriber to your magazine, but I never received my July 2014 or August 2014 issues. When my subscription expires at the end of this year, please extend it two more months at no charge to make up for this error. Originally, my last issue would have been the December 2014 magazine. Since I have missed two issues and since my subscription was paid in full almost a year ago, please send me the January and February 2015 issues of *Home Design* at no additional charge.

Thank you for your attention.

Sincerely,
J. Humbert
John Humbert

Letterhead is preprinted stationery carrying the return address of the writer or institution. It may also include a corporate logo.

Allow two or three spaces between the date and address.

Allow one line space above and below the salutation. A colon follows the greeting.

The letter is in block form, with all major elements aligned with the left margin.

COVER LETTER

In modified-block form, return address, date, closing, and signature are centered.

1001 Harold Circle #10
Austin, TX 78712
June 28, 20--

Mr. Josh Greenwood
ABC Corporate Advisers, Inc.
9034 Brae Rd., Suite 1111
Austin, TX 78731

Dear Mr. Greenwood:

Opening paragraph clearly states thesis of letter: Nancy Linn wants this job.

Rita Weeks, a prelaw adviser at the University of Texas at Austin, e-mailed me about an internship opportunity at your firm. Working at ABC Corporate Advisers sounds like an excellent chance for me to further my interests in finance and corporate law. I would like to apply for the position.

Letter highlights key accomplishments succinctly and specifically.

As my attached résumé demonstrates, I have already interned at an estate-planning law firm, where I learned to serve the needs of an office of professionals and clients. I also have a record of achievement on campus: I used my skills as a writer and speaker to obtain funding for the Honors Business Association at UT-Austin, for which I serve as vice president and financial director. By contacting corporate recruiters, I raised $5,500 from Microsoft, ExxonMobil, Deloitte, and other companies.

Candidate repeatedly explains how internship fits career goals.

I am ready for a job that more closely relates to my academic training and career goal: becoming a certified financial analyst and corporate lawyer. Please contact me at 210-555-0000 or NLINN@abcd.com to schedule an interview. Thank you for considering me as a potential intern. I look forward to meeting you.

Additional contact information provided.

Sincerely,
N. Linn
Nancy Linn

Courtesy copy of letter sent to adviser mentioned in first paragraph; can be contacted as reference.

Enclosure: Résumé
CC: Rita Weeks

Your Turn Have you received a business letter recently? If so, pull it out and take a moment to note the specific features described in this chapter. They are easy to overlook: letterhead, date, inside address, greeting, closing, attachments, spacing. Are their functions obvious and do they make sense? Now take a look at a recent e-mail you may have received from an institution or business (rather than a friend or classmate). What features does the business e-mail have in common with a business letter? In what ways are they different?

15

record
professional
achievements

Résumés

A one-page résumé usually accompanies any letter of application you send for a position or job. The résumé gathers and organizes details about your experiences at school, on the job, and in the community. In some careers, you may recap years of work and achievements in a longer, but similarly organized, document called a CV (curriculum vitae).

● Applying for a part-time position at a local day-care center, you assemble a résumé that chronicles your relevant experience.

● For an application to graduate school, you prepare a résumé that gives first priority to your accomplishments as a dean's list dual major in government and English.

● You modify your résumé slightly to highlight your internships with several law firms because you are applying for a paralegal clerk position at Baker Botts LLP.

● For a campus service scholarship, you tweak your résumé to emphasize activities more likely to interest college administrators than potential employers.

UNDERSTANDING RÉSUMÉS.   The point of a résumé is to provide a quick, easy-to-scan summary of your accomplishments to someone interested in hiring you. The document must be readable at a glance, meticulously accurate, and reasonably handsome. Think of it this way: A résumé is your one- or two-page chance to make a memorable first impression.

Résumés do vary enormously in design—though they often resemble outlines without the numbers or letters. You have to decide on everything from fonts and headings to alignments and paper. You can pay companies to craft your résumé or use widely available templates to design it and then post it online. But your word processor has all the power you need to create a competent résumé on your own. Here's some advice.

At a Walt Disney Company job fair for returning veterans, experts help vets polish their résumés. Associated Press/Reed Saxon.

For a tutorial on job searches, see **macmillanhighered.com/howtowrite3e.**
Tutorials › Digital Writing › Job Search/Personal Branding

Gather the necessary information. You'll have to collect this career data sooner or later. It's much simpler if you start in college and gradually build a full résumé. Don't guess or rely on memory for résumé information: Get the data right. Verify your job titles and your months or years of employment; give your major as it is identified in your college catalog; make an accurate list of your achievements and activities without embellishing them. Don't turn an afternoon at a sandlot into "coaching high school baseball." Focus on attainments during your college years and beyond. Grade school and high school achievements don't mean much, unless you're LeBron James.

Decide on appropriate categories. Contrary to what you may think, there's no standard form for résumés, but they do usually contain some mix of the following information:

- Basic contact data or heading: your name, address, phone number, and e-mail address
- Educational attainments (usually college and above, once you have a BA, BS, or other postsecondary credential): degrees earned, where, and when
- Work experience: job titles, companies, and dates of employment, with a brief list of skills you used in specific jobs (such as customer service, sales, software programs, language proficiencies, and so on)
- Other accomplishments: extracurricular activities, community service, volunteer work, honors, awards, and so on. These may be broken into subcategories.

Depending on the situation, you might also include the following elements:

- A brief statement of your career goals
- A list of people willing to serve as references (with their contact information)

You can add categories to a résumé too, whenever they might improve your chances for a position. As your career evolves, for instance, your résumé may eventually include items such as administrative appointments, committee service, awards, patents, publications, lectures, participation in business organizations, community service, and so on. But keep the document compact. Ordinarily, a first résumé shouldn't exceed one page—though it may have to run longer if you are asked to provide references.

Arrange the information within categories in reverse chronological order.   The most recent attainments come first in each of your categories. If such a list threatens to bury your most significant items, you have several options: Cut the lesser achievements from the list, break out special achievements in some consistent way, or highlight those special achievements in the cover letter that should always accompany a résumé. O

Design pages that are easy to read.   Basic design principles aren't rocket science: Headings and key information should stand out and individual items should be clearly separated. The pages should look substantive but not cluttered. White space makes any document friendly, but too much in a résumé can suggest a lack of achievement. O

    In general, treat the résumé as a conservative document. This is not the time to experiment with fonts and flash or curlicues. Don't include a photograph either, even a good one.

want to ◄
get a job?

Applying for a job need not be as dreary as it once was—or as sexist.
© Hulton-Deutsch Collection/Corbis.

understand business letters p. 288

think visually p. 557

Getting the details right

With its fussy dates, headings, columns, and margins, a résumé is all about the details. Fortunately, it is brief enough to make a thorough going-over easy. Here are some important considerations.

Proofread every line in the résumé several times.   Careful editing isn't a minor "detail" when it comes to résumés: It can be the whole ball game. When employers have more job candidates than they can handle, they may look for reasons to dismiss weak cases. Misspelled words, poor design of headings and text, and incomplete or confusing chronology are the kinds of mistakes that can terminate your job quest. ○

Don't leave unexplained gaps in your education or work career.   Readers will wonder about blanks in your history (Are you hiding something?) and so may dismiss your application in favor of candidates whose career paths raise no red flags. Simply account for any long periods (a year or so) you may have spent wandering the capitals of Europe or flipping burgers. Do so either in the résumé or in the job-application/cover letter—especially if the experiences contributed to your skills.

Be consistent.   Keep the headings and alignments the same throughout the document. Express all dates in the same form: For example, if you abbreviate months, do so everywhere. Use hyphens between dates.

Protect your personal data.   You don't have to volunteer information about your race, gender, age, or sexual orientation on a job application or résumé. Neither should you provide financial data, Social Security or credit card numbers, or other information you don't want in the public domain and that is not pertinent to your job search. However, you do need to be accurate and honest about the relevant job information: Any disparity about what you state on a résumé and your actual accomplishments may be a firing offense down the road.

Look for help.   Check whether your campus career center or writing center offers help with résumés. Online employment sites such as Headhunter.com and Monster also offer useful tips and tools for preparing and posting a résumé.

help with common
errors p. 566

Examining a model

The following résumé, by Andrea Palladino, is arranged in reverse chronological order. Palladino uses a simple design that aligns the major headings and dates in a column down the left-hand margin and indents the detailed accomplishments to separate them, making them highly readable.

Contact information centered at top of page for quick reference. If necessary, give both school and permanent addresses.

Andrea Palladino
600 Oak St.
Austin, TX 78705
(281) 555-1234

CAREER OBJECTIVE   Soon-to-be college graduate seeking full-time position that allows for regular interpersonal communication and continued professional growth.

Optional "career objective" functions like thesis.

EDUCATION
8/10-5/15   University of Texas at Austin – Psychology, BA

EXPERIENCE
3/13-Present   Writing Consultant
University of Texas at Austin Undergraduate Writing Center – Austin, TX
Tutor students at various stages of the writing process. Work with a variety of assignments. Attend professional development workshops.

Alignments further emphasize headings and dates.

5/13-Present   Child Care Provider
CoCare Children's Services – Austin, TX
Care for infants through children aged ten, including children with physical and mental disabilities. Change diapers, give food and comfort, engage children in stimulating play, and clean/disinfect toys after child care. Work on standby and substitute for coworkers when needed.

Ample, but not excessive, white space enhances readability.

5/12-12/13   Salesperson/Stockperson
Eloise's Collectibles – Katy, TX
Unpacked new shipments, prepared outgoing shipments, and kept inventory. Interacted with customers and performed the duties of a cashier.

ACCOMPLISHMENTS

2012-Present	College Scholar for three years—acknowledgment of in-residence GPA of at least 3.50
10/14-Present	Big Brothers Big Sisters of Central Texas
Fall 2012	University of Texas at Austin Children's Research Lab—Research Assistant

Your Turn If you already have a résumé, open it up and check its features against the suggestions offered in this chapter. Consider how you might modify it for the different kinds of positions you may be applying for over the next several years. And if you don't yet have a résumé, now is an excellent time to draft one. You will more likely need it sooner than later.

How to start ● **Feeling lost?**

Gather your material. See page 306.

16 Personal Statements

explain a person's experiences and goals

Preparing a short personal statement has become almost a ritual among people applying for admission to college, professional school, or graduate school, or for jobs, promotions, scholarships, internships, or even elective office.

- An application for an internship asks for an essay in which you explain how your career goals will contribute to a more tolerant and diverse society.

- All candidates for the student government offices you're interested in must file a personal statement explaining their positions. Your statement, limited to three hundred words, will be printed in the campus newspaper and posted online.

- You dust off the personal statement you wrote to apply to college to see what portions you can use in an essay required for admission to upper-division courses in the College of Communication.

UNDERSTANDING PERSONAL STATEMENTS.   Institutions that ask for
personal statements are rarely interested in who you are. Rather, they want to
see whether you can *represent* yourself as a person with whom they might want
to be affiliated. That may seem harsh, but consider the personal statements you
have already written. At best, they are a slice of your life—the verbal equivalent
of you all dressed up for the prom.

   If you want a sense of what a school, business, or other institution expects
in the essays it requests from applicants, read whatever passes for that group's
core values or mission statement, often available online. If the words sound a
bit solemn, inflated, and unrealistic, you've got your answer—except that you
shouldn't actually sound as pretentious as an institution. A little blood has to
flow through the veins of your personal statement, just not so much that someone in an office gets nervous about your emotional shape.

Associated Press/Susan Walsh.

Hitting the right balance between displaying overwhelming competence and admitting human foibles in a personal statement is tough. Here's some advice for composing a successful essay.

Read the essay prompt carefully.   Essay topics are often deliberately open-ended to give you some freedom in pursuing a topic, but only answer the question actually posed, not one you'd prefer to deal with. Ideally, the question will focus on a specific aspect of your work or education; try to write about this even if the question is more general.

Don't repeat in your personal statement what's already on record in an application letter or résumé. Instead, look for incidents that will bring your résumé lines to life. If the prompt encourages personal reminiscences (e.g., *the person who influenced you the most*), think hard about how to give your story a clear direction.

▶ feeling lost?

Decide on a focus or theme.   Personal statements are short, so make the best use of a reader's time. Don't ramble about summer jobs or vague educational opportunities. Instead, find a theme that focuses on the strongest aspects of your application. If you're driven by a passion for research, arrange the elements of your life to illustrate this. If your best work is extracurricular, explain in a scholarship application how your specific commitments to people and organizations make you a more well-rounded student. In other words, turn your life into a thesis statement and make a clear point about yourself. ◯

Above all be honest and forthright. Here's good advice from a woman who worked with high school students who were composing college admission statements:

> In my years handling applications to elite schools, from Harvard to Haverford, Davidson to Dickinson and everything in between, I was often surprised by where students did gain acceptance. But in every case it was a student who wrote a fabulously independent essay. Not necessarily hyper-sophisticated. But true.
>
> My students always asked me, What should I write about?
>
> I'd answer: You are a student of the world. What is it that moves you? What incites you, enrages you? The first-person pronoun is a mighty tool. Use it.

develop a
statement p. 362

I have had successful students write about the virtues of napping (Middlebury), failing a course (Harvard), and having to shoot a farm dog because it couldn't work stock (Princeton). Once a student came out to me in his fifth (and best) draft. His parents probably still don't know, but they got the Ivy Leaguer they wanted (Penn).

— Lacy Crawford, "Writing the Right College-Entrance Essay"

When you apply for professional programs, scholarships, and internships, your audiences will be different, but the basic principles outlined here still hold.

Be realistic about your audience.   Your personal statements are read by strangers. That's scary, but you can usually count on them to be reasonable people willing to give you a fair hearing. They measure you against other applicants—not unreachable standards of perfection. How might you overcome the initial anxiety? Experienced writing tutor Jacob Pietsch suggests that you address a statement to a real person in your life who doesn't know you very well: "Visualize them, and get ready to write them a letter."

Organize the piece strategically.   Many personal statements take a narrative form, though they may also borrow some elements of reports and even proposals. Malia Hamilton, a writing center consultant, offers a structure to consider: "Whenever I read a personal statement, I look to see if the writer has told me three things: (1) who they were, (2) who they are, and (3) who they want to be. If the writer has effectively incorporated these three stages of themselves into their personal statement, it's almost always an effective one." Whatever structures you adopt for your essay, pay attention to transitions: You cannot risk readers getting confused or lost. O

Try a high or middle style.   You don't want to be breezy or casual in an essay for law school or medical school, but a *personal* statement does invite a human voice. So a style that marries the correctness and formal vocabulary of a high style with the occasional untailored feel of the middle style might be perfect for many personal statements. O

connect ideas
p. 387

define your
style p. 400

Getting the details right

As with résumés, there's no room for errors or slips in personal statements. ○ They are a test of your writing skills, plain and simple, so you need to get the spelling, mechanics, and usage correct. In addition, consider the following advice.

Don't get too artsy.   A striking image or two may work well in the statement, as may the occasional metaphor or simile. But don't build your essay around a running theme, an extended analogy, or a pop-culture allusion that a reader might dismiss as hokey or simply not get. If a phrase or feature stands out too noticeably, change it, even though you may like it.

Use common sense.   You probably already have the good grace not to offend gender, racial, religious, and ethnic groups in your personal statement. You should also take the time to read your essay from the point of view of people from less protected groups who may take umbrage at your dismissal of *old folks, fundamentalists*, or even *Republicans*. You don't know who may be reading your essay.

Compose the statement yourself.   It's the ethical thing to do. If you don't and you're caught, you're toast. You might ask someone to review your essay or take a draft to a writing center for a consultation. ○ This review or any help from a parent or English-major roommate should not purge your voice from the essay. Remember, too, that when you arrive at a job or internship, you'll be expected to write at the level you display in the statement that got you there.

> **Your Turn**   Amused by the thought of your life as a thesis statement? Give it a try. Compose *three* thesis sentences that might be plausibly used to organize three different personal statements, emphasizing varying aspects of your life and career. Which statement do you think describes you best? Would it always be the best thesis for a personal statement? Why or why not?

help with common
errors p. 566

peer review
p. 428

Examining a model

The Academic Service Partnership Foundation asked candidates for an internship to prepare an essay addressing a series of questions. The prompt and one response to it follow.

ASPF NATIONAL INTERNSHIP PROGRAM

Please submit a 250- to 500-word typed essay answering the following three questions:

1. Why do you want an internship with the ASPF?
2. What do you hope to accomplish in your academic and professional career goals?
3. What are your strengths and skills, and how would you use these in your internship?

Specific questions limit reply, but also help organize it.

Michael Villaverde

April 14, 20--

Opening sentence states writer's thesis or intent; first two paragraphs address first question.

The opportunity to work within a health-related government agency alongside top-notch professionals initially attracted me to the Academic Service Partnership Foundation (ASPF) National Internship Program. Participating in the ASPF's internship program would enable me to augment the health-services research skills I've gained working at the VERDICT Research Center in San Antonio and the M. D. Anderson Cancer Center in Houston. This internship could also help me gain experience in health policy and administration.

    I support the ASPF's mission to foster closer relations between formal education and public service and believe that I

Essay uses first person (*I, me*) but is fairly formal in tone and vocabulary, between high and middle style.

Personal note slips through in enthusiasm author shows for internship opportunity.

could contribute to this mission. If selected as an ASPF intern, I will become an active alumnus of the program. I would love to do my part by advising younger students and recruiting future ASPF interns. Most important, I make it a point to improve the operations of programs from which I benefit. Any opportunities provided to me by the ASPF will be repaid in kind.

This statement transitions smoothly into second issue raised in prompt.

Other strengths I bring to the ASPF's National Internship Program are my broad educational background and dedication. My undergraduate studies will culminate in two honors degrees (finance and liberal arts) with additional premed course work. Afterward, I wish to enroll in a combined MD/PhD program in health-services research. Following my formal education, I will devote my career to seeing patients in a primary-care setting, researching health-care issues as a university faculty member, teaching bioethics, and developing public policy at a health-related government agency.

Formidable and specific goals speak for themselves in straightforward language.

Another transition introduces third issue raised by the prompt.

The course work at my undergraduate institution has provided me with basic laboratory and computer experience, but my strengths lie in oral and written communication. Comparing digital and film-screen mammography equipment for a project at M. D. Anderson honed my technical-writing skills and comprehension of statistical analysis. The qualitative analysis methods I learned at VERDICT while evaluating strategies used by the Veterans Health Administration in implementing clinical practice guidelines will be a significant resource to any prospective employer. By the end of this

Qualifications offered are numerous and detailed.

semester, I will also possess basic knowledge of Statistical Package for the Social Sciences (SPSS) software.

During my internship I would like to research one of the following topics: health-care finance, health policy, or ethnic disparities in access to high-quality health care. I have read much about the Patient Protection and Affordable Care Act of 2010 and anticipate studying its implications. I would learn a great deal from working with officials responsible for the operation and strategic planning of a program like Medicare (or a nonprofit hospital system). The greater the prospects for multiple responsibilities, the more excited I will be to show up at work each day.

Special interest/concern is noted and is likely to impress reviewers of statement.

Final sentence affirms enthusiasm for technical internship.

● **First time assembling a portfolio?**
Think about what you should include.
See page 313.

17 Writing Portfolios

gather samples of your work

Professionals in creative fields—art, architecture, photography, modeling—have long used portfolios to inventory their achievements or display their skills to potential clients or employers. The practice has spread to other fields because these careful collections of work provide an in-depth look at what people have actually accomplished over time. Not surprisingly, many schools now encourage (or require) students to assemble writing portfolios of various kinds to demonstrate what they have learned and to assist them in the job market.

- For a first-year writing course, you put together a portfolio that traces your composing process for two major assignments, from brainstorming, research, and topic proposal through draft and final versions.

- For an writing internship course that qualifies you to work at a writing center, you introduce your course portfolio with a "literacy narrative" and offer midterm and final self-assessments of your progress.

- For a portfolio that qualifies you to begin apprentice teaching, you compile a set of reflections on all the proficiencies of your training program.

UNDERSTANDING WRITING PORTFOLIOS. As assignments, portfolios vary enormously in what they aim to do and how they achieve their goals. Some collections serve as learning tools for particular courses, supporting students as they develop sound writing habits; not incidentally, they also provide material for helpful assessments of writing skills. Portfolios in writing classes, which are now usually compiled online, typically include some of the following elements:

first time ◀
assembling
a portfolio?

- Literacy narratives or statements of goals
- Brainstorming/prewriting activities for individual assignments
- Research logs and maps or annotated bibliographies
- Topic proposals and comments
- First drafts and revisions, with the writer's reflections
- Peer and instructor comments
- Final drafts, with the writer's reflections
- Writer's midcourse and/or final assessments of learning goals
- Additional documents or media materials selected by the writer
- A holistic assessment of the portfolio by the teacher (rather than grading of individual items)

Instructors and classmates may play a role at every stage of the composing process, especially when the portfolio is developed online.

In other situations, materials collected in a portfolio provide evidence that a student has mastered specific writing, research, or even media proficiencies required for a job or professional advancement. Such career portfolios (for example, for prospective teachers) may stretch across a sequence of courses, whole degree programs, or college careers. Owners of the portfolio usually have some responsibility for shaping their collection, but certain elements may be recommended or mandated, such as the following:

- A personal statement or profile describing accomplishments and learning trajectory as well as career goals

- Work that illustrates mastery of a subject matter
- Evidence of proficiency in specific technical or research skills
- Written reflections on specific issues in a field, such as philosophy, diversity, or professional ethics
- Assessments, evaluations, and outsider comments
- Documents that illustrate skills in writing, media, technology, or other areas

This list is partial. College programs that require career or degree portfolios typically offer detailed specifications, criteria of evaluation, templates, and lots of support.

Take charge of the portfolio assignment.   Many students are intimidated by the prospect of assembling a writing portfolio. But you won't have a problem if, right from the start, you study the instructions for the assignment, ask any nagging questions, figure out your responsibilities, and get hands-on experience with the required technology. Since most writing portfolios now

Here's where you can start: the dashboard screen of a typical online portfolio program. Clippings.me.

come together online, sit down with the platform and learn how it works. In many cases, you'll be expected not only to post your own work and reflections but also to respond regularly to your classmates' materials.

If you are submitting a portfolio in paper form, study the specifications carefully. Then, right from the start, settle on a template for all your submissions: consistent margins, fonts, headings, headers, pagination, captions, and so on. (You might simply adhere to MLA or APA guidelines.) Your work will be more impressive if you give careful attention to design.

Appreciate the audiences for a portfolio.   Portfolios are usually mandated by instructors or institutions, and the work you present is likely to influence a grade, certification, or even a job opportunity. Fortunately, such readers will typically offer clear-cut rubrics for measuring your performance. Study those standards carefully to find out what exactly a teacher or program expects in a portfolio.

You'll often prepare a portfolio in the company of classmates and you should be grateful when that is the case. Since they are in the same boat, they can keep you grounded and you can usually count on them for timely feedback and even encouragement. Respond in kind. In the long run, you may learn as much from these rough-and-tumble peer interactions as from your instructor.

One important audience for a portfolio remains: yourself. Creating a portfolio will underscore what it takes to be a writer, highlighting all your moves and making you more conscious of these choices. By discovering strengths and confronting weaknesses, you'll really learn the craft. So treat the portfolio as an opportunity, not just another long assignment.

Present authentic materials.   A writing portfolio demonstrates a process of learning, not a glide path to perfection. So be honest about what you post there, from topic proposals that feel reckless to first drafts that flop grandly. Your instructor will probably be more interested in your development as a writer than in any particular texts you produce: It's your overall performance that will be assessed, not a single, isolated assignment. Think of your portfolio as a movie, not a snapshot.

When you are allowed to choose what to include, look for materials that tell an important or illustrative story, from topic proposal to first draft to final version. Remember, too, that you can control this narrative (somewhat) through your reflections on these pieces. Here's how one student takes up that self-evaluative challenge in the first paragraph of an end-of-term assessment:

> Honestly, on the first day of English 109, I was not a happy student; I had failed the University of Waterloo English Proficiency Exam. Although I told everyone it was not a big deal after it happened, deep down I was bitter. So, signing up for this class to avoid retaking the proficiency exam, I decided to use the course to prove I was not illiterate. The Writing Clinic was wrong to think I was incompetent — a fifty-minute test would not define my writing abilities.

Take reflections seriously.   Several times during a semester or at various stages in the writing process, an instructor may require you to comment on your own work. Here, for example, is a brief reflective paragraph that accompanied the first draft of Susan Wilcox's "Marathons for Women," a report that appears in Chapter 2 (see p. 39):

> I focused my paper on the evolution of women in marathoning and the struggle for sporting equality with men. I had problems in deciding which incidents to include and which to ignore. Additionally, I'm expecting to hear back from some marathoners so I can possibly include their experiences in my paper; however, none of them have gotten back to me yet. When they do return the interview questions, I'll have to decide what, if anything, to remove from the paper to make room for personal anecdotes. Finally, I need some work on my introduction and conclusion. What do the current versions lack?

Like Susan, you might use the reflection to ask classmates for specific advice or for editing suggestions.

Most reflections for a portfolio will be lengthier and more evaluative. An instructor might ask for an explanatory comment after the final version of a paper is submitted. You can talk about items such as the following:

- Your goals in writing a paper and how well you have met them
- How you have defined your audience/readers and how you've adjusted your paper for them
- The strategies behind your organization or style
- How you have addressed problems pointed out by your instructor or peer editors

- What you believe succeeds and what you'd like to have handled better
- What specifically you learned from composing the paper

Don't try to answer all these questions. Give your reflection a point or focus. But your comments should be candid: An instructor will want to know both what you have learned and what you intend to work on more in subsequent assignments.

If asked to compose a midcourse evaluation or a final reflection, broaden your scope and think about the trajectory of your learning across a series of activities and assignments. Again, your instructor may specify what form this comprehensive reflection should take. Some instructors will ask focused questions, others may tie your responses to a specific learning rubric, and still others may even encourage you to write a letter. Here are some questions to think about on your own:

- What were your original goals for the writing course, and how well have you met them?
- What types of audiences do you expect to address in the future, and how prepared are you now to deal with them?
- What strategies of organization and style have you mastered?
- What did you gain from the responses and advice of classmates?
- What exactly did you learn during the term?
- What goals do you have for the writing you expect to do in the future?

If space permits, illustrate your points with examples from your papers or from comments you have received from classmates. For a sample midsemester course reflection, see "Examining a model" on page 320.

Getting the details right

Some parts of a writing portfolio may be more heavily edited than others: Midterm reflections might go through several drafts while topic proposals are often tentative and open-ended. And a writing portfolio might contain peer editing and other fairly off-the-cuff items. Yet the overall project should look competent, feel conscientious, and show attention to design.

With a career portfolio, plan on submitting nothing less than your best work—from cover to cover.

Polish your portfolio.   If you complain that pop quizzes or one-shot finals don't reflect your true abilities, what can you say when you turn in a bungled course portfolio? This is not an assignment to do at the last minute. So keep up with all prompts and activities—and that includes giving timely feedback to the work of your classmates. Online portfolio platforms may help keep you on track, but you'll still need to meet due dates and submit important documents.

Understand the portfolio activities.   You may be unfamiliar with some of the specific features of a writing portfolio. If you've never done a literacy narrative or a topic proposal, ask your instructor for models (or see p. 7 and p. 440). If your instructor suggests brainstorming activities, look to Chapter 19. If you have questions about peer editing, see Chapter 36. Other questions? Ask your instructor *and* talk with classmates.

Give honest feedback to classmates.   Most students seriously underestimate the value of the comments they make on their classmates' work. Simply because you are an experienced reader, you will recognize when ideas are unclear, arguments are hard to follow, evidence seems unconvincing, sentences are confusing, and so on. You don't have to fix the problems you point to; writers just need to know where they are and how you are reacting to them. Be as clear as you can and focus on big issues: content, organization, audience, style. It's fine to point out problems in grammar and mechanics, but they shouldn't be your first priority when you are a peer editor. And don't forget to mention what in a paper strikes you as distinctive and successful. Writers need to know that as well. You'll be surprised how much you'll gain from peer editing.

Here's a screen from a portfolio program that allows students to highlight a passage and comment on it.

Take advantage of multimedia. Portfolios routinely include examples of whatever genres of writing are important to a field or discipline (lesson plans, field reports, problem-solving logs, etc.). They may also display important kinds of media and can do so easily in electronic platforms. You can display and get feedback on digital images, podcasts, slide presentations, and videos you produce as part of your course work.

> **Your Turn** Search for the term "portfolio" on the Web sites for several post-secondary schools in your area. (You might exclude references to business and investment portfolios.) What kinds of portfolio programs or activities do you find described there? What do they have in common and how do they differ?

Examining a model

In the following brief midterm reflection, student Desiree Lopez describes her work in an internship class designed to train tutors for a campus writing center.

Describes initial course expectations.

When I first began the internship course, I was apprehensive and anxious about what was to come. To be honest, I had never been to the writing center and so I had little knowledge about the work the Undergraduate Writing Center (UWC) tutors did. My expectation was that writing tutors were people who helped polish student papers. I thought of the writing center as not so much a one-stop fix-it shop, but rather a center that anticipated what university professors were looking for in their students' papers and knew how to guide those students in the right direction.

Offers a revised point of view.

However, now that the semester is halfway completed and I have had the opportunity to observe tutors in action, my perception of the work done by campus writing centers has completely changed. I now see that, rather than polishing papers that are rough around the edges, the UWC helps students realize their potential while giving them the skills to polish their own papers.

I have learned how to help students identify what they are trying to do and organize their writing in ways appropriate to an assignment by asking simple questions such as "What are you trying to say here?" and "What do you want your readers to take from this?" I am happy to say that these tools have helped me hone my own skills as well. I have learned to ask myself those same questions while writing, and I now have a class of more than twenty peers to help me improve when I can't seem to figure out on my own what needs tweaking. Lastly, I have learned (mainly from the grammar quizzes) that my first instincts are generally right; if the sentence sounds correct, it probably is correct and I am just overthinking.

I know I still have more to learn about the writer-tutor relationship that can only be acquired through practice and hands-on experience. I am confident that I now have some of the tools I need and I know that, given the opportunity, I can tailor consultations to individual students and help them perceive their strengths and weaknesses. However, I am still nervous about the idea of conducting a consultation on my own. I worry that I have not yet perfected the art of nondirective/nonevaluative tutoring and that I will slip up—telling students I believe that their papers are interesting or really good or better than something I might have written on the subject. But I'll resist that temptation and simply ask them, "What do *you* think you've done well?"

Lists specific techniques and skills already learned.

Explains concerns that still remain.

How to start ● **Adapting material?**
Organize your presentation. See page 323.

Oral Reports

present
information
to a live
audience

In an oral report, you present material you have researched to an audience listening and watching rather than reading. So you must organize information clearly and find ways to convey your points powerfully, memorably, and sometimes graphically.

● For a psychology course, you use presentation software to review the results of an experiment you and several classmates designed to test which types of music were most conducive to studying for examinations.

● In a Shakespeare class, you use slides to give an oral report on Elizabethan theaters that draws upon research you are doing for your end-of-semester term paper.

● Prepping a crowd for a protest march, you use a bullhorn and a little humor to review the very serious ground rules for staging a peaceful demonstration on the grounds of the state capitol.

UNDERSTANDING ORAL REPORTS.   Oral reports can be deceptive. When watching someone give an effective five-minute talk, you may assume the speaker spent less time preparing it than he or she would a ten-page paper. But be warned: Oral presentations require all the research, analysis, and drafting of any other type of assignment, and then some. After all the background work is done, the material needs to be trimmed to its most important points and sold to an audience. Here is some advice for preparing effective oral reports.

Know your stuff.   Having a firm grasp on your subject will make a presentation more effective—which is why you need to do serious research. Knowledge brings you confidence that will ease some anxieties about public speaking. You'll appear believable and persuasive to an audience. And you'll feel more comfortable when improvising or taking questions. When you are in command of a subject, you'll survive even if equipment fails or you misplace a note card.

Organize your presentation.   If your report is based on material you've already written, reduce the text to an outline, memorize its key points (or put them on cards), and then practice speaking about each one. ○ If it helps, connect the main ideas to one or two strong examples listeners might later remember. Make the report seem spontaneous, but plan every move.

adapting ◄
material?

The process is similar for an oral report built from scratch. First, study your subject. Then list the points you want to cover and arrange them to engage listeners, choosing a pattern of organization that fits your topic. Use note cards or the outlining tools in programs like Word or PowerPoint to explore options for structuring the talk.

Cover only a limited number of points. You want an audience to walk away thinking about two or three key ideas.

The best equipment can't save a poorly prepared report. © Hulton-Deutsch Collection/Corbis.

order ideas
p. 377

Keep your audience on track.   At the beginning of your report, tell your audience briefly what you intend to cover and in what order. Then, at critical transitions in the report, remind listeners where you are simply by stating what comes next: *The second issue I wish to discuss . . . ; Now that we've examined the phenomenon, let's look at its consequences.* Don't be shy about making your main points this directly and don't worry about repetition. In an oral report, strategic repetition is your friend.

Stay connected to your listeners.   For about thirty seconds, you'll have the spontaneous goodwill of most audiences. After that, you've got to earn every minute of their attention. Begin by introducing yourself and your subject, if no one else performs that task. For longer reports, consider easing into your material with an anecdote that connects you, your subject, and your listeners. Self-deprecating humor usually works. (Short, in-class presentations won't need much, if any, warm-up.)

Establish eye contact with individual members of the group right from the start. Watch their reactions. When it's clear you've made a point, move on. If you see puzzled looks, explain more. No speaker charms everyone, so don't let a random yawn throw you. But if the whole crowd starts to snooze, you *are* the problem. Connect or lose 'em: Pick up your pace; move on to the next point; skip to your best material. O

Be sure to speak *to* your listeners, not to your notes or text. Arrange your materials and print them large enough so that you can read them easily from a distance and not lose your place. If you look downward too often or gaze at your own slides, you'll lose eye contact and your voice will be muffled, even with a microphone.

Use your voice and body.   Speak clearly and deliberately, and be sure people in the back of the room can hear you. Nervous speakers unconsciously speed up until they're racing to their conclusions. If you get skittish, calm yourself by taking a deep breath and smiling.

If the room is large and you're not confined by a fixed microphone, move around on the stage to address more of the audience. Use gestures too. They are a natural part of public speaking, especially for arguments and personal

connect ideas
p. 387

narratives. If you get stuck behind a podium, be sure to scan the entire audience (not just speak to the middle of the room) and modulate your voice. Keep your body steady too: Don't rock or sway as you speak.

Adapt your material to the time available.   If you know your subject well, don't worry about running out of things to say. Most speakers have the opposite problem: They talk too much. So be realistic about how much you can cover within an assigned time limit, especially if you have to take questions at the end. Tie your key ideas to fixed points on a clock. Know where you need to be at a quarter, half, and three-quarters of the way through the available time. If you're taking questions after your presentation, follow up with *Any questions?*

Practice your talk.   With any oral report, you need several dry runs to increase your confidence and identify potential problems. Speak your material aloud *exactly* as you intend to deliver it and go through all the motions, especially if you will use media such as slides or video clips. Have one or more friends or classmates observe you and offer feedback.

If your presentation is collaborative, choreograph the report with the full group in attendance, agreeing on the introductions, transitions, and interactions with the audience. Who manages the laptop? Who distributes the handouts and when? Who takes the questions? Handoffs like these seem minor until they are fumbled on game day.

Go through all your materials when you time the talk, including any audio and video clips. If you review the presentation only in your head, you will greatly underestimate its length.

Prepare for the occasion.   Before the report, check out the physical location if possible, as well as any equipment you will use. Be sure your laptop will connect to the multimedia projector in the room; know how to dim the lights; be sure a screen or electrical outlets are available.

Then dress up. A little spit and polish earns the goodwill of most audiences. Your classmates may razz you about the tie or skirt, but it just proves they're paying attention. And that's a good thing.

Viorika/E+ Collection/Getty Images.

Your Turn Given the number of oral presentations and lectures you've sat through, most of them using PowerPoint, you could probably write your own chapter on this special assignment. Working with a small group, list five hallmarks of an effective oral report and five characteristics of a dismal one. Annotate the list with examples that you may recall from particular reports. Then compare the features your group has come up with to those generated by other groups.

Getting the details right

There's nothing wrong with a report that relies on the spoken word alone. Still, audiences do appreciate supporting material, including flip charts, handouts, slides, and visual or audio samplings. All such materials, clearly labeled and handsomely reproduced, should also be genuinely relevant to the report. Resist the temptation to show something just because it's cool.

Most oral reports use presentation software of some kind such as the dominant player in this field, PowerPoint. With presentation software, you build the report upon a sequence of slides, designing them yourself or picking them from a gallery of ready-made items. You can choose slide layouts to accommodate text-only presentations, text and photos, text and charts, images only, and so on.

Presentation software offers so many bells and whistles that novices tend to overdo it, allowing the software to dominate their reports. Here's how to make PowerPoint, Keynote, or Prezi work for you.

Be certain you need presentation software. A short talk that makes only one or two points probably works better if viewers focus on you, not on a screen. Use presentation software to keep audiences on track through more complicated material, to highlight major issues or points, or to display images viewers really need to see. A little humor or eye candy is fine once in a while, but don't expect audiences to be impressed by glitz. What matters is the content of the report. O

Use slides to introduce points, not cover them. If you find yourself reading your slides, you've put too many words on-screen. Offer the minimum that viewers need: main points, important evidence, clear charts, and essential images (see the "Edenlawn Estates" slides on p. 329). It's fine, too, for a slide to outline your presentation at the beginning and to summarize key points at the end. In fact, it's helpful to have a slide that signals your conclusion.

Use a simple and consistent design. Select one of the design templates provided by your presentation software or create a design of your own that fits your subject. A consistent design scheme will unify your report and minimize distractions. O

For academic presentations, choose legible fonts in a size large enough for viewers at the back of the room to read easily. For reasons of legibility, avoid elegant, playful, or eccentric fonts, including Old English styles or those that

understand
reports p. 36

think visually
p. 557

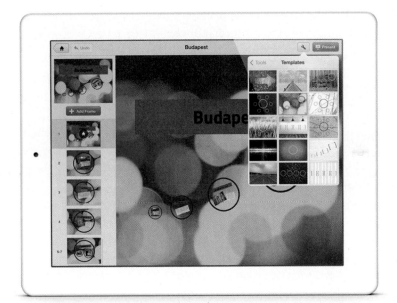

For presentations, Prezi offers a range of design templates, as shown here. Courtesy of Prezi, Inc.

resemble handwriting. Some experts prefer sans serif fonts for headlines and serif fonts for supporting text. But don't use more than two or, more rarely, three fonts within a presentation. Use boldface very selectively for emphasis. If you have to boldface a font to make it visible at a distance, simply find a thicker font. Italics are fine for occasional use, but in some fonts they are hard to read at a distance.

Consider alternatives to slide-based presentations. Anything you build on a laptop can be projected on-screen. So you need not use conventional slide-based presentation software for your oral report if you can create materials on your own. For example, various interactive Web 2.0 applications, from social-network software to blogs and wikis, can be configured for oral presentations, as can mind-mapping software and PowerPoint alternatives such as Prezi. In Prezi, for example, sequential slides are replaced by words, images, and media presented on an unending canvas; images move, rotate, and zoom in and out to provide different perspectives on a subject.

Examining a model

The following PowerPoint presentation was created by Terri Sagastume, a resident of a small Florida town who opposes a proposed real-estate development, Edenlawn Estates, on property near his home. J&M Investments, the real-estate developer that recently purchased the property, hopes to create a new multi-story condominium complex in place of the property's existing single-family homes. Sagastume's goal is to inform the public of the damage such a development would do to the surrounding area, and he is trying to convince his audience to sign a petition, which he will present to the local government in an effort to shut the project down.

The slides themselves are extremely simple and brief: They are merely the bullet points that Sagastume uses to anchor his presentation.

Edenlawn Estates

- What the developers want
- Why we should fight
- How we can win

What Developers Want

- Zoning variance
- Concrete seawall
- Four new traffic lights
- Height restriction exemption

Why We Should Fight

- Will cost taxpayers money
- Will harm environment
- Will increase traffic
- Will detract from quality of life

Stop Edenlawn Estates

Sign the petition today!

**Need more help?
Try these Visual Tutorials.**

reference

Ideas

part three

3

Brainstorming

a topic/
an idea

What do you do when you find yourself clueless, stuck, or just overwhelmed by the topic possibilities at the start of a writing project? Simple answer: Brainstorm. Put a notion on the table and see where it goes. Toy with an idea like a kitten with a catnip mouse. Push yourself to think through, around, over, and under a proposition. Dare to be politically incorrect or, alternatively, so conventional that your good behavior might scare your elders.

Naturally, you'll match brainstorming techniques to the type of writing you hope to produce. Beginning a personal tale about a trip to Wrigley Field, you might make a list of sensory details to jog your memory—the smell of hot dogs, the catcalls of fans, the green grass of the outfield. ○ But for an assigned report on DNA fingerprinting, your brainstorming might itemize things you still must learn about the subject: what DNA fingerprinting is, how it is done, when it can be used, how reliable it is, and so on. ○

Find routines that support thinking. Use whatever brainstorming techniques get you interested in a project. Jogging, swimming, knitting, or sipping brew at the coffeehouse may be your stimulus of choice. Such routine activities keep the body occupied, allowing insights to emerge. Be sure to capture and record those ideas in notes or, perhaps, voice memos.

understand
narratives p. 4

understand
reports p. 36

fin
ge

Need help organizing or drafting? See p. 360.

Whiteboards, flip charts, and even sticky notes can help you rapidly record your ideas. Image Source/Getty Images.

One warning: Passive brainstorming routines can easily slip into procrastination. That comfortable corner at Starbucks might become a spot too social for much thinking or writing. When your productivity drops, change tactics.

Build from lists.   Write down every plausible topic or, if you already have a subject, the major points you might cover. Don't be picky at this stage: List everything that comes to mind. One idea will lead to another, then another. Even grocery lists work this way.

For instance, preparing a letter to the editor in defense of collegiate sports, you can first itemize arguments you've heard from friends or have made yourself. List the counterarguments you come up with too—as well as any relevant examples, news events, or people. Then pick out the more intriguing or plausible items, and arrange them tentatively, perhaps sequencing them by time or pairing arguments and counterarguments.

Map your ideas.   If you find a list too static as a prompt for writing, another way may be to explore the relationships between your ideas *visually*. Some writers use logic trees to represent their thinking, starting with a single general concept and breaking it into smaller and smaller parts. Others begin with a key concept (just a word or two), circle it, and then begin to free-associate, quickly writing down more circled concepts and linking them by lines of relationship. When a page is full, writers look for interesting patterns, connections, and ideas.

Try freewriting. This is a technique of nonstop composing designed to loosen restraints we sometimes impose on our own thinking. Typically, free-writing sessions begin slowly, with a few disconnected phrases and words. But, suddenly, there's a spark and words stream onto the paper. Although freewriting comes in many forms, the basic formula is simple.

—Alfred North Whitehead

© Hulton-Deutsch Collection/Corbis.

> Ideas won't keep; something must be done about them.

STAGE ONE

- Start with a blank screen or sheet of paper.
- Put your subject or title at the top of the page.
- Write on that subject nonstop for ten minutes.
- Don't stop typing or lift your pen from the paper during that time.
- Write nonsense if you must, but keep writing.

STAGE TWO

- Stop at ten minutes and review what you have written.
- Underscore or highlight the most intriguing idea, phrase, or sentence.
- Put the highlighted idea at the top of a new screen or sheet.
- Freewrite for another ten minutes on the new, more focused topic.

Like other brainstorming techniques, freewriting works best when you already know something about a subject. You might freewrite successfully about standardized testing or working at fast-food restaurants if you've experienced both; you'll stumble trying to compose freely on subjects you know next to nothing about, such as, perhaps, thermodynamics or the career of Maria Callas. Freewriting tends to work best for personal narratives, personal statements, arguments, ○ and proposals, ○ and less well for reports and technical projects.

Use memory prompts. When writing personal narratives, institutional his-tories, or even résumés, you might trigger ideas with photographs, yearbooks, Facebook pages, or perhaps a Twitter feed. An image from a vacation may bring

understand
arguments p. 66

understand
proposals p. 160

events worth writing about flooding back to you. Even checkbooks or credit card statements may help you reconstruct past events or see patterns in your life worth exploring in writing.

Search online for your ideas.   You can get lots of ideas by simply exploring most topics online (or in a library catalog) through keywords. Indeed, determining those initial keywords and then following up with new terms you discover while browsing is in itself a potent form of brainstorming.

A photo album is a great place to look for writing ideas because we tend to document meaningful moments. *Left:* Allie Goldstein. *Center:* Courtesy of Ellen Darion. *Right:* Courtesy of Sid Darion.

Your Turn   If you have never used freewriting as a brainstorming activity, give it a try. Pick a general topic from among courses you are currently studying, news events that interest you, or activities you are deeply involved in: for example, the Japanese concept of Bushido, immigration reform, or unpaid internships. (You want a topic about which you have *some* knowledge or opinions.) Then follow the preceding directions. See what happens.

How to... Browse for ideas

Uncle Bob, who's a cop, complains about the "*CSI* effect." What is that?

I found a study by professors of law and psychology. What do they think?

Google | CSI effect

About 20,600,000 results (0.15 seconds)

▶ Scholarly articles for **CSI effect**
CSI Effect: Popular Fiction about Forensic Scien
... Concerning Scientific Evidence: Does the "**CS**
The **CSI effect**: fact or fiction - Thomas - Cited b

CSI effect - Wikipedia, the free encyclopedia
en.wikipedia.org/wiki/**CSI_effect** - Cached
The **CSI effect**, also known as the CSI syndrome and th
in which the exaggerated portrayal of forensic science o
Background - Manifestations - Trials - References

The '**CSI Effect**': Does It Really Exist? | Natio
www.nij.gov/journals/259/**csi-effect**.htm - Cached
by DE Shelton - Cited by 12 - Related articles
Mar 17, 2008 - Do law-related television shows like '**CS**
influence juror expectations and demands for forensic e

/archive/csieffect.pdf

108% | Find

ARTICLE

THE *CSI* EFFECT: POPULAR FICTION ABOUT FORENSIC SCIENCE AFFECTS THE PUBLIC'S EXPECTATIONS ABOUT REAL FORENSIC SCIENCE

N.J. Schweitzer
Michael J. Saks*

ABSTRACT: Two of a number of hypotheses loosely referred to as the CSI Effect suggest that the television program and its spin-offs, which wildly exaggerate and glorify forensic science, affect the public, and in turn affect trials either by (a) burdening the prosecution by creating greater expectations about forensic science than can be delivered or (b) burdening the defense by creating exaggerated faith in the capabilities and reliability of the forensic sciences. The present study tested these hypotheses by presenting to mock jurors a simulated trial transcript that included the testimony of a forensic scientist. The case for conviction was relatively weak, unless the expert testimony could carry the case across the threshold of reasonable doubt. In addition to reacting to the trial evidence, respondents were asked about their television viewing habits. Compared to non-CSI viewers, CSI viewers were more critical of the forensic evidence presented at the trial, finding it less believable. Regarding their verdicts, 29% of non-CSI viewers said they would convict, compared to 18% of CSI viewers (not a statistically significant difference). Forensic science viewers expressed more confidence in their verdicts than did non-viewers. Viewers of general crime programs, however, did not differ significantly from their non-viewing counterparts on any of the other dependent measures, suggesting that skepticism toward the forensic science testimony was specific to those whose diet consisted of heavy doses of forensic science television programs.

*N.J. Schweitzer is a Ph.D. candidate, Department of Psychology, Arizona State University. el J. Saks is Professor of Law and Psychology and Faculty Fellow, Center for the Study of

1 Find reliable sources.

Wikipedia isn't an academic source, but it will help me get a sense of the big picture.

This article comes from a government publication—does that automatically mean it's not biased?

WIKIPEDIA
The Free Encyclopedia

Article Discussion

CSI effect

From Wikipedia, the free encyclopedia

The **CSI effect**, also known as the **CSI syndrome**[1] and the **CSI** public perception. The term most often refers to the belief that ju American legal professionals, several studies have shown that cr

There are several other manifestations of the CSI effect. Greater and popularity of forensic science programs at the university leve forensic science shows teach criminals how to conceal evidence

Contents [hide]
1 Background
2 Manifestations
   2.1 Trials
   2.2 Academia
   2.3 Crimes
   2.4 Police investigations
3 References

Main page
Contents
Featured content
Current events
Random article
Donate to Wikipedia

▼ Interaction
   Help
   About Wikipedia
   Community portal
   Recent changes
   Contact Wikipedia

▶ Toolbox

▶ Print/export

▼ Languages
   Česky
   Deutsch
   Español
   Français
   Italiano

Background

The CSI effect is named for *CSI: Crime Scene Investigation*, a te discovery of a dead body leads to a criminal investigation by men which debuted in 2002, and *CSI: NY*, first aired in 2004. The *CS* Bones, Cold Case, Cold Case Files, Cold Squad, Criminal Minds

2 Stay alert to differing perspectives.

OFFICE OF JUSTICE PROGRAMS

NATIONAL INSTITUTE OF JUSTICE
Research • Development • Evaluation

HOME | FUNDING | PUBLICATIONS & MULTIMEDIA | EVENTS | TRAINING |

NIJ Home Page > NIJ Journal > NIJ Journal No. 259

NIJ JOURNAL NO. 259

Director's Message

The 'CSI Effect': Does It Really Exist?

Voice Stress Analysis: Only 15 Percent of Lies About Drug Use Detected in Field Test

Shopping Malls: Are They Prepared to Prevent and Respond to Attack?

Software Defined Radios Help Agencies Communicate

The 'CSI Effect': Does It Really Exist?

by Honorable Donald E. Shelton

Crime and courtroom proceedings have long been fodder f scriptwriters. In recent years, however, the media's use of for drama has not only proliferated, it has changed focus. our criminal justice process, many of today's courtroom dr cases. *Court TV* offers live gavel-to-gavel coverage of trial month. Now, that's "reality television"!

Reality and fiction have begun to blur with crime magazine *Hours Mystery, American Justice*, and even, on occasion, portray actual cases, but only after extensively editing the narration for dramatic effect. Presenting one 35-year-old c *Hours Mystery* filmed for months to capture all pretrial hea trial; the program, however, was ultimately edited to a 1- the crime remained a "mystery" . . . notwithstanding the j

3 Question claims.

20 Smart Reading

read closely

There's probably no better strategy for generating ideas than reading. Reading can deepen your impressions of any subject you are exploring, provide necessary background information, sharpen your critical acumen, and introduce you to alternative views. Reading also places you within a community of writers who have already thought about a subject.

Of course, not all reading serves the same purposes.

- You check out a dozen scholarly books to do research for a paper and then look for journal articles online.

- You consult stock market quotes and baseball box scores because you want numbers *now*.

- You interpret an organization chart to figure out who actually controls the student government budget.

- You read an old diary to discover what life was like before photocopiers, air-conditioning, and (*gulp!*) smartphones.

- You pack a *Divergent* series novel for pleasure reading on the Jersey Shore.

Yet any of these reading experiences, as well as thousands of others, might lead to ideas for projects.

You've probably been thoroughly schooled in basic techniques of academic reading: Survey the table of contents, preread to get a sense of the whole, look up terms or concepts you don't know, summarize what you've read, and so on. Such suggestions are practical, especially

READ is registered trademark of the American Library Association. Image courtesy of ALA Graphics, alastore.ala.org. Used with permission from the American Library Association, www.ala.org.

For a tutorial on active reading, see **macmillanhighered.com/howtowrite3e.**
Tutorials > Critical Reading > Active Reading Strategies

for difficult scholarly or professional texts. The following advice about reading can help you sharpen your college-level writing.

Read to deepen what you already know.   Whatever your interests or experiences in life, you're not alone. Others have explored similar paths and have probably written about them. Reading their work may give you the confidence to bring your own thoughts to public attention. Whether your passion is tintype photography, skateboarding, or film fashions of the 1930s, you'll find excellent books on the subject by browsing library catalogs or checking online bookstores.

For example, if you have worked at a fast-food franchise and know what goes on there, you might find a book like Eric Schlosser's classic *Fast Food Nation: The Dark Side of the All-American Meal* engrossing. You'll be drawn in because your experience makes you an informed critic. You can agree and disagree intelligently with Schlosser and, perhaps, see how to extend or amend his arguments. At a minimum, you'll walk away from the book knowing the titles of dozens of additional sources, should you want to learn more.

Read above your level of knowledge.   It's easy to connect with people online who share your interests, but they often don't know much more about a topic than you do. To find fresh ideas, push your reading to a more demanding level. Spend time with experts whose books and articles you can't blow right through. You'll know you are there when you find yourself looking up names, adding terms to your vocabulary, and feeling humbled by what you still need to learn about a subject. That's when invention occurs and ideas germinate.

Read what makes you uncomfortable.   Most of us today have access to devices that connect us to endless sources of information. But all those voices also mean that we can choose to read (or watch) only materials that confirm our existing beliefs and prejudices—and many people do. Such narrowness will be exposed, however, whenever you write on a controversial subject and find readers arguing back with facts you never considered before. Surprise! The world is more complicated than you thought. The solution is simple: Get out of the echo chamber and read more broadly, engaging with those who see the world differently.

Read against the grain.   Skeptics and naysayers may be no fun at parties, but their habits may be worth emulating whenever you are reading. It makes

> If you don't have the time to read, you don't have the time or tools to write.

—Stephen King
© Dick Dickinson.

For an activity on critical reading, see **macmillanhighered.com/howtowrite3e.**
Tutorials > LearningCurve Activities > Critical Reading

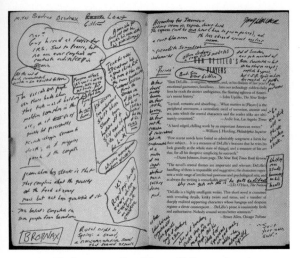

The late writer David Foster Wallace took copious notes when he read—in this case, the Don DeLillo novel *Players*. *PLAYERS* by Don DeLillo. Copyright © 1977 by Don DeLillo. Used by permission of the Wallace Literary Agency, Inc. David Foster Wallace notes used by permission of the David Foster Wallace Literary Trust and the Harry Ransom Center, The University of Texas at Austin.

sense to read with an open mind, giving reputable writers and their ideas a fair hearing. But you always want to raise questions about the assumptions writers make, the logic they use, the evidence they present, and the authorities and sources upon which they build their arguments.

Reading against the grain does not mean finding fault with everything, but rather letting nothing slip by without scrutiny. Treat the world around you as a text to be read and analyzed. ○ Ask questions. Why do so few men take liberal-arts courses? What topics does your campus paper avoid and why? How do friendships change when they are mostly online? Notice such phenomena, ponder their meaning, and write about them.

Read slowly.   Browsing online has made many of us superficial readers. For serious texts, forget speed-reading and your own Web habits. Settle in for the duration. Find the thesis; look up unfamiliar words and names; don't jump to another article until you've finished the one in hand.

Annotate what you read.   Find some way to record your reactions to whatever you read. If you own the text and don't mind marking it, use highlighting pens to flag key ideas. Then converse with them and leave a record. Electronic media and e-readers offer a range of built-in commenting tools. Even Post-it notes work in some circumstances.

> **Your Turn**   Working with a small group, make a list of the newspapers, Web sites, magazines, TV shows or networks, or other resources that you use to gather news and information about politics, society, and culture. Then try to locate these media resources along a ribbon that moves from the political far left to the political far right. Be prepared for considerable disagreement. When you are done, compare your placements with those of other groups working on the same project. What may account for your differences?
>
> Far left _____ Left _____ Center _____ Right _____ Far right

think critically
p. 343

Critical Thinking 21

think critically/ avoid fallacies

We all get edgy when our written work is criticized (or even edited) because the ideas we put on a page emerge from our own thinking—writing is *us*. Granted, our words rarely express *exactly* who we are or what we've been imagining, but such distinctions get lost when someone points to our work and says, "That's stupid" or "What crap!" The criticism cuts deep; it feels personal.

Fortunately, there's a way to avoid embarrassing gaffes in your work: *critical thinking*, a term that describes mental habits that reinforce logical reasoning and analysis. There are lots of ways to develop good sense, from following the strategies of smart reading described in Chapter 20 to using the rhetorical tactics presented throughout the "Guide" section of this book.

Here we focus on specific dimensions of critical thinking that you will find useful in college writing.

Think in terms of claims and reasons.   Whenever you read reports, arguments, or analyses, chances are you begin by identifying the claims writers make and assessing the evidence that supports them. Logically, then, when you write in these genres, you should expect the same scrutiny.

Claims are the passages in a text where you make an assertion, offer an argument, or present a hypothesis for which you intend to provide evidence.

> Using a cell phone while driving is dangerous.
>
> Playing video games can improve intelligence.
>
> Worrying about childhood obesity is futile.

Claims may occur almost anywhere in a paper: in a thesis statement, in the topic sentences of paragraphs, in transitional passages, or in summaries or conclusions. (An exception may be formal scientific writing, in which the hypothesis, results, and discussion will occur in specific sections of an article.)

Make sure that all your major claims in a paper are accompanied by plausible supporting *reasons* either in the same sentence or in adjoining material. Such reasons are usually introduced by expressions as straightforward as *because, if, to,* and *so.* Once you attach reasons to a claim, you have made a deeper commitment to it. You must then do the hard work of providing readers with convincing evidence, logic, or conditions for accepting your claim. Seeing your ideas fully stated on paper early in a project may even persuade you to abandon an implausible claim—one you cannot or do not want to defend.

> Using a cell phone while driving is dangerous *since* distractions are a proven cause of auto accidents.
>
> Playing video games can improve intelligence *if* they teach young gamers to make logical decisions quickly.
>
> ~~Worrying about childhood obesity is futile because there's nothing we can do about it.~~

Think in terms of premises and assumptions. Probe beneath the surface of key claims and reasons that writers offer, and you will discover their core principles, usually only implied but sometimes stated directly: These are called *premises* or *assumptions.* In oral arguments, when people say *I get where you're coming from,* they signal that they understand your assumptions. You want to achieve similar clarity, especially whenever the claims you make in a report or argument are likely to be controversial or argumentative. Your assumptions can be general or specific, conventional or highly controversial, as in the following examples.

> Improving human safety and well-being is a desirable goal. [general]
>
> We should discourage behaviors that contribute to traffic accidents. [specific]

Improving intelligence is desirable. [conventional]

Play should train children to think quickly. [controversial]

When writing for readers who mostly share your values, you usually don't have to explain where you're coming from. But be prepared to explain your values to more general or hostile readers: *This is what I believe and why.* Naturally—and here's where the critical thinking comes in—you yourself need to understand the assumptions upon which your claims rest. Are they logical? Are they consistent? Are you prepared to stand by them? Or is it time to rethink some of your principles?

Think in terms of evidence.   A claim without evidence attached is just that—a barefaced assertion no better than a child's "Oh, yeah?" So you should choose supporting material carefully, always weighing whether it is sufficient, complete, reliable, and unbiased. ○ Has an author you want to cite done solid research? Or does the evidence provided seem flimsy or anecdotal? Can you offer enough evidence yourself to make a convincing case—or are you cherry-picking only those facts that support your point of view? Do you even have the expertise to evaluate the evidence you present? These are questions to ask routinely and persistently.

Anticipate objections.   Critical thinkers understand that serious issues have many dimensions—and rarely just two sides. That's because they have done their homework, which means trying to understand even those positions with which they strongly disagree. When you start writing with this kind of inclusive perspective, you'll hear voices of the loyal opposition in your head and you'll be able to address objections even before potential readers make them. At a minimum, you will enhance your credibility. But more important, you'll have done the kind of thinking that makes you smarter.

Avoid logical fallacies.   Honest, fair-minded writers have nothing to hide. They name names, identify sources, and generate appropriate emotions. They acknowledge weaknesses in their arguments and concede graciously when the opposition scores a point. These are qualities you want to display in your serious academic and professional work.

refine your
search p. 442

One way to enhance your reputation as a writer and critical thinker is to avoid logical fallacies. *Fallacies* are rhetorical moves that corrupt solid reasoning—the verbal equivalent of sleight of hand. The following classic, but all too common, fallacies can undermine the integrity of your writing.

- **Appeals to false authority.** Be sure that any experts or authorities you cite on a topic have real credentials in the field and that their claims can be verified. Similarly, don't claim or imply knowledge, authority, or credentials yourself that you don't have. Be frank about your level of expertise. Framing yourself as an honest, if amateur, broker on a subject can even raise your credibility.

- *Ad hominem* **attacks.** In arguments of all kinds, you may be tempted to bolster your position by attacking the personal integrity of your opponents when character really isn't an issue. It's easy to resort to name-calling (*socialist, racist*) or character assassination, but it usually signals that your own case is weak.

- **Dogmatism.** Writers fall back on dogmatism whenever they want to give the impression, usually false, that they control the party line on an issue and have all the right answers. You are probably indulging in dogmatism when you begin a paragraph, *No serious person would disagree* or *How can anyone argue . . .*

- **Either/or choices.** A shortcut to winning arguments, which even Socrates abused, is to reduce complex situations to simplistic choices: good/bad, right/wrong, liberty/tyranny, smart/dumb, and so on. If you find yourself inclined to use some version of the *either/or* strategy, think again. Capable readers see right through this tactic and demolish it simply by pointing to alternatives that haven't been considered.

- **Scare tactics.** Avoid them. Arguments that make their appeals by preying on the fears of audiences are automatically suspect. Targets may be as vague as "unforeseen consequences" or as specific as particular organizations or groups of people who pose various threats. When such fears may be legitimate, make sure you provide evidence for the danger and don't overstate it.

- **Sentimental or emotional appeals.** Maybe it's fine for the Humane Society to decorate its pleas for cash with pictures of sad puppies, but you can see how the tactic might be abused. In your own work, be wary of

"Either you left the TV on downstairs or we have whales again."

using language that pushes buttons the same way, *oohing* and *aahing* readers out of their best judgment.

● **Hasty or sweeping generalizations.** Drawing conclusions from too little evidence or too few examples is a *hasty generalization* (*Climate change must be a fraud because we sure froze last winter*); making a claim apply too broadly is a *sweeping generalization* (*All Texans love pickups*). Competent writers avoid the temptation to draw conclusions that fit their preconceived notions—or pander to those of an intended audience. But the temptation is powerful, so you might find examples, even in college reading assignments.

● **Faulty causality.** Just because two events or phenomena occur close together in time doesn't mean that one caused the other. (The Red Sox didn't start winning *because* you put on the lucky boxers.) People are fond of leaping to such easy conclusions, and many pundits and politicians do routinely exploit this weakness, particularly in situations involving economics, science, health, crime, and culture. Causal relationships are almost always complicated, and you will get credit for dealing with them honestly. ○

- **Evasions, misstatements, and equivocations.** Evasions are utterances that avoid the truth, misstatements are untruths excused as mistakes, and equivocations are lies made to seem like truths. Skilled readers know when a writer is using these slippery devices, so avoid them.

- **Straw men.** *Straw men* are easy or habitual targets that writers aim at to win an argument. Often the issue in such an attack has long been defused or discredited: for example, middle-class families abusing food stamps, immigrants taking jobs from hardworking citizens, the rich not paying a fair share of taxes. When you resort to straw-man arguments, you signal to your readers that you may not have much else in your arsenal.

- **Slippery-slope arguments.** Take one wrong step off the righteous path and you'll slide all the way down the hill: That's the warning that slippery-slope arguments make. They aren't always inaccurate, but they are easy to overstate. Will using plastic bags really doom the planet? Maybe or maybe not. If you create a causal chain, be sure that you offer adequate support for every step and don't push beyond what's plausible.

© Ariel Molvig/The New Yorker/Condé Nast.

understand causal
analyses p. 128

Your Turn   Working in a group, find an example of a short argument that impresses most of you. (Your instructor might suggest a particular article.) Carefully locate the claims within the piece that all of you regard as its most important, impressive, or controversial statements. Then see if you can formulate the premises or values upon which these claims rest. Try to state these premises as clearly as you can in a complete, declarative sentence. Are the assumptions you uncovered statements that you agree with? If the assumptions are controversial, does the piece explain or defend them? Be prepared to present your group's analysis and conclusions in class.

- **Bandwagon appeals.** You haven't made an argument when you simply tell people it's time to cease debate and get with popular opinion. Too many bad decisions and policies get enacted that way. If you order readers to jump aboard a bandwagon, expect them to resist.

- **Faulty analogies.** Similes and analogies are worth applauding when they illuminate ideas or make them comprehensible or memorable. But seriously analyze the implications of any analogies you use. Calling a military action either "another Vietnam" or a "crusade" might raise serious issues, as does comparing one's opponents to "Commies" or the KKK. Readers have a right to be skeptical of writers who use such ploys.

22 Experts

ask for help

Forget about *expert* as an intimidating word. When you need help with your writing, seek advice from authorities who either know more about your subject than you do or have more experience developing such a project. Advice may come from different sources, but that's not a problem: The more people you talk to, the better.

Talk with your instructor.   Don't be timid. Instructors hold office hours to answer your questions, especially about assignments. Save yourself time and, perhaps, much grief by getting early feedback on your ideas and topic. It's better to learn that your thesis is unworkable before you compose a first draft.

Just as important, your instructor might help you see aspects of a topic you hadn't noticed or direct you to essential sources. Don't write a paper just to please instructors, but you'd be foolish to ignore their counsel.

Take your ideas to the writing center.   Many student writers think the only time to use a campus writing center is when their instructor returns a draft on life support. Most writing-center tutors prefer not to be seen as EMTs. So they are eager to help at the start of a project, when you're still developing ideas. Tutors may not be experts on your subject, but they have reviewed enough papers to offer sensible advice for focusing a topic, shaping a thesis, or adapting a subject to an audience. ○ They also recognize when you're so clueless that you need to talk with your instructor pronto.

develop a
statement p. 362

Find local experts.   Don't trouble an expert for information you could find easily yourself in the library or online: Save human contacts for when you need serious help on a major writing project—a senior thesis, an important story for a campus periodical, a public presentation on a controversial subject. But, then, do take advantage of the human resources around you. Campuses are teeming with knowledgeable people and that doesn't just include faculty in their various disciplines. Staff and administrative personnel at your school can advise you on everything from trends in college admissions to local crime statistics.

Look to the local community for expertise and advice as well. Is there a paper to be written about declining audiences for Hollywood blockbusters? You couldn't call J. J. Abrams and get through, but you could chat with a few local theater owners or managers to learn what they think about the business. Their insights might change the direction of your project.

Check with librarians.   Campus librarians have lots of experience helping writers find information, steering them toward feasible projects and away from ideas that may not have much intellectual standing. Librarians can't be as specific or directive as, for example, your instructor, but they know what sorts of topics the library's resources will and will not support.

Chat with peers.   Peers aren't really experts, but an honest classroom conversation with fellow students can be an eye-opening experience. You'll probably see a wide spectrum of opinions (if the discussion is frank) and even be surprised by objections you hadn't anticipated to your topic idea or first draft. Peers often have a surprising range of knowledge and, if the group is diverse, your classmates might bring enlightening life experiences to the conversation.

Departmental lists of academic faculty and staff often include information on their areas of special expertise. Women's Studies Department, Kansas State University.

KANSAS STATE
UNIVERSITY

Search web, people, directories

Browse A-Z   Sign in ▼

K-State home » Arts and Sciences » Women's Studies Department » Faculty

Women's Studies Department

About Women's Studies

Position Opening

Information for Alumni

Courses

Faculty

   Information for Affiliated
   Faculty

Undergraduate Studies

Graduate Studies

Scholarships & Awards

Study Abroad

News & Events

Links

Women's Studies
Department
Kansas State University
3 Leasure Hall
Manhattan, KS 66506

(t) 785-532-5738
785-532-3299 fax
womst@k-state.edu

[f]

Women's Studies Faculty

Core Faculty:

Diaz de Sabates, Gabriela, Instructor of Women's Studies. BS 1989, University of Buenos Aires; MA 1994, Harvard University. Research interests: gender, ethnicity and race; Latinas' cultural and gender identity, academic achievement and oral stories.

Dickinson, Torry, Professor of Women's Studies. BA 1975, Livingston College, Rutgers University; MA 1977, PhD 1983, State University of New York, Binghamton. Research interests: global sociology of women; women and work; women and public policy.

Hubler, Angela, Associate Professor of Women's Studies. BA 1985, College of Wooster; MA 1986, PhD 1992, Duke University. Research interests: Marxism, Feminism, Literature, and Girls' Studies.

Janette, Michele, Department Head, Women's Studies & Associate Professor of English, BA 1988, MA 1991, MPhil 1993, PhD 1997, Yale University. Research interests: Vietnamese American Literature and film; Asian American literature; cultural studies; film.

Padilla Carroll, Valerie, Assistant Professor of Women's Studies, BA 1994, University of Texas at San Antonio; MA 1997, PhD 2005, St. Louis University. Research interests: Intersections of gender, race/ethnicity and class, environmental justice and environmentalism, gender and popular culture.

Tushabe, Assistant Professor of Women's Studies, 2008. M.A., Texas Woman's University, Women's Studies, 2005; Ph.D., SUNY Binghamton, Philosophy, 2008, Graduate Certificate in Feminist Theory. Research interests: Global sexual identities, African cultures and philosophy, colonialism and post-colonial theories, critical race theory.

Affiliated Faculty:

BAIRD, CHARDIE, Associate Professor of Sociology, Anthropology and Social Work. BS 1996, Sociology, College of Charleston; MS 2000, Sociology, Florida State University; PhD 2005, Sociology, Florida State University. Research interests: Youth and the Life course, gender and work; work and the family.

BHATTACHARYA, KAKALI, Associate Professor of Educational Leadership. BS 1995, McMaster University, Hamilton, Canada; MS 2000, Southern Illinois University of Carbondale, IL; PhD 2005, University of Georgia, Athens. Research interests: De/colonizing epistemologies, social and organizational context of transnational education and gender, qualitative inquiry, social foundation of higher education in the U.S., gender, race and ethnic studies in education, technology-integrated learning and social environments.

Your Turn   If you were asked to identify yourself as an expert on a subject, what would it be? Don't consider academic subjects only. Think about any areas or activities about which you could confidently offer reliable advice. Make a list and share it with your classmates. Do their lists give you additional ideas about the kinds of expertise you may possess?

How to... Use the writing center

1 Bring materials with you, including the assignment, previous drafts or outlines, comments from your instructor if you have any, a pen, and a notebook.

2 Be actively involved during the session, and arrive with specific goals in mind. Your tutor may ask questions about your writing process and your paper. Be prepared to think about and respond to your tutor's suggestions.

3 Keep revising. While the tutor may be able to help you with some aspects of your writing, you are ultimately responsible for the finished paper — and your grade.

Writer's Block

Waiting until the last minute to write a paper hasn't been defined as a medical problem yet. But give it time. Already a condition called *executive dysfunction* describes the inability of some children and adults to plan, organize, pace, and complete tasks. No doubt we've all experienced some of its symptoms, describing the state as *procrastination* when it comes to doing the laundry and *writer's block* when it applies to finishing papers on time.

Getting writing done isn't hard because the process is painful, but rather because it is so fragile and vulnerable to ridiculous excuses and distractions. Who hasn't vacuumed a floor or washed a car rather than compose a paragraph? Writing also comes with no guarantees, no necessary connection between labor put in and satisfactory pages churned out.

Like baseball, writing is a game without time limits. When a paper isn't going well, you can stretch into fruitless twelfth and

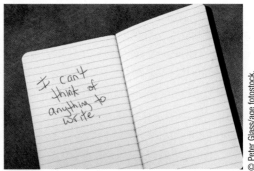

© Peter Glass/age fotostock.

thirteenth innings with no end in sight. And if you do finish, readers may not like what you have done—even when you know your work is solid and is based on honest reading, observation, and research. Such concerns are enough to give anyone writer's block.

So what do you do when you'd rather crack walnuts with your teeth than write a term paper?

Break the project into parts.   Getting started is usually the hard part for writers simply because the project taken as a whole seems overwhelming. Even a simple one-page position paper can ruin a whole weekend, and a term paper—with its multiple drafts, abstract, notes, bibliography, tables, and graphs—stretches beyond the pale.

But what if, instead of stewing over how much time and energy the whole project will absorb, you divide it into manageable stages? Then you can do the work in chunks and enjoy the success that comes from completing each part. That position paper might be broken down into two, maybe three, less daunting steps: doing the assigned reading; brainstorming the paper; writing the page required. The same procedure makes a research paper less intimidating: You have more elements to manage, but you also have a strategy to finish them.

Set manageable goals.   Unless you are very disciplined, writing projects sop up all the time available for them. Worse, you'll probably expend more energy fretting than working. To gain control, set levelheaded goals for completing the project and stick to them. In other words, don't dedicate a whole Saturday to preparing your résumé or working up a lab report; instead, commit yourself to the full and uninterrupted two hours the task will really take if you sit down and concentrate.

If you have trouble estimating how much time a project may require, consider that it is better to set a goal than to face an open-ended commitment. That's one good reason both instructors and publishers set deadlines.

> Inspiration is wonderful when it happens, but the writer must develop an approach for the rest of the time. . . . The wait is simply too long.

—Leonard Bernstein

Photo by Marion S. Trikusko, *U.S. News & World Report* Magazine Photograph Collection/ Library of Congress, Prints and Photographs Division, LC-U9-24858- 17 (P & P).

Create a calendar.   For complicated assignments that extend over weeks or even months, create a calendar or timeline and stick with it. ○ First break the task into parts and estimate how much time each stage of the paper or other project will take. Knowing your own work habits, you can draw on past experiences with similar assignments to construct a feasible plan. You'll feel better once you've got a road map that leads to completion.

Don't draw up a schedule so elaborate that you build in failure by trying to manage too many events. Assume that some stages, especially research or drafting, may take more time than you originally expect. But do stick to your schedule, even if it means starting a draft with research still remaining or cutting off the drafting process to allow time for necessary revisions.

Limit distractions.   Put yourself in a place that encourages writing and minimizes any temptations that might pull you away from your work. Schedule a specific time for writing and give it priority over all other activities, from paying your bills to feeding the dog. (On second thought, feed that dog to stop the barking.) Log off your Facebook and Twitter accounts, turn off your cell phone, start writing, and don't stop for an hour. Really.

Do the parts you like first.   Movies aren't filmed in sequence and papers don't have to be written that way either. Compose those sections of a project that feel ready to go or interest you most. You can fix the transitions later to make the paper feel seamless, the way movie editors cut diverse scenes into coherent films. Once you have whole pages in hand, you'll be more inclined to keep working on a paper: The project suddenly seems manageable.

Write a zero draft.   When you are *really* blocked, try a zero draft—that is, a version of the paper composed in one sitting, virtually nonstop. The process may resemble freewriting, but this time you aren't trawling for topic ideas. You've already done the necessary background reading and research, and so you're primed to write. You might even have a thesis and an outline. All you lack is the confidence to turn all this preparation into coherent sentences. Repress your inhibitions by writing relentlessly, without pausing to reread and

plan a
project p. 436

review your stuff. Keep at it for several *hours* if need be. You can do it—just imagine you're writing a timed exam. ○

The draft you produce won't be elegant (though you might surprise yourself) and some spots will be rough indeed. But keep pushing until you've finished a full text, from introduction to conclusion. Set this version aside, delaying any revision for a few hours or even days. Then, instead of facing an empty tablet or screen, you will have full pages of prose to work with.

Reward yourself.   People respond remarkably well to incentives, so promise yourself some prize correlated to the writing task you face. Finishing a position paper is probably worth a pizza. A term paper might earn you dinner and a movie. A dissertation is worth a used Honda Civic.

Peter Dazeley/Getty Images.

> **Your Turn**   Do you have a good writer's block story to share? You might describe an odd thing you have done rather than start a paper — especially one that might seem far more arduous than putting words down on a page. Or maybe you have figured out an infallible method for overcoming procrastination. Or you have endured a roommate's endless excuses for failing to complete a writing assignment. Tell your story in a paragraph or two, which you will start writing *now*.

understand essay
exams p. 252

Shaping & Drafting

part four

4

Need help developing your ideas? See p. 329. / Need style help? See p. 398.

24 Thesis

make a claim

Offering a thesis is a move as necessary and, eventually, as instinctive to writers as stepping on a clutch before shifting used to be to drivers. No thesis, no forward motion.

A *thesis* is a statement in which a writer identifies or suggests the specific idea that will give focus to a paper. Typically, the thesis appears in an opening paragraph or section, but it may also emerge as the paper unfolds. In some cases, it may not be stated in classic form until the very conclusion. A thesis can be complex enough to require several sentences to explain, or a single sentence might suffice. But a thesis will be in the writing somewhere.

How do you write and frame a thesis? Consider the following advice.

Compose a complete sentence.   Simple phrases might identify topic areas, even intriguing ones, but they don't make specific claims that provoke thinking and then require support. Sentences do. ○ Neither of the following phrases comes close to providing direction for a paper.

> Human trafficking in the United States
>
> Reasons for global warming

Make a significant claim or assertion.   *Significant* here means that the statement stimulates discussion or inquiry. You want to give an audience a reason to spend time with your writing by making a point or raising an issue worth exploring.

help with common
errors p. 566

Until communities recognize that human trafficking persists in parts of the United States, immigrant communities will be exploited by the practice.

Global warming won't stop until industrial nations either lower their standards of living or admit the need for more nuclear power.

Write a declarative sentence, not a question.   Questions do focus attention, but they are often too broad to give direction to a paper. A humdrum question acting as a thesis can invite superficial or even sarcastic responses. So, while you might use a question to introduce a topic (or to launch your own research), don't rely on it to carry a well-developed and complex claim in a paper. There are exceptions to this guideline: Provocative questions often give direction to personal and exploratory writing.

Expect your thesis to mature.   Your initial thesis will usually expand and grow more complicated as you learn more about a subject. That's natural. But don't believe the myth that a satisfactory thesis must be a statement that breaks a subject into three parts. Theses that follow this pattern often read like shopping lists, with only vague connections between the ideas presented.

ORIGINAL THESIS

Crime in the United States has declined because more people are in prison, the population is growing older, and DNA testing has made it harder to get away with murder.

When you slip into an easy pattern like this, look for connections between the points you have identified and then explore the truth. The result can sometimes be a far more compelling thesis.

REVISED THESIS

It is **much more likely** that crime in the United States has declined because more people are in prison **than because** the population is growing older or DNA testing has made it harder to get away with murder.

Introduce a thesis early in a project.   This sound guideline applies especially to academic projects and term papers. Instructors usually want to know up front what the point of a report or argument will be. Whether phrased as a single sentence or several, a thesis typically needs one or more paragraphs to provide background and contexts for its claim. Here's the thesis (highlighted in yellow) of Andrew Kleinfeld and Judith Kleinfeld's essay "Go Ahead, Call Us Cowboys," following several sentences that offer the necessary lead-in.

> Everywhere, Americans are called *cowboys*. On foreign tongues, the reference to America's Western rural laborers is an insult. Cowboys, we are told, plundered the earth, arrogantly rode roughshod over neighbors, and were addicted to mindless violence. So some of us hang our heads in shame. We shouldn't. The cowboy is in fact our Homeric hero, an archetype that sticks because there's truth in it.

Or state a thesis late in a project.   In high school, you may have heard that the thesis statement is *always* the last sentence in the first paragraph. That may be so in conventional five-paragraph essays, but you'll rarely be asked to follow so predictable a pattern in college or elsewhere.

In fact, it is not unusual, especially in some arguments, for a paper to build toward a thesis—and that statement may not appear until the final paragraph or sentence. ○ Such a strategy makes sense when a claim might not be convincing or rhetorically effective if stated baldly at the opening of the piece. Bret Stephens uses this strategy in an essay titled "Just Like Stalingrad" to debunk frequent comparisons between former President George W. Bush and either Hitler or Stalin. Stephens's real concern turns out to be not these exaggerated comparisons themselves but rather what happens to language when it is abused by sloppy writers. The final two paragraphs of his essay summarize this case and, arguably, lead up to a thesis in the very last sentence of the piece—more rhetorically convincing there because it comes as something of a surprise.

> Care for language is more than a concern for purity. When one describes President Bush as a fascist, what words remain for real fascists? When one describes Fallujah as Stalingrad-like, how can we express, in the words that remain to the language, what Stalingrad was like?
>
> George Orwell wrote that the English language "becomes ugly and inaccurate because our thoughts are foolish, but the slovenliness of our language makes it easier for us to have foolish thoughts." In taking care with language, we take care of ourselves.
>
> — *Wall Street Journal*, June 23, 2004

understand
argument p. 66

Write a thesis to fit your audience and purpose.   Almost everything you write will have a purpose and a point (see the following table), but not every piece will have a formal thesis. In professional and scientific writing, readers want to know your claim immediately. For persuasive and exploratory writing, you might prefer to keep readers intrigued or have them track the path of your thinking, and delay the thesis until later.

Type of Assignment	Thesis or Point
Narratives	Thesis is usually implied, not stated.
Reports	Thesis usually previews material or explains its purpose. (See thesis example on p. 59.)
Arguments	Thesis makes an explicit and arguable claim. (See thesis example on p. 72.)
Evaluations	Thesis makes an explicit claim of value based on criteria of evaluation. (See thesis example on p. 123.)
Causal analyses	Thesis asserts or denies an explanatory or causal relationship, based on an analysis of evidence. (See thesis example on p. 147.)
Proposals	Thesis offers a proposal for action. (See thesis example on p. 165.)
Literary analyses	Thesis explains the point of the analysis. (See thesis example on p. 207.)
Rhetorical analyses	Thesis explains the point of the analysis. (See thesis example on p. 233.)
Essay examinations	Thesis previews the entire answer, like a mini-outline. (See thesis example on p. 257.)
Position papers	Thesis makes specific assertion about reading or issue raised in class. (See thesis example on p. 262.)
Annotated bibliographies	Each item may include a statement that describes or evaluates a source. (See example on p. 270.)
Synthesis papers	Thesis summarizes and paraphrases different sources on a specific topic. (See thesis example on p. 280.)
E-mails	Subject line may function as thesis or title. (See thesis example on p. 287.)
Business letters	Thesis states the intention for writing. (See thesis example on p. 293.)
Résumés	"Career objective" may function as a thesis. (See thesis example on p. 301.)
Personal statements	May state an explicit purpose or thesis or lead readers to inferences about qualifications. (See thesis example on p. 309.)
Portfolios	Various items may include a thesis, especially any summary reflections on work presented or done. (See thesis example on p. 320.)
Oral reports	Introduction or preview slide describes purpose. (See thesis example on p. 329.)

Your Turn   Transform two or three of the following song titles into full-blown thesis statements that might be suitable in an academic paper or newspaper op-ed piece. If these titles don't inspire you, start with several song, album, or movie titles of your own choosing. Be sure that your theses are full, declarative sentences that make a significant assertion.

"Taxman"	"Lost in the Supermarket"
"Stand by Your Man"	"Bleed American"
"Share the Ride"	"Especially in Michigan"
"Waiting on the World to Change"	"I Turn My Camera On"
"This Land Is Your Land"	"Someone Else's Problem"
"Concrete and Barbed Wire"	"Let the Idiot Speak"
"The Times They Are A-Changin'"	"Be True to Your School"

Strategies 25

develop a
draft

Strategies are patterns of writing that you will use in many situations and across many genres. This chapter looks at some of these essential tools, such as description, division, classification, definition, and comparison/contrast. While you may sometimes write "descriptions" for their own sake, or you may "compare and contrast" movies, smartphones, or college majors just for the heck of it, mostly you will draw upon these modes of writing to serve some larger purpose: to tell a story, clarify a point, or move an argument forward.

Use description to set a scene. Descriptions, which use language to re-create physical scenes and impressions, can be impressive enough to stand on their own. But you'll often use them to support other kinds of writing—perhaps you'll write a descriptive sentence to set the scene in a narrative or you'll develop a cluster of paragraphs full of concrete details to enliven a historical event in a term paper. Writers adapt descriptions to particular situations. Your depiction of an apparatus in a lab report might be cold and technical, while a novelist might describe a scene just as factually yet suggest a whole lot more, as in the following paragraph.

> *Malpais*, translated literally from the Spanish, means "bad country." In New Mexico, it signifies specifically those great expanses of lava flow which make black patches on the map of the state. The malpais of the Checkerboard country lies just below Mount Taylor, having been produced by the same volcanic fault that, a millennium

earlier, had thrust the mountain fifteen thousand feet into the sky. Now the mountain has worn down to a less spectacular eleven thousand feet and relatively modern eruptions from cracks at its base have sent successive floods of melted basalt flowing southward for forty miles to fill the long valley between Cebolleta Mesa and the Zuni Mountains.

—Tony Hillerman, *People of Darkness*

Descriptions like this always involve selection. Just as a photographer carefully frames a subject, you have to decide which elements (visual, aural, tactile, and so on) in a scene will convey the situation most accurately, efficiently, or memorably and then turn them into words. Think nouns first, and only then modifiers: Adjectives and adverbs are essential, but it's easy to ruin a description by overdressing it. Be specific, tangible, and honest. ○

A smart procedure is to write down everything you want to include in a descriptive passage and then cut out any words or phrases not pulling their weight. Be sure to sketch a scene that a reader can imagine easily, providing directions for the eyes and mind. The following descriptive paragraphs are from the opening of a student's account of a trip she made to South Africa: Notice how lean and specific her sentences are, full of details that tell a story all on their own.

> In Soweto, I am seventeen, curious, and in the largest shantytown in the world, so many thousands of miles away from my home. Streets are dusty, houses are made of cinderblock, and their yards are pressed-flat dirt. If there is grass, there is no way to see the trails of a snake.
>
> Doors to homes are rare and inside I can see tired grandmothers with babies on their curved backs making spicy *potjieko* over smoky, single-burner stoves. Skinny cats stretch out in the sunshine. Every few homes has a flat-screen TV, shockingly out of place, wearing a veil of dust. They were stolen.
>
> Soweto spreads over forty miles and nearly one million people call it home. It is a striking sight to see so close to the upscale suburbs of Johannesburg. There are row upon row of homemade houses, punctuated by schools and churches with fresh coats of paint from well-meaning Westerners. Lean-to shacks on the corner sell cucumbers and *naartjes*. The ground is flat for as far as I can see.
>
> —Lily Parish, "Sala Kahle, South Africa"

improve your
sentences p. 412

Use division to divide a subject.   This strategy of writing is so common you might not notice it. A division involves no more than breaking a subject into its major components or enumerating its parts. In a report for an art history class, you might present a famous cathedral by listing and then describing its major architectural features, one by one: facade, nave, towers, windows, and so on. Or in a sports column on the Big Ten's NCAA football championship prospects, you could just run through its roster of twelve teams. That's a reasonable structure for a review, given the topic.

Division also puts ideas into coherent relationships that make them easier for readers to understand and use. The challenge comes when a subject doesn't break apart as neatly as a tangerine. Then you have to decide which parts are essential and which are subordinate. Divisions of this sort are more than mechanical exercises: They require your clear understanding of a subject. For example, in organizing a Web site for your school or student organization, you'd probably start by deciding which aspects of the institution merit top-tier placement on the home page. ○ Such a decision will then shape the entire project.

Left: Provided by Binghamton University. *Right:* Oklahoma State University.

learn media
conventions p. 542

Use classification to sort objects or ideas by consistent principles.
Classification divides subjects up not by separating their parts but by clustering
their elements according to meaningful or consistent principles. Just think of
all the ways by which people can be classified:

> **Body type:** endomorph, ectomorph, mesomorph
>
> **Hair color:** black, brown, blond, red, gray, other
>
> **Weight:** underweight, normal, overweight, obese
>
> **Sexual orientation:** straight, bisexual, gay/lesbian, transgender
>
> **Race:** black, Asian, white, other
>
> **Religion:** Hindu, Buddhist, Muslim, Christian, Jew, other, no religion

Ideally, a principle of classification should apply to every member of the general
class studied (in this case, people), and there would be no overlap among the
resulting groups. But almost all useful efforts to classify complex phenomena—
whether people, things, or ideas—have holes, gaps, or overlaps. Classifying
people by religious beliefs, for instance, usually means mentioning the major
groups and then lumping tens of millions of other people in a convenient
category called "other."

Even scientists who organize everything from natural elements to species of
birds run into problems with creatures that cross boundaries (plant or animal?)
or discoveries that upset familiar categories. You'll wrestle with such problems
routinely when, for instance, you argue about social policy.

Use definition to clarify meaning.   Definitions don't appear only in
dictionaries. Like other strategies in this chapter, they occur in many genres. A
definition might become the subject of a scientific report (*What is a planet?*),
the bone of contention in a legal argument (*How does the statute define* life*?*), or
the framework for a cultural analysis (*Can a comic book be a serious novel?*). In all
such cases, writers need to know how to construct valid definitions.

Though definitions come in various forms, the classic dictionary definition
is based on principles of classification discussed in the previous section. Typically a term is defined first by placing it in a general class. Then its distinguishing features or characteristics are enumerated, separating it from other members
of the larger class. You can see the principle operating in this comic paragraph,

which first fits "dorks" into the general class of "somebody," that is to say, a *person*, and then claims two distinguishing characteristics.

> It's important to define what I truly mean by "dork," just so he or she doesn't get casually lumped in with "losers," "burnouts" and "lone psychopath bullies." To me, the dork is somebody **who didn't fit in at school** and who **therefore sought consolation in a particular field**—computers, *Star Trek*, theater, heavy metal, medieval war reenactments, fantasy, sports trivia, even isolation sports like cross-country and ice skating.
> —Ian R. Williams, "Twilight of the Dorks?" *Salon.com*, October 23, 2003

In much writing, definitions become crucial when a question is raised about whether a particular object does or does not fit into a particular group. You engage in this kind of debate when you argue about what is or isn't a sport, a hate crime, an act of terrorism, and so on. In outline form, the structure of such a discussion looks like this:

Defined group:
— General class
— Distinguishing characteristic 1
— Distinguishing characteristic 2 . . .

Controversial term
—**Is / is not in the general class**
—**Does / does not share characteristic 1**
—**Does / does not share characteristic 2 . . .**

Controversial term is/is not in the defined group

Use comparison and contrast to show similarity and difference.   We seem to think better when we place ideas or objects side by side. So it's not surprising that comparisons and contrasts play a role in all sorts of writing, especially reports, arguments, and analyses. Paragraphs are routinely organized to show how things are alike or different.

Adam Zyglis, *The Buffalo News* (blogs.buffalonews/adam-zyglis).

> The late 1960s and early 1970s were a time of cultural conflict, a battle between what I have called the beautiful people and the dutiful people. While Manhattan glitterati thronged Leonard Bernstein's apartment to celebrate the murderous Black Panthers, ordinary people in the outer boroughs and the far-flung suburbs of New Jersey like Hamilton Township were going to work, raising their families, and teaching their children to obey lawful authority and work their way up in the world.
>
> — Michael Barone, "The Beautiful People vs. the Dutiful People,"
> *U.S. News & World Report*, January 16, 2006

Much larger projects can be built on similar structures of comparison and/or contrast.

To keep extended comparisons on track, the simplest structure is to evaluate one subject at a time, running through its features completely before moving on to the next. Let's say you decided to contrast economic conditions in France and Germany. Here's how such a paper might look in a scratch outline if you focused on the countries one at a time. ○

France and Germany: An Economic Report Card
I.   France
     A. Rate of growth
     B. Unemployment rate
     C. Productivity

order ideas
p. 377

       D. Gross national product
       E. Debt
  II. Germany
       A. Rate of growth
       B. Unemployment rate
       C. Productivity
       D. Gross national product
       E. Debt

The disadvantage of evaluating subjects one at a time is that actual comparisons, for example, of rates of employment in the outline above, might appear pages apart. So in some cases, you might prefer a comparison/contrast structure that looks at features point by point. ○

France and Germany: An Economic Report Card
  I.   Rate of growth
       A. France
       B. Germany
  II.   Unemployment rate
       A. France
       B. Germany
  III. Productivity
       A. France
       B. Germany
  IV. Gross national product
       A. France
       B. Germany
  V.   Debt
       A. France
       B. Germany

Your Turn   In a paper you have recently written (or an article you've been asked to read), point out all the examples you can find of the strategies described in this chapter: description, division, classification, definition, and comparison/contrast. Does the strategy dominate the piece — as comparison/contrast might in an essay evaluating different smartphones or describing law schools? Or is the use of the strategy incidental, for example, just a line or two of description or a quick definition offered to clarify a point?

understand
evaluations p. 100

26 Organization

shape your work

To describe the structure of their projects, writers often use metaphors or other figures of speech. They visualize their work in terms of links, frames, templates, maps, or even skeletons. Such images help writers keep their emerging ideas on track. Just as important, familiar patterns of organization make life easier for readers who come to a project wondering how its ideas and elements will fit together.

In Parts 1 and 2, you'll find specific suggestions for structuring a wide variety of writing genres. The following advice on organization applies more generally.

Examine model documents.   Many types of writing are highly conventional—which simply means that they follow predictable patterns and formulas. So when you are asked to compose in a new genre, study the arrangement of several examples. Some structural features are immediately obvious, such as headings or introductory and concluding sections. But look for more subtle moves too—for example, many editorials first describe a problem, then blame someone for it, and finally make a comment or offer a comparison. Good models will point you in the right direction.

Sketch out a plan or sequence.   To give direction to a new project, try starting with a scratch (or informal) outline, even a rough one. You will probably discover relationships between your ideas (sequence, similarity, difference) or quickly note gaps or flaws in your thinking. Just as important, creating a structure makes a writing project suddenly seem more doable because you've broken a complex task into smaller, more manageable parts.

Technology can also make it easier to organize a project. Consider how effortlessly you can move the slides in a PowerPoint presentation until you find the most effective order. Yet pen and paper work almost as well, whether you use note cards to map out a senior thesis or draw an outline to clarify matters in a comparison/contrast piece. ○

Provide cues or signals for readers.   Just because you understand how the parts of your project fit together, don't assume readers will. You have to give them cues—which come in various forms, including titles, headings, captions, and, especially, transitional words and phrases. For example, in a narrative you might include transitional words to mark the passage of time (*next*, *then*, *before*, *afterward*). Or, if you organize a project according to a principle of magnitude,

How many patterns of organization can you find in this storeroom of a hospital intensive care unit? © Justin Paget/ Corbis.

think
visually p. 557

you might give readers signals that clearly show a change from *best* to *worst, cheapest* to *most expensive, most common species* to *endangered species*. And if you are writing to inform or report, you might also rely heavily on visuals to help make your point. O

Deliver on your commitments.   This is a basic principle of organization. If, for example, you promise in an introductory paragraph to offer two reasons in support of a claim, you need to offer two clearly identifiable reasons in that paper or readers will feel that they missed something. But commitments are broader than that: Narratives ordinarily lead somewhere, perhaps to a climax; editorials offer opinions; proposals offer and defend new ideas; evaluations make judgments. You can depart from these structural expectations, but you should do so knowing what readers expect and anticipating how they might react to your straying from the formula.

order
ideas p. 377

Outlines

Despite what you may believe, outlines are designed to make writing easier, not harder. You'll feel more confident when you begin a project with a plan. The trick is to start simple and let outlines evolve to fit your needs.

Start with scratch outlines.   After researching a topic, many writers sketch out a quick, informal outline—the verbal equivalent of the clever mechanical idea hastily drawn on a cocktail napkin. Good ideas do often emerge from simple, sometimes crude, notions that suddenly make sense when seen on paper. Both the Internet and the structure of the DNA molecule can be traced to such visualizations.

order ideas

Bob Metcalfe's original sketch of the Ethernet concept. Courtesy of PARC, Inc., a Xerox company.

List key ideas.   Scratch outlines usually begin with ragged lists. You simply write down your preliminary thoughts and key ideas so you can see exactly how they relate, merging any that obviously overlap. Keep these notes brief but specific, using words and phrases rather than complete sentences. At this point, you might find yourself posing questions too. In fact, your initial scratch outline might resemble a mildly edited brainstorming list (see Chapter 19). Here's the first stage of a scratch outline addressing a topic much discussed in academia: the impact that massive open online courses (MOOCs) may have on higher education. (If you are unfamiliar with the term, you might do a quick Web search.)

Massive open online courses (MOOCs)

Taught by top-notch professors from prestigious schools

First-rate MOOCs are complex — expensive to produce

Rely on "superstar" professors

Can reach unlimited numbers of students across the country

How different from old-style correspondence or online courses?

Cheap: no classrooms; less administration; less "brick and mortar"

Less interaction with faculty

No face-to-face work with classmates

Available anytime and anywhere

Education through watching slick videos

Promise equal access to first-rate educational opportunities

Could replace large core courses at many schools

Use interactive online activities

Might drive down the high cost of postsecondary education

Differences between learning facts and gaining knowledge?

Very high attrition rate in early MOOCs

Depersonalized and dehumanizing: no real faculty-student interaction

A sprawling list like this could easily grow even longer, so you need to get it under control. To do that, you can apply the three principles that make outlining such a powerful tool of organization: *relationship*, *subordination*, and *sequence*.

Look for relationships.   Examine the initial items on your list and try grouping *like* with *like*—or look for opposites and contrasts. Experiment with various arrangements or clusters. In the scratch outline above, for example, you might decide that the items fall into three basic categories. A first cluster explains what MOOCs do, a second cluster focuses on their advantages, while a third and lengthier cluster considers their weaknesses.

<u>What MOOCs do</u>

Taught by top-notch professors from prestigious schools

Use video lectures and interactive online activities

Available anytime and anywhere

Can reach unlimited numbers of students across the country

<u>Strengths of MOOCs</u>

Cheap: no classrooms; less administration; less "brick and mortar"

Promise equal access to first-rate educational opportunities

Could replace large core courses at many schools

Might drive down the high cost of postsecondary education

<u>Weaknesses of MOOCs</u>

How different from old-style correspondence or online courses?

Less interaction with faculty

No face-to-face work with classmates

First-rate MOOCs are complex—expensive to produce

Rely on "superstar" professors

Equate education to watching slick videos

Differences between learning facts and gaining knowledge?

Very high attrition rate in early MOOCs

Depersonalized and dehumanizing: no real faculty-student interaction

Subordinate ideas.   In outlines, you routinely divide subjects into topics and subtopics. This means that some ideas belong not only grouped with others but also grouped under them—which is to say, they become a subset within a larger group.

For instance, looking again at the lengthy group of "Weaknesses of MOOCs," you might notice that MOOCs seem to differ from old-style correspondence or online courses chiefly because more money is spent to develop them—an idea you connect to several supporting points, some of which you modify and amplify.

> MOOCs are high-class correspondence courses
>> Rely on well-paid "superstar" professors
>> Require slick videos to keep students entertained
>> Cost more to produce than most schools can afford
>> Narrow the range of academic experiences

Then you notice a second cluster within the "Weaknesses of MOOCs" grouping, one related to your claim that MOOCs are "depersonalized and dehumanizing." Once again, you subordinate some initial points to a broader claim, enlarging and connecting them.

> MOOCs are depersonalized and dehumanizing
>> Support little interaction between online faculty and students
>> Minimize face-to-face work with peers: no true classmates
>> Equate learning facts with gaining knowledge
>> [Consequently?] have a high attrition rate

At this point, you have pushed well beyond a list. You are using the outlining process to explore your ideas and turn them into, in this case, an argument.

Decide on a sequence.   Once you have sorted out the patterns within an initial list of ideas, you are ready to arrange them to support a thesis. At this point, you have a great many options, depending on what type of project you are developing—a narrative, a report, an argument, or something else. You might sequence the items chronologically or by magnitude (for example, least to most important). Or you might determine your order rhetorically—by how you want readers to respond.

Continuing to pursue the MOOC project, you could, for example, do a detailed report on these new types of courses, focusing on what MOOCs do—the first cluster in your initial list of relationships. But, given the number of criticisms you generated of this technology, perhaps your heart is in writing an evaluation, one that weighs the strengths of MOOCs against the more numerous weaknesses you have identified. Your working outline, now considerably more formal than a scratch version, might look like the following:

A. What MOOCs are
　1. Highly evolved, technologically sophisticated online college courses
　2. Top professors from prestigious schools
B. What MOOCs aim to do
　1. Offer first-rate course material
　2. Lower the cost of college education
　3. Provide equal access to education for more students
C. What MOOCs really do
　1. Update old-style correspondence courses
　　a. Rely on "superstar" model
　　b. Use slick videos to keep students entertained
　　c. Narrow the range of academic experiences
　2. Depersonalize and dehumanize learning
　　a. Support little interaction between online faculty and students
　　b. Minimize face-to-face encounters with classmates
　　c. Equate learning facts with gaining knowledge

Needless to say, this is but one of many possible takes on this subject, as proponents of MOOCs would be quick to point out.

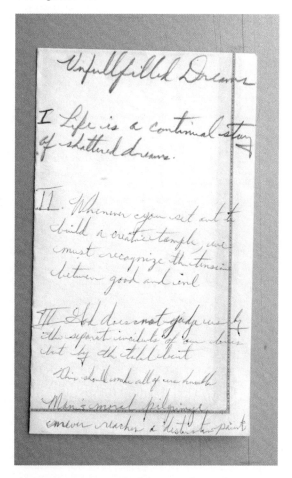

Here's an outline for a sermon titled "Unfulfilled Dreams" from a notebook of Rev. Martin Luther King, Jr.
Frances M. Roberts/Newscom.

Move up to a formal outline.   You may be required to submit a formal outline with your final paper. When that's the case, be sure to follow the following
guidelines—which may help you to detect even more relationships between
your ideas:

- Carefully align the headings at every level (see example).

- Be sure to have at least two items at every heading level (I, A, and 1). If you
  can't find a second item to match the first in a new level of heads, perhaps
  the new level isn't needed.

- Express all items (except the thesis) as complete and parallel statements
  (not questions), properly punctuated.

- Position your thesis sentence above the outline, underlined or italicized.
  Seeing the thesis there may keep you from wandering off-subject.

  Thesis: <u>Though massive open online courses (MOOCs) promise to solve the
  problems of higher education, they are just upgraded versions of older
  correspondence courses that will dehumanize learning.</u>

  I.   MOOCs represent the latest trend in higher education.
       A. They use advanced video and Web 2.0 technologies to make sophisti-
          cated online college courses widely available.
       B. They feature distinguished faculty from top-tier colleges and universities.
  II. MOOCs aim to improve higher education.
       A. They make top-rated courses available to vastly more students.
       B. They claim to lower the cost of education.
          1. They reduce the number of faculty required.
          2. They eliminate many "brick and mortar" costs on campus.
       C. They equalize educational opportunity.
  III. MOOCs depersonalize and dehumanize the process of education.
       A. Online lectures remove faculty from the lives of students.
          1. Professors in MOOCs become performers for students, not mentors.
          2. Students cannot personally question or challenge instructors.
       B. Students take MOOCs in isolation, without interaction with classmates.
       C. MOOCs encourage students to equate learning facts with becoming
          educated.

Paragraphs 28

Paragraphs are a practical invention, created to make long blocks of prose easier to read by dividing them up. Here are some helpful ways to think about them.

Make sure paragraphs lead somewhere.   Typically, you'll place a topic sentence at the beginning of a paragraph to introduce a claim that the rest of the paragraph will develop. Ron Rosenbaum's opener leaves little doubt about the direction his paragraph will take. ○

develop ideas

> **The hysterical crusade against fat has become a veritable witch hunt.** With New York City Mayor Michael Bloomberg's ban on supersize sodas (now temporarily thwarted) and the first lady's campaign to push leaves and twigs (i.e., salad) on reluctant school children — all in the name of stamping out obesity — it is fat-shaming time in America. Yes, there are countertrends, like the pro-fat TV shows of Paula Deen and Guy Fieri. But in the culture at large, eating that kind of fat has become a class-based badge of shame: redneck food (which I say as someone who likes rednecks and redneck food). It isn't food for someone who drives a Prius to Pilates class.
>
> — Ron Rosenbaum, "Let Them Eat Fat," *Wall Street Journal*, March 15, 2013

Sometimes, however, you may wait until the concluding sentences to divulge your point, or you may even weave a key idea into the fabric of the entire paragraph. Whatever your strategy, all

develop a
statement p. 362

paragraphs should do serious work: introduce a subject, move a narrative forward, offer a new argument or claim, provide support for a claim already made, contradict another point, amplify an idea, furnish more examples, even bring discussion to an end. A paragraph has to do something that readers see as purposeful and connected to what comes before and after.

Develop ideas adequately.   Instructors who insist that paragraphs run a minimum number of sentences (say 6–10) are usually just tired of students who don't back up claims with enough evidence. ⃝ In fact, experienced writers don't count sentences when they build paragraphs. Instead, they develop a sense for paragraph length, matching the swell of their ideas to the habits of their intended readers.

Consider the following paragraph, which describes the last moments of the final Apollo moon mission in December 1972. The paragraph might be reduced to a single sentence: *All that remained of the 363-foot* Apollo 17 *launch vehicle was a 9-foot capsule recovered in the ocean.* But what would be lost? The pleasure of the full paragraph resides in the details the writer musters to support the final sentence, which reveals his point.

> A powerful Sikorsky Sea King helicopter, already hovering nearby as they [the *Apollo 17* crew] hit the water, retrieved the astronauts and brought them to the carrier, where the spacecraft was recovered shortly later. The recovery crew saw not a gleaming instrument of exotic perfection, but a blasted, torn, and ragged survivor, its titanic strength utterly exhausted, a husk now, a shell. The capsule they hauled out of the ocean was all that remained of the *Apollo 17* Saturn V. The journey had spent, incinerated, smashed, or blistered into atoms every other part of the colossal, 363-foot white rocket, leaving only this burnt and brutalized 9-foot capsule. A great shining army had set out over the horizon, and a lone squadron had returned, savaged beyond recognition, collapsing into the arms of its rescuers, dead. Such was the price of reaching for another world.
>
> — David West Reynolds, *Apollo: The Epic Journey to the Moon*

Organize paragraphs logically.   It would be surprising if paragraphs didn't use the same structures found in full essays: thesis and support, division, classification, narrative. But it's ideas that drive the shape of paragraphs, not patterns

understand
arguments p. 66

of organization. Writers don't puzzle over whether their next paragraph should follow a comparison/contrast or cause/effect plan. They just write it, making sure it makes a point and appeals to readers.

In fact, individual paragraphs in any longer piece can be organized many different ways. And because paragraphs are relatively short, you usually see their patterns unfold right before your eyes. The following two passages are from an essay by Jon Katz titled "Do Dogs Think?" The paragraphs within them follow structures Katz needs at that given moment.

Blue, Heather's normally affectionate and obedient Rottweiler, began tearing up the house shortly after Heather went back to work as an accountant after several years at home. The contents of the trash cans were strewn all over the house. A favorite comforter was destroyed. Then Blue began peeing all over Heather's expensive new living-room carpet and systematically ripped through cables and electrical wires.

Narrative paragraph describes changes in Blue's behavior.

Lots of dogs get nervous when they don't know what's expected of them, and when they get anxious, they can also grow restless. Blue hadn't had to occupy time alone before. Dogs can get unnerved by this. They bark, chew, scratch, destroy. Getting yelled at and punished later doesn't help: The dog probably knows it's doing something wrong, but it has no idea what. Since there's nobody around to correct behaviors when the dog is alone, how could the dog know which behavior is the problem? Which action was wrong?

Katz uses *causal* pattern to explore Blue's behavioral problem.

I don't believe that dogs act out of spite or that they can plot retribution, though countless dog owners swear otherwise. To punish or deceive requires the perpetrator to understand that his victim or object has a particular point of view and to consciously work to manipulate or thwart it. That requires mental processes dogs don't have.

A simple *statement/ proof* structure organizes this paragraph.

Why will Clementine come instantly if she's looking at me, but not if she's sniffing deer droppings? Is it because she's being stubborn or, as many people tell me, going through "adolescence"? Or because, when following her keen predatory instincts, she simply doesn't hear me? Should my response be to tug at her leash or yell? Maybe I should be sure we've established eye contact before I give her a command, or better yet, offer a liver treat as an alternative to whatever's distracting her. But how do I establish eye contact when her nose is buried? Can I cluck or bark? Use a whistle or hoot like an owl?

Taken together, the two paragraphs in this passage follow a *problem/solution* structure common in proposal arguments.

> I've found that coughing, of all things, fascinates her, catches her attention, and makes her head swivel, after which she responds. If you walk with us, you will hear me clearing my throat repeatedly. What can I say? It works. She looks at me, comes to me, gets rewarded.
>
> — *Slate.com*, October 6, 2005

Use paragraphs to manage transitions. Paragraphs often give direction to a paper. An opening paragraph, for example, can outline the content of a report or set the scene for a narrative. ○ In lengthy projects, you might need full paragraphs at critical junctures to summarize what has been covered and then send readers off in new directions.

You might even use very brief paragraphs—sometimes just a sentence or two long—to punctuate a piece by drawing attention to a turn in your thinking or offering a strong judgment. You've probably seen paragraphs that consist of nothing more than an indignant "Nonsense!" or a sarcastic "Go figure." There's a risk in penning paragraphs with so much attitude, but it's an option when the subject calls for it.

Design paragraphs for readability. It's common sense: Paragraph breaks work best when they coincide with shifts of thought within the writing itself. When they meet a new paragraph, readers assume that your ideas have moved in some (sometimes small) way. But paragraphs are often at the mercy of a text's physical environment as well. When you read a news items on the Web, the short paragraphs used in those single-column stories look fine. But hit the "print this article" button and the text suddenly sprawls across the screen, becoming difficult to read.

The point? You should adjust the length and shape of paragraphs to the space where your words will appear.

shape a
beginning p. 391

Transitions 29

What exactly makes words, sentences, and ideas flow from paragraph to paragraph as fluidly as Michael Phelps slipping through the water? *Transitional words and phrases*, many writers would reply—thinking of words such as *and*, *but*, *however*, *neither . . . nor*, *first . . . second . . . third*, and so on. Placed where readers need them, these connecting words make a paper read smoothly. But they are only part of the story.

Almost any successful piece of writing is held together by more devices than most writers can consciously juggle. A few of the ties—such as connections between pronouns and their referents—are almost invisible and seem to take care of themselves. Here are some guidelines for making smooth transitions between ideas in paragraphs and sections of your writing.

© Steve Terrill/Corbis.

Common Transitions

Connection or Consequence	Contrast	Correlation	Sequence or Time	Indication
and	but	if . . . then	first . . . second	this
or	yet	either . . . or	and then	that
so	however	from . . . to	initially	there
therefore	nevertheless		subsequently	for instance
moreover	on the contrary		before	for example
consequently	despite		after	in this case
hence	still		until	
	although		next	
			in conclusion	

Use appropriate transitional words and phrases.   There's nothing complicated or arcane about them: You'll recognize every word in any list of transitions. But be aware that they have different functions and uses, with subtle distinctions even between words as close in meaning as *but* and *yet*.

   Transitional words are often found at the beginnings of sentences and paragraphs simply because that's the place where readers expect a little guidance. There are no rules, per se, for positioning transitions—though they can be set off from the rest of the sentence with commas.

Use the right word or phrase to show time or sequence.   Readers often need specific words or phrases to help keep events in order. Such expressions can simply mark off stages: *first, second, third.* Or they might help readers keep track of more complicated passages of time.

Use sentence structure to connect ideas.   When you build sentences with similar structures, readers will infer that the ideas in them are related. Devices you can use to make this kind of linkage include *parallelism* ○ and *repetition*.

   In the following example, the first three paragraphs of James P. Gannon's "America's Quiet Anger," you can see both strategies at work, setting up an emotional argument that continues in this pattern for another three paragraphs. Parallel items are highlighted.

parallelism
p. 597

> There is a quiet anger boiling in America.
> It is the anger of millions of hardworking citizens who pay their bills, send in their income taxes, maintain their homes, and repay their mortgage loans — and see their government reward those who do not.
> It is the anger of small town and Middle American folks who have never been to Manhattan, who put their savings in a community bank and borrow from a local credit union, who watch Washington lawmakers and presidents of both parties hand billions in taxpayer bailouts to the reckless Wall Street titans who brought down the economy in 2008.
>
> —*American Spectator*, March 20, 2010

Pay attention to nouns and pronouns.   Understated transitions in a piece can occur between pronouns and their antecedents, but make sure the relationships between the nouns and pronouns are clear. ○ And, fortunately, readers usually don't mind encountering a pronoun over and over—except maybe *I*. Note how effortlessly Adam Nicolson moves between *George Abbot, he*, and *man* in the following paragraph from *God's Secretaries* (2003), in which he describes one of the men responsible for the King James translation of the Bible:

> George Abbot was perhaps the ugliest of them all, a morose, intemperate man, whose portraits exude a sullen rage. Even in death, he was portrayed on his tomb in Holy Trinity, Guilford, as a man of immense weight, with heavy, wrinkled brow and coldly open, staring eyes. He looks like a bruiser, a man of such conviction and seriousness that anyone would think twice about crossing him. What was it that made George Abbot so angry?

Use synonyms.   Simply by repeating a noun from sentence to sentence, you make an obvious and logical connection within a paper—whether you are naming an object, an idea, or a person. To avoid monotony, vary terms you have to use frequently. But don't strain with archaic or inappropriate synonyms that will distract the reader.

Note the sensible variants on the word *trailer* in the following paragraph.

> Hype and hysteria have always been a part of movie advertising, but the frenzy of film trailers today follows a visual style first introduced by music videos in the 1980s. The quick cut is everything, accompanied by a deafening soundtrack. Next time you go to a film, study the three

help with common
errors p. 566

PART 4   SHAPING & DRAFTING

or four previews that precede the main feature. How are these teasers constructed? What are their common features? What emotions or reactions do they raise in you? What might trailers say about the expectations of audiences today?

Use physical devices for transitions.   You know all the ways movies manage transitions between scenes, from quick cuts to various kinds of dissolves. Writing has fewer visual techniques to mark transitions, but they are important. Titles and headings in lab reports, for instance, let your reader know precisely when you are moving from "Methods" to "Results" to "Discussion." In books, you'll encounter chapter breaks as well as divisions within chapters, sometimes marked by asterisks or perhaps a blank space. Seeing these markers, readers expect that the narration is changing in some way. Even the numbers in a list or shaded boxes in a magazine can be effective transitional devices, moving readers from one place to another.

Read a draft aloud to locate weak transitions.   The best way to test your transitions in a paper or project may be to listen to yourself. As you read, mark every point in the paper where you pause, stumble, or find yourself adding a transitional word or phrase not in the original text. Record even the smallest bobble because tiny slips have a way of cascading into bigger problems.

Simone End/Getty Images.

Introductions and Conclusions

Introductions and conclusions are among the most important parts of a project. An introduction has to grab and hold a reader's attention while identifying topic and purpose and setting a context. A conclusion has to bring all the parts of a paper together and seal the deal with readers. None of these tasks—which vary according to genre—are easy.

Shape an introduction.   The opening of some projects must follow a template. Writing a story for a newspaper, you begin by providing essential facts, identifying *who*, *what*, *where*, and *when*. You'll also follow conventions with technical materials (lab reports, research articles, scholarly essays). To get such introductions right, study models of these genres and then imitate their structures.

When not constrained by a template, you have many options for an opening, the most straightforward being simply to announce your project. This blunt approach is common in academic papers where it makes sense to identify a subject and preview your plan for developing it. Quite often, the introductory material leads directly into a thesis or a hypothesis, as in the following student paper:

shape a beginning and an ending

Paper opens by
identifying its general
topic or theme.

In her novel *Wuthering Heights* (1847), Emily Brontë presents the
story of the families of Wuthering Heights and Thrushcross Grange
through the seemingly impartial perspective of Nelly Dean, a servant who
grows up with the families. Upon closer inspection, however, it becomes
apparent that Nelly acts as much more than a bystander in the tragic
events taking place around her. In her status as an outsider with influence
over the families, Nelly strikingly resembles the Byronic hero Heathcliff and
competes with him for power. Although the author depicts Heathcliff as the
more overt gothic hero, Brontë allows the reader to infer from Nelly's story

Detailed thesis states
what paper will prove.

her true character and role in the family. The author draws a parallel
between Nelly Dean and Heathcliff in their relationships to the Earnshaw
family, in their similar roles as tortured heroes, and in their competition for
power within their adoptive families.

—Manasi Deshpande, "Servant and Stranger: Nelly and Heathcliff in *Wuthering Heights*"

Reports and arguments may open more slowly, using an introductory
section that helps readers appreciate why an issue deserves attention. You
might, for example, present an anecdote, describe a trend, or point to some
phenomenon readers may not have noticed. Then you can thrash out its
significance or implications.

Opening paragraphs can also deliver necessary background information.
The trick is always to decide what exactly readers need to know about a subject.
Provide too little background information on a subject and readers may find
the project confusing. Supply too much context and you lose fans quickly.

And yet, even when readers know a subject well, be sure to supply basic
facts about the project. Name names in your introduction, provide accurate
titles for works you are discussing, furnish dates, and explain what exactly your
subject is. Imagine readers from just slightly outside your target audience who
might not instantly recall, for instance, that it was Shakespeare who wrote a
play titled *Henry V* or that Edwin "Buzz" Aldrin was the *second* person to walk
on the surface of the moon. Don't leave readers guessing. But it's fair game to
intrigue them.

So give them reasons to enter your text. Invite them with a compelling
incident or provocative story, with a recitation of surprising or intriguing
facts, with a dramatic question, with a memorable description or quotation.
Naturally, any opening has to be in sync with the material that follows—not

outrageously emotional if the argument is sober, not lighthearted and comic if the paper has a serious theme.

Typically, readers use an introduction to determine whether they belong to the audience of the piece. A paper that opens with highly technical language says "specialists only," while a more personal or colloquial style welcomes a broader group. Readers are also making judgments about you in those opening lines, so you can't afford errors of fact or even grammar and usage there. Such slips-ups cloud their impression of all that follows.

One last bit of advice: Don't write an introduction until you're ready. The opening of a project can be notoriously difficult to frame because it does so much work. If you are blocked at the beginning of a project, plunge directly into the body of the paper and see what happens. You can even write the opening section last, after you know precisely where the paper goes. No one will know.

Draw a conclusion.   Like introductions, conclusions serve different purposes and audiences. An e-mail to a professor may need no more of a sign-off than a signature, while a senior thesis could require a whole chapter to wrap things up. In reports and arguments, you typically use the concluding section to summarize what you've covered and draw out the implications. The following is the no-nonsense conclusion of a college report on a childhood developmental disorder, cri du chat syndrome (CDCS). Note that this summary paragraph also leads where many other scientific and scholarly articles do: to a call for additional research.

Even towns sometimes need introductions. Yee haw! Andre Jenny/Newscom.

Major point

Major point

Conclusion ties together
main points made in
paper, using transitional
words and phrases.

Though research on CDCS remains far from abundant, existing studies prescribe early and ongoing intervention by a team of specialists, including speech-language pathologists, physical and occupational therapists, various medical and educational professionals, and parents. Such intervention has been shown to allow individuals with CDCS to live happy, long, and full lives. The research, however, indicates that the syndrome affects all aspects of a child's development and should therefore be taken quite seriously. Most children require numerous medical interventions, including surgery (especially to correct heart defects), feeding tubes, body braces, and repeated treatment of infections. Currently, the best attempts are being made to help young children with CDCS reach developmental milestones earlier, communicate effectively, and function as independently as possible. However, as the authors of the aforementioned studies suggest, much more research is needed to clarify the causes of varying degrees of disability, to identify effective and innovative treatments/interventions (especially in the area of education), and to individualize intervention plans.

—Marissa Dahlstrom, "Developmental Disorders: Cri du Chat Syndrome"

On other occasions, you will want to finish dramatically and memorably, especially in arguments and personal narratives that seek to influence readers and change opinions. Since final paragraphs are what readers remember, it makes sense to use powerful language. Here's the conclusion of a lengthy personal essay by Shane McNamee on gay marriage that leads up to a poignant political appeal.

Deliberate repetition
focuses readers on
serious point.

Conclusion makes direct
appeal to readers,
addressed as *you.*

Final sentence appeals
emotionally through
both images and
language.

Forget for the moment the rainbow flags and pink triangles. Gay pride is not about being homosexual; it's about the integrity and courage it takes to be honest with yourself and your loved ones. It's about spending life with whomever you want and not worrying what the government or the neighbors think. Let's protect that truth, not some rigid view of sexual orientation or marriage. Keep gay marriage out of your church if you like, but if you value monogamy as I do, give me an alternative that doesn't involve dishonesty or a life of loneliness. Many upstanding gay citizens yearn for recognition of their loving, committed relationships. Unless you enjoy being lied to and are ready to send your gay friends and family on a Trail of Queers to a state where gay marriage is legal then consider letting them live as they wish.

—"Protecting What Really Matters"

Titles **31**

Titles may not strike you as an important aspect of writing, but they can be. Sometimes the struggle to find a good title helps a writer shape a piece or define its main point. Of course, a proper title tells readers what a paper is about and makes searching for the document easier.

Use titles to focus documents.   A title that is too broad early on in a project is a sure sign that you have yet to find a manageable topic. If all you have is "Sea Battles in World War II" or "Children in America," you need to do more reading and research. If no title comes to mind at all, it means you don't have a subject. ○ You're still exploring ideas.

For academic papers, titles need be descriptive. Consider these items culled at random from one issue of the *Stanford Undergraduate Research Journal*. As you might guess, scientific papers aimed at knowledgeable specialists have highly technical titles. Titles in the social sciences and humanities are less intimidating but just as focused on providing information about their subjects.

> "Molecular and Morphological Characterization of Two Species of Sea Cucumber, *Parastichopus parvimensis* and *Parastichopus californicus*, in Monterey, CA"
>
> —Christine O'Connell, Alison J. Haupt, Stephen R. Palumbi

name your
work

develop a
statement p. 362

"Justifiers of the British Opium Trade: Arguments by Parliament, Traders, and the *Times* Leading Up to the Opium War"

—Christine Su

"The Incongruence of the Schopenhauerian Ending in Wagner's *Götterdämmerung*"

—James Locus

Create searchable titles. For academic or professional papers, a thoughtful title makes sense standing on its own and out of context. It should also include keywords by which it might be searched for in a database or online. For example, an essay titled "Smile!" wouldn't offer many clues about its content or purpose; far more useful is the title of a real journal article by Christina Kotchemidova, "From Good Cheer to 'Drive-By Smiling': A Social History of Cheerfulness." When Professor Kotchemidova's paper winds up in someone's bibliography or in an online database, readers know what its subject is.

If you must be clever or allusive, follow the cute title with a colon and an explanatory subtitle.

"'Out, Damn'd Spot!': Images of Conscience and Remorse in Shakespeare's *Macbeth*"

"Out, Damn'd Spot: Housebreaking Your Puppy"

Avoid whimsical or suggestive titles. A bad title will haunt you like a silly screen name. At this point, you may not worry about publication, but documents take on a life of their own when uploaded to the Web or listed on a résumé. Any document posted where the public can search for it online needs a levelheaded title, especially when you enter the job market.

Titles tell readers what to expect. *Top:* Columbia Pictures/Photofest. *Center:* Federal Emergency Management Agency/Ready Campaign. *Bottom:* By permission. From *Merriam-Webster's Collegiate Dictionary* © 2014 by Merriam-Webster, Inc. (www.Merriam-Webster.com).

Capitalize and punctuate titles carefully. The guidelines for capitalizing titles vary between disciplines. See Chapters 46 and 47 for the MLA and APA guidelines, or consult the style manual for your discipline.

Your titles should avoid all caps, boldface, underscoring, and, with some exceptions, italics (titles within titles and foreign terms may be italicized; see examples above). For Web sites, newsletters, PowerPoint presentations, and so on, you can be bolder graphically. **O**

think visually
p. 557

32

High, Middle, and Low Style

define your style/refine your tone

We all have an ear for the way words work in sentences and paragraphs, for the distinctive melding of voice, tone, rhythm, and texture some call *style*. You might not be able to explain exactly why one paragraph sparkles and another is as flat as day-old soda, but you know when writing feels energetic, precise, and clear or stodgy, lifeless, and plodding. Choices you make about sentence type, sentence length, vocabulary, pronouns, and punctuation *do* create distinctive verbal styles—which may or may not fit particular types of writing. ○

In fact, there are as many styles of writing as of dress. In most cases, language that is clear, active, and economical will do the job. But even such a bedrock style has variations. Since the time of the ancient Greeks, writers have imagined a "high" or formal style at one end of a scale and a "low" or colloquial style at the other, bracketing a just-right porridge in the middle. Style is more complex than that, but keeping the full range in mind reveals some of your options.

Even dining has distinct levels of style and formality you grasp immediately. *Top:* Anna Brykhanova/Getty Images. *Center:* Steve Debenport/E+ Collection/ Getty Images. *Bottom:* Mary Altaffer/ Associated Press.

improve your sentences p. 412

Use high style for formal, scientific, and scholarly writing. You will find high style in professional journals, scholarly books, legal briefs, formal addresses, many newspaper editorials, some types of technical writing, and even traditional wedding invitations. Use it yourself when a lot is at stake—in a scholarship application, for example, or a job letter, term paper, or thesis. High style is signaled by some combination of the following features—all of which can vary.

John Cole, courtesy Cagle Cartoons.

- Serious or professional subjects
- Knowledgeable or professional audiences
- Impersonal point of view signaled by dominant, though not exclusive, third-person (*he, she, it, they*) pronouns
- Relatively complex and self-consciously patterned sentences (that display *parallelism, balance, repetition*)
- Sophisticated or professional vocabulary, often abstract and technical
- Few contractions or colloquial expressions
- Conventional grammar and punctuation; standard document design
- Formal documentation, when required, often with notes and a bibliography

The following example is from a scholarly journal. The article uses a formal scientific style, appropriate when an expert in a field is writing for an audience of his or her peers.

Temperament is a construct closely related to personality. In human research, temperament has been defined by some researchers as the inherited, early appearing tendencies that continue throughout life and serve as the foundation for personality (A. H. Buss, 1995; Goldsmith et al., 1987). Although this definition is not adopted uniformly by human researchers (McCrae et al., 2000), animal researchers agree even less about how to define temperament (Budaev, 2000). In some cases, the word *temperament* appears to be used purely to avoid using the word *personality*, which some animal researchers associate with anthropomorphism. Thus, to ensure that my review captured all potentially relevant reports, I searched for studies that examined either personality or temperament.

— Sam D. Gosling, "From Mice to Men: What Can We Learn About Personality from Animal Research?" *Psychological Bulletin*

> Technical terms introduced and defined.

> Sources documented.

> Perspective generally impersonal — though *I* is used.

For an activity on appropriate language, see **macmillanhighered.com/howtowrite3e.**
Tutorials > LearningCurve Activities > Appropriate Language

The following excerpt from a 2013 Presidential Proclamation marking National Arts and Humanities Month also uses a formal style. The occasion calls for an expressive reflection on a consequential subject.

Opening is general and serious—with carefully balanced sentences.

Throughout our history, America has advanced not only because of our people's will or our leaders' vision, but also because of paintings and poems, stories and songs, dramas and dances. These works open our minds and nourish our souls, helping us understand what it means to be human and what it means to be American. . . .

Vocabulary is learned and dignified.

Our history is a testament to the boundless capacity of the arts and humanities to shape our views of democracy, freedom, and tolerance. Each of us knows what it is like to have our beliefs changed by a writer's perspective, our understanding deepened by a historian's insight, or our waning spirit lifted by a singer's voice. These are some of the most striking and memorable moments in our lives, and they reflect lasting truths — that

Ideas expressed are abstract and uplifting.

the arts and humanities speak to everyone and that in the great arsenal of progress, the human imagination is our most powerful tool.

Ensuring our children and our grandchildren can share these same experiences and hone their own talents is essential to our Nation's future. Somewhere in America, the next great author is wrestling with a sentence in her first short story, and the next great artist is doodling in the pages of

Voice is "presidential," speaking for the nation.

his notebook. We need these young people to succeed as much as we need our next generation of engineers and scientists to succeed. And that is why my Administration remains dedicated to strengthening initiatives that not only provide young people with the nurturing that will help their talents grow, but also the skills to think critically and creatively throughout their lives.

Final paragraph evokes well-calibrated emotions.

This month, we pay tribute to the indelible ways the arts and humanities have shaped our Union. Let us encourage future generations to carry this tradition forward. And as we do so, let us celebrate the power of artistic expression to bridge our differences and reveal our common heritage.

—Presidential Proclamation, National Arts and Humanities Month, September 20, 2013

Use middle style for personal, argumentative, and some academic writing.   This style, perhaps the most common, falls between the extremes and, like the other styles, varies enormously. It is the language of journalism, popular books and magazines, professional memos and nonscientific reports, instructional guides and manuals, and most commercial Web sites. Use this style in position papers, letters to the editor, personal statements, and business e-mails and memos—even in some business and professional work, once you are comfortable with the people to whom you are writing. Middle style doesn't so much claim features of its own as walk a path between formal and everyday language. It may combine some of the following characteristics:

- Full range of topics, from serious to humorous
- General audiences
- Range of perspectives, including first-person (*I*) and second-person (*you*) points of view
- Typically, a personal rather than an institutional voice
- Sentences in active voice that vary in complexity and length
- General vocabulary, more specific than abstract, with concrete nouns and action verbs and with unfamiliar terms or concepts defined
- Informal expressions, occasional dialogue, slang, and contractions, when appropriate to the subject or audience
- Conventional grammar and reasonably correct formats
- Informal documentation, usually without notes

In the following excerpt from an article that appeared in the popular magazine *Psychology Today*, Ellen McGrath uses a conversational but serious middle style to present scientific information to a general audience.

> Families often inherit a negative thinking style that carries the germ of depression. Typically it is a legacy passed from one generation to the next, a pattern of pessimism invoked to protect loved ones from disappointment or stress. But in fact, negative thinking patterns do just the opposite, eroding the mental health of all exposed.
>
> When Dad consistently expresses his disappointment in Josh for bringing home a B minus in chemistry although all the other grades are A's, he is exhibiting a kind of cognitive distortion that children learn to deploy

Vocabulary is sophisticated but not technical.

Familiar example (fictional son is even named) illustrates technical term: *cognitive distortion*.

Phrase following dash offers further clarification helpful to educated, but nonexpert, readers.

on themselves — a mental filtering that screens out positive experience from consideration.

Or perhaps the father envisions catastrophe, seeing such grades as foreclosing the possibility of a top college, thus dooming his son's future. It is their repetition over time that gives these events power to shape a person's belief system.

—"Is Depression Contagious?," July 1, 2003

The middle style works especially well for speakers addressing actual audiences. Compare the informal and personal style of Michelle Obama, in her role as first lady, advocating for arts education at an awards luncheon to the more stately language her husband uses in his presidential proclamation, also on the subject of the arts (p. 402):

Style is personal, with feelings close to the surface.

So for every Janelle Monae [an artist recognized at the luncheon], there are so many young people with so much promise [that] they never have the chance to develop. And think about how that must feel for a kid to have so much talent, so much that they want to express, but it's all bottled up inside because no one ever puts a paintbrush or an instrument or a script into their hand.

Sentences and clauses are parallel, rhythmic, and evocatively short.

Think about what that means for our communities, that frustration bottled up. Think about the neighborhoods where so many of our kids live — neighborhoods torn apart by poverty and violence. Those kids have no good outlets or opportunities, so for them everything that's bottled up — all that despair and anger and fear — it comes out in all the wrong places. It comes out through guns and gangs and drugs, and the cycle just continues.

Vocabulary choices are crisp and varied. Note the use of "kids" throughout.

But the arts are a way to channel that pain and frustration into something meaningful and productive and beautiful. And every human being needs that, particularly our kids. And when they don't have that outlet, that is such a tremendous loss, not just for our kids, but for our nation. And that's why the work you all are doing is so important.

—Remarks by the First Lady at the Grammy Museum's Jane Ortner Education Award Luncheon, July 14, 2014

Use a low style for personal, informal, and even playful writing.
Don't think of "low" here in a negative sense: A colloquial or informal style is perfect when you want or need to sound more open and at ease. Low style can be right for your personal e-mails and instant messaging, of course, as well as in advertisements, magazines trying to be hip, personal narratives, humor writing, and many blogs. Low style has many of the following features:

- Everyday or off-the-wall subjects, often humorous or parodic
- In-group or specialized readers
- Highly personal and idiosyncratic points of view; lots of *I*, *me*, *you*, *us*, and dialogue
- Shorter sentences and irregular constructions, especially fragments
- Vocabulary from pop culture and the street—idiomatic, allusive, and obscure to outsiders
- Colloquial expressions resembling speech
- Unconventional grammar and mechanics and alternative formats
- No systematic acknowledgment of sources

Here's a movie review from *Rolling Stone* written in the easy, informal style expected by (and probably used by) its readers.

JOBS
PETER TRAVERS
AUGUST 15, 2013

Casting Ashton Kutcher as Apple's mercurial trailblazer, Steve Jobs, could have backfired big-time. It's one thing being the highest-paid sitcom star on TV, another for Charlie Sheen's replacement on *Two and a Half Men* to find the gravitas to play a computer-and-marketing visionary pursued by personal and professional demons. Kutcher nails the genius and narcissism. It's a quietly dazzling performance.

> Opening paragraph flirts with middle-style vocabulary: *mercurial, gravitas, narcissism.*

As a movie, *Jobs* is a decidedly mixed bag. Director Joshua Michael Stern (*Swing Vote*) and newbie screenwriter Matt Whiteley check off boxes in Jobs's life like they're connecting the dots. Oddly, the film doesn't include Jobs's 2011 death from pancreatic cancer at fifty-six. The film kicks off in 2001 (Jobs intro'ing the iPod) and works back to his career start. It's as if Kutcher were starring in the thinking man's version of *That '70s Show.*

> Tone shifts in a more colloquial second paragraph: *mixed bag, newbie, connecting the dots.*

Sentence structures imitate informal talk.

Jobs, the barefoot hippie and Reed College dropout, sets up shop with his geek buds in the California garage of his adoptive parents. That's where he and Steve "The Woz" Wozniak (Josh Gad) create Apple and start a revolution. Jobs loses the business. Then he wins it back. It plays like a Jobs Wiki page, including young Steve kicking his girlfriend Chrisann (Ahna O'Reilly) to the curb and initially disowning their daughter.

Travers renders a verdict in the final sentence.

The kick comes in watching the man at work, where his blunt style wins few friends but real respect. Kutcher, rising to the occasion, makes every moment count. The skilled Gad looks eager to take him on, but the Woz is a painfully underwritten role. *Jobs* is a one-man show that needed to go for broke and doesn't. My guess is that Jobs would give it a swat.

> **Your Turn**   Over the next day, look for three pieces of writing that seem to you to represent examples of high, middle, and low style. Then study several paragraphs or a section of each in detail, paying attention to the features listed in the checklists for the three styles. How well do the pieces actually conform to the descriptions of high, middle, and low style? Where would you place your three examples on a continuum that moves from high to low? Do the pieces share some stylistic features? Do you find any variations of style within the individual passages you examined?

The very serious story told in the *9/11 Commission Report* was retold in *The 9/11 Report: A Graphic Adaptation* (p. 407). Creators Sid Jacobson and Ernie Colón use the colloquial visual style of a comic book to make the formidable data and conclusions of a government report accessible to a wider audience. For more on choosing a genre, see the Introduction.

Panels combine verbal and visual elements to tell a story.

Political figures become characters in a real-life drama.

Sounds (*Shoom!*) are represented visually — as in superhero tales.

Real images (the photograph on the left) are sometimes juxtaposed with cartoon panels as part of the collage.

Excerpt from "Heroism and Horror" from *THE 9/11 REPORT: A GRAPHIC ADAPTATION* by Sid Jacobson and Ernie Colón. Copyright © 2006 by Castlebridge Enterprises, Inc. Reprinted by permission of Hill and Wang, a division of Farrar, Straus and Giroux LLC.

33 Inclusive and Culturally Sensitive Style

respect your readers

Remember Polish jokes? Let's hope not, and that's a good thing. Slowly, we're all learning to avoid offensive racial, ethnic, and gender stereotypes in our public lives and the bigoted language that propagated them. Thanks to electronic media, the world is smaller and more diverse today: When you compose any document electronically, it may sail quickly around the Web, conveying not only ideas but also your attitudes and prejudices. You can't please every reader in this vast potential audience, but you can at least write respectfully, accurately, and, yes, honestly. Language that is both inclusive and culturally sensitive can and should have the qualities described in the following guidelines.

Avoid expressions that stereotype genders or sexual orientation.   Largely purged from contemporary English usage are job titles that suggest that they are occupied exclusively by men or women. Gone are *stewardess* and *poetess*, *policeman* and *chairman*, *male nurse* and *woman scientist*. When referring to professions, even those still dominated by one gender or another, avoid using a gendered pronoun.

Don't strain sense to be politically correct. *Nun* and *NFL quarterback* are still gendered, as are *witch* and *warlock*—and *surrogate mother*. Here are some easy solutions.

STEREOTYPED	The postman came up the walk.
INCLUSIVE	The letter carrier came up the walk.
STEREOTYPED	Among all her other tasks, a nurse must also stay up-to-date on her medical education.
INCLUSIVE	Among all their other tasks, nurses must also stay up-to-date on their medical education.

Outdated Terms	Alternatives
fireman	firefighter
mankind	humankind, people, humans
congressman	congressional representative
chairman	chair
policewoman	police officer
stewardess	flight attendant
actress, poetess	actor, poet

Avoid expressions that stereotype races, ethnic groups, or religious groups.   Deliberate racial slurs these days tend to be rare in professional writing. But it is still not unusual to find clueless writers (and politicians) noting how "hardworking," "articulate," "athletic," "well-groomed," or "ambitious" members of minority and religious groups are. The praise rings hollow because it draws on old and brutal stereotypes. You have an obligation to learn the history and nature of such ethnic caricatures and grow beyond them. It's part of your education, no matter what group or groups you belong to.

Refer to people and groups by the expressions used in serious publications, understanding that almost all racial and ethnic terms are contested: *African American, black* (or *Black*), *Negro, people of color, Asian American, Hispanic, Mexican American, Cuban American, Native American, Indian, Inuit, Anglo, white* (or *White*). Even the ancient group of American Indians once called Anasazi now goes by the more culturally and historically accurate Native Puebloans. While shifts of this sort may seem fussy or politically correct to some, it costs little to address people as they prefer, acknowledging both their humanity and our differences.

Be aware, too, that being part of an ethnic or racial group usually gives you license to say things about the group not open to outsiders. Anjelah Johnson and Hari Kondabolu can joke about topics that Jimmy Fallon can't touch, using epithets that would cost the *Tonight Show* host his job. In academic and professional settings, show similar discretion in your language—though not in your treatment of serious subjects. Sensitivities of language should not become an excuse for avoiding open debate, nor a weapon to chill it. In the following table are suggestions for inclusive, culturally sensitive terms.

Outdated Terms	Alternatives
Eskimo	Inuit
Oriental	Asian (better to specify country of origin)
Hispanic	Specify: Mexican, Cuban, Nicaraguan, and so on
Negro (acceptable to some)	African American, black
colored	people of color
a gay, the gays	gay, lesbian, gays and lesbians, the LGBT community
cancer victim	cancer survivor
boys, girls (to refer to adults)	men, women

Treat all people with respect.   This policy makes sense in all writing. Some slights may not be intended—against the elderly, for example. But writing that someone drives *like an old woman* manages to offend two groups. In other cases—such as when you are describing members of campus groups, religious groups, the military, gays and lesbians, athletes, and so on—you might mistakenly use language that implies most readers share your own prejudices or narrow vision. You know the derogatory terms and references well enough, and you should avoid them if for no other reason than the Golden Rule. Everyone is a member of some group that has at one time or another been mocked or stereotyped. So writing that is respectful will itself be treated with respect.

Avoid sensational language.   It happens every semester. One or more students ask the instructor whether it's okay to use four-letter words in their papers. Some instructors tolerate expletives in personal narratives, but it is difficult to make a case for them in academic reports, research papers, or position papers unless they are part of quoted material—as they may be in writing about contemporary literature or song lyrics.

Your Turn   Write a paragraph or two about any pet peeve you may have with language use. Your problem may address a serious issue like insensitivities in naming your ethnicity, community, or beliefs. Or you may just be tired of a friend insisting that you describe Sweetie Pie as your "animal companion" rather than use that demeaning and hegemonic term "pet." You'll want to share your paragraph and also read what others have written.

34

Vigorous, Clear, Economical Style

improve your sentences

Ordinarily, tips and tricks don't do much to enhance your skills as a writer. But a few guidelines, applied sensibly, can improve your sentences and paragraphs noticeably—and upgrade your credibility as a writer. You sound more professional and confident when every word and phrase pulls its weight.

Always consider the big picture in applying the following tips: Work with whole pages and paragraphs, not just individual sentences. Remember, too, that these are guidelines, not rules. Ignore them when your good sense suggests a better alternative.

Build sentences around specific and tangible subjects and objects. Scholar Richard Lanham famously advised writers troubled by tangled sentences to ask, "Who is kicking who?" This question expresses the principle that readers shouldn't have to puzzle over what they read. They are less likely to be confused when they can identify the people or things in a sentence that act upon other people and things. Answering Professor Lanham's question often leads to stronger verbs and tighter sentences too.

CONFUSING	Current tax policies necessitate congressional reform if the reoccurrence of a recession is to be avoided.
BETTER	Congress needs to reform current tax policies to avoid another recession.
CONFUSING	In the Prohibition era, tuning cars enabled the bootleggers to turn ordinary automobiles into speed machines

for the transportation of illegal alcohol by simply altering certain
components of the cars.

BETTER   In the Prohibition era, bootleggers modified their cars to turn them
into speed machines for transporting illegal alcohol.

Both of the confusing sentences here work better with subjects capable of
action: *Congress* and *bootleggers*. Once identified, these subjects make it easy to
simplify the sentences, giving them more power.

**Look for opportunities to use specific nouns and noun phrases rather
than general ones.**   This advice depends very much on context. Academic
reports and arguments often require broad statements and general terms. But
don't ignore the power and energy of specific words and phrases; they create
more memorable images for readers, so they may have more impact.

GENERAL	SPECIFIC
bird	roadrunner
cactus	prickly pear
lawbreaker	mugger
business	pizzeria
jeans	501s

Many writers are fond of generic terms and the impenetrable phrases they
inspire because they sound serious and sophisticated. But such language can
be hard to figure out or even suggest a cover-up. What better way to hide an
inconvenient truth than to bury it in words? So revise those ugly, unreadable,
inhuman sentences:

ABSTRACT   All of the separate constituencies at this academic institution must
be invited to participate in the decision-making process under the
current fiscal pressures we face.

BETTER   Faculty, students, and staff at this school must all have a say during
this current budget crunch.

Avoid sprawling phrases.   These constructions give readers fits, especially
when they thicken, sentence after sentence, like limescale or sludge. Be alert
whenever your prose shows any combination of the following features:

> Don't use words
> too big for the
> subject. Don't
> say "infinitely"
> when you mean
> "very"; otherwise
> you'll have no
> word left when
> you want to talk
> about something
> really infinite.

—C. S. Lewis

- Strings of prepositional phrases
- Verbs turned into nouns via endings such as -*ation* (*implement* becomes *implementation*)
- Lots of articles (*the*, *a*)
- Lots of heavily modified verbals

Such expressions are not inaccurate or wrong, just tedious. They make readers work hard for no good reason. Fortunately, they are also easy to clean up once you notice the accumulation.

WORDY members of the student body at Arizona State

BETTER students at Arizona State

WORDY the producing of products made up of steel

BETTER steel production

WORDY the prioritization of decisions for policies of the student government

BETTER the student government's priorities

Avoid sentences with long windups. The more stuff you pile up ahead of the main verb, the more readers have to remember. Very skillful writers can pull off complex sentences of this kind because they know how to build interest and manage clauses. But a safer strategy in academic and professional writing is to get to the point of your sentences quickly. Here's a sentence from the Internal Revenue Service Web site that keeps readers waiting far too long for a verb. Yet it's simple to fix once its problem is diagnosed:

ORIGINAL A new scam e-mail that appears to be a solicitation from the IRS and the U.S. government for charitable contributions to victims of the recent Southern California wildfires has been making the rounds.

REVISED A new scam e-mail making the rounds asks for charitable contributions to victims of the recent Southern California wildfires. Though it appears to be from the IRS and the U.S. government, it is a fake.

Favor simple, active verbs. When a sentence, even a short one, goes off track, consider whether the problem might be a nebulous, strung-out, or unimaginative verb. Replace it with a verb that does something:

For an activity on active and passive voice, see **macmillanhighered.com/howtowrite3e.** **Tutorials** > LearningCurve Activities > Active and Passive Voice

WORDY VERB PHRASE	We must make a decision soon.
BETTER	We must decide soon.
WORDY VERB PHRASE	Students are absolutely reliant on federal loans.
BETTER	Students need federal loans.
WORDY VERB PHRASE	Engineers proceeded to reinforce the levee.
BETTER	Engineers reinforced the levee.

You'll be a better writer the instant you apply this guideline.

Avoid strings of prepositional phrases.   Prepositional phrases are simple structures, consisting of prepositions and their objects and an occasional modifier: *from the beginning; under the spreading chestnut tree; between you and me; in the line of duty; over the rainbow*. You can't write much without prepositional phrases. But use more than two or, rarely, three in a row and they drain the energy from a sentence. When that's the case, try turning the prepositions into more compact modifiers or moving them into different positions within the sentence. Sometimes you may need to revise the sentence even more substantially.

TOO MANY PHRASES	We stood in line at the observatory on the top of a hill in the mountains to look in a huge telescope at the moons of Saturn.
BETTER	We lined up at the mountaintop observatory to view Saturn's moons through a huge telescope.
TOO MANY PHRASES	To help first-year students in their adjustment to the rigors of college life, the Faculty Council voted for the creation of a new midterm break during the third week of October.
BETTER	To help first-year students adjust better to college life, the Faculty Council endorsed a new break in mid-October.

Don't repeat key words close together.   You can often improve the style of a passage just by making sure you haven't used a particular word or phrase too often—unless you repeat it deliberately for effect (*government of the people, by the people, for the people*). Your sentences will sound fresher after you have eliminated pointless repetition; they may also end up shorter.

REPETITIVE   Students in writing courses are often assigned common readings, which they are expected to read to prepare for various student writing projects.

BETTER   Students in writing courses are often assigned common readings to prepare them for projects.

This is a guideline to apply sensibly: Sometimes for clarity, you must repeat key expressions over and over—especially in technical writing.

The *New Horizons* payload is incredibly power efficient, with the instruments collectively drawing only about 28 watts. The payload consists of three optical instruments, two plasma instruments, a dust sensor, and a radio science receiver/radiometer.

—NASA, "*New Horizons* Spacecraft Ready for Flight"

Avoid doublings.   In speech, we tend to repeat ourselves or say things two or three different ways to be sure listeners get the point. Such repetitions are natural, even appreciated. But in writing, the habit of doubling may irritate readers. And it is very much a habit, backed by a long literary tradition comfortable with pairings such as *home and hearth, friend and colleague, tried and true, clean and sober, neat and tidy,* and so on.

Sometimes, writers will add an extra noun or two to be sure they have covered the bases: *colleges and universities, books and articles, ideas and opinions.* There may be good reasons for a second (or third) item. But the doubling is often just extra baggage that slows down the train. Leave it at the station.

The same goes for redundant expressions. For the most part, they go unnoticed, except by readers who crawl up walls when someone writes *young* **in age,** *bold* **in character,** **totally** *dead,* **basically** *unhappy,* **current** *fashion,* **empty** *hole,* **extremely** *outraged, later* **in time,** *mix* **together,** *reply* **back,** and so on. (In each case, the boldfaced words restate what is already obvious.) People precise enough to care about details deserve respect: They land rovers on Mars. Cut the dumb redundancies. (Is *dumb* unnecessary here?)

Turn clauses into more direct modifiers.   If you are fond of *that, which,* and *who* clauses, be sure you need them. You can sometimes save a word or two by pulling the modifiers out of the clause and moving them directly ahead of the words they explain. Or you may be able to tighten a sentence just by cutting *that*, *which*, or *who*.

WORDY	Our football coach, who is nationally renowned, expected a raise.
BETTER	Our nationally renowned football coach expected a raise.
WORDY	Our football coach, who is nationally renowned and already rich, still expected a raise.
BETTER	Our football coach, nationally renowned and already rich, still expected a raise.

Cut introductory expressions such as *it is* and *there is/are* when you can.   These slow-moving expressions, called *expletives*, are fine when they are conventional, as in the following sentences, which would be difficult to rephrase.

> *It's* going to rain today.
>
> *It was* her first Oscar.
>
> *There is* a tide in the affairs of men.

But don't default to easy expletives at the beginning of every other sentence. Your prose will suffer. Fortunately, revision is easy.

WORDY	It is necessary that we reform the housing policies.
BETTER	We need to reform the housing policies.
WORDY	There were many incentives offered by the company to its sales force.
BETTER	The company offered its sales force many incentives.

Expletives in a sentence often attract other wordy and vague expressions. Then the language swells like a blister. Imagine having to read paragraph after paragraph of prose like the following sentence.

SLOW	It is quite evident that an argument sociologist Annette Lareau supports is that it is important to find the balance between authoritarian and indulgent styles of parenting because it contributes to successful child development.
BETTER	Clearly, sociologist Annette Lareau believes that balancing authoritarian and indulgent styles of parenting contributes to successful child development.

Vary your sentence lengths and structures.   Sentences, like music, have rhythm. If all your sentences run about the same length or rarely vary from a predictable subject-verb-object pattern, readers will grow bored without knowing why. Every so often, surprise them with a really short statement. Or begin with a longer-than-usual introductory phrase. Or try compound subjects or verbs, or attach a series of parallel modifiers to the verb or object. Or let a sentence roll toward a grand conclusion, as in the following example.

> [Carl] Newman is a singing encyclopedia of pop power. He has identified, cultured, and cloned the most buoyant elements of his favorite Squeeze, Raspberries, Supertramp, and Sparks records, and he's pretty pathological about making sure there's something unpredictable and catchy happening in a New Pornographers song every couple of seconds — a stereo flurry of *ooohs*, an extra beat or two bubbling up unexpectedly.
>
> — Douglas Wolk, "Something to Talk About," *Spin*, August 2005

Read what you have written aloud.   Then fix any words or phrases that cause you to pause or stumble, and rethink sentences that feel *awkward*—a notoriously vague reaction that should still be taken seriously. Reading drafts aloud is a great way to find problems. After all, if you can't move smoothly through your own writing, a reader won't be able to either. Better yet, persuade a friend or roommate to read your draft to you. Take notes.

Understand, though, that prose never sounds quite like spoken language— and thank goodness for that. Accurate transcripts of dialogue are almost unreadable, full of gaps, disconnected phrases, pauses, repetitions, and the occasional obscenity. And yet written language, especially in the middle style, should resemble the human voice, with all its cadences and rhythms pulling readers along, making them want to read more.

Cut a first draft by 25 percent — or more.   If you tend to be wordy, try to cut your first drafts by at least one-quarter. Put all your thoughts down on the page when drafting a paper. But when editing, cut every unnecessary expression. Think of it as a competition. However, don't eliminate any important ideas and facts. If possible, ask an honest friend to read your work and point out where you might tighten your language.

If you ~~are aware that you~~ tend to ~~say more than you need to in your writing,~~ *be wordy,* then ~~get in the habit of~~ trying to cut ~~the~~ *your* first drafts ~~that you have written~~ by at least one-quarter. ~~There may be good reasons for you to~~ *P*ut all your thoughts ~~and ideas~~ down on the page when ~~you are in the process of~~ drafting a paper ~~or project~~. But when ~~you are in the process of~~ editing, ~~you should be sure to~~ cut every unnecessary ~~word that is not needed or necessary.~~ *expression.* ~~You may find it advantageous to~~ *T*hink of it as a competition ~~or a game.~~ ~~In making your cuts, it is important that you~~ *However,* don't eliminate any important ideas ~~that may be essential or~~ facts ~~that may be important.~~ *and* If ~~you find it~~ possible, ~~you might consider~~ asking an honest friend ~~whom you trust~~ to read your ~~writing~~ *work* and ~~ask them to~~ point out ~~those places in your writing~~ where you might ~~make~~ your language ~~tighter.~~ *tighten*

> I believe more in the scissors than I do in the pencil.

— Truman Capote

Roger Higgins/New York World-Telegram and the Sun Newspapers Photograph Collection/ Library of Congress, Prints and Photographs Division, LC-USZ62-119336.

Your Turn   Even if you think your prose is as tight as Scrooge, take a first draft you have written and try the 25 percent challenge. Count the words in the original version (or let your software do it for you) and then pare away until you come in under quota. And, while you are at it, turn abstract nouns and strung-out verbs into livelier expressions and eliminate long windups and boring chains of prepositional phrases. When you are done, read the revised version aloud — and then revise one more time.

35

Revising Your Own Work

**revise
and edit**

How much time should you spend revising a draft? That depends on the importance of the document and the time available to complete it. A job-application letter, résumé, or term paper had better be impressive. But you shouldn't send even an e-mail without a quick review, if only to make certain you're directing it to the right people and that your tone is spot-on. Errors might not bother you, but don't assume that other readers are just as easygoing. A well-edited piece always trumps sloppy work.

How you revise your work is a different matter. Some people edit line by line, perfecting every sentence before moving on to the next. Others write whole drafts quickly and then revise, and others combine these methods.

In most cases, it makes sense to draft a project fairly quickly and then edit it. Why? Because revising is hierarchical: Some issues matter more to your success than others. You might spend hours on a draft, getting each comma right and deleting every unneeded word. But then you read the whole thing and get that sinking feeling: The paper doesn't meet the assignment or is aimed at the wrong audience. So you trash paragraph after carefully edited paragraph and reorganize many of your ideas. Maybe you even begin from scratch.

Wouldn't it have been better to discover those big problems early on, before you put in so many hours polishing the punctuation? With major projects, consider revising and editing sequentially, starting with the top-tier issues like content and organization. Think of *revising* as making sweeping changes, and *editing* as finessing the details.

Revise to see the big picture.   Be willing to overhaul a whole project, if necessary. Of course, you'll need a draft first and it should be a real one with actual words on the page, not just good intentions. Revisions at this top level may require heavy rewrites of the paper, even starting over. Whatever it takes.

- **Does the project meet the assignment?** You really can get so wrapped up in a paper that you forget the original assignment. If you received an assignment sheet, go back and measure your first draft against its specifications. If it asks for a report and you have offered an argument, prepare for a major overhaul. Review, too, any requirements set for length, format, or use of sources.

- **Does the project reach its intended audience?** Who will read your paper? Are its tone and level of vocabulary right for these people? Have you used the type of sources readers expect: scholarly articles and books for an academic audience? Adjustments to satisfy the assigned audience may ripple throughout the piece.

- **Does the project do justice to its subject?** This is a tough question and you may want to get another reader's input. It might also help to review successful models of the assignment before you revise your paper. Look for such work in magazines, newspapers, and textbooks. How well does yours compare?

Edit to make the paper flow.   There are different opinions as to exactly what *flow* means when applied to writing, but everyone agrees that it's a good thing. With the major requirements of an assignment met, check how well you have put the piece together.

- **Does the organization work for the reader?** You may understand the paper, but will its structure be obvious to readers? Is a thesis statement, when one is required, clearly in place? Do your paragraphs develop coherent points? Pay particular attention to the opening sentences in those paragraphs: They must both connect to what you just wrote and preview the upcoming material.

- **Does the paper have smooth and frequent transitions?** Transitional words and phrases are road signs to help keep readers on track. Make sure they appear not only at the beginning of paragraphs but also throughout the project.

- **Is the paper readable?** Tinker to your heart's content with the language, varying sentence structures, choosing words to match the level of style you want, and paring away clumsy verbiage (which almost rhymes with *garbage*). Review Part 5 on style and apply those suggestions to the paper at this stage.

Edit to get the details right.   When editing a paper, nothing clears your mind as much as putting a draft aside for a few days and then looking at it with fresh eyes. You will be amazed at all the changes you will want to make. But you have to plan ahead to take advantage of this unsurpassed editing technique. Wait until the last minute to complete a project and you lose that opportunity.

- **Is the format correct right down to the details?** Many academic and professional projects follow templates from which you cannot vary. In fact, you may be expected to learn these requirements as a condition for entering a profession or major. So if you are asked to prepare a paper in Modern Language Association (MLA) or American Psychological Association (APA) style, for instance, invest the few minutes it takes to get the titles, margins, headings, and page numbers right. ○ Give similar attention to the formats for lab reports, e-mails, Web sites, and so on. You'll look like a pro if you do.

- **Are the grammar and mechanics right?** Word-processing programs offer a surprising amount of help in these areas. But use this assistance only as a first line of defense, not as a replacement for carefully rereading every word yourself. Even then, you still have to pay close attention to errors you make habitually. You know what they are. ○

- **Is the spelling correct?** Spell-checkers pick up some obvious gaffes but may not be any help with proper nouns or other special items—such as your professor's last name. They also don't catch correctly spelled words that simply aren't the ones you meant to use: *the* instead of *then*, *rein* instead of *reign*, and so on.

understand citation styles p. 470

help with common errors p. 566

Your Turn   Advice about revising can sound abstract, but the process is a real one you engage in regularly—or should. In a discussion with your classmates (or in a paragraph or two), describe your habits of revision. Explore questions such as the following:

- Do you revise as you write, or do you prefer to wait until you have a full draft?

- How willing are you to make big changes in a draft?

- Have you ever been embarrassed or hurt by what seemed like minor errors?

- Do you know your specific areas of weakness, and how do you address them?

- Do you allow yourself enough time to give your projects a close second look? Should you?

- Have you ever had a surprising success with a paper you wrote at the last minute and turned in almost unrevised?

1 Put the paper aside for a few days (or at least a few hours) before revising.

2 Print out the paper, clear space on your desk, and read with fresh eyes. Does the paper respond to the assignment? Will it make sense to readers?

3 Read your paper aloud to yourself, your roommate, your goldfish — anyone who will listen. Mark the parts that confuse you or your audience.

36

Peer Editing

Many people get nervous when asked to play editor, though such requests come all the time: "Read this for me?" Either they don't want to offend a friend or classmate with their criticisms or they have doubts about their own abilities. These are predictable reactions, but you need to get beyond them.

Your job in peer editing drafts is not to criticize other writers but to help them. And you will accomplish that best by approaching a project honestly, from the perspective of a typical reader. You may not grasp all the finer points of grammar, but you will know if a paper is boring, confusing, or unconvincing. Writers need this response.

And yet most peer editors in college or professional situations focus on tiny matters, such as misspellings or commas, and ignore arguments that completely lack evidence or paragraphs dull enough to make accountants yawn. Of course, spelling and punctuation errors are easy to catch. It's much tougher to suggest that whole pages need to be redone or that a colleague should do better research. But there's nothing charitable about ignoring these deeper issues when a writer's grade or career may be on the line. So what should you do?

First, before you edit any project, agree on ground rules for making comments. It is painless to annotate electronic drafts since you don't have to touch or change the original file. But writers may be more protective of paper copies of their work. Always ask whether you may write comments on a paper and then make sure that your handwriting is legible and your remarks are identified.

Peer edit the same way you revise your own work. As suggested in Chapter 35, pay attention to global issues first. ○ Examine the purpose, audience, and subject matter of the project before dealing with its sentence structure, grammar, or mechanics. Deal with these major issues in a thoughtful and supportive written comment at the end of the paper. Use marginal comments and proofreading symbols (see pp. 431–32) to highlight mechanical problems. But don't correct these items. Leave it to the writer to figure out what is wrong.

Be specific in identifying problems or opportunities. For instance, it doesn't help a writer to read "organization is confusing." Instead, point to places in the draft that went off track. If one sentence or paragraph exemplifies a particular problem—or strength—highlight it in some fashion and mention it in the final comment. Nothing helps a writer less than vague complaints or cheerleading:

> *You did a real good job, though I'm not sure you supported your thesis.*

It's far better to write something like the following:

> *Your thesis on the opening page is clear and challenging, but by the second page, you have forgotten what you are trying to prove. The paragraphs there don't seem connected to the original claim, and I don't find strong evidence to support the points you do make. Restructure these opening pages?*

Too tough? Not at all. The editor takes the paper seriously enough to explain why it's not working.

Offer suggestions for improvement. You soften criticism when you follow it up with reasonable suggestions or strategies for revision. It's fine, too, to direct writers to resources they might use, from better sources to more effective software. Avoid the tendency, however, to revise the paper for your classmate or to recast it to suit your own opinions.

> No passion in the world is equal to the passion to alter someone else's draft.

—H. G. Wells

Library of Congress, Prints and Photographs Division, LC-DIG-ggbain-21320.

Praise what is genuinely good in the paper.   An editor can easily over-look what's working well in a paper, yet a writer needs that information as much as any apt criticism. Find something good to say, too, even about a paper that mostly doesn't work. You'll encourage the writer, who may be facing some lengthy revisions. But don't make an issue of it. Writers will know immediately if you are scraping bottom to find something to praise. Here's a detailed com-ment at the end of a first draft that makes many helpful moves, from encourag-ing a writer to making quite specific criticisms.

> *Whit,*
>
> *I liked your draft and the direction your paper is going. Your use of imagery throughout was spot-on. I've never seen the movie* Mad Max, *but I can see the post-apocalyptic setting in my head.*
>
> *Your thesis is clear and concise, but as we discussed, perhaps you can do away with the low-budget innovation portion? That way you can focus on the film's themes and social impact, both of which relate more to why* Mad Max *should be treated as a film classic. . . . Also, focus more of your energy on the movie's influence because I think that is the best argument to support your claim.*
>
> *I do think your paper could benefit from more personal ethos: Say you are an avid film watcher and a humble fan of the movie so that the reader can trust your opinion easily.*
>
> *In terms of style, I found some of your sentences to be long and overbearing. Switch up short and long sentences so the reader can move through the paper easily.*
>
> *I think that's it. I can't wait to read the final draft of this paper, because I know it's going to be good. Good luck.*
>
> *— Stefan*

Use proofreading symbols.   Proofreading marks may seem fussy or imper-sonal, but they can be a useful way of quickly highlighting some basic errors or omissions. Here are some you might want to remember and use when editing a paper draft.

SP	Word misspelled (not a standard mark, but useful)
X	Check for error here (not a standard mark)
ℐ	Delete marked item
⌒	Close up space
∧	Insert word or phrase
⌄	Insert comma
⸌⸍ ⸌⸍	Insert quotation marks
≡	Capitalize
⊙	Insert period
⎵	Transpose or reverse the items marked
¶	Begin new paragraph
#	Insert or open up space
(ital)	Italicize word or phrase

Keep comments tactful.   Treat another writer's work the way you'd like to have your own efforts treated. Slips in writing can be embarrassing enough without an editor tweeting about them.

Your Turn   Anderson Cooper of CNN reported on a teacher in North Carolina suspended without pay for two weeks for writing "Loser" on a sixth-grader's papers. Apparently the student wasn't offended because the teacher was known to be a "jokester," but administrators were. Did they overreact with the suspension (without pay), or should teachers and editors show discretion when commenting on something as personal as writing? Is there any room for sarcasm when peer editing? Make the case, one way or the other, in an exploratory paragraph.

How to... Insert a comment in a Word document

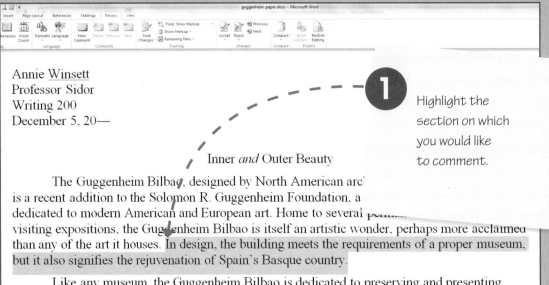

1 Highlight the section on which you would like to comment.

2 On the "Review" tab, click "New Comment."

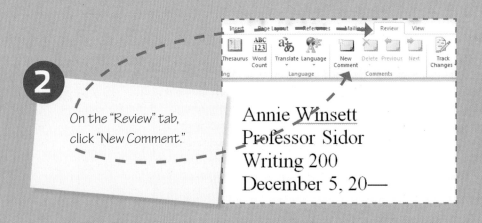

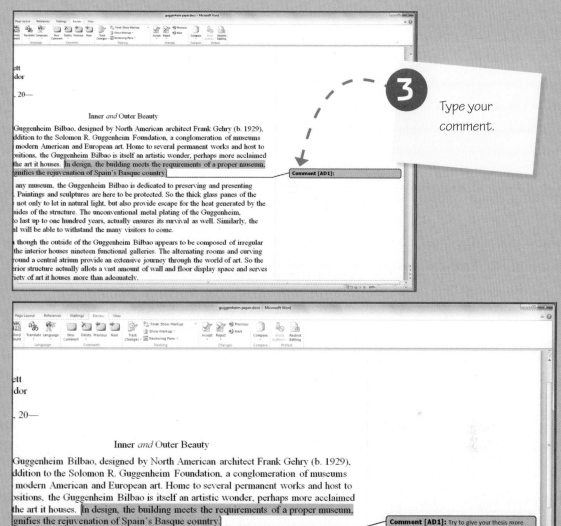

3 Type your comment.

4 ✓ Done.

Comment [AD1]: Try to give your thesis more context. Is this unique? How have other structures failed in comparison, either as functional museums or as cultural emblems?

Research & Sources

part seven

37 Beginning Your Research

Research can be part of any writing project. When doing research, you examine what is already known about a topic and then, sometimes, push the boundaries of knowledge forward. For humanities courses, this typically involves examining a wide range of books, articles, and Web sources. In the social and natural sciences, you might perform experiments or do field research and then share new data you have collected on a topic. For more on choosing a genre, see the Introduction.

plan a project

Quality Research

So where do you begin your research project, and how do you keep from being swamped by the sheer quantity of information available? You need smart research strategies.

Research Organizations

Know your assignment. When one is provided, review the assignment sheet for any project to establish exactly the kinds of research the paper requires. You may need to use only the reference section of the library for a one-page position paper related to a class discussion. An argument about current events will usually send you to newspapers, magazines, and Web sites, while a full-length term paper will need references drawn from academic books and journals. (For details and advice on a wide variety of assignments, refer to Parts 1 and 2.)

Come up with a plan. Research takes time because you have to find sources, read them, record your findings, and then write about them. Most research projects also require full documentation and some type of formal presentation, either as a research paper or, perhaps, an oral report. This stuff cannot be thrown together the night before. One way to avoid mayhem is to prepare a project calendar that ties specific tasks to specific dates. Simply creating the schedule (and you should keep it *simple*) might even jump-start your actual research. At a minimum, record important due dates in your phone or day planner. Here's a full schedule for a serious research paper with three key deadlines.

Research is formalized curiosity. It is poking and prying with a purpose.

—**Zora Neale Hurston**

Photo by Carl Van Vechten/ Library of Congress, Prints and Photographs Division, LC-USZ62-79898.

Schedule: Research Paper

February 20: Topic proposal due
____ Explore and select a topic
____ Do preliminary library/Web research
____ Define a thesis or hypothesis
____ Prepare an annotated bibliography
March 26: First draft due
____ Read, summarize, paraphrase, and synthesize sources
____ Organize the paper
____ Draft the paper
April 16: Final draft due
____ Get peer feedback on draft
____ Revise the project
____ Check documentation
____ Edit the project

Find a manageable topic.   For a research project, this often means defining a problem you can solve with available resources. (For advice on finding and developing topics, see Part 3.) Look for a question within the scope of the assignment that you can answer in the time available.

When asked to submit a ten- or twenty-page term paper, some writers panic, thinking they need a massive, general topic to fill up all those blank pages. But the opposite is true. You will have more success finding useful sources if you break off small but intriguing parts of much larger subjects.

not Military Aircraft, *but* The Development of Jet Fighters in World War II

not The History of Punk Rock, *but* The Influence of 1970s Punk Rock on Nirvana

not Developmental Disorders in Children, *but* Cri du Chat Syndrome

It's fine to read widely at first to find a general subject. But you have to narrow the project to a specific topic so that you can explore focused questions in your preliminary research. At this early stage in the research process, your goal is to turn a topic idea into a claim at least one full sentence long. ○

In the natural and social sciences, topics sometimes evolve from research problems already on the table in various fields. Presented with such a research agenda, do a "review of the literature" to find out what represents state-of-the-art thinking on the topic. You do this by reading what others have published on this subject in major journals. Then create an experiment in which your specific research question—offered as a claim called a *hypothesis*—either confirms the direction of ongoing work in the field or advances or changes it. In basic science courses, get plenty of advice from your instructor about formulating workable research questions and hypotheses.

Ask for help.   During preliminary research, you'll quickly learn that not all sources are equal. ○ They differ in purpose, method, media, audience, and authority. Until you get your legs as a researcher, never hesitate to ask questions about research tools and strategies: Get recommendations about the best available journals, books, and authors from instructors and reference librarians. Ask them which publishers, institutions, and experts carry the most intellectual weight in their fields. If your topic is highly specialized, expect to spend additional time tracking down sources from outside your own library.

Distinguish between primary and secondary sources.   A *primary source* is a document that provides an eyewitness account of an event or phenomenon; a *secondary source* is a step or two removed, an article or book that interprets or reports on events and phenomena described in primary sources. The famous Zapruder film of the John F. Kennedy assassination in Dallas (November 22, 1963) is a memorable primary historical document; the many books or articles that draw on the film to comment on the assassination are secondary sources. Both types of sources are useful to you as a researcher.

develop a
statement p. 362

find reliable
sources p. 451

Use primary sources when doing research that breaks new ground. Primary sources represent raw data—letters, journals, newspaper accounts, official documents, laws, court opinions, statistics, research reports, audio and video recordings, and so on. Working with primary materials, you generate your own ideas about a subject, free of anyone else's opinions or explanations. Or you can review the actual evidence others have used to make their claims and arguments, perhaps reinterpreting their findings, correcting them, or bringing a new perspective to the subject.

Use secondary sources to learn what others have discovered or claimed about a subject. In many fields, you spend most of your time reviewing secondary materials, especially when a subject is new to you. Secondary sources include scholarly books and articles, encyclopedias, magazine pieces, and many Web sites. In academic assignments, you may find yourself moving between different kinds of materials, first reading a primary text like _Hamlet_ and then reading various commentaries on it.

Record every source you examine.   Whether you examine sources in libraries or look at them online, _you must_ accurately list, right from the start, every research item you encounter, gathering the following information:

- Authors, editors, translators, sponsors (of Web sites), or other major contributors
- Titles, subtitles, edition numbers, and volumes

Web sites featuring government resources, such as Thomas or FedStats, and corporate annual reports provide primary material for analysis. _Left:_ Thomas/Library of Congress, http://thomas.loc.gov. _Center:_ FedStats, http://fedstats.gov. _Right:_ Courtesy, General Motors.

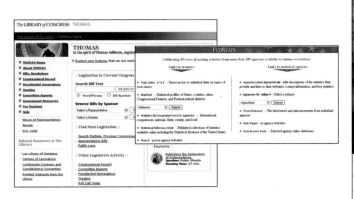

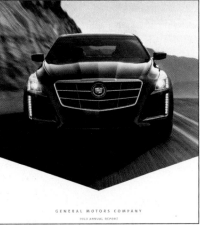

- Publication information, including places of publication and publishers (for books); titles of magazines and journals, as well as volume and page numbers; dates of publication and access (the latter for online materials)

- Page numbers, URLs, electronic pathways, keywords, DOI (digital object identifier), or other locators

You'll need this information later to document your sources.

It might seem obsessive to collect so much data on books and articles you may not even use. But when you spend weeks or months on an assignment, you don't want to have to backtrack, wondering at some point, "Did I read this source?" A log tells you whether you have.

Prepare a topic proposal.   Your instructor may request a topic proposal. Typically, this includes a topic idea, a draft thesis or hypothesis, potential sources, your intended approach, and a list of potential problems. It may also include an annotated bibliography of the books, articles, and other materials you anticipate using in your project—see Chapter 11 for more on annotated bibliographies.

Remember that such proposals are written to get feedback about your project's feasibility and that even a good idea raises questions. The following sample proposal for a short project is directed chiefly at classmates, who must respond via electronic discussion board as part of the assignment.

Books and magazines often provide secondary, not primary, information. *Top:* Book-cover from the book *Through the Language Glass: Why the World Looks Different In Other Languages* by Guy Deutscher. Book-cover design by Steve Attardo and Rodrigo Corral. Book-cover design copyright © 2011 by Steve Attardo and Rodrigo Corral. Used by permission of Henry Holt and Company, LLC. All rights reserved. *Bottom:* Reprinted by permission from Macmillan Publishers Ltd: *Nature*, copyright © 2008.

Eades 1

Micah Eades

Professor Kurtz

English 201

March 20, 20--

Causal Analysis Proposal: Awkward Atmospheres

People don't like going to the doctor's office. You wait in an office room decorated from the 1980s reading *Highlights* or last year's *Field & Stream* and listen to patients in the next room talking about the details of their proctology exam. Since I am planning a future as a primary care physician, I don't want people to dread coming to see me.

My paper will propose that patient dissatisfaction with visits to their physicians may be due not entirely to fear of upcoming medical examinations but rather to the unwelcoming atmosphere of most waiting and treatment rooms. More specifically, I will examine the negative effect that noise, poor interior design, and unsympathetic staff attitudes may have on patient comfort. I will propose that these factors have a much larger impact on patient well-being than previously expected. Additionally, I will propose possible remedies and ways to change these negative perceptions.

My biggest problem may be finding concrete evidence for my claims. For evidence, I do intend to cite the relatively few clinical studies that have been conducted on patient satisfaction and atmosphere. My audience will be a tough crowd: doctors who have neither an awareness of the problems I describe nor much desire to improve the ambience of their offices.

Title indicates that proposal responds to a specific assignment.

Opening paragraph offers a rationale for subject choice.

Describes planned content and structure of paper.

Has done enough research to know that literature on subject is not extensive.

Paper will be directed to a specific audience.

38

Finding Print and Online Sources

refine your
search

When writing an academic paper that requires facts, data, and reputable research or opinion, look to three resources in this order: local and school libraries, informational databases and indexes, and the Internet. Libraries remain your first resource because they have been set up specifically to steer you toward materials appropriate for academic projects. Informational databases and indexes are usually available to you only through libraries and their Web sites, so they are a natural follow-up. And the Internet places third on this list, an undeniably useful resource but still a rugged frontier when it comes to reliable information, particularly for a novice.

Search libraries strategically.   At the library you'll find books, journals, newspapers, and other materials, both print and electronic, in a collection expertly overseen by librarians and information specialists, who are, perhaps, the most valuable resources in the building. They are specifically trained to help you find what you need. Get to know them.

Of course, the key to navigating a library is its catalog. All but the smallest or most specialized libraries now organize their collections electronically (rather than with printed cards), but there's still a learning curve. The temptation will be to plunge in and start searching. After all, you can locate most items by author, title, subject, keywords, and even call number. But spend a few minutes reading the available Help screens to discover the features and protocols of the catalog. Most searches tell you immediately if the library has a book or journal you need, where it is on the shelves or in data collections, and whether it is available.

Do not ignore, either, the advanced features of a catalog (such as searches by language, by date, by type of content); these options help you find just the items you need or can use. And since you will often use a library not to find specific materials but to choose and develop topics, pay attention to the keywords or search terms the catalog uses to index the subject you're exploring: You can use index terms for sources you find to look for other similar materials—an important way of generating leads on a subject.

Explore library reference tools.   In the age of Wikipedia, it's easy to forget that libraries still offer truly authoritative source materials in their reference rooms or online reference collections. Such standard works include encyclopedias, almanacs, historical records, maps, archived newspapers, and so on.

Quite often, for instance, you will need reliable biographical facts about important people—dates of birth, countries of origin, schools attended, career paths, and so on. You *might* find enough data from a Web search or a Wikipedia entry for people currently in the news. But to get accurate and substantial materials on historical figures, consult library tools such as the *Oxford Dictionary of National Biography* (focusing on the United Kingdom) or the *Dictionary of American Biography*. The British work is available in an up-to-date online version. Libraries also have many more specialized biographical tools, both in print and online. Ask about them.

If you want information from old newspapers, you may need ingenuity. Libraries don't store newspapers, so local and a few national papers will be available only in clumsy (though usable) microfilm or microfiche form. Just as discouraging, very few older newspapers are indexed. So, unless you know the approximate date of an event, you may have a tough time finding a particular story in the microfilmed copies of newspapers. Fortunately, both the *New York*

In addition to author, title, and publication information, the full entry for an item in a library catalog will also include subject headings. These terms may suggest additional avenues of research. Chicago Public Library.

Times and *Wall Street Journal* are indexed and available in most major libraries. You'll also find older magazines on microfilm. These may be indexed (up to 1982) in print bibliographies such as the *Readers' Guide to Periodical Literature*. Ask a librarian for assistance.

When your local library doesn't have resources you need, ask the people at the checkout or reference desks about interlibrary loan. If cooperating libraries have the books or materials you want, you can borrow them at minimal cost. But plan ahead. The loan process takes time.

Use professional databases.   Information databases and indexes—our second category of research materials—are also found at libraries, among their electronic resources. These tools give you access to professional journals, magazines, and newspaper archives, in either summary or full-text form. Your library or school purchases licenses to make these valuable, often password-protected, resources available—services such as *EBSCOhost*, *InfoTrac*, and *Lexis-Nexis*. And, once again, librarians can teach you how to navigate such complex databases efficiently.

Many academic research projects, for instance, begin with a search of multi-disciplinary databases such as *LexisNexis Academic*, *Academic OneFile*, or *Academic Search Premier*. These über-indexes cover a wide range of materials, including newspapers, reputable magazines, and many academic periodicals. Most libraries subscribe to one or more of these information services, which you can search online much like library catalogs, using basic and advanced search features.

For even more in-depth research, you need to learn to use databases within your specific field or major, tools such as *Ei* in engineering or the *MLA International Bibliography* in language and literature studies. There are, in fact, hundreds of such databases, far too many to list here, and some of them may be too specialized or technical for projects early in a college career. Librarians or instructors can direct you to the ones you can handle and, when necessary, explain how to use them. Such databases are sometimes less accessible than they seem at first glance.

Explore the Internet.   As you well know, you can find information simply by exploring the Web from your laptop or tablet, using search engines such as Google and Bing to locate data and generate ideas. The territory may seem familiar because you spend so much time there, but don't overestimate your ability to find what you need online. Browsing the Web daily to check sports scores and favorite blogs is completely different from using the Web for academic work.

For a tutorial on online research, see **macmillanhighered.com/howtowrite3e**.
Tutorials > Digital Writing > Online Research Tools

Research suggests that many students begin their projects by simply typing obvious terms into Web browsers, ignoring the advanced capabilities of search engines. To take more control of searches, follow the links on search engine screens that you now probably ignore: Learn to use the tools such as Advanced Search; Search Help; Help; Fix a Problem; Tips & Tricks; Useful Features; and More. You'll be amazed what you discover.

Then exercise care with Web sources. Always be sure you know who is responsible for the material you are reading (for instance, a government agency, a congressional office, a news service, a corporation), who is posting it, who is the author of the material or sponsor of the Web site, what the date of publication is, and so on. ○ A site's information is often skewed by those who pay its bills or run it; it can also be outdated if no one regularly updates the resource.

Keep current with Web developments too. Web companies such as Google are making more books and journal articles both searchable and available through their sites. Examine these resources as they come online. For instance, a tool such as Google Scholar will direct you to academic studies and scholarly papers on a given topic—exactly the kind of material you want to use in term papers or reports.

As an experiment, you might compare the hits you get on a topic with a regular Google search with those that turn up when you select the Scholar option. You'll quickly notice that the Scholar items are more serious and technical—and also more difficult to access. In some cases, you may see only an abstract of a journal article or the first page of the item. Yet the materials you locate may be worth a trip to the library to retrieve in their entirety.

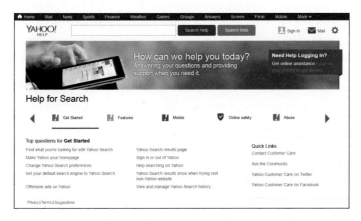

The Yahoo! Help screen provides tips on how to search the Internet. Reproduced with permission of Yahoo. © 2014 Yahoo. YAHOO! and the YAHOO! logo are registered trademarks of Yahoo.

find reliable
sources p. 451

Resources to Consult When Conducting Research

Source	What It Provides	Usefulness in Academic Research	Where to Find It
Scholarly Books	Fully documented and detailed primary research and analyses by scholars	Highly useful if not too high-level or technical	Library, Google Scholar
Scholarly Journals	Carefully documented primary research by scientists and scholars	Highly useful if not too high-level or technical	Library, databases
Newspapers	Accounts of current events	Useful as starting point	Library, microfilm, databases (*LexisNexis*), Internet
Magazines	Wide topic range, usually based on secondary research; written for popular audience	Useful if magazine has serious reputation	Libraries, newsstands, databases (*EBSCOhost*, *InfoTrac*), Internet
Encyclopedias (General or Discipline-Specific)	Brief articles	Useful as starting point	Libraries, Internet
Wikipedia	Open-source encyclopedia: entries written/edited by online contributors	Not considered reliable for academic projects	Internet: www.wikipedia.org
Special Collections	Materials such as maps, paintings, artifacts, etc.	Highly useful for specialized projects	Libraries, museums; images available via Internet
Government, Academic, or Organization Web Sites	Vast data compilations of varying quality, some of it reviewed	Highly useful	Internet sites with URLs ending in *.gov*, *.edu*, or *.org*
Commercial Web Sites	Information on many subjects; quality varies	Useful if possible biases are known	Internet sites
Blogs	Controlled, often highly partisan discussions of specialized topics	Useful when affiliated with reputable sources such as newspapers	Internet
Personal Web Sites	Often idiosyncratic information	Rarely useful; content varies widely	Internet

Doing Field Research

39

While most writing you do will be built on the work of others—
that is, their books, articles, and fact-finding—you can do research
of your own in many situations. For instance, you might interview
people with experiences or information related to the subject you're
exploring. ○ Or you could support a claim for a psychology or
marketing paper by carefully observing and recording how people
actually think or behave.

interview
and observe

Field research is done
in many ways and with
different tools and media.
Left: TopFoto/The Image Works.
Center: TopFoto/The Image Works.
Right: PA Photos/Landov.

ask for
help p. 350

Interview people with unique knowledge of your subject.   When considering whether an interview makes sense for your project, ask yourself this important question: "What do I expect to learn from the interviewee?" If the information you seek is easily available online or in print, don't waste everyone's time going through with an interview. If, on the other hand, this person offers a fresh perspective on your topic, a personal interview could advance your research.

Interviews can be written or spoken. Written interviews, whether by e-mail or letter, instant messaging or online chat, allow you to keep questions and answers focused and provide a written record of the interviewee's responses. But spoken interviews, both in person and via Skype, allow in-depth discussion of a topic and may lead to more memorable reactions and deeper insights. Be flexible in setting up the type of interview most convenient for your subject. For oral interviews, keep the following suggestions in mind:

- Request an interview formally by phone, confirming it with a follow-up message.

- Give your subjects a compelling reason for meeting or corresponding with you; briefly explain your research project and why their knowledge or experience is important to your work.

- Let potential interviewees know how you chose them as subjects. If possible, identify a personal reference—that is, a professor or administrator who can vouch for you.

- Prepare a set of purposeful interview questions. Don't try to wing it.

- Think about how to phrase questions to open up the interview. Avoid queries that can be answered in one word. Don't ask, *Did you enjoy your years in Asia?* Instead, lead with, *What did you enjoy most about the decade you spent in Tokyo?*

- Start the interview by thanking the interviewee for his or her time and providing a very brief description of your research project.

- Keep a written record of material you intend to quote. If necessary, confirm the exact wording with your interviewee.

- End the interview by again expressing your thanks.

● Follow up with a thank-you note or e-mail and, if the interviewee's contributions were substantial, send him or her a copy of the final research
  paper.

● In your paper, give credit to any people interviewed by documenting the
  information they provided. ○

For an interview conducted in person, arrive at the predetermined meeting
place on time and dressed professionally. If you wish to record the interview, be
sure to ask permission first.

If you conduct your interview in writing, request a response by a certain
date—one or two weeks is reasonable for ten questions. Refer to Chapter 13 for
e-mail etiquette and Chapter 14 for guidelines on writing business letters.

For telephone interviews, call from a place with good reception, where you
will not be interrupted. Your cell phone should be fully charged or plugged in.

> **Your Turn**   Prepare a full set of questions you would use to interview a
> classmate about some *academic* issue—for example, study habits, methods
> for writing papers, or career objectives. Think about how to sequence your
> questions, how to avoid one-word responses, and how to follow up on pos-
> sible replies (if the interview is oral). Write your questions down and then
> pair up with a classmate for a set of mutual interviews.
>
> When you are done, write a one-page report based on what you learn
> and share the results with classmates.

Make careful and verifiable observations.   The point of systematic observation is to provide a reliable way of studying a narrowly defined activity or
phenomenon. But in preparing reports or arguments that focus on small groups
or local communities, you might find yourself without enough data to move
your claims beyond mere opinion.

For example, an anecdote or two won't persuade administrators that
community rooms in the student union are being scheduled inefficiently. But
you could conduct a simple study of these facilities, showing exactly how many
student groups use them and for what purposes, over a given period of time.

understand citation
styles p. 470

This kind of evidence usually carries more weight with readers, who can decide whether to accept or challenge your numbers.

Some situations can't be counted or measured as readily as the one described above. If you wanted, let's say, to compare the various community rooms to determine whether those with windows encouraged more productive discussions than rooms without, your observations would be "softer" and more qualitative. You might have to describe the tone of speakers' voices or the general mood of the room. But numbers might play a part; you could, for instance, track how many people participated in the discussion or the number of tasks accomplished during the meeting.

To avoid bias in their observations, many researchers use double-column notebooks. In the first column, they record the physical details of their observation as objectively as possible—descriptions, sounds, countable data, weather, time, circumstances, activity, and so on. In the second column, they record their interpretations and commentaries on the data.

In addition to careful and objective note-taking techniques, devices such as cameras, video recorders, and tape recorders provide reliable backup evidence about an event. Also, having more than one witness observe a situation can help verify your findings.

Learn more about fieldwork.   In those disciplines or college majors that use fieldwork, you will find guides or manuals to explain the details of such research procedures. You will also discover that fieldwork comes in many varieties, from naturalist observations and case studies to time studies and market research.

A double-column notebook entry.

OBSERVABLE DATA	COMMENTARY
9/12/11 2 P.M. Meeting of Entertainment Committee Room MUB210 (no windows) 91 degrees outside Air conditioning broken People appear quiet, tired, hot	Heat and lack of a/c probably making everyone miserable.

Evaluating Sources

40

In Chapter 38, you were directed to the best possible print and online sources for your research. But the fact is, all sources, no matter how prestigious, have strengths and weaknesses, biases and limitations. Even the most well-intentioned instructors, librarians, and experts have their preconceptions too. So evaluating the sources you've either found or been directed to is a necessary part of the research process. Here are some strategies for making those judgments.

find reliable sources

Preview source materials for their key features and strategies.
Give any source a quick once-over, looking for clues to its aim, content, and structure. Begin with the title and subtitle, taking seriously its key terms and qualifiers. A good title tells what a piece is—and is not—about. For many scholarly articles, the subtitle (which typically follows a colon) describes the substance of the argument.

Then scan the introduction (in a book) or abstract (in an article). From these items, you should be able to quickly grasp what the source covers, what its methods are, and what the author hopes to prove or accomplish.

Inspect the table of contents in a book or the headings in an article methodically, using them to figure out the overall structure of the work or to find specific information. Briefly review charts, tables, and illustrations, too, to discover what they offer. If a book has an index—and a serious book should—look for the key terms or subjects you are researching to see how well they are covered.

If the work appears promising, read its final section or chapter. Knowing how the material concludes gives insight into its value for your research. Finally, look over the bibliography. The list of sources indicates how thorough the author has been and, not incidentally, points you to other materials you might want to examine.

Check who published or produced the source.   In general, books published by presses associated with colleges and universities (Harvard, Oxford, Stanford, etc.) are reputable sources for college papers. So are articles from professional journals described as *refereed* or *peer-reviewed*. These terms are used for journals in which the articles have been impartially evaluated by panels of experts prior to publication. Instructors and librarians can help you grasp these distinctions.

You can also usually rely on material from reputable commercial publishers and from established institutions and agencies. The *New York Times*; the *Wall Street Journal*; Random House; Farrar, Straus & Giroux; Simon & Schuster; and the U.S. Government Printing Office make their ample share of mistakes, of course, but are generally considered to be far more reliable than most blogs or personal Web sites. But you always need to be cautious.

Check who wrote a work.   Ordinarily, you should cite recognized authorities on your topic. Look for authors who are mentioned frequently and favorably within a field or whose works appear regularly in notes or bibliographies. Get familiar with them.

The Web makes it possible to examine the careers of other authors whom you might not recognize. Search for their names online to confirm that they are reputable journalists or recognized experts in their field. Avoid citing authors working too far beyond their areas of professional expertise. Celebrities especially like to cross boundaries, sometimes mistaking their passion for an issue (environmentalism, diet, public health) for genuine mastery of a subject.

Consider the audience for a source.   What passes for adequate information in the general marketplace of ideas may not cut it when you're doing academic research. Many widely read books and articles that popularize a subject—such as climate change or problems with education—may, in fact, be based on more technical scholarly books and articles. For academic projects, rely primarily on those scholarly works themselves, even if you were inspired to choose a subject by reading respectable nonfiction. Glossy magazines shouldn't play a role in your research either, though the lines can get blurry. *People, O, Rolling Stone,* or *Spin* might be important if you are writing about popular culture or music. Similarly, Wikipedia is invaluable for a quick introduction to a subject, but don't cite it as an authority in an academic paper.

Establish how current a source is.   Scholarly work doesn't come with an expiration date, but you should base your research on the latest information. For fields in which research builds on previous work, the date of publication may even be highlighted within its system of documentation. For books, you'll find the date of publication on the copyright page, which is the reverse side of the title page (see p. 487).

Check the source's documentation.   All serious scholarly and scientific research is documented. Claims are based on solid evidence backed up by formal notes, data are packed into charts and tables, and there is a bibliography at the end. All of this is done so that readers can verify the claims an author makes.

In a news story, journalists may establish the credibility of their information by simply naming their sources or, at a minimum, attributing their findings to reliable unnamed sources—and usually more than one. The authors of serious magazine pieces don't use footnotes and bibliographies either, but they, too, credit their major sources somewhere in the work. No serious claim should be left hanging. O

For your own academic projects, avoid authors and sources with undocumented assertions. Sometimes you have to trust authors when they are writing about personal experiences or working as field reporters, but let readers know when your claims are based on uncorroborated personal accounts.

Entertainer Jenny McCarthy has disturbed many public health officials by her claims of a connection between childhood vaccination and autism. She has a personal connection to the issue but no medical or scientific credentials. Dennis Van Tine/Newscom.

think critically
p. 343

You can learn a lot about a
source by previewing a few
basic elements.

Available online at www.sciencedirect.com

SCIENCE @ DIRECT®

ACADEMIC
PRESS

Journal of Research in Personality 36 (2002) 607–614

JOURNAL OF
RESEARCH IN
PERSONALITY

www.academicpress.com

Brief report

Are we barking up the right tree?
Evaluating a comparative approach
to personality

Samuel D. Gosling * and Simine Vazire

Department of Psychology, University of Texas, Austin, TX, USA

Playful title nonetheless
fits: Article is about
animals.

Abstract

Animal studies can enrich the field of human personality psychology by addressing questions that are difficult or impossible to address with human studies
alone. However, the benefits of a comparative approach to personality cannot be
reaped until the tenability of the personality construct has been established in animals. Using criteria established in the wake of the person–situation debate (Kenrick & Funder, 1988), the authors evaluate the status of personality traits in
animals. The animal literature provides strong evidence that personality does exist
in animals. That is, personality ratings of animals: (a) show strong levels of inte-
robserver agreement, (b) show evidence of validity in terms of predicting behaviors and real-world outcomes, and (c) do not merely reflect the implicit theories of
observers projected onto animals. Although much work remains to be done,
the preliminary groundwork has been laid for a comparative approach to personality.
© 2002 Elsevier Science (USA). All rights reserved.

Abstract previews entire
article.

Introduction

Personality characteristics have been examined in a broad range of non-
human species including chimpanzees, rhesus monkeys, ferrets, hyenas, rats,

Headings throughout
signal this is a research
article.

* Corresponding author. Fax: 1-512- 471-5935.
E-mail address: gosling@psy.utexas.edu (S.D. Gosling).

0092-6566/02/$ - see front matter © 2002 Elsevier Science (USA). All rights reserved.
PII: S0092-6566(02)00511-1

608   *Brief report / Journal of Research in Personality 36 (2002) 607–614*

sheep, rhinoceros, hedgehogs, zebra finches, garter snakes, guppies, and oc-
topuses (for a full review, see Gosling, 2001). Such research is important because animal studies can be used to tackle questions that are difficult or
impossible to address with human studies alone. By reaping the benefits
of animal research, a comparative approach to personality can enrich the
field of human personality psychology, providing unique opportunities to
examine the biological, genetic, and environmental bases of personality,
and to study personality development, personality-health links, and personality perception. However, all of these benefits hinge on the tenability of the
personality construct in non-human animals. Thus, the purpose of the present paper is to address a key question in the animal domain: is personality
real? That is, do personality traits reflect real properties of individuals or are
they fictions in the minds of perceivers?

Thirty years ago, the question of the reality of personality occupied the
attention of human-personality researchers, so our evaluation of the comparative approach to personality draws on the lessons learned in the human domain. Mischel's (1968) influential critique of research on human
personality was the first of a series of direct challenges to the assumptions
that personality exists and predicts meaningful real-world behaviors. Based
on a review of the personality literature, Mischel (1968) pointed to the lack
of evidence that individuals' behaviors are consistent across situations (Mischel & Peake, 1982). Over the next two decades, personality researchers
garnered substantial empirical evidence to counter the critiques of personality. In an important article, Kenrick and Funder (1988) carefully analyzed the various arguments that had been leveled against personality
and summarized the theoretical and empirical work refuting these arguments.

The recent appearance of studies of animal personality has elicited renewed debate about the status of personality traits. Gosling, Lilienfeld,
and Marino (in press) proposed that the conditions put forward by Kenrick
and Funder (1988) to evaluate the idea of human personality can be mobi-
lized in the service of evaluating the idea of animal personality. Gosling et
al. (in press) used these criteria to evaluate research on personality in non-
human primates. In the present paper, we extend their analysis to the broader field of comparative psychology, considering research on nonhuman
animals from several species and taxa. Kenrick and Funder's paper delin-
eates three major criteria that must be met to establish the existence of personality traits: (1) assessments by independent observers must agree with
one another; (2) these assessments must predict behaviors and real-world
outcomes; and (3) observer ratings must be shown to reflect genuine attributes of the individuals rated, not merely the observers' implicit theories
about how personality traits covary. Drawing on evidence from the animal-
behavior literature, we evaluate whether these three criteria have been met
with respect to animal personality.

Point of this brief study is
defined at end of opening
paragraph.

This page reviews literature
on studies of animal
personality.

41 Annotating Sources

analyze
claims and
evidence/
take notes

Once you locate trustworthy sources, review them to zero in on the best ideas and most convincing evidence for your project. During this process of critical reading, you annotate, summarize, ○ synthesize, ○ and paraphrase ○ your sources—in effect creating the notes you need to compose your paper.

Annotate sources to understand them.   Examine important sources closely enough to figure out not only what they say but also how the authors reached their conclusions or gathered their data. Think of it as becoming an expert on the sources you cite. To preserve your ideas, mark up key texts with tools that work for you—notes in the margins, Post-it notes, electronic comments, and so forth. Simply writing these comments will draw you deeper into source materials and make you think more about them.

Read sources to identify claims.   Begin by highlighting any specific claims, themes, or thesis statements a writer offers early in a text. Then pay attention to the way these ideas recur throughout the work, especially near the conclusion. At a minimum, decide whether a writer has made reasonable claims, developed them consistently, and delivered on promised evidence. In the example on pages 457–59, claims and reasons are highlighted in yellow.

Read sources to understand assumptions.   Finding and annotating the assumptions in a source can be *much* trickier than

sum up
ideas p. 460

understand
synthesis p. 272

restate
ideas p. 463

locating claims. Highlight any assumptions stated outright in the source; they will be rare. More often, you have to infer a writer's assumptions, put them into your own words, and perhaps record them in marginal notes. Identifying controversial or debatable assumptions is particularly important. For instance, if a writer makes the claim that *America needs tighter border security to prevent terrorist attacks*, you draw the inference that the writer believes that terrorism is caused by people crossing inadequately patrolled borders. Is that assumption accurate? Should the writer explain or defend it? Raise such questions. The one key assumption in the example that follows is highlighted in orange.

Read sources to find evidence.   Look for evidence that an author uses to support both the claims and assumptions in a text. Evidence can come in the form of data, examples, illustrations, or logical inferences. Since most academic materials you read will be thick with evidence, highlight only key items— especially any facts or materials you intend to mention in your own project. Make sure no crucial point goes unsupported; if you find one, make a note of it. In the following example, key evidence is highlighted in blue.

Record your personal reactions to source material.   When reading multiple sources, you'll want a record of what you favored or objected to in them. To be certain you don't later mistake your personal comments for observations *from* the source, use first person or pose questions as you respond. Use personal annotations, as well, to draw connections to other source materials you have read. In the following example, personal reactions appear on the left.

SANITY 101

Parents of adolescents usually strive for an aura of calm and reason. But just two words can trigger irrational behavior in parent and child alike: "college admissions."

It's not an unreasonable response, actually, given the list of exasperating questions facing parents seeking to maximize their children's prospects: Do I tutor my child to boost college admissions test scores? Do I

CLAIM AND REASON: Fear of college admissions procedures is key point in editorial.

rely on the school admissions counselor or hire a private adviser? Do I hire a professional editor to shape my child's college essay?

CLAIM

EVIDENCE

The price tags behind those decisions drive up the angst. A testing tutor "guaranteeing" a 200-point score boost on the SAT admissions test will charge roughly $2,400. Hiring a private college counselor can cost from $1,300 to $10,000. And hiring an essay editor can cost between $60 and $1,800. Wealthy suburbs are particularly lucrative for the college prep industry. Less affluent families are left with even greater reason to fret: Their children face an unfair disadvantage.

EVIDENCE:
Specific concerns support initial claim. They are the issues troubling parents most.

READER'S REACTION:
Why don't colleges realize how unfair their admissions policies might be to poorer applicants?

Now, private employers are stepping in to help out.

In a front-page article on Tuesday, *USA Today's* education reporter Mary Beth Marklein revealed a range of counseling packages that companies are offering parents of college applicants, from brown-bag discussion lunches to Web-based programs that manage the entire admissions process.

CLAIM

EVIDENCE

It's thoughtful of the employers, but it shouldn't be necessary.

READER'S REACTION:
Might there be a parallel here to out-of-control sports programs? Why are schools so poorly administered?

Thanks to overanxious parents, aggressive college admissions officials, and hustling college prep entrepreneurs, the admissions system has spun out of control. And the colleges have done little to restore sanity.

Take just one example, the "early decision" process in which seniors apply to a college by November 1 and promise to attend if admitted.

CLAIM:
This assertion, midway through editorial, may in fact be its thesis.

EVIDENCE

Early decision induces students to cram demanding courses into their junior year so they will appear on the application record. That makes an already stressful year for students and parents even more so. Plus, students must commit to a college long before they are ready. The real advantages of early decision go to colleges, which gain more control over their student mix and rise in national rankings by raising their acceptance rates.

Parents and students can combat the stress factor by keeping a few key facts in mind. While it's true that the very top colleges are ruthlessly selective — both Harvard and Yale accept slightly less than 10 percent of applicants — most colleges are barely selective. Of the 1,400 four-year colleges in the United States, only about 100 are very selective, and they aren't right for every student. Among the other 1,300, an acceptance rate of about 85 percent is more the norm.

And the best part of all: Many of those 1,300 colleges are more interested in educating your child than burnishing their rankings on lists of the "top" institutions. So the next time you hear the words "college admissions," don't instantly open your wallet. First, take a deep breath.

—Editorial/Opinion, *USA Today*, January 19, 2006

CLAIM AND REASON: Parents are worrying too much.

EVIDENCE: Statistics offer reasons not to fear college admissions procedures.

ASSUMPTION: Change "are" to "should be" and you have the assumption underlying this entire argument.

Your Turn   Exchange a draft of a paper you are developing with that of a classmate. Then read your colleague's paper closely, as outlined in this chapter, imagining how you might use it as a source. First highlight its major claims and reasons; then identify any key assumptions in the paper. Bracket the sections of the project that primarily offer evidence. Finally, offer your personal reactions to various parts of the paper.

You might use highlighting pens of different colors to separate claims/reasons from assumptions and evidence, as in the sample essay.

Summarizing Sources

sum up ideas

Once you determine which materials deserve closer attention and you have read these articles, books, and other texts critically—with an eye toward using their insights and data in your research project—you're ready to summarize the individual items, putting ideas you've found into your own words. These brief summaries or fuller paraphrases can become the springboard for composing your paper. ○

Prepare a summary for every item you examine in a project. This advice seems self-evident, but it is not. A quick look may tell you that an article or book has no bearing on your project. Even so, describe it very briefly on a note card or in an electronic file (with complete bibliographic data). Such a record reminds you that you have, in fact, seen and reviewed that item—which can be no small comfort when working on projects that stretch over several weeks or months. After you've examined dozens and dozens of sources, it's easy to forget what exactly you've read.

Use a summary to recap what a writer has said. When a source is clearly relevant to your project, look carefully for its main point and build your summary on it, making sure that this state-ment *does* reflect the actual content of the source, not your opinion of it. Be certain that the summary is *entirely* in your own words. Include the author and title of the work, too, so you can easily cite

restate
ideas p. 463

it later. The following is one summary of the *USA Today* editorial reprinted on pages 457–59, with all the required citation information:

> In "Sanity 101," the editors of *USA Today* (January 19, 2006) criticize current college admission practices, which, they argue, make students and parents alike fear that getting into an appropriate school is harder than it really is.
>
> Source: "Sanity 101." Editorial. *USA Today* 19 Jan. 2006: 10A. Print.

Be sure your summary is accurate and complete.   Even when a source makes several points, moves in contradictory directions, or offers a complex conclusion, your job is simply to describe what the material does. Don't embellish the material or blur the distinction between the source's words and yours. Include all bibliographical information (title, author, and date) from the source. The following summary of "Sanity 101" shows what can go wrong if you are not careful.

> According to *USA Today*, most students get into the colleges they want. But admission into most colleges is so tough that many parents blow a fortune on tutors and counselors so that their kids can win early admission. But the paper's advice to parents is don't instantly open your wallet. First, take a deep breath.

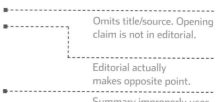

Omits title/source. Opening claim is not in editorial.

Editorial actually makes opposite point.

Summary improperly uses source's exact words. Might lead to inadvertent plagiarism later on.

Use a summary to record your take on a source.   In addition to reporting the contents of the material accurately, note also how the source might (or might not) contribute to your paper. But make certain that your comments won't be confused with claims made in the summarized article itself. The following are two acceptable sample summaries for "Sanity 101."

> In "Sanity 101," *USA Today* (January 19, 2006) describes the efforts of college applicants and parents to deal with the progressively more competitive admissions policies of elite institutions. The editorial claims that most schools, however, are far less selective. The article includes a reference to another *USA Today* piece by Mary Beth Marklein on the support some companies offer employees to assist them with college admissions issues.
>
> Source: "Sanity 101." Editorial. *USA Today* 19 Jan. 2006: 10A. Print.

In an editorial (January 19, 2006) entitled "Sanity 101," *USA Today* counsels parents against worrying too much about hypercompetitive current college admission practices. In reality, only a small percentage of schools are highly selective about admissions. The editorial doesn't provide the schools' side of the issue.

Source: "Sanity 101." Editorial. *USA Today* 19 Jan. 2006: 10A. Print.

Use summaries to prepare an annotated bibliography.   In an annotated bibliography, brief summaries are provided for every item in an alphabetical list of sources. These summaries help readers understand the content and scope of materials. For more about annotated bibliographies, see Chapter 11. ○

Your Turn   Practice writing summaries by pairing up with a classmate and finding (probably online) a newspaper or blog page with a variety of opinion-oriented articles. For instance, check out the "Opinion" page in the *New York Times* or the home page of *Arts & Letters Daily* or the *Huffington Post*.

Agree on one or two pieces that both of you will recap separately. Then write the paired summaries, being careful to identify the items, describe them accurately, and separate your recaps from any comments you make about the material you have read. When you are done, compare your summaries. Discuss their accuracy and make certain that neither of you has inadvertently borrowed language from the original articles.

understand annotated
bibliographies p. 266

Paraphrasing Sources

Paraphrases provide more complete records of the research materials you examine than do summaries. ○ Like a summary, a paraphrase records a book or article's main point, but it also recaps the reasons and key evidence supporting that conclusion. Paraphrase any materials you expect to use extensively in a project. Then consider how the research materials you have gathered stand in relationship to each other.

Identify the major claims and the structure of the source. Determine the main points made by the article, chapter, or text you are paraphrasing, and examine how the work organizes information to support its claims. ○ Then follow the same structure when you paraphrase the source. For example, your paraphrase will probably be arranged sequentially when a work has a story to tell, be arranged topic by topic when you're dealing with reported information, or be structured logically—by claims and evidence—when you take notes from arguments or editorials.

Track the source faithfully. A paraphrase should move through an article, chapter, or book succinctly while remaining faithful to its purpose, organization, tone, and, to some extent, style. In effect, you are preparing an abstract of the material, complete and readable on its own. Take concise and practical notes, adapting the paraphrase to your needs—understanding that materials especially valuable to your project will need to be described thoroughly. ○

restate
ideas

sum up
ideas p. 460

think
critically p. 343

take notes
p. 456

Record key pieces of evidence.   Thanks to photocopies and downloaded files, you don't usually have to copy data laboriously into your notes—and you probably shouldn't. (Chances of error greatly multiply whenever you transcribe information by hand.) Be certain, though, that your paraphrase sets down supporting reasons for all major claims in the source, as well as key evidence and facts. Key evidence is whatever proves a point or seals the deal in an argument. Keep track of page numbers for all the important data so you can cite this material in your paper without having to return to the original source.

Be certain your notes are entirely in your own words.   If you copy the language of sources as you paraphrase them, you risk plagiarism. Deliberately or not, you could transfer big chunks of someone else's writing into your project. But if you have paraphrased by the rules, setting all borrowed words between quotation marks, it's safe to import those notes directly into your project— giving the original writers due credit for their ideas, of course. When you write competent paraphrases, you've already started to compose your own paper. There is no lost motion.

The following is a possible paraphrase of "Sanity 101," the complete, fully annotated text of which appears in Chapter 41 (pp. 457–59). Compare the paraphrase here to the briefer summaries of the article that appear in Chapter 42 (pp. 461–62).

> In an editorial entitled "Sanity 101" (January 19, 2006), the editors of *USA Today* worry that many fearful parents are resorting to costly measures to help assure their child's college admission, some hiring private counselors and tutors that poorer families can't afford. Companies now even offer college admission assistance as part of employees' job packages. Colleges themselves are to blame for the hysteria, in part because of "early admission" practices that benefit them more than students. But parents and students should consider the facts. Only a handful of colleges are truly selective; most have acceptance rates near 85 percent. In addition, most schools care more about students than about their own rankings.

Avoid misleading or inaccurate paraphrasing.   Your notes won't be worth much if your paraphrases of sources distort the content of what you read. Don't rearrange the information, give it a spin you might prefer, or offer your own opinions on a subject. Make it clear, too, whenever your comments focus just on particular sections or chapters of a source, rather than on the entire piece. That way, you won't misread your notes days later and give readers a wrong impression about an article or book. The following is a paraphrase of "Sanity 101" that gets almost *everything* wrong.

> Parents of teens usually try to be reasonable, the editors of *USA Today* complained on January 19, 2006. But the words "college admission" can make both child and parent irrational. The response is not unreasonable, given all the irritating questions facing parents seeking to improve their children's prospects. But the fact is that just a few colleges are highly selective. Most of the four-year schools in the country have acceptance rates of 85 percent. So high school students and parents should just chill and not blow their wallets on extra expenses. Rely on the school admissions counselor; don't hire a private adviser or professional editor to shape your child's college essay. A testing tutor might charge $2,400; a private college counselor can cost from $1,300 to $10,000. This is unfair to poorer families too, especially when companies start offering special admissions services to their employees. As always, the colleges are to blame, with their pushy "early admissions" programs, which make them look good in rankings but just screw their students.

Opening sentences follow language of editorial too closely and also distort structure of editorial.

Paraphrase shifts tone, becoming much more colloquial than editorial.

Paraphrase borrows words and phrases too freely from original.

Opinion offered here distorts what is in the editorial.

Use your paraphrases to synthesize sources.   If you are asked to prepare a literature review or synthesis paper on a subject, begin that work by carefully summarizing and paraphrasing a range of reputable sources. For more about synthesis and synthesis papers, see Chapter 12. ○

> **Your Turn**   Practice writing paraphrases by pairing up with a classmate and choosing a full essay to paraphrase from Part 1 of this book.
>
>   Write your paraphrases of the agreed-upon essay separately, just as if you intended to cite the piece later in a report, research paper, or argument yourself. When both of you are done, compare your paraphrases. What did you identify as the main point(s) or thesis of the piece? What kind of structure did the article follow: for example, narrative, report, comparison/contrast, argument, and so on? What evidence or details from the article did you include in your paraphrases? How do your paraphrases compare in length?
>
>   Discuss the differences. How might you account for them?

understand synthesis
papers p. 272

44 Incorporating Sources into Your Work

avoid
plagiarism/
use
quotations

When you incorporate sources into your research projects cogently, you give readers information they need to appraise the thinking you've done. They discover what you've read and learned and how much purchase you have on ideas. Yet introducing borrowed ideas and quoted passages into papers is far from easy. You have to help readers identify paraphrased or quoted items, and you need to clearly identify any edits you made to quotations for accuracy or clarity.

Cue the reader in some way whenever you introduce borrowed material.   Readers *always* need to know what words and ideas are yours and what you have culled from other authors. So give them a verbal signal whenever you summarize, paraphrase, or quote directly from sources. Think of it as *framing* these borrowed materials to set them off from your own work. Such frames offer many options for introducing either ideas or direct quotes drawn from sources:

EXACT WORDS

Michelle Obama argued on *The View* that "... [quotation]."

"[Quotation] ... ," says Jack Welch, former CEO of General Electric, pointing out that "... [more quotation]."

SUMMARIZED FACTS

According to a report in *Scientific American* (October 2012), the Mars rover *Curiosity* will soon ... [your own words].

PARAPHRASED IDEA

Can a person talk intelligently about books even without reading them? Pierre Bayard, for one, suggests that . . . [your own words].

YOUR SUMMARY WITH QUOTATION

In *Encounters with the Archdruid*, author John McPhee introduces readers to conservationist David Brower, whom he credits with [your own words], calling him " . . . [quotation]."

As you see, a frame can introduce, interrupt, follow, or even surround the words or ideas taken from sources, but be sure that your signal phrases are grammatical and lead smoothly into the material.

Select an appropriate "verb of attribution" to frame borrowed material.

These "signal verbs" influence what readers think of borrowed ideas or quoted material. Use neutral verbs of attribution in reports; save descriptive or even biased terms for arguments. Note that, by MLA convention, verbs of attribution are usually in the present tense when talking about current work or ideas. (In APA, these verbs are generally in the past or present perfect tense.)

Verbs of Attribution

Neutral	Descriptive	Biased
adds	acknowledges	admits
explains	argues	charges
finds	asserts	confesses
notes	believes	confuses
offers	claims	derides
observes	confirms	disputes
says	disagrees	evades
shows	responds	impugns
states	reveals	pretends
writes	suggests	smears

MLA and APA Style

The examples in this section follow MLA (Modern Language Association) style, covered in Chapter 46. For information on APA (American Psychological Association) style, see Chapter 47.

Use ellipsis marks [. . .] to shorten a lengthy quotation.   When quoting a source in your paper, it's not necessary to use every word or sentence, as long as the cuts you make don't distort the meaning of the original material. An ellipsis mark, formed from three spaced periods, shows where words, phrases, full sentences, or more have been removed from a quotation. The mark doesn't replace punctuation within a sentence. Thus, you might see a period or a comma immediately followed by an ellipsis mark.

ORIGINAL PASSAGE

Although gift giving has been a pillar of Hopi society, trade has also flourished in Hopi towns since prehistory, with a network that extended from the Great Plains to the Pacific Coast, and from the Great Basin, centered on present-day Nevada and Utah, to the Valley of Mexico. Manufactured goods, raw materials, and gems drove the trade, supplemented by exotic items such as parrots. The Hopis were producers as well, manufacturing large quantities of cotton cloth and ceramics for the trade. To this day, interhousehold trade and barter, especially for items of traditional manufacture for ceremonial use (such as basketry, bows, cloth, moccasins, pottery, and rattles), remain vigorous.

— Peter M. Whiteley, "Ties That Bind: Hopi Gift Culture and Its First Encounter with the United States," *Natural History*, November 2004, p. 26

Highlighting shows words to be deleted when passage is quoted.

PASSAGE WITH ELLIPSES

Whiteley has characterized the practice this way:

Although gift giving has been a pillar of Hopi society, trade has also flourished in Hopi towns since prehistory. . . . Manufactured goods, raw materials, and gems drove the trade, supplemented by exotic items such as parrots. The Hopis were producers as well, manufacturing large quantities of cotton cloth and ceramics for the trade. To this day, interhousehold trade and barter, especially for items of traditional manufacture for ceremonial use, . . . remain vigorous. (26)

Ellipses show where words have been deleted.

Use brackets [ ] to insert explanatory material into a quotation.   By convention, readers understand that the bracketed words are not part of the original material.

Writing in the *London Review of Books* (January 26, 2006), John Lancaster describes the fears of publishers: "At the moment Google says they have no intention of providing access to this content [scanned books still under copyright]; but why should anybody believe them?"

Use ellipsis marks, brackets, and other devices to make quoted materials fit the grammar of your sentences.   Sometimes, the structure of sentences you want to quote won't quite match the grammar, tense, or perspectives of your own surrounding prose. If necessary, cut up a quoted passage to slip appropriate sections into your own sentences, adding bracketed changes or explanations to smooth the transition.

ORIGINAL PASSAGE

Among Chandler's most charming sights are the business-casual dads joining their wives and kids for lunch in the mall food court. The food isn't the point, let alone whether it's from Subway or Dairy Queen. The restaurants merely provide the props and setting for the family time. When those kids grow up, they'll remember the food court as happily as an older generation recalls the diners and motels of Route 66 — not because of the businesses' innate appeal but because of the memories they evoke.

—Virginia Postrel, "In Defense of Chain Stores," *The Atlantic*, December 2006

> Words to be quoted are highlighted.

MATERIAL AS QUOTED

People who dislike chain stores should ponder the small-town America that cultural critic Virginia Postrel describes, one where "business-casual dads [join] their wives and kids for lunch in the mall food court," a place that future generations of kids will remember "as happily as an older generation recalls the diners and motels of Route 66."

> Words quoted from source are highlighted.

Use [sic] to signal an obvious error in quoted material.   You don't want readers to blame a mistake on you, and yet you are obligated to reproduce a quotation exactly—including blunders in the original. You can highlight an error by putting *sic* (the Latin word for "thus") in brackets immediately following the mistake. The device says, in effect, that this is the way you found it.

The late Senator Edward Kennedy once took Supreme Court nominee Samuel Alito to task for his record: "In an era when America is still too divided by race and riches, Judge Alioto [sic] has not written one single opinion on the merits in favor of a person of color alleging race discrimination on the job."

45 Documenting Sources

understand
citation
styles

Required to document your research paper? It seems simple in theory: List your sources and note where and how you use them. But the practice can be intimidating. For one thing, you have to follow rules for everything from capitalizing titles to captioning images. For another, documentation systems differ between fields. What worked for a Shakespeare paper won't transfer to your psychology research project. Bummer. What do you need to do?

Understand the point of documentation. Documentation systems differ to serve the writers and researchers who use them. Modern Language Association (MLA) documentation, which you probably know from composition and literature classes, highlights author names, books, and article titles and assumes that writers will be quoting a lot—as literature scholars do. American Psychological Association (APA) documentation, gospel in psychology and social sciences, focuses on publication dates because scholars in these fields value the latest research. Council of Science Editors (CSE) documentation, used in the hard sciences, provides predictably detailed advice for handling formulas and numbers.

So systems of documentation aren't arbitrary. Their rules simply reflect the specialized needs of writers in various fields.

Understand what you accomplish through documentation. First, you clearly identify the sources you have used. In a world awash with information, readers really do need to have reliable information about titles, authors, data, media of publication, and so on.

 For a tutorial on documentation, see **macmillanhighered.com/howtowrite3e.**
Tutorials > Documentation and Working with Sources > Do I Need to Cite That?

In addition, by citing your sources, you certify the quality of your research and, in turn, receive credit for your labor. You also provide evidence for your claims. An appreciative reader or instructor can tell a lot from your bibliography alone.

Finally, when you document a paper, you encourage readers to follow up on your work. When you've done a good job, serious readers will want to know more about your subject. Both your citations and your bibliography enable them to take the next step in their research.

Style Guides Used in Various Disciplines

Field or Discipline	Documentation and Style Guides
Anthropology	*AAA Style Guide* (2009) and *Chicago Manual of Style* (16th ed., 2010)
Biology	*Scientific Style and Format: The CSE Manual for Authors, Editors, and Publishers* (8th ed., 2014)
Business and management	*The Business Style Handbook: An A-to-Z Guide for Writing on the Job* (2nd ed., 2012)
Chemistry	*The ACS Style Guide: Effective Communication of Scientific Information* (3rd ed., 2006)
Earth sciences	*Geowriting: A Guide to Writing, Editing, and Printing in Earth Science* (rev. ed., 2004)
Engineering	Varies by area; *IEEE Standards Style Manual* (online)
Federal government	*United States Government Printing Office Manual* (30th ed., 2008)
History	*Chicago Manual of Style* (16th ed., 2010)
Humanities	*MLA Handbook for Writers of Research Papers* (7th ed., 2009)
Journalism	*The Associated Press Stylebook and Briefing on Media Law* (2013); *UPI Stylebook and Guide to Newswriting* (4th ed., 2004)
Law	*The Bluebook: A Uniform System of Citation* (19th ed., 2010)
Mathematics	*A Manual for Authors of Mathematical Papers* (8th ed., 1990)
Music	*Writing about Music: An Introductory Guide* (4th ed., 2008)
Nursing	*Writing for Publication in Nursing* (2nd ed., 2010)
Political science	*The Style Manual for Political Science* (2006)
Psychology	*Publication Manual of the American Psychological Association* (6th ed., 2010)
Sociology	*American Sociological Association Style Guide* (4th ed., 2010)

MLA Documentation and Format

The style of the Modern Language Association (MLA) is used in many humanities disciplines. For complete details about MLA style, consult the *MLA Handbook for Writers of Research Papers*, 7th ed. (2009). The basic details for documenting sources and formatting research papers in MLA style are presented below.

cite in MLA

Document sources according to convention.   When you use sources in a research paper, you are required to cite the source, letting readers know that the information has been borrowed from somewhere else and showing them how to find the original material if they would like to study it further. An MLA-style citation includes two parts: a brief in-text citation and a more detailed works cited entry to be included in a list at of the end of your paper.

In-text citations must include the author's name as well as the number of the page where the borrowed material can be found. The author's name (shaded in orange) is generally included in the signal phrase that introduces the passage, and the page number (shaded in yellow) is included in parentheses after the borrowed text.

> Frazier points out that the Wetherill-sponsored expedition to explore Chaco Canyon was roundly criticized (43).

Alternatively, the author's name can be included in parentheses along with the page number.

> The Wetherill-sponsored expedition to explore Chaco Canyon was roundly criticized (Frazier 43).

At the end of the paper, in the works cited list, a more detailed citation includes the author's name as well as the title (shaded in green) and publication information about the source (shaded in blue).

Frazier, Kendrick. *People of Chaco: A Canyon and Its Culture.* Rev. ed. New York: Norton, 1999. Print.

Both in-text citations and works cited entries can vary greatly depending on the type of source cited (book, periodical, Web site, etc.). The following pages give specific examples of how to cite a wide range of sources in MLA style.

Directory of MLA In-Text Citations

1. Author named in signal phrase 474
2. Author named in parentheses 474
3. With block quotations 474
4. Two or three authors 475
5. Four or more authors 475
6. Group, corporate, or government author 475
7. Two or more works by the same author 475
8. Authors with same last name 476
9. Unidentified author 476
10. Multivolume work 476
11. Work in an anthology 476
12. Entry in a reference book 477
13. Literary work 477
14. Sacred work 478
15. Entire work 478
16. Secondary source 478
17. No page numbers 478
18. Multiple sources in the same citation 479

MLA in-text citation

1. Author Named in Signal Phrase

Include the author's name in the signal phrase that introduces the borrowed material. Follow the borrowed material with the page number of the source in parentheses. Note that the period comes after the parentheses. For a source without an author, see item 9; for a source without a page number, see item 17.

> According to Seabrook, "astronomy was a vital and practical form of knowledge" for the ancient Greeks (98).

2. Author Named in Parentheses

Follow the borrowed material with the author and page number of the source in parentheses, and end with a period. For a source without an author, see item 9; for a source without a page number, see item 17.

> For the ancient Greeks, "astronomy was a vital and practical form of knowledge" (Seabrook 98).

Note: Most of the examples below follow the style of item 1, but naming the author in parentheses (as shown in item 2) is also acceptable.

3. With Block Quotations

For quotations of four or more lines, MLA requires that you set off the borrowed material indented one inch from the left-hand margin. Include the author's name in the introductory text (or in the parentheses at the end). End the block quotation with the page number(s) in parentheses, *after* the end punctuation of the quoted material.

> Jake Page, writing in *American History*, underscores the significance of the well-organized Pueblo revolt:
>
> > Although their victory proved temporary, in the history of Indian-white relations in North America the Pueblo Indians were the only Native Americans to successfully oust European invaders from their territory. . . . Apart from the Pueblos, only the Seminoles were able to retain some of their homeland for any length of time, by waging war from the swamps of the Florida Everglades. (36)

4. Two or Three Authors

If your source has two or three authors, include all their names in either the signal phrase or parentheses.

> Muhlheim and Heusser assert that the story "analyzes how crucially our actions are shaped by the society . . . in which we live" (29).

> According to some experts, "Children fear adult attempts to fix their social lives" (Thompson, Grace, and Cohen 8).

5. Four or More Authors

If your source has four or more authors, list the first author's name followed by "et al." (meaning "and others") in the signal phrase or parentheses.

> Hansen et al. estimate that the amount of fish caught and sold illegally worldwide is between 10 and 30 percent (974).

6. Group, Corporate, or Government Author

Treat the name of the group, corporation, or government agency just as you would any other author, including the name in either the signal phrase or the parentheses.

> The United States Environmental Protection Agency states that if a public water supply contains dangerous amounts of lead, the municipality is required to educate the public about the problems associated with lead in drinking water (3).

7. Two or More Works by the Same Author

If your paper includes two or more works by the same author, add a brief version of the works' titles (shaded in green) in parentheses to help readers locate the right source.

> Mills suggests that new assessments of older archaeological work, not new discoveries in the field, are revising the history of Chaco Canyon ("Recent Research" 66). She argues, for example, that new analysis of public spaces can teach us about the ritual of feasting in the Puebloan Southwest (Mills, "Performing the Feast" 211).

8. Authors with Same Last Name

If your paper includes two or more sources whose authors have the same last name, include a first initial with the last name in either the signal phrase or the parentheses.

> According to T. Smith, "[A]s much as 60 percent of the computers sold in India are unbranded and made by local assemblers at about a third of the price of overseas brands" (12).

9. Unidentified Author

If the author of your work is unknown, include a brief title of the work in parentheses.

> Though a single language, Spanish varies considerably, a fact that "befuddles advertisers who would aim to sell to the entire Spanish-speaking world, like the shampoo-maker who discovered that *cabello chino* ("Chinese hair") means curly hair in almost all Latin America save Ecuador, where it means straight hair" ("The Rise of Spanish" 1).

10. Multivolume Work

If you cite material from more than one volume of a multivolume work, include in the parentheses the volume number followed by a colon before the page number. (See also item 11, on p. 485, for including multivolume works in your works cited list.)

> Odekon defines *access-to-enterprise zones* as "geographic areas in which taxes and government regulations are lowered or eliminated as a way to stimulate business activity and create jobs" (1: 2).

11. Work in an Anthology

Include the author of the work in the signal phrase or parentheses. There is no need to refer to the editor of the anthology in the in-text citation; this and other details will be included in the works cited list at the end of your paper.

> Vonnegut suggests that *Hamlet* is considered such a masterpiece because "Shakespeare told us the truth, and [writers] so rarely tell us the truth" (354).

12. Entry in a Reference Book

In the signal phrase, include the author of the entry you are referring to, if there is an author. In the parentheses following the in-text citation, include the title of the entry and the page number(s) on which the entry appears.

> Willis points out that the Empire State Building, 1,250 feet tall and built in just over one year, was a record-breaking feat of engineering ("Empire State Building" 375-76).

For reference entries with no author (such as dictionaries), simply include the name of the article or entry in quotation marks along with the page reference in parentheses.

> Supersize—one of the newest pop culture terms added to the dictionary— is a verb meaning "to increase considerably the size, amount, or extent of" ("Supersize" 714).

13. Literary Work

Include as much information as possible to help readers locate your borrowed material. For classic novels, which are available in many editions, include the page number, followed by a semicolon, and additional information such as book ("bk."), volume ("vol."), or chapter ("ch.") numbers.

> At the climax of Brontë's *Jane Eyre,* Jane fears that her wedding is doomed, and her description of the chestnut tree that has been struck by lightning is ominous: "it stood up, black and riven: the trunk, split down the center, gaped ghastly" (274; vol. 2, ch. 25).

For classic poems and plays, include division numbers such as act, scene, and line numbers; do not include page numbers. Separate all numbers with periods. Use Arabic (1, 2, 3, etc.) numerals instead of Roman (I, II, III, etc.) unless your instructor prefers otherwise.

> In Homer's epic poem *The Iliad,* Agamemnon admits that he has been wrong to fight with Achilles, but he blames Zeus, whom he says "has given me bitterness, who drives me into unprofitable abuse and quarrels" (2.375-76).

14. Sacred Work

Instead of page numbers, include book, chapter, and verse numbers when citing material from sacred texts.

> Jesus's association with the sun is undeniable in this familiar passage from the Bible: "I am the light of the world. Whoever follows me will not walk in darkness, but will have the light of life" (John 8.12).

15. Entire Work

When referring to an entire work, there is no need to include page numbers in parentheses; simply include the author's name(s) in the signal phrase.

> Dobelli claims that cognitive errors tend to be ingrained in us, making it likely we'll stumble over the same mistakes again and again unless we alter our way of thinking.

16. Secondary Source

To cite a source you found within another source, include the name of the original author in the signal phrase. In the parentheses, include the term "qtd. in" and give the author of the source where you found the quote, along with the page number. Note that your works cited entry for this material will be listed under the secondary source name (Pollan) rather than the original writer (Howard).

> Writing in 1943, Howard asserted that "artificial manures lead inevitably to artificial nutrition, artificial food, artificial animals, and finally to artificial men and women" (qtd. in Pollan 148).

17. No Page Numbers

If the work you are citing has no page numbers, include only the author's name (or the brief title, if there is no author) for your in-text citation.

> According to Broder, the Federal Trade Commission has begun to police and crack down on false company claims of producing "environmentally friendly" or "green" merchandise.

18. Multiple Sources in the Same Citation

If one statement in your paper can be attributed to multiple sources, alphabetically list all the authors with page numbers, separated by semicolons.

> Two distinct Harlems coexisted in the late 1920s: one a cultural and
> artistic force—the birthplace of a renaissance of literature, music, and
> dance—and the other, a slum and profit center for organized crime
> (Giddins and DeVeaux 132; Gioia 89).

Directory of MLA Works Cited Entries

(Continued)

Directory of MLA Works Cited Entries (*Continued*)

General Guidelines for MLA Works Cited Entries

AUTHOR NAMES

- Authors listed at the start of an entry should be listed last name first and should end with a period.
- Subsequent author names, or the names of authors or editors listed in the middle of the entry, should be listed first name first.

DATES

- Format dates as day month year: 27 May 2014.
- Use abbreviations for all months except for May, June, and July, which are short enough to spell out: Jan., Feb., Mar., Apr., Aug., Sept., Oct., Nov., Dec. (Months should always be spelled out in the text of your paper.)

TITLES

- Italicize the titles of long works — such as books, plays, periodicals, entire Web sites, and films. (Underlining is an acceptable alternative to italics, but note that whichever format you choose, you should be consistent throughout your paper.)
- Titles of short works — such as essays, articles, poems, and songs — should be placed in quotation marks.

PUBLICATION INFORMATION

- Include only the city .name.
- Abbreviate familiar words such as "University" ("U") and "Press" ("P") in the publisher's name. Leave out terms such as "Inc." and "Corp."
- Include the medium of publication for each entry ("Print," "Web," "DVD," "Radio," etc.).

MLA works cited entries

AUTHOR INFORMATION

1. Single Author

> Author's Last Name, First Name. *Book Title*. Publication City: Publisher, Year of
> Publication. Medium.

Bazelon, Emily. *Sticks and Stones: Defeating the Culture of Bullying and
Rediscovering the Power of Character and Empathy*. New York:
Random, 2013. Print.

2. Two or Three Authors

List the authors in the order shown on the title page.

> First Author's Last Name, First Name, and Second Author's First Name Last Name.
> *Book Title*. Publication City: Publisher, Year of Publication. Medium.

Power, Michael L., and Jay Schulkin. *The Evolution of Obesity*. Baltimore:
Johns Hopkins UP, 2009. Print.

Michaels, Ed, Helen Handfield-Jones, and Beth Axelrod. *The War for Talent*.
Boston: Harvard Business School, 2001. Print.

3. Four or More Authors

When a source has four or more authors, list only the name of the first author
(last name first) followed by a comma and the Latin term "et al." (meaning
"and others").

> First Author's Last Name, First Name, et al. *Book Title*. Publication City: Publisher,
> Year of Publication. Medium.

Roark, James L., et al. *The American Promise: A History of the United
States*. 5th ed. Boston: Bedford, 2012. Print.

4. Corporate Author

If a group or corporation rather than a person appears to be the author, include
that name as the work's author in your list of works cited.

Name of Corporation. *Book Title.* Publication City: Publisher, Year of Publication. Medium.

World Health Organization. *Technical Report of the TDR Thematic Reference Group on Environment, Agriculture, and Infectious Diseases of Poverty.* Geneva: WHO, 2013. Print.

5. Unidentified Author

If the author of a work is unknown, begin the works cited entry with the title of the work.

Note that in the example given, "The New Yorker" is not italicized because it is a title within a title (see item 19).

Book Title. Publication City: Publisher, Year of Publication. Medium.

The New Yorker *Top 100 Cartoons.* New York: Cartoon Bank, 2004. Print.

6. Multiple Works by the Same Author

To cite two or more works by the same author in your list of works cited, organize the works alphabetically by title (ignoring introductory articles such as *The* and *A*). Include the author's name only for the first entry; for subsequent entries by this same author, type three hyphens followed by a period in place of the author's name.

Author's Last Name, First Name. *Title of Work.* Publication City: Publisher, Year of Publication. Medium.

---. *Title of Work.* Publication City: Publisher, Year of Publication. Medium.

Krakauer, Jon. *Under the Banner of Heaven: A Story of Violent Faith.* Harpswell: Anchor, 2004. Print.

---. *Three Cups of Deceit: How Greg Mortenson, Humanitarian Hero, Lost His Way.* Harpswell: Anchor, 2011. Print.

BOOKS

7. Book: Basic Format

The example here is the basic format for a book with one author. For author variations, see items 1–6. For more information on the treatment of authors, dates, titles, and publication information, see the box on page 481. After listing the author's name, include the title (and subtitle, if any) of the book, italicized. Next give the publication city, publisher's name, and year. End with the medium of publication.

> Author's Last Name, First Name. *Book Title: Book Subtitle.* Publication City: Publisher, Publication Year. Medium.

> Seeling, Charlotte. *Fashion: 150 Years of Couturiers, Designers, Labels.* Potsdam: Ullmann, 2012. Print.

8. Author and Editor

Include the author's name first if you are referring to the text itself. If, however, you are citing material written by the editor, include the editor's name first, followed by a comma and "ed."

> Author's Last Name, First Name. *Book Title.* Year of Original Publication. Ed. Editor's First Name Last Name. Publication City: Publisher, Year of Publication. Medium.

> Editor's Last Name, First Name, ed. *Book Title.* Year of Original Publication. By Author's First Name Last Name. Publication City: Publisher, Year of Publication. Medium.

> Dickens, Charles. *Great Expectations.* 1861. Ed. Janice Carlisle. Boston: Bedford, 1996. Print.

> Carlisle, Janice, ed. *Great Expectations.* 1861. By Charles Dickens. Boston: Bedford, 1996. Print.

9. Edited Collection

> Editor's Last Name, First Name, ed. *Book Title.* Publication City: Publisher, Year of Publication. Medium.

> Abbott, Megan, ed. *A Hell of a Woman: An Anthology of Female Noir.* Houston: Busted Flush, 2007. Print.

10. Work in an Anthology or a Collection

Author's Last Name, First Name. "Title of Work." *Book Title*. Ed. Editor's First Name
   Last Name. Publication City: Publisher, Year of Publication. Page Numbers
   of Work. Medium.

Okpewho, Isidore. "The Cousins of Uncle Remus." *The Black Columbiad:*
   Defining Moments in African American Literature and Culture. Ed.
   Werner Sollors and Maria Diedrich. Cambridge: Harvard UP, 1994.
   15-27. Print.

11. Multivolume Work

To cite one volume of a multivolume work, include the volume number after
the title. Including the volume number in your list of works cited means that
you do not need to list it in your in-text citation. To cite two or more volumes,
include the number of volumes after the title. In this case, you would need to
include the specific volume number in each of your in-text citations for this
source.

Author or Editor's Last Name, First Name. *Title of Work*. Vol. Number.
   Publication City: Publisher, Year of Publication. Medium.

Odekon, Mehmet, ed. *Encyclopedia of World Poverty*. Vol. 2. Thousand
   Oaks: Sage, 2006. Print.

Author or Editor's Last Name, First Name. *Title of Work*. Number of vols.
   Publication City: Publisher, Year of Publication. Medium.

Odekon, Mehmet, ed. *Encyclopedia of World Poverty*. 3 vols. Thousand
   Oaks: Sage, 2006. Print.

12. Part of a Series

After the title of the book, include the series title and number (if any) from the
title page.

Author or Editor's Last Name, First Name. *Title of Work*. Title and Number of
   Series. Publication City: Publisher, Year of Publication. Medium.

Haugen, David M. *Illegal Immigration*. Opposing Viewpoints Ser.
   Farmington Hills: Greenhaven, 2011. Print.

How to...
Cite from a book (MLA)

BOOK COVER

TITLE PAGE

Andrews McMeel Publishing, LLC
Kansas City · Sydney · London

1 author

2 book title and subtitle

3 city of publication and publisher

When a publisher lists more than one city, use the first one.

For a video tutorial, see **macmillanhighered.com/howtowrite3e**.
Tutorials › Documentation and Working with Sources › How to Cite a Book in MLA Style

COPYRIGHT PAGE

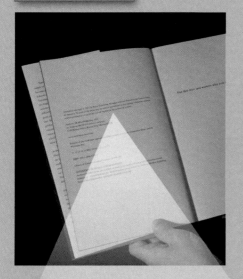

Tomatoland copyright © 2011 by Barry Estabrook.

QUOTED PAGE

145

4 year of publication

5 page number

6 medium

MLA in-text citation

Describing his vision for the new tomato breed, the seed company owner explained, "We were going to start with roadside growers and chefs. People who were interested in good flavor and good quality" (Estabrook 145).

1 **5**

MLA works cited entry

1 **2**

Estabrook, Barry. *Tomatoland: How Modern Industrial Agriculture Destroyed*

3 **4** **6**

Our Most Alluring Fruit. Kansas City: Andrews McMeel, 2011. Print.

13. Republished Book

If the book you are citing was previously published, include the original publication date after the title. If the new publication includes additional text, such as an introduction, include that, along with the name of its author, before the current publication information.

> Author's Last Name, First Name. *Title of Work.* Original Year of Publication. New Material Author's First Name Last Name. Publication City: Publisher, Year of Publication. Medium.

> Davidson, Bruce. *Subway.* 1986. Introd. Fred Brathwaite. New York: Aperture, 2011. Print.

14. Later Edition

Include the edition number as a numeral with letters ("2nd," "3rd," "4th," etc.) followed by "ed." after the book's title. If the edition is listed on the title page as "Revised," without a number, include "Rev. ed." after the title of the book.

> Author(s). *Title of Work.* Number ed. Publication City: Publisher, Year of Publication. Medium.

> Bodley, John H. *Anthropology and Contemporary Human Problems.* 6th ed. Lanham: AltaMira, 2012. Print.

15. Sacred Work

Include the title of the work as it is shown on the title page. If there is an editor or a translator listed, include the name after the title with either "Ed." or "Trans."

> *Title of Work.* Editor or Translator. Publication City: Publisher, Year of Publication. Medium.

> *The King James Bible: 400th Anniversary Edition.* New York: Oxford UP, 2010. Print.

> *The Qur'an.* Trans. M. A. S. Abdel Haleem. New York: Oxford UP, 2008. Print.

16. Translation

Original Author's Last Name, First Name. *Title of Work*. Trans. Translator's First
Name Last Name. Publication City: Publisher, Year of Publication. Medium.

Alighieri, Dante. *Inferno: A New Translation*. Trans. Mary Jo Bang.
Minneapolis: Graywolf, 2012. Print.

17. Article in a Reference Book

If there is no article author, begin with the title of the article.

Article Author's Last Name, First Name. "Title of Article." *Book Title*.
Publication City: Publisher, Year of Publication. Medium.

Dirr, Michael A. "Brunfelsia." *Dirr's Encyclopedia of Trees and Shrubs*.
Portland: Timber, 2011. Print.

"Supreme Court Decisions." *The World Almanac and Book of Facts 2013*.
New York: World Almanac, 2013. Print.

18. Introduction, Preface, Foreword, or Afterword

Book Part Author's Last Name, First Name. Name of Book Part. *Book Title*. Ed. Book
Author or Editor's First Name Last Name. Publication City: Publisher, Year of
Publication. Page Numbers. Medium.

Gladwell, Malcolm. Foreword. *The Book of Basketball: The NBA According to
The Sports Guy*. Bill Simmons. New York: Ballantine, 2009. xi-xiii. Print.

19. Title within a Title

If a book's title includes the title of another long work (play, book, or periodical) within it, do not italicize the internal title.

Author's Last Name, First Name. *Book Title* Title within Title. Publication City:
Publisher, Year of Publication. Medium.

Mayhew, Robert, ed. *Essays on Ayn Rand's* Atlas Shrugged. Lanham:
Lexington, 2009. Print.

PERIODICALS

20. Article in a Scholarly Journal

List the author(s) first, and then include the article title, the journal title (in italics), the volume number, the issue number, the publication year, the page numbers, and the publication medium.

> Author's Last Name, First Name. "Title of Article." *Title of Journal* Volume
>   Number.Issue Number (Year of Publication): Page Numbers. Medium.

> Dorson, James. "Demystifying the Judge: Law and Mythical Violence in
>   Cormac McCarthy's *Blood Meridian.*" *Journal of Modern Literature*
>   36.2 (2013): 105-21. Print.

21. Article in a Scholarly Journal with No Volume Number

Follow the format for scholarly journals (as shown in item 20), but list only the issue number before the year of publication.

> Author's Last Name, First Name. "Title of Article." *Title of Journal* Issue
>   Number (Year of Publication): Page Numbers. Medium.

> Leow, Joanne. "Mis-mappings and Mis-duplications: Interdiscursivity
>   and the Poetry of Wayde Compton." *Canadian Literature* 214 (2012):
>   47-66. Print.

22. Magazine Article

Include the date of publication rather than volume and issue numbers. (See abbreviation rules in the box on p. 481.) If page numbers are not consecutive, add "+" after the initial page.

> Author's Last Name, First Name. "Title of Article." *Title of Magazine* Date of
>   Publication: Page Numbers. Medium.

> Wasik, Bill. "Welcome to the Programmable World." *Wired* June 2013:
>   202-9. Print.

23. Newspaper Article

If a specific edition is listed on the newspaper's masthead, such as "Late Edition" or "National Edition," include an abbreviation of this after the date. If page numbers are not consecutive, add "+" after the initial page.

Author's Last Name, First Name. "Title of Article." *Title of Newspaper* Date of
    Publication: Page Numbers. Medium.

Birnbaum, Michael. "Autobahn Speed Limit Proposal Revs Up Debate in
    Germany." *Washington Post* 20 May 2013: A1+. Print.

Author's Last Name, First Name. "Title of Article." *Title of Newspaper* Date of
    Publication, Spec. ed.: Page Numbers. Medium.

Kaminer, Ariel. "On a College Waiting List? Sending Cookies Isn't Going
    to Help." *New York Times* 11 May 2013, natl ed.: 2. Print.

If a newspaper numbers each section individually, without attaching letters to
the page numbers, include the section number in your citation.

Author's Last Name, First Name. "Title of Article." *Title of Newspaper* Date of
    Publication, sec. Section Number: Page Numbers. Medium.

Bowley, Graham. "Keeping Up with the Windsors." *New York Times* 15
    July 2007, sec. 3: 1+. Print.

24. Editorial

For a newspaper editorial, do not include an author, but do include the word
"Editorial," followed by a period, after the title of the article.

"Title of Article." Editorial. *Title of Newspaper* Date of Publication: Page Number(s).
    Medium.

"Do Teachers Really Discriminate against Boys?" Editorial. *Time* 6 Feb.
    2013: 37. Print.

25. Letter to the Editor

Letter Writer's Last Name, First Name. Letter. *Title of Newspaper* Date of
    Publication: Page Number. Medium.

Le Tellier, Alexandra. Letter. *Los Angeles Times* 18 Apr. 2013: 12. Print.

26. Unsigned Article

"Title of Article." *Title of Newspaper* Date of Publication: Page Number. Medium.

"An Ounce of Prevention." *The Economist* 20 Apr. 2013: 27. Print.

How to...
Cite from a magazine (MLA)

MAGAZINE COVER

ARTICLE

March 2010

By Marcus E. Raichle

1 magazine title

2 publication date

3 author

4 article title

 For a video tutorial, see **macmillanhighered.com/howtowrite3e.**
Tutorials › Documentation and Working with Sources › How to Cite an Article in MLA Style

48

5 page number of quoted passage

44 **49**

6 first and last page numbers of article

7 medium

MLA
in-text
citation

As early as 1929, Hans Berger proposed that "we have to assume that the central nervous system is always, and not only during wakefulness, in a state of considerable activity" (Raichle 48).

3 **5**

3 **4** **1** **2**

MLA
works cited
entry

Raichle, Marcus E. "The Brain's Dark Energy." *Scientific American* Mar.

6 **7**

2010: 44-49. Print.

27. Review

Add "Rev. of" before the title of the work being reviewed.

> Review Author's Last Name, First Name. "Title of Review." Rev. of *Title of Work Being Reviewed*, by Author of Work Being Reviewed First Name Last Name. *Title of Publication in Which Review Appears* Date of Publication: Page Numbers. Medium.

> Gogolak, Emily. "*The Unchangeable Spots of Leopards* Review: How to Become a Person." Rev. of *The Unchangeable Spots of Leopards*, by Kristopher Jansma. *Village Voice* 20 Mar. 2013: 9. Print.

ELECTRONIC SOURCES

28. Short Work from a Web Site

> Short Work Author's Last Name, First Name. "Title of Short Work." *Title of Web Site*. Name of Sponsoring Organization, Date of Publication or Most Recent Update. Medium. Date of Access.

> Frick, Kit. "On Heroism and The Oregon Trail." *Booth*. Butler University, 8 Feb. 2013. Web. 7 July 2014.

29. Entire Web Site

> Web Site Author's Last Name, First Name. *Title of Web Site*. Name of Sponsoring Organization, Date of Publication or Most Recent Update. Medium. Date of Access.

> Zaretsky, Staci. *Above the Law*. Breaking Media, 28 May 2013. Web. 2 Jan. 2014.

30. Entire Blog (Weblog)

Include any of the following elements that are available. If there is no publisher or sponsoring organization, use the abbreviation "N.p."

Blog Author's Last Name, First Name. *Title of Blog.* Name of Sponsoring Organization
(if any), Date of Most Recent Post. Medium. Date of Access.

Asher, Levi. *Literary Kicks*. N.p., 18 May 2013. Web. 23 Sept. 2014.

31. Entry in a Blog (Weblog)

Entry Author's Last Name, First Name. "Title of Blog Entry." *Title of Blog.* Name
of Sponsoring Organization (if any), Date of Entry. Medium.
Date of Access.

Smith, Alisa. "How College Students Can Eat Locally When Held Captive
to a Meal Plan." *The Daily Green*. Hearst Communications, 4 Sept.
2007. Web. 5 Dec. 2014.

32. Online Book

Book Author's Last Name, First Name. *Title of Book.* Book Publication City:
Book Publisher, Book Publication Year. *Title of Web Site.* Medium.
Date of Access.

Wells, H. G. *A Short History of the World*. New York: MacMillan, 1922.
Bartleby.com: Great Books Online. Web. 7 Aug. 2014.

33. Work from a Library Subscription Service (such as *InfoTrac* or *FirstSearch*)

Follow the format for periodical articles as shown in items 20–27, above. If page
numbers are not available, use the abbreviation "n. pag." End the citation with
the database name (in italics), the publication medium ("Web"), and the date of
access.

Article Author(s). "Title of Article." *Title of Periodical* Volume Number.Issue Number
(Year of Publication): Page Numbers. *Name of Database*. Medium.
Date of Access.

Waters, Mary C., et al., eds. "Coming of Age in America: The Transition to
Adulthood in the Twenty-First Century." *American Journal of Sociology*
118.2 (2012): 517-19. *InfoTrac*. Web. 7 Oct. 2014.

How to...
Cite from a Web site (MLA)

TOP OF WEB PAGE

1 Web site title

2 article title

JAD ABUMRAD and
ROBERT KRULWICH

3 author

August 17, 2010

4 update date

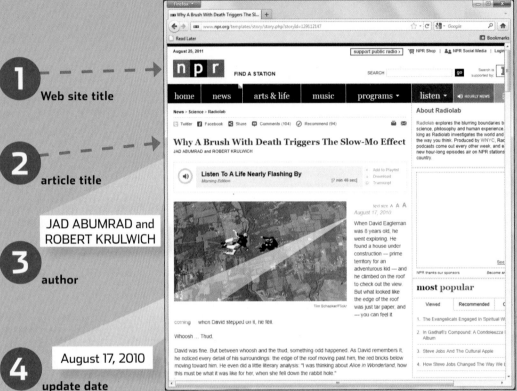

For a video tutorial, see **macmillanhighered.com/howtowrite3e.**
Tutorials > Documentation and Working with Sources > How to Cite a Web Site in MLA Style

BOTTOM OF WEB PAGE

7 medium

Copyright 2011 NPR

5 Web site sponsor

August 25, 2011

6 date of access

MLA in-text citation

Dr. Eagleman suggests that moments of near-death panic prompt the brain to form memories of otherwise-ignored stimuli, and "when you read that back out, the experience feels like it must have taken a very long time" (Abumrad and Krulwich).

3

3 **2**

MLA works cited entry

Abumrad, Jad, and Robert Krulwich. "Why a Brush with Death Triggers the

1 **5** **4** **7** **6**

Slow-Mo Effect." *NPR*. NPR, 17 Aug. 2010. Web. 25 Aug. 2011.

5 volume and issue number

6 publication date

7 name of database

DATABASE SCREEN

1 journal title

2 article title

3 author

4 page numbers

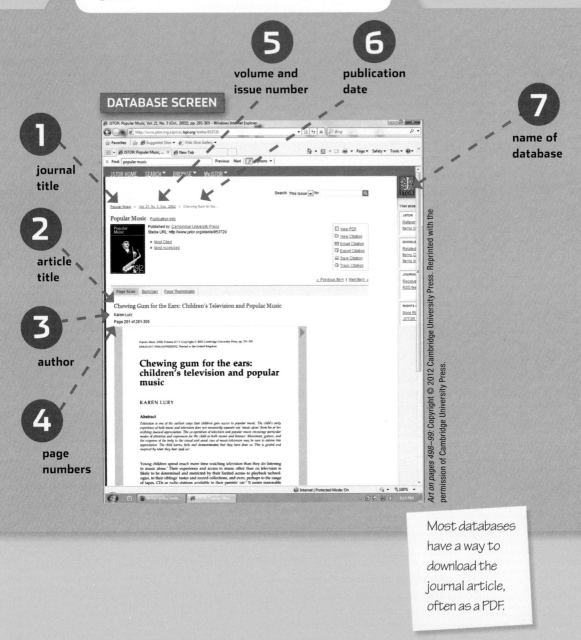

Most databases have a way to download the journal article, often as a PDF.

PDF VIEW

Use the PDF to double-check your citation elements. If you print the PDF, the medium is still Web, not print.

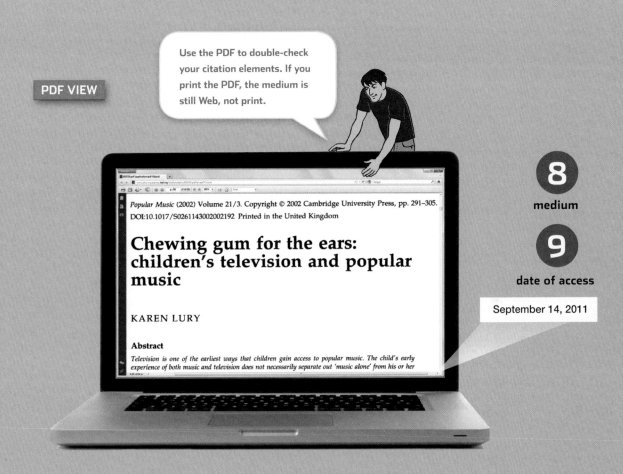

8

medium

9

date of access

September 14, 2011

MLA
in-text
citation

Children accept even nonsensical lyrics as legitimate musical expression, and one researcher calls their tolerance "a mode of engagement carried productively into the adult's experience of popular songs" (Lury 300).

MLA works
cited entry

Lury, Karen. "Chewing Gum for the Ears: Children's Television and Popular Music." *Popular Music* 21.3 (2002): 291-305. *JSTOR*. Web. 14 Sept. 2011.

34. Work from an Online Periodical

Follow the format for periodical articles as shown in items 20–27, above, listing the Web site name, in italics, as the periodical title. For articles in scholarly journals, include page numbers (or the abbreviation "n. pag." if page numbers are unavailable). End the citation with the publication medium ("Web") and the date of access.

> Journal Article Author(s). "Title of Article." *Title of Online Journal* Volume Number.Issue Number (Year of Publication): Page Numbers (or "n. pag."). Medium. Date of Access.

> Clarke, Laura Hurd, and Erica Bennett. "'You Learn to Live with All the Things That Are Wrong with You': Gender and the Experience of Multiple Chronic Conditions in Later Life." *Ageing and Society* 33.2 (2013): 342-60. Web. 27 Dec. 2014.

For articles appearing in online magazines and newspapers, list the publisher's name after the online periodical title. Page numbers are not required for nonscholarly articles published online.

> Magazine or Newspaper Article Author(s). "Title of Article." *Title of Online Periodical.* Periodical Publisher, Publication Date. Medium. Date of Access.

> Gogoi, Pallavi. "The Trouble with Business Ethics." *BusinessWeek.* McGraw, 25 June 2007. Web. 3 Oct. 2014.

35. Online Posting

> Post Author's Last Name, First Name. "Title (or Subject) of Post." *Title of Message Board or Site Name.* Date of Post. Medium. Date of Access.

> Cravens, Jayne. "Can a 6 Second Video Make a Difference?" *TechSoup Forum.* 5 May 2013. Web. 18 Nov. 2014.

36. E-mail

> E-mail Author's Last Name, First Name. "Subject of E-mail." Message to the author (or Name of Recipient). Date Sent. Medium.

> Jobs, Steve. "HarperCollins." Message to James Murdoch. 22 Jan. 2010. E-mail.

37. CD-ROM

CD-ROM Author's (if any) Last Name, First Name. *Title of CD-ROM.* Publication City: Publisher, Publication Year. Medium.

Car Talk: 25 Years of Lousy Car Advice. Minneapolis: HighBridge, 2013. CD-ROM.

38. Podcast

For downloaded podcasts, include the file type, such as "MP3 file," as the medium. If the file type is unknown, use the term "MP3 file."

"Title of Podcast." Names and Function of Pertinent Individual(s). *Title of Web Site.* Name of Sponsoring Organization, Date of Publication. Medium.

"Are Humans Meant for Monogamy?" Prod. Ben Valsler and Meera Senthilingam. *The Naked Scientists.* Cambridge University, 14 Feb. 2013. MP3 file.

For podcasts that were listened to directly from the host Web site, list "Web" as the medium and include an access date at the end.

39. Entry in a Wiki

Wiki content is continually edited by its users, so there is no author to cite.

"Title of Entry." *Title of Wiki.* Name of Sponsoring Organization, Date of Publication or Most Recent Update. Medium. Date of Access.

"Selfie." *Wikipedia.* Wikimedia Foundation, 24 May 2013. Web. 7 June 2013.

OTHER

40. Dissertation

For unpublished dissertations, put the title in quotation marks.

Author's Last Name, First Name. "Dissertation Title." Diss. Name of University, Year. Medium.

Yadav, Lekha. "The Effect of Ozone on the Growth and Development of Selected Food Spoilage Fungi." Diss. Newcastle Univ., 2009. Print.

If the dissertation is published as a book, italicize the title and include the publication information.

> Author's Last Name, First Name. *Dissertation Title*. Diss. Name of University, Year. Publication City: Publisher, Publication Year. Medium.

> Dugas, Kevin. "Can You Keep a Secret?": *The Effects of Coaching and Moral Stories on Children's Concealment of an Adult's Transgression.* Diss. McGill University, 2012. Montreal: McGill Univ., 2012. Print.

41. Published Conference Proceedings

List the name(s) of the editor(s), followed by "ed." or "eds.," and italicize the title of the proceedings. Before the conference information, add "Proc. of" and follow with the conference title, date, and location.

> Editor(s), ed(s). *Title of Proceedings*. Proc. of Conference Title, Conference Date, Conference Location. Publication City: Publisher, Year. Medium.

> Frischer, Bernard, Jane Webb Crawford, and David Koller, eds. *Making History Interactive: Computer Applications and Quantitative Methods in Archaeology.* Proc. of the Conference of Computer Applications and Quantitative Methods in Archaeology, March 2010, Williamsburg. Oxford: Archaeopress, 2010. Print.

42. Government Document

List the government (usually a country or state) that issued the document, and then list the department or agency. Most U.S. government documents are published by the Washington-based Government Printing Office (GPO).

> Government. Department or Agency. *Title of Document*. Publication City: Publisher, Date of Publication. Medium.

> United States. National Cancer Institute. *Clear Pathways: Winning the Fight against Tobacco.* Bethesda: National Institutes of Health, Jan. 2013. Print.

43. Pamphlet

> *Pamphlet Title*. Publication City: Publisher, Year of Publication. Medium.

> *Weathering the Storm: Financial Education Resources for Hurricane Recovery. Gulf Coast Edition: Alabama, Florida, Louisiana, Mississippi, Texas.* Washington: U.S. Dept. of the Treasury, 2012. Print.

44. Letter (Personal and Published)

For personal letters that you received, give the name of the letter writer, followed by the description "Letter to the author." For publication medium, list "TS" ("typescript") for typed letters or "MS" ("manuscript") for handwritten letters. For e-mail, see item 36.

> Letter Writer's Last Name, First Name. Letter to the author. Date of Letter. Medium.

> Warren, Elizabeth. Letter to the author. 10 Feb. 2013. TS.

For published letters, list the letter writer as well as the recipient.

> Letter Writer's Last Name, First Name. Letter to First Name Last Name. Date of Letter. *Title of Book.* Ed. Editor's First Name Last Name. Publication City: Publisher, Year. Medium.

> Lincoln, Abraham. Letter to T. J. Pickett. 16 Apr. 1859. *Wit & Wisdom of Abraham Lincoln: As Reflected in His Letters and Speeches.* Ed. H. Jack Lang. Mechanicsburg: Stackpole, 2006. Print.

45. Legal Source

List the names of laws or acts (with no underlining or quotation marks), followed by the Public Law number and the date. Also give the Statutes at Large cataloging number and the medium. For other legal sources, refer to *The Bluebook: A Uniform System of Citation*, 19th ed. (Cambridge: Harvard Law Review Assn., 2010).

> Title of Law. Pub. L. number. Stat. number. Date of Enactment. Medium.

> Violence against Women Reauthorization Act. Pub. L. 113-114. Stat. 47. 7 Mar. 2013. Print.

46. Lecture or Public Address

For the medium, describe the type of speech ("Reading," "Address," "Lecture," etc.).

> Speaker's Last Name, First Name. "Title of Speech." Name of Sponsoring Institution. Location of Speech. Date of Speech. Medium.

> Brooks, David. "What Not to Worry About." Indiana University. Bloomington. 3 May 2013. Address.

47. Interview

For published or broadcast interviews, give the title (if any), followed by the publication or broadcast information for the source that aired or published the interview. If there is no title, use "Interview" followed by a period.

> Interviewee's Last Name, First Name. "Title of Interview." *Book, Periodical, Web Site, or Program Title.* Publication or Broadcast Information (see specific entry for guidance). Medium.

> Biden, Joe. "Joe Biden: The *Rolling Stone* Interview." *Rolling Stone* 9 May 2013: 33-36. Print.

> Brooks, Mel. Interview. *Fresh Air.* Natl. Public Radio. WBEZ, Chicago. 20 May 2013. Radio.

For interviews that you conduct yourself, include the name of the interviewee, interview type ("Personal interview," "E-mail interview," "Telephone interview," etc.), and date.

> Dean, Howard. E-mail interview. 3 May 2011.

48. Television or Radio Program

If you access an archived show online, include the access date after the medium.

> "Episode Title." *Program Title. or Series Title.* Network. Local Channel's Call Letters, City (if any). Air Date. Medium. Date of Access.

> "Mr. Selfridge: Episode 2." *Masterpiece.* PBS. KCTS, Seattle. 13 Jan. 2014. Television.

> "The Future of Marriage." *On Being.* Amer. Public Media. 4 Apr. 2013. Web. 1 June 2014.

49. Film or Video Recording

If you accessed the film via videocassette or DVD, include the distributor name and release date.

> *Film Title.* Dir. Director's First Name Last Name. Original Release Date. Distributor, Release Date of Recording. Medium.

> *3:10 to Yuma.* Dir. Delmer Daves. 1957. Criterion, 2013. DVD.

To highlight a particular individual's performance or contribution, begin with that person's name, followed by a descriptive label (for example, "perf." or "chor.").

> Ford, Glenn, perf. *3:10 to Yuma*. Dir. Delmer Daves. 1957. Criterion, 2013. DVD.

50. Sound Recording

> Performer's Last Name, First Name or Band's Name. "Title of Song." *Title of Album*. Record Label, Year. Medium.

> Benson, George. "Unforgettable." *Inspiration: A Tribute to Nat King Cole*. Concord Jazz, 2013. CD

51. Musical Composition

Long works such as operas, ballets, and named symphonies should be italicized. Additional information, such as key or movement, may be added at the end.

> Composer's Last Name, First Name. *Title of Long Work*. Artists' names. Orchestra. Conductor. Manufacturer, Date. Medium.

> Bellini, Vincenzo. *I Capuleti e i Montecchi*. Perf. Beverly Sills, Janet Baker, Nicolai Gedda, Raimund Herincx, and Robert Lloyd. New Philharmonia Orchestra. Cond. Giuseppe Patanè. EMI Classics, 2005. CD.

> Mozart, Wolfgang Amadeus. *Sonata for 2 Pianos in D Major, K. 448*. Perf. Radu Lupu and Murray Perahia. Sony, 2003. CD.

52. Live Performance

> *Performance Title*. By Author Name. Dir. Director Name. Perf. Performer Name(s). Theater or Venue Name, City. Date of Performance. Medium.

> *Lucky Guy*. By Nora Ephron. Dir. George C. Wolfe. Perf. Tom Hanks and Peter Scolari. Broadhurst Theatre, New York. 3 Jul. 2013. Performance.

53. Work of Art

> Artist's Last Name, First Name. *Title of Artwork*. Date. Institution, City.

> Picasso, Pablo. *Les Demoiselles d'Avignon*. 1907. Museum of Modern Art, New York.

A publication medium is required only for reproduced works, such as in books or online. For works accessed on the Web, include an access date.

> Opie, Catherine. *Untitled #1 (Michigan Womyn's Music Festival)*. 2010. Institute of Contemporary Art, Boston. ICA Online. Web. 22 Mar. 2014.

54. Map or Chart

> Title of Map. Map. Publication City: Publisher Name, Year. Medium.

> *West Coast Trail and Carmanah Valley*. Map. Vancouver: Intl. Travel Maps, 2010. Print.

If you accessed the map online, include an access date.

> *Cambodia*. Map. Google Maps. 2014. Web. 15 April 2014.

55. Cartoon or Comic Strip

> Artist's Last Name, First Name. "Cartoon Title" (if given). Cartoon. *Title of Periodical* Date: Page Number. Medium.

> Crawford, Michael. "Effective Catcalls." Cartoon. *New Yorker* 11 Feb. 2013: 109. Print.

56. Advertisement

> Product Name. Advertisement. *Title of Periodical* Date: Section Number: Page Number(s). Medium.

> Pictionary. Advertisement. *Reader's Digest* 23 Nov. 2011, 12-13. Print.

If you accessed the advertisement online, include an access date.

> iPhone 5. Advertisement. Apple YouTube Channel. Web. 18 Sept. 2014.

Format an MLA paper correctly. You can now find software to format your academic papers in MLA style, but the key alignments for such documents are usually simple enough for you to manage on your own.

- Set up a header on the right-hand side of each page, one-half inch from the top. The header should include your last name and the page number.

- In the upper left on the first—or title—page, include your name, the instructor's name, the course title and/or number, and the date.

- Center the title above the first line of text.

- Use one-inch margins on all sides of the paper.

- Double-space the entire paper (including your name and course information, the title, and any block quotations).

- Indent paragraphs one-half inch.

- Use block quotations for quoted material of four or more lines. Indent block quotations one inch from the left margin.

- Do not include a separate title page unless your instructor requires one.

- When you document using MLA style, you'll need to create an alphabetically arranged works cited page at the end of the paper so that readers have a convenient list of all the books, articles, and other data you have used.

Wilcox 1

Susan Wilcox

Professor Longmire

Rhetoric 325M

March 7, 20--

Marathons for Women

Today in America, five women are running. Two of them live in Minnesota, one in Virginia, and two in Texas. Their careers are different, their political views are divergent, and their other hobbies are irrelevant, for it is running that draws these women together. They are marathoners. Between them, they are eighteen-time veterans of the 26.2-mile march of exhaustion and exhilaration.

These five women are not alone; over 205,000 women in the United States alone ran a marathon in 2010 (RunningUSA). They sacrifice sleeping late, watching TV, and sometimes even toenails (lost toenails are a common malady among marathon runners) for the sake of their sport. Why do these women do this to themselves? Karin Warren explains, "It started out being about losing weight and getting fit again. But I enjoyed running so much—not just how physically fit I felt afterward, but the actual act of running and how it cleared my mind and made me feel better about myself in all aspects of my life—that it became a part of who I am." The other women agree, using words like "conquer," "powerful," and "confident" to describe how

Wilcox 2

running makes them feel.

However, these women know that only a generation ago, marathons weren't considered suitable for women. Tammy Moriearty and Wendy Anderson remember hearing that running could make a woman's uterus fall out; Tammy adds, "It floors me that medical professionals used to believe that." Michelle Gibson says that her friends cautioned her against running when she was pregnant (she ran anyway; it's safe). Naomi Olson has never heard a specific caution, but "lots of people think I am crazy," she says. Female runners, like their male counterparts, do have to maintain adequate nutrition during training (Third Age), but "there are no inherent health risks involved with marathon preparation and participation" (Dilworth). Unfortunately, scientists were not researching running health for women when the marathon was born, and most people thought women were too fragile to run that far. The myth that marathoning is dangerous for women was allowed to fester in the minds of race organizers around the world.

Legend holds that the original marathon runner, Pheidippides, ran from the Battle of Marathon to Athens to bring news of the Athenian victory over Persia. Pheidippides died of exhaustion after giving the news, and the marathon race today is held in honor of his final journey (Lovett x). Historians doubt all the details of this legend, including that a professional runner in Greece would die after what would have been a relatively short distance for him (x–xi) Nevertheless, the myth

Wilcox 8

Works Cited

Anderson, Wendy. Facebook interview. 25 Feb. 2012.

Associated Press. "Paula Radcliffe to Keep Marathon Record."
    ESPN Olympic Sports. ESPN, 9 Nov. 2011. Web. 19 Feb.
    2012.

Brown, Gwilym S. "A Game Girl in a Man's Game." *Sports
    Illustrated*. SI Vault, 2 May 1966. Web. 19 Feb. 2012.

Dilworth, Mark. "Women Running Marathons: Health Risks."
    EmpowHER. EmpowHER Media, 23 Apr. 2010. Web.
    19 Feb. 2012.

ESPN. "Paula Radcliffe to Keep Marathon Record." *ESPN
    Olympic Sports*. ESPN, n.d. Web. 9 Nov. 2012.

Gibb, Roberta. "A Run of One's Own." *Running Past*. Running
    Past, 2011. Web. 19 Feb. 2012.

Gibson, Michelle. Facebook interview. 20 Feb. 2012.

Longman, Jeré. "Still Playing Catch-Up." *New York Times*. New
    York Times, 5 Nov. 2011. Web. 19 Feb. 2012.

Lovett, Charles C. *Olympic Marathon: A Centennial History
    of the Games' Most Storied Race*. Westport: Praeger-Green-
    wood, 1997. Print.

Moriearty, Tammy. Facebook interview. 21 Feb. 2012.

Olson, Naomi. Facebook interview. 21 Feb. 2012.

Run Like a Girl. "History of Women's Distance Running." *Run
    Like a Girl Film*. Run Like a Girl, n.d. Web. 20 Feb. 2012.

"Works Cited" centered at top of page.

Begins on separate page.

Entries arranged alphabetically.

Entire page is double-spaced: no extra spaces between entries.

Second and subsequent lines of entries indent five spaces or one-half inch.

Wilcox 9

RunningUSA. "RunningUSA's Annual Marathon Report."

    RunningUSA. RunningUSA, 16 Mar. 2011. Web.

    19 Feb. 2012.

Switzer, Kathrine. *Marathon Woman: Running the Race*

    to Revolutionize Women's Sports. New York: Avalon,

    2007. Print.

Third Age. "Women Running Marathons: Do Benefits

    Outweigh Risks?" *Third Age*. Third Age Media,

    1 July 2008. Web. 19 Feb. 2012.

Warren, Karin. Facebook interview. 21 Feb. 2012.

47 APA Documentation and Format

APA (American Psychological Association) style is used in many social science disciplines. For full details about APA style and documentation, consult the *Publication Manual of the American Psychological Association*, 6th ed. (2010). The basic details for documenting sources and formatting research papers in APA style are presented below.

cite in APA

Document sources according to convention. When you use sources in a research paper, you are required to cite the source, letting readers know that the information has been borrowed from somewhere else and showing them how to find the original material if they would like to study it further. Like MLA style, APA includes two parts: a brief in-text citation and a more detailed reference entry.

In-text citations should include the author's name, the year the material was published, and the page number(s) that the borrowed material can be found on. The author's name and year of publication are generally included in a signal phrase that introduces the passage, and the page number is included in parentheses after the borrowed text. Note that for APA style, the verb in the signal phrase should be in the past tense (*reported*, as in the following example) or present perfect tense (*has reported*).

> Millman (2007) reported that college students around the country are participating in Harry Potter discussion groups, sports activities, and even courses for college credit (p. A4).

Alternatively, the author's name and year can be included in parentheses with the page number.

> College students around the country are participating in Harry Potter discussion groups, sports activities, and even courses for college credit (Millman, 2007, p. A4).

The list of references at the end of the paper contains a more detailed citation that repeats the author's name and publication year and includes the title and additional publication information about the source. Inclusive page numbers are included for periodical articles and parts of books.

> Millman, S. (2007). Generation hex. *The Chronicle of Higher Education,* *53*(46), A4.

Both in-text citations and reference entries can vary greatly depending on the type of source cited (book, periodical, Web site, etc.). The following pages give specific examples of how to cite a wide range of sources in APA style.

Directory of APA In-Text Citations

1. Author named in signal phrase 515
2. Author named in parentheses 515
3. With block quotations 515
4. Two authors 515
5. Three to five authors 516
6. Six or more authors 516
7. Group, corporate, or government author 516
8. Two or more works by the same author 517
9. Authors with the same last name 517
10. Unknown author 517
11. Personal communication 518
12. Electronic source 518
13. Musical recording 518
14. Secondary source 519
15. Multiple sources in same citation 519

For an activity on APA style, see **macmillanhighered.com/howtowrite3e.**
Tutorials › LearningCurve Activities › Working with Sources (APA)

General Guidelines for In-Text Citations in APA Style

AUTHOR NAMES

- Give last names only, unless two authors have the same last name (see item 9 on p. 517) or the source is a personal communication (see item 11 on p. 518). In these cases, include the first initial before the last name ("J. Smith").

DATES

- Give only the year in the in-text citation. The one exception to this rule is personal communications, which should include a full date (see item 11 on p. 518).
- Months and days for periodical publications should not be given with the year in in-text citations; this information will be provided as needed in the reference entry at the end of your paper.
- Add a small letter to the common date to differentiate between the items. See item 8 on page 517 and item 6 on p. 523.
- If you can't locate a date for your source, include the abbreviation "n.d." (for "no date") in place of the date in parentheses.

TITLES

- Titles of works generally do not need to be given in in-text citations. Exceptions include two or more works by the same author and works with no author. See items 8 and 10 on page 517 for details.

PAGE NUMBERS

- Include page numbers whenever possible in parentheses after borrowed material. Put "p." (or "pp.") before the page number(s).
- When you have a range of pages, list the full first and last page numbers (for example, "311-320"). If the borrowed material isn't printed on consecutive pages, list all the pages it appears on (for example, "A1, A4-A6").
- If page numbers are not available, use section names and/or paragraph (written as "para.") numbers when available to help a reader locate a specific quotation. See items 7 and 12 on pages 517 and 518 for examples.

APA in-text citation

1. Author Named in Signal Phrase

> While McWilliams (2010) acknowledged not only the growing popularity but also the ecological and cultural benefits of the locavore diet, he still maintained that "eating local is not, in and of itself, a viable answer to sustainable food production on a global level" (p. 2).

2. Author Named in Parentheses

For a source without an author, see item 10; for an electronic source without a page number, see item 12.

> "Eating local is not, in and of itself, a viable answer to sustainable food production on a global level" (McWilliams, 2010, p. 2).

3. With Block Quotations

For excerpts of forty or more words, indent the quoted material one-half inch and include the page number at the end of the quotation after the end punctuation.

> Pollan (2006) suggested that the prized marbled meat that results from feeding corn to cattle (ruminants) may not be good for us:
>> Yet this corn-fed meat is demonstrably less healthy for us, since it contains more saturated fat and less omega-3 fatty acids than the meat of animals fed grass. A growing body of research suggests that many of the health problems associated with eating beef are really problems with corn-fed beef. . . . In the same way ruminants are ill adapted to eating corn, humans in turn may be poorly adapted to eating ruminants that eat corn. (p. 75)

4. Two Authors

Note that if you name the authors in the parentheses, connect them with an ampersand (&).

> Sharpe and Young (2005) reported that new understandings about tooth development, along with advances in stem cell technology, have brought researchers closer to the possibility of producing replacement teeth from human tissue (p. 36).

New understandings about tooth development, along with advances in stem cell technology, have brought researchers closer to the possibility of producing replacement teeth from human tissue (Sharpe & Young, 2005, p. 36).

5. Three to Five Authors

The first time you cite a source with three to five authors, list all their names in either the signal phrase or parentheses. If you cite the same source again in your paper, use just the first author's name followed by "et al."

Frueh, Anouk, Elhai, and Ford (2010) identified the homecoming of Vietnam veterans as the advent for PTSD's eventual inclusion in the DSM, pointing out that "in the immediate, post-Vietnam era, compensation for significant functional impairment was difficult to obtain other than for observable physical injuries, and access to Veterans Administration (VA) medical services were possible only via a 'war-related' disorder" (p. 3).

Frueh et al. (2010) presented data to combat the assumption that although most people who endure a trauma will develop PTSD, "only a small minority of people will develop distress and functional impairment that rises to the level of a psychiatric disorder. Instead, long-term resilience is actually the norm rather than the exception for people after trauma" (p. 7).

6. Six or More Authors

List the first author's name only, followed by "et al."

While supportive parenting has not been found to decrease the incidence of depression in bullied adolescents, Bilsky et al. (2013) have insisted that parental support can still offset or counterbalance the negative effects of peer victimization (p. 417).

7. Group, Corporate, or Government Author

Treat the name just as you would any other author, and include the name in either the signal phrase or the parentheses.

The resolution called on the United States to ban all forms of torture in interrogation procedures (American Psychological Association

[APA], 2007, para. 1). It also reasserted "the organization's absolute opposition to all forms of torture and abuse, regardless of circumstance" (APA, 2007, para. 5).

8. Two or More Works by the Same Author

Two or more works by the same author will be differentiated by the publication year of the work being referenced, unless you're citing two works by the same author that were published in the same year. In this case, add a lowercase letter after the year to indicate which entry in the references list is being cited. To see reference list entries for these sources, see item 6 on page 523.

> Shermer (2005a) has reported that false acupuncture (in placebo experiments) is as effective as true acupuncture (p. 30).

> Shermer (2005b) has observed that psychics rely on vague and flattering statements, such as "You are wise in the ways of the world, a wisdom gained through hard experience rather than book learning," to earn the trust of their clients (p. 6).

9. Authors with the Same Last Name

Distinguish the authors in your in-text citations by including initials of their first names.

> S. Harris (2012) argued that free will is actually an illusion—a by-product of our past experiences, over which we believe we have more control than we actually do (p. 64).

10. Unknown Author

Identify the item by its title. However, if the author is actually listed as "Anonymous," treat this term as the author in your citation.

> Tilapia provides more protein when eaten than it consumes when alive, making it a sustainable fish ("Dream Fish," 2007, p. 26).

> The book *Go Ask Alice* (Anonymous, 1971) portrayed the fictional life of a teenager who was destroyed by her addiction to drugs.

11. Personal Communication

If you cite personal letters or e-mails or your own interviews for your research paper, cite these as personal communication in your in-text citation, including the author of the material (with first initial), the term "personal communication," and the date. Personal communications should not be included in your reference list.

> One instructor has argued that it is important to "make peer review a lot more than a proofreading/grammar/mechanics exercise" (J. Bone, personal communication, July 27, 2007).

To include the author of a personal communication in the signal phrase, use the following format:

> C. Garcia (personal communication, December 11, 2013) has argued that "while it's important to accept criticism of your writing, you should be able to distinguish between a valid suggestion and an opinion that your target audience does not share."

12. Electronic Source

If page numbers are not given, use section names or paragraph numbers to help your readers track down the source.

> Our natural feelings of disgust—for example, at the sight of rotten food or squirming maggots—are "evolutionary messages telling us to get as far away as possible from the source of our discomfort" ("How Our Brains Separate Empathy from Disgust," 2013, para. 15).

13. Musical Recording

> In an ironic twist, Mick Jagger sang backup on the song "You're So Vain" (Simon, 1972, track 3).

14. Secondary Source

Include the name of the original author in the signal phrase. In the parentheses, add "as cited in," and give the author of the quoted material along with the date and page number. Note that your end-of-paper reference entry for this material will be listed under the secondary source name (Pollan) rather than the original writer (Howard).

> Writing in 1943, Howard asserted that "artificial manures lead inevitably to artificial nutrition, artificial food, artificial animals, and finally to artificial men and women" (as cited in Pollan, 2006, p. 148).

15. Multiple Sources in Same Citation

If one statement in your paper can be attributed to multiple sources, alphabetically list all the authors with dates, separated by semicolons.

> Black Sabbath, considered the originators of heavy metal music, used their bleak upbringing in the failing industrial town of Birmingham, England, to power the darkness and passion in a sound that wowed the masses and disgusted the critics (Christe, 2004; Widerhorn & Turman, 2013).

Directory of APA Reference Entries

(Continued)

Directory of APA Reference Entries (*continued*)

General Guidelines for Reference Entries in APA Style

AUTHOR NAMES

- When an author's name appears *before* the title of the work, list it by last name followed by a comma and first initial followed by a period. (Middle initials may also be included.)
- If an author, editor, or other name is listed *after* the title, then the initial(s) precede the last name (see examples on pp. 523, 524–25, 527).
- When multiple authors are listed, their names should be separated by commas, and an ampersand (&) should precede the final author.

DATES

- For scholarly journals, include only the year (2014).
- For monthly magazines, include the year followed by a comma and the month (2014, May).
- For newspapers and weekly magazines, include the year followed by a comma and the month and the day (2014, May 27).
- Access dates for electronic documents use the month-day-year format: "Retrieved May 27, 2014."
- Months should not be abbreviated.
- If a date is not available, use "n.d." (for "no date") in parentheses.

TITLES

- Titles of periodicals should be italicized, and all major words capitalized (*Psychology Today; Journal of Archaeological Research*).
- Titles of books, Web sites, and other nonperiodical long works should be italicized. Capitalize the first word of the title (and subtitle, if any) and proper nouns only (*Legacy of ashes: The history of the CIA*).
- For short works such as essays, articles, and chapters, capitalize the first word of the title (and subtitle, if any) and proper nouns only (The black sites: A rare look inside the CIA's secret interrogation program).

PAGE NUMBERS

- Reference entries for periodical articles and sections of books should include the range of pages: "245-257." For material in parentheses, include the abbreviation "p." or "pp." before the page numbers ("pp. A4-A5").
- If the pages are not continuous, list all the pages separated by commas: "245, 249, 301-306."

APA reference entries

AUTHOR INFORMATION

1. One Author

Golden, E. (2013). *John Gilbert: The last of the silent film stars*. Lexington, KY: University Press of Kentucky.

2. Two Authors

Cox, B., & Cohen, A. (2011). *Wonders of the universe*. New York, NY: HarperCollins.

3. Three or More Authors

List every author up to and including seven; for a work with eight or more authors, give the first six names followed by three ellipsis dots and the last author's name.

Holstein, M. B., Parks, J., & Waymack, M. (2010). *Ethics, aging, and society: The critical turn*. New York, NY: Springer.

Barry, A. E., Stellefson, M. L., Piazza-Gardner, A. K., Chaney, B. H., & Dodd, V. (2013). The impact of pre-gaming on subsequent blood alcohol concentrations: An event-level analysis. *Addictive Behaviors, 38*(8), 2374-2377.

4. Group, Corporate, or Government Author

In many cases, the group name is the same as the publisher. Instead of repeating the group name, use the term "Author" for the publisher's name.

Scientific American Editors. (2012). *Storm warnings: Climate change and extreme weather*. New York, NY: Author.

5. Unidentified Author

If the author is listed on the work as "Anonymous," list that in your reference entry, alphabetizing accordingly. Otherwise, start with and alphabetize by title.

Anonymous. (1996). *Primary colors: A novel of politics*. New York, NY: Random House.

Quantum computing: Faster, slower—or both at once? (2013, May). *The Economist*, 57-58.

6. Multiple Works by the Same Author

Shermer, M. (2003). I knew you would say that [Review of the book *Intuition: Its powers and perils*]. *Skeptic, 10*(1), 92-94.

Shermer, M. (2005a, August). Full of holes: The curious case of acupuncture. *Scientific American, 293*(2). 30.

Shermer, M. (2005b). *Science friction*. New York, NY: Henry Holt, 6.

BOOKS

7. Book: Basic Format

Author. (Publication Year). *Book title: Book subtitle.* Publication City, State (abbreviated) or Country of Publication: Publisher.

O'Neil, S. K. (2013). *Two nations indivisible: Mexico, the United States, and the road ahead*. New York, NY: Oxford University Press.

8. Author and Editor

Author. (Publication Year). *Book title: Book subtitle* (Editor's Initial(s). Editor's Last Name, Ed.). Publication City, State (abbreviated) or Country of Publication: Publisher.

Faulkner, W. (2004). *Essays, speeches, and public letters* (J. B. Meriwether, Ed.). New York, NY: Modern Library.

9. Work in an Anthology or a Collection

Begin with the author and date of the short work and include the title as you would a periodical title (no quotations and minimal capitalization). Then list "In" and the editor's first initial and last name followed by "Ed." in parentheses. Next give the anthology title and page numbers in parentheses. End with the publication information. If an anthology has two editors, connect them with an ampersand (&) and use "Eds."

Author. (Publication Year). Title of short work. In Editor's initials. Editor's Last
    Name (Ed.), *Title of anthology* (pp. Page Numbers). Publication City, State
    (abbreviated) or Country of Publication: Publisher.

Keller, H. (2008). I go adventuring. In P. Lopate (Ed.), *Writing New York: A
    literary anthology* (pp. 505-508). New York, NY: Library of America.

For more than two editors, connect them with commas and an ampersand. For
large editorial boards, give the name of the lead editor followed by "et al."

J. Smith, L. Hoey, & R. Burns (Eds.)

N. Mallen et al. (Eds.)

10. Edited Collection

Editor. (Ed.). (Publication Year). *Book title: Book subtitle.* Publication City, State
    (abbreviated) or Country of Publication: Publisher.

McKibben, B. (Ed.). (2008). *American Earth: Environmental writing since
    Thoreau.* New York, NY: Library of America.

11. Multivolume Work

Author(s) or Editor(s) (Eds.). (Publication Year). *Book title: Book subtitle* (Vols. volume
    numbers). Publication City, State (abbreviated) or Country of Publication:
    Publisher.

Wright, W., Gardner, S., Graves, J., & Ruffin, P. (Eds.). (2011). *The southern
    poetry anthology* (Vols. 1-5). Huntsville, TX: Texas Review Press.

12. Later Edition

In parentheses include the edition type (such as "Rev." for "Revised" or "Abr."
for "Abridged") or number ("2nd," "3rd," "4th," etc.) as shown on the title
page, along with the abbreviation "ed." after the book title.

Author. (Publication Year). *Book title* (Edition Type or Number ed.). Publication
    City, State (abbreviated) or Country of Publication: Publisher.

Akmajian, A., Demers, R. A., Farmer, A. K., & Harnish, R. M. (2010).
    Linguistics: An introduction to language and communication
    (6th ed.). Cambridge, MA: MIT Press.

13. Translation

List the translator's initial, last name, and "Trans." in parentheses after the title. After the publication information, list "Original work published" and year in parentheses. Note that the period is omitted after the final parenthesis.

> Author. (Publication Year of Translation). *Book title* (Translator Initial(s). Last Name, Trans.). Publication City, State (abbreviated) or Country of Publication: Publisher. (Original work published Year)

> Camus, A. (1988). *The stranger* (M. Ward, Trans.). New York, NY: Knopf. (Original work published 1942)

14. Article in a Reference Book

> Article Author. (Publication Year). Article title. In Initial(s). Last Name of Editor (Ed.), *Reference book title* (pp. Page Numbers). Publication City, State (abbreviated) or Country of Publication: Publisher.

> Stroud, S. (2013). Value theory. In H. LaFollette (Ed.), *The international encyclopedia of ethics* (pp. 789-790). Malden, MA: John Wiley & Sons.

If a reference book entry has no author, begin with the title of the article.

> Article title. (Publication Year). In *Book title.* Publication City, State (abbreviated) or Country of Publication: Publisher.

> Top 10 news topics of 2012. (2012). In *The world almanac and book of facts 2013*. New York, NY: World Almanac Books.

PERIODICALS

15. Article in a Journal Paginated by Volume

> Article Author. (Publication Year). Title of article. *Title of Journal, Volume Number,* Page Numbers.

> Mace, B. L., Corser, G. C., Zitting, L., & Denison, J. (2013). Effects of overflights on the national park experience. *Journal of Environmental Psychology, 35*, 30-39.

16. Article in a Journal Paginated by Issue

> Article Author. (Publication Year). Title of article. *Title of Journal, Volume Number*(Issue Number), Page Numbers.

> Clancy, S., & Simpson, L. (2002). Literacy learning for indigenous students: Setting a research agenda. *Australian Journal of Language and Literacy, 25*(2), 47-64.

17.   Magazine Article

> Article Author. (Publication Year, Month). Title of article. *Title of Magazine, Volume Number*(Issue Number), Page Number(s).

> Doll, J. (2013, June). The evolution of hand gestures: Why do some die out and others endure? *The Atlantic, 200*(1167): 58-60.

18. Newspaper Article

> Article Author. (Publication Year, Month Day). Title of article. *Title of Newspaper,* p. Page Number.

> Tobar, H. (2013, May 28). Tech-savvy parents prefer print over e-books for kids, PEW reports. *Los Angeles Times,* p. 24.

19. Letter to the Editor

Include "Letter to the editor" in brackets after the letter title (if any) and before the period.

> Author. (Publication Year, Month Day). Title of letter [Letter to the editor]. *Title of Newspaper,* p. Page Number.

> Murray, M. (2013, April 24). Giving cash to panhandlers is the wrong way to help [Letter to the editor]. *Denver Post,* p. A17.

20. Review

After the review title (if any), include in brackets "Review of the" and the medium of the work being reviewed ("book," "film," "CD," etc.), followed by the title of the work in italics. If the reviewed work is a book, include the author's name after a comma; if it's a film or other media, include the year of release.

Author Name. (Publication Year, Month Day). Title of review [Review of the book *Book title,* by Author Name]. *Title of Periodical, Volume Number,* Page Number.

Abramson, J. (2012, November 11). Grand bargainer [Review of the book *Thomas Jefferson: The art of power,* by J. Meacham]. *The New York Times Book Review, 3,* 1.

ELECTRONIC SOURCES

21. Article with a DOI

A DOI (digital object identifier) is a unique number assigned to specific content, such as a journal article. Include the DOI but not the database name or URL. Note that there is no period after the DOI.

DiGangi, J., Jason, L. A., Mendoza, L., Miller, S. A., & Contreras, R. (2013). The relationship between wisdom and abstinence behaviors in women in recovery from substance abuse. *The American Journal of Drug and Alcohol Abuse, 39*(1), 33-37. doi: 10.3109/00952990.2012.702172

22. Article without a DOI

Give the exact URL or the URL for the journal's home page if access requires a subscription. Do not give the database name. Note that there is no period after the URL.

McDermott, L. A., & Pettijohn, T. F., II (2011). The influence of clothing fashion and race on the perceived socioeconomic status and person perception of college students. *Psychology & Society, 4*(2), 64-75. Retrieved from http://www.psychologyandsociety.org/__assets /__original/2012/01/McDermott_Pettijohn.pdf

23. Article in Internet-Only Periodical

An article published exclusively online is unlikely to have page numbers.

> Palmer, B. (2013, May 24). How accurate are AAA's travel forecasts? *Slate.*
> *com.* Retrieved from http://www.slate.com/articles/health_and
> _science/explainer/2013/05/aaa_memorial_day_travel_forecast_are
> _holiday_driving_predictions_accurate.html

24. Multipage Web Site

Include a retrieval date before the URL if the material is likely to be changed or updated or if it lacks a set publication date. Do not add a period at the end of the entry.

> Web Site Author or Sponsor. (Date of Most Recent Update). *Title of Web site.*
> Retrieved date, from URL

> Department of Homeland Security. (2013). *Disasters.* Retrieved January 14,
> 2014, from http://www.dhs.gov/topic/disasters

> Linder, D. O. (2013). *Famous trials.* Retrieved March 2, 2014, from
> http://law2.umkc.edu/faculty/projects/ftrials/ftrials.htm

25. Part of a Web Site

> Short Work Author. (Date of Most Recent Update). Title of short work. *Title of*
> *Web site.* Retrieved date, from URL

> Slate, M., & Sestan, N. (2012, September 18). The emerging biology of
> autism spectrum disorders. *Autism speaks.* Retrieved from http://
> www.autismspeaks.org/blog/2012/09/18/emerging-biology-autism
> -spectrum-disorders

26. Online Posting

For detailed advice on citing social media, see http://blog.apastyle.org/apastyle
/social-media.

> Post Author. (Year, Month Day of post). Title of post [Description of post].
> Retrieved date, from URL

> Parkin, G. (2011, December 5). Mobile learning platforms and tools [Online
> forum comment]. Retrieved from http://community.astd.org/eve
> /forums/a/tpc/f/6401041/m/142107851

27. Computer Software or App

If the software or app has an author or editor listed, the reference begins with that.

Title of software [Computer software]. (Publication Year). Publication City, State (abbreviated) or Country of Publication: Publisher.

History: The French revolution [Computer software]. (2009). San Jose, CA: Innovative Knowledge.

When citing an app, look at the most recent update for the publication date.

Title of app. (Publication Year). Creator and version number [Mobile application software]. Retrieval information.

Medscape. (2014). WebMD Health (Version 4.4.1) [Mobile application software]. Retrieved from http://itunes.apple.com

28. Entry in a Blog (Weblog)

Hasselbrink, K. (2013, February 5). Chai [Web log post]. Retrieved from http://theyearinfood.com/2013/02/chai.html

29. Podcast

Fogarty, M. (Producer). (2013, May 10). How texting is changing English. [Audio podcast]. *Grammar Girl*. Retrieved from http://grammar .quickanddirtytips.com/how-texting-is-changingenglish.aspx

30. Entry in a Wiki

Article title. Posting date (if any). Retrieved date, from URL

Selfie. (n.d.). Retrieved July 27, 2013, from http://en.wikipedia.org/wiki /Selfie

How to...
Cite from a Web site (APA)

2 publisher of report (if not named as author)

1 publication date

3 report number

4 title of online report

5 author

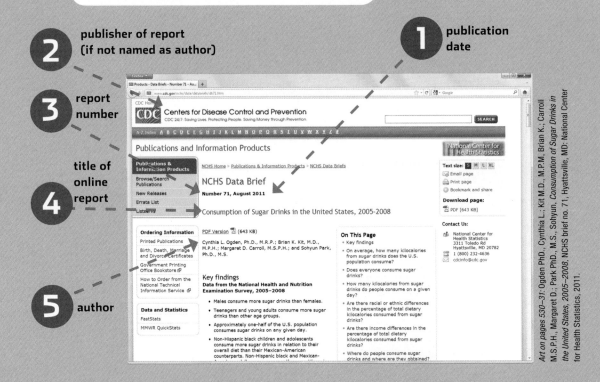

Art on pages 530–31: Ogden PhD, Cynthia L.; Kit M.D., M.P.M, Brian K.; Carroll M.S.P.H., Margaret D.; Park PhD, M.S., Sohyun, Consumption of Sugar Drinks in the United States, 2005–2008, NCHS brief no. 71, Hyattsville, MD: National Center for Health Statistics, 2011.

If you cite a source with three or more authors more than once in text, only list all of the authors the first time. Subsequent times only need the first author's last name, like this: (Ogden et al.).

For a video tutorial, see **macmillanhighered.com/howtowrite3e.**
Tutorials > Documentation and Working with Sources > How to Cite a Web Site in APA Style

SECTION BEING CITED

6 **URL of section**

7 **section title**

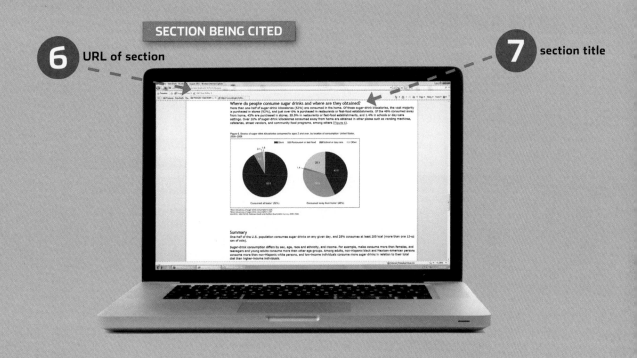

APA
in-text
citation

A nutrition survey of U.S. behavior between 2005 and 2008 found that an overwhelming 92% of sugar-drink kilocalories consumed outside the home were from drinks purchased in stores, not restaurants (Ogden, Kit, Carroll, & Park, 2011).

1   5

1   5   1   7

Ogden, C. L., Kit, B. K., Carroll, M. D., & Park S. (2011, August). Where do

4

APA
references
list entry

people consume sugar drinks and where are they obtained? In Consumption

3

of sugar drinks in the United States, 2005–2008 (NCHS Data Brief No. 71).

2

Retrieved from Centers for Disease Control and Prevention website:

6

http://www.cdc.gov/nchs/data/databriefs/db71.htm#people

How to...
Cite from a database (APA)

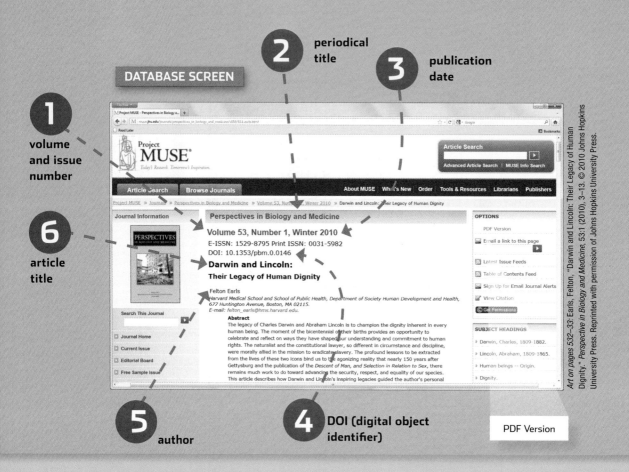

DATABASE SCREEN

1 volume and issue number

2 periodical title

3 publication date

6 article title

5 author

4 DOI (digital object identifier)

Art on pages 532–33: Earls, Felton, "Darwin and Lincoln: Their Legacy of Human Dignity," *Perspective in Biology and Medicine,* 53:1 (2010), 3–13. © 2010 Johns Hopkins University Press. Reprinted with permission of Johns Hopkins University Press.

PDF Version

For a video tutorial, see **macmillanhighered.com/howtowrite3e.**
Tutorials > Documentation and Working with Sources > How to Cite a Database in APA Style

If you're reading an article in an Internet browser and aren't sure where to find the information you need, try viewing the article as a PDF, which usually shows what originally appeared in the print journal.

PDF VIEW (FIRST PAGE)

7 page range

IT IS WITH A SENSE of intellectual excitement that this year we celebrate the bicentennial of two extraordinary men who just happened to be born on the same day, February 12, 1809. Charles Darwin was born into a learned and landed family in Shropshire, England. Quite a different social and economic setting prevailed in Abraham Lincoln's home in Kentucky. His father was a poor and une-

Harvard Medical School and School of Public Health , Department of Society Human Development and Health, 677 Huntington Avenue, Boston, MA 02115.
E-mail: felton_earls@hms.harvard.edu.

*Max Perutz Memorial Lecture, Ninth Biennial Meeting, International Human Rights Network of Academies and Scholarly Societies, Rabat, Morocco, May 21, 2009.

Perspectives in Biology and Medicine, volume 53, number 1 (winter 2010):3–15
© 2010 by The Johns Hopkins University Press

3

APA in-text citation

It's important to note the contributions of Darwin and Lincoln to modern conceptions of human rights, "particularly the beliefs that scientists are free to pursue knowledge, no matter how different from or risky to the prevailing wisdom, and that one of the responsibilities of modern governments is to protect this right to rationality and critical inquiry" (Earls, 2011, 4).

5 **3** **7**

APA references list entry

5 **3** **6**

Earls, F. (2011, Winter). Darwin and Lincoln: Their legacy of human dignity.

2 **1** **7** **4**

Perspectives in Biology and Medicine, 53(1), 3-15. doi:10.1353/pbm.0.0146

OTHER

31. Group, Corporate, or Government Document

List the group or agency as the author, and include any identifying numbers. Many federal agencies' works are published by the U.S. Government Printing Office. If the group is also the publisher, use the word "Author" rather than repeating the group name at the end of the entry.

> Name of Group, Corporation, or Government Agency. (Publication Year). *Title of document* (Identifying number, if any). Publication City, State (abbreviated) or Country of Publication: Publisher.

> National Equal Pay Task Force. (2013). *Fifty years after the Equal Pay Act: Assessing the past, taking stock of the future* (PREX 1.2:EQ 2). Washington, DC: U.S. Government Printing Office.

> Maine Department of Health and Human Services. (2011). *Connections: A guide for family caregivers in Maine*. Augusta, ME: Author.

32. Published Conference Proceedings

> Editor(s). (Eds.). (Publication Year). *Proceedings of the Conference Name: Book title*. Publication City, State (abbreviated) or Country of Publication: Publisher.

> Contreras, F., Farjas, M., & Melero, F. J. (Eds.). (2013). *Proceedings of the 38th annual Conference on Computer Applications and Quantitative Methods in Archaeology: Fusion of cultures*. Oxford, United Kingdom: Archaeopress.

33. Dissertation Abstract

For dissertations abstracted in Dissertation Abstracts International, include the author's name, date, and dissertation title. Then include the volume, issue, and page number. If you access the dissertation from an electronic database, identify the type of work ("Doctoral dissertation") before giving the database name and any identifying number. If you retrieve the abstract from the Web, include the name of the institution in the parentheses, and then give the URL.

Author. (Year of Publication). *Title of dissertation. Dissertation Abstracts International, Volume Number*(Issue Number), Page Number.

Hand, J. A. (2011). *Making sense of change: Sexuality transformation at midlife. Dissertation Abstracts International, 72*(9), 8745B.

Hand, J. A. (2011). *Making sense of change: Sexuality transformation at midlife* (Doctoral dissertation). Available from ProQuest Dissertations and Theses database. (9347727101).

Hand, J. A. (2011). *Making sense of change: Sexuality transformation at midlife* (Doctoral dissertation. Temple University). Retrieved from http://cdm16002.contentdm.oclc.org/cdm/compoundobject/collection /p245801coll10/id/108810/rec/14

34. Film

Writer(s), Producer(s), Director(s). (Release year). *Film title* [Motion picture]. Country of Origin: Movie Studio.

Terrio, C. (Writer), Affleck, B. (Director/Producer), & Clooney, G., & Heslov, G. (Producers). (2012). *Argo* [Motion picture]. United States: GK Films.

35. Television Program

Writer(s), Producer(s), Director(s). (Year of Release). Title of episode [Television series episode]. In Producer Initials. Last Name (Producer), *Title of series.* City, State (abbreviated) or Country of Publication: Broadcast Company.

Zwonitzer, M. (Writer/Producer/Director). (2013). Jesse James [Television series episode]. In M. Samels (Producer), *American Experience.* Boston, MA: WGBH.

36. Musical Recording

Writer. (Copyright Year). Title of song [Recorded by Artist Name]. On *Album title* [Recording medium]. City of Recording, State (abbreviated) or Country of Publication: Record Label. (Recording Year).

Lennon, J., & McCartney, P. (1967). With a little help from my friends [Recorded by The Beatles]. On *Sgt. Pepper's Lonely Hearts Club Band: Remastered* [CD]. Los Angeles, CA: Capitol. (2009).

Format an APA paper correctly.   The following guidelines will help you prepare a manuscript using APA style.

- Set up a header on each page, one-half inch from the top. The header should include a brief title (shortened to no more than fifty characters) in all capital letters and should align left. Page numbers should appear in the upper right corner.

- Margins should be set at one inch on all sides of the paper.

- Check with your instructor to see if a title page is preferred. If so, at the top of the page, you need the short title you'll use in your header, in all capital letters, preceded by the words "Running head" and a colon. The page number appears on the far right. Next, the full title of your paper, your name, and your affiliation (or school) appear in the middle of the page, centered.

- If you include an abstract for your paper, put it on a separate page, immediately following the title page.

- All lines of text (including the title page, abstract, block quotations, and the list of references) should be double-spaced.

- Indent the first lines of paragraphs one-half inch or five spaces.

- Use block quotations for quoted material of four or more lines. Indent block quotations one inch from the left margin.

- When you document a paper using APA style, you'll need to create an alphabetically arranged references page at the end of the project so that readers have a convenient list of all the books, articles, and other data you have used in the paper or project.

Running head: CRI DU CHAT SYNDROME   1

Short title in all capitals is aligned left. Arabic numerals are used for page numbers.

Developmental Disorders:

Cri du Chat Syndrome

Marissa Dahlstrom

University of Texas at Austin

Full title, writer's name, and affiliation are all centered in middle of page.

CRI DU CHAT SYNDROME   2

Developmental Disorders: Cri du Chat Syndrome

Developmental disorders pose a serious threat to young children. However, early detection, treatment, and intervention often allow a child to lead a fulfilling life. To detect a problem at the beginning of life, medical professionals and caregivers must recognize normal development as well as potential warning signs. Research provides this knowledge. In most cases, research also allows for accurate diagnosis and effective intervention. Such is the case with cri du chat syndrome (CDCS), also commonly known as cat cry syndrome and 5p– (5p minus) syndrome.

Cri du chat syndrome, a fairly rare genetic disorder first identified in 1963 by Dr. Jerome Lejeune, affects between 1 in 15,000 to 1 in 50,000 live births (Campbell, Carlin, Justen, & Baird, 2004). The syndrome is caused by partial deletion of chromosome number 5, specifically the portion labeled as 5p; hence the alternative name for the disorder (5P– Society). While the exact cause of the deletion is unknown, it is likely that "the majority of cases are due to spontaneous loss . . . during development of an egg or sperm. A minority of cases result from one parent carrying a rearrangement of chromosome 5 called a translocation" (Sondheimer, 2005). The deletion leads to many different symptoms and outcomes. Perhaps the most noted characteristic of children affected by this syndrome—a high-pitched cry resembling the mewing of a cat— explains Lejeune's choice of the name cri du chat. Pediatric nurse Mary Kugler writes that the cry is caused by "problems with the

CRI DU CHAT SYNDROME 6

References

Campbell, D., Carlin M., Justen, J., III, & Baird, S. (2004).

Cri-du-chat syndrome: A topical overview. *5P– Society*

Retrieved from http://www.fivepminus.org/online.htm

Denny, M., Marchand-Martella, N., Martella, R., Reilly, J. R., &

Reilly, J. F. (2000). Using parent-delivered graduated

guidance to teach functional living skills to a child with

cri du chat syndrome. *Education & Treatment of Children*,

23(4), 441.

5P– Society. (n.d.). About 5P–syndrome. *5P– Society Web site*.

Retrieved from http://www.fivepminus.org/about.htm

Kugler, M. (2006). Cri-du-chat syndrome: Distinctive kitten-

like cry in infancy. *About.com Rare Diseases*. Retrieved

from http://rarediseases.about.com/cs/criduchatsynd

/a/010704.htm

McClean, P. (1997). Genomic analysis: *In situ* hybridization.

Retrieved from http://www.ndsu.nodak.edu/instruct

/mcclean/plsc431/genomic/genomic2.htm

Sarimski, K. (2003). Early play behavior in children with 5p–

syndrome. *Journal of Intellectual Disability Research,*

47(2), 113-120. doi: 10.1046/j.1365-2788.2003.00448.x

Sondheimer, N. (2005). Cri du chat syndrome. In *MedlinePlus*

medical encyclopedia. Retrieved from http://www.nlm

.nih.gov/medlineplus/ency/article/001593.htm

Media & Design

part eight

48 Understanding Digital Media

go
multimodal

Schools, businesses, and professional organizations are finding innovative uses for new media tools and services such as blogs, wikis, digital video, Web-mapping software, social networks, and more. The resulting texts—often spun from Web 2.0 interactive media technologies—represent genres much in flux. And yet they already

Plotting Flickr and Twitter locations in Europe produces this luminous map of the continent, suggesting the sweep of new media activity. Eric Fischer.

play a role in many classrooms. You are employing new media if you contribute to a college service project hosted on a blog, schedule study sessions with classmates via Facebook, use slide software to spiff up a report to the student government, or find yourself enrolled in a MOOC (massive open online course).

Choose a media format based on what you hope to accomplish. A decision to compose with digital tools or to work in environments such as Facebook, Twitter, or Instagram should be based on what these media offer you. An electronic tool may support your project in ways that conventional printed texts simply cannot—and that's the reason to select it. Various media writing options are described in the following table.

Format	Elements	Purpose	Software Technology/Tools
Social networks, blogs	Online discussion postings; interactive; text; images; video; links	Create communities (fan, political, academic); distribute news and information	Facebook; Twitter; Reddit; Blogger; Instagram; Tumblr; WordPress
Web sites	Web-based information site; text; images; video; links; interactive posts	Compile and distribute information; establish presence on Web; sell merchandise, etc.	Dreamweaver; Drupal; WordPress, Google Sites
Wikis	Collaboratively authored linked texts and posts; Web-based; information; text; images; data	Create and edit collaborative documents based on community expertise; distribute and share information	DokuWiki; MediaWiki; Tiki Wiki
Podcasts, music	Digital file-based audio or (sometimes) video recording; downloadable; voice; music; episodic	Distribute mainly audio texts; document or archive audio texts and performances	Audacity; GarageBand
Maps	Interactive image maps; text; data; images; mind maps	Give spatial or geographical dimension to data, texts, ideas; help users locate or visualize information	iMapBuilder; Google Earth; Google Maps; NovaMind
Video	Recorded images; live-action images; enhanced slides; animation; sound; music	Record events; provide visual documentation; create presentations; furnish instructions, etc.	Animoto; Camtasia; iMovie; Movie Maker; Blender; Soundslides

Use social networks and blogs to create communities.   You know, of course, that Facebook and Twitter have transformed the way people share their lives and ideas. Social networks such as these are vastly more interactive versions of the online exchanges hosted by groups or individuals on blogs—which typically focus on topics such as politics, news, sports, technology, and entertainment. Social networks and blogs integrate comments, images, videos, and links in various ways; they are constantly updated, most are searchable, and some are archived.

College courses might use social networks and blogs to spur discussion of class materials, to distribute information, and to document research activities: Students in courses often set up their own social media groups. When networking or blogging is part of a course assignment, understand the ground rules. Instructors often require a defined number of postings/comments of a specific length. Participate regularly by reading and commenting on other students' posts; by making substantive comments of your own on the assigned topic; and by contributing relevant images, videos, and links.

Keep your academic postings focused, title them descriptively, and make sure they reflect the style of the course—most likely informal, but not quite as colloquial as public online groups. Pay attention to grammar and mechanics too. Avoid the vitriol you may encounter on national sites: Remember that anyone—from your mother to a future employer—might read your remarks.

Create Web sites to share information.   Not long ago, building Web sites was at the leading edge of technological savvy in the classroom. Today, social

This masthead appears on a Web site created by a college professor for his students and colleagues at McDaniel College in Maryland. Dr. Paul Muhlhauser, McDaniel College, English Department.

networks, blogs, and wikis are far more efficient vehicles for academic com-munication. Still, Web sites remain useful because of their capacity to organize large amounts of text and information online. A Web site you create for a course might report research findings or provide a portal to information on a complex topic.

When creating a site with multiple pages, plan early on how to organize that information; the structure will depend on your purpose and audience. A simple site with sequential information (e.g., a photo-essay) might lead readers through items one by one. More complicated sites may require a complex, hierarchical structure, with materials organized around careful topic divisions. The more comprehensive the site, the more deliberately you will need to map out its structure, allowing for easy navigation and growth.

Use wikis to collaborate with others.   If you have ever looked at Wiki-pedia, you know what a wiki does: It enables a group to collaborate on the development of an ongoing online project—from a comprehensive encyclo-pedia to focused databases on just about any imaginable topic. Such an effort combines the knowledge of all its contributors, ideally making the whole greater than its parts.

In academic courses, instructors may ask class members to publish articles on an existing wiki—in which case you should read the site guidelines, examine its current entries and templates, and then post your item. More likely, though, you will use wiki software to develop a collaborative project for the course itself—bringing together research on a specific academic topic. A wiki might even be used for a service project in which participants gather useful informa-tion about nutrition, jobs, or arts opportunities for specific communities.

As always with electronic projects, you need to learn the software—which will involve not only uploading material to the wiki but also editing and developing texts that classmates have already placed there.

Make videos and podcasts to share information.   With most cell phones now equipped with cameras, digital video has become the go-to medium these days for recording just about any event or for sharing ideas and information. In a sociology or government course, you might want to record important interviews; in a biology or engineering course, a video might be the best way to demonstrate a complex procedure. Software such as Movie Maker or iMovie can help you tell a

For a tutorial on audio editing, see **macmillanhighered.com/howtowrite3e.**
Tutorials › Digital Writing › Audio Editing with Audacity

story or make an argument; you can edit and mix digital scenes, refine the sound, add special effects and captions, and so on. If your subject is better served by animation, software such as Blender gives you different choices. You can construct nonnarrative kinds of video writing by combining text, film clips, still photos, and music using software such as Animoto, Soundslides, or Camtasia.

Podcasts remain a viable option for sharing downloadable audio or video files. Playable on various portable devices from MP3 players to tablets, podcasts are often published in series. Academic podcasts usually need to be scripted and edited. Producing a podcast is a two-step process. First you must record the podcast; then you need to upload it to a Web site for distribution. Software such as GarageBand can do both.

Hill Street Studios/Getty Images.

Use maps to position ideas.   You use mapping services such as Google Maps whenever you search online for a restaurant, store, or hotel. The service quickly provides maps and directions to available facilities, often embellished with links, information, and images. Not surprisingly, Google Maps, the related Google Earth, and other mapping software are finding classroom applications.

Multimedia maps also make it possible to display information such as economic trends, movements of people, climate data, and other variables graphically and dynamically, using color, text, images, and video/audio clips to emphasize movement and change across space and time. Even literary texts can be mapped so that scholars or readers may track events or characters as they move in real or imaginary landscapes. Mapping thus becomes a vehicle for reporting and sharing information, telling personal stories, revealing trends, exploring causal relationships, or making arguments.

Use appropriate digital formats.   Digital documents come in many forms, but you will use familiar word-processing, presentation, or spreadsheet software for most of your academic work. Compatibility is rarely an issue today when you move materials across computer platforms (PC to Mac) or download a presentation in a classroom for an oral report. Still, it never hurts to check ahead of time if, for example, you use Keynote or Prezi for a report rather than the more common PowerPoint.

Occasionally you need to save digital files in special formats. Sharing a file with someone using an older version of Word or Office may require saving a document in compatibility mode (.doc) rather than the now-standard .docx mode. Or moving across different applications may be easier if you use a plain text (.txt) or rich text format (.rtf)—in which case your document will lose some features, though the text will be preserved. When you want to share a document exactly as you wrote it and send it successfully across platforms, choose the .pdf mode. Files in .pdf form arrive exactly as you sent them, without any shifts in headings, alignments, or image locations; just as important, they cannot be easily altered.

Even if you have only a limited knowledge of differing image file formats (such as JPG, GIF, or TIFF), you probably understand that digital files come in varying sizes. The size of a digital-image file is directly related to the quality, or resolution, of the image. Attach a few high-resolution 26-megapixel photos to an e-mail and you'll clog the recipient's mailbox (or the e-mail will bounce back).

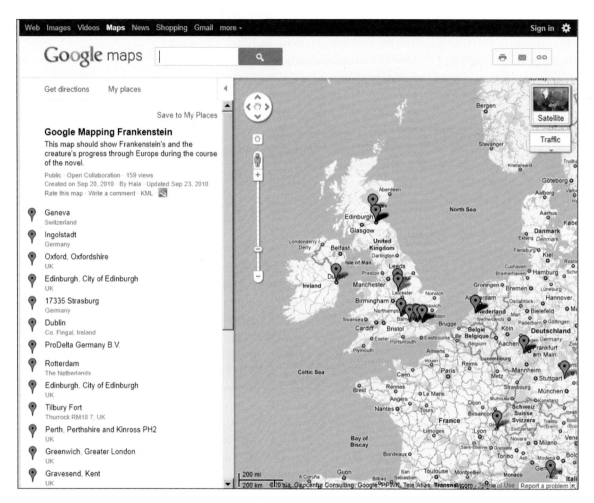

English instructor Hala Herbly asked students to map the movements across Europe of the monster from Mary Shelley's novel *Frankenstein.* © 2010 Google. Google and the Google logo are registered trademarks of Google, Inc., used with permission. Map data © 2010 Europa Technologies, PPWK. TeleAtlas-Hala Herbly.

For most Web pages and online documents, compressed or lower-resolution images will be acceptable. On the other hand, if you intend to print an image—in a paper or brochure, for example—use the highest-resolution image (the greatest number of pixels) available to assure maximum sharpness and quality.

Edit and save digital elements.   Nonprint media texts often require as much revising and editing as traditional written ones. In fact, the tools for manipulating video, audio, and still-image files are among the most remarkable accomplishments of the digital age. Even the simplest image-editing software, for example, enables users to adjust the tint, contrast, saturation, and sharpness of digital photographs or crop them as needed. If you are developing a podcast, an audio file can be tweaked a dozen ways using an audio editor like GarageBand or Audacity; such programs can also be used to create or refine musical clips. Comparable software is available for editing video clips.

Do keep careful tabs on any electronic content you collect for a project. Create a dedicated folder on your desktop, hard drive, or online storage and save each item with a name that will remind you where it came from. Keeping a printed record of images, with more detailed information about copyrights and sources, will pay dividends later, when you are putting your project or paper together and need to give proper credit to contributors.

Image-editing software offers numerous options for enhancing picture files. Look for these options on format tabs, palettes, or dropdown menus.
John J. Ruszkiewicz.

Respect copyrights.   The images you find, whether online or in print, belong to someone. You cannot use someone else's property—photographs, Web sites, brochures, posters, magazine articles, and so on—for commercial purposes without permission. You may use a reasonable number of images in academic papers, but you must be careful not to go beyond "fair use," especially for any work you put online. Search the term "academic fair use" online for detailed guidelines. Be prepared, too, to document images in academic research papers.

Your Turn   Most of the software programs mentioned in this chapter have Web sites that describe their features, and some sites even include sample projects. Explore one or two of these programs online to learn about their capabilities. Then describe a new media project you would like to create using the software.

---

e   For a tutorial on photo editing, see **macmillanhighered.com/howtowrite3e.**
Tutorials > Digital Writing > Photo Editing Basics with GIMP

49

Tables, Graphs, and Infographics

display data

> Often the most effective way to describe, explore, and summarize a set of numbers — even a very large set — is to look at pictures of those numbers.

—Edward R. Tufte

Inge Druckrey.

Just as images and photographs are often the media of choice for conveying visual information, tables, graphs, and other "infographics" are essential tools for displaying numerical and statistical data. They take raw data and transform it into a story or picture readers can interpret.

Most such items are created in spreadsheet programs such as Excel that format charts and graphs and offer numerous design templates — though you will find basic graphics tools in Word and PowerPoint as well. More elaborate charts and graphs can be drawn with software such as Adobe Illustrator.

Creating effective tables and graphs is an art in itself, driven as always by purpose and audience. A table in a printed report that a reader will study can be rich in detail; a bar graph on screen for only a few moments must make its point quickly and memorably. Function always trumps appearance. Yet there's no question that handsome visual texts appeal to audiences. So spend the time necessary to design effective items. Use color to emphasize and clarify graphs, not just to decorate them. Label items clearly (avoiding symbols or keys that are hard to interpret), and don't add more detail than necessary.

In academic projects, be sure to label (*Fig.*, *Table*), number, and caption your important graphic items, especially any that you mention in your text. Both MLA and APA style offer guidelines for handling labels; the APA rules are particularly detailed and specific.

Use tables to present statistical data.   Tables can do all kinds of work. They are essential for organizing and recording information as it comes in, for example, daily weather events: temperature, precipitation, wind velocities, and so on. A table may also show trends or emphasize contrasts. In such cases, tables may make an argument (in a print ad, for example) or readers may be left to interpret complex data on their own—one of the pleasures of studying such material.

Tables typically consist of horizontal rows and vertical columns into which you drop data. The axes of the chart provide different and significant ways of presenting data, relating x to y: for example, in Table 1, lifetime earnings are connected to education level.

In designing a table, determine how many horizontal rows and vertical columns are needed, how to label them, and whether to use color or shading to enhance the readability of the data. Software templates will provide options. Good tables can be very plain. In fact, many of the tables on federal government Web sites, though packed with information, are dirt simple and yet quite clear.

Use line graphs to display changes or trends.   Line graphs are dynamic images, visually plotting and connecting variables on horizontal x- and vertical

Table 1
Expected Lifetime Earnings Relative to High School Graduates, by Education Level

	Total Lifetime Earnings	Total Earnings Relative to High School Graduates	Present Value of Total Lifetime Earnings (3% Discount Rate)	Present Value Earnings Relative to HS Graduates (3% Discount Rate)
Not a High School Graduate	$941,370	0.74	$551,462	0.75
High School Graduate	1,266,730	1.00	738,609	1.00
Some College, No Degree	1,518,300	1.20	878,259	1.19
Associate Degree	1,620,730	1.28	943,181	1.28
Bachelor's Degree	2,054,380	1.62	1,189,836	1.61
Master's Degree	2,401,565	1.90	1,427,392	1.93
Doctoral Degree	3,073,240	2.43	1,748,716	2.37
Professional Degree	3,706,910	2.93	2,123,309	2.87
Bachelor's Degree or Higher	2,284,110	1.80	1,312,316	1.78

Sources: U.S. Census Bureau, 2006, PINC-03; calculations by the authors.

From College Board, *Education Pays: The Benefits of Higher Education for Individuals and Society*, 2007. Copyright © 2007 The College Board. www.collegeboard.org. Reproduced with permission.

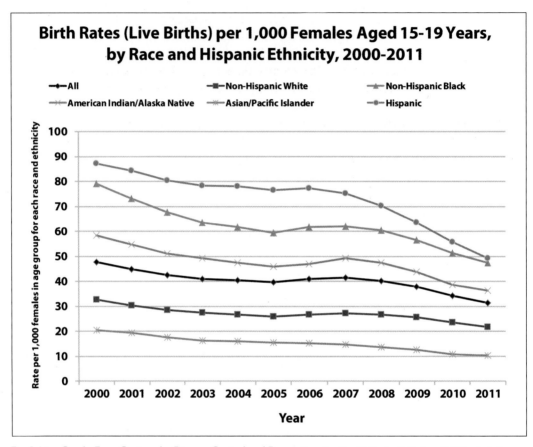

Fig. 1. Line Graph. From Centers for Disease Control and Prevention. Hamilton BE, Martin JA, Ventura SJ. *Births: Preliminary data for 2010.* National Vital Statistics Reports, 2011; 60(2): Table S-2.* Hamilton BE, Martin JA, Ventura SJ. *Births: Preliminary data for 2011.* National Vital Statistics Reports. 2012; 61(5). Table 2, Hyattsville, MD: National Center for Health Statistics, 2012.

y-axes so that readers can see how relationships change or trends emerge, usually over time. As such, line graphs often contribute to political or social arguments by tracking fluctuations in income, unemployment, educational attainment, stock prices, and so on.

Properly designed, line graphs are easy to read and informative, especially when just a single variable is presented. But it is possible to plot several items on an axis, complicating the line graph but increasing the amount of information it offers (see fig. 1).

Use bar and column graphs to plot relationships within sets of data.
Column and bar graphs use rectangles to represent information either horizontally (bar graph) or vertically (column graph). In either form, these graphs
emphasize differences and can show changes over time; they enable readers to
grasp relationships that would otherwise take many words to explain. Bar and
column graphs present data precisely, if their *x*- and *y*-axes are carefully drawn
to scale. In Figure 2, for example, a reader can determine the number of major

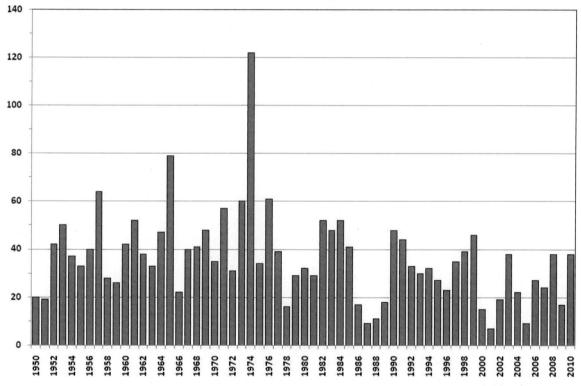

*Beginning in 2007, NOAA switched from the Fujita scale
to the Enhance Fujita scale for rating tornado strength.*

Fig. 2. Number of Strong to Violent (EF3–EF5) Tornadoes. From NOAA Satellite and Information Service. National Oceanic and
Atmospheric Administration and the Department of Commerce.

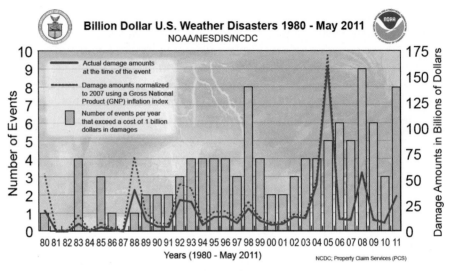

Fig. 3. Billion Dollar U.S. Weather Disasters 1980–2011. From NOAA Satellite and Information Service. National Oceanic and Atmospheric Administration, National Environmental Satellite, Data and Information Service, and the National Climatic Data Center.

tornadoes in any of more than fifty years and also note a slight trend toward fewer severe storms.

But it is easy to ask a single graphic image to do too much. For example, many readers probably find Figure 3 hard to interpret. Is the chart about the number of storms, their growing frequency, or their actual and adjusted costs? Storm effects in the background of the graphic just add to the clutter.

Use pie charts to display proportions.   A typical pie chart is a circle broken into segments that represent some proportion of a whole. Such charts illustrate which parts of that whole have greater or lesser significance, but they do not display precise numbers well. Note in Figure 4, for example, that without the actual sales percentages attached to the chart, you could not easily tell which auto brand sold the most cars in the United States in 2012—Mercedes or BMW. Since the segments in a typical pie chart need to total 100 percent, you sometimes have to include a segment called "Others / Don't know" to account for items not actually present in the major categories.

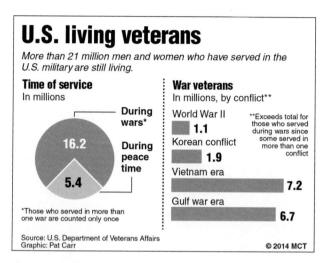

Fig. 4. A combined pie and bar chart uses pale green, a color associated with military fatigue uniforms, to show numbers of veterans in terms of their time of service, as well as the conflicts in which they served. Carr/MCT/Newscom.

Pie-chart sections can be cut only so thin before they begin to lose clarity. Figure 4, for instance, uses a pie chart for double-digit figures, and a bar chart for smaller numbers. If you wanted to use a pie chart to depict dozens of items—say the payrolls of all thirty major league baseball teams—you'd find yourself with slivers readers couldn't interpret confidently. Better to transfer the data to a bar graph that could incorporate more detailed information.

Explore the possibilities of infographics.   Under the rubric of "infographics," many organizations and information specialists create data-driven visual texts about subjects from climate change to trends in music. Such presentations part ways with traditional academic conventions to tell lively but information-rich stories (see fig. 5). One writer calls these focused presentations—freely combining charts, tables, timelines, maps, and other design elements—"visual essays." But many infographics are, in fact, "visual arguments" that use the medium to support particular claims or points of view: They combine images and data to dramatize an issue.

Various tools are available online to support the creation of infographics, including Many Eyes, Google Public Data Explorer, Wordle, and StatPlanet. For more about infographics and many examples, search the term online.

Fig. 5. The Summer Surge. From Georgetown University Center on Education and the Workforce. Georgetown Center on Education and the Workforce, the Summer Surge.

Your Turn   Study Figure 5, "The Summer Surge." Then look online for additional examples of infographics. (They are readily available on sites such as VizWorld or Cool Infographics.) When you have sampled enough such items to have a sense of what the genre does, try to define the term "infographics" on your own. What do these charts have in common? What are their distinctive features?

Designing Print and Online Documents

50

Much advice about good visual design is common sense: *Of course*, academic and professional documents should look uncluttered, consistent, and harmonious. But it is not always easy to translate principles into practice. Nor are any visual guidelines absolute. A balanced and consistent design is exactly what you want for research reports and government documents, but brochures or infographics may need more snap.

think
visually

Understand the power of images. Most of us realize how powerful images can be, particularly when they perfectly capture a moment or make an argument that words alone struggle to express. The famous "Blue Marble" shot of the Earth taken by *Apollo 17* in 1972 is one such image—conveying both the wonder and fragility of our planet hanging in space.

Visual texts can be important elements in your own work. Use photographs to tell arresting stories or use videos to underscore important points in an argument. In fact, you can craft the style of any page or screen—its colors, shapes, headings, type fonts, and so on—to make a text more visually appealing, focused, and accessible.

Be sure, though, to identify or caption any photos, videos, or audio files in your project. Captions, in particular, help readers appreciate the significance of the specific texts you have included. If you also number these items in longer papers (e.g., *Fig. 1*; *Table 4*), you can direct readers to them unambiguously.

Science Source.

For a tutorial on using Word and similar tools, see **macmillanhighered.com/howtowrite3e.**
Tutorials › Digital Writing › Word Processing

557

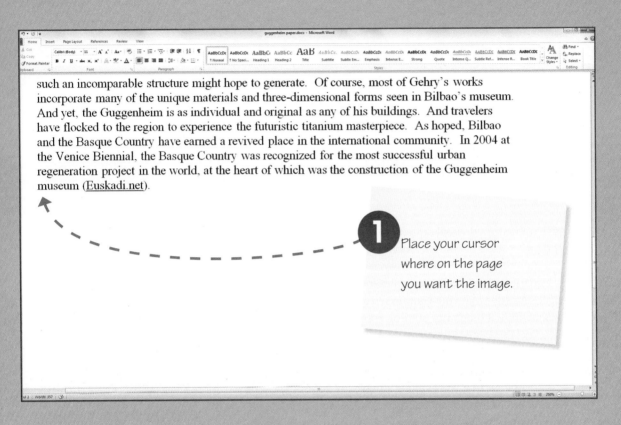

such an incomparable structure might hope to generate. Of course, most of Gehry's works incorporate many of the unique materials and three-dimensional forms seen in Bilbao's museum. And yet, the Guggenheim is as individual and original as any of his buildings. And travelers have flocked to the region to experience the futuristic titanium masterpiece. As hoped, Bilbao and the Basque Country have earned a revived place in the international community. In 2004 at the Venice Biennial, the Basque Country was recognized for most successful urban regeneration project in the world, at the heart of which was the construction of the Guggenheim museum (Euskadi.net).

1 Place your cursor where on the page you want the image.

2 On the "Insert" tab, click "Picture."

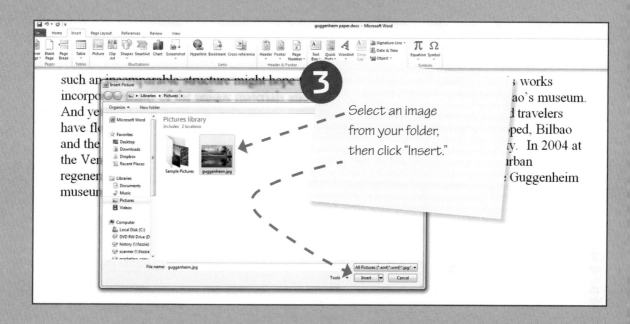

Select an image from your folder, then click "Insert."

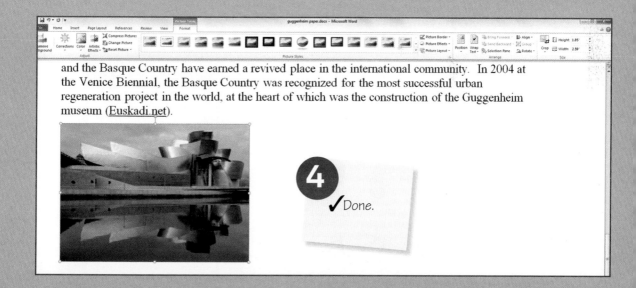

and the Basque Country have earned a revived place in the international community. In 2004 at the Venice Biennial, the Basque Country was recognized for the most successful urban regeneration project in the world, at the heart of which was the construction of the Guggenheim museum (Euskadi.net).

4 ✓Done.

Keep page designs simple and uncluttered.   Simple doesn't mean a design should be simplistic, only that you shouldn't try to do more on a page than it (or your design skills) can handle. You want readers to find information they need, navigate your document without missteps, and grasp the structure of your project. Key information should stand out. If you make the basic design intuitive, you can present lots of information without a page feeling cluttered.

Consider, for example, how cleverly Anthro Technology Furniture uses design cues as simple as *Step 1*, *Step 2*, and *Step 3* to guide consumers on a Web page through the complex process of configuring a workstation. Readers simply move left to right across a page, making specific choices. They don't feel overwhelmed by the options, even though the material is detailed.

Horizontal header guides reader across page.

Configuring the piece of furniture is broken into four easy steps.

Thumbnail images depict wide range of possible accessories.

Special box keeps track of consumer's decisions.

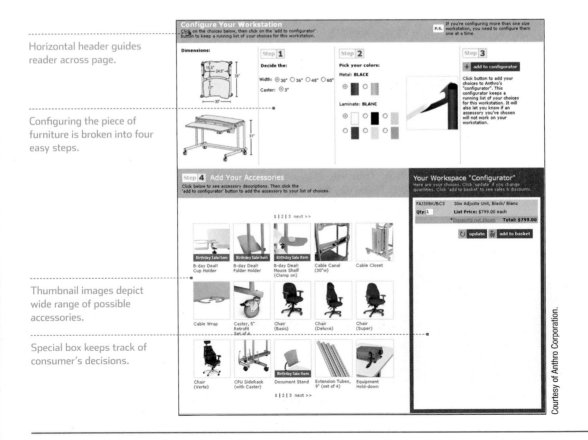

Courtesy of Anthro Corporation.

Keep the design logical and consistent. Readers should grasp the logic of a design quickly and then understand how its elements operate throughout a document—especially on Web sites, in PowerPoint presentations, and in long papers.

Look to successful Web sites for models of logical and consistent design. Many sites build their pages around distinct horizontal and vertical columns that help readers find information. A main menu generally appears near the top of the page, more detailed navigational links are usually located in a narrow side column, and

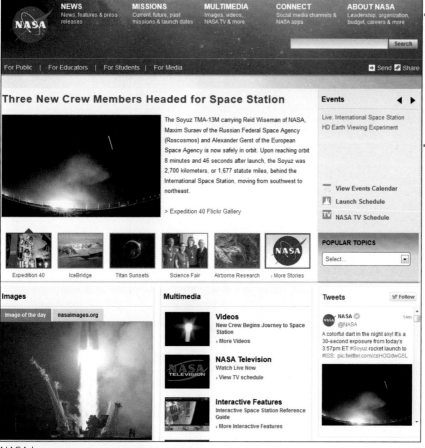

NASA's information-rich page has a consistent horizontal orientation. The eye moves left to right to explore major options. Yet distinct horizontal sections also break the page into visually coherent segments.

Images (many of them thumbnail sized) are carefully aligned to convey information appealingly.

Full screen (not reproduced here) offers more than sixty links or options. Color scheme throughout the site is consistent: white, black, and shades of blue.

NASA home page. Courtesy NASA/JPL-Caltech.

Home page of the *Pittsburgh Post-Gazette,* July 17, 2014. Copyright ©, *Pittsburgh Post-Gazette,* 2014, all rights reserved. Reprinted with permission.

To attract readers, interior section previews top the simple masthead.

Larger headline size gives impact to this international story.

Local human-interest story dominates the news, its importance signaled by its special headline, its placement, and a large color photo.

Below the fold, a unique headline style is used to set off an interesting color photo of a local event.

featured stories often appear in wide columns in the center. To separate columns as well as individual items, the site designers use headlines, horizontal rules, images, or some combination of these devices. Handled well, pages are easy to navigate and thick with information, yet somehow they seem uncluttered.

Keep the design balanced.   Think of balance as an operative term—what you hope to achieve *overall* in a design. You probably don't want many pages that, if split down the middle, would show mirror images. Strive instead for dynamic designs, in which, for example, a large photograph on one side of a document is offset on the other by blocks of print and maybe several smaller images. The overall effect achieved is rough symmetry, even though various page elements may all differ in size and shape.

You can see conventional design principles at work on the front pages of most newspapers (print or online), where editors try to come up with a look that gives impact to the news. They have many elements to work with, including their paper's masthead, headlines of varying size, photographs and images, columns of copy, screened boxes, and much more. The pages of a newspaper can teach you a lot about design.

But you can learn, too, from the boundaries being pushed by designers of Web infographics (see Chapter 49), who use elaborate media effects to present information efficiently yet imaginatively. Unlike newspapers, magazines, or full Web sites, which must follow consistent specifications for page after page, a typical infographic focuses on a single theme or subject, and its creator chooses the media tools best suited to the topic, whether graphs, flowcharts, maps, images, diagrams, or cutaways.

Use templates sensibly.   If you have the time and talent to design all your own documents, that's terrific. But for many projects, you could do worse than to begin with the templates offered by many software products. The Project Gallery in Microsoft Office, for example, helps you create business letters, brochures, PowerPoint presentations, and more. It sets up a generic document, placing the document's margins, aligning key elements and graphics, and offering an array of customizations. No two projects based on the same template need look alike.

If you resist borrowing such materials from software, not wanting yet another part of your life packaged by corporate types, know that it is tough to design documents from scratch. Even if you intend to design an item yourself, consider examining a template to figure out how to assemble a complex document. Take what you learn from the model and then strike out on your own.

Coordinate your colors.   Your mother was right: Pay attention to shades and patterns when you dress and when you design color documents. To learn elementary principles of color coordination, try searching "color wheel" on the Web, but recognize that the subject is both complicated and more art than science. As an amateur, keep your design palettes relatively conventional and model your work on documents that you find particularly attractive.

For academic papers, the text is always black and the background is white. Color is fine in graphs and illustrations if the paper will be reviewed onscreen or printed in color. But be sure that no important elements are lost if the document is printed in black and white: A bar graph that relies on color to display differences might become unreadable. For Web sites and other projects, keep background shades light, if you use them at all, and maintain adequate contrast between text and background. Avoid either bright or pale fonts for passages of text.

Use headings if needed.   Readers appreciate headings as pathways through a text. In academic work, they should be descriptive rather than clever. If you have prepared a good scratch or topic outline, the major points may provide you with almost ready-made headings. ○ Like items in an outline, headings at the same level in a project should be roughly parallel in style. ○

A short paper (three to five pages) doesn't require much more than a title. For longer papers (ten to twenty pages), it's possible to use top-level items from your outline as headings. For some projects, especially in the sciences, you must use the headings you're given. This is especially true for lab reports and scientific articles, and you shouldn't vary from the template.

Choose appropriate fonts.   There are probably dozens or even hundreds of fonts to work with on your computer, but simple is generally best. Here is some basic information to help you choose an appropriate font for your needs.

order ideas
p. 377

help with common
errors p. 566

Serif fonts, such as Times New Roman, show thin flares and embellishments (called serifs; circled in the illustration on p. 565) at the tops and bottoms of their letters and characters. These fonts have a traditional look. In contrast, *sans serif* fonts, such as Helvetica, lack the decorations of serif fonts. They are smoother and more contemporary. On the sample newspaper front page (see p. 562), serif fonts dominate, but sans serif fonts are used for several minor items.

Serif fonts are more readable than sans serif for extended passages of writing, such as papers. Headings in a sans serif font can offer welcome contrast in a document that uses a serif font for its text. Some designers prefer sans serif fonts for Web sites and PowerPoint presentations, especially for headings.

For typical academic projects, all text, headings, and other elements— including the title—are set in one font size, either 10 or 12 point. The standard font is Times New Roman. In professional or business projects, however, such as résumés, newsletters, or PowerPoint slides, you may want to vary fonts and type sizes in order to set off headings, captions, and headlines from other elements.

You can boldface words and phrases selectively to make them stand out clearly on a page. But boldfaced items or headings close together can make a page look heavy and cluttered. Such items should be rare. Never use boldface as the regular text throughout a project. If you want an emphatic font, find one that looks that way in its regular form.

Fonts described as *display* and *decorative* are designed to attract attention (see, for example the masthead of the *Pittsburgh Post-Gazette* on p. 562). You should avoid them for academic and professional writing, but you may want to explore their use when creating posters, brochures, or special PowerPoint presentations. Never use them for extended passages of writing.

Times New Roman

Times New Roman, a serif font.

Helvetica

Helvetica, a sans serif font.

Common Errors

part nine

51 Capitalization

Spring or
spring?

In principle, the guidelines for capitalizing seem straightforward. You surely know to capitalize most proper nouns (and the proper adjectives formed from them), book and movie titles, the first words of sentences, and so on. But the fact is that you make many judgment calls when capitalizing, some of which will require a dictionary. Here are just a few of the special cases that can complicate your editing.

Capitalize the names of ethnic, religious, and political groups.   The names of these groups are considered proper nouns. Nonspecific groups, however, are lowercase.

South Korean	Native Americans	native peoples
Buddhists	Muslims	true believers
Tea Party	Democrats	political parties
the Miami City Council		the city council

Capitalize modifiers formed from proper nouns.   In rare cases, such as *gargantuan* or *french* (in *fry* or *toast*), the expressions have become so common that the adjective is not routinely capitalized. When in doubt, consult a dictionary.

PROPER NOUN	PROPER NOUN USED AS MODIFIER
French	French thought
Navajo	Navajo rug
Jew	Jewish lore
American	American history

Capitalize all words in titles except prepositions, articles, or conjunctions.
This is the basic rule for the titles of books, movies, long poems, and so on.

Dickens and the Dream of Cinema

In the Company of Cheerful Ladies

The variations and exceptions to this general rule, however, are numerous. MLA style specifies that the first and last words in titles always be capitalized, including any articles or prepositions.

The Guide to National Parks of the Southwest

To the Lighthouse

Such Stuff as Dreams Are Made Of

APA style doesn't make that qualification, but does specify that all words longer than four letters be capitalized in titles—even prepositions. (Note that this rule applies to titles mentioned within articles and essays themselves not titles in APA-style documentation, discussed below.)

A Walk Among the Tombstones

Sleeping Through the Night and Other Lies

In all major styles, any word following a colon (or, much rarer, a dash) in a title is capitalized, even an article or preposition:

True Blood: All Together Now

The Exile: An Outlander Graphic Novel

Finally, note that in APA style *documentation*—that is, within the in-text citations and on the references page, titles are capitalized differently. Only the first word in most titles, any proper nouns or adjectives, and any word following a colon are capitalized. All other words are lowercase:

Bat predation and the evolution of frog vocalizations in the neotropics

Human aging: Usual and successful

Take care with compass points, directions, and specific geographical areas.   Points of the compass and simple directions are not capitalized when referring to general locations.

north	southwest
northern Ohio	eastern Canada
southern exposure	western horizons

But these same terms *are* capitalized when they refer to specific regions that are geographically, culturally, or politically significant (keep that dictionary handy!). Such terms are often preceded by the definite article, *the*.

the West	the Old South
the Third Coast	Southern California
Middle Eastern politics	the Western allies

Understand academic conventions.   Academic degrees are not capitalized, except when abbreviated.

bachelor of arts	doctor of medicine
MA	PhD

Specific course titles are capitalized, but they are lowercase when used as general subjects. Exception: Languages are always capitalized when referring to academic subjects.

Organic Chemistry 101	Contemporary British Poetry
an organic chemistry course	an English literature paper

Capitalize months, days, holidays, and historical periods.   But don't capitalize the seasons.

January	winter
Monday	spring
Halloween	summer
the Enlightenment	fall

Apostrophes  52

Like gnats, apostrophes are small and irritating. They have two major functions: to signal that a noun is possessive and to indicate where letters have been left out in contractions. Apostrophes always need careful review.

Use apostrophes to form the possessive.   The basic rules for forming the possessive aren't complicated: For singular nouns, add 's to the end of the word:

it's or
its?

> the wolf's lair
>
> the photographer's portfolio
>
> IBM's profits
>
> Bush's foreign policy

Some possessives, while correct, look or sound awkward. In these cases, try an alternative:

ORIGINAL	REVISED
the class's photo	the class photo; the photo of the class
Alicia Keys's latest hit	the latest hit by Alicia Keys
Kansas's budget	in the Kansas budget; in the budget of Kansas

For plural nouns that do not end in *s*, also add *'s* to the end of the word:

men's shoes   the mice's tails   the geese's nemesis

For plural nouns that do end in *s*, add an apostrophe after that terminal *s*:

the wolves' pups

the Bushes' foreign policies

three senators' votes

Use apostrophes in contractions.   An apostrophe in a contraction takes the place of missing letters. Edit carefully, keeping in mind that a spell-checker doesn't help you with such blunders. It catches only words that make no sense without apostrophes, such as *dont* or *Ive*.

DRAFT	Its a shame that its come to this.
CORRECTED	It's (It is) a shame that it's (it has) come to this.
DRAFT	Whose got the list of whose going on the trip?
CORRECTED	Who's (Who has) got the list of who's (who is) going on the trip?

Don't use apostrophes with possessive pronouns.   The following possessives do not take apostrophes: *its, whose, his, hers, ours, yours,* and *theirs.*

DRAFT	We photographed the tower at it's best angle.
CORRECTED	We photographed the tower at its best angle.
DRAFT	The book is her's, not his.
CORRECTED	The book is hers, not his.
DRAFT	Their's may be an Oscar-winning film, but our's is still better.
CORRECTED	Theirs may be an Oscar-winning film, but ours is still better.

There is, inevitably, an exception. Indefinite pronouns such as *everybody, anybody, nobody,* and so on do show possession via *'s*.

House of Cards was everybody's favorite.

Why it was so successful is anybody's guess.

Commas  53

The comma has more uses than any other punctuation mark—uses that can seem complex. The following guidelines will help you handle commas in academic writing.

Use a comma and a coordinating conjunction to join two independent clauses.   An independent clause can stand on its own as a sentence. To join two of them, you need both a coordinating conjunction *and* a comma. A comma alone is not enough.

> Fiona's car broke down. She had to walk two miles to the train station.

> Fiona's car broke down, so she had to walk two miles to the train station.

need to connect ideas?

There are several points to remember here. Be certain that you truly have two independent clauses, and not just a compound subject or verb. Also, make sure to include both a comma and a coordinating conjunction (*and, but, for, nor, or, so, yet*). Leaving out the coordinating conjunction creates an error known as a comma splice (see p. 577).

Use a comma after an introductory word group.   Introductory word groups are descriptive phrases or clauses that open a sentence. Separate these introductions from the main part of the sentence with a comma.

e For an activity on commas, see **macmillanhighered.com/howtowrite3e.**
Tutorials > LearningCurve Activities > Commas

573

> Within two years of getting a degree in journalism, Ishan was writing for the *Wall Street Journal*.

For very brief introductory phrases, the comma may be omitted, but it is not wrong to leave it in.

> After college I plan to join the Marines.
>
> After college, I plan to join the Marines.

Use commas with common connective words and phrases.   These would include items such as the following: *however; therefore; consequently; finally; furthermore; nonetheless; specifically; as a result; in addition; for instance; in fact; on the other hand; that is*. If a transitional word or phrase opens a sentence, it is usually followed by a comma.

> Furthermore, medical reports suggest that trans fats lower the amount of good cholesterol found in the body.
>
> On the other hand, studies of cholesterol have been notoriously controversial.

When used within a sentence, expressions such as *however* and *for example* should be set off by a pair of commas.

> Big payrolls mean success in professional sports. In baseball, for example, teams from New York and Boston are almost always competitive. There are, however, notable exceptions.

Be especially careful with punctuation around *however* and *therefore*. A common error is to place commas around these connective words to link a pair of related sentences. This move produces an error called a comma splice (see Chapter 54 for more details). Here's what that error looks like:

COMMA SPLICE   In baseball, teams with big payrolls are almost always competitive, however, there are notable exceptions.

To correct this type of comma splice, you can place a semicolon before *however* or create two separate sentences:

> In baseball, teams with big payrolls are almost always competitive; however, there are notable exceptions.
>
> In baseball, teams with big payrolls are almost always competitive. However, there are notable exceptions.

Put commas around nonrestrictive (that is, nonessential) elements.
You'll know that a word or phrase is functioning as a nonrestrictive modifier if
you can remove it from the sentence without obscuring the overall meaning of
the sentence.

> Cicero, ancient Rome's greatest orator and lawyer, was a self-made man.
>
> Cicero was a self-made man.

The second sentence is less informative but still makes sense. See also the
guideline on page 576, "Do not use commas to set off restrictive elements."

Use commas to separate items in a series.   Commas are necessary when
you have three or more items in a series.

> American highways were once ruled by powerful muscle cars such as GTOs,
> Road Runners, and Gran Sports.

Do not use commas to separate compound verbs.   Don't confuse a true
compound sentence (which has two independent clauses) with a sentence that
simply has two verbs.

DRAFT	They rumbled through city streets, and smoked down drag strips.
CORRECTED	They rumbled through city streets and smoked down drag strips.

They rumbled through city streets is an independent clause, but *and smoked down
drag strips* is not, because it doesn't have its own subject. To join two verbs that
share a common subject (in this case, *they*), all you need is *and*. When you have
three or more verbs, however, treat them as items in a series and do separate
them with commas. Compare the following examples:

TWO VERBS	Muscle cars guzzled gasoline and burned rubber.
THREE VERBS	Muscle cars guzzled gasoline, burned rubber, and drove parents crazy.

Do not use a comma between subject and verb.   Perhaps it's obvious
why such commas don't work when you notice one in a short sentence.

DRAFT	Keeping focused, can be difficult.
CORRECTED	Keeping focused can be difficult.

When a subject gets long and complicated, however, you might be more tempted to insert the comma. It would still be both unnecessary and wrong. The commas in the following sentences should be omitted.

UNNECESSARY COMMA   Keeping focused on driving while simultaneously trying to operate a cell phone, can be difficult.

The excuses that some people come up with to defend their bad habits on the road, sound pathetic.

Do not use commas to set off restrictive elements.   Phrases you cannot remove from a sentence without significantly altering meaning are called *restrictive* or *essential*. They are modifiers that provide information needed to understand the subject.

Only nations that recognize a right to free speech and free press should be eligible for seats on international human rights commissions.

Students who have a perfect attendance record will earn three points for class participation.

Delete the blue phrases in the above examples and you are left with sentences that are vague or confusing. Put commas around the phrases and you create the false impression that they could be removed.

Comma Splices, Run-Ons, and Fragments

The sentence errors marked most often in college writing are comma splices, run-ons, and fragments.

Identify comma splices and run-ons.   A *comma splice* occurs when only a comma is used to join two independent clauses (an independent clause contains a complete subject and verb).

Identify a comma splice simply by reading the clauses on either side of a doubtful comma. If *both* clauses stand on their own as sentences (with their own subjects and verbs), it's a comma splice.

need a complete sentence?

COMMA SPLICES   Officials at many elementary schools are trying to reduce childhood obesity on their campuses, research suggests that few of their strategies will work.

Some schools emphasize a need for more exercise, others have even gone so far as to reinstate recess.

A *run-on* sentence resembles a comma splice, but this somewhat rarer mistake doesn't even include the comma to mark a break between independent clauses. The clauses just slam together, confusing readers.

For an activity on run-ons and comma splices, see **macmillanhighered.com/howtowrite3e.**
Tutorials > LearningCurve Activities > Run-Ons and Comma Splices

577

Common Coordinating
Conjunctions

and	or
but	so
for	yet
nor	

RUN-ON SENTENCES   Officials at many elementary schools are trying to reduce childhood obesity on their campuses research suggests that few of their strategies will work.

Some schools emphasize a need for more exercise others have even gone so far as to reinstate recess.

Fix comma splices and run-ons.   To repair comma splices and run-ons, you have many options. The first is to connect the two independent clauses by inserting *both* a comma and a coordinating conjunction between them.

> Officials at many elementary schools are trying to reduce childhood obesity on their campuses, but research suggests that few of their strategies will work.

> Some schools emphasize a need for more exercise, and others have even gone so far as to reinstate recess.

A second fix is to use a semicolon alone to join the two clauses.

> Officials at many elementary schools are trying to reduce childhood obesity on their campuses; research suggests that few of their strategies will work.

> Some schools emphasize a need for more exercise; others have even gone so far as to reinstate recess.

Less frequently, colons or dashes may be used as connecting punctuation when the second clause summarizes or illustrates the main point of the first clause.

> Some schools have taken extreme measures: They have banned cookies, snacks, and other high-calorie foods from their vending machines.

Along with the semicolon (or colon or dash), you may wish to add a transitional word or phrase (such as *however* or *in fact*). If you do, set off the transitional word or phrase with commas. ○

> Officials at many elementary schools are trying to reduce childhood obesity on their campuses; research, however, suggests that few of their strategies will work.

> Some schools emphasize a need for more exercise — in fact, some have even gone so far as to reinstate recess.

Alternatively, you can rewrite the sentence to make one of the clauses clearly subordinate to the other. To do that, introduce one of the clauses with a

connect ideas
p. 387

subordinating conjunction so that it can no longer stand as a sentence on its own. Compare the two corrected versions to see your options:

Common Subordinating Conjunctions	
after	once
although	since
as	that
because	though
before	unless
except	until
if	when

DRAFT   Officials at many elementary schools are trying to reduce childhood obesity on their campuses, research suggests that few of their strategies will work.

CORRECTED   Although officials at many elementary schools are trying to reduce childhood obesity on their campuses, research suggests that few of their strategies will work.

CORRECTED   Officials at many elementary schools are trying to reduce childhood obesity on their campuses, even though research suggests that few of their strategies will work.

Finally, you can simply use end punctuation to create two independent sentences. Here, a period between the clauses eliminates either a comma splice or a run-on.

Officials at many elementary schools are trying to reduce childhood obesity on their campuses. Research suggests that few of their strategies will work.

Identify sentence fragments.   A sentence fragment is a word group that lacks a subject, verb, or possibly both. As such, it is not a complete sentence and is usually not appropriate for academic and professional writing. (You will find fragments routinely in fiction and popular writing.)

FRAGMENT   Climatologists see much physical evidence of climate change. Especially in the receding of glaciers around the world.

Fix sentence fragments in your work.   You have two options for fixing sentence fragments. Attach the fragment to a nearby sentence with appropriate punctuation, often a comma:

COMPLETE   Climatologists see much physical evidence of climate change, especially
SENTENCE   in the receding of glaciers around the world.

For an activity on fragments, see **macmillanhighered.com/howtowrite3e.**
Tutorials > LearningCurve Activities > Fragments

Turn the fragment into its own sentence:

COMPLETE SENTENCE   Climatologists see much physical evidence of climate change.
They are especially concerned by the receding of glaciers
around the world.

Watch for fragments in the following situations.   Often a fragment will follow a complete sentence and start with a subordinating conjunction.

FRAGMENT   Climate change seems to be the product of human activity.
Though some scientists believe sun cycles may explain the
changing climate.

COMPLETE SENTENCE   Climate change seems to be the product of human activity,
though some scientists believe sun cycles may explain the
changing climate.

Participles (such as *breaking, seeking, finding*) and infinitives (such as *to break, to seek, to find*) can also lead you into fragments.

FRAGMENT   Of course, many people welcome the warmer weather. Upsetting scientists who fear governments will not act until global
warming becomes irreversible.

COMPLETE SENTENCE   Of course, many people welcome the warmer weather. Their
attitude upsets scientists who fear governments will not act
until global warming becomes irreversible.

Use deliberate fragments only in appropriate situations.   You'll find that fragments are common in advertising, fiction, and informal writing. In personal e-mail or on social networking sites, for example, expressions or clichés such as the following would probably be acceptable to your audience.

In your dreams.	Excellent!
Not on your life.	When pigs fly.

Subject/Verb Agreement

55

Verbs take many forms to express changing tenses, moods, and voices. To avoid common errors in choosing the correct verb form, follow these guidelines.

Be sure the verb agrees with its real subject. It's tempting to link a verb to the noun(s) closest to it (in purple below) instead of the subject, but that's a mistake.

none are or
none is?

DRAFT	Cameras and professional lenses that cost as much as a small **car** makes photography an expensive hobby.
CORRECTED	Cameras and professional lenses that cost as much as a small car make photography an expensive hobby.
DRAFT	Bottled water from convenience **stores** or **groceries** usually cost far more per ounce than gasoline.
CORRECTED	Bottled water from convenience stores or groceries usually costs far more per ounce than gasoline.

Some of the indefinite pronouns described as variable (see chart on p. 583) are exceptions to the rule. Whether they are singular or plural depends on the nouns that follow them (see p. 583).

For an activity on subject/verb agreement, see **macmillanhighered.com/howtowrite3e.**
Tutorials › LearningCurve Activities › Subject-Verb Agreement

581

In most cases, treat multiple subjects joined by *and* as plural.   But when a subject with *and* clearly expresses a single notion, that subject is singular.

> Hip-hop, rock, and country are dominant forms of popular music today. [subject is plural]
>
> Blues and folk have their fans too. [subject is plural]
>
> Rock and roll often strikes a political chord. [subject is singular]
>
> Peanut butter and jelly is the sandwich of choice in our house. [subject is singular]

When singular subjects are followed by expressions such as *along with*, *together with*, or *as well as*, the subjects may feel plural, but technically they remain singular.

DRAFT	James Blake, as well as Kendrick Lamar, Macklemore & Ryan Lewis, Kacey Musgraves, and Ed Sheeran, were competing for Best New Artist at the 2014 Grammys.
CORRECTED	James Blake, as well as Kendrick Lamar, Macklemore & Ryan Lewis, Kacey Musgraves, and Ed Sheeran, was competing for Best New Artist at the 2014 Grammys.

If the corrected version sounds awkward, try revising the sentence.

CORRECTED	James Blake, Kendrick Lamar, Macklemore & Ryan Lewis, Kacey Musgraves, and Ed Sheeran were all competing for Best New Artist at the 2014 Grammys.

When compound subjects are linked by *either . . . or* or *neither . . . nor*, make the verb agree with the nearer part of the subject.   Knowing this rule will make you one person among a thousand.

> Neither my sisters nor my mother is a fan of Kanye West.

When possible, put the plural part of the subject closer to the verb to make it sound less awkward.

> Neither my mother nor my sisters are fans of Kanye West.

Indefinite Pronouns

Singular	Plural	Variable
anybody	both	all
anyone	few	any
anything	many	more
each	others	most
everybody	several	none
everyone		some
everything		
nobody		
no one		
nothing		
one		
somebody		
someone		
something		

Confirm whether an indefinite pronoun is singular, plural, or variable.

Most indefinite pronouns are singular, but consult the chart on this page to double-check.

> Everybody complains about politics, but nobody does much about it.

> Each of the women expects a promotion.

> Something needs to be done about the budget crisis.

A few indefinite pronouns are obviously plural: *both, few, many, others, several*.

> Many complain about politics, but few do much about it.

And some indefinite pronouns shift in number, depending on the prepositional phrases that modify them.

> All of the votes are in the ballot box.

> All of the fruit is spoiled.

> Most of the rules are less complicated.
>
> Most of the globe is covered by oceans.
>
> None of the rules make sense.
>
> On the Security Council, none but the Russians favor the resolution.

Be consistent with collective nouns.   Many of these words describing a group can be treated as either singular or plural: *band, class, jury, choir, group, committee.*

> The jury seems to resent the lawyer's playing to its emotions.
>
> The jury seem to resent the lawyer's playing to their emotions.
>
> The band was unhappy with its latest release.
>
> The band were unhappy with their latest release.

A basic principle is to be consistent throughout a passage. If *the band* is singular the first time you mention it, keep it that way for the remainder of the project. Be sensible too. If a sentence sounds odd to your ear, modify it:

AWKWARD   The band were unhappy with their latest release.

BETTER   The members of the band were unhappy with their latest release.

Irregular Verbs

Verbs are considered regular if the past and past participle—which you use to construct various tenses—are formed by simply adding -*d* or -*ed* to the base of the verb. Below are several regular verbs.

Base Form	Past Tense	Past Participle
smile	smiled	smiled
accept	accepted	accepted
manage	managed	managed

lie or *lay*?

Unfortunately, the most common verbs in English are irregular. The chart on page 586 lists some of them. When in doubt about the proper form of a verb, check a dictionary.

Base Form	Past Tense	Past Participle
be	was, were	been
become	became	become
break	broke	broken
buy	bought	bought
choose	chose	chosen
come	came	come
dive	dived, dove	dived
do	did	done
drink	drank	drunk
drive	drove	driven
eat	ate	eaten
get	got	gotten
give	gave	given
go	went	gone
have	had	had
lay (to put or place)	laid	laid
lie (to recline)	lay	lain
ride	rode	ridden
ring	rang, rung	rung
rise	rose	risen
see	saw	seen
set	set	set
shine	shone, shined	shone, shined
sing	sang, sung	sung
sink	sank, sunk	sunk
speak	spoke	spoken
swear	swore	sworn
throw	threw	thrown
wake	woke, waked	woken, waked
write	wrote	written

Pronoun/Antecedent Agreement

57

You already know that pronouns take the place of nouns. Anteced-ents are the words pronouns refer to. Pronouns share some of the same markers with nouns, such as gender and number.

SINGULAR/FEMININE	The nun merely smiled because **she** had taken a vow of silence.
SINGULAR/MASCULINE	The NASCAR champion complained that **he** got too little media attention.
SINGULAR/NEUTER	The chess team took **itself** too seriously.
PLURAL	Members of the chess team took **themselves** too seriously.
PLURAL	**They** seemed awfully subdued for pro athletes.
PLURAL	The bride and groom wrote **their** own marriage vows.
PLURAL	Many in the terminal resented searches of **their** luggage.

their or *his* or *hers?*

The basic rule for managing pronouns and antecedents couldn't be simpler: Make sure pronouns you select have the same number and gender as the words they stand for.

DRAFT	When a student spends too much time on sorority activities, **they** may suffer academically.
CORRECTED	When a student spends too much time on sorority activities, **she** may suffer academically.

As always, though, there are confusing cases and numerous exceptions. The following guidelines can help you avoid common problems.

Check the number of indefinite pronouns.   Some of the most common singular indefinite pronouns—especially *anybody, everybody, everyone*—may seem plural, but they should be treated as singular in academic or formal writing. (For the complete list of indefinite pronouns, see the chart on p. 583 in Chapter 55.)

DRAFT   Has everybody completed **their** assignment by now?

CORRECTED   Has everybody completed **his or her** assignment by now?

If using *his or her* sounds awkward (and it almost always does), revise the sentence.

    Have all students completed **their** assignments by now?

Correct sexist pronoun usage.   Using either *his* or *her* alone (instead of *his or her*) to refer to an indefinite pronoun can be considered sexist unless the pronoun clearly refers only to males or females. The principle also applies to *he* and *she* when the pronouns are similarly exclusionary. ○ You usually have several options for avoiding sexist usage.

DRAFT   Don't trust a driver using her cell phone on the freeway.

CORRECTED   Don't trust a driver using **his or her** cell phone on the freeway.

CORRECTED   Don't trust drivers using **their** cell phones on the freeway.

Treat collective nouns consistently.   Collective nouns—such as *team, herd, congregation, mob,* and so on—can be treated as either singular or plural.

    The Roman legion marched until **it** reached **its** camp in Gaul.

    The Roman legion marched until **they** reached **their** camp in Gaul.

Just be consistent and sensible in your usage. Treat a collective noun the same way, as either singular or plural, throughout a paper or project. And don't hesitate to modify a sentence when even a correct usage sounds awkward.

AWKWARD   The team smiled as **it** received **its** championship jerseys.

BETTER   Members of the team smiled as **they** received **their** championship jerseys.

respect your
readers p. 408

Pronoun Reference

58

A pronoun should refer back clearly to a noun or pronoun (its *antecedent*), usually the one nearest to it that matches it in number and, when necessary, gender.

> Consumers will buy a **Rolex** because they covet its snob appeal.
>
> Nancy Pelosi spoke at the news conference instead of **Harry Reid** because she had more interest in the legislation than **he** did.

sure what it means?

If connections between pronouns and antecedents wobble within a single sentence or longer passage, readers will struggle. The following guidelines can help you avoid three common problems.

Clarify confusing pronoun antecedents. Revise sentences in which readers will find themselves wondering who is doing what to whom. Multiple revisions are usually possible, depending on how the confusing sentence could be interpreted.

CONFUSING	The batter collided with the first baseman, but he wasn't injured.
BETTER	The batter collided with the first baseman, who wasn't injured.
BETTER	The batter wasn't injured by his collision with the first baseman.

Make sure a pronoun has a plausible antecedent.   Sometimes the problem is that the antecedent doesn't actually exist—it is only implied. In these cases, either reconsider the antecedent/pronoun relationship or replace the pronoun with a noun.

CONFUSING   Grandmother had hip-replacement surgery two months ago, and it is already fully healed.

In the above sentence, the implied antecedent for *it* is *hip*, but the noun *hip* isn't in the sentence (*hip-replacement* is an adjective describing *surgery*).

BETTER   Grandmother had her hip replaced two months ago, and she is already fully healed.

BETTER   Grandmother had hip-replacement surgery two months ago, and her hip is already fully healed.

Be certain that the antecedent of *this*, *that*, or *which* isn't vague.   In the following example, a humble *this* is asked to shoulder the burden of a writer who hasn't quite figured out how to pull together all the ideas raised in the preceding sentences. What exactly might the antecedent for *this* be? It doesn't exist. To fix the problem, the writer needs to replace *this* with a more thoughtful analysis.

FINAL SENTENCE VAGUE

The university staff is underpaid, the labs are short on equipment, and campus maintenance is neglected. Moreover, we need two or three new parking garages to make up for the lots lost because of recent construction projects. Yet students cannot be expected to shoulder additional costs because tuition and fees are high already. This is a problem that must be solved.

FINAL SENTENCE CLARIFIED

How to fund both academic departments and infrastructure needs without increasing students' financial outlay is a problem that must be solved.

Pronoun Case

In spoken English, you know it when you run into a problem with pronoun case.

> "Let's just keep this matter between **you** and . . . *ummmm* . . . **me**."

> "To **who** . . . I mean, uh . . . **whom** does this letter go?"

> "Hector is more of a people person than **her** . . . than **she** is."

Like nouns, pronouns can act as subjects, objects, or possessives in sentences, so their forms vary to show which case they express.

I or *me*? *who* or *whom*?

Subjective Pronouns	Objective Pronouns	Possessive Pronouns
I	me	my, mine
you	you	your, yours
he, she, it	him, her, it	his, her, hers, its
we	us	our, ours
they	them	their, theirs
who	whom	whose

Unfortunately, determining case isn't always easy. Here are some strategies for dealing with these common situations.

Use the subjective case for pronouns that are subjects.   When a pronoun is the lone subject in a clause, it rarely causes a problem. But double the subject and suddenly there's trouble.

> Sara and me . . . , or is it Sara and I? . . . wrote the report.

To make the right choice, try answering the question for each subject separately, one at a time. You will then probably recognize that *Sara* wrote the report, and so did the subjective form of the pronoun, *I: I* wrote the report. (*Me*, the objective pronoun, sure didn't.) So the revision is simple:

> Sara and I wrote the report.

Use the objective case for pronouns that are objects.   Again, choosing one objective pronoun is generally easy, but with two objects, the choice becomes less clear. How do you decide what to do in the following sentence?

> The corporate attorney will represent both Geoff and I . . . Geoff and me?

Again, deal with one object at a time.

> The corporate attorney will represent Geoff.
> The corporate attorney will represent me.

The sentence needs the objective form of the pronoun:

> The corporate attorney will represent Geoff and me.

Or, to be more concise:

> The corporate attorney will represent us.

Note that *us* is also an objective form of the pronoun. The subjective form *we* would not work here at all.

Use *whom* when appropriate.   One pronoun choice brings many writers to their knees: *who* or *whom*. The rule, however, is the same as for other pronouns: Use the subjective case (*who*) for subjects and the objective case (*whom*) for objects. In some cases, the choice is obvious.

DRAFT   Whom wrote the report?

CORRECTED   Who wrote the report?

DRAFT   By who was the report written?

CORRECTED   By whom was the report written?

But this choice becomes tricky when you're dealing with subordinate clauses.

DRAFT   The shelter needs help from whomever can volunteer three hours per week.

The previous example may sound right because *whomever* immediately follows the preposition *from*. But, because the pronoun is the subject of a subordinate clause, it needs to be in the subjective case.

CORRECTED   The shelter needs help from whoever can volunteer three hours per week.

When in doubt, prefer *who* to *whom*. Even when you err, you won't sound ridiculous.

Finish comparisons to determine the right case.   Many times when writers make comparisons, they leave out some understood information.

> I've always thought John was more talented than Paul.
>
> (I've always thought John was more talented than Paul *was*.)

But leaving this information out can lead to confusion when it comes to choosing the correct pronoun case. Try the sentence, adding *him*.

DRAFT   I've always thought John was more talented than him.

   I've always thought John was more talented than him *was*.

CORRECTED   I've always thought John was more talented than he.

If it sounds strange to use the correct pronoun, just complete the sentence.

CORRECTED   I've always thought John was more talented than he was.

Don't be misled by an appositive.   An *appositive* is a word or phrase that amplifies or renames a noun or pronoun. In the example below, *Americans* is the appositive. First, try reading the sentence without it.

DRAFT	Us Americans must defend our civil rights.
APPOSITIVE CUT	Us must defend our civil rights. [*Us* can't be a subject.]
CORRECTED	We Americans must defend our civil rights.

Note that when the pronoun is contained within the appositive, as in the examples that follow, the pronoun uses the case of the word or words it stands in for. This rule makes more sense when seen in an example.

SUBJECTIVE	The runners leading the marathon, Matt, Luci, and I, all had trained at Central High School.
OBJECTIVE	The race was won by the runners from Central High, Matt, Luci, and me.

In the first example, *runners* is the subject of the sentence. Since *Matt, Luci, and I* merely rename that subject, they share its subjective case. In the second example, *the runners* have become the object of a preposition: *by the runners*. So the threesome now moves into the objective case as well: *Matt, Luci, and me*.

Misplaced and Dangling Modifiers

In general, modifiers need to be close and obviously connected to the words they modify. When they aren't, readers may become confused—or amused.

Position modifiers close to the words they modify.

| MISPLACED | Layered like a wedding cake, Mrs. DeLeon unveiled her model for the parade float. |

Mrs. DeLeon is not layered like a wedding cake; the model for the parade float is.

| REVISED | Mrs. DeLeon unveiled her model for the parade float, which was layered like a wedding cake. |

Place adverbs such as *only, almost, especially,* and *even* carefully.
If these modifiers are placed improperly, their purpose can be vague or ambiguous.

| VAGUE | The speaker almost angered everyone in the room. |
| CLEARER | The speaker angered almost everyone in the room. |

AMBIGUOUS	Joan only drove a pickup.
CLEARER	Only Joan drove a pickup.
CLEARER	Joan drove only a pickup.

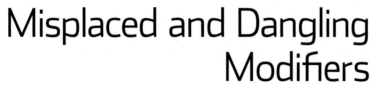

are your
descriptions
clear?

Don't allow a modifier to dangle.   A modifying word or phrase at the beginning of a sentence should usually be followed by a subject to which it connects clearly. When it doesn't, the modifier is said to dangle, especially when there is no other word in the sentence it can logically describe.

DANGLING   Arriving at sunset, the Grand Canyon was awash in golden light.

Nothing in the sentence is actually modified by the opening phrase. Revision is necessary.

REVISED   Arriving at sunset, we beheld the Grand Canyon awash in golden light.

Don't, however, confuse dangling modifiers with *absolutes*, which are phrases that can, in fact, modify entire sentences without connecting to particular words or subjects. Here are some examples:

All things considered, the vacation was a success.

To be honest, our hotel room at the park left much to be desired.

Parallelism

61

When items in sentences follow similar patterns of language, they are described as parallel. Parallel structure makes your writing easier to read and understand.

When possible, make compound items parallel.   Don't confuse your readers by requiring them to untangle subjects, verbs, modifiers, or other items that could easily be parallel.

making a list?

NOT PARALLEL	Becoming a lawyer and to write a novel are Casey's goals.
PARALLEL	Becoming a lawyer and writing a novel are Casey's goals.
NOT PARALLEL	The college will demolish its aging stadium and bricks from it are being sold.
PARALLEL	The college will demolish its aging stadium and sell the bricks.
NOT PARALLEL	The TV anchor reported the story thoroughly and with compassion.
PARALLEL	The TV anchor reported the story thoroughly and compassionately.

Keep items in a series parallel.   This means that once you start a series, all the items in it should share the same form or structure. You might have a series of adjectives (*tough, smart,* and *aggressive*), adverbs (*slowly* and *carefully*), participles (*kicking, screaming,* and *giggling*), infinitives (*to break the siege* and *to free the hostages*), and so on.

NOT PARALLEL	She was a fine rookie teacher — eager, very patient, and gets her work done.
PARALLEL	She was a fine rookie teacher — eager, very patient, and conscientious.
NOT PARALLEL	We expected to rehabilitate the historic property, breaking even on the investment, and earn the goodwill of the community.
PARALLEL	We expected to rehabilitate the historic property, to break even on the investment, and to earn the goodwill of the community.
PARALLEL	We expected to rehabilitate the historic property, break even on the investment, and earn the goodwill of the community.

Keep headings and lists parallel.   If you use headings to break up the text of a document, use a similar language pattern and design for all of them. It may help to type the headings out separately from the text to make sure you are keeping them parallel. Items in a printed list should be parallel as well.

reader

Readings

10

Need help with critical reading? See page 340. / Need help analyzing claims and evidence? See page 456.

62 Narratives: Readings

Literacy Narrative

AMY TAN

From "Mother Tongue"

I later decided I should envision a reader for the stories I would write. And the reader I decided upon was my mother, because these were stories about mothers. So with this reader in mind — and in fact she did read my early drafts — I began to write stories using all the Englishes I grew up with: the English I spoke to my mother, which for lack of a better term might be described as "simple"; the English she used with me, which for lack of a better term might be described as "broken"; my translation of her Chinese, which could certainly be described as "watered down"; and what I imagined to be her translation of her Chinese if she could speak in perfect English, her internal language, and for that I sought to preserve the essence, but neither an English nor a Chinese structure. I wanted to capture what language ability tests can never reveal: her intent, her passion, her imagery, the rhythms of her speech and the nature of her thoughts.

Use lists.

Though we might think that lists should only be included in genres like reports or proposals, lists in narrative essays can be very powerful. Lists allow writers to create a sense of rhythm and momentum; they allow us to acknowledge many possibilities within a story, even if we can't explore all of them; they can mirror the stream of our thoughts. In the passage above, Amy Tan concludes her essay with two lists, one divided by semicolons, one divided by commas. Importantly, because this is a literacy narrative about "Englishes," the lists allow her to catalog and honor the diversity of the language as she knows it. By ending the essay with these lists, she offers more than one conclusion or lesson.

▶

Try ending your own narrative with a list of things you learned from experiencing your story or a list of things you hope your readers learned from reading it. Experiment with long lists, short lists, and different styles of punctuation. Reread your list and look back to make sure your narrative has effectively communicated all the things you have listed—this is a good test to see if your narrative is as complete as you'd intended. Then you may choose to use this list as part of your conclusion, or you might cut it. Regardless, developing the ability to effectively write lists can help you write in nearly any genre.

NARRATIVE   Actor and comedian Patton Oswalt is perhaps best known as the voice of Remy, the lead character in the animated Pixar film *Ratatouille*. This short essay comes from his book of the same name: *Zombie Spaceship Wasteland* (2011), which, as in his standup comedy, mixes personal history with pop culture. In addition to standup, Oswalt has written essays for publications such as *The Believer* and *The Huffington Post*, and stories for comics. His latest book, *Silver Screen Fiend*, is a memoir that also chronicles his obsession with classic movies.

PATTON OSWALT

Zombie Spaceship Wasteland

Are you a Zombie, a Spaceship, or a Wasteland?

For my group of friends, after seeing *Star Wars* in 1977, around age eight, and then *Night of the Living Dead* and all the eighties slasher films once VCRs sprouted on top of our TVs, and *The Road Warrior* in 1981, the answer to that question decided our destinies.

I know there have been a thousand parsings of the pop subculture — comic books, video games, horror movies, heavy metal, science fiction, Dungeons and Dragons. There are hundreds more categories. They can be laid out in overlapping Venn diagrams — a tub full of lonely bubbles. Burnouts who are into heavy metal got there through Dungeons and Dragons, maybe some glam rock, probably horror movies. Hard-core comic book readers often became film snobs later in life (they spent their adolescence reading, essentially, storyboards). Even sports freaks[1] — with their endless, exotic game stats — overlapped into metal and, yeah, maybe comic books.

But for me, and my circle of high school friends, it came down to *Zombies*, *Spaceships*, or *Wastelands*. These were the three doors out of the Vestibule of Adolescence, and each opened onto a dark, echoing hallway. The corridors twisted and intertwined, like a DNA helix. Maybe those paths were a rough reflection of the DNA we were born with, which made us more likely to cherish and pursue one corridor over another.

I'm going to try to explain each of these categories (and will probably fail). And then I'll figure out where I came out, on the other end, once the cards were played. I think this essay is more for me than for you.

Each of these categories represents different aspects of a shared teen experience — not fully understanding how the world works, socially or economically. The early outcasts — like me — were late to sex and careers. If we did find a vocation, it usually involved drawing or writing or *something* creative — work that's done in the home, and usually alone. The real-world experience we're going to need, as writers or artists or filmmakers, will come later, when we actually have to get a real job to support whatever creative thing we're hoping to do.

So until then, anything we create has to involve *simplifying*, *leaving*, or *destroying* the world we're living in.

Zombies simplify. They don't understand the world any better than Spaceships or Wastelands, but they sure like the houses and highways. Every zombie story is fundamentally about a breakdown of order, with the infrastructure intact. That infrastructure might be on fire, yes. And it's great fun to crash a bus through a department store window as the driver finds himself torn to shreds by the suddenly zombified passengers. But the world, appearance-wise, survives. It might eventually become a wasteland (more advanced Zombies begin their stories far in the future, where the world is already a wasteland), but for now, it's a microcosm of archetypes, fighting for survival against the undead hordes. Usually this small group is made up of the archetypes that the teen has met thus far into his short existence — the Hero, the Unattainable Hottie, the Loudmouth Douchebag, and the Brainiac Who Knows What's Going On. Consistent with an awkward teen's roiling sense of vengeance and self-hatred, it's usually only the Loudmouth Douchebag and the Brainiac who get killed.

Usually, but not often. Since Zombies follow their path into horror, Goth, slasher films, some punk rock, and most metal, Zombies tend to be the most nihilistic of the three. Thus, most zombie movies — including the classic *Night of the Living Dead* — end with every single character dead.

A friend of mine from high school — more of a passing acquaintance, now that I think of it — was a hard-core zombie before he even knew it. He had an unshakable love for the awkward and outcast and a quiet, final disgust with the slick and false. And he divided everyone into one of these two categories, with maybe three subsets for each (Physically Awkward, Mentally Awkward, Sports Slick, Republican Slick — you get the idea).

Years later, when I'd moved to L.A., he sent me a zombie script he'd written. Not a bad effort. Not a great one.

At one point in the script, one of the characters knocks a zombie off of a boat. The zombie struggles for a moment, trying to stay afloat, and then sinks.

I asked him, innocently, "It never occurred to me — would a zombie care if it were underwater or not? They don't breathe. Would they even know?"

This was his terse answer: "For your information, zombies can live underwater, *they just don't like it.*"

He was a Zombie who'd long ago taken a zombie-eyed view of the world. You see them everywhere — rolling their eyes outside a rock club at how lame the band was, shaking their heads over a newspaper in a coffee shop, resentful under office lighting. Zombies can't believe the energy we waste on nonfood pursuits.

Night of the Living Dead (and most zombie films) is about *Zombies* who are in the process of turning the world into a *Wasteland*, and who've been brought back to life by radiation on a crashed *Spaceship*.

Spaceships leave. No surviving infrastructure for them. No Earth, period. *That* would still involve people.

Better to not only leave the world, but to create a new one and decide how the creatures (or human-looking aliens) act. Often, the alien planet they populate is a glorified wasteland. But even in that wasteland, Spaceships figure it's easier for them to build a world and know its history or, better yet, choose the limited customs and rituals that fit the story. Every Spaceship kid I knew growing up now works in computers. They got there through New Wave, post-punk, video games, and science fiction. Why bother reading subtle facial cues and emotional signals when there's a vast (yet finite) map of a motherboard to tinker with?

But, being Spaceships, they describe in the most loving detail the spaceships that zoom between worlds. "Laser cannons" take the place of conversation, "deflector shields" are emotional nuance, and "warp drive" is story exposition. The opening shot of *Star Wars*, with the sleek rebel ship and then the massive Imperial Star Destroyer, barreling across the screen like the pan across a party in an Altman film, permanently doomed a generation of Spaceships to their insular, slightly muted lives. Spaceships have the hallway with the most gravity, firmly pulling its victims down a cool tunnel of romantic vacuum. In their bodies, skulls, and spirits, a chunk of my peers became Spaceships, skimming over the surface of the world, maneuvering through their own lives. Deflector shields up.

Spaceships are the ones most likely to get married and have kids. They treat their houses like spaceships that have landed on earth, and their spouses and kids like crew members. Which makes them pretty good parents—they've always got emergency kits, lists of most-used numbers, backup supplies of ointment, painkillers, and bottled water. The two guys I spent my youth building Lego spaceships with are two of the greatest dads I've ever known—a good captain knows how to treat his crew.

Darth Vader is, essentially, a *Zombie*, born in a *Wasteland*, who works on a *Spaceship*.

Wastelands destroy. They're confused but fascinated by the world. So the idea of zooming off in a self-contained spaceship, no matter how lovingly described or sensually evoked,[2] smacks of retreat. But the blandness of the world we've built — a lot of Wastelands come from the suburbs — frustrates and frightens them as much as the coldness of space. Aliens would bring wonder, and zombies bring the surviving humans together — Wastelands aren't comfortable with either of those ideas.

The solution? Wasteland. Post-nuke, post–meteor strike, or simply a million years into the future — that's the perfect environment for the Wasteland's imagination to gallop through. The wasteland is inhabited by people or, for variety, mutants. At least mutants are outgrowths of humans. Mutants — the main inhabitants of post-apocalyptic environments — are more familiar. Variations of the human species grown amok — isn't that how some teenage outcasts already feel? Mutants bring comfort. You don't have to figure out alien biology or exotic, inhuman cultures or religions. At the most, mutants will have weird mental powers or practice cannibalism. The heroes are unmutated humans, wandering across deserts (always, weirdly, wearing leather or tattered overcoats — suburban teens are accustomed to air-conditioning, so it's not until they're older that they learn the importance of fabrics that breathe) and carrying what they need. Wastelands are great at stocking belt pouches, backpacks, and pockets. At any time, Wastelands suspect they're going to need to grab whatever's at hand and head for the horizon.

Wastelands are almost always swallowed up by punk rock and science fiction. They're also the most likely to keep journals and usually the first to get menial jobs. The Wasteland tarot card should come with a pay stub.

Weirdly, Wastelands are the most hopeful and sentimental of the bunch. Because even though they've destroyed the world as we know it, they conceive of stories in which a core of humanity — either in actual numbers of survivors or in the conscience of a lone hero — survives and endures. Wastelands, in college, love Beckett.

The monster in *Alien* was discovered on a *Spaceship* that had crashed in a *Wasteland*, and reproduced by temporarily turning its victims into alien-incubating *Zombies*.

Leatherface, Michael Myers, Jason Voorhees, Pinhead, and Freddy Krueger are, essentially, *Zombies* who want to turn our world into a *Wasteland*. Jason and Pinhead each, at one point, end up on a *Spaceship*.

The *Matrix* films are about a hero, Neo, who doesn't realize he's a *Zombie*, and also doesn't realize he's living in a *Wasteland*, until he's awoken by Morpheus, who dezombifies Neo by bringing him on board a *Spaceship*.

Every teen outcast who pursues a creative career has, at its outset, either a Zombie, Spaceship, or Wasteland work of art in them.

Looking back on it now, I realize I'm a Wasteland. A lot of comedians are Wastelands—what is stand-up comedy except isolating specific parts of culture or humanity and holding them up against a stark, vast background to approach at an oblique angle and get laughs? Or, in a broader sense, pointing out how so much of what we perceive as culture and society is disposable waste? Plus, comedians have to work the Road. We wander the country, seeking outposts full of cheap booze, nachos, and audiences in order to ply our trade. I'm amazed we all don't wear sawed-off shotguns on our hips.

The Zombie, Spaceship, or Wasteland "work" is conceived of during the nadir of puberty—a grim, low-budget film about the undead; a vast space opera; or a final battle for civilization in a blasted wasteland, where the fate of mankind is decided by a shotgun blast or a crossbow.

Turns out I had two Wasteland works in me, and I wrote them both freshman year of high school. The first was called *The Shadow Dogs*, which I figured I'd publish in paperback, like a Stephen King novel.[3] It involved—I'm not kidding—a future where mutant dogs had taken over. They were basically tall people with dog heads. The hero—I can't even remember his name—wandered the wasteland with a cool wrist gun and another sidearm that I basically swiped from *Blade Runner*, which I still think has one of the coolest movie guns.

Hey—why do the heroes always "wander" the wasteland? Wouldn't you at least have a plan to get somewhere with water or food before you started hoofing it? Even desert nomads don't "wander" around pell-mell, assuming they'll hit an oasis just before dropping dead of thirst. Is it the alliteration of it? "Wander the wasteland"? I guess "Take a well-thought-out, purposeful trek through the wasteland" lacks that movie-trailer punch.

Anyway, *The Shadow Dogs.* I spent the first eighty pages of the novel equipping my main character. I'm not kidding—he started with a bolt-action rifle and a knife, and then he killed some people and took enough canned food and other trinkets from them to trade for the wrist gun and *Blade Runner* gun. Once I realized I couldn't think of any cooler guns for him to acquire, I lost interest in the book.

The other one was called *Cholly Victor and the Wasteland Blues,* which I wrote in installments and planned to do as a massive graphic novel. Cholly Victor was a near-plotless library of everything I was obsessed with at the time—*The Road Warrior, El Topo, Eraserhead,* Richard Corben, nuclear fears, and spaghetti westerns. Holy God, was it a piece of crap. But I got it out of my system. It ends with my hero, Cholly, a shotgun-wielding wasteland scavenger, defeating a mutant, flayed-lamb robot warlord, and then continuing on down a piece of broken highway to the mythical "Westcoast."[4]

My own life didn't even come close to my defeating a robot warlord and setting out for Westcoast. In reality, I got sick of doing jokes in front of the zombies at the local comedy clubs. I moved to San Francisco. In a used Jetta, not a spaceship. And driving cross-country wasn't "wandering the wasteland," but Utah came close enough.

Notes

1. Not to be confused with jocks or athletes—a distinction beautifully laid out by Sarah Vowell in *Take the Cannoli*, a book very much worth your time.
2. The spaceship in *Battle beyond the Stars* has huge breasts and a woman's voice!
3. Stephen King, who was the first person I ever read who could meld perfectly felt, mundane life with cosmic horror, later published the *Dark Tower* series, a huge Wasteland epic that tied together most of his novels, which take place in our "real" world. And I'm pretty sure he got the idea in high school. If he didn't, I would like him to lie about it to support my thesis. Thanks, Steve!
4. Cormac McCarthy won the Pulitzer for *The Road*, about a father and son making their way for a mythical coast after an unnamed global cataclysm. But Cormac's hero didn't have a four-armed, bandolier-wearing mutant Kodiak bear sidekick, did he?

Reading the Genre

1. Think about the categories Oswalt sets up. Are you a zombie, a spaceship, or a wasteland? Or are you some parts of each? Explain why you do or don't fit into these categories. Don't be afraid to make up your own category if none of these works for you.

2. This is a narrative essay, but it also lays out its own taxonomy (a taxonomy is a way to sort or classify things). How does this classification system help Oswalt tell stories? What does this taxonomy do for his structure, organization, and characterization, and how does it help him to reflect on past experiences?

3. An anthropologist might suggest that what Oswalt is doing in this narrative is also ethnography (a way to describe groups of people through close observation and writing). Some of the goals of ethnography are that the text should help the reader better understand social life, that its authors must be sufficiently conscious of their own role in the society they study, and that the account should feel true and revealing. How does Oswalt's essay measure up to these standards?

4. **WRITING:** Develop your own classification system for you and your friends. As Oswalt does, use stories to illustrate why you and those you know fit in these invented categories. If it helps, you could choose one of your favorite books, films, or TV shows and then show how you and your friends align with the characters from that text.

5. **COMPOSING VISUALLY:** Using YouTube, find examples of a zombie, spaceship, or wasteland character from a movie or television show (or from other media). Write about how the character fits this category, and embed relevant video or images in your Word document or blog. Then think about how this character also reflects aspects of your own personality or the personality of someone you know. How does this fictional character (and his or her zombieness, spaceship-ness, or wasteland-ness) help you to better understand yourself or people you know?

GRAPHIC NARRATIVE (EXCERPT)   Lynda Barry writes the weekly comic strip *Ernie Pook's Comeek*, which can be found in many alternative weekly newspapers. Barry's work is often funny but serious, sad but optimistic. When she writes about herself, as she does in this excerpt from the book *One! Hundred! Demons!* (2002), she is very honest about her own past. She currently teaches a popular writing workshop called Writing the Unthinkable. Barry has written seventeen books; her most recent is the collection *Blabber Blabber Blabber: Volume 1 of Everything* (2011).

Lost and Found

Lynda Barry

"Lost and Found" from *One! Hundred! Demons!* by Lynda Barry (Sasquatch Books, 2002). © 2002 by Lynda Barry. Courtesy of Darhansoff & Verrill.

AFTER I LEARNED TO READ, I LOVED GETTING HOME FROM SCHOOL AND WAITING FOR THE AFTERNOON PAPER. WE DIDN'T HAVE BOOKS IN THE HOUSE, BUT THE PAPER GAVE ME PLENTY TO WORK WITH.

THE FIRST SECTION I TURNED TO WAS THE CLASSIFIEDS. I ALWAYS READ THE "LOST AND FOUND" ADS, TRYING TO MEMORIZE DESCRIPTIONS OF DOGS AND CATS WHO WERE OUT THERE ALONE AND SCARED.

2 YR OLD M BRN+WHT CHIHUAHUA MIX. RD COLLAR. ANS TO "HENRY." REWARD.

"JINGLES" LOST 10/2. F GRAY TABBY. BLIND RT EYE NEEDS MEDICATION.

POOR JINGLES.

EACH QUARTER-INCH AD WAS LIKE A CHAPTER IN A BOOK. I'D IMAGINE THE WHOLE STORY: THE FREAKED-OUT PEOPLE, THE FREAKED-OUT ANIMALS, AND ME, ALWAYS COMING TO THE RESCUE AND NEVER ACCEPTING THE REWARD.

NO, KEEP THE FIVE HUNDRED DOLLARS, SIR. ALL I CARE ABOUT IS THAT HENRY IS HOME.

PLEASE, MA'AM, WHAT MY NAME IS DOESN'T MATTER. AND NEITHER DOES THE TEN THOUSAND DOLLARS. ALL THAT MATTERS IS JINGLES.

LIKE MOST WRITERS, I LOVED TO READ WHEN I WAS LITTLE, BUT UNTIL RECENTLY, I NEVER REALLY THOUGHT ABOUT SOME OF THE THINGS I ENJOYED READING MOST. THE CLASSIFIED ADS FASCINATED ME.

CRYPT IN MAUSOLEUM. PRIME LOC. EYE-LEVEL. BEST OFFER. EVENINGS.

SZ. 12 WEDDING DRESS. NEVER WORN. MUST SACRIFICE.

FILL DIRT, VERY CLEAN.

PARTY PIANIST. MY PIANO OR YOURS.

THEY GAVE ME SO MANY WEIRD BLANKS TO FILL IN. LIKE WHO WAS SELLING THEIR CRYPT? I ONLY KNEW THE WORD FROM HORROR MOVIES. ZOMBIES AND VAMPIRES CAME OUT OF THEM. THE AD SAID "EVENINGS." IT SEEMED LIKE SUCH AN OBVIOUS TRICK.

DING DONG

WHO IS IT?

UH, I'M HERE ABOUT THE CRYPT?

AAHHHH!!

SAME WITH THE WEDDING DRESS AD. WHO ELSE WAS GOING TO CALL ABOUT IT EXCEPT A MAIDEN? IT SAID "MUST SACRIFICE." WHO ELSE GOT SACRIFICED BUT MAIDENS? THE POLICE WOULD BE BAFFLED BY HOW MAIDENS KEPT DISAPPEARING.

HELLO?

YES?

YOU'VE GOT TO BE KIDDING.

OK.

NOT ANOTHER MAIDEN!

I'M AFRAID SO.

DANG!

WHEN I CAME FORWARD WITH THE SOLUTION TO THESE CRIMES, AT FIRST NO ONE WOULD BELIEVE ME. I EXPECTED THAT. I WATCHED A LOT OF MOVIES. NO ONE EVER BELIEVES KIDS AT FIRST. YOU HAVE TO WAIT UNTIL ALMOST THE END. YOU HAVE TO WAIT 'TIL YOUR LIFE IS IN DANGER.

CALLING ALL CARS! THAT KID WAS RIGHT ABOUT THE WANT ADS!

BUT NOW THE CRYPT-VAMPIRE AND THE WEDDING DRESS-ZOMBIE HAVE HER IN THEIR CLUTCHES! WE WERE SO STUPID! REPEAT! VERY STUPID!

MOSTLY I DIED IN MY CLAS-SIFIED STORIES. EVEN THEN I LOVED TRAGIC ENDINGS. PEO-PLE WOULD BE CRYING SO HARD. THEY'D COVER MY COFFIN WITH FILL DIRT, VERY CLEAN. THE PARTY PIANIST WOULD PLAY.

CHERISH IS THE WORD I USE TO DIS-CRI-IBE..

WHEN I READ ABOUT WRITER'S LIVES, THERE ARE USUALLY STORIES ABOUT WRITING FROM THE TIME THEY WERE LITTLE. I NEVER WROTE ANYTHING UN-TIL I WAS A TEENAGER, AND THEN IT WAS ONLY A DIARY THAT SAID THE SAME THING OVER AND OVER.

I thought Bill liked me but turns out he doesn't. I'm so depressed about Bill. He didn't call me. I can't stop thinking about Bill.

WRITERS TALK ABOUT ALL THE BOOKS THEY LOVED WHEN THEY WERE CHILDREN. CLASSIC STORIES I NEVER READ, BUT I LIED ABOUT BECAUSE I WAS SCARED IT WAS PROOF I WASN'T REALLY A WRITER.

AND WIND IN THE WILLOWS?

AH, YES.

AMAZING.

"THE LION, THE WITCH AND THE WARDROBE?"

INCREDIBLE. SAME WITH "WATERHEAD DOWN".

YOU MEAN "WATERSHIP".

UH, YEAH.

SUPER DRAMATICALLY EDUCATED. KNOWS ABOUT "STORY STRUC-TURE" AND "ARC" AND "PLOT POINTS"

JIVE-ASS FAKER WHO CAN'T SPELL AND HAS NO IDEA WHAT "STORY STRUCTURE" EVEN MEANS

BUT ONLY CERTAIN PEOPLE WERE "ADVANCED" ENOUGH FOR WRITING AND LITERATURE. IN COLLEGE IT GOT EVEN WORSE. I LOVED THE WRONG KIND OF WRITING AND I NEVER COULD BREAK A STORY DOWN TO FIND THE SYMBOLIC MEANING, ALTHOUGH I SURE TRIED TO FAKE IT.

(3:30 AM)

In "The Bell Jar," Plath profounds her enumerated existential parthenogenesis using subvertible intra-mural insight on the dissimulation of her classic bummer of the 20th century.

MY TROUBLE ENDED WHEN I STARTED MAKING COMIC-STRIPS. IT'S NOT SOMETHING A PERSON HAS TO BE VERY "ADVANCED" TO DO. AT LEAST NOT IN THE MINDS OF LITERARY TYPES.

SO YOU'RE A CARTOONIST! HOW ADORABLE!

POLITICAL? NO. HUMOROUS? KINDA.

WE'RE BOTH WRITERS.

SAY, MAYBE WE COULD COLLABORATE! WE WRITE IT AND YOU DRAW IT! HOW FUN!

NOBODY FEELS THE NEED TO PROVIDE DEEP CRITICAL IN-SIGHT TO SOMETHING WRITTEN BY HAND. MOSTLY THEY KEEP IT AS SHORT AS A WANT AD. THE WORST I GET IS, "TOO MANY WORDS. NOT FUNNY. DON'T GET THE JOKE." I CAN LIVE WITH THAT.

GALS, EVER FELT SO intimidated by the IDEA OF writing THAT you've never even given it a try? Think writing IS only "FOR "writers"? Sure IS common!

ESPECIALLY BECAUSE I'M SURE THAT THE NINE-YEAR-OLD VERSION OF ME WHO MADE UP ALL THOSE "CLASSI-FIED STORIES" WOULD THINK THAT THIS ONE HAD A VERY HAPPY ENDING.

(and YES, Gals- the first thing I read in the paper IS still the "lost and found")

LOST. SOMEWHERE AROUND PUBERTY. ABILITY TO MAKE UP STORIES. HAPPINESS DEPENDS ON IT. PLEASE WRITE.

Reading the Genre

1. Even though this essay is in comic form, it also addresses literacy directly, discussing the author's early reading experiences. As a literacy narrative, what does "Lost and Found" teach us about the author's approach to reading and writing? (For another example of a literacy narrative, see Allegra Goodman's "O.K., You're Not Shakespeare. Now Get to Work" on p. 7.)

2. Unlike many other comic authors, Lynda Barry provides descriptions for some of her pictures. Why do you think she does this, and how do these descriptions contribute to the essay?

3. How is Barry's artistic and storytelling style different from that of Marjane Satrapi in the excerpt from *Persepolis* (pp. 27–34)?

4. If Barry had presented her story without images, do you think your response to it would be different? How do comics present information, and why might a writer or artist choose this medium? (See Chapter 32, "High, Middle, and Low Style," p. 400.)

5. **WRITING:** Craigslist might be the online equivalent of the newspaper's classified section. Go to www.craigslist.org and find an advertised item that suggests a story to you. (Hint: Try looking at the lost-and-found section or the ads for free items.) Draw a picture of this item and write a short imaginative narrative about it. (See "Finding and developing materials," p. 13.)

6. **COMPOSING VISUALLY:** This essay comes from the book *One! Hundred! Demons!* The concept for the book comes from an ancient Japanese painting exercise in which artists painted about things that worried or challenged them. As she began painting and writing about her demons, Barry explains that "at first the demons freaked me, but then I started to love watching them come out of my paintbrush." Try drawing or writing about memories from your own past as a student. What have you struggled with? In writing about these memories, have you also come to better understand them?

REFLECTION   Poet and novelist Naomi Shihab Nye has written or edited more than twenty books and has won dozens of awards for her writing. Nye's mother is American and her father is Palestinian, and much of her writing is focused on helping people understand the similarities and differences between Middle Eastern and American cultures, and specifically on dispelling stereotypes about the Middle East. This piece appeared in Nye's 2001 collection *Mint Snowball*.

NAOMI SHIHAB NYE

Mint Snowball

My great-grandfather on my mother's side ran a drugstore in a small town in central Illinois. He sold pills and rubbing alcohol from behind the big cash register and creamy ice cream from the soda fountain. My mother remembers the counter's long polished sweep, its shining face. She twirled on the stools. Dreamy fans. Wide summer afternoons. Clink of nickels in anybody's hand. He sold milkshakes, cherry Cokes, old-fashioned sandwiches. What did an old-fashioned sandwich look like? Dark wooden shelves. Silver spigots on chocolate dispensers.

My great-grandfather had one specialty: a Mint Snowball which he invented. Some people drove all the way in from Decatur just to taste it. First he stirred fresh mint leaves with sugar and secret ingredients in a small pot on the stove for a very long time. He concocted a flamboyant elixir of mint. Its scent clung to his fingers even after he washed his hands. Then he shaved ice into tiny particles and served it mounded in a glass dish. Permeated with mint syrup. Scoops of rich vanilla ice cream to each side. My mother took a bite of minty ice and ice cream mixed together. The Mint Snowball tasted like winter. She closed her eyes to see the Swiss village my great-grandfather's parents came from. Snow frosting the roofs. Glistening, dangling spokes of ice.

Before my great-grandfather died, he sold the recipe for the mint syrup to someone in town for one hundred dollars. This hurt my grandfather's feelings. My grandfather thought he should have inherited it to carry on the tradition. As far as the family knew, the person who bought the recipe never used it. At least not in public. My mother had watched my grandfather make the syrup so often she thought she could replicate it. But what did he have in those little unmarked bottles? She experimented. Once she came close. She wrote down what she did. Now she has lost the paper.

Perhaps the clue to my entire personality connects to the lost Mint Snowball. I have always felt out-of-step with my environment, disjointed in the modern world. The crisp flush of cities makes me weep. Strip centers, poodle grooming, and take-out Thai. I am angry over lost department stores, wistful for something I have never tasted or seen.

Although I know how to do everything one needs to know—change airplanes, find my exit off the interstate, charge gas, send a fax—there is something missing. Perhaps the stoop of my great-grandfather over the pan, the slow patient swish of his spoon. The spin of my mother on the high stool with her whole life in front of her, something fine and fragrant still to happen. When I breathe a handful of mint, even pathetic sprigs from my sunbaked Texas earth, I close my eyes. Little chips of ice on the tongue, their cool slide down. Can we follow the long river of the word "refreshment" back to its spring? Is there another land for me? Can I find any lasting solace in the color green?

Reading the Genre

1. Nye uses sentence fragments in this essay. Examine these incomplete sentences, particularly in the first two paragraphs of the essay. How is the content of each of these shorter sentences similar, and how does this work within the essay? (See Chapter 32, "High, Middle, and Low Style," p. 400; Chapter 53, "Commas," p. 573; and Chapter 54, "Comma Splices, Run-Ons, and Fragments," p. 577.)

2. This narrative is divided into two parts. The perspective in the second part of the story radically shifts. How would you describe the perspective, or point of view, in the first half and in the second? What can the author do in the second half that she can't in the first? Why? (See Chapter 29, "Transitions," p. 387, and Chapter 31, "Titles," p. 395.)

3. **WRITING:** Consider the work history of your own family: What kind of work do your parents do, and what kind of work did their parents do? What kind of work does your extended family do? Are there specific skills or lessons, or even ways of looking at the world, that have been passed down in your family because of the sort of work your family has done? Write a short personal reflection on this topic.

4. **WRITING:** Visit a local business and interview the owner about the history of this business. Then write a short narrative that tells the story of the business — how it began, what it specializes in, what makes it unique, how it has changed over the years, and so on. (See "Develop the setting to set the context and mood," p. 19.)

MEMOIR Ira Sukrungruang writes and teaches creative nonfiction. He is the author of *Talk Thai: The Adventures of Buddhist Boy* (2010), a memoir of growing up Thai American, and the coeditor of *What Are You Looking At? The First Fat Fiction Anthology* (2003) and *Scoot Over, Skinny: The Fat Nonfiction Anthology* (2005). This story comes from the online journal *Brevity* (www.brevitymag.com), which collects very short creative nonfiction.

Brevity

Posted: Fall 2005
From: Ira Sukrungruang

Chop Suey

My mother was a champion bowler in Thailand. This was not what I knew of her. I knew only her expectations of me to be the perfect Thai boy. I knew her distaste for blonde American women she feared would seduce her son. I knew her distrust of the world she found herself in, a world of white faces and mackerel in a can. There were many things I didn't know about my mother when I was ten. She was what she was supposed to be. My mother.

At El-Mar Bowling Alley, I wanted to show her what I could do with the pins. I had bowled once before, at Dan Braun's birthday party. There, I had rolled the ball off the bumpers, knocking the pins over in a thunderous crash. I liked the sound of a bowling alley. I felt in control of the weather, the rumble of the ball on the wood floor like the coming of a storm, and the hollow explosion of the pins, distant lightning. At the bowling alley, men swore and smoked and drank.

My mother wore a light pink polo, jeans, and a golf visor. She put on a lot of powder to cover up the acne she got at fifty. She poured Vapex, a strong smelling vapor rub, into her handkerchief, and covered her nose, complaining of the haze of smoke that floated over the lanes. My mother was the only woman in the place. We were the only non-white patrons.

I told her to watch me. I told her I was good. I set up, took sloppy and uneven steps, and lobbed my orange ball onto the lane with a loud thud. This time there were no bumpers. My ball veered straight for the gutter.

My mother said to try again. I did, and for the next nine frames, not one ball hit one pin. Embarrassed, I sat next to her. I put my head on her shoulder. She patted it for a while and said bowling wasn't an easy game.

dpa/Landov.

My mother rose from her chair and said she wanted to try. She changed her shoes. She picked a ball from the rack, one splattered with colors. When she was ready, she lined herself up to the pins, the ball at eye level. In five concise steps, she brought the ball back, dipped her knees, and released it smoothly, as if her hand was an extension of the floor. The ball started on the right side of the lane and curled into the center. Strike.

She bowled again and knocked down more pins. She told me about her nearly perfect game, how in Thailand she was unbeatable.

I listened, amazed that my mother could bowl a 200, that she was good at something beyond what mothers were supposed to be good at, like cooking and punishing and sewing. I clapped. I said she should stop being a mother and become a bowler.

As she changed her shoes, a man with dark hair and a mustache approached our lane. In one hand he had a cigarette and a beer. He kept looking back at his buddies a few lanes over, all huddling and whispering. I stood beside my mother, wary of any stranger. My mother's smile disappeared. She rose off the chair.

"Hi," said the man.

My mother nodded.

"My friends over there," he pointed behind him, "well, we would like to thank you." His mustache twitched.

My mother pulled me closer to her leg, hugging her purse to her chest.

He began to talk slower, over-enunciating his words, repeating again. "We . . . would . . . like . . . to . . . thank . . ."

I tugged on my mother's arm, but she stood frozen.

". . . you . . . for . . . making . . . a . . . good . . . chop . . . suey. You people make good food."

The man looked back again, toasted his beer at his friends, laughing smoke from his lips.

My mother grabbed my hand and took one step toward the man. In that instant, I saw in her face the same resolve she had when she spanked, the same resolve when she scolded. In that instant, I thought my mother was going to hit the man. And for a moment, I thought the man saw the same thing in her eyes, and his smile disappeared from his face. Quickly, she smiled — too bright, too large — and said, "You're welcome."

Reading the Genre

1. This story begins as a pleasant memory of the author's youth but ends with a difficult and awkward encounter. This development comes as a surprise to readers, just as it did to Sukrungruang and his mother. When the story ends, what emotions are you left with as a reader? What would you have wanted to do if you had been in the bowling alley that day? (See Chapter 30, "Introductions and Conclusions," p. 391.)

2. At the end of this story, in the dialogue between Sukrungruang's mother and the man with "dark hair and a mustache," Sukrungruang uses ellipses to insert pauses in the discussion. What effect do these pauses have on the story and on you as a reader? (See "Develop major characters through action and dialogue," p. 18, and "Pace the story," p. 12.)

3. It's not easy to realistically depict action in a personal narrative, but using just a few details, Sukrungruang does a good job of capturing the act of throwing a bowling ball. Reread his descriptions of his own bad bowling and his mother's excellent bowling. Try and identify the adjectives and adverbs he uses, as well as the metaphors. (See "Use figures of speech," p. 17.)

4. **WRITING:** The events Sukrungruang recounts in this story reveal a turning point in his life, a moment when he learns something important. Can you identify the turning points in your life when you discovered important things you hadn't known before? Choose one of these moments and write a narrative about this event.

5. **WRITING:** Sukrungruang's narrative comes from a journal that publishes only nonfiction stories shorter than 750 words, and Naomi Shihab Nye's narrative (pp. 621–22) was published in an anthology of very short essays. *Smith* magazine has recently taken the concept of brevity many steps further by asking writers to create six-word memoirs. Read some examples of these memoirs at www.smithmag.net/sixwords/, and then write a personal narrative in six words. You might also try writing your story as a 140-character "tweet."

LITERACY NARRATIVE   An award-winning essayist, journalist, and fiction writer, Jonathan Franzen is best known for his novels *Freedom* (2010) and *The Corrections* (2001). This essay was published in the November 29, 2004, issue of the *New Yorker*. It can be considered a literacy narrative because it is organized around reading (comics, especially *Peanuts*), writing (a grade-school play), and other related activities (the "Homonym Spelldown"). Every scene seems to be about developing literacy in some way.

The Comfort Zone
Growing Up with Charlie Brown

JONATHAN FRANZEN

In May, 1970, a few nights after the Kent State shootings, my father and my brother Tom, who was nineteen, started fighting. They weren't fighting about the Vietnam War, which both of them opposed. The fight was probably about a lot of different things at once. But the immediate issue was Tom's summer job. He was a good artist, with a meticulous nature, and my father had encouraged him (you could even say forced him) to choose a college from a short list of schools with strong programs in architecture. Tom had deliberately chosen the most distant of these schools, Rice University, and he had just returned from his second year in Houston, where his adventures in late-sixties youth culture were pushing him toward majoring in film studies, not architecture. My father, however, had found him a plum summer job with Sverdrup & Parcel, the big engineering firm in St. Louis, whose senior partner, General Leif Sverdrup, had been a United States Army Corps of Engineers hero in the Philippines. It couldn't have been easy for my father, who was shy and morbidly principled, to pull the requisite strings at Sverdrup. But the office gestalt was hawkish and buzz-cut and generally inimical to bell-bottomed, lefty film-studies majors; and Tom didn't want to be there.

Up in the bedroom that he and I shared, the windows were open and the air had the stuffy wooden-house smell that came out every spring. I preferred the make-believe no-smell of air-conditioning, but my mother, whose subjective experience of temperature was notably consistent with low gas and electric bills, claimed to be a devotee of "fresh air," and the windows often stayed open until Memorial Day.

On my night table was the *Peanuts Treasury*, a large, thick hardcover compilation of daily and Sunday funnies by Charles M. Schulz. My mother had given it to me the previous Christmas, and I'd been rereading it at bedtime ever since. Like most of the nation's ten-year-olds, I had an intense, private relationship with Snoopy, the cartoon beagle. He was a solitary not-animal animal who lived among larger creatures of a different species, which was more or less my feeling in my own house. My brothers, who are nine and twelve years older than I, were less like siblings than like an extra, fun pair of quasi-parents. Although I had friends and was a Cub Scout in good standing, I spent a lot of time alone with talking animals. I was an obsessive rereader of A. A. Milne and the Narnia and Doctor Dolittle novels, and my involvement with my collection of stuffed animals was on the verge of becoming age-inappropriate. It was another point of kinship with Snoopy that he, too, liked animal games. He impersonated tigers and vultures and mountain lions, sharks, sea monsters, pythons, cows, piranhas, penguins, and vampire bats. He was the perfect sunny egoist, starring in his ridiculous fantasies and basking in everyone's attention. In a cartoon strip full of children, the dog was the character I recognized as a child.

Tom and my father had been talking in the living room when I went up to bed. Now, at some late and even stuffier hour, after I'd put aside the *Peanuts Treasury* and fallen asleep, Tom burst into our bedroom. He was shouting with harsh sarcasm. "You'll get over it! You'll forget about me! It'll be so much easier! You'll get over it!"

My father was offstage somewhere, making large abstract sounds. My mother was right behind Tom, sobbing at his shoulder, begging him to stop, to stop. He was pulling open dresser drawers, repacking bags he'd only recently unpacked. "You think you want me here," he said, "but you'll get over it."

What about me? my mother pleaded. *What about Jon?*

"You'll get over it!"

I was a small and fundamentally ridiculous person. Even if I'd dared sit up in bed, what could I have said? "Excuse me, I'm trying to sleep"? I lay still and followed the action through my eyelashes. There were further dramatic comings and goings, through some of which I may in fact have slept. Finally I heard Tom's feet pounding down the stairs and my mother's terrible cries, now nearly shrieks, receding after him: "Tom! Tom! Tom! Please! Tom!" And then the front door slammed.

Things like this had never happened in our house. The worst fight I'd ever witnessed was between Tom and our older brother, Bob, on the subject of Frank Zappa, whose music Tom admired and Bob one day dismissed with such patronizing disdain that Tom began to sneer at Bob's own favorite group, the Supremes, which led to bitter hostilities. But a scene of real wailing and doors slamming in the night was completely off the map. When I woke up the next morning, the memory of it already felt decades-old and semi-dreamlike and unmentionable.

My father had left for work, and my mother served me breakfast without comment. The food on the table, the jingles on the radio, and the walk to school all were unremarkable; and yet everything about the day was soaked in dread. At school that week, in Miss Niblack's class, we were rehearsing our fifth-grade play. The script, which I'd written, had a large number of bit parts and one very generous role that I'd created with my own memorization abilities in mind. The action took place on a boat, involved a taciturn villain named Mr. Scuba, and lacked the most rudimentary comedy, point, or moral. Not even I, who got to do most of the talking, enjoyed being in it. Its badness—my responsibility for its badness—became part of the day's general dread.

There was something dreadful about springtime itself, the way plants and animals lost control, the *Lord of the Flies* buzzing, the heat indoors. After school, instead of staying outside to play, I followed my dread home and cornered my mother in our dining room. I asked her about my upcoming class performance. Would Dad be in town for it? What about Bob? Would he be home from college yet? And what about Tom? Would Tom be there, too? This was quite plausibly an innocent line of questioning—I was a small glutton for attention, forever turning conversations to the subject of myself—and, for a while, my mother gave me plausibly innocent answers. Then she slumped into a chair, put her face in her hands, and began to weep.

"Didn't you hear anything last night?" she said.

"No."

"You didn't hear Tom and Dad shouting? You didn't hear doors slamming?"

"No!"

She gathered me in her arms, which was probably the main thing I'd been dreading. I stood there stiffly while she hugged me. "Tom and Dad had a terrible fight," she said. "After you went to bed. They had a terrible fight, and Tom got his things and left the house, and we don't know where he went."

"Oh."

"I thought we'd hear from him today, but he hasn't called, and I'm frantic, not knowing where he is. I'm just frantic!"

I squirmed a little in her grip.

"But this has nothing to do with you," she said. "It's between him and Dad and has nothing to do with you. I'm sure Tom's sorry he won't be here to see your play. Or maybe, who knows, he'll be back by Friday and he will see it."

"O.K."

"But I don't want you telling anyone he's gone until we know where he is. Will you agree not to tell anyone?"

"O.K.," I said, breaking free of her. "Can we turn the air-conditioning on?"

I was unaware of it, but an epidemic had broken out across the country. Late adolescents in suburbs like ours had suddenly gone berserk, running away to other cities to have sex and not attend college, ingesting every substance they could get their hands on, not just clashing with their parents but rejecting and annihilating everything about them. For a while, the parents were so frightened and so mystified and so ashamed that each family, especially mine, quarantined itself and suffered in isolation.

When I went upstairs, my bedroom felt like an overwarm sickroom. The clearest remaining vestige of Tom was the *Don't Look Back* poster that he'd taped to a flank of his dresser where Bob Dylan's psychedelic hairstyle wouldn't always be catching my mother's censorious eye. Tom's bed, neatly made, was the bed of a kid carried off by an epidemic.

In that unsettled season, as the so-called generation gap was rending the cultural landscape, Charles Schulz's work was almost uniquely beloved. Fifty-five million Americans had seen *A Charlie Brown Christmas* the previous December, for a Nielsen share of better than 50 percent. The musical *You're a Good Man, Charlie Brown* was in its second sold-out year on Broadway. The astronauts of *Apollo X*, in their dress rehearsal for the first lunar landing, had christened their orbiter and landing vehicle *Charlie Brown* and *Snoopy*. Newspapers carrying *Peanuts* reached more than 150 million readers, *Peanuts* collections were all over the best-seller lists, and if my own friends were any indication there was hardly a kid's bedroom in America without a *Peanuts* wastebasket or *Peanuts* bedsheets or a *Peanuts* gift book. Schulz, by a luxurious margin, was the most famous living artist on the planet.

To the countercultural mind, a begoggled beagle piloting a doghouse and getting shot down by the Red Baron was akin to Yossarian paddling a dinghy to Sweden. The strip's square panels were the only square thing about it. Wouldn't the country be better off listening to Linus Van Pelt than Robert McNamara? This was the era of flower children, not flower adults. But the strip appealed to older Americans as well. It was unfailingly inoffensive (Snoopy never lifted a leg) and was set in a safe, attractive suburb where the kids, except for Pigpen, whose image Ron McKernan of the Grateful Dead pointedly embraced, were clean and well spoken and conservatively dressed. Hippies and astronauts, the Pentagon and the antiwar movement, the rejecting kids and the rejected grown-ups were all of one mind here.

An exception was my own household. As far as I know, my father never in his life read a comic strip, and my mother's interest in the funnies was limited to a single-panel feature called *The Girls,* whose generic middle-aged matrons, with their weight problems and stinginess and poor driving skills and weakness for department-store bargains, she found just endlessly amusing.

I didn't buy comic books, or even *Mad* magazine, but I worshipped at the altars of Warner Bros. cartoons and the funnies section of the *St. Louis Post-Dispatch*. I read the section's black-and-white page first, skipping the dramatic features like *Steve Roper* and *Juliet Jones* and glancing at *Li'l Abner* only to satisfy myself that it was still trashy and repellent. On the full-color back page I read the strips strictly in reverse order of preference, doing my best to be amused by Dagwood Bumstead's midnight snacks and struggling to ignore the fact that Tiger and Punkinhead were the kind of messy, unreflective kids I disliked in real life, before treating myself to my favorite strip, *B.C.* The strip, by Johnny Hart, was caveman humor. Hart wrung hundreds of gags from the friendship between a flightless bird and a long-suffering tortoise who was constantly attempting unturtlish feats of agility and flexibility. Debts were always paid in clams; dinner was always roast leg of something. When I was done with *B.C.*, I was done with the paper.

The comics in St. Louis's other paper, the *Globe-Democrat,* which my parents didn't take, seemed bleak and foreign to me. *Broom Hilda* and *Animal Crackers* and *The Family Circus* were off-putting in the manner of the kid whose partially visible underpants, which had the name Cuttair hand-markered on the waistband, I'd stared at throughout my family's tour of the Canadian parliament. Although *The Family Circus* was resolutely unfunny, its panels clearly were based on some actual family's life and were aimed at an audience that recognized this life, which compelled me to posit an entire subspecies of humanity that found *The Family Circus* hilarious.

I knew very well, of course, why the *Globe-Democrat's* funnies were so lame: The paper that carried *Peanuts* didn't *need* any other good strips. Indeed, I would have swapped the entire *Post-Dispatch* for a daily dose of Schulz. Only *Peanuts*, the strip we didn't get, dealt with stuff that really mattered. I didn't for a minute believe that the children in *Peanuts* were really children — they were so much more emphatic and cartoonishly *real* than anybody in my own neighborhood — but I nevertheless took their stories to be dispatches from a universe of childhood that was somehow more substantial and convincing than my own. Instead of playing kickball and foursquare, the way my friends and I did, the kids in *Peanuts* had real baseball teams, real football equipment, real fistfights. Their interactions with Snoopy were far richer than the chasings and bitings that constituted my own relationships with neighborhood dogs. Minor but incredible disasters, often involving new vocabulary words, befell them daily. Lucy was "blackballed from the Bluebirds." She knocked Charlie Brown's croquet ball so far that he had to call the other players from a phone booth. She gave Charlie Brown a signed document in which she swore not to pull the football away when he tried to kick it, but the "peculiar thing about this document," as she observed in the final frame, was that "it was never notarized." When Lucy smashed the bust of Beethoven on Schroeder's toy piano, it struck me as odd and funny that Schroeder had a closet full of identical replacement busts, but I accepted it as humanly possible, because Schulz had drawn it.

To the *Peanuts Treasury* I soon added two other equally strong hardcover collections, *Peanuts Revisited* and *Peanuts Classics*. A well-meaning relative once also gave me a copy of Robert Short's national best seller, *The Gospel According to Peanuts,* but it couldn't have interested me less. *Peanuts* wasn't a portal to the Gospel. It was my gospel.

Chapter 1, verses 1–4, of what I knew about disillusionment: Charlie Brown passes the house of the Little Red-Haired Girl, the object of his eternal fruitless longing. He sits down with Snoopy and says, "I wish I had two ponies." He imagines offering one of the ponies to the Little Red-Haired Girl, riding out into the countryside with her, and sitting down with her beneath a tree. Suddenly, he's scowling at Snoopy and asking, "Why aren't you two ponies?" Snoopy, rolling his eyes, thinks, "I knew we'd get around to that."

Or Chapter 1, verses 26–32, of what I knew about the mysteries of etiquette: Linus is showing off his new wristwatch to everyone in the neighborhood. "New watch!" he says proudly to Snoopy, who, after a hesitation, licks it. Linus's hair stands on end. "You licked my watch!" he cries. "It'll rust! It'll turn green! He's ruined it!" Snoopy is left looking mildly puzzled and thinking, "I thought it would have been impolite not to taste it."

Or Chapter 2, verses 6–12, of what I knew about fiction: Linus is annoying Lucy, wheedling and pleading with her to read him a story. To shut him up, she grabs a book, randomly opens it, and says, "A man was born, he lived and he died. The End!" She tosses the book aside, and Linus picks it up reverently. "What a fascinating account," he says. "It almost makes you wish you had known the fellow."

The perfect silliness of stuff like this, the koanlike inscrutability, entranced me even when I was ten. But many of the more elaborate sequences, especially the ones about Charlie Brown's humiliation and loneliness, made only a generic impression on me. In a classroom spelling bee that Charlie Brown has been looking forward to, the first word he's asked to spell is "maze." With a complacent smile, he produces "M-A-Y-S." The class screams with laughter. He returns to his seat and presses his face into his desktop, and when his teacher asks him what's wrong he yells at her and ends up in the principal's office. *Peanuts* was steeped in Schulz's awareness that for every winner in a competition there has to be a loser, if not twenty losers, or two thousand, but I personally enjoyed winning and couldn't see why so much fuss was made about the losers.

In the spring of 1970, Miss Niblack's class was studying homonyms to prepare for what she called the Homonym Spelldown. I did some desultory homonym drilling with my mother, rattling off "sleigh" for "slay" and "slough" for "slew" the way other kids roped softballs into center field. To me, the only halfway interesting question about the Spelldown was who was going to come in second. A new kid had joined our class that year, a shrimpy black-haired striver, Chris Toczko, who had it in his head that he and I were academic rivals. I was a nice enough little boy as long as you didn't compete on my turf. Toczko was annoyingly unaware that I, not he, by natural right, was the best student in the class. On the day of the Spelldown, he actually taunted me. He said he'd done a lot of studying and he was going to beat me! I looked down at the little pest and did not know what to say. I evidently mattered a lot more to him than he did to me.

For the Spelldown, we all stood by the blackboard, Miss Niblack calling out one half of a pair of homonyms and my classmates sitting down as soon as they had failed. Toczko was pale and trembling, but he knew his homonyms. He was the last kid standing, besides me, when Miss Niblack called out the word "liar." Toczko trembled and essayed, "L . . . I . . ." And I could see that I had beaten him. I waited impatiently while, with considerable anguish, he extracted two more letters from his marrow: "E . . . R?"

"I'm sorry, Chris, that's not a word," Miss Niblack said.

With a sharp laugh of triumph, not even waiting for Toczko to sit down, I stepped forward and sang out, "L-Y-R-E! *Lyre*. It's a stringed instrument."

I hadn't really doubted that I would win, but Toczko had got to me with his taunting, and my blood was up. I was the last person in class to realize that Toczko was having a meltdown. His face turned red and he began to cry, insisting angrily that "lier" *was* a word, it *was* a word.

I didn't care if it was a word or not. I knew my rights. Toczko's tears disturbed and disappointed me, as I made quite clear by fetching the classroom dictionary and showing him that "lier" wasn't in it. This was how both Toczko and I ended up in the principal's office.

I'd never been sent down before. I was interested to learn that the principal, Mr. Barnett, had a Webster's International Unabridged in his office. Toczko, who barely outweighed the dictionary, used two hands to open it and to roll back the pages to the "L" words. I stood at his shoulder and saw where his tiny, trembling index finger was pointing: *lier, n., one that lies (as in ambush)*. Mr. Barnett immediately declared us co-winners of the Spelldown—a compromise that didn't seem quite fair to me, since I would surely have murdered Toczko if we'd gone another round. But his outburst had spooked me, and I decided it might be O.K., for once, to let somebody else win.

A few months after the Homonym Spelldown, just after summer vacation started, Toczko ran out into Grant Road and was killed by a car. What little I knew then about the world's badness I knew mainly from a camping trip, some years earlier, when I'd dropped a frog into a campfire and watched it shrivel and roll down the flat side of a log. My memory of that shriveling and rolling was sui generis, distinct from my other memories. It was like a nagging, sick-making atom of rebuke in me. I felt similarly rebuked now when my mother, who knew nothing of Toczko's rivalry with me, told me that he was dead. She was weeping as she'd wept over Tom's disappearance some weeks earlier. She sat me down and made me write a letter of condolence to Toczko's mother. I was very much unaccustomed to considering the interior states of people other than myself, but it was impossible not to consider Mrs. Toczko's. Though I never met her, in the ensuing weeks I pictured her suffering so incessantly and vividly that I could almost see her: a tiny, trim, dark-haired woman who cried the way her son did.

"Everything I do makes me feel guilty," says Charlie Brown. He's at the beach, and he has just thrown a pebble into the water, and Linus has commented, "Nice going. . . . It took that stone four thousand years to get to shore, and now you've thrown it back."

I felt guilty about Toczko. I felt guilty about the little frog. I felt guilty about shunning my mother's hugs when she seemed to need them most. I felt guilty about the washcloths at the bottom of the stack in the linen closet, the older, thinner washcloths that we seldom used. I felt guilty for preferring my best shooter marbles, a solid-red agate and a solid-yellow agate, my king and my queen, to marbles farther down my rigid marble hierarchy. I felt guilty about the board games that I didn't like to play—Uncle Wiggily, U.S. Presidential Elections, Game of the States—and sometimes, when my friends weren't around, I opened the boxes and examined the pieces in the hope of making the games feel less forgotten. I felt guilty about neglecting the stiff-limbed, scratchy-pelted Mr. Bear, who had no voice and didn't mix well with my other stuffed animals. To avoid feeling guilty about them, too, I slept with one of them per night, according to a strict weekly schedule.

We laugh at dachshunds for humping our legs, but our own species is even more self-centered in its imaginings. There's no object so Other that it can't be anthropomorphized and shanghaied into conversation with us. Some objects are more amenable than others, however. The trouble with Mr. Bear was that he was more realistically bearlike than the other animals. He had a distinct, stern, feral persona; unlike our faceless washcloths, he was assertively Other. It was no wonder I couldn't speak through him. An old shoe is easier to invest with comic personality than is, say, a photograph of Cary Grant. The blanker the slate, the more easily we can fill it with our own image.

Our visual cortexes are wired to quickly recognize faces and then quickly subtract massive amounts of detail from them, zeroing in on their essential message: Is this person happy? Angry? Fearful? Individual faces may vary greatly, but a smirk on one is a lot like a smirk on another. Smirks are conceptual, not pictorial. Our brains are like cartoonists—and cartoonists are like our brains, simplifying and exaggerating, subordinating facial detail to abstract comic concepts.

Scott McCloud, in his cartoon treatise *Understanding Comics*, argues that the image you have of yourself when you're conversing is very different from your image of the person you're conversing with. Your interlocutor may produce universal smiles and universal frowns, and they may help you to identify with him emotionally, but he also has a particular nose and particular skin and particular hair that continually remind you that he's an Other. The image you have of your own face, by contrast, is highly cartoonish. When you feel yourself smile, you imagine a cartoon of smiling, not the complete skin-and-nose-and-hair package. It's precisely the simplicity and universality of cartoon faces, the absence of Otherly particulars, that invite us to love them as we love ourselves. The most widely loved (and profitable) faces in the modern world tend to be exceptionally basic and abstract cartoons: Mickey Mouse, the Simpsons, Tintin, and, simplest of all—barely more than a circle, two dots, and a horizontal line—Charlie Brown.

Schulz only ever wanted to be a cartoonist. He was born in St. Paul in 1922, the only child of a German father and a mother of Norwegian extraction. As an infant, he was nicknamed Sparky, after a horse in the then popular comic strip *Barney Google*. His father, who, like Charlie Brown's father, was a barber, bought six different newspapers on the weekend and read all the era's comics with his son. Schulz skipped a grade in elementary school and was the least mature kid in every class after that. Much of the existing Schulzian literature dwells on the Charlie Brownish traumas in his early life: his skinniness and pimples, his unpopularity with girls at school, the inexplicable rejection of a batch of his drawings by his high-school yearbook, and, some years later, the rejection of his marriage proposal by the real-life Little Red-Haired Girl, Donna Mae Johnson. Schulz himself spoke of his youth in a tone close to anger. "It took me a long time to become a human being," he told *Nemo* magazine in 1987.

> I was regarded by many as kind of sissified, which I resented because I really was not a sissy. I was not a tough guy, but . . . I was good at any sport where you threw things, or hit them, or caught them, or something like that. I hated things like swimming and tumbling and those kinds of things, so I was really not a sissy. [But] the coaches were so intolerant and there was no program for all of us. So I never regarded myself as being much and I never regarded myself as being good looking

and I never had a date in high school, because I thought, who'd want to date me? So I didn't bother.

Schulz "didn't bother" going to art school, either—it would only have discouraged him, he said, to be around people who could draw better than he could. You could see a lack of confidence here. You could also see a kid who knew how to protect himself.

On the eve of Schulz's induction into the army, his mother died of cancer. She was forty-eight and had suffered greatly, and Schulz later described the loss as an emotional catastrophe from which he almost did not recover. During basic training, he was depressed, withdrawn, and grieving. In the long run, though, the army was good for him. He went into the service, he recalled later, as "a nothing person" and came out as a staff sergeant in charge of a machine-gun squadron. "I thought, by golly, if that isn't a man, I don't know what is," he said. "And I felt good about myself and that lasted about eight minutes, and then I went back to where I am now." After the war, Schulz returned to his childhood neighborhood, lived with his father, became intensely involved in a Christian youth group, and learned to draw kids. For the rest of his life, he virtually never drew adults. He avoided adult vices—didn't drink, didn't smoke, didn't swear—and, in his work, he spent more and more time in the imagined yards and sandlots of his childhood. But the world of *Peanuts* remained a deeply motherless place. Charlie Brown's dog may (or may not) cheer him up after a day of failures; his mother never does.

Although Schulz had been a social victim as a child, he'd also had the undivided attention of two loving parents. All his life, he was a prickly Minnesotan mixture of disabling inhibition and rugged self-confidence. In high school, after another student illustrated an essay with a watercolor drawing, Schulz was surprised when a teacher asked him why he hadn't done some illustrations himself. He didn't think it was fair to get academic credit for a talent that most kids didn't have. He never thought it was fair to draw caricatures. ("If somebody has a big nose," he said, "I'm sure that they regret the fact they have a big nose and who am I to point it out in gross caricature?") In later decades, when he had enormous bargaining power, he was reluctant to demand a larger or more flexible layout for *Peanuts*, because he didn't think it was fair to the papers that had been his loyal customers. His resentment of the name *Peanuts,* which his editors had given the strip in 1950, was still fresh in the eighties, when he was one of the ten highest-paid entertainers in America (behind Bill Cosby, ahead of Michael Jackson). "They didn't know when I walked in there that here was a fanatic," he told *Nemo*. "Here was a kid totally dedicated to what he was going to do. And to label then something that was going to be a life's work with a name like *Peanuts* was really insulting." To the suggestion that thirty-seven years might have softened the insult, Schulz said, "No, no. I hold a grudge, boy."

I never heard my father tell a joke. Sometimes he reminisced about a business colleague who ordered a "Scotch and Coke" and a "flander" fillet in a Dallas diner in July, and he could smile at his own embarrassments, his impolitic remarks at the office and his foolish mistakes on home-improvement projects, but there wasn't a silly bone in his body. He responded to other people's jokes with a wince or a grimace. As a boy, I told him a story I'd made up about a trash-hauling company cited for "fragrant violations." He shook his head, stone-faced, and said, "Not plausible."

In another archetypal *Peanuts* strip, Violet and Patty are abusing Charlie Brown in vicious stereo: "Go on home! We don't want you around here!" As he trudges away with his eyes on the ground, Violet remarks, "It's a strange thing about Charlie Brown. You almost never see him laugh."

My father only ever wanted not to be a child anymore. His parents were a pair of nineteenth-century Scandinavians caught up in a Hobbesian struggle to prevail in the swamps of north-central Minnesota. His popular, charismatic older brother drowned in a hunting accident when he was still a young man. His nutty and pretty and spoiled younger sister had an only daughter who died in a one-car accident when she was twenty-two. My father's parents also died in a one-car accident, but only after regaling him with prohibitions, demands, and criticisms for fifty years. He never said a harsh word about them. He never said a nice word, either.

The few childhood stories he told were about his dog, Spider, and his gang of friends in the invitingly named little town, Palisade, that his father and uncles had constructed among the swamps. The local high school was eight miles from Palisade. To attend, my father lived in a boarding house for a year and later commuted in his father's Model A. He was a social cipher, invisible after school. The most popular girl in his class, Romelle Erickson, was expected to be the valedictorian, and the school's "social crowd" was "shocked," my father told me many times, when it turned out that "the country boy," "Earl Who," had claimed the title.

When he registered at the University of Minnesota, in 1933, his father went with him and announced, at the head of the registration line, "He's going to be a civil engineer." For the rest of his life, my father was restless. He was studying philosophy at night school when he met my mother, and it took her four years to persuade him to have children. In his thirties, he agonized about whether to study medicine; in his forties, he was offered a partnership in a contracting firm which he almost dared to accept; in his fifties and sixties, he admonished me not to waste my life working for a corporation. In the end, though, he spent fifty years doing exactly what his father had told him to do.

My mother called him "oversensitive." She meant that it was easy to hurt his feelings, but the sensitivity was physical as well. When he was young, a doctor gave him a pinprick test that showed him to be allergic to "almost everything," including wheat, milk, and tomatoes. A different doctor, whose office was at the top of five long flights of stairs, greeted him with a blood-pressure test and immediately declared him unfit to fight the Nazis. Or so my father told me, with a shrugging gesture and an odd smile (as if to say, "What could I do?"), when I asked him why he hadn't been in the war. Even as a teenager, I sensed that his social awkwardness and sensitivities had been aggravated by not serving. He came from a family of pacifist Swedes, however, and was very happy not to be a soldier. He was happy that my brothers had college deferments and good luck with the lottery. Among his patriotic colleagues and the war-vet husbands of my mother's friends, he was such an outlier on the subject of Vietnam that he didn't dare talk about it. At home, in private, he aggressively declared that, if Tom had drawn a bad number, he personally would have driven him to Canada.

Tom was a second son in the mold of my father. He got poison ivy so bad it was like measles. He had a mid-October birthday and was perennially the youngest kid in his classes. On his only date in high school, he was so nervous that he forgot his baseball tickets and left the car idling in the street while he ran back inside; the car rolled down the hill, punched through an asphalt curb, and cleared two levels of a terraced garden before coming to rest on a neighbor's front lawn.

To me, it simply added to Tom's mystique that the car was not only still drivable but entirely undamaged. Neither he nor Bob could do any wrong in my eyes. They were expert whistlers and chess players, phenomenal wielders of tools and pencils, sole suppliers of whatever anecdotes and cultural data I was able to impress my friends with. In the margins of Tom's school copy of *A Portrait of the Artist,* he drew a two-hundred-page riffle-animation of a stick-figure pole-vaulter clearing a hurdle, landing on his head, and being carted away on a stretcher by stick-figure EMS personnel; this seemed to me a masterwork of filmic art and science. But my father had told Tom: "You'd make a good architect, here are three schools to choose from." He said: "You're going to work for Sverdrup."

Tom was gone for five days before we heard from him. His call came on a Sunday after church. We were sitting on the screen porch, and my mother ran the length of the house to answer the phone. She sounded so ecstatic with relief I felt embarrassed for her. Tom had hitchhiked back to Houston and was doing deep-fry at a Church's Fried Chicken, hoping to save enough money to join his best friend in Colorado. My mother kept asking him when he might come home, assuring him that he was welcome and that he wouldn't have to work at Sverdrup; but there was something toxic about us now which Tom obviously wanted nothing to do with.

Charles Schulz was the best comic-strip artist who ever lived. When *Peanuts* débuted, in October 1950 (the same month Tom was born), the funny pages were full of musty holdovers from the thirties and forties. Even with the strip's strongest precursors, George Herriman's *Krazy Kat* and Elzie Segar's *Popeye*, you were aware of the severe constraints under which newspaper comics operated. The faces of Herriman's characters were too small to display more than rudimentary emotion, and so the burden of humor and sympathy came to rest on Herriman's language; his work read more like comic fable than like funny drawing. Popeye's face was proportionately larger than Krazy Kat's, but he was such a florid caricature that much of Segar's expressive budget was spent on nondiscretionary items, like Popeye's distended jaw and oversized nose; these were good jokes, but the same jokes every time. The very first *Peanuts* strip, by contrast, was all white space and big funny faces. It invited you right in. The minor character Shermy was speaking in neat letters and clear diction: "Here comes ol' Charlie Brown! Good ol' Charlie Brown . . . Yes, sir! Good ol' Charlie Brown . . . How I hate him!"

This first strip and the 759 that immediately followed it have recently been published, complete and fully indexed, in a handsome volume from Fantagraphics Books. (This is the first in a series of twenty-five uniform volumes that will reproduce Schulz's entire daily oeuvre.) Even in Schulz's relatively primitive early work, you can appreciate what a breakthrough he made in drawing characters with large, visually uncluttered heads. Long limbs and big landscapes and fully articulated facial features—adult life, in short—were unaffordable luxuries. By dispensing with them, and by jumping from a funnies world of five or ten facial expressions into a world of fifty or a hundred, Schulz introduced a new informational dimension to the newspaper strip.

Although he later became famous for putting words like "depressed" and "inner tensions" and "emotional outlets" in the mouths of little kids, only a tiny percentage of his strips were actually drawn in the mock-psychological vein. His most important innovations were visual—he was all about *drawing funny*—and for most of my life as a fan I was curiously unconscious of this fact. In my imagination, *Peanuts* was a narrative, a collection of locales and scenes and sequences. And, certainly, some comic strips do fit this description. Mike Doonesbury, for example, can be translated into words with minimal loss of information. Garry Trudeau is essentially a social novelist, his topical satire and intricate family dynamics and elaborate camera angles all serving to divert attention from the monotony of his comic expression. But Linus Van Pelt consists, first and foremost, of pen strokes. You'll never really understand him without seeing his hair stand on end. Translation into words inevitably diminishes Linus. As a cartoon, he's already a perfectly efficient vector of comic intention.

The purpose of a comic strip, Schulz liked to say, was to sell newspapers and to make people laugh. Although the formulation may look self-deprecating at first glance, in fact it is an oath of loyalty. When I. B. Singer, in his Nobel address, declared that the novelist's first responsibility is to be a storyteller, he didn't say "mere storyteller," and Schulz didn't say "merely make people laugh." He was loyal to the reader who wanted something funny from the funny pages. Just about anything—protesting against world hunger; getting a laugh out of words like "nooky"; dispensing wisdom; dying—is easier than real comedy.

Schulz never stopped trying to be funny. Around 1970, though, he began to drift away from aggressive humor and into melancholy reverie. There came tedious meanderings in Snoopyland with the unhilarious bird Woodstock and the unamusing beagle Spike. Certain leaden devices, such as Marcie's insistence on calling Peppermint Patty "sir," were heavily recycled. By the late eighties, the strip had grown so quiet that younger friends of mine seemed baffled by my fandom. It didn't help that later *Peanuts* anthologies loyally reprinted so many Spike and Marcie strips. The volumes that properly showcased Schulz's genius, the three hardcover collections from the sixties, had gone out of print. There were a few critical appreciations, most notably by Umberto Eco, who argued for Schulz's literary greatness in an essay written in the sixties and reprinted in the eighties (when Eco got famous). But the praise of a "low" genre by an old semiotic soldier in the culture wars couldn't help carrying an odor of provocation.

Still more harmful to Schulz's reputation were his own kitschy spinoffs. Even in the sixties, you had to fight through cloying Warm Puppy paraphernalia to reach the comedy; the cuteness levels in latter-day *Peanuts* TV specials tied my toes in knots. What first made *Peanuts Peanuts* was cruelty and failure, and yet every *Peanuts* greeting card and tchotchke and blimp had to feature some-body's sweet, crumpled smile. (You should go out and buy the new Fantagraph-ics book just to reward the publisher for putting a scowling Charlie Brown on the cover.) Everything about the billion-dollar *Peanuts* industry, which Schulz himself helped create, argued against him as an artist to be taken seriously. Far more than Disney, whose studios were churning out kitsch from the start, Schulz came to seem an icon of art's corruption by commerce, which sooner or later paints a smiling sales face on everything it touches. The fan who wants to see an artist sees a merchant instead. Why isn't he two ponies?

It's hard to repudiate a comic strip, however, when your memories of it are more vivid than your memories of your own life. When Charlie Brown went off to sum-mer camp, I went along in my imagination. I heard him trying to make conversation with the fellow-camper who sat on his bunk and refused to say anything but "Shut up and leave me alone." I watched when he finally came home again and shouted to Lucy "I'm back!" and Lucy gave him a bored look and said, "Have you been away?"

I went to camp myself, in the summer of 1970. But, aside from an alarm-ing personal-hygiene situation that seemed to have resulted from my peeing in some poison ivy, and which, for several days, I was convinced was either a fatal tumor or puberty, my camp experience paled beside Charlie Brown's. The best part of it was coming home and seeing Bob's new yellow Karmann Ghia waiting for me at the YMCA.

Tom was also home by then. He'd managed to make his way to his friend's house in Colorado, but the friend's parents weren't happy about harboring somebody else's runaway son, and so they'd sent Tom back to St. Louis. Of-ficially, I was very excited that he was back. In truth, I was embarrassed to be around him. I was afraid that if I referred to his sickness and our quarantine I might trigger a relapse. I wanted to live in a *Peanuts* world where rage was funny and insecurity was lovable. The littlest kid in my *Peanuts* books, Sally Brown, grew older for a while and then hit a glass ceiling. I wanted everyone in my family to get along and nothing to change; but suddenly, after Tom ran away, it was as if the five of us looked around, asked why we should be spending time together, and failed to come up with many good answers.

For the first time, in the months that followed, my parents' conflicts became audible. My father came home on cool nights to complain about the house's "chill." My mother countered that the house wasn't cold if you were *doing housework all day*. My father marched into the dining room to adjust the thermostat and dramatically point to its "Comfort Zone," a pale-blue arc between 72 and 78 degrees. My mother said that she was *so hot*. And I decided, as always, not to voice my suspicion that the Comfort Zone referred to air-conditioning in the summer rather than heat in the winter. My father set the temperature at seventy-two and retreated to the den, which was situated directly above the furnace. There was a lull, and then big explosions. No matter what corner of the house I hid myself in, I could hear my father bellowing, "Leave the god-damned thermostat alone!"

"Earl, I didn't touch it!"

"You did! Again!"

"I didn't think I even moved it, I just *looked* at it, I didn't mean to change it."

"Again! You monkeyed with it again! I had it set where I wanted it. And you moved it down to seventy!"

"Well, if I did somehow change it, I'm sure I didn't mean to. You'd be hot, too, if you worked all day in the kitchen."

"All I ask at the end of a long day at work is that the temperature be set in the Comfort Zone."

"Earl, it is so hot in the kitchen. You don't know, because you're never *in* here, but it is *so* hot."

"The *low end* of the Comfort Zone! Not even the middle! The low end! It is not too much to ask!"

I wonder why "cartoonish" remains such a pejorative. It took me half my life to achieve seeing my parents as cartoons. And to become more perfectly a cartoon myself: What a victory that would be.

My father eventually applied technology to the problem of temperature. He bought a space heater to put behind his chair in the dining room, where he was bothered in winter by drafts from the bay window. Like so many of his appliance purchases, the heater was a pathetically cheap little thing, a wattage hog with a stertorous fan and a grinning orange mouth which dimmed the lights and drowned out conversation and produced a burning smell every time it cycled on. When I was in high school, he bought a quieter, more expensive model. One evening, my mother and I started reminiscing about the old model, caricaturing my father's temperature sensitivities, doing cartoons of the little heater's faults, the smoke and the buzzing, and my father got mad and left the table. He thought we were ganging up on him. He thought I was being cruel, and I was, but I was also forgiving him.

Reading the Genre

1. What kind of research did Franzen do to write this narrative? Make a list of the nonpersonal details he includes in the story — such as biographical information, historical facts, and other writers' literary analyses — and then comment on what this research adds to Franzen's own memories. (See Chapter 7, "Literary Analyses," p. 184.)

2. Franzen seems to jump from one scene to another, but this narrative does have a plot. Map the story along a timeline. What is the major action that moves the narrative along? How does Franzen tie the different scenes together? (See "Use physical devices for transitions," p. 390.)

3. This essay blends three genres: memoir, literary analysis, and literacy narrative. Focusing first on Franzen's literary analysis, what arguments does he make about Schulz's work? What evidence does he include to support his arguments?

4. **WRITING:** Franzen draws on close readings of his favorite comic strip to explain how he saw the world when he was young. Looking back at a favorite book, television show, or movie from your childhood, explore how you might have developed an understanding of the world through its characters. What truths about life did you learn from fiction? Write a narrative based on your reflections.

63

Reports:
Readings

N. SCOTT MOMADAY
From *The Way to Rainy Mountain*

A single knoll rises out of the plain in Oklahoma, north and west of the Wichita Range. For my people, the Kiowas, it is an old landmark, and they gave it the name Rainy Mountain. The hardest weather in the world is there. Winter brings blizzards, hot tornadic winds arise in the spring, and in summer the prairie is an anvil's edge. The grass turns brittle and brown, and it cracks beneath your feet. There are green belts along the rivers and creeks, linear groves of hickory and pecan, willow and witch hazel. At a distance in July or August the steaming foliage seems almost to writhe in fire. Great green and yellow grasshoppers are everywhere in the tall grass, popping up like corn to sting the flesh, and tortoises crawl about on the red earth, going nowhere in the plenty of time. Loneliness is an aspect of the land. All things in the plain are isolate; there is no confusion of objects in the eye, but one hill or one tree or one man.

Give life to scenes and settings.

For many descriptive reports, it is important for authors to *show* their readers vivid scenes and settings, so readers can fully understand where the report takes place and can thus better imagine the action. But creating an authentic experience of the scene or setting requires more than just observing a few details. If N. Scott Momaday had simply described the size and color of the knoll, this passage might not have been very successful. What makes the knoll vivid is Momaday's description of the life of this scene over the course of a year. He describes the weather, the vegetation, and the creatures that populate the space, using metaphors to bring these details alive. The result is that the reader receives not just a view of this landscape but a feel for this world.

If you are writing a report in which location matters (such as a report on a local school), consider not only giving your reader a thorough description of the place, but describing it over the course of time. Momaday offers a view of one specific knoll, but he describes what happens to this space over the course of the seasons. Consider not just the objects and static details of the place you are reporting on—but also how that space has been filled with life. Describe the place by taking on Momaday's perspective: Imagine that you are standing or sitting still in front of it at the time when you first encountered it, and describe what you see. But then imagine the days and months streaming past, as though in fast-forward. Write about how that space is animated by the people who inhabit it and the actions and changes that occur there.

INFORMATIONAL REPORT   Kamakshi Ayyar is a journalist based in Mumbai, India, and a graduate of Columbia University's Graduate School of Journalism. This essay was published in 2013 on Project Wordsworth (www.projectwordsworth.com), an experimental site created by Ayyar and a large group of her fellow Columbia graduate students. Project Wordsworth is designed to assess what the value of a good story is by inviting the reader to pay what the story is worth to them, with all proceeds going to the authors.

Cosmic Postcards: The Adventures of an Armchair Astronaut

KAMAKSHI AYYAR

My eye was jammed to the biggest telescope that I've seen in my life, up on the roof of Columbia University's Pupin Hall. I was looking at three absurdly bright points of light in a nebulous gas cloud that I was told represented stars. Stars being born, to be precise. After I heard that I lingered a little longer and had the indentation of the eyepiece mold around my eye when I stepped back.

It was just another instance of the universe blowing me away and the start of my mission to learn more about space.

Brian Cox is the man responsible for my fixation with space. He's the host of many BBC television and radio programs, including the spectacular *Wonders of the Universe* and *Wonders of the Solar System* series.

Until he came around, I was somewhat interested in the cosmos. I'd read all five Douglas Adams books in *The Hitchhiker's Guide to the Galaxy* series (don't roll your eyes, fiction still counts), I'd look up at the sky trying to pick out stars in the halo of Bombay's orange lights, and I'd sort of follow the space shuttle launches. But growing up in India, with a nascent though promising space program, I wasn't spellbound by the universe.

Then I watched *Wonders of the Solar System*. Somehow, through my TV, Cox managed to get me as enamored as he was with what's up there. Being a space ignoramus, everything he said was new to me.

Using an abandoned prison in Rio de Janeiro as a metaphor for a dying star, he broke down the chemical reactions that take place during the penultimate stages. What comes out of these reactions is carbon and oxygen, among other things—the same carbon that's in you, in me, in our iPads, and in everything else on this planet. So Carl Sagan was right when he said, "We are made of star-stuff."

Cox explained how Saturn's rings are made up of ice particles, some smaller than a centimeter. He talked about *Cassini*, NASA's robotic probe sent to study Saturn and its surroundings. And I was hooked.

How couldn't I be? The thirty-five-year-old *Voyager* spacecraft, older than me, has almost reached the end of our solar system and is still going farther out into the unknown. And some of the stars we see at night might already be dead, but they're so far away that their light is still traveling to reach us.

The possibilities are endless. We're never going to know everything about space; we're never going to explore every part of it. Given how controlling humans as a species are, that should put us off exploration. And yet, its vastness and secrets inspire awe, intrepidness, and serious courage in a few.

Sadly, I'm lacking in the last component. But that doesn't mean I can't stay down here and soak up everything I can find on the subject. Even though I have a Google alert for "Space" and my Twitter feed is filled with cosmological tweets, I still wanted to know more.

So I set out on a mission that began with the telescope at Columbia. I spoke to an astronaut who's had so many memorable moments in space he couldn't pick one. And to a research psychologist who thinks about what color to paint the signs around the docking ports of the International Space Station. Then there was the anthropologist in Canada who studies the science of looking for extraterrestrials.

I interviewed an artist who set up installations that captured the sounds of the Sun and Jupiter, a NASA trainer who prepares astronauts for space by creating simulations in an underwater habitat, and a food scientist who worries about vegan astronauts on long-term missions to Mars.

And what I learned from them only made me more curious about the Big Black Beyond.

Kathryn Denning spends a lot of time studying scientists who think about aliens. Denning, an anthropologist at York University in Canada, is fascinated by the idea of The Other in relation to humans. Her recent research has focused on how scientists think about the evolution of intelligence in relation to hypothetical extraterrestrials, ethical difficulties, and the future of the human colonization of space.

A big reason we're so drawn to space, she told me, is "its importance in traditional culture." We all share the experience of looking up at the stars and trying to make sense of it all. "It tends to get intertwined with the heavens and Heaven and we think of it as a place of revelations and knowledge and dreams," Denning said.

What is behind the search for those from other worlds varies with who is doing the searching. Scientists, for instance, search for what they consider extensions of theories of evolution, while others search for spiritual reasons. Denning and her colleagues think a lot about how humans would react when confronted with extraterrestrials. Carl Sagan, for one, thought interacting with aliens would be a character-building experience. "And then there are those who believe it could become an Earth versus Aliens situation," she said. To say nothing of the realization that humans are not the center of the universe.

There is also the enduring wonder of what those beings might actually look like and how intelligent they might be, which Denning and her colleagues have thought about. Denning noted that the usual SETI (Search for Extraterrestrial Intelligence, an exploratory science) expectation is that because the only way of communicating across interstellar distances is via radio signals or laser pulses, the only kind of distant life form we could detect would be one who could build a transmitter—and that this suggests that they'd have to have hands or the functional equivalent.

Aliens with appendages building radios. Allow that to sink in for a minute.

Our visual system evolved to help us navigate on foot, but we've moved on from carts and cars to planes and now spaceships. On Earth, our inner ear helps us differentiate between up and down. But in space, in zero gravity, humans must rely on their eyes to orient themselves. Which works only up to a point. That's where Dr. Mary Kaiser comes in.

Kaiser, a research psychologist with NASA, works with engineers to develop better ways to share important information, like distance and acceleration, and make it easier for astronauts to process during missions. One of the problems Kaiser faced occurred in the earliest moments of space travel—during the colossally powerful vibrations of lift-off, when astronauts struggled to read information on a computer screen.

Kaiser was working on the booster rockets for the Orion capsule, when she discovered that although each astronaut reacted differently during lift-off, based on their head shapes and neck muscles, "whatever they were doing was around the frequency of the vibration, about twelve times a second," she told me. "So we came up with a display that would strobe at the same frequency so that your head would be in the same position every cycle and the blur of the display disappears."

Then there is the problem of harsh illumination in space. On Earth we can still see what's in the shadows, even dimly. But in space, like on the Moon, if something's in the shadows it's pretty much invisible. Kaiser told me how careful consideration was given to the Sun's angle when astronauts were landing on the Moon. "You wanted an angle that gave you enough of a definition of all the craters and rocks, so you didn't want the Sun right overhead. But then you didn't want it so low that you got only shadows."

These deliberations were in addition to things like where windows on space shuttles should be placed and what color the signs around docking ports should be, which just goes to show how much planning goes into planning a mission.

Vickie Kloeris worries about keeping astronauts happily fed. As a NASA food scientist and manager of the Flight Food Systems, her job is to devise ways to extend the shelf life of, say, shrimp cocktail—and by extend, I mean for up to six months and longer.

Then there's the matter of making food taste good in an environment with little or no gravity. In space shuttles, for instance, astronauts live for extended periods in microgravity, which means their bodily fluids move to their head and upper parts of the body. This makes them congested, as if they have colds. And that, in turn, affects the way the food tastes.

The fact that the astronauts are eating from packages rather than plates impedes the way the food smells, which plays a big part in its taste. Add to that a closed setting with many other odors and a microgravity environment that keeps heat from rising and carrying aromas to the nose. Given these circumstances and astronaut reports that their sense of taste is numbed, Kloeris isn't surprised by the requests for hot sauce, garlic paste, and wasabi.

While taste is always on her mind, the nutritional effects of the food matter, too. Kloeris's most recent project was trying to reduce the content of sodium in the astronauts' diets. While it was known that a high-sodium diet aggravates bone loss, a common side effect of spaceflight, "We've had reports of some crew members on the International Space Station saying they experienced increased intercranial pressure. That has manifested itself as vision issues for some," Kloeris told me, because of pressure on the optic nerve. While the bone loss, per se, doesn't especially worry Kloeris's team—astronauts regain what they lose once they come back to Earth—that isn't the case with vision. Whatever visual acuity is lost in space stays lost.

As if these challenges weren't enough, Kloeris has had to deal with the personal dietary preferences of astronauts too. Kosher and halal are out of the question since the NASA food facilities aren't designed to support these religiously based diets. The vegetarians and vegans on shorter space shuttles haven't been too difficult, although their choice was restricted. So far, there hasn't been a vegetarian astronaut who stayed for six months on the International Space Station. But, Kloeris said, when the day comes that would be a "huge, huge challenge." And as for vegans—"that would be even worse."

You may not know it, but at some point in your life you've heard the Sun. Yes, heard the Sun. Before today's fancy digital radios, in the days of physically turning knobs to tune to the right station, you'd encounter a lot of static or white noise. That is usually attributed to interference from other electronic and radio signals in the vicinity, but a part of that is from a little farther away.

Thanks to a field of science called radio astronomy, space now has a soundtrack. As if the pictures weren't enough to blow your mind, you can now hear the Sun and Jupiter and in the future, possibly even black holes.

My introduction to radio astronomy was through a TED talk given by New Zealand artist Honor Harger a couple of years ago. She was part of a group of artists called radioqualia, who created sound sculptures and sound art compositions during most of the first decade of the 2000s. In 2004, the group set up installations that allowed people to hear objects in space. But the first space sounds were heard a little over 135 years ago. By accident, as Harger explained in her talk.

In 1876, Alexander Graham Bell and Thomas Watson were working on the telephone. Part of their setup was a length of charged wire, draped over the roofs of Boston that carried the telephone signal. Only, it caught something else, too. When Watson was listening, he heard a whole array of snaps, crackles, pops, whistles, and hisses.

The reason this was so strange was because it wasn't coming from humans. We were still a little over twenty years away from Marconi's first radio transmission, so these sounds were coming from nature. Some of it was lightning and other surrounding sounds, but there were certain noises that Watson correctly guessed were coming from elsewhere. He had, in fact, inadvertently "dialed into space," Harger said.

As time went on, technological advancements helped spawn the field of radio astronomy and refined it to today's age where we can pick out solar flares on the Sun and hear *Cassini* being bombarded by the ice particles that make up Saturn's rings.

"The Sun is, by far, the loudest radio object in our sky," Harger told me over Skype. It's a big nuclear furnace that emits frequencies that can be picked up in all parts of the electromagnetic spectrum. "It's very loud on the shortwave band of the radio, which is what we use for communications on Earth," she said. Hence, you've heard it as part of the white noise between tuning radio stations. Advanced radio telescopes now allow scientists to eliminate the noise coming from local disturbances and focus on just the Sun.

Jupiter isn't as noisy. Harger explained, "What we pick up is conversations between Jupiter and its moon, Io." Usually, two types of radiations are picked up in these noise storms—long bursts that sound like ocean waves breaking on a beach and short bursts that sound like popcorn popping or "someone throwing pebbles onto a tin roof," she said.

The reason we can hear these faraway objects better than, say, sounds from neighboring Mars, is because they're made up of gases. Mars is described as a "rocky planet" while Jupiter is a "gas giant, made up of really hot, swirling gas," Harger said. What this gas emits is energized particles and radio waves, much more than what a rocky planet would send out.

The sounds are audible through any good radio antenna and a shortwave receiver that can pick up waves in the frequency of 20MHz. It helps to be away from a city to avoid terrestrial electronic interference.

And since radio waves travel like light waves, you might be able to pick up sounds from the Big Bang, just like the scientists at the Bell Laboratory who, in 1965, first heard the cosmic radiation left over from about 13.8 billion years ago. If you're lucky, that'll be the oldest sound you'll ever hear.

NASA does its best to train astronauts for every possible scenario they could face up in space. A boring mission is a successful mission because everything goes according to plan.

As part of his role with the Analog Project Office, Marc Reagan creates simulations and scenarios that test crew members and flight teams to their limits. With just their imagination and discussions with the scientific community to work with, Reagan and his team build exercises that focus on the crew's weaknesses to "ultimately increase the odds of a successful flight," in his words.

The closest thing NASA had to a zero-G environment was the Neutral Buoyancy Lab at the Johnson Space Center in Houston. It's a pool that holds 6.2 million gallons of water and allows astronauts to practice scheduled procedures on submerged mockups of orbiting structures in safety. But it wasn't exactly like the real thing.

One thing that stumped Reagan was how crew members, who performed complex procedures to perfection multiple times during their training, experienced a moment of forgetfulness during an actual mission. He always wondered why they chose the day they were in space to make a mistake. "When you have tasks going on in extreme environments, a portion of your brain has to be dedicated to everyone's safety," he told me. "That means you're operating on less capacity on the tasks at hand, which leads to errors." Those elements of a real mission were missing from the training.

Reagan and his colleague Bill Todd, the NASA Extreme Environment Missions Operations (NEEMO) Project Manager, saw this vacuum and brainstormed ways to fill it. "Bill observed that this is just a simulation and the lessons may not sink in," Reagan said. At the end of the day you go home and there's no real consequence. This is very different from a real mission where you don't get to choose your fellow crew members, or get a second shot to try something.

Todd was aware of a U.S. underwater habitat, Aquarius, owned by the National Oceanic and Atmospheric Administration under the waters of the Florida Keys. He proposed that astronauts be allowed to live in the habitat to get a complete feel for what the mission might be like—social dynamics and all.

The first underwater mission was a success, with astronauts and authorities, and led to several more. It fit NASA's requirements perfectly, since the habitat already had the infrastructure in place like computer networks, high-speed communication links, and boats to carry equipment out to Aquarius. And so the NEEMO program was born.

"What a NEEMO mission teaches you is how to live off a timeline every day, how to finish one event on time to get to the next one and then the next one on schedule," Reagan said. "There's very little margin for error . . . and if there's a malfunction then you have to deal with that on top of your timeline, having to completely replan your day," he explained. The pace of living like that, day after day, can become exhausting and stressful. Just what astronauts can expect on a real mission.

Reagan shared an anecdote of what it is trainers try and do—anticipate the improbable and be as prepared as they can be: For the *Apollo 11* mission, the first one to land on the moon, the computers experienced situations during training when an information overload would cause them to release an abort code. Most of the time when the computers said to abort the landing, that was the prudent and correct thing to do. But in this one exception, it was safe to continue. Granted these computers were not even as powerful as most cell phones today, but the last thing you want when you're about to create history is a hiccup.

Fortunately, an enterprising training instructor at NASA studied the problem, and presented it during a simulation. Though at first it was treated as far-fetched, the flight controller responsible for the computers during landing took the time to study the case in detail.

As luck would have it, during the actual landing "they got one of these codes and the obvious thing to do was to say we have to abort the landing," Reagan narrated. But because of the training, the flight controller could confidently tell the flight director to proceed and the rest is history. "It was that close to calling off the first moon landing," he said, "and you would never know the name Neil Armstrong."

Once you get used to the floating that is life in space, you start worrying about more mundane things. Like losing stuff.

"Flat surfaces and gravity keep us organized; it's a wonderful thing," Dr. Stephen Robinson, a veteran of four space shuttle missions, told me. The organizational overload in space, having to keep track of every tiny instrument for long periods of time, can be mentally tiring and frustrating.

But that is more than offset by the singular thrill of going around the Earth every ninety minutes. One thing that caught Robinson by surprise was how stars are colored slightly differently. He knew that they're of different temperatures and compositions, but no one had ever told him to expect the different colors. "There are pockets of darkness but the Milky Way is just amazing, very well named," he recalled.

Another thing Robinson saw a lot of was the Northern Lights. "I've only ever seen it from space and it is the most amazing, beautiful, and spooky-looking thing," he said. That isn't hard to believe—imagine seeing a blanket of dancing green waves over miles of the Earth, like a force field.

Robinson's childhood heroes were the early astronauts. Now fifty-seven, he used to build and test his own gliders as a boy. They often crashed a lot, but luckily he never ended up in the emergency room.

The greater risks, of course, came as he prepared to venture into space. "Finding a place in your brain where you can accept that risk and then use it to your advantage," he said, "to make yourself sharper and quicker thinking, that's the trick." In the moments before lift-off, he recalls feeling "like the luckiest person ever—my dream was about to come true. It wasn't a time to be worried but a time to be thankful."

He laughed when I asked how space made him feel. "It makes you realize that no matter how big your burden is the universe doesn't really care that much," he said. "That kind of makes you more relaxed."

I wanted to know about his first moments in space, whether he recalled unbuckling his safety belt. "Oh heck yeah!" he said. "Everyone remembers that." Multiple training flights on reduced-gravity aircrafts, less affectionately called vomit comets by those with a queasy disposition, had given Robinson a feel for a zero-G environment, but it wasn't very similar to the real thing.

"You aren't in a big open airplane, but a cramped spaceship. And it doesn't last thirty seconds but two weeks," he told me. The space suit now floats on your body and that ladder that you used to climb during training? You can just float up and down it now. This is sort of what you'd experience when you enter a zero-G environment. First you take off your helmet and take a few seconds to process that the helmet is floating in front of you instead of falling like a rock. When you unbuckle you'd probably be popped out of your seat, "like a spring."

The first thing Robinson did was get hold of his camera. He slowed down when he was sharing this part, as if he were reliving the moment—"The shuttle was upside down facing the Earth's oceans in the daylight. When I looked up that ladder at the two windows on the top of the shuttle, there was this intense blue light that was reflecting off the ocean and coming down like a shaft of light that I just floated right up into. It was like a dream."

Even after all these experiences Robinson is still spellbound by the cosmos, saying, "I guess humans just want what they can see but can't experience. When you see a mountain you want to know what's on the other side. It's just the way we are."

I'm back on the roof of Columbia. The queue to the biggest telescope was long; it seemed like people were taking their own time with this one. Finally I got my turn and looked at a huge ball of light surrounded by two or three tinier lights. I prepared myself for the astronomer's description of what I was looking it. Just Jupiter and its moons, he said.

Just Jupiter and its moons. Wow.

Reading the Genre

1. How is this report organized? What are the benefits and the drawbacks of the unique organization of this essay? Does this organization work better for a report than it would for an argument or a narrative? What would happen if you took one of your own essays and reorganized it in this way? (For more on organizing reports, see p. 52.)

2. Ayyar clearly has enthusiasm for the mysteries of outer space. What strategies does she use to pass that enthusiasm on to the reader? How does the tone of her writing encourage the reader to share her interest in astronomy? Can you find specific words, phrases, or constructions that seem to convey her interest and seem likely to inspire her readers?

3. How does Ayyar describe complicated ideas in simple language? Are there some concepts that could be better or more carefully described? Identify two such concepts and try revising the description. (For more on using language strategically, see Part 5, "Style," p. 398.)

4. **WRITING:** Just as Ayyar does for astronomy, choose a career that interests you—then create "postcards" by profiling eight to ten people who you feel stand out in that particular career. The profile postcards should be short, just like Ayyar's, but each should reveal something intriguing about this person's life and work and should show your reader why you are fascinated with this career. Your profiles can be based on Internet research, but if people you'd like to profile are approachable enough to actually interview, go for it!

5. **MULTIMODALITY—POSTCARDS:** Create images to accompany each of your written "postcards" from question 4, and then create each as an actual postcard, with a front and back. In your class, trade these postcards around and then discuss the different insights you gained about these different careers.

DEFINITIONAL REPORT   Steve Silberman writes about science for *Wired* magazine, which published his influential article "The Geek Syndrome" about people with autism in 2001. Silberman hosts several "conferences" on the online community site The Well, and his Twitter account has made *Time*'s list of best feeds. He has a forthcoming book on autism and neurodiversity.

Wired

Posted: April 16, 2013, at 6:30 AM
From: Steve Silberman

Neurodiversity Rewires Conventional Thinking about Brains

In the late 1990s, a sociologist named Judy Singer — who is on the autism spectrum herself — invented a new word to describe conditions like autism, dyslexia, and ADHD: *neurodiversity*. In a radical stroke, she hoped to shift the focus of discourse about atypical ways of thinking and learning away from the usual litany of deficits, disorders, and impairments. Echoing positive terms like *biodiversity* and *cultural diversity*, her neologism called attention to the fact that many atypical forms of brain wiring also convey unusual skills and aptitudes.

Autistic people, for instance, have prodigious memories for facts, are often highly intelligent in ways that don't register on verbal IQ tests, and are capable of focusing for long periods on tasks that take advantage of their natural gift for detecting flaws in visual patterns. By autistic standards, the "normal" human brain is easily distractible, is obsessively social, and suffers from a deficit of attention to detail. "I was interested in the liberatory, activist aspects of it," Singer explained to journalist Andrew Solomon in 2008, "to do for neurologically different people what feminism and gay rights had done for their constituencies."

The new word first appeared in print in a 1998 *Atlantic* article about *Wired* magazine's Web site, HotWired, by journalist Harvey Blume. "Neurodiversity may be every bit as crucial for the human race as biodiversity is for life in general," he declared. "Who can say what form of wiring will prove best at any given moment? Cybernetics and computer culture, for example, may favor a somewhat autistic cast of mind."

Thinking this way is no mere exercise in postmodern relativism. One reason that the vast majority of autistic adults are chronically unemployed or underemployed, consigned to make-work jobs like assembling keychains in sheltered workshops, is because HR departments are hesitant to hire workers who look, act, or communicate in non-neurotypical ways — say, by using a keyboard and text-to-speech software to express themselves, rather than by chattering around the water cooler.

One way to understand neurodiversity is to remember that just because a PC is not running Windows doesn't mean that it's broken. Not all the features of atypical human operating systems are bugs. We owe many of the wonders of modern life to innovators who were brilliant in non-neurotypical ways. Herman Hollerith, who helped launch the age of computing by inventing a machine to tabulate and sort punch cards, once leaped out of a school window to escape his spelling lessons because he was dyslexic. So were Carver Mead, the father of very large-scale integrated circuits, and William Dreyer, who designed one of the first protein sequencers.

Singer's subversive meme has also become the rallying cry of the first new civil rights movement to take off in the twenty-first century. Empowered by the Internet, autistic self-advocates, proud dyslexics, unapologetic Touretters, and others who think differently are raising the rainbow banner of neurodiversity to encourage society to appreciate and celebrate cognitive differences, while demanding reasonable accommodations in schools, housing, and the workplace.

A nonprofit group called the Autistic Self Advocacy Network is working with the U.S. Department of Labor to develop better employment opportunities for all people on the spectrum, including those who rely on screen-based devices to communicate (and who doesn't these days?). "Trying to make someone 'normal' isn't always the best way to improve their life," says ASAN cofounder Ari Ne'eman, the first openly autistic White House appointee.

Neurodiversity is also gaining traction in special education, where experts are learning that helping students make the most of their native strengths and special interests, rather than focusing on trying to correct their deficits or normalize their behavior, is a more effective method of educating young people with atypical minds so they can make meaningful contributions to society. "We don't pathologize a calla lily by saying it has a 'petal deficit disorder,'" writes Thomas Armstrong, author of a new book called *Neurodiversity in the Classroom*. "Similarly, we ought not to pathologize children who have different kinds of brains and different ways of thinking and learning."

In forests and tide pools, the value of biological diversity is resilience: the ability to withstand shifting conditions and resist attacks from predators. In a world changing faster than ever, honoring and nurturing neurodiversity is civilization's best chance to thrive in an uncertain future.

Reading the Genre

1. What key terms does Silberman define in this short report? Read through the text, and when he defines a key term or theory, underline it. How important are these definitions to Silberman's report?

2. This short report might also be seen as a long definition of "neurodiversity." How does the report center on the term, and how does the focus on one term help the reader to understand a larger issue like autism in new ways? (For more on organizing reports by definition, see p. 55.)

3. It is notable that Silberman does not just reference doctors or scientists in this report, though those are the people who most often define autism in our culture. Discuss the significance of the sources that Silberman *does* cite in this report, and comment on how he establishes the authority of each source. Why do you think he focuses on the sources he does? (For more on where and how to find sources, see pp. 436, 442, and 451.)

4. **WRITING:** Neurodiversity is a neologism, an invented word. Every year, the *Washington Post* publishes a list of the best neologisms of the year. Search through some of these lists and find a word that intrigues you. Then write a report about where exactly this word came from and the cultural impact it has had.

INFORMATIONAL REPORT   Ross Perlin is the author of *Intern Nation: How to Earn Nothing and Learn Little in the Brave New Economy* (2012), from which this article is adapted. His writing has appeared in the *New York Times*, the *Guardian* (UK), the *Washington Post*, and *Time* magazine, among other publications. In an interview with *Academe Blog*, Perlin suggested, "For interns who are already saddled with college debt, unpaid internships can be the straw that breaks the camel's back, forcing young people to go still deeper into debt." This article explores the structure of internships at Disney and the problems they pose for students and colleges. Since its publication, Perlin's book has influenced three large and very visible class-action lawsuits on behalf of interns against Fox Entertainment Group, Hearst Corporation, and Charlie Rose, Inc.

Down and Out in the Magic Kingdom

ROSS PERLIN

At Disney World, interns are everywhere. The bellboy carrying luggage up to your room, the monorail "pilot" steering a train at forty miles per hour, the smiling young woman scanning tickets at the gate. They corral visitors into the line for Space Mountain, dust sugar over funnel cakes, sell mouse ears, sweep up candy wrappers. Mickey, Donald, Pluto, and the gang may well be interns, boiling in their furry costumes in the Florida heat. Visiting the Magic Kingdom recently, I tried to count them, scanning for the names of colleges on the blue and white name tags that all "cast members" wear. They came from public and private schools, community colleges and famous research universities, from across America. International interns, hailing from at least nineteen different countries, were also out in force. A sophomore from Shanghai greeted customers at the Emporium on Main Street, U.S.A. She was one of hundreds of Chinese interns, she told me, and she was looking forward to "earning her ears." Disney runs one of the world's largest internship programs. Each year, between seven thousand and eight thousand college students and recent graduates work full-time, minimum-wage, menial internships at Disney World. Typical stints last four to five months, but the "advantage programs" may last up to seven months.

Rather than offer traditional summer internships, Disney determines its schedule based on the company's manpower needs, requiring students to temporarily suspend their schooling or continue it on Disney property and on Disney terms. The interns work entirely at the company's will without sick days or time off, without grievance procedures, without guarantees of workers' compensation or protection against harassment or unfair treatment. Twelve-hour shifts are typical, many beginning at 6 AM or stretching past midnight. Interns sign up without knowing their assignments or their compensation, though it typically hovers near minimum wage. "Do any of these guests know that if not for these students their vacations would not exist?" former intern Wesley Jones asked in his book *Mousecatraz*.

© Melvyn Longhurst/Corbis.

At Disney World, labor is meant to have an almost invisible quality. Except for the name tags, nothing distinguishes interns for the visitor; in certain parts of the park, at certain times of day, they comprise more than 50 percent of staff. Their work is identical to what permanent employees do, and there's no added supervision, training, or mentoring on the job. The internship's educational component is a three- or four-hour class each week, offering some of the easiest college credits in the land. Students are also encouraged to obtain credit through networking, distance learning, and "individualized learning opportunities."

Many interns do nothing scholastic, given that Disney doesn't require it and that twelve-hour shifts are exhausting enough.

Like other employers, Disney has mastered how to rebrand ordinary jobs as exciting opportunities. "We're not there to flip burgers or to give people food," a fast-food intern told the Associated Press. "We're there to create magic." Should the magic fail, the program at least seems to promise professional development and the prestige of the Disney name. Yet training and education are afterthoughts: The kids are brought in to work. Having traveled thousands of miles and barely breaking even financially, they find themselves cleaning hotel rooms, performing custodial work, and parking cars in the guise of an academic exercise. A small number of College Program "graduates" are offered full-time positions at Disney. The housing is designed to scale the program to massive proportions, where the savings of not employing full-timers, who demand benefits and have unions, kick in. Mandatory communal housing, the cost of which is deducted from their paychecks, may make the experience fun and memorable, like college, but it also looks like a term of indenture: living on company property, eating company food, and working when the company says so.

In its scale, the Disney program is unusual, if not unique. Although technically legal, the program has grown up over thirty years to become an eerie model, a microcosm of an internship culture gone haywire. The word "internship" has no set meaning, but at Disney World it signifies cheap, flexible labor for one of the world's best-known companies—magical, educational burger-flipping in the Happiest Place on Earth.

Disney would not respond to these charges or comment on anything else for this piece, despite repeated requests. Like many a corporate titan, Disney likes to give the impression it's in the education business. Disney University, born in 1955 as the company's training division, predated McDonald's Hamburger University, Motorola University, and others, prefiguring what Andrew Ross has called "the quasi-convergence of the academy and the knowledge corporation." Since 1996, the Disney Institute has charged "millions of attendees representing virtually every sector of business from every corner of the globe" for the privilege of learning about Disney's "brand of business excellence." The Disney Career Start Program attracts high school dropouts and graduates, promising a custom-designed "learning curriculum." The Disney Dreamers Academy targets one hundred high school students each year. Interns are not the only ones on the receiving end of a dubious Disney degree. The company has every demographic, every part of the life cycle, covered.

With some sixty-three thousand people now working on the property, Disney World is the largest single-site employer in the United States. With the 1978 announcement of the building of EPCOT (Experimental Prototype Community of Tomorrow), the big question for Duncan Dickson and his fellow managers in Disney's "Casting Department" (Human Resources) was, "Where were we going to get these five to six thousand people?" Dickson and his colleague John Brownley thought of Harry Purchase, head of the Hotel Management Department at Paul Smith's College in upstate New York. Purchase had been bringing his students to the Magic Kingdom since 1972 to work in food service and take classes off-site. Then in 1978 came a year-round arrangement with the much larger Johnson and Wales College in Rhode Island, which wanted to increase its enrollment. As Dickson remembers, the school proposed that "they would send an instructor down, they would have classes off-site . . . and the students would work." Disney agreed.

Dickson and Brownley wondered if these initiatives could be magnified. In early 1980, they hosted a three-day meeting in Orlando with a few dozen educators—"department heads of various programs and directors of cooperative education from different universities"—with the goal of setting out "a blueprint for the College Program." The educators were strongly supportive, stressing only that Disney should handle housing and provide some sort of classroom experience. The senior Disney executive in charge of all the theme parks approved; Disney parks had always employed some number of college students and young people. The College Program would institutionalize this on a massive scale, tapping colleges as recruiters and controlling the entire process. "To build it to any size, we had to have the academic piece," said Dickson. "Besides scale, the other impetus was to provide a flexible labor force that can adjust to [seasonal] operating fluctuations."

The Magic Kingdom College Program launched in the summer of 1980, restricted at first to some two hundred students from three universities in the southeastern United States. The immediate plan was to ramp the intake up to four hundred interns in spring and summer (then the busiest times in the park) and drop it to two hundred interns in the fall. Until 1988, interns lived in the Snow White Village Campground, a mobile home park set amidst the strip malls and discount motels in nearby Kissimmee. The College Program has employed more than fifty thousand interns in Florida and California over the thirty years of its existence, and has spawned imitations at the Disney parks in Hong Kong and France.

From the late 1980s through the 1990s, more than ten thousand new hotel rooms were built at Disney World. Interns were rushed in to fill a large number of the new positions, although hotel work had not originally been part of the program. The earlier focus on students majoring in hospitality, theme park management, or culinary arts disappeared as Disney ceased to require or seek out students studying particular majors: Now history majors dunk fries in hot oil and psychology majors work as lifeguard interns. The loosening of immigration regulations in the late 1990s prompted the massive recruitment of ICPs (International College Program interns), more than one thousand of whom now come to work at Disney World each year, under the J-1 "cultural exchange" and H-2B "seasonal work" visas.

If Disney's motives are transparent and readily grasped, more surprising is the passionate support of Disney's many cheerleaders at colleges and universities. For example, Kent Phillips, Educator Relations and New Market Development Specialist for the internship program, recently received a major award for his good offices from the Cooperative Education and Internship Association.

In a promotional video aimed at students, over a dozen college internship coordinators, career counselors, and professors of experiential education bless the program:

> "Disney is not just a place to work—it's an experience, and it's an experience you can't get anywhere else."

> "We tell students that the Disney College Program is for students of all majors, from engineers to business to students in the liberal arts."

> "The best thing . . . is what it does for the students' self-esteem."

> "They've learned people skills, they've learned accountability, they've learned how to be creative decision makers."

> "By far the best intern program I've seen in the nation."

More troubling is that so many colleges offer academic credit for what is essentially a summer job devoid of academic content. The thousands of students who do receive academic credit pay their schools for the privilege—a financial windfall for schools.

Purdue and Tulane both have arrangements with Disney, as does Central Michigan University, which charges up to $2,630 in any given semester. If an institution refuses to award credit, Disney will help its interns find a more accommodating college or university. And, in order for its legions of international interns to secure J-1 visas, Disney has also helped forge relationships between American schools and foreign counterparts, such that—to take a single example—Montclair State University can charge thousands of dollars in tuition for a student from Beijing to work for Disney at minimum wage. Educators acknowledge that Disney's name recognition alone can help break the ice during a job interview.

According to Dickson, educators who endorse the program are "absolutely" aware that the majority of interns work in fast-food and sit-down restaurants, park cars, clean up after guests, and perform other routine maintenance tasks, which are indistinguishable from the work performed by regular employees. Jerry Montgomery, another member of Disney's HR team who was involved in managing the program, defended it as helping to manage students' career expectations. Not everyone in life gets to be "the CFO's assistant," says Montgomery, and young people trying to get ahead often need a reality check, someone to "slap them upside the head." Dickson pointed to "guest contact," along with the requirement that interns show up on time neatly attired, as educational components.

Disney boasts that eight of the courses are recommended for credit by the American Council on Education. Standard course offerings include "Corporate Communication," "Experiential Learning," and "Marketing You." The "professors" have traditionally been Disney managers, but there is now a dedicated staff of instructors, some with master's degrees. Interns commonly complain about feeling "mouse-washed"—brainwashed by Disney. In *Mousecatraz*, another former intern had this to say of the Disney Practicum, the core course for credit-seeking interns: "All we heard about in the class was how wonderful Lee Cockerell, the Executive Vice President of Walt Disney World Operations, was. It was Lee this, and Lee that and then more Lee. Perhaps Lee should have taught the course because most of the students walked away with the impression that it was all about Lee." During peak periods, classes may be canceled so students can work longer hours.

As one former intern put it, "Despite taking Disney courses, there was absolutely no connection between my [internship] experience and my academic progress. . . . Folks that just wanted to learn were disappointed." But those who wanted to network "loved" it. Those who complete a course earn their "Ducktorate."

The Rolling Stones' "Start Me Up" is the ringtone on Ed Chambers's cell phone and he answers it with a friendly growl: "Big Ed." His desk is weighed down by a massive Rolodex. He wears a sports jersey to work. Over the past few decades, Chambers has brought an aggressive brand of "Yankee politics" to union-building in Florida. "I'm an organizer—that's what I do," says Chambers. "I was the organizer who organized Disney World."

He is the head of the United Food & Commercial Workers Union (UFCW), Local 1625, and represents six thousand full-time employees at Disney World. He is one of six major union presidents in the Service Trades Council, whose contracts cover the majority of workers at Disney World, but not interns. For union members, the debate about Disney's College Program is about more than academic worthiness: It's about their livelihood. As one worker told me, "We're trying to make a living, and they're here to play." Ironically, unions came to central Florida in part thanks to Disney. When [Roy Disney] broke ground on the Magic Kingdom in 1969, says Chambers, "the building trades came down [from California] and pressured [Roy Disney], so it became union—[Disney World] was built with union construction. They chased him," he adds with a smile. "[Roy] sat down and said, 'Fine, you can be union.'" Four decades later, the area covered by Local 1625 now has the highest concentration of union members in Florida. In 1997, Chambers's union won a battle to organize at the Lakeland Regional Medical Center, setting off a domino effect: "Then we won the LPNs [licensed practical nurses] and the lab techs, then the police went union and the firefighters went union, then the sergeants of the police went union. Then we started picking off nursing homes around here, and the electric company just went union."

But handling a massive influx of intern labor at Disney has proven to be an unusual challenge. "Unfortunately, Walt would probably be rolling in his grave with some of the things they do," says Chambers. Back in 1980, the unions made a handshake agreement over the tiny pilot program, understanding that it would relieve full-timers during the year's busiest periods. But they have been powerless to stop the program's massive, year-round expansion. "They just went ahead and did it," says Eric Clinton, a former Disney worker who is now president of UNITE HERE Local 362, another of the six major unions. "This is totally and purely about labor costs. . . . The College Program is almost as good as subcontracting. They've found a way to 'insource,'" given that Disney World itself can't be moved offshore.

Disney World has never seen a strike before. But union membership has climbed to over 60 percent of the workforce, in response to company attacks on wages and benefits. Still, says Clinton, "There's a lot of internal organizing that has to go on. Disney will only take us seriously when we have 75 percent membership."

Chambers and Clinton agree, as do many Disney-watchers, that the company changed in the decades after Michael Eisner became CEO in 1984. Free family health care disappeared, along with the defined benefit pension plan for new employees. The pension plan for older employees may soon be gone as well, replaced by nonmatching 401(k) plans to which few of these low-paid hourly employees can afford to contribute. The unions were also powerless to stop the imposition of a new two-tier wage system, which has meant much lower pay raises for all new workers. After five years at Disney World, a typical worker would now be lucky to make $9 an hour, and even twenty-year veterans are likely to have their salaries "top out" below $13 an hour.

According to a report by economists Bruce Nissen, Eric Schutz, and Yue Zhang, Disney's move to a two-tier wage structure saved the company close to $20 million in 2006. The economists estimated that, as a result, $23.4 million was lost in goods and services in Orange and Osceola counties in that year, bringing about further ripple effects: job losses, depressed wages, lower tax receipts for local governments. Between wage squeezes, benefit cuts, and the broad casualization of the Disney World workforce, the company has clearly saved itself hundreds of millions of dollars over the years, if not more. With Disney the largest employer in the region, these changes do significant damage to the local economy.

There is also the issue of safety. According to one long-time employee, the Animal Kingdom's "Asia" attraction had approximately sixty-five full-time employees and just under thirty interns before the most recent recession. Since then, with a virtual hiring freeze on full-timers, the number of interns shot up to almost equal the number of full-timers. "It's a revolving door," he commented, and both the visitors' experience and the running of the theme park suffer as result.

In a single hour, running at full throttle, the full-time staff can put some two thousand visitors through a major ride like the Mount Everest Rollercoaster, but "when you get a whole bunch of new folks, those numbers plummet, and the managers ride us, saying we've got to work on our OHRC, our Operational Hourly Ride Capacity. . . . Collective lack of experience on the ride systems is kind of scary." If this hasn't actually put visitors in danger yet, it has certainly translated into longer wait times for rides.

In the beginning, Dickson and his HR team had to convince executives that the internship program would bring serious savings in labor costs: "We fought that battle all the way up to the Chief Financial Officer." No one questions it any longer. In Dickson's words, anyone who "looked at having to replace the College Program employees with full-time employees" would realize that the savings from having interns instead are "substantial." Who could doubt that this perpetual minimum wage machine would bring big returns? Besides having no benefits and being a captive audience for Disney paraphernalia, Disney rent, and Disney food, the interns never get genuine raises. Any changes in salary have closely followed adjustments in the minimum wage. In the meantime, the price of admission to Disney World has risen over 100 percent since 1990, around when the College Program started to take off.

With interns guaranteed at least thirty hours per week, and many working closer to forty, it is universally acknowledged that the interns are taking what would otherwise be full-time jobs. Departing or fired full-timers are often replaced with one or more interns, according to many people I interviewed.

"They've done it through attrition," says Clinton. A small recruiting project, supposedly intended to relieve workers during peak periods, has turned into a monster. One overcast night I slipped into Vista Way, home to a thousand Disney interns. I half expected I would have to scale over fences or dart past the intimidating security gate, where interns are required to show their name tags every time they enter. As I approached, a caravan of American Coach buses was discharging a slew of exhausted interns. Following an intern's friendly nod, I quickly made my way inside. The buses are an endless source of grief for the interns, I learned later. They don't run all the time, often leaving interns assigned to the earliest or latest shifts stranded. The few interns who bring their own cars become gods among men. Interns violating any of a long list of rules can be forced to leave the property within twenty-four hours. Regular searches of cars and rooms are conducted, with a policy of collective responsibility often applying: Groups of interns can be "terminated" for the infraction of a single roommate.

Within walking distance there's only a Wendy's, a Chevron gas station, a 7-Eleven, and a Walgreens (with a liquor store annex). The place has been mythologized as "Vista Lay" and received honors from Playboy as home of the world's sexiest internship—but the reality is less glamorous. I saw interns doing laundry, sharing cigarettes, shooting hoops, recovering from their shift, and getting ready for the next one. The grounds are filled with nondescript stucco apartment buildings in white and red. Most interns live four or six to an apartment, two to a bedroom, all sharing a kitchen. Interstate 4 roars behind the complex. There's a "clubhouse" used for College Program events, with massive, painted mouse ears emblazoned at the entrance. The apartment blocks surround tired-looking lawns, a basketball court, large sumps filled with brackish water. Any bustle in the complex is around a fitness center and the hot tub. Who are the interns and how did they get here?

"I had the [Disney College Program] on my radar since I was about ten years old," one of them told me. "I even went to a recruiting presentation at a nearby college while in middle school." Others said they'd been "Disney kids" as long as they could remember: just being able to inhale a little of the pixie dust was enough for them. Many simply had dropped by a recruiting presentation on their college campus and decided to give it a shot.

In a world of competitive, often unpaid internship programs, Disney's is easy to get—and at least it's paid. "Candidates rarely inquire about the dirty details such as the long hours, low pay, and tight living conditions," Wesley Jones wrote in *Mousecatraz*.

On the other hand, Disney isn't hiding anything. It provides detailed and basically accurate information about the program. At a campus recruiting event that I attended, there were three featured presentations with upbeat orchestral jingles and inspiring testimony, from clean-cut, attractive young people. The conference room was strewn with glitter, along with Mickey Mouse stickers and photo-heavy brochures. The cheery recruiter cajoled a distracted student audience into his call and response shtick: "Help me help —" "You!" In one of the promotional videos, we hear from Stephanie (the perky blonde with a nause-ating smile) and Tenoccus (the sensitive, soft-spoken African American male): "We're here to tell you about what we think is the coolest paid internship in the entertainment business." Disney is "the place where dreams come true" and "every morning is a magical morning." Disney internship applicants list their work preferences, but they don't receive their assignments until they arrive.

As one intern wrote on a message board: "You have virtually no say in your hours or work location." Interns often have no regular schedule—they are expected to take whatever shifts are left over and to work at multiple locations. During his internship, Wesley Jones reported to five different supervisors.

Bureaucratic snafus, overbooking, and health problems can all prevent interns from getting their guaranteed thirty hours of work per week, which can cause them financial problems. A shop steward sees interns struggling to make ends meet all the time and provides free food to tide them over. "She didn't work her thirty hours because they switched her schedule," the steward said of a new merchandising intern. "She's pushed into three different jobs. For one of them they had hired too many people, so they had to transfer thirteen people out . . . So on this paycheck she got two dollars, after they took out the rent." The steward has seen a number of interns leave the program early because "they're not making any money, they can't make their bills," and schedulers avoid giving them overtime.

Unless you consistently work long shifts for a number of months, many interns told me, almost all of your earnings will go toward rent and basic expenses. Parental support is common. "I needed my parents to wire me money just to make it through the first two months," said one former intern.

Like workers without rights everywhere, the interns vote with their feet. There are no official statistics on dropout or termination rates, but they appear to be uncommonly high. "I would wager a 20–30 percent termination/dropout rate just based on my own observations," Kyle told me, adding that he had enjoyed the program. During his first internship, four of his five roommates left. Clearly, some of the attrition has to do with college kids being college kids, but there are also many who hightail it home after they see the actual work. "I didn't travel clear across the country to work in a store," said one such intern. "I was cast as a Custodial Host, but I wasn't going to spend my hot summer days cleaning up people's crap," said another.

If few of these problems seem visible in the smiling faces of housekeeping and fast-food interns, you can thank the Disney Look. A College Program recruiter calls it a "clean, classic, timeless look [that] goes back to Walt Disney himself," where "timeless" apparently means 1950s suburban America. An extensive literature covers the regulations for hair: short for men, long for women, and "extremes in dying, bleaching, or coloring" are not permitted. Mustaches are permitted under certain conditions, as well as sideburns that extend to the bottom of the earlobe but no further. The frames and lenses of eyeglasses must be "neutral" in color, any makeup should be "applied in a blended manner and in colors complementary to the skin tone," and so on. "Intentional body alteration or modification" (visible tattoos, piercings, etc.) is out, except for "traditional ear piercing for women." Good "stage presence" means no chewing gum, no smoking on the job, no sleepiness, no moodiness, and no eating or drinking. Along with the Disney Look, there is Disneyspeak. Customers are "guests," positions are "roles," and a crowd is "an audience." Vomit is a "protein spill."

Nonetheless, many interns love their experience. Free access to the parks and employee discounts are more than enough for some of these Disney kids who have grown up to be Disney interns and may yet become Disney parents. "I'm a Disney slave and I wouldn't have it any other way," tweeted one intern proudly.

Walt Disney's original vision for EPCOT was a modernist utopia in the Florida swamps, half Le Corbusier and half Fordlandia, "a planned, controlled community, a showcase for American industry and research, schools, cultural and educational opportunities." But the reality is just another theme park, albeit one employing an abundance of slogans about progress and national stereotypes. Wesley Jones jokes in *Mousecatraz* that the Disney College Program might justifiably be called "the Experimental Prototype 'College' of Tomorrow." One of the world's largest internship programs—touted as a massive and wondrous experiment in experiential education—is a minimum-wage, corporate paradise, endorsed by schools and accepted by students, as much a mirage as the original EPCOT.

Reading the Genre

1. Perlin doesn't write about himself in this report at all—he never tells us how he has access to people or information, or what his role is at Disney. How does this approach differ from the approach an individual worker might take when writing a report centered on his or her own experience? What forms of evidence and what arguments can Perlin use because he remains an outside observer rather than a participant?

2. How does Perlin move back and forth between primary research on the ground at Disney World and secondary research about Disney's policies and history? Go through the text and make note of secondary research and primary research, and discuss how the two types of research work together. Which of Perlin's points are better made with evidence from primary sources? Which are better made with evidence from secondary sources? (See "Distinguish between primary and secondary sources," p. 438.)

3. What does Perlin want this report to accomplish? He may not make an overt argument in this report, but what sense do you get of his assessment of these internships? Where can you find evidence of his opinions in the text? (See "Aim for objectivity," p. 38.)

4. **WRITING:** Write a report on your own worst work or internship experience, using your own stories as a form of primary research. Then combine this personal narrative with secondary research into the employment or internship policies of this employer or others like it, so that your own experiences can lead you to answer bigger questions about why this experience might have been so memorably bad.

5. **MULTIMODALITY—VISUAL DICTIONARY:** This essay is full of interesting Disney neologisms (made-up words) like "Ducktorate" and euphemisms like "protein spill." Create a visual dictionary for a few of these words: Draw pictures that reveal or describe the definition of these strange new words.

LEGAL REPORT   Philip Deloria, a descendant of the famous Sioux (Dakota) leader Tipi Sapa, is a well-known and highly regarded scholar. He teaches history, American culture, and Native American studies at the University of Michigan. Both of his books, *Playing Indian* (1998) and *Indians in Unexpected Places* (2004), were awarded prizes for academic excellence. The following essay appears in the book *A New Literary History of America* by Greil Marcus and Werner Sollors (2009).

PHILIP DELORIA

The *Cherokee Nation* Decision

This is a story about the law. For me, however, it begins elsewhere, with a cryptic little book, measuring three by five inches and covered with a crumbling leather binding. Open it to the title page—*A History of the Black Hawk War* by "An Old Resident of the Military Tract" (1832)—and you will think it a historical memoir, published locally at Fort Armstrong, Iowa. The Black Hawk War, which "opened up" the Mississippi Midwest to white settlement, did indeed take place in 1832. Continue reading, however, and you will find not history, but sixty-three pages of ciphered and mnemonic figures:

Indian

1. (I) g t t e a g o * w c t chief o # # t o o a t p
2. (I) # I I - -
3. (I) a a p Indians- - (II) I w a a r * - -# VI- -%
4. (II) y w s y t a p a Indians

And so it continues, through four tantalizing sections (Indian, Squaw, Warrior, and Braves). The book feels a bit like Poe, dark, desperate, and strange. Each section represents a role in the rituals of a white fraternal group that pretended, in its secret ceremonies, to be the Indian people so recently dispossessed in the war. Holding it I

feel the 1830s, furtive and confused, a time of dark lanterns and sinister killings, treasure hunting and magic, secret ciphers, and houses (full of dead people and greasy
playing cards) floating intact on the cresting Mississippi, with plenty of sorry to go
around.

A fulcrum moment, these 1830s, of precarious cultural shifts, when the genera-
tive American contradiction between *killing Indians* and *becoming them* still lay close
to the surface. That contradiction, long embodied in captivity narratives, frontier
folk mythologies, and performances of Indian "American" identities, erupted in
the 1830s into the realm of law. The eruption came in response to the crisis of an
American nation that fully believed in its imperial destiny, yet spoke of its domi-
nations only haltingly. It structures the lives, literatures, and politics of American
Indian people—and thus *all* Americans—to the present day.

One phrase—"domestic dependent nations"—reordered the world of the 1830s.
Authored by John Marshall, the chief justice of the U.S. Supreme Court, the three
words translated the older cultural contradictions into new law and politics. If
killing the Indian had allowed settlers to claim land and proclaim independence,
"becoming" the Indian had let those same settlers incorporate themselves *into* the
land, and lodge the ancient memory of Indian aboriginality in American souls. The
new words applied (in reverse) the same contradictory structure of logic to Indian
people themselves: Somehow, they could be distinct nations—and yet be simultaneously incorporated within the American body politic. As nations, they might claim
to be independent—and yet they were in fact dependent on the federal government.

John Marshall named Indian people as "domestic dependent nations" in the
second of three closely linked legal cases involving the Cherokees. In the first case,
Johnson v. M'Intosh (1823), Marshall wrote an unnecessarily elaborate opinion in
which he codified the "discovery doctrine." He argued that, in the wake of contact
between New World and Old, title to Indian lands no longer resided with Indian
people but accrued instead to the European nation claiming first discovery. Indian

people could sell the "claim" to their land, but only to the discovering sovereign—or a rightful successor, in most cases (conveniently) the United States. Marshall used this "discovery" argument carelessly, to prop up the land claims of Virginia militiamen, former comrades during the War for Independence. This set the legal terms for the second case, *Cherokee Nation v. Georgia.*

In 1828, the discovery of gold on Cherokee lands led the state of Georgia to try to eliminate the Cherokees. Earlier, Georgians had forsworn territorial claims in return for a federal promise to remove the Cherokees as soon as was practical. The passage in 1830 of the Indian Removal Act—which encouraged tribes to exchange their eastern land for territory west of the Mississippi—suggested that the time for Cherokee removal was at hand. President Andrew Jackson was more than sympathetic.

Before the violent dispossessions of Removal, however, Cherokees, Georgians, and the federal government fought over their respective sovereignties. The federal government claimed power over the individual states—which meant the continued validity of federally negotiated Indian treaties (with the Cherokees, for example). South Carolina and other states in the South claimed primacy for themselves, insisting that they could "nullify" federal laws they deemed unconstitutional. And within their state borders, Georgians confronted the Cherokee Nation, an independent society replete with a constitution, representative government, educational institutions, written language, and other appurtenances of "civilization," including chattel slavery.

Asserting its own state sovereignty, Georgia could hardly embrace the rising sovereign nation of the Cherokees. In 1828 the Georgia legislature passed an act to make Cherokee territory part of and subject to the laws of Georgia. The following year, a second act added a provision "to annul all laws and ordinances made by the Cherokee nation of Indians." In 1830 Georgia seized and sentenced to death George Tassells, a Cherokee man who had killed another Cherokee within the bounds of the Cherokee Nation—a case in which the Cherokee justice system had clear jurisdiction.

After a failed appeal at the state level (Georgians used the "doctrine of discovery" to insist on their own jurisdiction), the Cherokees sought help from the U.S. Supreme Court, and John Marshall ordered a stay of execution. Georgia defied the Court (and suddenly, a dry legal narrative turns sinister: emergency sessions of the legislature, a rushed message on horseback from the governor—probably a dark lantern involved somewhere—and a hasty Christmas Eve hanging from a tree in a lonely field).

The Supreme Court said little about the legalized murder of Tassells, however, preferring to concentrate on *Cherokee Nation v. Georgia*, filed only days before by Cherokee chief John Ross in an effort to overturn Georgia's assertions of sovereignty. In the debate over the Indian Removal Act, many advocates insisted that Indian people *did* hold title to their lands—and thus national and territorial sovereignty, recognized through treaties and land purchases. The basis for this understanding, however, had been effectively undermined by the discovery doctrine. Brandishing a Supreme Court decision, Removal advocates argued that Indians had no title to their land and could be evicted at the pleasure of the United States, inheritor of the European rights of discovery.

Marshall ignored both the discovery doctrine and the defiance of Georgia (which refused to appear before the court), focusing instead on the question of jurisdiction. He framed the case around a grand historical narrative, and situated the Cherokees at a decisive turning point, one that required political recalibration. "If courts were permitted to indulge their sympathies," he wrote,

> a case better calculated to excite them can scarcely be imagined. A people once numerous, powerful, and truly independent, found by our ancestors in the quiet and uncontrolled possession of an ample domain, gradually sinking beneath our superior policy, our arts and our arms, have yielded their lands by successive treaties, each of which contains a solemn guarantee of the residue, until they retain no more of their formerly extensive territory than is deemed necessary to their comfortable subsistence. To preserve this remnant, the present application is made.

The key words—"independent," "powerful," "uncontrolled possession"—make the beginnings of his narrative clear. Indians were distinct, autonomous peoples ("nations" in a European sense). They formed alliances and negotiated treaties. The proper executive-branch office for Indian affairs was the War Department and the proper political relation was diplomacy or formal conflict. In the 1830s, however, Americans began saying out loud that after decades of conflicts, land cessions, removals, and dislocations, those relations had changed. Witness the key terms that seemed to shift the ground: "sinking beneath," "yielded their lands," "preserve this remnant."

The first rhetoric reflects a distinct form of colonial practice, characterized by warfare, treaties, a nation-to-nation relationship, and a cultural imagination that played with Indian otherness. The second calls into being a new and different kind of colonialism. Indian people were consolidated and segregated in regional spaces—the so-called Indian territory—the better to manage, reeducate, and incorporate them. This segregation enabled the development of American imperial governance based on the demographic shift from Indian to white, and the political transitions from mixed territory to white state and from Indian "nation" to Indian "tribe." The militiamen hunting down Black Hawk in 1832 engaged in exactly this process of containment. The results were clear: the states of Iowa, Illinois, and Wisconsin, the removal of many Indians from the Midwest, and a secret fraternal order with a book of coded rituals.

In this new form of colonialism, Indian nations could be viewed as something like states, though vastly inferior. The proper executive branch office for their oversight was now the Department of the Interior (the shift from the War Department was made in 1849) and the proper relationship would be that of a paternalistic guardian to its immature ward. Marshall's historical narrative—and American cultural production in general—repositioned 1830s Indians; once a foreign affairs problem, they were now a domestic issue.

And that is how it played out. The third article of the Constitution gives the Supreme Court jurisdiction over "controversies between a state or the citizens thereof, and foreign states, citizens, or subjects." Were the Cherokees a foreign state? If they were, then the Court would have jurisdiction and Marshall might indulge his sympathies and perhaps undo the damage he had caused. And yet, as foreign states, Indian nations would also be able to sign treaties with other nations, establish trade alliances with American enemies, and subject U.S. citizens to Indian laws, all acts the United States would construe as hostile. Despite any sympathies, the Court proved unwilling to see the Cherokees as a foreign nation.

So what were they? Indian tribes were distinct nations—but they existed in relation to the United States and within the borders it claimed. And so Marshall wrote: "It may well be doubted whether those tribes which reside within the acknowledged boundaries of the United States can, with strict accuracy, be denominated foreign nations. They may, more correctly, perhaps, be denominated domestic dependent nations. . . . Their relation to the United States resembles that of a ward to his guardian." Lacking jurisdiction, John Marshall could not use the case to recall the unanticipated consequences of the discovery doctrine. But when the last of the three Cherokee cases came to the Court the following year, he reversed himself, ruling in *Worcester v. Georgia* that American Indian tribes were in fact sovereign nations and that they retained all sovereign rights not given up by treaty or lost in a just war. Cherokee claims to Cherokee homelands were guaranteed by those solemn federal treaties, and Georgia's claims to jurisdiction over those homelands were invalid.

It was too late. Southern courts responded to Marshall's decisions with their own cases—*Georgia v. Tassells* (1830), *Caldwell v. Alabama* (1831), and *Tennessee v. Forman* (1835)—each of which denied not only Marshall's belated assertion of tribal sovereignty but also the power of the Supreme Court itself. These Southern cases gave the doctrine of discovery new form, primarily around stark assertions of Indian racial inferiority. And, since Andrew Jackson's executive branch refused to enforce the Supreme Court's decision in *Worcester*, calling it "stillborn," it was the Southern decisions that structured Indian removal and the new colonialism of consolidation and reservation rule. They became the de facto legal precedents, even if *Worcester* theoretically dictated the rule of law.

The decision paved the way for the Trail of Tears, a forced migration to Indian territory in 1838 during which more than four thousand Cherokees died. Similar removals and consolidations of Indians would become central to American policy over the next six decades. The federal government stopped making treaties in 1871, began reeducating Indian children in boarding schools, chopped up reservation land, and restricted tribes' religious practices. In law and politics, the paternalist language of guardians and wards was everywhere; indeed, it seemed to take precedence over "domestic dependent nations"—not to mention the idea that a tribe might have sovereignty.

These displacements existed in complex relation to the omnipresent cultural trope of the "vanishing" Indian. James Fenimore Cooper's *Last of the Mohicans* (1826) ends with noble Chingachgook alone, with no legacy or future. John Augustus Stone's *Metamora* (1829)—one of the most popular plays of the nineteenth century—finishes with tragic Indian death and a promising white future. John Mix Stanley's evocative painting *Last of the Race* (1857) shows a sad remnant of different tribes at sunset on the shores of the Pacific. And white fraternal orders in Iowa and elsewhere gathered at night, pretending to be now-departed Indians in order to perpetuate their memory.

And yet, Indian people did not vanish but began slowly reworking John Marshall's words. Some emphasized "domestic" and "dependent," focusing on American treaty obligations and using the language of "guardian" and "ward" to press the federal government for support for education, health, economic development, and other forms of assistance enshrined in treaty agreements. Others went in a different direction, skipping over "domestic" and "dependent" to argue for Indian nationhood and autonomy. In 1972, for example, following the Trail of Broken Treaties march on Washington, D.C., Indian activists demanded that all Indian people be governed by treaty relations, that the government restore a nation-to-nation relationship, ratify unapproved treaties, and establish a commission to review violations of treaty rights. Contemporary movements have pushed for Indian sovereignty, and they emphasize the word with a range of adjectives: political, legal, economic, intellectual, cultural.

When you hear about Indian casino gaming or tribal taxing authority or license plates, you are hearing—through the word "sovereignty"—the echoes of the *Cherokee Nation* decision. That decision has come full circle with the efforts of some Cherokees to dis-enroll Cherokee freedmen, the descendants of Cherokee-owned slaves guaranteed tribal citizenship under a treaty signed in 1866. The issue plays out on the grounds of Cherokee sovereignty (in the tribe's Supreme Court cases and electoral processes), nation-to-nation relations (in the Treaty of 1866), and guardianship oversight (in federal membership lists, a federal Indian blood quantum card, and a congressional effort to strip the Cherokees of federal recognition and funding). The complications of the 1830s—and sometimes their mood and tone—have continuously erupted into a series of presents.

Bibliography

Tim Alan Garrison, *The Legal Ideology of Removal: The Southern Judiciary and the Sovereignty of Native American Nations* (Athens, GA, 2002).

Lindsay G. Robertson, *Conquest by Law: How the Discovery of America Dispossessed Indigenous Peoples of Their Lands* (New York, 2005).

David E. Wilkins, *American Indian Sovereignty and the U.S. Supreme Court: The Masking of Justice* (Austin, TX, 1997).

Robert A. Williams, *The American Indian in Western Legal Thought: The Discourses of Conquest* (New York, 1990).

Reading the Genre

1. Deloria identifies several key terms in this report. What are they? How does Deloria explain them and their importance?

2. What strategy does Deloria use to organize information? (Hint: Take another look at the key terms from question 1.) How does the structure of the report make it accessible and easy to read? How does Deloria's organization help readers follow his argument?

3. In his conclusion, Deloria asks readers to consider how this legal history reaches into "a series of presents." What are some of the ways this happens? Where can we see the impact of the *Cherokee Nation* decision today?

4. Deloria quotes several historical figures and summarizes the work of four legal researchers in this report. How does he manage to include so much information efficiently, and how does he use it to support his thesis, or main idea? (See "Find reliable sources," p. 38; "Finding and developing materials," p. 50; "Base reports on the best available sources," p. 50; and Chapter 40, "Evaluating Sources," p. 451.)

5. **WRITING:** Deloria begins his report by stating, "This is a story about the law." The same is true, in a way, of any legal report. Choose a brief legal report from the Pew Research Web site (http://www.pewtrusts.org/our_work_detail.aspx?id=306/) and rewrite it as a short story. Try to follow the simplest narrative structure you can: Once upon a time there was a legal problem; it affected this group of characters; they decided to do some things about it; there was a struggle and a series of compromises and resolutions; this was the conclusion.

GRAPHIC REPORT   Mark Graham and Stefano De Sabbata are fellows in the Information Geographies project at the Oxford Internet Institute, which is dedicated to "understanding life online." The Information Geographies project aims "to produce a comprehensive atlas of contemporary information and Internet geographies . . . in order to tell a story about three key facets of global information geographies (access, information production, and information representation)." Graham and De Sabbata's graphic report focuses on the most visited Web sites in different regions. Other graphic reports in the project reveal the geographically uneven coverage of Wikipedia and the varying affordability of broadband around the world.

Age of Internet Empires

Mark Graham and Stefano De Sabbata

Description

This map illustrates the most visited Web site in each country.

Data

The map uses freely available data retrieved from Alexa on August 12, 2013. The company has provided Web site analytics since 1996. Alexa collects data from millions of Internet users using one of over twenty-five thousand different browser extensions, and the data used for this visualization were calculated "using a combination of the estimated average daily unique visitors to a site and the estimated number of pageviews on that site from users in that country over the past month."

The data are visualized as a choropleth map, where the color indicates each country's most visited Web site. Starting from the evident dominance of two companies (Google and Facebook), whose colors (red and blue, respectively) cover most of the map, we styled the illustration as an old colonial map, and named it after the computer game series *Age of Empire*. A second map [on page 687] illustrates the same data, using the hexagonal cartogram of the Internet Population in 2011.

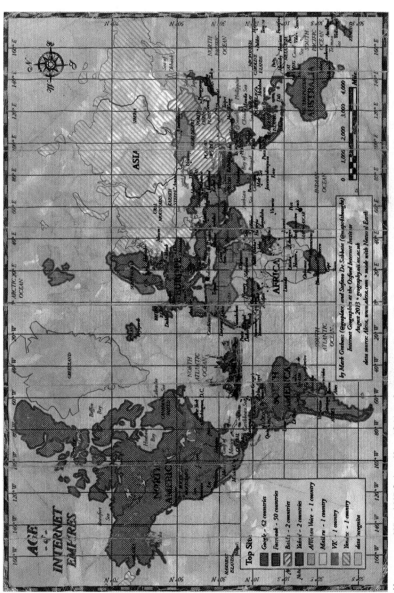

Maps on pages 685 and 687: Graham, M., and Sabbata, S. (2013), Age of Internet Empires, geography.oii.ox.ac.uk/?page=age-of-internet-empires, published by the Oxford Internet Institute of Oxford University.

Findings

The supremacy of Google and Facebook over any other site on the Web is clearly apparent. We also see an interesting geographical continuity of these two "empires." Google is the most visited Web site in most of Europe, North America, and Oceania. Facebook, in contrast, is the most visited Web site in most of the Middle East and North Africa, as well as much of the Spanish-speaking Americas.

The situation is more complex in Asia, as local competitors have been able to resist the two large American empires. Baidu is well known as the most used search engine in China, which is currently home to the world's largest Internet population at over half a billion users. At the same time, we see a puzzling fact that Baidu is also listed as the most visited Web site in South Korea (ahead of the popular South Korean search engine, Naver). We speculate that the raw data that we are using here are skewed. However, we may also be seeing the Baidu empire in the process of expanding beyond its traditional home territory.

The remaining territories that have escaped being subsumed into the two big empires include Yahoo! Japan in Japan (in joint venture with SoftBank) and Yahoo! In Taiwan (after the acquisition of Wretch). The *Al-Watan Voice* newspaper is the most visited Web site in the Palestinian Territories, the e-mail service Mail.ru is the most visited in Kazakhstan, the social network VK the most visited in Belarus, and the search engine Yandex the most visited in Russia.

Alexa does not provide much information about countries in Sub-Saharan Africa. However, most countries that have a significant Internet population are covered. Kenya, Madagascar, Nigeria, and South Africa fall within the sphere of Google's empire, whereas Ghana, Senegal, and Sudan have been subsumed within Facebook's dominion.

The power of Google on the Internet becomes starkly evident if we also look at the second most visited Web site in every country. Among the 50 countries that have Facebook listed as the most visited Web site, 36 of them have Google as the second most visited, and the remaining 14 countries list YouTube (currently owned by Google).

The countries where Google is the most visited Web site account for half of the entire Internet population, with over one billion people, as illustrated in the map below. Thanks to the large Internet population of China and South

Korea, Baidu is second in this rank, as these two countries account for more than half a billion Internet users, whereas the 50 countries where Facebook is the most visited Web site account for only about 280 million users, placing the social network Web site in third position.

We are likely still in the very beginning of the Age of Internet Empires. But, it may well be that the territories carved out now will have important implications for which companies end up controlling how we communicate and access information for many years to come.

Most visited website per Country
weighted by Internet Population

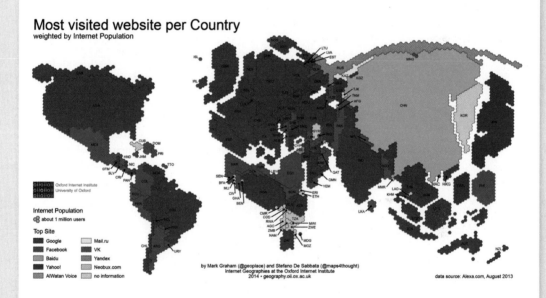

Oxford Internet Institute
University of Oxford

Internet Population
about 1 million users

Top Site

- Google
- Facebook
- Baidu
- Yahoo!
- AlWatan Voice
- Mail.ru
- VK
- Yandex
- Neobux.com
- no information

by Mark Graham (@geoplace) and Stefano De Sabbata (@maps4thought)
Internet Geographies at the Oxford Internet Institute
2014 • geography.oii.ox.ac.uk

data source: Alexa.com, August 2013

Reading the Genre

1. Graham and De Sabbata carefully explain the sources of their data and the inspiration for their visualization. Given that they borrowed the research from the company Alexa and borrowed the image idea from a game, what value are they really adding? Look carefully at the choices they have made and comment on the ways that these choices change your viewing of the map. (For more on data visualization, see Chapter 49, "Tables, Graphs, and Infographics," p. 550.)

2. This is a graphic report, even though it comes in the form of a map. Do you think the map also has an argument or thesis? How do Graham and De Sabbata want their audience to act on their report, and what do they want the audience to learn? (See Chapter 2, "Reports," p. 36.)

3. Looking at the goals of the Information Geographies project, what does this map tell us about "access, information production, and information representation"? Choose one of these "three key facets of global information geographies" and examine what the map reveals about that facet. How is information accessed, how is information produced, or how is information represented?

4. **WRITING:** While these maps chart modern-day "Internet empires," they don't really consider what some of the costs of empire are. Empires colonize, centralize power and resources, and create a lot of casualties. Look at one of these Internet empires and report on some of these costs and casualties. (For instance, we know that a key cost of Facebook's expansion is privacy.)

5. **MULTIMODALITY—INFORMATION GEOGRAPHY MAP:** Look at demographic information listing state-by-state (or province-by-province) Internet access, broadband cost, or even Facebook usage. These statistics can be found on the U.S. Census site or even on reference sites like Wikipedia. Map these statistics as if you were part of the Information Geographies team, using color carefully, choosing the right type of map, and considering how to explain the map with a legend, with captions, or with other forms of description.

Arguments: Readings

GENRE MOVES Argumentative Speech

SOJOURNER TRUTH
From "Ain't I a Woman?"

Well, children, where there is so much racket there must be something out of kilter. I think that 'twixt the negroes of the South and the women at the North, all talking about rights, the white men will be in a fix pretty soon. But what's all this here talking about?

Frame the problem.

This famous speech from 1851 begins when Sojourner Truth recognizes a "racket": disenfranchised groups talking about rights and advocating for themselves in a way that's perceived as disruptive by those in power. She then goes on to argue powerfully for women's rights. The "racket" provides framing for the argument. We know there is an issue, problem, or current event that requires our attention, giving Truth occasion to address the issue, and telling the audience how important it is to pay attention.

To generate ideas for your own arguments, think about what "racket" can be heard around rights issues in our current society. What, as Truth would put it, is "out of kilter" in the world around us? Or, more simply, what are people making a racket about in news media, or on Twitter, or on the street? By starting with a question that lots of people are asking, you lend your argument immediacy and importance, allowing you to easily draw your readers in.

Once you've found a topic and explored the arguments others have made about it, begin your own essay by identifying the problem, as Truth does. Frame the problem in a way that showcases its urgency and importance. Then, in your argument, show what can be done to respond to this racket—or what might be at stake if we ignore it.

EDITORIAL   Maureen Dowd is a prominent — if sometimes controversial — voice in American politics and culture. A Pulitzer Prize–winning journalist, she has been writing opinion columns and feature articles for the *New York Times* since 1995. Some of her favorites are collected in *Bushworld: Enter at Your Own Risk* (2004) and *Are Men Necessary? When Sexes Collide* (2005). This op-ed piece originally appeared in the *New York Times* in 2010.

Don't Send in the Clones

Maureen Dowd

For a time in college, I shared a dorm suite with three other girls.

We food shopped and ate dinner together but always squabbled over what groceries to buy. It got to the point where the only food we could agree on was corn, so that was what we got.

This upset my mother, who used to call me regularly to ominously demand: "Do you know why the Incas are extinct?"

This was B.G. (Before Google.) So I simply assumed that it either had to do with too much maize in the Inca diet or that Mom was just trying to scare me into healthier behavior — as when she attempted to ward off any tequila-tippling by calling to ask portentously: Do you know why so many tequila drinkers have nervous breakdowns?

Anyway, on one shopping expedition, I had a big fight with a roommate, no doubt over whether to get canned or frozen corn, creamed or whole kernel.

We were at a supermarket in a blighted part of D.C. My roommate got furious, stormed off in her car, and left me stranded. I called my brother Kevin to come get me. On the way back to school, he offered this advice: "Never pick a fight with the guy who's driving."

I took that to heart, literally and metaphorically. It has spared me plenty of problems since.

The serendipity of ending up with roommates that you like, despite your differences, or can't stand, despite your similarities, or grow to like, despite your reservations, is an experience that toughens you up and broadens you out for the rest of life.

So I was dubious when I read in the *Wall Street Journal* last week that students are relying more on online roommate matching services to avoid getting paired with strangers or peers with different political views, study habits, and messiness quotients.

A University of Florida official told the *Journal* that a quarter of incoming freshmen signed up to a Facebook application called RoomBug to seek out a roommate they thought would be more compatible than a random selection.

Other students are using URoomSurf. It makes matches with questions like these: How often do you shower? How neat are you? How outgoing are you? What's your study/party balance? Is it okay for your roommate to use your belongings?

I guess if I had used URoomSurf, I might have avoided those donnybrooks with one pill of a roommate, who yelled at me for such infractions as allegedly stretching out her sweater and eating a whole can of Campbell's Chunky Soup when I could have made do with half.

But cohabiting with snarly and moody roomies prepared me for the working world, where people can be outlandishly cantankerous over small stuff.

Just as rooming with Donna taught me humility. She was the sexiest girl on campus, an actress who would later brush off John Travolta in the Bee Gees–scored opening credits of *Saturday Night Fever*. And Susan, who wouldn't leave the room when it rained and who lost twenty pounds on an all-brownies diet, taught me to tolerate quirks.

I knew the lovely Susan would be my friend for life when I arrived in our freshman-year room shadowed by my mom, who was carrying a butcher knife, a can of Mace, and a letter opener.

Mom wanted us to be well armed against rapists — she wrote down instructions about how to insert the letter opener into an attacker's jugular — and Susan appreciated the gesture.

As in Darwinian evolution, cross-pollination with diverse strains promotes species development.

One young woman I know was appalled at first that the giggly cheerleader and former prom queen sharing her freshman room at the University of Pennsylvania put up 'N Sync posters "unironically." But in the end, she realized that just because her roommate loved 'N Sync and wore cute outfits did not necessarily mean she was shallow. And the prom queen realized that just because you hum when you write papers doesn't mean you're mentally ill. The prom queen lightened up the brooding, cynical, emo chick, and even got her to an 'N Sync concert — unironically.

Choosing roommates who are mirror images may fit with our narcissistic and microtargeted society, but it retards creativity and social growth. This reluctance to mix it up also has been reflected in the lack of full-throated political and cultural debates on campuses (as opposed to ersatz debates on cable TV), replaced by a quiet P.C. acceptance of differing views or an obnoxious stereotyping of anyone different.

As the *Times*'s Michiko Kakutani noted, the diminished debate syndrome at schools "suggests a closing off of the possibilities of growth and transformation."

Besides intensifying partisanship and conspiracy theories—think the birthers—the Internet divides the world more firmly into niches, birds of a feather avidly flocking together.

As you leave behind high school to redefine and even reinvent yourself as an adult, you need exposure to an array of different ideas, backgrounds, and perspectives—not a cordon of clones.

College is not only where you hit the books. It also should be where you learn not to judge a book by its cover.

Reading the Genre

1. This essay about roommate selection also addresses the political climate on college campuses and in American media. What is Dowd's point? How does she encourage readers to think beyond college relationships?

2. What life lessons has Dowd learned from her roommates? What life lessons have *you* learned from the people you've lived with?

3. Dowd uses puns, or plays on words, in her title and in the last line of her essay. What are they? What does clever word play add to, or take away from, the effectiveness of Dowd's argument? (See Chapter 31, "Titles," p. 395; "Frame arguments powerfully — and not in words only," p. 68, and Part 5, "Style," p. 398.)

4. This essay originally appeared on the "Opinion" page of the *New York Times*. Opinion sections of newspapers contain several short arguments, like this one, about current issues every day. How do you think the length restriction shapes the style, tone, and form of argumentation in this essay?

5. **WRITING:** Think of another aspect of college existence that you have found unexpectedly challenging, such as grades, tuition, intramural sports, Greek life, finals, cafeterias, laundry, campus parking, or part-time work. Write a short opinion column for your campus newspaper about this aspect of college life: What have you learned from the challenges, and how, if at all, have such difficulties prepared you for life after graduation? What can other students learn from your experience?

ARGUMENTATIVE REPORT   Jeff Wise is a contributing editor at *Popular Mechanics* and the author of *Extreme Fear: The Science of Your Mind in Danger*, as well as a contributor to magazines such as *Psychology Today*, where this article first appeared. He writes on the subjects of psychology, fear, aviation, and technology. Perhaps not surprisingly, Wise is also an airplane and glider pilot. From a quick Google Image search of his name, he doesn't appear to be a hipster.

Extreme Fear

Posted: September 8, 2010
From: Jeff Wise

The Sad Science of Hipsterism

The Psychology of Indie Bands, PBR, and Weird Facial Hair

Behold the hipster, the stylishly disaffected breed of twentysomethings whose fog of twee whimsy envelops Williamsburg and the East Village. Most who encounter the hipster in its natural habitat respond in one of two ways: derision or ridicule.

But science does not cast judgment. Its goal is to explore and explain dispassionately, whether the object of study be the noble eagle or the lowly nematode. So what does science have to tell us about this fascinatingly misunderstood breed, the indigenous North American hipster?

Yuri Arcurs/© Tetra Images/Alamy.

Surprisingly much.

In a paper in an upcoming issue of the *Journal of Consumer Research* entitled "Demythologizing Consumption Practices: How Consumers Protect Their Field-Dependent Identity Investments from Devaluing Marketplace Myths," authors Zeynep Arsel and Craig J. Thompson delve deep into the phenomenon of hipsterism, and in particular its most abiding mystery: If everyone hates hipsters, why would anyone want to be one?

The long and short of it is that they don't.

In general, psychologists who study consumers understand that people are largely motivated to spend money not just on things that they materially need, but that bolster their sense of identity. They purchase not just goods and services, but mythologies. Imagining themselves as rugged, rebellious patriots, they buy a Harley-Davidson. Imagining themselves as respected and well-heeled, they buy a Lexus.

Hipsters, though, follow a different paradigm. Their problem is that their purchases tend to place them within a category whose mythology they despise. That's right: Nobody likes hipsters, not even hipsters.

As Arsel and Thompson put it, the beats of the '50s and hippies of the '60s and '70s, both of which had an admirable authenticity about them even if you didn't care for the particulars, eventually gave rise to "the millennial hipster," which "came to be represented as an über-consumer of trends and as a new, and rather gullible, target market that consumes cool rather than creating it." As examples of the dorkification they cite online parodies of the iconic Mac v. PC ads and this viral YouTube video.[1]

The upshot being that any people who legitimately enjoy all the trappings of hipsterhood — the authors mention Pabst Blue Ribbon, Puma, and the trucker hat — must psychologically distance themselves from the demographic group of which they are so clearly a part. And so their subconscious brains have to work double time so that they can convince themselves that the things they buy do not reflect on their true character.

Arsel and Thompson interviewed hipsters and asked them how they dealt with the problem of being identified as such. The answer, they found, was to "demythologize" the hipster experience, that is, to psychologically reclassify their own behavior

---

[1] http://youtu.be/0tBH0E7A8BA

as being separate from the aggregate activity that the rest of the world lumps together as "hipster." They interviewed one consumer, identified as Scarlet, who told them:

> I'm not gonna lie, I shop at Urban [Outfitters] sometimes, only when it's on sale of course. . . . I like doing a lot of the things that are the hipster thing to do, but I do them because I like to do them, not because they're the cool thing to do. And because I am immersed in the social scene where there are a lot of hipsters, people mistake me for being one of them.

The deeper irony is that those who try to assert their independence from the commodification of identity wind up tapping into another marketplace myth, what the authors call "the myth of consumer sovereignty." This is the idea that by assiduously selecting from all the identity markers available for purchase, a person can assemble one that authentically reflects their true self independent of the marketplace. Some of the hipsters that Arsel and Thompson talked to are well aware of the futility of this project. Said one, identified as "Tom":

> I don't necessarily know every single weird obscure band. I don't necessarily want to. But I mean, yeah, who do I hang out with? I hang out with like a bunch of tattooed indie dorks. So, yeah, I guess I am but I wouldn't self-identify, I think. I'd listen to stuff that's outside the mainstream or it's like I dress weird compared to the majority of the population. I just try not to think about it too much. The minute you start identifying with a subculture . . . you kind of lose individuality, surrender part of your identity, and we don't wanna do that.

This, then, is the essence of being a hipster. Pretending you aren't one.

Reading the Genre

1. This essay starts out with an anthropological mission, to study a subculture: hipsters. But the article was published in *Psychology Today*, so it also has the goal of studying the hipster mentality. Read through the essay and identify the sections that seem anthropological and the sections that seem psychological.

2. Using your library's online databases, track down the research paper that Wise summarizes in this article. Compare the full paper with Wise's short report. What does Wise miss? Did he do a responsible job of representing the larger research study?

3. Wise seems to assume that most of his readers will see hipsters as objects of ridicule. What assumptions are built into Wise's writing and the research he cites, and how do these assumptions distract us from seeing the positives associated with hipsterism? How could Wise conduct further research to determine if these assumptions are valid? (For more on finding common ground with readers, see p. 80.)

4. **WRITING:** Wise writes that "people are largely motivated to spend money not just on things that they materially need, but that bolster their sense of identity." Write an analysis of one specific product that you believe has become a specific marker of identity—a product that people buy specifically to build their "identity." Explore how this identity building does or does not work in practice, and consider interviewing people about their reasons for making this purchase.

ARGUMENT FOR CHANGE   Emily Bazelon is a senior editor at the online magazine *Slate.com*, where she writes about legal affairs. She takes part in a weekly *Slate* podcast called "The Gabfest," talking about current political issues with colleagues David Plotz and John Dickerson. Bazelon has also written for the *Atlantic, Mother Jones,* and the *Yale Law Journal*. In this essay, Bazelon examines an age-old domestic issue: spanking.

slate.com

Posted: Thursday, January 25, 2007, at 6:16 PM ET
From: Emily Bazelon

Hitting Bottom:
Why America Should Outlaw Spanking

Sally Lieber, the California assemblywoman who proposed a ban on spanking last week, must be sorry she ever opened her mouth. Before Lieber could introduce her bill, a poll showed that only 23 percent of respondents supported it. Some pediatricians disparaged the idea of outlawing spanking, and her fellow politicians called her crazy. Anyone with the slightest libertarian streak seems to believe that outlawing corporal punishment is silly. More government intrusion, and for what — to spare kids a few swats? Or, if you're pro-spanking, a spanking ban represents a sinister effort to take a crucial disciplinary tool out of the hands of good mothers and fathers — and to encourage the sort of permissive parenting that turns kids ratty and rotten.

Why, though, are we so eager to retain the right to hit our kids? Lieber's ban would apply only to children under the age of four. Little kids may be the most infuriating; they are also the most vulnerable. And if you think that most spanking takes place in a fit of temper — and that banning it would gradually lead more parents to restrain themselves — then the idea of a hard-and-fast rule against it starts to seem not so ridiculous.

The purpose of Lieber's proposal isn't to send parents to jail, or children to foster care, because of a firm smack. Rather, it would make it easier for prosecutors to bring charges for instances of corporal punishment that they think are tantamount to child abuse. Currently, California law (and the law of other states) allows for spanking that is reasonable, age-appropriate, and does not carry a risk of serious injury. That forces judges to referee what's reasonable and what's not. How do they tell? Often, they may resort to looking for signs of injury. If a smack leaves a bruise or causes a fracture, it's illegal. If not, bombs away. In other words, allowing for "reasonable" spanking gives parents a lot of leeway to cause pain.

Who should we worry about more: the well-intentioned parent who smacks a child's bottom and gets hauled off to court, or the kid who keeps getting pounded because the cops can't find a bruise? A U.N. report on violence against children argues that "[t]he de minimis principle — that the law does not concern itself with trivial matters" will keep minor assaults on children out of court, just as it does almost all minor assaults between adults. The U.N. Committee on the Rights of the Child has been urging countries to ban corporal punishment since 1996. The idea is that by making it illegal to hit your kids, countries will make hurting them socially unacceptable.

The United Nations has a lot of converting to do in this part of the world. Its report cites a survey showing that 84 percent of Americans believe that it's "sometimes necessary to discipline a child with a good hard spanking." On this front, we are in the company of the Koreans, 90 percent of whom reported thinking that corporal punishment is "necessary." On the other side of the spanking map are nineteen countries that have banned spanking and three others that have partially banned it.

The grandmother of the bunch is Sweden, which passed a law against corporal punishment in 1979. The effects of that ban are cited by advocates on both sides of the spanking debate. Parents almost universally used corporal punishment on Swedish children born in the 1950s; the numbers dropped to 14 percent for kids born in the late 1980s, and only 8 percent of parents reported physically punishing their kids in 2000. Plus, only one child in Sweden died as the result of physical abuse by a parent between 1980 and 1996. Those statistics suggest that making spanking illegal contributes to making it less prevalent and also to making kids safer. On the other hand, reports to police of child abuse soared in the decades after the spanking ban, as did the incidence of juvenile violence. Did reports rise because frustrated, spanking-barred parents lashed out against their kids in other ways, or because the law made people more aware of child abuse? The latter is what occurred in the United States when reports of abuse spiked following the enactment of child-protective laws in the 1970s. Is the rise in kids beating on each other evidence of undisciplined, unruly child mobs, or the result of other unrelated forces? The data don't tell us, so take your pick.

A similar split exists in the American social-science literature. In a 2000 article in the *Clinical Child and Family Psychology Review*, Dr. Robert Larzelere (who approves of spanking if it's "conditional" and not abusive) reviewed thirty-eight studies and found that spanking posed no harm to kids under the age of seven, and reduced misbehavior when deployed alongside milder punishments like scolding and time-outs. By contrast, a 2002 article in *Psychology Bulletin* by Dr. Elizabeth Gershoff (not a spanking fan) reviewed eighty-eight studies and found an association between corporal punishment and a higher level of childhood aggression and a greater risk of physical abuse.

This is the sort of research impasse that leaves advocates free to argue what they will — and parents without much guidance. But one study stands out: an effort by University of California at Berkeley psychologist Diana Baumrind to tease out the effects of occasional spanking compared to frequent spanking and no spank-ing at all. Baumrind tracked about one hundred white, middle-class families in the East Bay area of northern California from 1968 to 1980. The children who were hit frequently were more likely to be maladjusted. The ones who were occasionally spanked had slightly higher misbehavior scores than those who were not spanked at all. But this difference largely disappeared when Baumrind accounted for the children's poor behavior at a younger age. In other words, the kids who acted out as toddlers and preschoolers were more likely to act out later, whether they were spanked occasionally or never. Lots of spanking was bad for kids. A little didn't seem to matter.

Baumrind concluded that it is "*reliance* on physical punishment, not whether it is used at all, that is associated with harm to the child." The italics are mine. While Baumrind's evidence undercuts the abolitionist position, it doesn't justify spanking as a regular punishment. In addition, Baumrind draws a telling distinction between "impulsive and reactive" spanking and punishments that require "some restraint and forethought." In my experience as a very occasional (once or twice) spanker, impul-sivity was what hitting my kid was all about. I know that I'm supposed to spank my sons more in sorrow than in anger. But does that really describe most parents, espe-cially occasional spankers, when they raise their hand to their children? More often, I think, we strike kids when we're mad — enraged, in fact. Baumrind's findings suggest that occasional spankers don't need to worry about this much. I hope she's right. But her numbers are small: Only three children in her study weren't spanked at all. That's a tiny control group.

Baumrind argues that if the social-science research doesn't support an outright ban on spanking, then we shouldn't fight over the occasional spank, because it diverts attention from the larger problems of serious abuse and neglect. "Professional advice that categorically rejects any and all use of a disciplinary practice favored and considered functional by parents is more likely to alienate than educate them," she argues. The extremely negative reaction to Lieber's proposed ban is her best proof.

It's always difficult and awkward — and arguably misguided — to use the law as a tool for changing attitudes. In the case of corporal punishment, though, I'm not sure we'd be crazy to try. A hard-and-fast rule like Sweden's would infuriate and frustrate some perfectly loving parents. It would also make it easier for police and prosecutors to go after the really bad ones. The state would have more power over parents. But then parents have near infinite amounts of power over their kids.

Reading the Genre

1. How does Bazelon look at the many arguments against a ban on spanking? How does she address these arguments with her own refutations and arguments for a ban? Do you think that she fairly considers counterarguments? (See "Understand opposing claims and points of view," p. 68, and "Anticipate objections," p. 345.)

2. Who are the key stakeholders in this debate — that is, whom does spanking directly affect, and who should care most about it? Make a list of people involved in this debate, and rank them in order of the impact that spanking has on their lives. How does Bazelon address these different stakeholders in the essay? Does she pay attention to the right people? How could identifying the stakeholders in an issue influence your own argumentative writing?

3. Bazelon uses hard evidence and other forms of research to support her arguments. Make an outline of her use of research: What kinds of research does she cite, what authority does it have, and how exactly does she use it to support her own claims? (See "Assemble your hard evidence," p. 83; "Creating a structure," p. 86; Chapter 40, "Evaluating Sources," p. 451; and Chapter 44, "Incorporating Sources into Your Work," p. 466.)

4. **WRITING:** Many people find it easy to criticize or second-guess parents. Write a short argument paper that makes a few suggestions to parents about how to best raise children. Keep in mind that your audience of parents might not want your advice, so write accordingly, considering possible counterarguments.

ANALYSIS OF CULTURAL VALUES   Poranee Natadecha-Sponsel teaches philosophy, sociology, and religion at Chaminade University of Honolulu, Hawaii, where she focuses on the interconnectedness of religion and the environment, or "spiritual ecology." In this essay, Natadecha-Sponsel reflects on her experiences as a newcomer to American culture.

PORANEE NATADECHA-SPONSEL

The Young, the Rich, and the Famous: Individualism as an American Cultural Value

"Hi, how are you?" "Fine, thank you, and you?" These are greetings that everybody in America hears and says every day—salutations that come ready-made and packaged just like a hamburger and fries. There is no real expectation for any special information in response to these greetings. Do not, under any circumstances, take up anyone's time by responding in depth to the programmed query. What or how you may feel at the moment is of little, if any, importance. Thai people would immediately perceive that our concerned American friends are truly interested in our welfare, and this concern would require polite reciprocation by spelling out the details of our current condition. We become very disappointed when we have had enough experience in the United States to learn that we have bored, amused, or even frightened many of our American acquaintances by taking the greeting "How are you?" so literally. We were reacting like Thais, but in the American context where salutations have a different meaning, our detailed reactions were inappropriate. In Thai society, a greeting among acquaintances usually requests specific information about the other person's condition, such as "Where are you going?" or "Have you eaten?"

One of the American contexts in which this greeting is most confusing and ambiguous is at the hospital or clinic. In these sterile and ritualistic settings, I have always been uncertain exactly how to answer when the doctor or nurse asks "How are you?" If I deliver a packaged answer of "Fine," I wonder if I am telling a lie. After all, I am there in the first place precisely because I am not so fine. Finally, after debating for some time, I asked one nurse how she expected a patient to answer the query "How are you?" But after asking this question, I then wondered if it was rude to do so. However, she looked relieved after I explained to her that people from different cultures have different ways to greet other people and that for me to be asked how I am in the hospital results in awkwardness. Do I simply answer, "Fine, thank you," or do I reveal in accurate detail how I really feel at the moment? My suspicion was verified when the nurse declared that "How are you?" was really no more than a polite greeting and that she didn't expect any answer more elaborate than simply "Fine." However, she told me that some patients do answer her by describing every last ache and pain from which they are suffering.

A significant question that comes to mind is whether the verbal pattern of greetings reflects any social relationship in American culture. The apparently warm and sincere greeting may initially suggest interest in the person, yet the intention and expectations are, to me, quite superficial. For example, most often the person greets you quickly and then walks by to attend to other business without even waiting for your response! This type of greeting is just like a package of American fast food! The person eats the food quickly without enjoying the taste. The convenience is like many other American accoutrements of living such as cars, household appliances, efficient telephones, or simple, systematic, and predictable arrangements of groceries in the supermarket. However, usually when this greeting is delivered, it seems to lack a personal touch and genuine feeling. It is little more than ritualized behavior.

I have noticed that most Americans keep to themselves even at social gatherings. Conversation may revolve around many topics, but little, if anything, is revealed about oneself. Without talking much about oneself and not knowing much about others, social relations seem to remain at an abbreviated superficial level. How could one know a person without knowing something about him or her? How much does one need to know about a person to really know that person?

After living in this culture for more than a decade, I have learned that there are many topics that should not be mentioned in conversations with American acquaintances or even close friends. One's personal life and one's income are considered to be very private and even taboo topics. Unlike my Thai culture, Americans do not show interest or curiosity by asking such personal questions, especially when one just meets the individual for the first time. Many times I have been embarrassed by my Thai acquaintances who recently arrived at the University of Hawaii and the East-West Center. For instance, one day I was walking on campus with an American friend when we met another Thai woman to whom I had been introduced a few days earlier. The Thai woman came to write her doctoral dissertation at the East-West Center where the American woman worked, so I introduced them to each other. The American woman greeted my Thai companion in Thai language, which so impressed her that she felt immediately at ease. At once, she asked the American woman numerous personal questions such as, How long did you live in Thailand? Why were you there? How long were you married to the Thai man? Why did you divorce him? How long have you been divorced? Are you going to marry a Thai again or an American? How long have you been working here? How much do you earn? The American was stunned. However, she was very patient and more or less answered all those questions as succinctly as she could. I was so uncomfortable that I had to interrupt whenever I could to get her out of the awkward situation in which she had been forced into talking about things she considered personal. For people in Thai society, such questions would be appropriate and not considered too personal, let alone taboo.

The way Americans value their individual privacy continues to impress me. Americans seem to be open and yet there is a contradiction because they are also aloof and secretive. This is reflected in many of their behavior patterns. By Thai standards, the relationship between friends in American society seems to be somewhat superficial. Many Thai students, as well as other Asians, have felt that they could not find genuine friendship with Americans. For example, I met many American classmates who were very helpful and friendly while we were in the same class. We went out, exchanged phone calls, and did the same things as would good friends in Thailand. But those activities stopped suddenly when the semester ended.

Privacy as a component of the American cultural value of individualism is nurtured in the home as children grow up. From birth they are given their own individual, private space, a bedroom separate from that of their parents. American children are taught to become progressively independent, both emotionally and economically, from their family. They learn to help themselves at an early age. In comparison, in Thailand, when parents bring a new baby home from the hospital, it shares the parents' bedroom for two to three years and then shares another bedroom with older siblings of the same sex. Most Thai children do not have their own private room until they finish high school, and some do not have their own room until another sibling moves out, usually when the sibling gets married. In Thailand, there are strong bonds within the extended family. Older siblings regularly help their parents to care for younger ones. In this and other ways, the Thai family emphasizes the interdependence of its members.

I was accustomed to helping Thai babies who fell down to stand up again. Thus, in America when I saw babies fall, it was natural for me to try to help them back on their feet. Once at a summer camp for East-West Center participants, one of the supervisors brought his wife and their ten-month-old son with him. The baby was so cute that many students were playing with him. At one point he was trying to walk and fell, so all the Asian students, males and females, rushed to help him up. Although the father and mother were nearby, they paid no attention to their fallen and crying baby. However, as the students were trying to help and comfort him, the parents told them to leave him alone; he would be all right on his own. The baby did get up and stopped crying without any assistance. Independence is yet another component of the American value of individualism.

Individualism is even reflected in the way Americans prepare, serve, and consume food. In a typical American meal, each person has a separate plate and is not supposed to share or taste food from other people's plates. My Thai friends and I are used to eating Thai style, in which you share food from a big serving dish in the middle of the table. Each person dishes a small amount from the serving dish onto his or her plate and finishes this portion before going on with the next portion of the same or a different serving dish. With the Thai pattern of eating, you regularly reach out to the serving dishes throughout the meal. But this way of eating is not considered appropriate in comparison to the common American practice where each person eats separately from his or her individual plate.

One time my American host, a divorcée who lived alone, invited a Thai girlfriend and myself to an American dinner at her home. When we were reaching out and eating a small portion of one thing at a time in Thai style, we were told to dish everything we wanted onto our plates at one time and that it was not considered polite to reach across the table. The proper American way was to have each kind of food piled up on your plate at once. If we were to eat in the same manner in Thailand, eyebrows would have been raised at the way we piled up food on our plates, and we would have been considered to be eating like pigs, greedy and inconsiderate of others who shared the meal at the table.

Individualism as a pivotal value in American culture is reflected in many other ways. Material wealth is not only a prime status marker in American society but also a guarantee and celebration of individualism—wealth allows the freedom to do almost anything, although usually within the limits of law. The pursuit of material wealth through individual achievement is instilled in Americans from the youngest age. For example, I was surprised to see an affluent American couple, who own a large ranch house and two BMW cars, send their nine-year-old son to deliver newspapers. He has to get up very early each morning to deliver the papers, even on Sunday! During summer vacation, the boy earns additional money by helping in his parents' gift shop from 10 AM to 5 PM. His thirteen-year-old sister often earns money by babysitting, even at night.

In Thailand, only children from poorer families work to earn money to help the household. Middle- and high-income parents do not encourage their children to work until after they have finished their education. They provide economic support in order to free their children to concentrate on and excel in their studies. Beyond the regular schooling, families who can afford it pay for special tutoring as well as training in music, dance, or sports. However, children in low- and middle-income families help their parents with household chores and the care of younger children.

Many American children have been encouraged to get paid for their help around the house. They rarely get any gifts free of obligations. They even have to be good to get Santa's gifts at Christmas! As they grow up, they are conditioned to earn things they want; they learn that "there is no such thing as a free lunch." From an early age, children are taught to become progressively independent economically from their parents. Also, most young people are encouraged to leave home at college age to be on their own. From my viewpoint as a Thai, it seems that American family ties and closeness are not as strong as in Asian families whose children depend on family financial support until joining the work force after college age. Thereafter, it is the children's turn to help support their parents financially.

Modern American society and economy emphasize individualism in other ways. The nuclear family is more common than the extended family, and newlyweds usually establish their own independent household rather than initially living with either the husband's or the wife's parents. Parents and children appear to be close only when the children are very young. Most American parents seem to "lose" their children by the teenage years. They don't seem to belong to each other as closely as do Thai families. Even though I have seen more explicit affectionate expression among American family members than among Asian ones, the close interpersonal spirit seems to be lacking. Grandparents have relatively little to do with the grandchildren on any regular basis, in contrast to the extended family, which is more common in Thailand. The family and society seem to be graded by age to the point that grandparents, parents, and children are separated by generational subcultures that are evidently alienated from one another. Each group "does its own thing." Help and support are usually limited to whatever does not interfere with one's own life. In America, the locus of responsibility is more on the individual than on the family.

In one case I know of, a financially affluent grandmother with Alzheimer's disease is taken care of twenty-four hours a day by hired help in her own home. Her daughter visits and relieves the helper occasionally. The mature granddaughter, who has her own family, rarely visits. Yet they all live in the same neighborhood. However, each lives in a different house, and each is very independent. Although the mother worries about the grandmother, she cannot do much. Her husband also needs her, and she divides her time between him, her daughters and their children, and the grandmother. When the mother needs to go on a trip with her husband, a second hired attendant is required to care for the grandmother temporarily. When I asked why the granddaughter doesn't temporarily care for the grandmother, the reply was that she has her own life, and it would not be fair for the granddaughter to take care of the grandmother, even for a short period of time. Yet I wonder if it is fair for the grandmother to be left out. It seems to me that the value of individualism and its associated independence account for these apparent gaps in family ties and support.

In contrast to American society, in Thailand older parents with a long-term illness are asked to move in with their children and grandchildren if they are not already living with them. The children and grandchildren take turns attending to the grandparent, sometimes with help from live-in maids. Living together in the same house reinforces moral support among the generations within an extended family. The older generation is respected because of the previous economic, social, and moral support for their children and grandchildren. Family relations provide one of the most important contexts for being a "morally good person," which is traditionally the principal concern in the Buddhist society of Thailand.

In America, being young, rich, and/or famous allows one greater freedom and independence and thus promotes the American value of individualism. This is reflected in the mass appeal of major annual television events like the Super Bowl and the Academy Awards. The goal of superachievement is also seen in more mundane ways. For example, many parents encourage their children to take special courses and to work hard to excel in sports as a shortcut to becoming rich and famous. I know one mother who has taken her two sons to tennis classes and tournaments since the boys were six years old, hoping that at least one of them will be a future tennis star like Ivan Lendl. Other parents focus their children on acting, dancing, or musical talent. The children have to devote much time and hard work as well as sacrifice the ordinary activities of youth in order to develop and perform their natural talents and skills in prestigious programs. But those who excel in the sports and entertainment industries can become rich and famous, even at an early age, as for example, Madonna, Tom Cruise, and Michael Jackson. Television and other media publicize these celebrities and thereby reinforce the American value of individualism, including personal achievement and financial success.

Although the American cultural values of individualism and the aspiration to become rich and famous have had some influence in Thailand, there is also cultural and religious resistance to these values. Strong social bonds, particularly within the extended family, and the hierarchical structure of the kingdom run counter to individualism. Also, youth gain social recognition through their academic achievement.

From the perspective of Theravada Buddhism, which strongly influences Thai culture, aspiring to be rich and famous would be an illustration of greed, and those who have achieved wealth and fame do not celebrate it publicly as much as in American society. Being a good, moral person is paramount, and ideally Buddhists emphasize restraint and moderation.

Beyond talent and skill in the sports and entertainment industries, there are many other ways that young Americans can pursue wealth. Investment is one route. One American friend who is only a sophomore in college has already invested heavily in the stock market to start accumulating wealth. She is just one example of the 1980s trend for youth to be more concerned with their individual finances than with social, political, and environmental issues. With less attention paid to public issues, the expression of individualism seems to be magnified through emphasis on lucrative careers, financial investment, and material consumption—the "Yuppie" phenomenon. This includes new trends in dress, eating, housing (condominiums), and cars (expensive European imports). Likewise, there appears to be less of a long-term commitment to marriage. More young couples are living together without either marriage or plans for future marriage. When such couples decide to get married, prenuptial agreements are made to protect their assets. Traditional values of marriage, family, and sharing appear to be on the decline.

Individualism as one of the dominant values in American culture is expressed in many ways. This value probably stems from the history of the society as a frontier colony of immigrants in search of a better life with independence, freedom, and the opportunity for advancement through personal achievement. However, in the beliefs and customs of any culture there are some disadvantages as well as advantages. Although Thais may admire the achievements and material wealth of American society, there are costs, especially in the value of individualism and associated social phenomena.

Reading the Genre

1. Natadecha-Sponsel, who is originally from Thailand, has lived in the United States for more than thirty years. What does she notice about America that people who have always lived in America might not notice? How does she get her readers to look more closely at American culture? (See "Understanding your audience," p. 80, and Chapter 33, "Inclusive and Culturally Sensitive Style," p. 408.)

2. How does the author set up her comparison of the United States and other cultures? Does she have an opinion about which culture is better? Is her purpose to help us choose which culture is best? (See "Compare and contrast," p. 113.)

3. Consider what this essay has to offer both an American reader and a non-American reader. How does Natadecha-Sponsel speak to both audiences?

4. How does Natadecha-Sponsel define the term *individualism*? Consider how she provides examples that illustrate what *individualism* means in America. How does each example help the reader understand what American individualism looks like to her? How does she connect these examples? (See Chapter 29, "Transitions," p. 387.)

5. **WRITING:** Create a "beginner's guide" to culture at your college or university. What would a new student (perhaps a foreign student) have to know to understand the cultural values at your school? Try to write about major cultural values — the big things that students believe in or assume to be inherently true — rather than cultural practices (like partying or studying). Which values would a new student find strange? Why?

6. **COMPOSE VISUALLY:** Look at your college's Web site and identify the key cultural values conveyed by the home page and other relevant sections. Do you feel comfortable with the site's portrayal of your school, its students, and their values? Create a sketch proposing a redesign of the Web site that reflects campus values as you understand them.

POLICY ARGUMENT   Daniel Engber writes a regular science column for *Slate.com* and has published articles in *Popular Mechanics, Popular Science, Salon.com,* and the *Chronicle of Higher Education*. A deliberately quirky writer, he has drawn on his graduate education in neuroscience to argue for distracting free-throw shooters at NBA games, for creating foolproof viral videos, and, in this article, for ending the backlash against obesity.

slate.com

Posted: Monday, October 5, 2009, at 6:02 PM ET
From: Daniel Engber

Glutton Intolerance

What If a War on Obesity Only Makes the Problem Worse?

Just about every discussion of obesity and health care begins with the same purported fact: The diseases associated with excess weight are impoverishing the nation with $147 billion in unnecessary medical bills every year.

In my last column ("Give Us Your Tired, Your Poor, Your Big Fat Asses . . ."), I argued that obesity can also make us poor individually, since fat people face rampant discrimination on the job and marriage markets.

A recent paper from Yale's Rudd Center for Food Policy & Obesity hints at the scope of this anti-fat prejudice. We know, for example, that if you're fat, you make less money. Lots of studies have shown how body size plays out in the working world: According to one, women who are two standard deviations (or sixty-four pounds) overweight suffer a wage penalty of 9 percent; another found that severely obese white women lose out on one-quarter of their potential income. There's also evidence that obese women are less likely to attend college or maintain romantic relationships, even controlling for socioeconomic background. (One survey found that a few extra pounds could reduce a woman's chance of getting married by 20 percent.)

Heavy people may face discrimination in medical settings, too. The authors of the review, Rebecca Puhl and Chelsea Heuer, cite numerous surveys of anti-fat attitudes among health-care workers, who tend to see obese patients as ugly, lazy, weak-willed, and lacking in motivation to improve their health. Doctors describe treating fatties as a waste of time, and the staff at teaching hospitals appear to single them out for derogatory jokes. Unsurprisingly, many obese people avoid seeing their primary care providers altogether, and those who do are less likely to be screened for breast, cervical, and colorectal cancers. (That's true even among those with health insurance and college degrees.)

These data points suggest a rather simple approach to America's obesity problem: Stop hating. If we weren't such unrepentant body bigots, fat people might earn more money, stay in school, and receive better medical care in hospitals and doctors' offices. All that would go a long way toward mitigating the health effects of excess weight — and its putative costs. But there's an even better reason to think that America's glutton intolerance is a threat to public health and the federal budget. Recent epidemiological research implies that the shame of being obese poses its own medical risk. Mental anguish harms the body; weight stigma can break your heart.

The victims of chronic stress or depression, whatever their size, tend to maintain higher levels of certain inflammatory chemicals in their bloodstream. Under normal circumstances — and over the short term — these cytokines help to control the body's response to dangerous situations like injury or illness. The chemicals create their own problems, though, when they stick around too long. A sustained or elevated stress response seems to increase your risk of heart disease, hypertension, and diabetes. That may explain some of the relationships between health and wealth: Blood tests show unusual cytokine activity among those of low socioeconomic status as well as patients with post-traumatic stress and panic disorders.

It turns out that obese people have unusual cytokine readings, too, and these are often taken as the cause of weight-related illness. According to one theory, the presence of visceral fat cells can set off a biochemical chain reaction that leads to the inflammatory response. (Fat cells may even secrete the cytokines themselves.) As a result, someone who's fat and someone who's chronically stressed will be at risk for many of the same diseases.

It may be that obesity and stress are independent risk factors that happen to affect the body in similar ways. Or maybe chronic stress leads to weight gain, which in turn causes inflammation.

According to epidemiologist Peter Muennig, there's another pathway from excess weight to disease. In his 2008 paper "The Body Politic: The Relationship between Stigma and Obesity-Associated Disease," Muennig argues that the stress and shame of being fat causes those cytokine abnormalities. In other words, obesity makes you sick by stressing you out.

According to Muennig's theory, the health effects of obesity should vary with the intensity of anti-fat bias — the more abuse you take, the worse the disease. Women are more likely than men to have eating disorders, and they face greater weight-based discrimination in the overweight range. (According to Puhl, men get harsher treatment when they're really obese.) And, sure enough, women are seven times more likely to experience significant illness or death as a result of being overweight. (Obese women are especially vulnerable to clinical depression, which is itself a risk factor for cardiovascular disease.)

White people also appear to suffer disproportionately from weight-related illness, as compared with black people. According to Muennig, a black woman who's 5 feet 5 inches and less than sixty years old won't develop any weight-related risk of early death until she reaches 225 lbs. Meanwhile, a white woman of the same height and age group would hit the same threshold at 170 lbs. That fits with the idea that body-size norms differ among blacks and whites. (Black people also tend to be less susceptible to eating disorders and weight-based wage discrimination.)

There are some alternative explanations for these disparities. They might, for example, be an artifact of the crude way in which we measure obesity. Black people tend to have less abdominal fat (associated with cardiovascular disease) than white people given the same BMI reading, and women also tend to have more adipose tissue, and smaller waist-to-hip ratios, than men. But even the most accurate measures of fatness — like dual energy X-ray absorptiometry — don't really improve our ability to predict health outcomes across the population. It may be that the exact volume of adipose tissue in someone's body is less important than the way they look to others. (Muennig suggests that merely having "big bones" could be bad for your health.)

That's not to say obesity won't affect your body, independent of any social factors. As Muennig points out, obese lab rodents aren't likely to suffer much emotional abuse from their fellow mice, but they seem to have higher levels of pro-inflammatory cytokines nonetheless. Still, there's plenty of evidence that body-shape discrimination plays a role in human disease outcomes. Shortness, for example, is associated with an increased risk of coronary heart disease, diabetes, and early death — as well as lower wages and fewer long-term relationships. For some reason, though, the health effects of being short are worse for men than they are for women. Could it be that the social consequences of height and weight go in opposite directions?

If anti-fat bias can affect our bodies, then it's worth considering how an all-out war on obesity plays out in terms of public health. When we reach out to poor communities and educate them about the risks of being overweight, we are, in effect, exporting the weight stigma that happens to be most prevalent among rich, white people. Indeed, Rebecca Puhl says the reported prevalence of weight discrimination has increased by two-thirds since the mid-1990s, while media coverage of the "obesity epidemic" has quintupled over roughly the same interval. (Meanwhile, the U.S. diet industry has just about doubled its annual revenues — to nearly $60 billion.)

We've worked hard to frame excess weight as a major health risk and a drain on the economy. The motivation is generous enough: Anti-obesity rhetoric encourages people to eat less and exercise more. But what if it also encourages discrimination? If that's the case, a war on obesity would come at a significant cost to the fattest Americans — in terms of lower wages, less education, and more stress-related illness.

Fat activists argue that the risks of such a policy far outweigh its potential benefits. (They say that doctors should encourage healthy lifestyles instead of trying to enforce an ideal body size.)

But few mainstream public-health advocates take such claims seriously. They point out that many interventions in poor communities focus on diet and exercise rather than weight per se. If BMI is used as a measure of success in these programs, that's because it's a quick way to see whether people really are pursuing a healthy lifestyle. For Kelly Brownell, director of the Rudd Center and a leading researcher on both health policy and weight bias, the dangers of discrimination are important but relatively modest. What about the idea that targeting obesity might be counterproductive for the fattest Americans? He doesn't buy it.

The fact is, very few researchers have tried to measure the combined health effects of anti-fat prejudice. Nor have legislators spent much effort on the social consequences of weight stigma. Only a handful of cities — Washington, D.C.; San Francisco; and Santa Cruz, Calif. — have passed laws to protect the rights of obese people, and there's only one state — Michigan — that forbids employers from discriminating on the basis of body size. If you're victimized for being fat anywhere else in the United States, good luck. You can sue your employer under the Americans with Disabilities Act, but you'll have to prove that your weight condition is something like being wheelchair-bound or mentally retarded — not such a good way to reduce weight stigma overall.

Given the risks associated with weight stigma, we should at least reconsider our tendency to blame obesity for the country's health crisis. (I suggested last week that we could target poverty instead.) If obesity prevention measures do end up in the health bill, let's make sure they'll do more good than harm. The Rudd Center has called for a new federal ban on weight discrimination or an expansion of the Civil Rights Act. Both would go a long way toward protecting the two-thirds of all Americans who are classified as overweight or obese.

Reading the Genre

1. Engber opens his argument with an overview of recent scientific research on the costs of obesity and then startles readers with his thesis — "Stop hating" — in the fifth paragraph. Reread the article and locate other instances when Engber switches between academic and conversational style. How does he want his audience to respond when he makes these shifts in style? (See Chapter 32, "High, Middle, and Low Style," p. 400.)

2. Find Engber's restatement of his thesis in the last paragraph. How does the thesis change between Engber's introduction and his conclusion? (See Chapter 24, "Thesis," p. 362.)

3. Engber tests the logic of several theories, offers a range of possible causes for obesity, and considers the effects of being obese on individuals and on society. What do these causal analyses contribute to his argument? (See Chapter 5, "Causal Analyses," p. 128.)

4. Engber's article is thoroughly researched. Choose a few of the sources he names in his text, find them online or through your library's databases, and create a list of works cited in MLA style or a references list in APA style. (See Chapter 46, "MLA Documentation and Format," p. 472, and Chapter 47, "APA Documentation and Format," p. 512.)

5. **WRITING:** Visit the Yale Rudd Center on Food Policy's "Hot Topics" Web page (www.yaleruddcenter.org/hot_topics.aspx) and select a food policy issue that interests you. Read five to ten of the articles and studies linked on the page, and then write an argumentative essay on your topic. Be sure to have a clearly expressed thesis and to document your sources as appropriate.

65

Evaluations:
Readings

GENRE MOVES Evaluation

NAOMI KLEIN
From *No Logo*

The most sophisticated culture jams are not stand-alone ad parodies but interceptions; counter-messages that hack into a corporation's own method of communication to send a message starkly at odds with the one that was intended. The process forces the company to foot the bill for its own subversion, either literally because the company is the one that paid for the billboard, or figuratively because anytime people mess with a logo, they are tapping into the vast resources spent to make that logo meaningful. Kalle Lasn, editor of Vancouver-based *Adbusters* magazine, uses the martial art of jujitsu as a precise metaphor to explain the mechanics of the jam: "In one simple deft move you slap the giant on its back. We use the momentum of the enemy." It's an image borrowed from Saul Alinsky, who, in his activist bible, *Rules for Radicals*, defines "mass political jujitsu" as "utilizing the power of one part of the power structure against another part[;] . . . the superior strength of the Haves become their own undoing."

Establish your own criteria by borrowing from others.

For any evaluation, a key task is to clearly establish the criteria you will use to evaluate. What makes the act or object that you are evaluating good or bad? How can it be fairly measured against other similar acts or objects? In "Culture Jamming," a chapter from her book *No Logo*, Naomi Klein lays out her own criteria: The best culture jams "intercept" and "hack." But then she uses ideas from Lasn and Alinsky to expand on these criteria by relating the best culture jams to jujitsu in terms of their deft maneuvers against powerful enemies. Expanding her criteria allows her, later in the chapter, to evaluate other groups' culture jams with a precise, critical eye. Her criteria are clear, but they are also supported by the criteria of other experts.

▶

As you develop criteria for evaluation in your own essay, look at how other experts have evaluated your object or objects like it. You can borrow some of their criteria and justifications to support your own. Or you can disagree with these experts, especially if their criteria show a bias or are based on unrealistic expectations. Don't be afraid to borrow and modify ideas from others, even as you develop your own unique evaluation. Just be sure to cite properly, as Klein does.

TELEVISION REVIEW   Emily Nussbaum writes about culture for the *New Yorker*. Nussbaum is quickly becoming one of the most influential voices discussing the roles and representations of gender on TV. This article, published in April 2013, focuses on subgenres of cooking shows and gives readers a glimpse of Nussbaum's critical thinking.

To Stir, with Love

The Modern Cooking Show, from *Hell's Kitchen* to *Barefoot Contessa*

EMILY NUSSBAUM

In 1968, Nora Ephron wrote a tart exposé of New York's backbiting food establishment; at the end, she asked its members if haute cuisine would survive. "Of course it will last," Poppy Cannon argued. "Just in the way sculpture will last." Nika Hazelton disagreed, sighing that "the old cuisine is gone for good and dying out." She predicted, "Ultimately, cooking will be like an indoor sport, just like making lace and handiwork."

The late sixties are not generally considered an age of innocence, but there you go. Neither Cannon nor Hazelton, nor Ephron herself, envisioned anything like today's gladiatorial, whirligig culinary culture, which has expanded far beyond the salons of the Upper East Side. Instead of a few competing cookbooks and restaurants, we have *Lucky Peach* and Chowhound and *Iron Chef*, not to mention Sandra Lee on YouTube making a baked potato out of ice cream, rolling it in cocoa powder, and garnishing it with "chives" (pistachios dyed deep green). Culinary taste now indicates not merely economic class but morality and environmental chic as well. Across the globe, celebrity chefs clash, like clans in *Game of Thrones*. Yet, even as whole channels of food programming have emerged, I've been a conscientious objector (or maybe a deserter). Unlike Ephron, I'm a subsistence cook at best: My specialty is a Turkish spinach-lentil soup from the cookbook *Sundays at Moosewood Restaurant* which I haven't actually prepared in three years.

Among the many options, two TV genres dominate: the traditional "stand-and-stir," popularized by Julia Child, and the reality competition, spearheaded by

Iron Chef. They suggest opposing food philosophies. Julia Child took an occult discipline, once reserved for men in tall hats, and made it accessible to all. Her show implied that food might, in fact, be easier than you ever imagined—and that cooking itself was no big deal. The reality show begs to differ. In these chef-versus-chef contests, food is a perpetual emergency. Every single contestant might, under more ordinary circumstances, be an excellent cook, capable of hosting relaxed weekly dinner parties. But, when they are faced with a rasher of kelp plus extra-virgin honey and a ticking timer, even the production of appetizers becomes something out of *24.*

Given my own culinary ineptitude, it might have been wiser to start in the welcoming bosom of Nigella Lawson. Instead, I walked straight into the wood-fired oven: the gleeful dystopia of Gordon Ramsay's *Hell's Kitchen.* Filmed in a Los Angeles soundstage-restaurant, the show has aired for eleven seasons and spawned several spinoffs, also Inferno-themed. In this iteration (Ramsay is apparently much nicer on *MasterChef*), the chef is a Scottish-accented Heat Miser, with forehead furrows that deepen into canyons when he screams. On *Hell's Kitchen,* he screams a lot, when not delivering Schwarzeneggerian wise-cracks like "Did you throw up on this plate?" One contestant gets booted each week; the grand prize this season is a job in Ramsay's employ, which seems like a mixed blessing. The drama is (as the participants point out with regularity) *intense,* with challenges such as extracting the meat from as many lobsters as possible in ten minutes. Praise is doled out in scraps, like liver pâté tossed to mongrels.

For all I know, this is actually a reasonable approximation of restaurant life, with a closer resemblance to the brutality of Orwell's *Down and Out in Paris and London* than to Bravo's likable, globe-trotting *Top Chef,* on which Padma Lakshmi might smile at your pasta. It's loud and it's ugly, but it's also refreshing to come across participants who are not telegenic Hollywood types, let alone celebrity chefs: Instead, they're fat and sweaty, male and female, line cooks and small-time chefs, from a wide range of backgrounds—ordinary mugs hoping for their big break. A few might be ringers, and it's hard not to suspect that some of the competition is rigged, but who cares? Food is pain, Princess.

Still, I learned almost nothing about cooking, other than that it's a bad idea to set asparagus on fire and that you must scream "Yes, Chef!" at your boss—a fact I already knew from *Treme.* For more depth, I checked out *Chopped,* on the Food Network. The formula here is as strict as a sonnet: Four contestants open mystery baskets, find four ingredients, and improvise dishes on deadline. A typical basket featured rack of antelope, stinging nettles, jicama, and port-wine cheese; the results included a luscious-looking Peruvian spiced antelope with polenta. Ted Allen, who made his name on *Queer Eye for the Straight Guy*, oversees the festivities. "I know the jicama wants to be a salsa," one contestant says—and then there's a knife accident. "That will definitely disqualify him," a judge observes. "If there's blood on the plates." That's as frightening as things get. Soothing in its repetitions, the show has the reliable charm of *Law & Order: Seared-Veal Unit*.

These shows—and other old reliables like *Iron Chef America*, currently in its eleventh season—are primarily about restaurant life. They concern the fantasies and fears of working in a professional kitchen, as the underling of a person with a tremendous ego, which you hope someday to replace with your own. Like much of TV drama, they glamorize workaholism, and on the better shows the gimmickry is half the appeal: If you can survive this obstacle course, no regular kitchen can defeat you. In contrast, the modern stand-and-stir is more about the dream of an idyllic home kitchen, with everything in its place and nothing burning. As a result, these shows tend to be as static as network news: There's a kitchen, there's a person, there are ingredients pre-prepped in bowls, and, often, a significant amount of purring while things sizzle. (You might imagine there is nothing more wholesome than a cooking show, but in my survey there were as many double-entendres as on *Archer*.)

A few shows do try to expand the genre's visual rhetoric, including the food-science series *Good Eats*, hosted by Alton Brown, which is no longer producing new episodes but is still on the air. Unlike the preening celebrity chefs, Brown is all shop-class enthusiasm and dorky competence. His show focuses on one food per episode, and it features quick-cut editing and puns, reminding me a bit of *Blue's Clues*. In one session, Brown bought some beef, defattified it, and then butterflied it, all while juggling props. He delivered an abstruse explanation of "reticulum" and "elastin" which I didn't quite catch, although I did absorb the fact that steaks should be at room temperature when cooking begins. Also that peppercorns were used as currency in the Middle Ages. By the final sequence, when Brown tore into some steak au poivre, I found myself wishing I could join him—the sign of success for any such show.

I cannot advise you on whose cooking tips are the most reliable, but then these shows are often more about the fantasy of one's perfect life. Which would you prefer: down-home southern cooking for the in-laws or dinners for ten elderly men from the U.N.? Of the fancier options, the one that drew me in most was *Barefoot Contessa*, which is set in East Hampton, a luxurious Narnia in which guests are due for cocktails in the new library. Despite the posh milieu, the Contessa, Ina Garten, seems down-to-earth and perpetually amused. She knows just how to handle fennel and zest. After twenty minutes, I gave in—and began to follow directions. "Fresh figs I save for eating just the way they are," she confided. I got on FreshDirect and ordered figs. "I love things that you can just assemble," she cooed. Nigella Lawson may be the planet's most sensuous food celebrity (and the woman does have a way with phrases like "sticky bits of caramelized scallop juice"), but the Contessa was clearly my soul mate.

You'll have to find your own, though. After hours of flipping between the Food Network and PBS, I was forced to admit the truth: I was never going to be able to tell a cassoulet from a cassava. The shows didn't bore me, exactly: As with sports, it can be fun to look at athletes, even if you can't throw a ball. But while I'd like to announce that my brief immersion inspired me to raise my game, the truth is I mostly learned that watching food TV makes me ravenous. So I ordered in.

Reading the Genre

1. Following the two main genres of cooking shows suggested by Nussbaum, list as many "stand-and-stir" and as many "reality competition" shows as you can. Can you also come up with any other genres of cooking shows that Nussbaum has neglected? For Nussbaum's two genres, and for any genres you can identify yourself, list as many rules or conventions as you can that define these types of shows. (For more on understanding genres, see the Introduction, p. xix.)

2. Nussbaum uses vivid similes and metaphors in her evaluation. Find as many metaphors and similes as you can, and think about what they each add to this essay. What work can figurative language do for an author trying to capture a visual medium like TV in a written essay?

3. Throughout the essay, Nussbaum alludes to the economics of cooking shows: Stand-and-stir shows are set in idealized kitchens; winners get jobs; the contestants are line cooks looking for a "big break." How could you respond to Nussbaum's article by further exploring the economics that food shows reveal? Consider the costs of eating out or preparing food, about the underpaid labor of those who cook, and other economic questions.

4. **WRITING:** Write your own evaluation of a television show, paying attention to how it fits into a popular "genre" or type of TV show. How does the show follow specific genre rules, how does it break them, and what is the intended impact on the audience? Are there any genre rules that the show has created and other shows now follow?

5. **MULTIMODALITY — STILL IMAGE ANALYSIS:** Nussbaum writes about the "visual rhetoric" of these cooking shows — the dominant settings, camera shots, and images. Choose one cooking show to watch, and look for opportunities to pause the video (whether on TV or online) in a key moment of "visual rhetoric." Choose just one still, describe it in detail, and evaluate what this one visual moment can teach us about the show. (See "Present evaluations visually," p. 116.)

SCIENTIFIC EVALUATION Michio Kaku is a theoretical physicist who specializes in string field theory—and in making scientific concepts understandable to a popular audience. This essay comes from his book *Physics of the Impossible* (2008), a collection of essays that examine the real science behind fictional ideas like death rays and invisibility cloaks.

MICHIO KAKU

Force Fields

I. When a distinguished but elderly scientist states that something is possible, he is almost certainly right. When he states that something is impossible, he is very probably wrong.

II. The only way of discovering the limits of the possible is to venture a little way past them into the impossible.

III. Any sufficiently advanced technology is indistinguishable from magic.

—Arthur C. Clarke's Three Laws

"**S**hields up!"

In countless *Star Trek* episodes this is the first order that Captain Kirk barks out to the crew, raising the force fields to protect the starship *Enterprise* against enemy fire.

So vital are force fields in *Star Trek* that the tide of the battle can be measured by how the force field is holding up. Whenever power is drained from the force fields, the *Enterprise* suffers more and more damaging blows to its hull, until finally surrender is inevitable.

So what is a force field? In science fiction it's deceptively simple: a thin, invisible yet impenetrable barrier able to deflect lasers and rockets alike. At first glance a force field looks so easy that its creation as a battlefield shield seems imminent. One expects that any day some enterprising inventor will announce the discovery of a defensive force field. But the truth is far more complicated.

In the same way that Edison's lightbulb revolutionized modern civilization, a force field could profoundly affect every aspect of our lives. The military could use force fields to become invulnerable, creating an impenetrable shield against enemy missiles and bullets. Bridges, superhighways, and roads could in theory be built by simply pressing a button. Entire cities could sprout instantly in the desert, with sky-scrapers made entirely of force fields. Force fields erected over cities could enable their inhabitants to modify the effects of their weather — high winds, blizzards, tornadoes — at will. Cities could be built under the oceans within the safe canopy of a force field. Glass, steel, and mortar could be entirely replaced.

Yet oddly enough a force field is perhaps one of the most difficult devices to create in the laboratory. In fact, some physicists believe it might actually be impossible, without modifying its properties.

Michael Faraday

The concept of force fields originates from the work of the great nineteenth-century British scientist Michael Faraday.

Faraday was born to working-class parents (his father was a blacksmith) and eked out a meager existence as an apprentice bookbinder in the early 1800s. The young Faraday was fascinated by the enormous breakthroughs in uncovering the mysterious properties of two new forces: electricity and magnetism. Faraday devoured all he could concerning these topics and attended lectures by Professor Humphrey Davy of the Royal Institution in London.

One day Professor Davy severely damaged his eyes in a chemical accident and hired Faraday to be his secretary. Faraday slowly began to win the confidence of the scientists at the Royal Institution and was allowed to conduct important experiments of his own, although he was often slighted. Over the years Professor Davy grew increasingly jealous of the brilliance shown by his young assistant, who was a rising star in experimental circles, eventually eclipsing Davy's own fame. After Davy died in 1829 Faraday was free to make a series of stunning breakthroughs that led to the creation of generators that would energize entire cities and change the course of world civilization.

The key to Faraday's greatest discoveries was his "force fields." If one places iron filings over a magnet, one finds that the iron filings create a spiderweb-like pattern that fills up all of the space. These are Faraday's lines of force, which graphically describe how the force fields of electricity and magnetism permeate space. If one graphs the magnetic fields of the Earth, for example, one finds that the lines emanate from the north polar region and then fall back to the Earth in the south polar region. Similarly, if one were to graph the electric field lines of a lightning rod in a thunderstorm, one would find that the lines of force concentrate at the tip of the lightning rod. Empty space, to Faraday, was not empty at all, but was filled with lines of force that could make distant objects move. (Because of Faraday's poverty-stricken youth, he was illiterate in mathematics, and as a consequence his notebooks are full not of equations but of hand-drawn diagrams of these lines of force. Ironically, his lack of mathematical training led him to create the beautiful diagrams of lines of force that now can be found in any physics textbook. In science a physical picture is often more important than the mathematics used to describe it.)

Historians have speculated on how Faraday was led to his discovery of force fields, one of the most important concepts in all of science. In fact, the *sum total of all modern physics* is written in the language of Faraday's fields. In 1831, he made the key breakthrough regarding force fields that changed civilization forever. One day, he was moving a child's magnet over a coil of wire and he noticed that he was able to generate an electric current in the wire, without ever touching it. This meant that a magnet's invisible field could push electrons in a wire across empty space, creating a current.

Faraday's "force fields," which were previously thought to be useless, idle doodlings, were real, material forces that could move objects and generate power. Today the light that you are using to read this page is probably energized by Faraday's discovery about electromagnetism. A spinning magnet creates a force field that pushes the electrons in a wire, causing them to move in an electrical current. This electricity in the wire can then be used to light up a lightbulb. This same principle is used to generate electricity to power the cities of the world. Water flowing across a dam, for example, causes a huge magnet in a turbine to spin, which then pushes the electrons in a wire, forming an electric current that is sent across high-voltage wires into our homes.

In other words, the force fields of Michael Faraday are the forces that drive modern civilization, from electric bulldozers to today's computers, Internet, and iPods.

Faraday's force fields have been an inspiration for physicists for a century and a half. Einstein was so inspired by them that he wrote his theory of gravity in terms of force fields. I, too, was inspired by Faraday's work. Years ago I successfully wrote the theory of strings in terms of the force fields of Faraday, thereby founding string field theory. In physics when someone says, "He thinks like a line of force," it is meant as a great compliment.

The Four Forces

Over the last two thousand years one of the crowning achievements of physics has been the isolation and identification of the four forces that rule the universe. All of them can be described in the language of fields introduced by Faraday. Unfortunately, however, none of them has quite the properties of the force fields described in most science fiction. These forces are

1. *Gravity*, the silent force that keeps our feet on the ground, prevents the Earth and the stars from disintegrating, and holds the solar system and galaxy together. Without gravity, we would be flung off the Earth into space at the rate of 1,000 miles per hour by the spinning planet. The problem is that gravity has precisely the opposite properties of a force field found in science fiction. Gravity is attractive, not repulsive; is extremely weak, relatively speaking; and works over enormous, astronomical distances. In other words, it is almost the opposite of

the flat, thin, impenetrable barrier that one reads about in science fiction or one sees in science fiction movies. For example, it takes the entire planet Earth to attract a feather to the floor, but we can counteract Earth's gravity by lifting the feather with a finger. The action of our finger can counteract the gravity of an entire planet that weighs over six trillion trillion kilograms.

2. *Electromagnetism* (EM), the force that lights up our cities. Lasers, radio, TV, modern electronics, computers, the Internet, electricity, magnetism—all are consequences of the electromagnetic force. It is perhaps the most useful force ever harnessed by humans. Unlike gravity, it can be both attractive and repulsive. However, there are several reasons that it is unsuitable as a force field. First, it can be easily neutralized. Plastics and other insulators, for example, can easily penetrate a powerful electric or magnetic field. A piece of plastic thrown in a magnetic field would pass right through. Second, electromagnetism acts over large distances and cannot easily be focused onto a plane. The laws of the EM force are described by James Clerk Maxwell's equations, and these equations do not seem to admit force fields as solutions.

3. & 4. *The weak and strong nuclear forces*. The weak force is the force of radioactive decay. It is the force that heats up the center of the Earth, which is radioactive. It is the force behind volcanoes, earthquakes, and continental drift. The strong force holds the nucleus of the atom together. The energy of the sun and the stars originates from the nuclear force, which is responsible for lighting up the universe. The problem is that the nuclear force is a short-range force, acting mainly over the distance of a nucleus. Because it is so bound to the properties of nuclei, it is extremely hard to manipulate. At present the only ways we have of manipulating this force are to blow subatomic particles apart in atom smashers or to detonate atomic bombs.

Although the force fields used in science fiction may not conform to the known laws of physics, there are still loopholes that might make the creation of such a force field possible. First, there may be a fifth force, still unseen in the laboratory. Such a force might, for example, work over a distance of only a few inches to feet, rather than over astronomical distances. (Initial attempts to measure the presence of such a fifth force, however, have yielded negative results.)

Second, it may be possible to use a plasma to mimic some of the properties of a force field. A plasma is the "fourth state of matter." Solids, liquids, and gases make up the three familiar states of matter, but the most common form of matter in the universe is plasma, a gas of ionized atoms. Because the atoms of a plasma are ripped apart, with electrons torn off the atom, the atoms are electrically charged and can be easily manipulated by electric and magnetic fields.

Plasmas are the most plentiful form of visible matter in the universe, making up the sun, the stars, and interstellar gas. Plasmas are not familiar to us because they are only rarely found on the Earth, but we can see them in the form of lightning bolts, the sun, and the interior of your plasma TV.

Plasma Windows

As noted above, if a gas is heated to a high enough temperature, thereby creating a plasma, it can be molded and shaped by magnetic and electrical fields. It can, for example, be shaped in the form of a sheet or window. Moreover, this "plasma window" can be used to separate a vacuum from ordinary air. In principle, one might be able to prevent the air within a spaceship from leaking out into space, thereby creating a convenient, transparent interface between outer space and the spaceship.

In the *Star Trek* TV series, such a force field is used to separate the shuttle bay, containing small shuttle craft, from the vacuum of outer space. Not only is it a clever way to save money on props, but it is a device that is possible.

The plasma window was invented by physicist Ady Herschcovitch in 1995 at the Brookhaven National Laboratory in Long Island, New York. He developed it to solve the problem of how to weld metals using electron beams. A welder's acetylene torch uses a blast of hot gas to melt and then weld metal pieces together. But a beam of electrons can weld metals faster, cleaner, and more cheaply than ordinary methods. The problem with electron beam welding, however, is that it needs to be done in a vacuum. This requirement is quite inconvenient, because it means creating a vacuum box that may be as big as an entire room.

Dr. Herschcovitch invented the plasma window to solve this problem. Only 3 feet high and less than 1 foot in diameter, the plasma window heats gas to 12,000°F, creating a plasma that is trapped by electric and magnetic fields. These particles exert pressure, as in any gas, which prevents air from rushing into the vacuum chamber, thus separating air from the vacuum. (When one uses argon gas in the plasma window, it glows blue, like the force field in *Star Trek*.)

The plasma window has wide applications for space travel and industry. Many times, manufacturing processes need a vacuum to perform microfabrication and dry etching for industrial purposes, but working in a vacuum can be expensive. But with the plasma window one can cheaply contain a vacuum with the flick of a button.

But can the plasma window also be used as an impenetrable shield? Can it withstand a blast from a cannon? In the future, one can imagine a plasma window of much greater power and temperature, sufficient to damage or vaporize incoming projectiles. But to create a more realistic force field, like that found in science fiction, one would need a combination of several technologies stacked in layers. Each layer might not be strong enough alone to stop a cannon ball, but the combination might suffice.

The outer layer could be a supercharged plasma window, heated to temperatures high enough to vaporize metals. A second layer could be a curtain of high-energy laser beams. This curtain, containing thousands of crisscrossing laser beams, would create a lattice that would heat up objects that passed through it, effectively vaporizing them. . . .

And behind this laser curtain one might envision a lattice made of "carbon nanotubes," tiny tubes made of individual carbon atoms that are one atom thick and that are many times stronger than steel. Although the current world record for a carbon nanotube is only about 15 millimeters long, one can envision a day when we might be able to create carbon nanotubes of arbitrary length. Assuming that carbon nanotubes can be woven into a lattice, they could create a screen of enormous strength, capable of repelling most objects. The screen would be invisible, since each carbon nanotube is atomic in size, but the carbon nanotube lattice would be stronger than any ordinary material.

So, via a combination of plasma window, laser curtain, and carbon nanotube screen, one might imagine creating an invisible wall that would be nearly impenetrable by most means.

Yet even this multilayered shield would not completely fulfill all the properties of a science fiction force field—because it would be transparent and therefore incapable of stopping a laser beam. In a battle with laser cannons, the multilayered shield would be useless.

To stop a laser beam, the shield would also need to possess an advanced form of "photochromatics." This is the process used in sunglasses that darken by themselves upon exposure to UV radiation. Photochromatics are based on molecules that can exist in at least two states. In one state the molecule is transparent. But when it is exposed to UV radiation it instantly changes to the second form, which is opaque.

One day we might be able to use nanotechnology to produce a substance as tough as carbon nanotubes that can change its optical properties when exposed to laser light. In this way, a shield might be able to stop a laser blast as well as a particle beam or cannon fire. At present, however, photochromatics that can stop laser beams do not exist.

Magnetic Levitation

In science fiction, force fields have another purpose besides deflecting ray-gun blasts, and that is to serve as a platform to defy gravity. In the movie *Back to the Future*, Michael J. Fox rides a "hover board," which resembles a skateboard except that it floats over the street. Such an antigravity device is impossible given the laws of phys-ics as we know them today. . . . But magnetically enhanced hover boards and hover cars could become a reality in the future, giving us the ability to levitate large objects at will. In the future, if "room-temperature superconductors" become a reality, one might be able to levitate objects using the power of magnetic force fields.

If we place two bar magnets next to each other with north poles opposite each other, the two magnets repel each other. (If we rotate the magnet, so that the north pole is close to the other south pole, then the two magnets attract each other.) This same principle, that north poles repel each other, can be used to lift enormous weights off the ground. Already several nations are building advanced magnetic levitation trains (maglev trains) that hover just above the railroad tracks using ordinary magnets. Because they have zero friction, they can attain record-breaking speeds, floating over a cushion of air.

In 1984 the world's first commercial automated maglev system began operation in the United Kingdom, running from Birmingham International Airport to the nearby Birmingham International railway station. Maglev trains have also been built in Germany, Japan, and Korea, although most of them have not been designed for high velocities. The first commercial maglev train operating at high velocities is the initial operating segment (IOS) demonstration line in Shanghai, which travels at a top speed of 268 miles per hour. The Japanese maglev train in Yamanashi prefecture attained a velocity of 361 miles per hour, even faster than the usual wheeled trains.

But these maglev devices are extremely expensive. One way to increase efficiency would be to use superconductors, which lose all electrical resistance when they are cooled down to near absolute zero. Superconductivity was discovered in 1911 by Heike Onnes. If certain substances are cooled to below 20 K above absolute zero, all electrical resistance is lost. Usually when we cool down the temperature of a metal, its resistance decreases gradually. (This is because random vibrations of the atom impede the flow of electrons in a wire. By reducing the temperature, these random motions are reduced, and hence electricity flows with less resistance.) But much to

Onnes's surprise, he found that the resistance of certain materials fell abruptly to zero at a critical temperature.

Physicists immediately recognized the importance of this result. Power lines lose a significant amount of energy by transporting electricity across long distances. But if all resistance could be eliminated, electrical power could be transmitted almost for free. In fact, if electricity were made to circulate in a coil of wire, the electricity would circulate for millions of years, without any reduction in energy. Furthermore, magnets of incredible power could be made with little effort from these enormous electric currents. With these magnets, one could lift huge loads with ease.

Despite all these miraculous powers, the problem with superconductivity is that it is very expensive to immerse large magnets in vats of supercooled liquid. Huge refrigeration plants are required to keep liquids supercooled, making superconducting magnets prohibitively expensive.

But one day physicists may be able to create a "room-temperature superconductor," the holy grail of solid-state physicists. The invention of room-temperature superconductors in the laboratory would spark a second industrial revolution. Powerful magnetic fields capable of lifting cars and trains would become so cheap that hover cars might become economically feasible. With room-temperature superconductors, the fantastic flying cars seen in *Back to the Future*, *Minority Report*, and *Star Wars* might become a reality.

In principle, one might be able to wear a belt made of superconducting magnets that would enable one to effortlessly levitate off the ground. With such a belt, one could fly in the air like Superman. Room-temperature superconductors are so remarkable that they appear in numerous science fiction novels (such as the Ringworld series written by Larry Niven in 1970).

For decades physicists have searched for room-temperature superconductors without success. It has been a tedious, hit-or-miss process, testing one material after another. But in 1986 a new class of substances called "high-temperature superconductors" was found that became superconductors at about 90 degrees above absolute zero, or 90 K, creating a sensation in the world of physics. The flood-gates seemed to open. Month after month, physicists raced one another to break the next world's record for a superconductor. For a brief moment it seemed as if the possibility of room-temperature superconductors would leap off the pages of science fiction novels and into our living rooms. But after a few years of moving at breakneck speed, research in high-temperature superconductors began to slow down.

At present the world's record for a high-temperature superconductor is held by a substance called mercury thallium barium calcium copper oxide, which becomes superconducting at 138 K ($-135\,°$C). This relatively high temperature is still a long way from room temperature. But this 138 K record is still important. Nitrogen liquefies at 77 K, and liquid nitrogen costs about as much as ordinary milk. Hence ordinary liquid nitrogen could be used to cool down these high-temperature superconductors rather cheaply. (Of course, room-temperature superconductors would need no cooling whatsoever.)

Embarrassingly enough, at present there is no theory explaining the properties of these high-temperature superconductors. In fact, a Nobel Prize is awaiting the enterprising physicist who can explain how high-temperature superconductors work. (These high-temperature superconductors are made of atoms arranged in distinctive layers. Many physicists theorize that this layering of the ceramic material makes it possible for electrons to flow freely within each layer, creating a superconductor. But precisely how this is done is still a mystery.)

Because of this lack of knowledge, physicists unfortunately resort to a hit-or-miss procedure to search for new high-temperature superconductors. This means that the fabled room-temperature superconductor may be discovered tomorrow, next year, or not at all. No one knows when, or if, such a substance will ever be found.

But if room-temperature superconductors are discovered, a tidal wave of commercial applications could be set off. Magnetic fields that are a million times more powerful than the Earth's magnetic field (which is .5 gauss) might become commonplace.

One common property of superconductivity is called the Meissner effect. If you place a magnet above a superconductor, the magnet will levitate, as if held upward by some invisible force. (The reason for the Meissner effect is that the magnet has the effect of creating a "mirror-image" magnet within the superconductor, so that the original magnet and the mirror-image magnet repel each other. Another way to see this is that magnetic fields cannot penetrate into a superconductor. Instead, magnetic fields are expelled. So if a magnet is held above a superconductor, its lines of force are expelled by the superconductor, and the lines of force then push the magnet upward, causing it to levitate.)

Using the Meissner effect, one can imagine a future in which the highways are made of these special ceramics. Then magnets placed in our belts or our tires could enable us to magically float to our destination, without any friction or energy loss.

The Meissner effect works only on magnetic materials, such as metals. But it is also possible to use superconducting magnets to levitate nonmagnetic materials, called paramagnets and diamagnets. These substances do not have magnetic properties of their own; they acquire their magnetic properties only in the presence of an external magnetic field. Paramagnets are attracted by an external magnet, while diamagnets are repelled by an external magnet.

Water, for example, is a diamagnet. Since all living things are made of water, they can levitate in the presence of a powerful magnetic field. In a magnetic field of about 15 teslas (30,000 times the Earth's field), scientists have levitated small animals, such as frogs. But if room-temperature superconductors become a reality, it should be possible to levitate large nonmagnetic objects as well, via their diamagnetic property.

In conclusion, force fields as commonly described in science fiction do not fit the description of the four forces of the universe. Yet it may be possible to simulate many of the properties of force fields by using a multilayered shield, consisting of plasma windows, laser curtains, carbon nanotubes, and photochromatics. But developing such a shield could be many decades, or even a century, away.

And if room-temperature superconductors can be found, one might be able to use powerful magnetic fields to levitate cars and trains and soar in the air, as in science fiction movies.

Given these considerations, I would classify force fields as a Class I impossibility—that is, something that is impossible by today's technology, but possible, in modified form, within a century or so.

Reading the Genre

1. Kaku explains concepts on the cutting edge of theoretical physics. What strategies does he use to make these ideas understandable for readers who can't count themselves among the smartest scientists in the world? (See "Write for novices," p. 108).

2. At several points in this essay, a scientist is evaluating science fiction. What is the effect of reading an evaluation of popular culture by a serious scientist? How does the writer establish ethos, or authority to analyze texts that are not in his field of expertise? How might you do the same in your own writing? (See "Consider and control your ethos," p. 80, and "Consider how well reasoned a piece is," p. 228.)

3. What qualities does Kaku suggest are necessary for force fields to become possible? How does he state these criteria and then apply them? How does he try to convince readers that these are valid criteria? (See "Finding and developing materials," p. 109.)

4. Aside from the idea that having a force field would be fun, what uses (good or evil) does Kaku envision for this technology? What additional uses can you imagine?

5. **WRITING:** Choose a technology you use every day. Then write an imaginary evaluation based not on what this technology is capable of now, but on what it might be capable of in the future. What might cell phones or televisions do ten years from now, for instance?

6. **WRITING:** Watch a science fiction movie and evaluate it purely on the basis of science. How realistically does this movie, and the science within it, follow the laws of physics? You may want or need to focus on just one specific scene or one specific technology in the film.

7. **MULTIMODALITY—SCIENCE FICTION ADVERTISEMENT:** Create an advertisement for a force field. Your advertisement should explain the technology and describe a way consumers might use the force field. You could make the advertisement in the form of a poster, a script for a television commercial, or an audio-recorded radio spot.

MUSIC REVIEW   Sasha Frere-Jones has been a pop critic for the *New Yorker* since 2004, and his Web site (www.sashafrerejones.com) collects his photographs, writing, and music. Frere-Jones is known for exploring issues of race in music, specifically indie rock and hip-hop. He appears in the bands The Sands and Ui. This 2013 essay examines the ways that the Internet is changing the music industry.

The Next Day

SASHA FRERE-JONES

Jay-Z's new track "Open Letter" is part of a trend that has little to do with new beat patterns, larger formal changes, regional shifts, or—gadzooks—money. Rappers have turned the Internet into a reliable, stable ally. Even those who work out tracks carefully for weeks ahead of time are creating old-fashioned, single-of-the-week buzz by feeding work through the Web. What does the Web allow for that no physical medium could match—aside from instant dissemination? Surprise.

David Bowie, the famous Bromley rapper, surprised the shit out of everyone a few months ago by leaking the single "Where Are We Now?" if only to announce a traditional, full-length album that absolutely nobody expected after Bowie's decade of what looked like reclusion. Big acts like Radiohead and Nine Inch Nails have taken release dates into their own hands, though nobody has matched Bowie's "gotcha" moment. Rappers generally don't have the luxury of seclusion to build up tension, so they have to catch you unaware with speed. This new method creates an excitement that may not be the same as kids lining up to buy *Thriller* at midnight, but it's potent.

© The New Yorker Magazine/Fido Nesti/Condé Nast.

On "Open Letter," produced by both Swizz Beats and Timbaland (though it sounds more like Swizz and features his ad-lib vocals), Jay-Z responds to suggestions that he is disconnecting from the Nets because, as Fox reports, he is selling his minor financial stake in the team. Since he's doing this, apparently, to become a scouting agent for the team, and remains deeply involved with them, his riposte seems entirely justified. The beat is low-key and weird, and stands up to repeated listening. Jay-Z namedrops "Idiot Wind," and does one of his favorite tricks, using one word to wring out two meanings. ("Cubans" are both Cuban people and Cuban cigars. Nice.)

Jay's wife, the little-known R&B singer Beyoncé, recently dropped an equally unexpected track, "Bow Down / I Been On," which felt as reactive as Jay's track. Following on the heels of her puzzling infomercial/Macbook-demonstration-as-documentary, "Life Is But a Dream," "Bow Down" seemed to be about putting the gloves back on, strapping on the heels, and acting anything but nice. It's a weird trifle that is most valuable for leading to an all-Houston remix of the second, slower half, "I Been On." Bun B—let's get you on the release schedule.

Kanye's team album *Cruel Summer* was a messy, minor work, but it was genuinely exciting to hear him leak "Mercy" and then "Clique," the album's two best tracks. Sacrificing those hits for the benefit of friends and business partners like Pusha T and Big Sean may have seemed profligate, but those tracks are still in the air, somehow. In April of 2009, Mike Skinner released close to an album's worth of tracks on Twitter, all of it better than his final studio album, *Computers and Blues*. Later that year, Freeway declared a "Month of Madness" and released a new song for every day of December. Collected, it all worked better than at least half of his more carefully created album. Maybe the immediacy of the Web is to the m.c. as a deadline is to a writer. Without them, we'd just slink around in our pajamas Googling walruses. (A friend of mine does that.)

Reading the Genre

1. While this essay presents itself as a music review, it contains elements of a report or even an argument. Go through the essay and highlight the sections that discuss the Jay-Z song, the sections that report on a new phenomenon in the music industry, and the sections that feel like an argument about the future. How do the sections work together? How would you classify the essay overall? (See Chapter 2, "Reports," p. 36; Chapter 3, "Arguments," p. 66; and Chapter 4, "Evaluations," p. 100.)

2. Frere-Jones discusses artists as varied as David Bowie, Radiohead, and of course Jay-Z. What similarities do you find in the ways these artists have seized control over the release of their music? How do the artists' release strategies fit with the differences in their musical styles and audiences? (See "Compare and contrast," p. 113.)

3. Jay-Z's song is titled "Open Letter." Though Frere-Jones doesn't comment on this particular genre, it is an intriguing form of public writing. An open letter is a way to address a letter to a certain individual or group, but to intend for a much wider audience to read it. Listen to Jay-Z's song and consider how it follows the conventions of the "open letter." How many other hip-hop songs can you identify that also follow the "open letter" genre? (For more on genre, see the Introduction, p. xix.)

4. **WRITING:** Instead of evaluating an album, evaluate one of the ways that you hear about new music or access it. Consider how this access point does or does not change the listening experience, expose you to new possibilities, or connect you to other fans.

5. **MULTIMODALITY—ONLINE EVALUATION TOOLS:** Consider the different ways that we can use online tools to evaluate. These tools can range from Facebook's "like" button, to GIFs and memes—think Grumpy Cat or Doge—to the reviews on sites like Amazon that can often serve as venues for satire. Using the visual language, strategies, rules, and conventions of one or more of these online phenomena, evaluate a product.

TELEVISION REVIEW
Nelle Engoron is a freelance writer and editor. She blogs about television, movies, and related topics for Open Salon, a reader forum hosted by *Salon.com* (http://open.salon.com/blog/silkstone). Engoron wrote this critique of *Mad Men* during its third season. In the seasons since this was written, depictions of women on the show have changed as the characters have grown and matured, but much of Engoron's critique still applies.

Salon.com

Posted: Friday, July 23, 2010, at 8:10 ET
From: Nelle Engoron

Why *Mad Men* Is Bad for Women

I've Championed the Show for Its Smart Depiction of Sexism — but as the Fourth Season Approaches, I'm Not So Sure

As a child of the 1950s and '60s who entered the workforce in the still-discriminatory '70s, I have deeply appreciated *Mad Men*'s frank and searing depiction of women's lives both at home and at work. Created by enormously talented and meticulous

© AMC/Courtesy: Everett Collection.

artists, *Mad Men* often feels so real and compelling to those of us who lived through those times that watching it sometimes revives painful memories.

But as we approach the start of the fourth season, I fear that I've been wrong about its treatment of womanhood. The message that many women, especially those under forty, seem to have taken from the show is not relief or gratitude at what's changed, nor an understanding of the past, but something quite different: Those fashions are cool! God, Don's hot! Are you a Joan or a Peggy? Let's dress up like them, have a *Mad Men* party, and drink martinis!

I'm also increasingly disturbed by the striking difference in how men and women are portrayed — all the more curious and distressing since, although it was created by a man (Matthew Weiner), *Mad Men* is notable for the number of women on its creative staff. Even as it depicts rampant sexism, the show sides with the men. The men get off scot-free (if not scotch-free) while the women are subjected to repeated humiliation and misfortune, which is invariably attributed to their own flaws and poor choices.

In the skilled hands of *Mad Men*'s writers, directors, and the actor Jon Hamm, Don Draper is a complex and alluring character who continues to win our sympathy despite his frequent affairs, excessive drinking, rough handling of women, and out-right desertions of his family. His callous treatment of his wife, whose suspicions he dismisses as paranoia, whose desires for connection he spurns, and whose grief at the loss of her mother he deems worthy of psychiatric treatment, is just short of despicable. Don doesn't merely deceive Betty; he also belittles her, playing mind games to get her to doubt herself rather than him.

And yet Don is the suave hero of the show, enjoying an uncanny creativity, a successful and lucrative career, a succession of beautiful women who fall into his arms, and a wife who initially forgives and embraces him when he spills all his secrets (although she does change her mind not long afterward). As the famous *Saturday Night Live* parody, "Don Draper's Guide to Women," astutely pointed out, his magnetism — despite the show's historical realism — is a James Bond fantasy. It is only in the penultimate episode of the third season that Don seems in any danger of being penalized for his transgressions.

The other men on the show are equally flawed and yet suffer very little. Roger Sterling is a raging alcoholic who abandons the loyal wife who stands up to him in order to marry a pretty young thing who lies down for him. Personifying the rich boy who is "born on third base and thinks he hit a triple," Roger's sole talent, for converting Stoli into lewd comments, is portrayed as catnip not just for clients but even put-upon secretaries. While Don's darkness is used to seduce the viewer, Roger provides comic relief, his open sexism and racism played strictly for laughs. So far Roger's only punishment has been a couple of heart attacks that not only didn't slow him down but actually rejuvenated him and drove him into the arms of a sultry young trophy wife.

Another rich boy, Pete Campbell, publicly demeans Peggy on her first day of work, a tactic that mysteriously causes her to sleep with him not long afterward, thus consigning her to a secret pregnancy and hidden torment. Pete thoughtlessly cheats on the wife who obviously loves him, apparently rapes a neighbor's au pair, breezes through his days in expense-account-fueled meetings with clients — while constantly whining about how life isn't fair to him. Upon finding out about his child with Peggy and having her reject his offer of love, he is temporarily dazed but then grows closer to the wife who adores him, forging what increasingly looks like a marriage of like-minded souls.

While some of the lesser male characters are more appealing — the gaffe-prone Harry in particular (although even he cheats on his wife) or even the terminally shallow but good-natured Ken Cosgrove (who we just know is headed for corporate success) — the only truly sympathetic male character is a gay man, Sal Romano, in large part because he is suffering oppression as well. Yet even Sal is guilty of marrying a woman under false pretenses and making her feel inadequate when he doesn't love her the way she does him.

Hardly an admirable portrait of manhood, and yet the costs to the men of their bad behavior seem minimal — other than of course for Sal, who loses his job due to sexual harassment (thus dramatically co-opting a fate usually endured by women). By contrast, the women not only suffer but also do so with the clear message that the fault lies not in society, but in themselves.

Betty has always represented the *Feminine Mystique*–era woman, privileged yet imprisoned by the restrictions of her life. Beautiful enough to have been a professional model, fluent in Italian, and possessing a degree from Bryn Mawr, she nonetheless knew she had to marry before her sell-by date arrived and to produce children even if she didn't really want them. After all, what were the alternatives? To stay single and be a waitress, teacher, or secretary? To have only furtive sexual relationships in order to avoid social disapproval and to constantly worry about an unwanted pregnancy? To give up on having children even if you wanted them but didn't want a husband? No, understandably enough, Betty made the same choice that most women did: selling her sexual appeal to gain financial security and ensure social approval.

But our sympathy for Betty is undermined by the extreme simplicity of her character, which is that of a child in a beautiful woman's body. How much more powerful would this show be if she were a smarter, more mature woman who found herself trapped in suburban hell, instead of a shallow princess who can't come up with more than "I have thoughts" when composing a love letter and who consistently behaves like a petulant five-year-old, albeit one armed with a cigarette and a glass of wine?

Being stuck in a life of mind-numbing domesticity is tragic only when the person is capable of — and desirous of — much more. But Betty seems less limited by her situation than by her intellect and character. We have no sense of what she'd do with her life if she hadn't married, other than perhaps be a Holly Golightly party girl in Europe. Even when she finally leaves Don, it's not to become independent but only to go to another man who wants to marry her and take care of her every little need.

While the pressures of the traditional maternal role deserve serious examination, Betty's coldness to her children (other than her new baby) repels any sympathy we might have. She takes no joy in her children, snapping at them to behave and thoughtlessly passing on her own repressive conditioning, like when she shuts down her daughter's grief at her beloved grandfather's death. Superficial and self-focused, Betty seems to enjoy very little, other than sex and the occasional party or jaunt to Italy — even her horseback riding is a clenched affair full of frustration and anger. Such unrelieved negativity undercuts the very real sufferings of women in her era, making Betty an ungrateful, whiny princess rather than an example of how even privilege can be a prison when it is challenge and autonomy that you desire instead.

Unlike Betty, Peggy chose a career, progressing from the "new girl in the office" to the New Woman just beginning to appear in the business world. But Peggy's success has been shrouded not only by what she has been given to endure — a secret pregnancy that left her nearly catatonic and locked in a mental ward, the surrender of her baby, the gibes of sexist coworkers, the fumbling and hostile attentions of Pete, and most humiliatingly of all, having sex with a man named Duck — but also by how her character has been constructed.

While smart, creative, and brave, Peggy isn't allowed to be a full, rounded person and is instead portrayed as socially inept, humorless, and utterly unable to connect with either men or women, remaining friendless and loveless. Her stiffness, introversion, and social missteps are painful to watch, and her awkward attempts to be more "feminine" fall flat. In the third season, she was finally allowed a measure of sexual satisfaction, but only in a tawdry, loveless connection with a repugnant older man. Denied a satisfying romantic life, she lives to work and is molding herself into a female Don Draper, but minus the spouse and kids.

Yet instead of being a biting commentary on the social strictures of the time — when women truly did have to choose between the rare opportunity of a professional career and marriage and family — Peggy's isolation is portrayed as the logical result of her social clumsiness and ambition. She's not penalized for her choices (a valid historical point) but instead seems to be making the best use of a stunted personality by forging a career rather than ending up a lonely old maid. Watching her, I've increasingly wondered why we can't have an attractive, happy, fully sexual, intelligent female character with a great personality on this show?

Which brings me to Joan.

There's no way around it: Joan starts out the show as a bitch. In the first episode, she suggests that Peggy go home, cut eyeholes in a paper bag, put it over her head, and figure out what she needs to change about herself. Ouch.

But Joan is also portrayed as the one woman who has power. The classic queen bee of a female workplace, Joan rules the secretarial pool with a manicured hand, her prow of a bust gliding through the office like a warship going into battle. She rules the waves, both permanent and rollered, and takes no crap from anyone. What has made Joan delicious to many women is the way she handles the men on the show, her honeyed tones belying the razor-sharp put-downs she doles out not just to dazzled office boys but to the firm's partners. And yet Joan is also impeccably professional, handling clients as adroitly as any accounts man, and keeping the office running as smoothly as Mussolini's trains.

Perhaps most satisfyingly of all, Joan is initially portrayed as being as fully in control of her sexuality as she is the rest of her life. Carrying on a secret affair with Roger, she resists his attempts to confine her (symbolized by that bird in a cage he gives her), insisting on staying a free woman who chooses what — or who — she wants to do. Unlike the other secretaries, she doesn't seem confined by her female-ghetto job, but triumphant in it. We believe her when she tells Peggy that she wouldn't want her copywriter position.

Joan's contentment is disturbed when she gets a chance to do media work and discovers that she's a natural at it. Yet as quickly as the opportunity to use her talents is given, it's taken away, and she faces the classic career bitch-slap of having to train a younger guy to do the same job, and for more money. So far, a great little history lesson about women's struggles at work to gain recognition.

But both Joan's discovery of her ambition and her disappointment are soon pushed to the side by the other development that's been scripted for her, which is to give up her satisfying single life and marry a handsome young doctor. In perhaps the most wrenching event of the entire series, not only is there no happy ending for Joan, but her supposedly "perfect" fiancé rapes her on the floor of Don's office in retaliation for what he senses about her sexual past. The free bird's wings have been clipped, if not broken.

At this point, Joan could have both retained her autonomy and restored her dignity by dumping the guy. But no, she married him. And continues to apparently love him as well as literally support him, after his promising career fizzles out. Many women have made the choice to stick with even more violent men, but this is "our Joanie" (as fans often call her), a strong woman who seemed the least likely person to take anything lying down, much less rape. We expected her to find the nearest letter opener and do a little surgery on Dr. Cut-Up, or failing that, at least leave the jerk. The one woman who had a career, autonomy, and a satisfying sex life is punished as surely as if we were reading *The Scarlet Letter*. Even worse, she embraces not only her punishment but also her punisher.

Of the minor female characters on the show — the vapid Jane who finds blackface hysterical, the hapless amateur chiropodist Lois, the succession of giggly secretaries so inept they can barely answer phones, the catty and racist housewives — the less said the better. Ironically, a show that has launched a slew of fashion trends has also made womanhood seem singularly unattractive. The men triumph despite who they are and what they do, while the women suffer as a result of both their character and their choices. The men are mad, all right, but the women on this show are increasingly crazy-making. I may need that martini, after all.

Reading the Genre

1. Engoron's evaluation begins with an appreciation of the positive qualities of the television series *Mad Men*. How does this strategy help establish her ethos? How does praising some parts of the show allow Engoron to be more critical in later parts of the essay? (See "Consider how well reasoned a piece is," p. 228, and Chapter 21, "Critical Thinking," p. 343.)

2. At what points in her essay does Engoron rely on literary analysis to evaluate the success of *Mad Men*? (See Chapter 7, "Literary Analyses," p. 184.) What other aspects of the show would lend themselves to this strategy? Pick one such aspect and write a paragraph analyzing it as though it were literature.

3. What is Engoron's underlying assumption about how television characters (especially women) should be depicted? What criteria does she use to determine if the depiction of characters is fair, and how does she support these criteria? (See "Establish and defend criteria," p. 102, and Chapter 21, "Critical Thinking," p. 343.)

4. Has your opinion of any television show changed over time? How has your opinion changed? Form a thesis statement that states how your opinion has changed about this television show. (See Chapter 24, "Thesis," p. 362, and "Expect your thesis to mature," p. 363.)

5. **WRITING:** Choose a television show that depicts your own generation and evaluate it based on what it says about gender roles. Concentrate on characters one at a time, as Engoron does. Does this show do a good or bad job of representing you and your peers? Why do you think so?

MEDIA EVALUATION   Leigh Alexander writes about video games, interactive entertainment, and contemporary culture for a wide variety of publications. This 2013 essay is part of *The Atlantic*'s "Object Lessons" series: essays that explore the "hidden lives of ordinary things." Perhaps nothing is more ordinary than bad pizza.

Domino's, the Pizza That Never Sleeps

The Imagined Community of Mediocre Delivery Pizza, an Object Lesson

LEIGH ALEXANDER

Speaking as a New Yorker, I have a confession. It's big.

Even though I once attended a reading by Colin "Slice Harvester" Hagendorf, the guy who spent a year trying every slice of pizza in New York City, and even though I bought his zine and I had it *signed*, and even though I can tell everyone *else* where to get a proper, broad-bellied and mozzarella-loaded slice of authentic New York pizza off the top of my head, and even though I gloat a little inside when my friends come to town and sigh eagerly over the opportunity to eat a Real Slice, even despite all that: I've eaten more Domino's Pizza than I have any other slice available on this island.

"You live in New York!" those same friends rejoin. "Why do you eat *Domino's*?!"

Because it's the only place that still delivers at 2 AM for one part. This may be the city that never sleeps, but what we do in the weird after-midnight hours rarely resembles work either. If you are a food delivery driver or an actuary or a bike messenger, you get to go do something else come 11 PM, as well you should.

But for another part, if you're a writer, or a Web designer, or an app programmer, or a member of any other precarious freelance professions named by the euphemism *creative class*, you might actually end up working at 1 AM. And maybe having a drink, and probably getting hungry. You check out GrubHub or Seamless, only to see a list of restaurants in your proximity that are utterly closed. They will begin taking orders at 11 AM tomorrow, the Web site says. In the wan quiet hours after midnight, when your head is buzzing and the sky is ruddy with Martian incandescence, hunger becomes surreal and urgent. What mortal will even be *alive* at 11 AM tomorrow, let alone hungry?

My initial impulse to start ordering Domino's came from such a desperate moment, one sufficient to make me overcome a brand aversion long baked into my discriminating cosmopolitan crust.

Memories of the Domino's of my childhood are dim: red-and-blue sense memories of cardboard box, cardboard flavor. Industrial food for school parties, the stuff harried parents fed to you at a weekend sleepover. There was also the Noid, a creepy and ill-thought mascot now relegated to the museum of puzzling relics for adult children of a certain age, the kind of thing that gets referenced on Family Guy. A simulation of pizza.

In 2009, Domino's came in last in a consumer taste survey alongside fellow pizza relic Chuck E. Cheese. The company could have gone all-out frat-boy retro and cornered the campus market, but instead it seemed genuinely stung, puzzled about the rejection, and committed to reversing its fortunes: "There comes a time when you know you've gotta make a

change," said CEO Patrick Doyle in a series of ads themed "Domino's Pizza Turnaround" (the company has a four and a half–minute video on its YouTube channel dedicated to the campaign).

The ad campaign was charmingly earnest, featuring apologetic pizza chefs expressing their commitment to developing better-tasting food, begging consumers to give Domino's another chance. It was so eager, so self-deprecatory, it was almost revolutionary (for a corporate chain). An obvious marketing trick, maybe, but a brave one.

Compare that with, say, my local pizza shop where surly men in stained aprons fling slices at me while trying to look down my shirt. I don't know. I started to feel a little sorry for the underdog. Maybe it's that this is a city where underdogs have enjoyed precious little sympathy—even if the underdog is a corporation. Maybe we've been waiting a long time for a corporation, any corporation, to make a self-flagellating apology to us, hat in hand.

In some of those Domino's ads, we cringe as the camera highlights ruthless feedback and complaint. You get the idea that the company kind of stumbled onto Twitter a little late, only to face the gut-knotting dread that all along, everyone had been making fun of it. Everyone and everything, from the mega-corporation to the individual writer, is a product to be stridently critiqued in the social media age. I thought about the Domino's CEO reading tweets about his "boring, bland" food, cardboard comparisons abundant, and thought, "I know that feel, bro."

The company's performance of embarrassing sincerity, complete with a trendy and try-hard box redesign, endeared me to Domino's in spite of myself. Four years later, has the pizza become honestly good, through this apparent committed self-reflection? I mean. I think it's good. I think it's good! I like to think Patrick Doyle continues to meticulously follow Domino's feedback, is reading this right now, maybe quietly says "*yesss*," with a subtle fist pump.

Still, it's entirely possible Domino's pizza has simply remained the kind of thing that you just *think* tastes good at 2 AM, when you've been not-sleeping during a New York weekend and feel like being fed by an over-earnest corporation at an absurd hour. It almost doesn't matter, because it's very easy for Domino's to start feeling like a pal on those nights when you tumble drunk and alone into a taxi and realize that you need to eat, urgently. You leave a party in Chelsea or a venue in Williamsburg, stumble into a car in a pile of your own unraveling frippery, mess clumsily with your iPhone for two minutes, and have a pizza ready to take to bed by the time you get home.

There are times in the life of a harried urbanite that such a thing feels like no lesser miracle. It's some idea you bring home routinely until, in true New York City fashion, you realize you've gotten a little attached to it.

The online ordering interface offers high design for the low-down. An utter lack of pretense and that impression of a meaningfully earnest desire for approval pervade the entire site. There's a ladleful of quaintness: "Awaiting your delicious selections," it promises underneath the "My Order" header. Popular items are placed front and center in case you have "no time to waste."

You can even build your own "Pizza Profile" so that Domino's will remember Your Location and Your Store. There are always coupons available so you can find the "perfect hot online deal," and the Build Your Own Pizza utility promises you can "watch the pizza of your wildest dreams come to life." And you can, through a visual simulation that lets you customize the amount and color of sauce, the density of your cheese, whether you place toppings only on half your pie or throughout.

It feels a little game-like, and it ought: In 2011, Domino's made waves with an iPad game called Domino's Pizza Hero, a complex touch-based simulation that challenged players to learn the demanding ropes of real pizza-making staffers. The game fits snugly among the kitchen sims popular on tablet devices, and aims to be genuinely difficult—to play it is to feel as if Domino's takes the craft of pizza-making incredibly seriously. It's also a subversive, avant-garde training and recruitment device where skilled players will be prompted to apply for jobs at their local franchise once their reward centers have been sufficiently flooded with a sense of success and importance.

Not only that, but the app allows you to submit the pizza you assemble in the game to your local franchise to be fulfilled as a proper order. As such, the company's use of game mechanics and social media has always felt admirably on-point, a success you kind of have to respect when you notice that most corporations have made a tacky mess of leveraging interactive entertainment and social media. Even beloved GrubHub made cynics of its consumers by wincingly offering up animal memes to consumers who lose its random-prize card game, and suggests recent orderers tweet "I just got Grub'd by the Hub."

"Where's the love?"—so a focus tester demands in Domino's 2009 "Pizza Turnaround" ad spot, as executives and line workers soberly accept a barrage of negative feedback. These days, the chain's online ordering tool makes a point of letting you know the names of the pizza professionals assembling and super-vising your meal ("Kenyatta is double-checking your order"), and encourages you to send them feedback from a pull-down menu. My personal favorite, fired frequently from the dizzy edges of late-night couches and lurching taxicabs? "I don't know what I would do without you."

Domino's also seems interested in soothing the uncertainty of shouting online orders into an inestimable ether. A third-party digital interface generally means a lot of unanswered questions, a leap of faith into the vague assumption that the human bodies that ultimately receive your transmission will fulfill it accurately and in reasonable time. The company has a unique antidote: its infamous Pizza Tracker, a five-chambered heart that glows red and pulsates gently on your screen to illuminate each stage of your order, from preparation to quality check to "out for delivery."

Whether the Pizza Tracker accurately tracks one's pizza journey is a subject of popular debate online, where it's frequently believed to be a hoax (anecdotal tales on forums point out that Domino's will claim your order is at the "oven" stage even if you've simply ordered soda bottles). It may not matter. Most Domino's fans would prefer not to know — the Pizza Tracker is among the most tangible, entertaining components of the Domino's mythos. In today's oversaturated media environment, Domino's has managed to make waiting for your pizza feel like better entertainment than social networks or television, and just as tweetable.

Once an order is placed, consumers can watch an unexpectedly innocent, winsome animated pizza chef named Pete the Pizzamaker putter around in a virtual coal oven as they wait for their orders to be completed. Dark disorientation descends on New York City while this little cartoon mimes making you a meal. You can choose other deeply uncool "themes" for the Pizza Tracker too: a calypso theme featuring a parrot, a "heavy metal" theme. Once I ordered one of Domino's new deep-dish pan pizzas, and while on the phone, was startled to realize a Barry White look-alike was cooing sensually at me from the Pizza Tracker, emphasizing the indulgent slow cooking the menu item proudly required. "There's people making babies to my pizza," I imagined him murmuring. The Pizza Tracker themes are so unfashionable that they reverse into trendiness.

It's strange. Of these various elements — accessible technology, over-earnestness, social media savvy — none is a particularly remarkable brand-building technique on its own. Yet together, the ordinariness of an effective online pizza-ordering routine stands in relief against the background of me-too social networks and superfluous photo filter apps.

Here in New York City, the ultimate behavioral ideal is to be *unavailable*—apology and accessibility alike are culturally unattractive things. You must always be very busy, very focused on what makes you special. Social success depends on an insufferable uniqueness coupled with an unforgiving drive and an obsession with authenticity and total responsibility. You must neither be corporate nor humiliated. And yet Domino's has carefully done both and somehow pulled it off.

All of its eagerness and dorky sincerity creates the impression that Domino's is, in violation of city norms, *making itself available*. It is apologetically present, quietly savvy but humble, seeming to sweetly hope for your patronage, promising that it'll be its own fault, not yours, if you're unsatisfied (I regularly receive 50 percent off coupons emblazoned big with SORRY! for Domino's perception that I experienced a delay in receiving my order, which of course I never even registered). In an unexpected way, this dinosaur corporation somehow stumbled into posing as the refreshing antithesis to our model of the too-busy, too-important, elusive, and infallible urban identity. We'd like to think that Domino's Pizza is antithetical to worldliness, and that embracing its earnest, dorky white-bread corporatism offers a shrewd rebellion staged quietly from within the walls of our brownstones. But maybe it's just a pretty good, easy meal you can get delivered late at night. A pizza touchstone, a way to connect one's solitary, lonely morning with all the others everywhere else.

Reading the Genre

1. Alexander admits, sheepishly, that she frequently eats Domino's "simulation of pizza." But this essay isn't really about pizza, is it? Discuss the ways that, while Domino's pizza is the object at the center of this essay, the lesson is about much more than food. How does Alexander show the "hidden life" of pizza in New York?

2. Alexander discusses Colin "Slice Harvester" Hagendorf and his zine evaluating New York pizza. On his Web site, in the section dedicated to his criteria for rating slices on a scale from 1–8, Hagendorf has placed a picture of a middle finger. He is clearly telling his readers not to expect solid and reasonable criteria. Likewise, in this essay about pizza, Alexander never specifically tells us what makes pizza good or bad. How could Alexander's analysis essay be rewritten as an evaluation or review of Domino's? What criteria does Alexander use to actually evaluate the Domino's "experience," even though the pizza itself might be terrible? (See "Decide on your criteria," p. 109.)

3. Can you think of other companies that do such a good job using media to shape the customer experience that you are likely to give them your business despite other shortcomings? Explore a few of these examples as a class.

4. **WRITING:** Choose one of the example businesses from question 3 and write a full media analysis essay about this company, as Alexander has done with Domino's. What does the company do to enhance its product or service — or to make up for what's wrong with it? What reasons do customers have for liking this company?

5. **MULTIMODALITY — APP CONCEPT:** Develop the concept for an app or social media campaign for a small business in your neighborhood. How could this small business use technology and new media to develop relationships with customers and to add value to the consumer experience?

Causal Analyses: Readings

GENRE MOVES Causal Analysis

JAMES BALDWIN

From "If Black English Isn't a Language, Then Tell Me, What Is?"

I say that the present skirmish is rooted in American history, and it is. Black English is the creation of the black diaspora. Blacks came to the United States chained to each other, but from different tribes: Neither could speak the other's language. If two black people, at that bitter hour of the world's history, had been able to speak to each other, the institution of chattel slavery could never have lasted as long as it did. Subsequently, the slave was given, under the eye, and the gun, of his master, Congo Square, and the Bible — or in other words, and under these conditions, the slave began the formation of the black church, and it is within this unprecedented tabernacle that black English began to be formed. This was not, merely, as in the European example, the adoption of a foreign tongue, but an alchemy that transformed ancient elements into a new language: A language comes into existence by means of brutal necessity, and the rules of the language are dictated by what the language must convey.

There was a moment, in time, and in this place, when my brother, or my mother, or my father, or my sister, had to convey to me, for example, the danger in which I was standing from the white man standing just behind me, and to convey this with a speed, and in a language, that the white man could not possibly understand, and that, indeed, he cannot understand, until today. He cannot afford to understand it. This understanding would reveal to him too much about himself, and smash that mirror before which he has been frozen for so long.

Now, if this passion, this skill, this (to quote Toni Morrison) "sheer intelligence," this incredible music, the mighty achievement of having brought a people utterly unknown to, or despised by "history" — to have brought this people to their present, troubled, troubling, and unassailable and unanswerable place — if this absolutely unprecedented journey does not indicate that black English is a language, I am curious to know what definition of language is to be trusted.

Offer a causal narrative.

One of the most effective ways to illustrate probable causes and effects is to tell a story. Here, to oppose claims that Black English isn't a language, James Baldwin focuses on how Black American English most likely came into being. For a causal analysis, you might not be able to *prove* cause and effect beyond a doubt, but if you can present a realistic and convincing chain of events supported by evidence, you will give your reader a compelling picture.

Baldwin could have focused on linguistic evidence to argue for the sophistication of Black English, but instead he focuses on social and cultural conditions that made the creation of a unique language inevitable. He also manages to very effectively show that the language cannot be separated from a history of oppression by explaining the exact nature of the situation and the dire necessity that created Black English. Creating a narrative, then, also allows Baldwin to avoid oversimplification, which is a common pitfall of causal analysis essays. Rather than reduce the analysis to its bare facts, Baldwin brings it to life.

In your own causal analysis research, look for the stories and the rich contexts that accompany causes and effects. For instance, if you are looking at how tuition costs have risen over time, why young people have stopped voting, or the effect of increased screen time on children, look for specific stories and examples that will help you illustrate probable causal relationships. While those stories won't make up the total of your evidence, they can provide a much-needed perspective.

CAUSAL ANALYSIS   Rita J. King is the executive vice president of Science House, a creative consultancy that connects science and business and funds science and math education projects for kids. King previously worked as a futurist at the National Institute of Aerospace and speaks internationally about creative collaboration. In this essay, King reflects on her own uses of Twitter and highlights the innovative ways others have used the platform.

Co.Exist

Posted: May 22, 2013, at 8:30 AM
From: Rita J. King

How Twitter Is Reshaping the Future of Storytelling

We might have fewer characters to work with, but we still hunger for narrative. New mediums aren't destroying fiction; they're allowing us to innovate even more in how we create and consume our stories.

Editor's Note: This post is part of *Co.Exist's* "Futurist Forum," a series of articles by some of the world's leading futurists about what the world will look like in the near and distant future, and how you can improve how you navigate future scenarios through better forecasting.

Every five days, a billion tiny stories are generated by people around the world. Those messages aren't just being lost in the ether, like the imaginary output of monkeys randomly attempting to produce the works of Shakespeare. Instead, the tweets are being archived by the Library of Congress as part of the organization's mission to tell the story of America. The archive now includes 170 billion posts and counting.

The patterns of human life will be stored in this Twitter archive like a form of digital sediment. Every meme and revelation will leave an imprint in the record constructed of posts by half a billion Twitter users around the world (and over 150,000 more signing up every day).

How has the future of storytelling been influenced by Twitter?

Sparking the Imagination

Writer and actor John Hodgman recalls how derisive many people were about Twitter when it first entered the public consciousness. "Many jokes were made," he said, "about 'why would I ever want to hear about what sandwich someone ate today?'"

"The early detractors failed to note that Twitter, while faddish, was not only a fad: It is a tool, one with almost as many unique uses as there are humans to take it up," Hodgman says. "Twitter offered a very restrictive set of protocols that awaken the imagination: What can I do with 140 characters that will be meaningful to others? The solution has proven to be pretty much endless. And do you know what? If the right person is telling the story, I'll read a tweet stream of sandwiches all day long."

We've gotten to know new characters through Twitter, Hodgman says, from Bigfoot to God, and their tweet streams are "more than just jokes, which themselves are the shortest stories of all." Instead, tweets are "a new kind of epistolary — postcards from a sensibility that over time, describe whole worlds."

"It is true," Hodgman says, "that this kind of storytelling is quick, even ephemeral, and largely improvised. It's really more like broadcasting than writing, and one of the things that makes Twitter so intimate, even in its rowdy, buzzing, crowd-y-ness, is that you are reading someone's work in real time."

A Future Biography

Prolific novelist Joyce Carol Oates recently tweeted:

Creating a Twitter-self is like constructing with tweezers & toothpicks. Much patience required, some sense of purpose, & a sense of humor.

While many people struggle to make sense of what identity looks like as the lines between personal and professional, private and public continue to blur, some just rely on straightforward candor.

Twitter has produced several celebrities, including Kelly Oxford, thirty-five, who transformed from a stay-at-home mother of three to the best-selling author of *Everything Is Perfect When You're a Liar*. Nicole Sperling of the *L.A. Times* noted: "Oxford's writing is marked by the same wry voice that's made her a social media sensation." "I always felt like the child actor playing myself in the biography from the future," Oxford told Sperling.

Twitter forces us to learn how to play compelling characters in a shared biography, a snapshot of this moment we are living and sharing right now, but I can't help thinking about a comment made by Noam Chomsky in *Manufacturing Consent*. He talks about context in the mainstream media, and the need for more space to explain ideas that go against the grain of the status quo. Twitter also has a context problem: When you come late to a conversation, for example, and only see a couple of previous tweets.

In the nearly six years since I've been using Twitter, I've generated over fourteen thousand tweets. How can these be used in the social mapping of a shared story that goes well beyond, but still includes, me?

Future Forms of Snippet Storytelling

Twitter itself is exploring ways to harness the power of future storytelling forms. The addition of Vine to the mix could be powerful — think of the difference between a "wheels up" tweet about a flight and a six-second video of floating above clouds. The Tribeca Film Festival just included Vine as a platform for a competition, posted through the #6secfilms hashtag.

Andrew Fitzgerald works for Twitter, driving experimentation in storytelling and looking for people doing it inventively. So many people post their favorite Taylor Swift lyrics, he said, that the singer could retweet an entire song based on found tweets, like W. W. Norton did for Hamlet's famous soliloquy.

The Twitter Fiction Festival was a successful experiment that featured authors from around the world in multiple languages. New forms of storytelling include Jennifer Egan's experimental "Black Box," tweeted out in blocks of 140 characters or less by the *New Yorker*. Fitzgerald, who loved the experiment, acknowledged that some criticized the serialized sentences because, they say, "that's not how you do fiction."

For people who love compelling writing, there's something tantalizing about lines being shared one at a time. A line on its own changes a reader's relationship to the very texture of the syllables and ideas. Twitter story experiments aren't shackled by the linear requirements of paper.

Elliott Holt's Twitter experiment grabbed readers and lured them into a heavily hashtagged mystery story, the first of its kind:

On November 28 at 10:13 pm EST a woman identified as Miranda Brown, 44, of Brooklyn, fell to her death from the roof of a Manhattan hotel.

So began Holt's story, followed by a second tweet:

Investigators are trying to determine whether Ms. Brown's death was an accident or if, as some speculate, she was pushed off that roof.

From there, Holt built a narrative through threaded Twitter feeds with distinct voices from each of three characters to reconstruct the party at which the character died.

"Holt embraces Twitter for what it is," Slate wrote, "rather than trying to bend it into some tool that it isn't. With its simultaneous narrators and fractured storyline, this is not the kind of tale that could march steadily across a continuous expanse of white space. It's actually made for the medium."

The medium is also remaking us.

Reading the Genre

1. Look for Twitter feeds that you think use Twitter as a "tool" in an innovative way, and discuss these examples in relation to King's essay. For instance, does the feed use Twitter's limitations to its advantage, or does it find a way to work around them?

2. Is the medium of Twitter actually "remaking us"? Are there ways that you think or interact differently because of Twitter? How will social media sites like Twitter change the shape of your future relationships and your future career?

3. **WRITING:** Consider turning your answer to question 2 into a full causal analysis essay. How has Twitter changed politics? Personal relationships? Marketing and advertising? Celebrity culture? For an example causal analysis, you can look online for several articles showing how Twitter has allowed people to make specific stock market predictions.

4. **MULTIMODALITY — TWITTER REWRITE:** How would you write King's essay over Twitter? Limit yourself to writing just ten to fifteen key 140-character tweets to summarize the essay. Consider using @s, hashtags, links, and images not only to add information to your summaries but also to engage others and encourage them to recirculate the essay and respond to it.

CULTURAL ANALYSIS   Pulitzer Prize–winning *New York Times* science writer Natalie Angier is the author of four critically acclaimed books, including the best seller *Woman: An Intimate Geography* (1999). Her most recent, *The Canon: A Whirligig Tour of the Beautiful Basics of Science* (2008), provides a guide to the major theories of science. The following article, published in 2005 in the *New York Times*, uses linguistic and psychological research to try to explain a very common phenomenon: swearing.

Almost Before We Spoke, We Swore

Natalie Angier

Incensed by what it sees as a virtual pandemic of verbal vulgarity issuing from the diverse likes of Howard Stern, Bono of U2, and Robert Novak, the United States Senate is poised to consider a bill that would sharply increase the penalty for obscenity on the air.

By raising the fines that would be levied against offending broadcasters some fifteenfold, to a fee of about $500,000 per crudity broadcast, and by threatening to revoke the licenses of repeat polluters, the Senate seeks to return to the public square the gentler tenor of yesteryear, when seldom were heard any scurrilous words, and famous guys were not foul-mouthed all day.

Yet researchers who study the evolution of language and the psychology of swearing say that they have no idea what mystic model of linguistic gentility the critics might have in mind. Cursing, they say, is a human universal. Every language, dialect, or patois ever studied, living or dead, spoken by millions or by a small tribe, turns out to have its share of forbidden speech, some variant on comedian George Carlin's famous list of the seven dirty words that are not supposed to be uttered on radio or television.

Young children will memorize the illicit inventory long before they can grasp its sense, said John McWhorter, a scholar of linguistics at the Manhattan Institute and the author of *The Power of Babel*, and literary giants have always constructed their art on its spine.

The Jacobean dramatist Ben Jonson peppered his plays with fackings and "peremptorie Asses," and Shakespeare could hardly quill a stanza without inserting profanities of the day like "zounds" or "sblood" — offensive contractions of "God's wounds" and "God's blood" — or some wondrous sexual pun.

The title *Much Ado about Nothing*, Dr. McWhorter said, is a word play on *Much Ado about an O Thing*, the *O thing* being a reference to female genitalia.

Even the quintessential Good Book abounds in naughty passages like the men in II Kings 18:27 who, as the comparatively tame King James translation puts it, "eat their own dung, and drink their own piss."

In fact, said Guy Deutscher, a linguist at the University of Leiden in the Netherlands and the author of *The Unfolding of Language: An Evolutionary Tour of Mankind's Greatest Invention*, the earliest writings, which date from five thousand years ago, include their share of off-color descriptions of the human form and its ever-colorful functions. And the written record is merely a reflection of an oral tradition that Dr. Deutscher and many other psychologists and evolutionary linguists suspect dates from the rise of the human larynx, if not before.

Some researchers are so impressed by the depth and power of strong language that they are using it as a peephole into the architecture of the brain, as a means of probing the tangled, cryptic bonds between the newer, "higher" regions of the brain in charge of intellect, reason, and planning, and the older, more "bestial" neural neighborhoods that give birth to our emotions.

Researchers point out that cursing is often an amalgam of raw, spontaneous feeling and targeted, gimlet-eyed cunning. When one person curses at another, they say, the curser rarely spews obscenities and insults at random, but rather will assess the object of his wrath, and adjust the content of the "uncontrollable" outburst accordingly.

Because cursing calls on the thinking and feeling pathways of the brain in roughly equal measure and with handily assessable fervor, scientists say that by studying the neural circuitry behind it they are gaining new insights into how the different domains of the brain communicate — and all for the sake of a well-venomed retort.

Other investigators have examined the physiology of cursing, how our senses and reflexes react to the sound or sight of an obscene word. They have determined that hearing a curse elicits a literal rise out of people. When electrodermal wires are placed on people's arms and fingertips to study their skin conductance patterns and the subjects then hear a few obscenities spoken clearly and firmly, participants show signs of instant arousal.

Their skin conductance patterns spike, the hairs on their arms rise, their pulse quickens, and their breathing becomes shallow.

Interestingly, said Kate Burridge, a professor of linguistics at Monash University in Melbourne, Australia, a similar reaction occurs among university students and others who pride themselves on being educated when they listen to bad grammar or slang expressions that they regard as irritating, illiterate, or déclassé.

"People can feel very passionate about language," she said, "as though it were a cherished artifact that must be protected at all cost against the depravities of barbarians and lexical aliens."

Dr. Burridge and a colleague at Monash, Keith Allan, are the authors of *Forbidden Words: Taboo and the Censoring of Language*, which will be published early next year [2006] by the Cambridge University Press.

Researchers have also found that obscenities can get under one's goosebumped skin and then refuse to budge. In one study, scientists started with the familiar Stroop test, in which subjects are flashed a series of words written in different colors and are asked to react by calling out the colors of the words rather than the words themselves.

If the subjects see the word *chair* written in yellow letters, they are supposed to say "yellow."

The researchers then inserted a number of obscenities and vulgarities in the standard lineup. Charting participants' immediate and delayed responses, the researchers found that, first of all, people needed significantly more time to trill out the colors of the curse words than they did for neutral terms like *chair.*

The experience of seeing titillating text obviously distracted the participants from the color-coding task at hand. Yet those risqué interpolations left their mark. In subsequent memory quizzes, not only were participants much better at recalling the naughty words than they were the neutrals, but that superior recall also applied to the tints of the tainted words, as well as to their sense.

Yes, it is tough to toil in the shadow of trash. When researchers in another study asked participants to quickly scan lists of words that included obscenities and then to recall as many of the words as possible, the subjects were, once again, best at rehashing the curses — and worst at summoning up whatever unobjectionable entries happened to precede or follow the bad bits.

Yet as much as bad language can deliver a jolt, it can help wash away stress and anger. In some settings, the free flow of foul language may signal not hostility or social pathology, but harmony and tranquillity.

"Studies show that if you're with a group of close friends, the more relaxed you are, the more you swear," Dr. Burridge said. "It's a way of saying: 'I'm so comfortable here I can let off steam. I can say whatever I like.'"

Evidence also suggests that cursing can be an effective means of venting aggression and thereby forestalling physical violence.

With the help of a small army of students and volunteers, Timothy B. Jay, a professor of psychology at Massachusetts College of Liberal Arts in North Adams and the author of *Cursing in America* and *Why We Curse*, has explored the dynamics of cursing in great detail.

The investigators have found, among other things, that men generally curse more than women, unless said women are in a sorority, and that university provosts swear more than librarians or the staff members of the university day-care center.

Regardless of who is cursing or what the provocation may be, Dr. Jay said, the rationale for the eruption is often the same.

"Time and again, people have told me that cursing is a coping mechanism for them, a way of reducing stress," he said in a telephone interview. "It's a form of anger management that is often underappreciated."

Indeed, chimpanzees engage in what appears to be a kind of cursing match as a means of venting aggression and avoiding a potentially dangerous physical clash.

Frans de Waal, a professor of primate behavior at Emory University in Atlanta, said that when chimpanzees were angry "they will grunt or spit or make an abrupt, upsweeping gesture that, if a human were to do it, you'd recognize it as aggressive."

Such behaviors are threat gestures, Professor de Waal said, and they are all a good sign.

"A chimpanzee who is really gearing up for a fight doesn't waste time with gestures, but just goes ahead and attacks," he added.

By the same token, he said, nothing is more deadly than a person who is too enraged for expletives — who cleanly and quietly picks up a gun and starts shooting.

Researchers have also examined how words attain the status of forbidden speech and how the evolution of coarse language affects the smoother sheets of civil discourse stacked above it. They have found that what counts as taboo language in a given culture is often a mirror into that culture's fears and fixations.

"In some cultures, swear words are drawn mainly from sex and bodily functions, whereas in others, they're drawn mainly from the domain of religion," Dr. Deutscher said.

In societies where the purity and honor of women is of paramount importance, he said, "it's not surprising that many swear words are variations on the 'son of a whore' theme or refer graphically to the genitalia of the person's mother or sisters."

The very concept of a swear word or an oath originates from the profound importance that ancient cultures placed on swearing by the name of a god or gods. In ancient Babylon, swearing by the name of a god was meant to give absolute certainty against lying, Dr. Deutscher said, "and people believed that swearing falsely by a god would bring the terrible wrath of that god upon them." A warning against any abuse of the sacred oath is reflected in the biblical commandment that one must not "take the Lord's name in vain," and even today courtroom witnesses swear on the Bible that they are telling the whole truth and nothing but.

Among Christians, the stricture against taking the Lord's name in vain extended to casual allusions to God's son or the son's corporeal sufferings — no mention of the blood or the wounds or the body, and that goes for clever contractions, too. Nowadays, the phrase "Oh, golly!" may be considered almost comically wholesome, but it was not always so. "Golly" is a compaction of "God's body" and, thus, was once a profanity.

Yet neither biblical commandment nor the most zealous Victorian censor can elide from the human mind its hand-wringing over the unruly human body, its chronic, embarrassing demands, and its sad decay. Discomfort over body functions never sleeps, Dr. Burridge said, and the need for an ever-fresh selection of euphemisms about dirty subjects has long served as an impressive engine of linguistic invention.

Once a word becomes too closely associated with a specific body function, she said, once it becomes too evocative of what should not be evoked, it starts to enter the realm of the taboo and must be replaced by a new, gauzier euphemism.

For example, the word *toilet* stems from the French word for "little towel" and was originally a pleasantly indirect way of referring to the place where the chamber pot or its equivalent resides. But *toilet* has since come to mean the porcelain fixture itself, and so sounds too blunt to use in polite company. Instead, you ask your tuxedoed waiter for directions to the ladies' room or the restroom or, if you must, the bathroom.

Similarly, the word *coffin* originally meant an ordinary box, but once it became associated with death, that was it for a "shoe coffin" or "thinking outside the coffin." The taboo sense of a word, Dr. Burridge said, "always drives out any other senses it might have had."

Scientists have lately sought to map the neural topography of forbidden speech by studying Tourette's patients who suffer from coprolalia, the pathological and uncontrollable urge to curse. Tourette's syndrome is a neurological disorder of unknown origin characterized predominantly by chronic motor and vocal tics, a constant grimacing or pushing of one's glasses up the bridge of one's nose or emitting a stream of small yips or grunts.

Just a small percentage of Tourette's patients have coprolalia — estimates range from 8 to 30 percent — and patient advocates are dismayed by popular portrayals of Tourette's as a humorous and invariably scatological condition. But for those who do have coprolalia, said Dr. Carlos Singer, director of the division of movement disorders at the University of Miami School of Medicine, the symptom is often the most devastating and humiliating aspect of their condition.

Not only can it be shocking to people to hear a loud volley of expletives erupt for no apparent reason, sometimes from the mouth of a child or young teenager, but the curses can also be provocative and personal, florid slurs against the race, sexual identity, or body size of a passerby, for example, or deliberate and repeated lewd references to an old lover's name while in the arms of a current partner or spouse.

Reporting in the *Archives of General Psychiatry*, Dr. David A. Silbersweig, a director of neuropsychiatry and neuroimaging at the Weill Medical College of Cornell University, and his colleagues described their use of PET scans to measure cerebral blood flow and identify which regions of the brain are galvanized in Tourette's patients during episodes of tics and coprolalia.

They found strong activation of the basal ganglia, a quartet of neuron clusters deep in the forebrain at roughly the level of the mid-forehead, that are known to help coordinate body movement along with activation of crucial regions of the left rear forebrain that participate in comprehending and generating speech, most notably Broca's area.

The researchers also saw arousal of neural circuits that interact with the limbic system, the wishbone-shape throne of human emotions, and, significantly, of the "executive" realms of the brain, where decisions to act or desist from acting may be carried out: the neural source, scientists said, of whatever conscience, civility, or free will humans can claim.

That the brain's executive overseer is ablaze in an outburst of coprolalia, Dr. Silbersweig said, demonstrates how complex an act the urge to speak the unspeakable may be, and not only in the case of Tourette's. The person is gripped by a desire to curse, to voice something wildly inappropriate. Higher-order linguistic circuits are tapped, to contrive the content of the curse. The brain's impulse control center struggles to short-circuit the collusion between limbic system urge and neocortical craft, and it may succeed for a time.

Yet the urge mounts, until at last the speech pathways fire, the verboten is spoken, and archaic and refined brains alike must shoulder the blame.

Reading the Genre

1. How does Angier manage to write an article about swearing with so little swearing in it? What effect does this have on you as a reader? Does it increase your "urge to speak the unspeakable"? If so, why?

2. At its simplest, a causal analysis asks *why something happens*. What claims does Angier make about why we swear? How does she support her claims?

3. Angier uses a range of sources to explore why people swear. List all her sources; then make notes about where each source gets his or her authority and how each source explains the predominance of swearing. Are some sources more persuasive? (See "Find reliable sources," p. 38; Chapter 21, "Critical Thinking," p. 343; Chapter 40, "Evaluating Sources," p. 451; and Chapter 41, "Annotating Sources," p. 456.)

4. In response to Angier's article, consider a causal analysis of an opposite inclination: Why do people refrain from swearing? What are some of the social, cultural, professional, familial, and personal forces that require people to speak politely? What are some good reasons for clean language? (See Chapter 21, "Critical Thinking," p. 343, and Chapter 32, "High, Middle, and Low Style," p. 400.)

5. **WRITING:** Do the media mold the way people speak? Watch a popular television show or listen to a song. Analyze the language of the television characters or that of the song lyrics. Can you make inferences about how these texts might influence audiences to speak similarly — using the same terms, dialects, and styles? Write a short causal analysis.

CAUSAL ANALYSIS   Robert W. Gehl is an assistant professor of New Media at the University of Utah, where he teaches critical studies of communication design and technology. His research centers on issues of technology and culture, and he is the author of *Reverse Engineering Social Media* (2014). In this essay, Gehl offers a genealogy and a critique of "liking" online.

The New Inquiry

Posted: March 27, 2013
From: Robert W. Gehl

A History of Like

The marketing field has long been obsessed with likability, but Facebook may be inadvertently revealing how shallow our liking goes.

If you blog, run a university home page, do e-commerce, write news articles for a local paper, have a local government site, or do nearly anything with the Internet, you're pretty much required to have users "like" your pages. Otherwise, you're going to be left out of the new economy of quantified affect. We live in what Carolin Gerlitz and Anne Helmond call a Like Economy, a distributed centralized Web of binary switches allowing us to signal if we like something or not, all powered by the now ubiquitous Facebook "Like" button.

But why "Like"? Why not "Love," or "I agree," or "This is awesome"? At first it seems like one of those accidents of popular culture, where an arbitrary boardroom decision eventually dictates our everyday language. In fact, one history of Facebook's Like button presents it in these very terms: Facebook engineer Adam Bosworth noted that the button began as an Awesome button but was later changed to Like because *like* is more universal. If it had stayed Awesome, perhaps we'd be talking about an economy of Awesomes binding together the social Web and we would sound more like Teenage Mutant Ninja Turtles than Valley Girls.

There's a deeper history to "like," though, that is far older than Facebook. The marketing subfield of Liking Studies, which began before Internet use became mainstream, is key to understanding how this somewhat bland, reductive signal of affect became central to the larger consumer economy we live in. It also explains why Facebook will never install a Dislike button.

What's the best way to predict whether an advertisement increases sales or not? The marketing field has searched for the answer to this question for decades. (If I knew,

I would be the head of some unctuous marketing firm instead of a state employee.) In the early 1990s, the Advertising Research Foundation's (ARF) "Copy Research Validity Project" proposed a simple answer: The advertisement is "likable." The massive study compared pairs of television ads in various settings and methods, against a wide range of accepted marketing measures: persuasive elements, how well the advertisement is recalled afterword, the clarity of the message, and (seemingly as an afterthought) how well the ad was "liked."

Of all the measures, "likability" was the surprise winner. "The average impression of the commercial, derived from a five-point liking scale, picked sales winners directionally 87 percent of the time and had an index of 300 (i.e., picked winners and was significant 60 percent of the time)." In other words, you like, you buy.

As the authors of the report, Russell Haley and Allan Baldinger, explain, "It appears probable that 'liking' is what Gordon Brown has called a 'creative magnifier' for both persuasive messages and for messages that are recalled." Likable ads, they conclude, are more persuasive and memorable than others. This triggered the development of Liking Studies, as academic and practicing marketers set out to further refine the contours of liking as an ad-copy-test measure.

Liking studies further decomposed likability into cognitive and affective elements. On the cognitive side, researchers theorized that viewers who like an ad pay attention and thus recall its message better. In terms of affect, a 1994 study by David Walker and Tony M. Dubinsky in the *Journal of Advertising Research* explores a "theory of 'affect transfer,'" which "asserts that if viewers experience positive feelings towards the advertising, they will associate those feelings with the advertiser or the advertised brand." A likable ad thus promises to encode brands into our bodies as precognive desire.

Of course, affect and cognition are complex phenomena. To be fair to academic marketers, there are repeated calls in the advertising research literature to resist reducing this complexity to liking and, at the very least, to continue to use other copy-testing measures in addition to likability to predict an ad's success. However, the underlying complexity of cognition and affect actually reinforces the value of likability as a measurable aspect of ads. The value of like is that it abstracts and condenses the complex thoughts and emotions it contains and, like any good abstraction, provides a simple and commensurable quantification of complexity. If a test subject says, "I like this ad!" it seems to stand in for the less cut-and-dried aspects of recall and emotion.

For a largely empirical, positivist field such as marketing — which has pretensions of being a science, not an art — independent variables such as likability have value because of their perceived universal predictive power. With globalization, marketing is in greater need of just such a universal measure capable of predicting the success of global branding campaigns across cultural contexts. Cultural variations might change how marketers go about getting us to like brands, but the goal is always likability.

One vertigo-inducing marketing moment illustrates this well. Since 1989, *USA Today* has published metrics on the most well-liked Super Bowl ads. These metrics partly inspired the makers of FedEx's 2005 "Perfect" Super Bowl ad, which combined the top ten likable elements of previous Super Bowl ads. (It featured Burt Reynolds getting kicked in the nuts by a dancing bear while a cute kid and sexy cheerleaders looked on. The bear talked to Reynolds about *Smokey and the Bandit* after Journey's "Don't Stop Believing" played. Oh, and somewhere in there is a message about how effective FedEx is at delivering things.) After this ad proved quite likable, the academic authors of a 2013 study of Super Bowl ad likability used many of its elements to measure the likability of other Super Bowl ads in the 2000s. Their discovery: Animals, cute kids, and humor are all elements of a likable ad. Their study also used data from, where else, *USA Today*'s Ad Meter likability measures. This self-referential loop will likely sentence us to ads featuring animals, cute kids, and bad humor for the rest of our Super Bowl watching lives.

Or maybe not. We are now allowed, even expected, to like other things than what's sold in Super Bowl ads. If you read even only the first two sentences of any given marketing paper today, you invariably learn that we are living in a new age where the user is in control. Social media in general, and Facebook in particular, are supposedly driving a brand-new world where marketers, editors, and other gatekeepers are marginalized and mass culture is dissolving into niche cultures and individual expression.

But if we keep the history of marketing in mind, including the development of Liking Studies, we see how Facebook is caught up in longer histories, specifically the history of the desire to dissect, study, and recompose a particular subject, the sovereign consumer.

Facebook's Like button has been lauded as a radically democratic tool allowing users to finally make their opinions heard, but the marketing field has always regarded the sovereign consumer's opinions the most important element in the circuit of production. After all, sovereign consumers realize the value locked away in commodities: When they buy, the corporation gets paid. In order to have us be better value-realization machines, marketers know they need to know what we like. The

Like button is a logical extension of the studies and practices developed by marketing since the 1990 ARF study and the *USA Today* Ad Meter system which, after all, have asked us to tell them what we like for decades.

Of course, the Facebook Like button does provide increased data about which ads are likable. With the Like button, marketers can constantly experiment with variations on ads with test audiences, seeing what works and then scaling up small experiments quickly. With a universal measure provided by Like, marketers can test ads across different segments, greatly aiding the globalization of marketing campaigns.

But this only begins to describe the continual monitoring of users who have clicked Like in Facebook. The choice to like an ad or brand in Facebook is seen as an affirmative interaction with that brand — and an agreement to have one's profile image associated with that brand and to have that approval follow you across the Web. If you like a brand, you must like to be a target for marketing messages, both from that brand and from others similar to it. You're providing just a bit more information to help Facebook build a profile of your tastes and desires, all of which is for sale.

But again, these things are not really all that new. Since even before the advent of Liking Studies, marketers have experimented with advertising messages and tracked users to determine ad effectiveness. Whether the branding happens on TV, in a magazine, or online, we like, we buy. We like, they know. The science of marketing has always been the science of placing us in taxonomies based on what we like.

So what is new about Facebook and the Like button? Oddly enough, it reveals too much. The great sin of Facebook is that it made "like" far too important and too obvious. Marketing is in part the practice of eliding the underlying complexity, messiness, and wastefulness of capitalist production with neat abstractions. Every ad, every customer service interaction, every display, and every package contributes to the commodity fetish, covering up the conditions of production with desire and fantasy. As such, Facebook may reveal too much of the underlying architecture of emotional capitalism. The Like button tears aside this veil to reveal the cloying, pathetic, Willy Lomanesque need of marketers to have their brands be well-liked. Keep liking, keep buying. Like us! Like us! Like us!

Liking in marketing was always meant to be a metonym for many other complex processes — persuasion, affect, cognition, recall — but it wasn't meant to be exposed to the public as such. In Facebook, however, the "Like" button further reduces this reduction and makes it visible, making the whole process somewhat cartoonish and tiresome. The consequences can be seen in "Like us on Facebook to enter to win!"

promotions and the obsession with Like counts among businesses large and small (not to mention the would-be "personal branded").

Because likability is now so visible, so prevalent as the preferred emotional response to brands and ideas, users have predictably called for the expansion of the emotional repertoire. They call for a Dislike button. At first glance, we might think this binary-emotional expansion would be welcome to marketers: It would add to their collected data on our desires. However, marketing's subfield of Liking Studies has already revealed that disliked ads poison everything they touch. Negative sentiment — disliking — is asymmetrical in its power to shape consumer's opinions of a brand: for every ten likes, one dislike could tear a brand apart. Such negative emotion requires much brand damage control. One thing Facebook will never do, then, is install a Dislike button.

This is not to say that Facebook won't introduce other binary-emotional switches. Facebook's flirtation with a Want button indicates their potential willingness to expand our binary-emotional repertoire. One could imagine users getting a Love button. But we are not allowed to dislike. And herein lies a way out of the Like Economy. Dissent, dissensus, refusal are not easily afforded in Facebook. Dissenters have to work for it: They have to write out comments, start up a blog, seek out other dislikers. They are not lulled into slackivism or "clickivism," replacing the work of activism with clicking "like" on a cause as if the sheer aggregate of sentiment will make someone somewhere change something.

Instead, frustrated dislikers must think through their negative affect and find ways to articulate it into networks of dislike. If dislike scares off brands, so be it. Brands aren't going to fix the world's problems — but the dislikers might.

Reading the Genre

1. This causal analysis examines the way that marketing has shaped the landscape of media, including social media. As a class, explore the ways that marketing has become a science, and discuss what this will mean for the future of commercials. How will marketing also change our communication on social media?

2. Whenever you are writing a causal analysis, it is important to consider a wide range of possible causes and causal relationships. What other factors do you think might have led to our current "like" economy and "like" culture? (See "Appreciate your limits," p. 129.)

3. Investigate Gerlitz and Helmond's "Like Economy," which Gehl discusses at the opening of his essay, and the connected concepts of the "hit economy" and the "link economy." What do you think might come next in this progression?

4. **WRITING:** Gehl's essay examines the history of the "like" button, analyzing how it has both reflected and shaped our attitudes toward culture, especially our consumer habits. Choose another element of social media — such as the hashtag, the share, the humblebrag, the vaguebook comment, the favorite, or the retweet — and explore how it both reflects and shapes attitudes.

5. **WRITING:** Write a short essay arguing for the addition of a new button on Facebook — for instance, a "dislike" button. Describe the button and discuss what would happen if this button were added to Facebook.

6. **MULTIMODALITY — LIKABLE ADVERTISEMENT:** Gehl recounts the story of a Super Bowl ad that was designed to incorporate all the elements of previously "liked" Super Bowl ads. As a class, develop a way to determine which four features of print advertisements the entire group "likes" most. Then, individually, create print advertisements that incorporate all four elements to advertise a product of your choice. The ad that the class finally "likes" the most, "wins."

EXPLORATORY ESSAY Tricia Rose teaches Africana studies at Brown University. Her first book, *Black Noise: Rap Music and Black Culture in Contemporary America* (1994), revolutionized academic study of popular music. The essay reprinted here originally appeared as a chapter in Rose's *The Hip Hop Wars: What We Talk about When We Talk about Hip Hop — and Why It Matters* (2008), a book that examines both sides of ten controversial issues surrounding hip-hop music and culture.

TRICIA ROSE

Hip Hop Causes Violence

I'm giving you my opinion that says he is not an artist, he's a thug.... [Y]ou can't draw a line in the sand and say Ludacris, because he is a subversive guy that, number one advocates violence, number two, narcotics selling and all the other things, he's not as bad as Pol Pot [Cambodian communist] so we'll put a Pepsi can in his hand.

> — Bill O'Reilly, on the subject of Ludacris as a Pepsi celebrity representative, *The O'Reilly Factor*, August 28, 2002

Ronald Ray Howard was executed Thursday [October 6, 2005] for fatally shooting a state trooper, a slaying his trial attorneys argued was prompted by Howard's listening to anti-police rap music.... Howard's trial attorney, Allen Tanner, told a reporter: "He grew up in the ghetto and disliked police, and these were his heroes . . . these rappers . . . telling him if you're pulled over, just blast away. It affected him." Howard didn't say for certain that rap music was responsible for his crime. [But he did say:] "All my experiences with police have never been good, whether I've been doing something bad or not."

> — David Carson (www.txexecutions.org/reports/350.asp, October 7, 2005)

> I would say to Radio 1, do you realize that some of the stuff you play on Saturday nights encourages people to carry guns and knives?
>
> — David Cameron, British politician, www.BBC.com, June 7, 2006

A key aspect of much of the criticism that has been leveled at hip hop is the claim that it glorifies, encourages, and thus causes violence. This argument goes as far back as the middle to late 1980s — the so-called golden age of hip hop — when politically radical hip hop artists, such as Public Enemy, who referred to direct and sometimes armed resistance against racism "by any means necessary," were considered advocates of violence. It is important to zero in on the specific issue of violence because this was the most highly visible criticism of hip hop for over a decade. The concern over hip hop and violence peaked in the early to mid-1990s when groups like N.W.A. from Los Angeles found significant commercial success through a gang-oriented repertoire of stories related especially to antipolice sentiment. N.W.A.'s 1989 song "*uck tha Police" — with lyrics boasting that when they are done, "it's gonna be a bloodbath of cops dyin' in L.A." — was at the epicenter of growing fears that rappers' tales of aggression and frustration (which many critics mistakenly perceived as simply pro-criminal statements of intent) were stirring up violent behavior among young listeners. The 1992 debut commercial single for Snoop Doggy Dogg, "Deep Cover" (from the film of the same name), garnered attention because of Snoop's laconic rap style, Dr. Dre's extra-funky beats, and the chorus phrase "187 on a undercover cop" ("187" is the police code for homicide). As what we now call gangsta rap began to move to the commercial center stage, the worry that increasing portrayals of violence in rap lyrics might encourage fans to imitate them evolved into a belief that the rappers were *themselves* criminals — representing their own violent acts in the form of rhyme. Snoop's own criminal problems authenticated his lyrics and added to the alarm about gangsta rap. As this shift in commercial hip hop has solidified, many vocal public critics have begun to characterize violence-portraying lyrics as autobiographical thuggery to a soundtrack. In turn, this link of violent lyrics in hip hop and behavior has been used in the legal arena by both defense and prosecuting attorneys. As the above epigraphs reveal, hip hop lyrics have indeed been considered strong influences. Increasingly, this connection has been extended into the realm of establishing character in murder trials. Prosecutors around the country have buttressed their cases with defendants' penned lyrics as evidence of their criminal-mindedness.

The criticism that hip hop advocates and thus causes violence relies on the unsubstantiated but widely held belief that listening to violent stories or consuming violent images *directly* encourages violent behavior. This concern was raised vis-à-vis violent video games during the 1980s, but also more recently, in relation to heavy metal music. Although the direct link between consumption and action may appear to be commonsensical, studies have been unable to provide evidence that confirms it. Recent challenges to the video game industry's sale of exceptionally gory and violent video games were stymied by the absence of such data and confirmation. Direct behavioral effect is, of course, a difficult thing to prove in scientific terms, since many recent and past factors — both individual and social — can contribute to a person's actions at any given time. The absence of direct proof doesn't mean that such imagery and lyrics are without negative impact. I am not arguing *for* the regular consumption of highly violent images and stories, nor am I saying that what we consume has no impact on us. Clearly, everything around us, past and present, has an impact on us, to one degree or another. Studies do show that violent music lyrics have been documented as increasing aggressive thoughts and feelings. High-saturation levels of violent imagery and action (in our simulated wars and fights in sports, film, music, and television but also, more significantly, in our real wars in the Middle East) clearly do not support patient, peaceful, cooperative actions and responses in our everyday lives.

However, the argument for one-to-one causal linking among storytelling, consumption, and individual action should be questioned, given the limited evidence to support this claim. And, even more important, the blatantly selective application of worries about violence in some aspects of popular culture and everyday life should be challenged for its targeting of individuals and groups who are already overly and problematically associated with violence. So, what may appear to be genuine concern over violence in entertainment winds up stigmatizing some expressions (rap music) and the groups with which they are associated (black youth). A vivid example of this highly selective application took place during the 1992 presidential campaign when George W. Bush said it was "sick" to produce a record that he said glorified the killing of police officers, but saw no contradiction between this statement and his acceptance of support and endorsement from Arnold Schwarzenegger. As one [*New York Times*] reporter put it: "I stand against those who use films or records or television or video games to glorify killing law enforcement officers," said Mr. Bush, who counts among his top supporters the actor Arnold Schwarzenegger, whose character in the movies *Terminator* and *Terminator II: Judgment Day* kills or maims dozens of policemen.

We live in a popular cultural world in which violent stories, images, lyrics, and performances occupy a wide cross-section of genres and mediums. Television shows such as *24* and *Law & Order*; Hollywood fare such as gangster, action, suspense, murder-driven, war, and horror films; video games; metal musics; and novels — together, these comprise a diverse and highly accessible palette of violent images attached to compelling characters and bolstered by high-budget realistic sets and backdrops. Although anti-violence groups mention many of these genres and mediums, the bulk of the popular criticism about violence in popular culture is leveled at hip hop, and the fear-driven nature of the commentary is distinct from responses to the many other sources of violent imagery. There are three important differences between the criticisms of hip hop and rappers and those leveled at other music, films, shows, and videos — most of which, unlike rap music, are produced (not just consumed) primarily by whites.

First, hip hop gets extra attention for its violent content, and the *perception* of violence is heightened when it appears in rap music form rather than in some other popular genre of music featuring violent imagery. Rappers such as Lil Jon, Ludacris, 50 Cent, and T.I. who claim that there is violence throughout popular culture and that they get overly singled out are right: Some violent imagery and lyrics in popular culture are responded to or perceived differently from others. Social psychologist Carrie B. Fried studied this issue and concluded that the perception of violence in rap music lyrics is affected by larger societal perceptions and stereotypes of African-Americans. In her study, she asked participants to respond to lyrics from a folk song about killing a police officer. To some of the participants the song was presented as rap; and to others, as country. Her study supports the hypothesis that lyrics presented as rap music are judged more harshly than the same lyrics presented as country music. She concluded that these identical lyrics seem more violent when featured in rap, perhaps because of the association of rap with the stereotypes of African-Americans.

Nevertheless, saying that there is violence elsewhere and that one is being unfairly singled out in connection with it isn't the best argument to make. Rappers' claims that violence is everywhere aren't a compelling case for hip hop's heightened investment in violent storytelling, especially for those of us who are worried about the extra levels of destructive forces working against poor black people. It is important, however, to pay close attention to the issue of unfair targeting, blame, and the compounded effect this perception of blacks as more violent has on black youth.

Second, many critics of hip hop tend to interpret lyrics literally and as a direct reflection of the artist who performs them. They equate rappers with thugs, see rappers as a threat to the larger society, and then use this "causal analysis" (that hip hop causes violence) to justify a variety of agendas: more police in black communities, more prisons to accommodate larger numbers of black and brown young people, and more censorship of expression. For these critics, hip hop is criminal propaganda. This literal approach, which extends beyond the individual to characterize an entire racial and class group, is rarely applied to violence-oriented mediums produced by whites.

Despite the caricature-like quality of many of hip hop's cultivated images and the similarity of many of its stories, critics often characterize rappers as speaking entirely autobiographically, implying that their stories of car-jacking, killing witnesses to crimes, hitting women, selling drugs, and beating up and killing opponents are statements of fact, truthful self-portraits. Thus, for instance, the rhyme in Lil Wayne's "Damage Is Done" that describes him as running away with a "hammer in my jeans, dead body behind me, cops'll never find me" would be interpreted by many critics as a description of actual events. This assumption—that rappers are creating rhymed autobiographies—is the result of both rappers' own investment in perpetuating the idea that everything they say is true to their life experience (given that the genre has grown out of the African-American tradition of boasting in the first person) and the genre's investment in the pretense of no pretense. That is, the genre's promoters capitalize on the illusion that the artists are not performing but "keeping it real"—telling the truth, wearing outfits on stage that they'd wear in the street (no costumes), remaining exactly as they'd be if they were not famous, except richer. Part of this "keeping it real" ethos is a laudable effort to continue to identify with many of their fans, who don't see their style or life experiences represented anywhere else, from their own points of view; part of it is the result of conformity to the genre's conventions. It makes rappers more accessible, more reflective of some of the lived experiences and conditions that shape the lives of some of their fans. And it gives fans a sense that they themselves have the potential to reach celebrity status, to gain social value and prestige while remaining "true" to street life and culture, turning what traps them into an imagined gateway to success.

But this hyper-investment in the fiction of full-time autobiography in hip hop, especially for those artists who have adopted gangsta personas, has been exaggerated and distorted by a powerful history of racial images of black men as "naturally" violent and criminal. These false and racially motivated stereotypes were promoted

throughout the last two centuries to justify both slavery and the violence, containment, and revised disenfranchisement that followed emancipation; and they persisted throughout the twentieth century to justify the development of urban segregation. In the early part of the twentieth century, well-respected scientists pursuing
the "genetic" basis of racial and ethnic hierarchy embraced the view that blacks were
biologically inferior, labeling them not only less intelligent but also more prone to
crime and violence. These racial associations have been reinforced, directly and indirectly, through a variety of social outlets and institutions and, even today, continue
to be circulated in contemporary scientific circles. In 2007, for example, Nobel laure-
ate biologist Jim Watson said that he was "inherently gloomy about the prospects
of Africa" because "all our social policies are based on the fact that their intelligence
is the same as ours, whereas all the testing says not really." He went on to say that
while he hoped everyone was equal, "people who have to deal with black employees
find this is not true." And in the now-infamous, widely challenged 1994 book *The Bell
Curve*, Richard J. Herrnstein and Charles Murray argued that it is highly likely that
genes partly explain racial differences in IQ testing and intelligence and also claimed
that intelligence is an important predictor of income, job performance, unwed pregnancy, and crime. Thus the pseudoscientific circle was closed: Blacks are genetically
less intelligent, and intelligence level predicts income, performance, criminality, and
sexually unsanctioned behavior; therefore, blacks are genetically disposed toward
poverty, crime, and unwed motherhood.

   This history of association of blacks with ignorance, sexual deviance, violence,
and criminality has not only contributed to the believability of hip hop artists' fic-
titious autobiographical tales among fans from various racial groups but has also
helped explain the excessive anxiety about the popularity and allure of these artists.
The American public has long feared black criminality and violence as particularly
anxiety-producing threats to whites—and the convincing "performance" of black
criminality taps into these fears. So, both the voyeuristic pleasure of believing that
hip hop artists are criminal minded and the exaggerated fear of them are deeply

connected. Hip hop has successfully traded on this history of scientific racism and its embedded impact on perceptions of poor black people, and has also been significantly criticized because of it.

A third central difference between the criticism of hip hop and rappers and the criticism leveled at other forms of popular culture has to do with the way the artists themselves are perceived in relation to their audiences and to society. Hip hop's violence is criticized at a heightened level and on different grounds from the vast array of violent images in American culture, and these disparities in perception are very important. While heavy metal and other nonblack musical forms that contain substantial levels of violent imagery are likewise challenged by anti-violence critics, the operative assumption is that this music and its violence-peddling creators will negatively influence otherwise innocent listeners. Therefore (according to these critics), metal, video games, and violent movies influence otherwise nonviolent teenagers, encouraging them to act violently. From this perspective, "our youth" must be protected from these outside negative, aggressive influences.

In the case of rap, the assumption is that the artists and their autobiographically styled lyrics represent an existing and already threatening violent black youth culture that must be prevented from affecting society at large. The quote from Bill O'Reilly at the outset of this chapter reflects this approach. For O'Reilly, Ludacris is advocating violence and selling narcotics. Allowing him to be a representative for Pepsi would, as O'Reilly's logic goes, be similar to giving power to Pol Pot, the Cambodian leader of the brutal Khmer Rouge government, allowing a "subversive" guy access to legitimate power. This difference in interpretation — such that black rappers are viewed as leaders of an invading and destructively violent force that undermines society — has a dramatic effect on both the nature of the criticism and the larger perceptions of black youth that propel the ways in which they are treated. It sets the terms of how we respond, whom we police, and whom we protect.

Tales of violence in hip hop share important similarities with the overall investment in violence as entertainment (and political problem solving) in American culture, but they have more localized origins as well—namely, the damaging and terrible changes in black urban America over the past forty or so years. Although hip hop's penchant for stories with violent elements isn't purely a matter of documentary or autobiography, these stories are deeply connected to real social conditions and their impact on the lives of those who live them, close up. My point here may be confusing: On the one hand, I am saying that rappers are not the autobiographers they are often believed to be and that seeing them that way has contributed to the attacks they specifically face. But, on the other hand, I am also saying that much of what listeners hear in hip hop stories of violence is reflective of larger real-life social conditions. How can both be true?

This is a crucial yet often improperly made distinction: Hip hop is not pure fiction or fantasy (such as might emerge from the mind of horror writer Stephen King), but neither is it unmediated reality and social advocacy for violence. Nor is rap a product of individual imagination (disconnected from lived experiences and social conditions) or sociological documentation or autobiography (an exact depiction of reality and personal action). Yet conversations about violence in hip hop strategically deploy both of these arguments. Defenders call it fiction, just like other artists' work, whereas critics want to emphasize rappers' own claims to be keeping it real as proof that these stories "advocate violence" or, as British politician David Cameron suggested, "[encourage] people to carry guns and knives."

Neither of these positions moves us toward a more empowering understanding of violent storytelling and imagery in hip hop or toward the fashioning of a productive, pro-youth position that recognizes the impact of these powerfully oppressive images without either accepting or excusing their negative effects. This is the line we must straddle: acknowledging the realities of discrimination and social policies that have created the conditions for the most dangerous and fractured black urban communities and, at the same time, not accepting or excusing the behaviors that are deeply connected to these local, social conditions.

The origins for the depth of investment in hip hop's myriad but context-specific stories involving guns, drugs, street culture, and crime are directly related to a combination of drastic changes in social life, community, and policies of neglect that destroyed neighborhood stability in much of black urban America. These local, social condition–based origins matter because the causal assumption that violent material when consumed increases violent actions underestimates the environmental forces at work. Although hip hop's violence has been marketed and exaggerated, its origins in violent urban communities and the reasons these communities became so violent must be understood. This context helps explain why hip hop's poorest inner-city fans and artists remain so invested in such stories. Rather than creating violence out of whole cloth, these stories are better understood as a distorted and profitable reflection of the everyday lives of too many poor black youth over the past forty or so years.

While context is crucial for explaining what we hear in a good deal of hip hop, context as justification for rap's constant repetition of violent storytelling is highly problematic. Rapper Tupac, for example, claimed that he was hoping to reveal the conditions in a powerful way to incite change: "I'm gonna show the most graphic details about what I see in my community and hopefully they'll stop it. Quick." Unfortunately, profits increased with increasingly violent, criminal-oriented rap while conditions remained and worsened. Despite the reality that these real conditions are not being changed because of rappers' stories and, instead, have become fodder for corporate profits, rappers continue to justify the use of black urban community distress and criminal icons along these lines, thus maintaining their value as a revenue stream. 50 Cent defended his lyrics, claiming that "[i]t's a reflection of the environment that I come from," and Jay-Z has confessed that "it's important for rappers to exaggerate 'life in the ghetto' because this is the only way the underclass can make its voice heard."

This context — the destruction of black community in urban America since the mid-1970s — has five central elements, each of which exacerbates the others, causing the serious dismantling of stable communities and resulting in several forms of social breakdown, one of which is increased violence.

High Levels of Chronic Joblessness

The issue of black and brown teen joblessness took on crisis proportions during the first two decades of hip hop's emergence. Unemployment and very low-paying, unstable employment have been concentrated in poor minority urban communities since the early part of the twentieth century, but this lengthy history of how race limits working-class opportunity took an especially pernicious turn in the 1980s and continued through the 1990s and beyond. What many scholars and economists call "permanent unemployment" or "chronic joblessness" began to plague poor black and brown communities, and the younger adults in these communities began to understand that traditional avenues for working-class job stability were becoming closed to them.

The effects of deindustrialization — the swift and extensive loss of unionized, well-paying manufacturing jobs out of urban areas to rural and nonunionized regions and out of the country entirely — hit all workers hard and dramatically undercut working-class economic mobility. This loss was accompanied by a growth in low-wage "service" jobs, which tended to be part-time and to offer limited or no benefits and few opportunities for upward mobility. Owing to both historical and contemporary forms of racial discrimination in the job market, these overall changes have been especially devastating for black communities. Indeed, blacks continued to be last hired and thus first fired when factories closed, and they were disproportionately kept in lower-level positions where upward advancement and skill-building (and thus job rehiring opportunities) are limited. During Ronald Reagan's second term, for example, more than one-third of black families earned incomes below the poverty line. By contrast, poverty rates hovered between 8 and 9 percent among white families. During the same period, black teenagers' already high levels of unemployment increased from 38.9 to 43.6 percent nationally, and in some regions, such as the Midwestern cities in the Great Lakes region, the figures were as high as 50 to 70 percent. By contrast, white teenage unemployment was around 13 percent.

Chronic and very high levels of unemployment and the poverty it creates, especially when magnified by long-standing injustice and discrimination, produce not only economic crisis but deep instabilities within families and across communities. These, in turn, result in higher levels of homelessness, street crime, and illegal income-generating activities (such as the drug trade), and alienation, rage, and violence.

Dramatic Loss of Affordable Housing/Urban Renewal

The legacies of thirty years of "urban renewal" began to bear rotten fruit in the middle to late 1970s. Dubbed "negro removal" by James Baldwin, the urban renewal programs designed to "clear slums" because they were considered "eyesores" proved to be terribly ill-conceived forms of neighborhood destruction that had a disproportionately negative impact on poor black urban communities. While the migration of millions of black people to cities in the twentieth century was met with forced urban housing segregation (producing what we now call black ghettos), those neighborhoods were also sources of community strength and general stability. Yes, poverty, discrimination, and other urban problems persisted, but areas like Watts in Los Angeles, Harlem in New York City, East St. Louis, and the Hill District in Pittsburgh became stable, multiclass communities where black people, as scholar Earl Lewis maintained, "turned segregation into congregation."

Urban renewal, especially during and after the 1960s, destroyed these low-income but highly network-rich and socially stable communities to make room for private development, sports arenas, hotels, trade centers, and high-income luxury buildings. Far from being a plan to create affordable housing, it created the massive housing crisis we still face today. By the summer of 1967, 400,000 residential units in urban renewal areas had been demolished; only 10,760 low-rent public housing units were built on these sites. In 1968, the Kerner Commission report pointed out that

> [i]n Detroit a maximum of 758 low-income units have been assisted through (federal) programs since 1956. . . . Yet, since 1960, approximately 8,000 low-income units have been demolished for urban renewal. . . . Similarly in Newark, since 1959, a maximum of 3,760 low-income housing units have been assisted through the programs considered. . . . [D]uring the same period, more than 12,000 families, mostly low income, have been displaced by such public uses of urban renewal, public housing, and highways.

This pattern of demolishing and not replacing thousands of units of existing affordable housing in poor black communities had a devastating impact in black communities all around the country, creating the constellation of symptoms in many major cities that we see today.

This was not just a housing problem, although the homeless crisis it produced was immense. The physical destruction of so many buildings was accompanied by the demolition of most of the adjacent venues and stores that served as community adhesive. Corner stores, music clubs, social clubs, beauty parlors, and barbershops were also displaced or destroyed, fraying community networks and patterns of connection. Social psychologist Mindy Fullilove refers to the destruction caused by urban renewal as "root shock," the "traumatic stress reaction to the destruction of all or part of one's emotional ecosystem." She astutely contextualizes this widespread destruction of housing and the social networks around it as one that destroyed communities, resulting in social disarray and increased levels of violence:

> Root shock, at the level of the individual, is a profound emotional upheaval. . . . [It] undermines trust, increases anxiety, . . . destabilizes relationships, destroys social, emotional, and financial resources, and increases the risk for every kind of stress-related disease, from depression to heart attack. Root shock, at the level of the local community, . . . ruptures bonds, dispersing people to all the directions of the

compass. . . . The great epidemics of drug addiction, the collapse of the black family, and the rise in incarceration of black men — all of these catastrophes followed the civil rights movement, they did not precede it. Though there are a number of causes of this dysfunction that cannot be disputed — the loss of manufacturing jobs, in particular — the current situation of Black America cannot be understood without a full and complete accounting of the social, economic, cultural, political, and emotional losses that followed the bulldozing of 1,600 neighborhoods.

Drug-Trade Expansion

The emergence of very cheap, addictive, and profitable drugs, such as PCP, but especially crack cocaine, in the mid-1980s made bad matters worse. The bleak economic reality of high levels of chronic joblessness and the loss of community networks produced by the destruction of black communities and massive housing demolition created not only a financial incentive for dealing hard drugs but an emotional one as well. The desire for drugs is directly linked to the longing to numb pain and suffering. Cheap, easily accessible, and highly addictive drugs like crack are especially alluring to the poor and others who face not only their own personal demons but also demons unleashed by society that are largely beyond their control. The affordability and profitability of crack created quick wealth for otherwise chronically unemployed people turned street dealers and fostered violent drug-gang turf wars and a whole generation of people in the clutches of a highly addictive drug.

This was at once a new phenomenon and part of a long history of black communities' serving as commercial shopping zones for all drug users from all class positions and racial backgrounds; crack's notoriously addictive qualities and low price — coupled with inattention to attacking drug distribution at higher levels — created a flourishing local and violent drug trade that spurred, expanded, and intensified gang activities in poor black and brown communities. The impact of drug addiction on the social public sphere was dramatic. The street sex trades became more linked to drugs; women especially, but also men who needed only a small amount of cash to get high, began selling themselves to support their crack habit. Drug addiction, which also fueled the spread of HIV/AIDS, was both a symptom and a cause of the extraordinary breakdown of poor black urban communities nationwide. Many rappers such as Jay-Z, 50 Cent, and T.I. are known for transforming themselves from drug dealers to rap moguls. Lyrics that reflect their history as drug dealers abound. Consider, for example, the chorus for 50 Cent's "Bloodhound": "I love to pump crack, I love to stay strapped."

But the crisis was so widespread that a whole generation of black comedians such as Chris Rock, David Chappelle, and others who grew up in and around this very dark period in black urban America came out with popular, biting, powerful routines and dark jokes about crack addiction and its impact on black communities. In a sense, the ground-level impact of crack, unemployment, and community destruction became a generational experience for many black youth. In a *Rolling Stone* interview, Chris Rock talked about the deep effects that crack had on the economic, social, and gender relations in black communities. The interviewer asked him: "How about crack? So many of your jokes and characters revolve around crack." Rock replies: "Basically, whatever was going on when you started getting laid will stick with you for the rest of your life. So crack was just a big part of my life, between my friends selling it or girls I used to like getting hooked on it. White people had the Internet; the ghetto had crack. . . . I have never been to war, but I survived that shit. I lost friends and family members. The whole neighborhood was kinda on crack. Especially living in Bed-Stuy [in Brooklyn], man." And in one of many David Chappelle skits featuring the memorable crack-head Tyrone Biggums, Biggums says: "Why do you think I car-jacked you, Rhonda?" Rhonda replies, "Cause the cops found you in it three hours later asleep, high on crack!" Biggums responds:

"That's impossible, Rhonda. How can you sleep when you're high on crack? Chinese riddle for you."

AK-47: Automatic Weapons and the Drug Economy

If this highly profitable illegal drug trade had been protected just by fists and knives, it would have been violent but not nearly as deadly. Instead, this always violent young men's drug trade was fueled by easy access to guns, especially high-powered automatic weaponry. Given the financial incentives of crack, drug dealers used the most powerful weapons available to protect their businesses. And, increasingly, those not involved in selling drugs, especially young black men who were considered part of the same age and gender demographic, felt they had to carry guns to protect themselves.

Neighborhood turf wars have a long bloody history in immigrant and working-class communities; tales of street peril among white male immigrant youth over one hundred years ago bear a striking resemblance to descriptions of today's invisible neighborhood boundaries and the dangerous street conflict they give rise to. But what really escalated this situation was the emergence of the highly lucrative crack trade and the flooding of poor urban communities with guns, especially semiautomatic ones. (Geoffrey Canada's book *Fist Stick Knife Gun* chronicles the impact of the availability of this increasingly deadly weaponry and its impact on adolescent male violence.) Few young men fifty years ago lost their lives in street skirmishes, bloody and frequent though they were, as access to deadly weapons was extremely limited then and the reasons for such turf battles were personal rather than wedded to the extremely lucrative high-stakes drug trade. Greedy high-level drug dealers and gun dealers, enabled both by the gun lobby and by terribly misguided and neglectful public policy, turned a long-standing problem into a life-threatening crisis of extraordinary proportions.

Government/Police Response: Incarceration over Rehabilitation

The 1980s "war on drugs" was really a war on the communities that bore the brunt of the drug crisis. The police and federal resource emphasis on low-level street dealers and the criminalization (rather than rehabilitation) of drug users resulted in the treatment of ravaged communities as war zones. The LAPD, for example, is considered legendary for its use of military strategies, developed during the war in Vietnam, on U.S. citizens in South Central Los Angeles. This slash-and-burn approach, one that failed to address the roots of the problem and barely distinguished between the drug dealers and the communities as a whole, turned poor black communities into occupied territories. Helicopter surveillance and small tanks equipped with battering rams were hallmarks of the LAPD policing in South Central L.A. in the middle to late 1980s. Housing projects were equipped with police substations, and young black males were routinely picked up for "potential gang activity." Their names were placed in a database; many were intimidated and brutalized. And yet the government failed to enact effective community-building responses such as rehabilitation, meaningful and stable jobs, well-supervised recreational outlets, and social services to enhance the support networks around children.

The criminal justice system reinforced this warlike strategy by defining crack offenses as more criminal than other drug offenses, applying and effectively justifying longer sentences (especially those dubbed "maximum minimum" sentences) for crack users and dealers, who were poor and predominantly black, than for users of cocaine, a drug more often consumed by middle-class and white drug users. In fact, although crack and cocaine possess the same active ingredient, crack cocaine is the only drug whereby the first offense of simple possession can initiate a federal mandatory minimum sentence. Possession of five grams of crack will trigger a five-year mandatory minimum sentence. By contrast, according to the U.S. Sentencing Commission, "simple possession of any quantity of any other substance by a first-time offender—including powder cocaine—is a misdemeanor offense punishable by a maximum of one year in prison." Owing to the designation of drug users as criminals rather than as people in need of rehabilitation (and given the special targeting of crack users and dealers over all other drug users), the black prison population skyrocketed and so did the parolee population. In 1986, before mandatory minimums for crack offenses went into effect, the average federal drug offense sentence for blacks was 11 percent higher than for whites; four years later—after these harsher and targeted laws were implemented, the average federal drug offense sentence was 49 percent higher for blacks. In 1997, the U.S. Sentencing Commission report found that "nearly 90 percent of the offenders convicted in federal court for crack cocaine distribution are African-American while the majority of crack cocaine users are white. Thus, sentences appear to be harsher and more severe for racial minorities than others as a result of this law." The extensive denial of the ways that race and racism shaped and consolidated violence, instability, and poverty continued to fuel misguided and mean-spirited policies that focused far more on emphasizing personal behavioral responsibility and punishment than on community support and collective responsibility.

The "war on drugs" policy that favored punishment over other social responses was singularly responsible for the incredible expansion of the prison industrial complex and the heavy impact this had on poor black communities. Between 1970 and 1982 the U.S. prison population doubled in size; between 1982 and 1999, it increased again threefold. Within the United States today are only 5 percent of the world's inhabitants but 25 percent of the world's prisoners. Of the 2 million Americans currently behind bars, black men and women, who comprise around 12 percent of the national population, are profoundly overrepresented. Currently, black men make up 40 percent of prisoners in federal, state, and local prisons. Researchers anticipate that this trend will continue; based on current policies and conditions, they say that 30 percent of black men born today can expect to spend some time in prison. Among current black male prisoners, a disproportionately high number come from a small number of predominantly or entirely minority neighborhoods in big cities where aggressive street-level policing and profiling are heavily practiced. Over half of the adult male inmates from New York City come from fourteen districts in the Bronx, Manhattan, and Brooklyn, even though men in those areas make up just 17 percent of the city's total population. Numbers like these inspired the Justice Mapping Center to examine prison spending by neighborhood and by city block. Center founders Eric Cadora and Charles Swartz discovered what they dubbed "million-dollar blocks," neighborhoods where "so many residents were sent to state prison that the total cost of their incarceration will be more than one million dollars." In Brooklyn alone, there were thirty-five such blocks. Rates of incarceration among black women have also risen dramatically and disproportionately. Almost half of the female prison population are black, and many of these women are locked up for nonviolent offenses (theft, forgery, prostitution, and drugs) that are directly linked to the forces of community destruction addressed in this chapter. The community-wide impact of these disproportionate and racially specific levels of policing and incarceration is staggering.

These are the architectural signposts of today's ghettos. The violence that takes place within them has been created not only by racial discrimination long ago but also by assaults on poor black communities since the 1960s. The high levels of crime, police brutality, violence, drugs, and instability that define poor black urban communities are the direct result of chronic and high levels of concentrated joblessness, loss of affordable housing, community demolition, the crack explosion, the impact of easily accessible and highly deadly weapons used to defend the lucrative drug trade, and incarceration strategies that have criminalized large swaths of the African-American population. While not all of these factors were unique to poor black urban America, some were, and others were highly concentrated there. These recent conditions, along with compounding factors such as the long-term effects of economic, social, and political forms of racial discrimination, intensified the dramatic demise of working-class and poor black urban communities.

Hip hop emerged in this context, and thus the tales of drug dealing, pimping, petty crime, dropping out of school, and joining a gang are more aptly seen as reflections of the violence experienced in these areas than as origins of the violence. The drive to point out and criticize violence in rappers' stories as the cause of violence in poor black communities is often a disgraceful extension of the overemphasis on individual (decontextualized) personal behavior and the deep denial of larger social responsibility for creating and fostering these contexts.

The violent stories that characterize many hip hop lyrics are tales from this landscape, told from the ground-level perspective of circumstances as lived experience, not historical or sociological analysis. When we understand the depths of this reality, the actual destruction and violence that these societally manufactured conditions have fostered, then the violent lyrics take on a different character.

Why is it so difficult to understand that this highly vulnerable and dismantled community of chronically poor and racially-discriminated-against young people is in need of protection and advocacy? Why are we turning youth (through attacks on rap) into the agents of their own demise, seeing black kids as the source of violence in America while denying the extraordinary violence done to them?

My foregoing summary of the five causes of destruction of black communities — *chronic joblessness, loss of affordable housing, drug-trade expansion, automatic weapons and the drug economy,* and *incarceration instead of rehabilitation* — is not meant to encourage a blithe reaction to violent stories in hip hop, nor to cause readers to say, "Well, this is their reality." The prevalence of such stories in hip hop and the fact that they too often valorize violence (sometimes even serving as seductive tales of predatory action against other poor black people) are signs of a crisis for which the nation as a whole is responsible; the stories and rhymes themselves are not the primary source of the crisis. Attacking the rappers individually — calling them thugs and criminals while studiously avoiding the state of poor black urban America, or, worse, blaming these conditions entirely or even primarily on black people themselves — is a disturbing aspect of the hip hop wars. This stance reflects a long-term drive to deny the continued power and influence of institutional racism, sustains a racialized "us" versus "them" philosophy that enables the maintenance of racial and class inequality, and, in effect, extends the very logic that drove many of these mean-spirited and disempowering urban policies in the first place.

Culture is a means by which we learn how to engage with the world, and thus constant depictions of violence can have a normative effect. While this effect is not direct and absolute, there is ample evidence that people are deeply influenced by their surroundings and the social conditions impinging on them. Compared to children growing up in secure and stable environments, those who live in violence- or crime-ridden communities are at greater risk for exhibiting criminal and violent behavior. Our visually mediated culture is a large part of the surroundings and social conditions that shape us. If we are treated in violent ways, if we are forced by circumstance to survive in places where violent conflict is a matter of everyday life, and if we consume many violent images, we are more at risk — not only for exhibiting higher levels of violent behavior but, more important, for experiencing less trust and intimacy, increased fear, and a greater need for self-protection.

So, hip hop's extensive repertoire of stories about violence, guns, drugs, crime, and prison is compounded by everyday life for those who have little or no option but to reside in the poorest and most troubled neighborhoods and communities. Such stories become more powerful in this context, providing an image of everyday realities that can overemphasize the worst of what young people in these places face. On behalf of these kids, not the ones who listen vicariously from afar, we should be concerned about how and how often street crime and the drug trade are depicted — not because they represent the infusion of violence in American culture but because they sound an alarm about the levels of violence and social decay created by policies, public opinion, and neglect.

We must pay close attention to violence in hip hop, but we should not treat the tales of violence in hip hop in dangerous isolation from the many crucial contexts for its existence. Decontextualization — taking the violence expressed in hip hop lyrics and storytelling and examining them out of context — has a number of problematic effects both for the art form and for black people in general. Not only are the larger nonblack cultural reasons for these violent themes ignored but, worse, these reasons are attributed to black people themselves. So, the issue, once decontextualized, becomes violence as a black cultural problem, not violence as a larger social problem with tragic consequences for the most vulnerable. This approach does nothing to help us think through and reduce violence in black communities or in American society more broadly, nor to reduce our collective appetite for violent entertainment or our use of violence as a means to achieve success and secure opportunity. It does, however, contribute to the further targeting and criminalization of poor black youth; it helps us imagine that this is "their problem," which only "they" can fix by acting right.

Another negative effect of taking hip hop's lyrical tales of violence out of social context is that their distinctive style of expression overshadows all similarities between them and other styles of violent storytelling. Because the particular *brand* of poor urban black and Latino male street culture that many rappers detail in their rhymes is unfamiliar to many whites (who because of continued patterns of residential segregation do not live in these overwhelmingly black and brown neighborhoods), these unfamiliar listeners often equate black style of expression with content. Although tales of violent street culture have various ethnic and racial origins, the fascination with black versions of such street culture creates the illusion that violent street culture is itself a black cultural thing.

Poor white ethnic neighborhoods have long had their own forms of violent street culture, but the fact that their slang, style, and rhetoric are not generally perceived as racially distinctive contributes to the misreading of black street crime and street culture as a cultural matter rather than as an outgrowth of larger social patterns. This lack of local familiarity with black style among white fans adds to the allure of its expression in hip hop. It also encourages a false sense of black ownership of street culture and crime among blacks. Thus, black language, clothing, and other distinctions in style override the deep similarities between black and other ethnic (white and nonwhite) forms of violent street culture. The lack of regular day-to-day contact between races (facilitated by sustained housing and school segregation) enhances this miscue. Many white fans come to "know" these neighborhoods and their residents through mass media portraits (Hollywood film, television programming, news coverage, rap music lyrics, and videos), which only reinforce the fixation and reduce the recognition of cross-racial examples of violent male street cultures.

These factors, when taken together, create a web that looks something like this: We support policies that destroy black communities, and communities with great instability often experience more violence. Then, we rely on long-standing racist perceptions of black men as more violent, fear them more, and then treat them with more violence in response, which results in both more violence and more incarceration. Next, because we associate these men with violence, the stories they tell about violence are perceived as "authentic black expression," which activates a familiar kind of racial voyeurism and expands the market for their particular stories of crime and violence, which, in turn, confirms the perception that black men are more violent. This creates economic opportunity for performing and celebrating violent storytelling. Round and round we go.

But what is the actual role of violence in lyrics written by young people who live in communities that are struggling to stem the tide of real violence? Are these lyrics celebrations of the violence that shapes their lives—statements in support of the gangs, drugs, and crime about which they rap and rhyme? Or do they reflect a process of emotional and social management—a means by which these young people manage the lived reality of violence by telling their stories (a well-known process of healing in therapeutic and psychological circles)? Do these stories contribute to the violence these young people experience? Or are their stories about violence an outgrowth of the day-to-day threats they face, and do such stories relieve or reduce actual violence by responding to real violence with metaphor?

Or can *both* be true? Can violent lyrics and imagery reflect a real condition and at the same time contribute to creating it? The nub of the problem is this: At what point do stories that emanate from an overly violent day-to-day life begin to encourage and support that aspect of everyday life and undercut the communities' anti-violent efforts?

The question remains as to how we should examine and respond to the images and stories about violence that emanate from people who live in communities plagued by violence. We must continue to discuss whether we should attack the lyrics and the lyricists as causing violence or the conditions that foster violence. Clearly, we should challenge artists who have profited handsomely by constantly reinforcing the worst forms of predatory behavior against poor black communities. But to do so while denying the reality of their circumstances is mean-spirited and ineffectual.

In the song "Trouble" on the CD *Kingdom Come* (Roc-A-Fella Records, 2006), Jay-Z raps about his desire to stop hustling, but says he's only "pretending to be different," praying to God, in the chorus, because he'll never change. Both his longing to change and the bravado that accompanies his return to the game heighten the impact of the song. Jay-Z, a consummate braggadocio-style rapper, reestablishes his dominance over all around him. At one point he raps: "The meek shall perish." He goes on to say, "I'll roof you little nigga, I'm a project terrorist." His unrepentant character (self?) brags about being a person who rules with violent disregard and terrorizes people who live in the projects, an already terrorizing place to be. How should black poor people respond to this character? With pride? Affirmatively? Supportively? Since the song does not offer a critique of this "project terrorist," and given the charisma that Jay-Z imparts through his rhymes, one could perceive it as a glorification of a person terrorizing the most vulnerable members of black American society and demanding that we support his creative rights to profit from it. Why aren't street-level rappers like Jay-Z fashioning countless tales of youthful outrage at such a predator? This is a powerful example of how the art of bragging wedded to the icon of the violent street hustler — in communities where street hustling is a vibrant and destructive force — ends up having the power to celebrate predatory behavior.

In a 2007 *Rolling Stone* interview, Jay-Z acknowledged that the drug wars of which he was a part are hostile to black people and black communities: "When dealers are in the middle of it, they don't realize what they're doing, they don't humanize the people that's using the drugs, they don't humanize the neighborhood. It's not until you mature, and then you look back on it like, 'I was causing a lot of destruction around the neighborhood.'" But where are all the highly commercially successful lyrics that make this crucial point, that de-glamorize the drug trade, that reject gangsta worldviews, that humanize black people? This is the central problem with the expressions of violence and drug-dealer-turned-rapper stories in hip hop: They do not publicly reinforce the transition from "project terrorist" to "project humanist." Far too much pleasure, fame, style, and celebration go to the game, to the hustle, to the dehumanizing rhetoric of taking advantage of black people.

Without making overly blanket, ill-informed generalizations about the creativity in hip hop, we need to be alarmed about storytelling that offers little critique of violence against black people. There are brilliant stories in hip hop that capture the day-to-day reality of dealing with violence but do not seem to glorify it. Consider, for example, the lyrics for Nas's "Gangsta Tears," which tap into the pain, loss, and seemingly permanent cycle of retribution. But such sorrowful tales are a decreasing proportion of what sells records in hip hop, serving instead as "alternative" fare on corporate radio. Far too many of the most financially successful lyricists in hip hop — Jay-Z, 50 Cent, T.I., and Lil Wayne, among others — overemphasize and glorify violent tales and gang personas because these are profitable. They no longer tell tales from the darkside, with the hopes of contributing to a devaluing of "the life" and producing radical, empowered youth. Instead, there is too much getting rich from the exploitation of black suffering.

Despite the wrong-headed, decontextualized, and unfairly targeted claims about hip hop causing violence, there is some truth to them. It is silly to claim that what we consume, witness, and participate in has no impact on us as individuals and as a society. When a society turns a blind eye to violent behavior and allows its culture and politics to be saturated in violence, it will normalize violence among its citizenry and perhaps also indirectly contribute to violent behavior among some of its citizens. And if we are going to rail about violence in hip hop, we should rail twice as hard about the depths of violence young black people experience, seeing them as the recipients and inheritors of violence rather than solely as its perpetrators. Where is all the media-supported outrage about this?

The combination of denial of the larger forces and the self-congratulatory story of hyper-individual responsibility most readily expressed by white middle-class leaders is more than dishonest; it is itself a form of social violence against the young people who are most vulnerable and who need all of us to make a real and serious commitment to restoring the kinds of institutions and opportunities that keep chaos, violence, and social root shock at bay. The refusal to acknowledge our national culpability for these conditions continues not only the legacy of denying the deep injuries done to African-Americans but also the long-standing use of the expression of black pain from these injuries as "evidence" of black people's own responsibility for these larger circumstances. The depths of the commercial success associated with violent, gang, and street culture as "authentic" hip hop has given violent black masculinity a seal of approval, thus encouraging these behaviors among the kids who are most at risk, and who "need" to embrace this model if manhood is to survive. What began as a form of releasing and healing has become yet another lucrative but destructive economy for young poor black men.

The day-to-day violence that plagues poor communities must be taken into account both as a crucial context for explaining some of what we hear in hip hop and as a reality that compounds the power of violent storytelling. The allure of celebrities whose cachet depends partly on their relationship to a criminal/drug underworld is surely a form of social idolization that might encourage already-vulnerable kids to participate in the lucrative drug trade in neighborhoods where good-paying jobs are nearly nonexistent. A good deal of 50 Cent's initial promotional campaign relied on the fact that he sold crack, that his mother was a crack user, that he was shot nine times and wore a bulletproof vest to protect him against enemies. We can't constantly make violence sexy for young people who find themselves mired in violent social spaces that are mostly not of their making and then expect them not to valorize violent action.

Some of this impact is going to be behavioral, and the behaviors in question should be vociferously challenged and rejected. Black people do not need "project terrorists"! The projects and "million-dollar blocks" are bad enough. Of course, the drive to pathologize black people (and to make pathologized blackness the only "true" and profitable blackness) makes such criticism of black behavior very tricky. But we must confront this dilemma with courage and honesty. Our efforts to support, sustain, and rebuild black communities must permanently join the five major causes of destruction I've listed above to their individual and collective consequences. Neither social responsibility nor individual responsibility should be talked about in isolation. Focusing on hip hop as a cause of violence is just as irresponsible as defending it by pointing to social conditions as a justification for perpetuating gang, gun, and drug slang, iconography, and lifestyles in the music. Despite the finger-pointing, both positions in the hip hop wars propagate the myth that black people are themselves violent, and both downplay the violence done to them. Both seem to accept the larger social context as it is; neither challenges American society to change the playing field.

Unbiased, socially just forms of concern about violence will and do focus on directly helping communities reduce violence rather than pointing the finger at and railing about lyrics and images as the cause. Working as many local leaders and community groups do in the communities most directly affected by street crime and other acts of daily violence, activists don't advocate more force, violence, and policing but, on the contrary, strongly advocate for nonviolent conflict resolution in schools, at home, and in other places where children spend a great deal of their time. They also call for access to resources for families to help resolve conflict. Indeed, our response to youth crimes should result in extensive conflict resolution counseling and other highly supervised programs designed to reverse their direction, not placement in ever more violent adult incarceration facilities.

The most effective way to enact concern over violence is to (1) express this concern for black youth, and the real violence they face, in the form of activist social change; and (2) stop being hypocritical about violence. In other words, we must avoid the duplicity involved in expressing outrage at hip hop's violence while remaining virtually silent about the ways that our society condones violence and uses it both as social policy (internationally and at home) and as entertainment. This effort would have to address head-on the social worlds this nation has formed by creating, maintaining, and exacerbating the conditions in ghettos. It would have to confront violence against black youth — direct and indirect — that is part of everyday life but all too often goes unchallenged as a crisis for *our* society unless it spills *out* of the ghetto. Until this happens, those who rail about hip hop's violence but refuse to take into account the forces working against these communities do so not on behalf of the thousands of kids and young adults who have been left to fend for themselves but, rather, against them.

Reading the Genre

1. Why, according to Rose, do critics blame hip-hop music for violence? How does she show that such concerns oversimplify cause and effect?

2. Rose cites other scholars to both ground and extend her causal analysis. To what effect? Find examples of her use of secondary sources, and consider what the use of each of these sources allows Rose to do as a writer. (See Chapter 40, "Evaluating Sources," p. 451.)

3. Find passages where it is obvious that Rose is carefully handling material that may be sensitive. How does she maintain her impartiality? How is she able to address readers across a range of perspectives? (See Chapter 33, "Inclusive and Culturally Sensitive Style," p. 408.)

4. This essay examines multiple causes of "the destruction of black communities." What are these causes? How does Rose use five separate causal analyses to argue that contributing factors have had a greater negative impact on urban life than hip-hop has? (See "Finding and developing materials," p. 140, and "Creating a structure," p. 142.)

5. In addition to discussing the causes of urban violence, Rose addresses the effects of interpreting hip-hop music out of context. What does she say those effects are? Why is it so important to understand the context surrounding this genre of music?

6. **WRITING:** Rose offers Nas's "Gangsta Tears" as an example of a hip-hop song that critiques violence instead of glorifying it. Using this song, or another example from your listening experience, write a short essay arguing that hip-hop music can have a beneficial effect. In your analysis, investigate the lyrics closely and consider the ways they might promote positive change.

Proposals: Readings

GENRE MOVES Proposal

RACHEL CARSON
From "The Obligation to Endure"

The history of life on earth has been a history of interaction between living things and their surroundings. To a large extent, the physical form and the habits of the earth's vegetation and its animal life have been molded by the environment. Considering the whole span of earthly time, the opposite effect, in which life actually modifies its surroundings, has been relatively slight. Only within the moment of time represented by the present century has one species — man — acquired significant power to alter the nature of his world.

During the past quarter century this power has not only increased to one of disturbing magnitude but it has changed in character. . . .

It took hundreds of millions of years to produce the life that now inhabits the earth — eons of time in which that developing and evolving and diversifying life reached a state of adjustment and balance with its surroundings. The environment, rigorously shaping and directing the life it supported, contained elements that were hostile as well as supporting. Certain rocks gave out dangerous radiation; even within the light of the sun, from which all life draws its energy, there were short-wave radiations with power to injure. Given time — time not in years but in millennia — life adjusts, and a balance has been reached. For time is the essential ingredient; but in the modern world there is no time.

The rapidity of change and the speed with which new situations are created follow the impetuous and heedless pace of man rather than the deliberate pace of nature.

Zoom out.

As Neil deGrasse Tyson does in his proposal essay (p. 822), Rachel Carson urges her readers to take a much wider, broader perspective on human life. What both authors understand is that proposals very often focus on the way a new course of action can create change. Proposal essays often ask their audience to *stop* behaving or acting in one way and instead take a different path. For Tyson, this means taking a "cosmic" perspective. For Carson, this means looking at time ecologically — "time not in years but in millennia." Both perspectives urge humans to take a more humble stance and then to act as though they *don't* own this place.

In many proposals, the trick is to convince readers to put someone else's, or something else's, interests before their own. Writers can accomplish this by showing readers the broader impact of their actions or by changing perspective — by zooming out. In your own proposal, examine what the wider impact of your proposed actions might be — or the broader implications of *not* acting. For instance, if you are proposing something like mandatory voting laws, think about how this will affect the next two or three generations, not just your own. If you are proposing higher taxes on petroleum, investigate what this will mean to nonhuman animals or the environment, or imagine how this will change the world by 2100. Such imagining might not be the central focus of an evidence-based proposal, but it could make for a compelling introduction or conclusion.

PROPOSAL FOR CHANGE   Michael Todd writes on environmental issues for the *Pacific Standard,* a publication devoted to studying "the science of society." This 2013 essay is based on a short proposal put forward by two scientific researchers in the journal *Nature*. In his essay, Todd interviews these researchers and explores their ideas, putting them into conversation with other movements to ban plastic or to regulate its disposal.

Is That Plastic in Your Trash a Hazard?

MICHAEL TODD

There are medical, chemical, and environmental issues associated with some pretty common plastic products. Is it time to label these as hazardous waste?

Plastic has taken its lumps of late. Plastic bags are being chased from store checkouts around the world. Bisphenol A, or BPA, in plastic containers has been linked to a Pandora's box of hormonal and genetic problems. And the Pacific, Atlantic, and Indian oceans each have a gigantic soupy concoction of plastic waste at their centers[1]—the Pacific and Atlantic have one such patch in both the Northern and Southern Hemispheres.

Despite this, the world's general attitude to plastic has been pretty cavalier. And since we're not sweating the advent of peak oil as much, at least not in North America, that plastics are made from petrochemicals doesn't seem so problematic. In fact, if current trends continue, the 280 million tons of plastic produced in 2012 will grow to 33 billion tons in 2050.

How cavalier would we be if plastics, always assumed to be chemically inert, were a hazardous waste?

A group of researchers led by ecologists Chelsea M. Rochman and Mark Anthony Browne, commenting in the journal *Nature*,[2] call for governments around the world to classify some plastics, such as PVC, polystyrene, polyurethane, and polycarbonate, as hazardous waste. Such a move, if undertaken by major producers like the United States, China, and the European Union, would—in the researchers' view—foster a virtuous circle of less waste, resulting in less potentially toxic material that ends up in oceans or leaches harmful chemicals from landfills, and could even create new jobs as industry sought safer replacement materials.

Neither Rochman or Browne are anti-plastic. There's a time and place for the petrochemical-based product, they explained recently over hot drinks at a Starbucks. (The toll? Two throwaway cups, one plastic and unused takeaway lid, and one battered plastic travel mug.) But the present overreliance on plastic, from food containers to fleece clothing to cheap housewares and electronics, is a concern.

Browne points to an increase in plastic milk containers in Britain as a prime example of plastic's overreach. For a century milk had been delivered in reusable glass containers, which were chemically inert, sustainable, and fostered local production. To use some jargon, it was a "closed-loop system." Then plastic swept in. It was cheap and weighed less, making it easier to move longer distances, which tended both to erase the smaller carbon footprint gains from its lightness and allow dairies to be further and further from their customers. Then, of course, once the plastic jug was empty, it either had to be broken down for recycling or just trashed.

In the United States, the EPA estimates 45 percent of plastics[3] were used as containers or for packaging, and just 12 percent of that gets recycled. In New York City, it's estimated the average citizen tosses out 107 pounds of different kinds of plastic waste each year, and only 17 pounds[4] of that was even designed for recycling,[5] much less recycled. "We create things just so we can throw them away," Browne laments.

But while recycling is a positive outcome, declaring some plastics as hazardous waste isn't an end run, the ecologists say, but a necessary step based on reality. Many plastics can be toxic in themselves in some contexts, or can absorb a surprising array of pollutants. "Yet," reads the commentary in *Nature*, "in the United States, Europe, Australia, and Japan, plastics are qualified as solid waste—so are treated the same way as food scraps or glass clippings."

And, both Browne and Rochman aver, no way is plastic that innocent, even as they admit they're still trying to get a grip on both the size of the issue and plastic's ecological impacts.

For example, some plastics that are seen as benign in their consumer forms can have nasty attributes when they break down. Rochman has studied how different kinds of plastic absorb pollutants in the oceans[6]—she calls plastic-filled seas "cocktails of contaminants." The kinds of plastic used in detergent bottles and shopping bags, for example, after breaking down into waterborne pellets, can continue to suck up pollutants for months and even years. The *Nature*

Mikadun/Shutterstock.

piece points to an unpublished analysis that found that at least 71 percent of priority pollutants listed by the EPA and 61 percent listed by the European Union are associated with plastic debris.

These poisonous pellets can then bob around in the water or settle and concentrate in the sediment; or they can get eaten by animals or microorganisms and enter the food web.

Rochman's work shows that not all plastics are equal. Those used in water bottles, or PVC, used in clear-food packaging, aren't as powerful at absorbing pollutants. On the other hand, vinyl chloride, a component in polyvinyl chloride (PVC), has been identified as carcinogenic.

In fact, while many plastics in their final form are considered safe, many of the chemicals used to make them are known to be hazardous to health, or conversely, individual chemical compounds may have received a green light for safety but haven't been tested as they interact with other compounds. Plus, as plastics degrade into smaller pieces, their properties can change. The particles that come from polyester or acrylic clothing — think of that warm fleece jacket made out of recycled two-liter soda bottles — can be ingested or inhaled with malign effects at the cellular level.

Again, says Browne, a lack of research has hampered the ability to make definitive statements, but not, he hopes, from invoking the precautionary principle. He and his coauthors would like producers and packagers to have to show that their products are safe.

"Our goal is to provide information. We're not telling people what to do but allowing them to make choices. But they should know that plastic is not an inert material."

While government and industry haven't necessarily embraced the idea of declaring plastic waste as hazardous, in some cases they've supported basic research—one of Rochman's experiments had funding from the American Chemistry Council—or started phasing out the most likely serious offenders.

There are laws from the local to international level that could help. In the European Union, regulations (described as the most complex sets of rules in the EU's history[7]) are in place to test out the hazards of chemicals in everyday use,[8] although the effects of these findings aren't expected to hit industry and consumers for years. And even long-standing rules may not effectively address long-standing problems. For example, the International Convention for the Prevention of Pollution from Ships[9] has banned disposing of plastic at sea since 1988, but since then things like the so-called "Great Pacific Garbage Patch" have gotten worse.

But there are stronger efforts afoot. The Center for Biological Diversity, for example, has petitioned the U.S. Environmental Protection Agency[10] to develop rules, using the Clean Water Act, to reverse the tide of plastic pollution in the oceans.

"We hope to be able to use existing laws—which industry wants us to do—to foster closed-loop systems," Browne says. That still leaves the door open to some plastics, especially those that can easily be reused and recycled, and to other materials that are benign by design.

Notes

1. Skenazy, Matt. "Ocean Garbage Patches: A Scientific Sifting." *Pacific Standard.* April 26, 2012.
2. Rochman, Chelsea M., Mark Anthony Browne, et al. "Policy: Classify Plastic Waste as Hazardous." *Nature* 494, 169–171. February 14, 2013.
3. "Plastics." EPA.gov. http://www.epa.gov/osw/conserve/materials/plastics .htm

4. "Quantities of Different Plastics in NYC's Waste." NYC.gov. http://www.nyc
    .gov/html/nycwasteless/html/resources/plastics_quantities.shtml

5. "What Plastics to Recycle in NYC." NYC.gov. http://www.nyc.gov/html
    /nycwasteless/html/resources/plastics_nycrecycles.shtml

6. Rochman, Chelsea M., Eunha Hoh, et al. "Long-Term Field Measurement
    of Sorption of Organic Contaminants to Five Types of Plastic Pellets: Im-
    plications for Plastic Marine Debris." *Environmental Science & Technology* 47
    (3), 1646–1654. December 27, 2012.

7. Rettman, Andrew. "EU's REACH Chemicals Law Begins Life in Helsinki."
    EUObserver. May 31, 2007.

8. "REACH." European Commission. http://ec.europa.eu/environment
    /chemicals/reach/reach_en.htm

9. "International Convention for the Prevention of Pollution from Ships
    (MARPOL)." International Maritime Organization. http://www.imo.org
    /About/Conventions/listofconventions/pages/international-convention-for
    -the-prevention-of-pollution-from-ships-%28marpol%29.aspx

10. "Petition for Water Quality Criteria for Plastic Pollution under the Clean
    Water Act, 33 USC § 1314." The Center for Biological Diversity. August 22,
    2012.   http://www.biologicaldiversity.org/campaigns/ocean_plastics/pdfs
    /Petition_Plastic_WQC_08-22-2012.pdf

Reading the Genre

1. Todd bases this essay around the work of Chelsea M. Rochman and Mark Anthony Browne, whose short and provocative proposal to label plastic hazardous was intended to get other scientists and commentators to explore the issue further. Do you feel that Todd does a good job exploring and researching the issue? What further evidence does Todd provide to support his proposal?

2. Look into some of the laws and regulations that Todd discusses at the very end of his proposal. What would happen if these laws or regulations were passed in your own country? Pick one of the laws and discuss how it might affect your daily life. (For more help with research, see Chapter 38, "Finding Print and Online Sources," p. 442)

3. **MULTIMODALITY — PUBLIC AWARENESS POSTER:** Create a public awareness poster that might be put on garbage cans across your campus to warn students what happens when they throw plastics in the trash instead of recycling. Use words and images carefully to grab people's attention and to persuade them. (For help with thinking about design and images, see Chapter 50, "Designing Print and Online Documents," p. 557.)

4. **WRITING:** Create a list of products that you consider "hazardous." The products could be hazardous to health, or they could be hazardous to self-esteem, or they could pose dangers to families and relationships, or to society more broadly. Write a proposal that suggests a way to "label" one of these products so that people fully understand its danger and can either avoid it or develop ways to use it more carefully.

PROPOSAL FOR CHANGE   Jane McGonigal designs alternate reality games intended to "improve real lives or solve real problems." She is the author of the best-selling book *Reality Is Broken: Why Games Make Us Better and How They Can Change the World* (2011) and serves as creative director for the group Social Chocolate and director of game research and development at the Institute for the Future. This article first appeared in the *Huffington Post* in February 2011. In this essay, McGonigal offers a modest and perhaps counterintuitive proposal about gaming.

The Huffington Post

Posted: February 15, 2011, at 7:05 AM
From: Jane McGonigal

Video Games:
An Hour a Day Is Key to Success in Life

The single biggest misconception about games is that they're an escapist waste of time. But more than a decade's worth of scientific research shows that gaming is actually one of the most productive ways we can spend time.

No, playing games doesn't help the GDP — our traditional measure of productivity. But games help us produce something more important than economic bottom line: powerful emotions and social relationships that can change our lives — and potentially help us change the world.

Currently there are more than half a billion people worldwide playing online games at least an hour a day — and 183 million in the U.S. alone. The younger you are, the more likely you are to be a gamer — 97 percent of boys under eighteen and 94 percent of girls under eighteen report playing video games regularly. And the average young person racks up ten thousand hours of gaming by the age of twenty-one. That's almost exactly as much time as they spend in a classroom during all of middle school and high school if they have perfect attendance. Most astonishingly, 5 million gamers in the U.S. are spending more than forty hours a week playing games — the same as a full-time job!

Why are we increasingly turning to games? According to my research, it's because games do a better job than ordinary life of provoking our most powerful positive emotions — like curiosity, optimism, pride, and a desire to join forces with others to achieve something extraordinary. Games also, increasingly, are a particularly effective way to bond with our friends and family — strengthening our real-life and online social networks in ways that no other kind of social interaction can.

That's what I mean when I say — in the title of my new book — that *Reality Is Broken*. The fact that so many people of all ages, all over the world, are choosing to spend so much time in game worlds is a sign of something important, a truth that we urgently need to recognize.

The truth is this: In today's society, computer and video games are fulfilling *genuine human needs* that the real world is currently unable to satisfy. Games are providing rewards that reality is not. They are teaching and inspiring and engaging us in ways that reality is not. They are bringing us together in ways that reality is not. And unless something dramatic happens to reverse the resulting exodus, we're fast on our way to becoming a society in which a substantial portion of our population devotes its greatest efforts to playing games, creates its best memories in game environments, and experiences its biggest successes in game worlds.

Fortunately, however, this temporary exodus is not a complete waste of time! When we play a good game, we get to practice being the best version of ourselves: We become more optimistic, more creative, more focused, more likely to set ambitious goals, and more resilient in the face of failure. And when we play multiplayer games, we become more collaborative and more likely to help others. In fact, we like and trust each other more after we play a game together — even if we lose! And more importantly, playing a game with someone is an incredibly effective way to get to know their strengths and weaknesses — as well as what motivates them. This is exactly the kind of social knowledge we need to be able to cooperate and collaborate with people to tackle real-world challenges.

The good news about games is that recent scientific research shows that all of these feelings and activities can trickle into our real lives.

For example: Kids who spend just thirty minutes playing a "pro-social" game like *Super Mario Sunshine* (in which you clean up pollution and graffiti around an island) are more likely to help friends, family, and neighbors in real life for a full week after playing the game.

People of all ages who play musical games like *Rock Band* and *Guitar Hero* report spending more time learning and playing real musical instruments than before they started playing the video game.

And just ninety seconds of playing a game like *World of Warcraft* — where you have a powerful avatar — can boost the confidence of college students so much that for up to twenty-four hours later, they're more likely to be successful taking a test at school and more outgoing in real-world social situations.

This "spill-over" effect of games means that young people who identify strongly as gamers have real-world talents and strengths that will undoubtedly serve them well in the future — if they understand that these are real skills and abilities, not just virtual ones. That's why I wanted to write *Reality Is Broken* to show gamers (and parents of gamers) exactly how playing games can prepare us to tackle challenges like curing cancer, ending world hunger, and stopping climate change. (Yes, it's true! There are games to help players do all of these things.)

Of course, there can always be too much of a good thing. Studies by both university researchers and the U.S. Army Mental Health Assessment Team show that playing games up to twenty-one hours a week can produce positive impacts on your health and happiness — especially if you're playing games face-to-face with friends and family, or playing cooperative games (rather than competitive games). That's why I personally recommend that parents of gamers spend as much time as they can playing, too. In fact, just this week, a new study by Brigham Young University's School of Family Life revealed that daughters who play video games with their parents report feeling much closer to their parents — and demonstrate significantly lower levels of aggression, behavior problems, and depression.

But when you hit twenty-eight hours a week of gaming or more, the time starts to distract you from real-life goals and other kinds of social interaction that are essential to leading a good life. Multiple studies have shown it's the twenty-one-hour mark that really makes the difference — more than three hours a day, and you're not going to get those positive impacts. Instead, you'll be at risk for negative impacts — like depression and social anxiety.

So what's the optimal level of gaming? For most people, an hour a day playing our favorite games will power up our ability to engage wholeheartedly with difficult challenges and strengthen our relationships with the people we care about most — while still letting us notice when it's time to stop playing in virtual worlds and bring our gamer strengths back to real life.

Reading the Genre

1. McGonigal argues for something that is counterintuitive, because many people think games are not good for us at all. How does she organize her own arguments and her research to respond to popular arguments against video games?

2. McGonigal is arguing for the positive effects of gaming for one to three hours a day, but she doesn't necessarily discuss the other things we might do with that time—things that might actually be even better for us. For instance, she cites studies that show that students perform better on tests after gaming. Yet wouldn't they be better off studying? Propose counterarguments or qualify the arguments that McGonigal makes in this essay to account for these other possibilities.

3. Look at how McGonigal takes risks with style in this essay, using exclamation points, short sentences, and a conversational tone. How could some of these strategies help her connect with some audiences but not others?

4. **WRITING:** Create a short "how-to" manual for gaming in college, using the arguments in McGonigal's proposal, in addition to your own personal opinions and some secondary research on the impact of gaming on college students. How can you play video games *and* do well in school?

5. **MULTIMODALITY—ADVERTISING POSTER:** Look for some examples of the "pro-social" games that McGonigal references in this proposal. Create a poster advertising the benefits of one of these games, utilizing the research McGonigal mentions in this article as evidence. Aim your advertisement at both young people and their parents.

PROPOSAL   Neil deGrasse Tyson is an astrophysicist, the current director of the Hayden Planetarium in New York, and an author dedicated to communicating scientific ideas to the public. Tyson used to host a science program, *Nova Science Now*, on PBS, and he continues to be a guest on *The Daily Show, Jeopardy*, and other programs. Tyson has also recently appeared as the host of the new version of the show *Cosmos*. In this proposal, which appeared in *Natural History* magazine in 2007, he considers what might happen if humans felt a little less significant.

The Cosmic Perspective

NEIL DEGRASSE TYSON

Of all the sciences cultivated by mankind, Astronomy is acknowledged to be, and undoubtedly is, the most sublime, the most interesting, and the most useful. For, by knowledge derived from this science, not only the bulk of the Earth is discovered . . . ; but our very faculties are enlarged with the grandeur of the ideas it conveys, our minds exalted above [their] low contracted prejudices.

—James Ferguson, *Astronomy Explained upon Sir Isaac Newton's Principles, and Made Easy to Those Who Have Not Studied Mathematics* (1757)

Long before anyone knew that the universe had a beginning, before we knew that the nearest large galaxy lies two and a half million light-years from Earth, before we knew how stars work or whether atoms exist, James Ferguson's enthusiastic introduction to his favorite science rang true. Yet his words, apart from their eighteenth-century flourish, could have been written yesterday.

But who gets to think that way? Who gets to celebrate this cosmic view of life? Not the migrant farmworker. Not the sweatshop worker. Certainly not the homeless person rummaging through the trash for food. You need the luxury of time not spent on mere survival. You need to live in a nation whose government values the search to understand humanity's place in the universe. You need a society in which intellectual pursuit can take you to the frontiers of discovery, and in which news of your discoveries can be routinely disseminated. By those measures, most citizens of industrialized nations do quite well.

Yet the cosmic view comes with a hidden cost. When I travel thousands of miles to spend a few moments in the fast-moving shadow of the Moon during a total solar eclipse, sometimes I lose sight of Earth.

When I pause and reflect on our expanding universe, with its galaxies hurtling away from one another, embedded within the ever-stretching, four-dimensional fabric of space and time, sometimes I forget that uncounted people walk this Earth without food or shelter, and that children are disproportionately represented among them.

When I pore over the data that establish the mysterious presence of dark matter and dark energy throughout the universe, sometimes I forget that every day—every twenty-four-hour rotation of Earth—people kill and get killed in the name of someone else's conception of God, and that some people who do not kill in the name of God kill in the name of their nation's needs or wants.

When I track the orbits of asteroids, comets, and planets, each one a pirouetting dancer in a cosmic ballet choreographed by the forces of gravity, sometimes I forget that too many people act in wanton disregard for the delicate interplay of Earth's atmosphere, oceans, and land, with consequences that our children and our children's children will witness and pay for with their health and well-being.

And sometimes I forget that powerful people rarely do all they can to help those who cannot help themselves.

I occasionally forget those things because, however big the world is—in our hearts, our minds, and our outsize atlases—the universe is even bigger. A depressing thought to some, but a liberating thought to me.

Consider an adult who tends to the traumas of a child: a broken toy, a scraped knee, a schoolyard bully. Adults know that kids have no clue what constitutes a genuine problem, because inexperience greatly limits their childhood perspective.

As grown-ups, dare we admit to ourselves that we, too, have a collective immaturity of view? Dare we admit that our thoughts and behaviors spring from a belief that the world revolves around us? Apparently not. And the evidence abounds. Part the curtains of society's racial, ethnic, religious, national, and cultural conflicts, and you find the human ego turning the knobs and pulling the levers.

Now imagine a world in which everyone, but especially people with power and influence, holds an expanded view of our place in the cosmos. With that perspective, our problems would shrink—or never arise at all—and we could celebrate our earthly differences while shunning the behavior of our predecessors who slaughtered each other because of them.

Back in February 2000, the newly rebuilt Hayden Planetarium featured a space show called *Passport to the Universe*, which took visitors on a virtual zoom from New York City to the edge of the cosmos. En route the audience saw Earth, then the solar system, then the 100 billion stars of the Milky Way galaxy shrink to barely visible dots on the planetarium dome.

Within a month of opening day, I received a letter from an Ivy League professor of psychology whose expertise was things that make people feel insignificant. I never knew one could specialize in such a field. The guy wanted to administer a before-and-after questionnaire to visitors, assessing the depth of their depression after viewing the show. *Passport to the Universe*, he wrote, elicited the most dramatic feelings of smallness he had ever experienced.

How could that be? Every time I see the space show (and others we've produced), I feel alive and spirited and connected. I also feel large, knowing that the goings-on within the three-pound human brain are what enabled us to figure out our place in the universe.

Allow me to suggest that it's the professor, not I, who has misread nature. His ego was too big to begin with, inflated by delusions of significance and fed by cultural assumptions that human beings are more important than everything else in the universe.

In all fairness to the fellow, powerful forces in society leave most of us susceptible. As was I . . . until the day I learned in biology class that more bacteria live and work in one centimeter of my colon than the number of people who have ever existed in the world. That kind of information makes you think twice about who—or what—is actually in charge.

From that day on, I began to think of people not as the masters of space and time but as participants in a great cosmic chain of being, with a direct genetic link across species both living and extinct, extending back nearly 4 billion years to the earliest single-celled organisms on Earth.

I know what you're thinking: We're smarter than bacteria.

No doubt about it, we're smarter than every other living creature that ever walked, crawled, or slithered on Earth. But how smart is that? We cook our food. We compose poetry and music. We do art and science. We're good at math. Even if you're bad at math, you're probably much better at it than the smartest chimpanzee, whose genetic identity varies in only trifling ways from ours. Try as they might, primatologists will never get a chimpanzee to learn the multiplication table or do long division.

If small genetic differences between us and our fellow apes account for our vast difference in intelligence, maybe that difference in intelligence is not so vast after all.

Imagine a life-form whose brainpower is to ours as ours is to a chimpanzee's. To such a species our highest mental achievements would be trivial. Their toddlers, instead of learning their ABCs on *Sesame Street*, would learn multivariable calculus on Boolean Boulevard. Our most complex theorems, our deepest philosophies, the cherished works of our most creative artists, would be projects their schoolkids bring home for Mom and Dad to display on the refrigerator door. These creatures would study Stephen Hawking (who occupies the same endowed professorship once held by Newton at the University of Cambridge) because he's slightly more clever than other humans, owing to his ability to do theoretical astrophysics and other rudimentary calculations in his head.

If a huge genetic gap separated us from our closest relative in the animal kingdom, we could justifiably celebrate our brilliance. We might be entitled to walk around thinking we're distant and distinct from our fellow creatures. But no such gap exists. Instead, we are one with the rest of nature, fitting neither above nor below, but within.

Need more ego softeners? Simple comparisons of quantity, size, and scale do the job well.

Take water. It's simple, common, and vital. There are more molecules of water in an eight-ounce cup of the stuff than there are cups of water in all the world's oceans. Every cup that passes through a single person and eventually rejoins the world's water supply holds enough molecules to mix 1,500 of them into every other cup of water in the world. No way around it: Some of the water you just drank passed through the kidneys of Socrates, Genghis Khan, and Joan of Arc.

How about air? Also vital. A single breathful draws in more air molecules than there are breathfuls of air in Earth's entire atmosphere. That means some of the air you just breathed passed through the lungs of Napoleon, Beethoven, Lincoln, and Billy the Kid.

Time to get cosmic. There are more stars in the universe than grains of sand on any beach, more stars than seconds have passed since Earth formed, more stars than words and sounds ever uttered by all the humans who ever lived.

Want a sweeping view of the past? Our unfolding cosmic perspective takes you there. Light takes time to reach Earth's observatories from the depths of space, and so you see objects and phenomena not as they are but as they once were. That means the universe acts like a giant time machine: The farther away you look, the further back in time you see—back almost to the beginning of time itself. Within that horizon of reckoning, cosmic evolution unfolds continuously, in full view.

Want to know what we're made of? Again, the cosmic perspective offers a bigger answer than you might expect. The chemical elements of the universe are forged in the fires of high-mass stars that end their lives in stupendous explosions, enriching their host galaxies with the chemical arsenal of life as we know it. The result? The four most common chemically active elements in the universe—hydrogen, oxygen, carbon, and nitrogen—are the four most common elements of life on Earth. We are not simply in the universe. The universe is in us.

Yes, we are stardust. But we may not be of this Earth. Several separate lines of research, when considered together, have forced investigators to reassess who we think we are and where we think we came from.

First, computer simulations show that when a large asteroid strikes a planet, the surrounding areas can recoil from the impact energy, catapulting rocks into space. From there, they can travel to—and land on—other planetary surfaces. Second, microorganisms can be hardy. Some survive the extremes of temperature, pressure, and radiation inherent in space travel. If the rocky flotsam from an impact hails from a planet with life, microscopic fauna could have stowed away in the rocks' nooks and crannies. Third, recent evidence suggests that shortly after the formation of our solar system, Mars was wet, and perhaps fertile, even before Earth was.

Those findings mean it's conceivable that life began on Mars and later seeded life on Earth, a process known as panspermia. So all earthlings might—just might—be descendants of Martians.

Again and again across the centuries, cosmic discoveries have demoted our self-image. Earth was once assumed to be astronomically unique, until astronomers learned that Earth is just another planet orbiting the Sun. Then we presumed the Sun was unique, until we learned that the countless stars of the night sky are suns themselves. Then we presumed our galaxy, the Milky Way, was the entire known universe, until we established that the countless fuzzy things in the sky are other galaxies, dotting the landscape of our known universe.

Today, how easy it is to presume that one universe is all there is. Yet emerging theories of modern cosmology, as well as the continually reaffirmed improbability that anything is unique, require that we remain open to the latest assault on our plea for distinctiveness: multiple universes, otherwise known as the multiverse, in which ours is just one of countless bubbles bursting forth from the fabric of the cosmos.

The cosmic perspective flows from fundamental knowledge. But it's more than just what you know. It's also about having the wisdom and insight to apply that knowledge to assessing our place in the universe. And its attributes are clear:

- The cosmic perspective comes from the frontiers of science, yet it's not solely the province of the scientist. The cosmic perspective belongs to everyone.
- The cosmic perspective is humble.
- The cosmic perspective is spiritual—even redemptive—but not religious.
- The cosmic perspective enables us to grasp, in the same thought, the large and the small.
- The cosmic perspective opens our minds to extraordinary ideas but does not leave them so open that our brains spill out, making us susceptible to believing anything we're told.
- The cosmic perspective opens our eyes to the universe, not as a benevolent cradle designed to nurture life but as a cold, lonely, hazardous place.
- The cosmic perspective shows Earth to be a mote, but a precious mote and, for the moment, the only home we have.
- The cosmic perspective finds beauty in the images of planets, moons, stars, and nebulae but also celebrates the laws of physics that shape them.
- The cosmic perspective enables us to see beyond our circumstances, allowing us to transcend the primal search for food, shelter, and sex.
- The cosmic perspective reminds us that in space, where there is no air, a flag will not wave—an indication that perhaps flag waving and space exploration do not mix.
- The cosmic perspective not only embraces our genetic kinship with all life on Earth but also values our chemical kinship with any yet-to-be discovered life in the universe, as well as our atomic kinship with the universe itself.

At least once a week, if not once a day, we might each ponder what cosmic truths lie undiscovered before us, perhaps awaiting the arrival of a clever thinker, an ingenious experiment, or an innovative space mission to reveal them. We might further ponder how those discoveries may one day transform life on Earth.

Absent such curiosity, we are no different from the provincial farmer who expresses no need to venture beyond the county line, because his forty acres meet all his needs. Yet if all our predecessors had felt that way, the farmer would instead be a cave dweller, chasing down his dinner with a stick and a rock.

During our brief stay on planet Earth, we owe ourselves and our descendants the opportunity to explore—in part because it's fun to do. But there's a far nobler reason. The day our knowledge of the cosmos ceases to expand, we risk regressing to the childish view that the universe figuratively and literally revolves around us. In that bleak world, arms-bearing, resource-hungry people and nations would be prone to act on their low contracted prejudices. And that would be the last gasp of human enlightenment—until the rise of a visionary new culture that could once again embrace the cosmic perspective.

Reading the Genre

1. Tyson offers a series of "ego softeners" in this proposal. How important is it to the success of this proposal for Tyson to soften the audience's egos, without shattering them or making readers defensive? How effectively does he do so?

2. Does Tyson consider counterarguments in this essay? Suggest some counterarguments to his proposal. What do we lose by embracing the cosmic perspective? (For more on counterpoints, see pp. 84, 86, and 87.)

3. **WRITING:** Identify a current problem or crisis in your community that a "cosmic perspective" could help solve. Propose how the public could be encouraged and educated to take such a perspective, and how that new perspective might lead to tangible actions to solve the problem.

4. **MULTIMODALITY — COSMIC CALENDAR:** Look at the "cosmic perspective" that Tyson outlines at the end of his proposal. He also suggests, "At least once a week, if not once a day, we might each ponder what cosmic truths lie undiscovered before us." Create a calendar that is at least one month long, and on every day in your calendar, add a fact or a question, a statistic or an image, that could help us to develop a more cosmic perspective.

SATIRICAL PROPOSAL   Kembrew McLeod is an activist, music critic, and documentary film producer. He focuses his work on issues of copyright and intellectual property and famously made an ironic point in 1997 by registering the phrase "Freedom of Expression" as a U.S. trademark. McLeod's books include *Freedom of Expression: Resistance and Repression in the Age of Intellectual Property* (2005), *Creative License: The Law and Culture of Digital Sampling* (2011), and *Pranksters: Making Mischief in the Modern World* (2014). He teaches communication at the University of Iowa and enjoys playing pranks.

The Huffington Post

Posted: June 29, 2010, at 12:58 PM
From: Kembrew McLeod

A Modest Free Market Proposal for Education Reform

Times are tough for public universities. Over the past quarter century, state legislatures have slashed college budgets — cuts that have only accelerated during this economic meltdown. We have been told to do more with less, make sacrifices, and be self-sufficient — and I couldn't agree more. Unlike those socialists lining up to mainline milk from the nanny state, there are many of us who favor fiscally sound solutions. We should teach our children well by following dogmatically free market principles that reject government meddling.

My modest proposal is multipronged and forward thinking. It would hand over all aspects of academic life to private companies, creating a university system that is more efficient, profitable even. In reimagining how higher education can be rebooted, we need to ask ourselves, "What would a liberal arts education look like if McDonald's funded it?" Killing many birds with one lethal stone, we can simultaneously solve the problems created by overstuffed state budgets, overpaid professors, and — as an added, unexpected bonus — plagiarism. Let me explain.

The first part of the plan involves the sponsorship of classes, in which companies would exchange cash and services for the prominent placement of their logos on syllabi and in teaching spaces. This is a no-brainer, especially because on-campus branding has expanded in recent years. Under this plan, rational economic decisions would play a greater role in determining course offerings; less popular, unprofitable classes would necessarily fall by the wayside.

My second proposal will be more controversial, for it involves radically rethinking the way undergraduate students approach their course work. These days, professors fret over undergrads using the services of "research assistance" companies — businesses that sell finished papers on every imaginable subject. Rather than siding with these fuddy-duddies, we should instead embrace this shift in student work habits. After all, the free market is influencing the decisions our students make, and it would be disastrous to regulate an emerging marketplace during these uncertain times.

It also seems morally wrong to force undergrads to waste their time on reading, researching, writing, and revising when their labor could be better spent working service jobs and other entry-level positions. This will allow them to buy prepackaged papers and still have spending money left over to inject into the economy — a win-win.

Only lazy students who are not gainfully employed would lose out. Additionally, those who carefully manage their money (or whose families have already done so) can purchase higher-quality papers that will earn them better grades: a one-dollar, one-vote approach to learning. While it is true that this shift in pedagogy will hurt some businesses — such as companies that produce plagiarism-detecting software such as TurnItIn.com — the overall fiscal impact for society will be positive.

The third and final part of my plan takes the economic potential of education to the next level, offering great rewards with virtually no risk. Still, I anticipate that some old-school professors will be alarmed by my suggestion that we should use this new education/business model to train future faculty. It's only fair that if we allow undergraduates to use research assistance companies, grad students should be allowed to do so as well. One such business, PhD-Dissertations.com, is leading the charge on this front. (When I first came across this Web site, I thought, Why hasn't anyone thought of this before? Talk about an untapped market!)

By no longer having to conduct original research themselves, graduate students will have more hours to spend in the classroom as adjunct instructors. Let's do the math. PhD-Dissertations.com charges $17.00 per page, which adds up to $3,400 for a 200-page dissertation (plus, their Web site states, "A discount of 10% applies to orders of 75+ pages!"). Although this might seem like a lot of money, consider the fact that most colleges pay adjuncts roughly the same, between $3,000 and $4,000, for each course taught per semester. Therefore, by just adding one extra course to his or her roster, a graduate student can pay for an entire dissertation in less than one academic year — while at the same time serving the university's undergraduate teaching needs. Once this new generation of scholar/project managers enters the profession, there will be no more need for traditional professors.

Following this course of action, universities can be transformed into a well-oiled machine that will generate more credit hours and, therefore, more tuition dollars. For years, college deans have argued that we need to find cheaper ways to process more students through the system. Predictably, many tenured radicals derisively use the phrase "credit factory" to describe this approach, but I think the industrial process is an apt metaphor for how universities should conduct their business. Fast food is another good model to follow, a point that is underscored on PhD-Dissertations .com's "Frequently Asked Questions" page:

> Will the material be one-of-a-kind and unique? Yes, of course. As they say at Jack in the Box, "We don't make it until you order it." We write all custom research materials from scratch, based on the specifications provided to us. Unlike other services with no sense of academic integrity, we do not copy-and-paste from writings that are freely available on the Internet.

Some will surely complain about this approach's "intellectually corrosive" effects, but these people — who have a practically medieval, pre-capitalist concept of what universities should do — are wrong. In fact, a legitimized research assistance industry will most definitely improve the quality of scholarly research and writing. Because these companies exist in the private sector, they naturally do a more efficient job than researchers in bloated college bureaucracies, which have extensive, wasteful workforce redundancies. In today's universities, some scholars examine similar topics, but using different perspectives. In other words, they hire multiple people to do a job fit for one!

Corporate research factories, on the other hand, can maximize the resources needed to produce top-notch scholarship better than any state-funded school. This is because research assistance companies have a streamlined division of labor: One specialized staff researcher writes, another proofreads, a different employee fact-checks, and another administrator can manage the whole project. As is noted on the home page for Student Network Resources, which owns PhD-Dissertations .com, "We created a highly advanced project management system for clients and writers to connect on a large scale"; only in the private sector can you achieve this level of efficiency.

Hard times call for tough choices and new ideas, which my plan will deliver. By creating synergistic links between universities and corporate sponsors — and by privatizing the work done by undergraduate student/workers and professors-in-training — we can create a lighter, leaner educational system that can better adapt to the realities of a changing world. More importantly, this approach will foster economic growth by turning the process of learning into a frictionless series of commodity exchanges. After all, what could go wrong?

Reading the Genre

1. This proposal essay is actually made up of three connected proposals. What are they, and how seriously does McLeod expect readers to take them?

2. Satire — the use of wit and irony to make a serious point — is a form of social commentary. What is McLeod criticizing with his use of satire?

3. Look up the meaning of *hyperbole* and consider how McLeod uses overstatement as a persuasive tool. How might this strategy work in a proposal that is not a satire? (See "Defend the proposal," p. 171).

4. **WRITING:** Because this is a satirical proposal, McLeod doesn't expect readers to follow through on his suggestions. Try to imagine real solutions to the problems McLeod addresses, and write a serious proposal for change.

5. **WRITING:** Using McLeod's satirical approach for inspiration, propose an outlandish change to another aspect of university life, beyond academics.

PROPOSAL FOR CHANGE   Peter Singer is a Princeton philosopher whose views on bioethics — animal rights, euthanasia, and reproduction, specifically — have been highly controversial. Singer is a utilitarian: He judges the morality of an action by its outcome. This essay first appeared in *People and Place*, a blog about "ideas that connect us."

People and Place

Posted: March 25, 2009, at 9:40 PM
From: Peter Singer

"One Person, One Share" of the Atmosphere

For most of human existence, people living only short distances apart might as well have been living in separate worlds. A river, a mountain range, a stretch of forest or desert: These were enough to cut people off from each other.

As a result, our moral intuitions evolved to deal with problems within our community, rather than with the impact of our actions on those far away. Resources like the atmosphere and the oceans seemed unlimited, and we have had no inhibitions against making the fullest use of them.

Over the past few centuries the isolation has dwindled, and now people living on opposite sides of the world are linked in ways previously unimaginable. Problems like climate change have revealed that by driving your car, you could be releasing carbon dioxide that is part of a causal chain leading to lethal floods in Bangladesh.

How can our ethics take account of this new situation?

"Enough and as Good"

Imagine that we live in a village in which everyone puts their wastes down a giant sink. The capacity of the sink to dispose of our wastes seems limitless, and as long as that situation continues, it is reasonable to believe that we are leaving "enough and as good" for others. No matter how much we pour down the sink, others can do the same.

This phrase "enough and as good" comes from John Locke's *Second Treatise on Civil Government*, published in 1690. In that work Locke says that the earth and its contents "belong to mankind in common." How, then, can there be private property? Because our labor is our own, and hence when we mix our labor with the land and its products, we make them our own. It has this effect, Locke says, as long as our appropriation does not prevent there being "enough and as good left in common for others."

Locke's justification of the acquisition of private property is the classic historical account of how property can be legitimately acquired, and it has served as the starting point for more recent discussions.

Now imagine that conditions change, so that the sink's capacity to carry away our wastes is used to the full. At this point, when we continue to throw our wastes down the sink we are no longer leaving "enough and as good" for others, and hence our right to unchecked waste disposal becomes questionable.

Think of that giant sink as our atmosphere and our wastes as carbon dioxide and other greenhouse gases. Once we have used up the atmosphere's capacity to absorb our gases without harmful consequences, it has become a finite resource on which various parties have competing claims. The problem is to allocate those claims justly.

Defining Equitable Distribution

During the 2000 U.S. presidential election, when the candidates were asked in a televised debate what they would do about global warming, George W. Bush said:

> I'll tell you one thing I'm not going to do is I'm not going to let the United States carry the burden for cleaning up the world's air, like the Kyoto treaty would have done. China and India were exempted from that treaty. I think we need to be more evenhanded.

As president, Bush frequently repeated this line of reasoning. Indeed, the issue of what constitutes evenhandedness, or fairness or equity, is perhaps the greatest hurdle to international action on climate change. But was Bush right to say that it is not evenhanded to expect the United States to restrict its emissions before China and India begin to restrict theirs?

There are various principles that people use to judge what is fair or evenhanded. In political philosophy, it is common to follow Robert Nozick, who distinguished between *historical principles* and *time-slice principles*.

A historical principle is one that says: To understand whether a given distribution of goods is just or unjust, we must ask how the situation came about; we must know its history. Are the parties entitled, by an originally justifiable acquisition and a chain of legitimate transfers, to the holdings they now have? If so, the present distribution is just. If not, rectification or compensation will be needed to produce a just distribution.

Looking at data for 1900 to 1999, we find that the United States, for example, with about 5 percent of the world's population, was responsible for about 30 percent of carbon dioxide emissions from fossil fuels, the primary source of greenhouse gases. Most of this carbon dioxide is still up in the atmosphere, contributing to global warming.

In this case, the application of the historical principle might be called "the polluter pays" or "you broke it, you fix it." It would assign responsibility proportionate to the amount that each country has contributed, a view that puts a heavy burden on the developed nations.

In their defense, it might be argued that at the time when the developed nations contributed most of their greenhouse gases into the atmosphere, they could not know of its limits in absorbing those gases. It would therefore be fairer to make a fresh start now and set standards that look to the future, rather than to the past.

This is the idea behind the time-slice principle. It looks at the existing distribution at a particular moment in time and asks whether that distribution satisfies some idea of fairness — irrespective of any preceding sequence of events.

An Equal Share for Everyone

If we begin by asking, "Why should anyone have a greater claim to part of the global atmospheric sink than any other?" then the first, and simplest response is: "No reason at all." Everyone has the same claim to part of the atmospheric sink as everyone else. This kind of equality seems self-evidently fair, at least as a starting point for discussion.

The Kyoto Protocol aimed to achieve a level for developed nations that was 5 percent below 1990 levels. Suppose that we focus on emissions for the entire planet and aim just to stabilize them. If we choose a target of 1996 emissions levels, then the allocation per person works out conveniently to about 1 metric ton of carbon per year. This becomes the basic equitable entitlement for every human being on the planet. (Note that emissions are sometimes expressed in terms of tons of carbon dioxide, rather than tons of carbon. One ton of carbon is equivalent to 3.7 tons of carbon dioxide.)

Now compare actual emissions for some key nations. In 2004, the United States produced 5.61 tons of carbon per person per year, while Japan, Germany, and the UK each produced less than 3 tons. China was at 1.05 and India at 0.34. This means that to reach an equal per capita annual emission limit of 1 ton, India would be able to increase its emissions three times. China, on the other hand, would need to stabilize its current emissions, and the United States would have to reduce its emissions to one-fifth of present levels.

One objection to this approach is that it gives countries an insufficient incentive to do anything about population growth. We can meet this objection by setting national allocations that are tied to a specified population, rather than letting them rise with an increase in population.

But since different countries have different proportions of young people about to reach reproductive age, this provision might produce greater hardship in countries that have younger populations. To overcome this, the per capita allocation could be based on an estimate of a country's population at some future date. Countries would then receive a reward in terms of an increased emission quota per citizen if they achieved a lower population than had been expected.

A Proposal

Each of these principles of fairness, or others, could be defended as the best one to take. I propose, both because of its simplicity, and hence its suitability as a political compromise, and because it seems likely to increase global welfare, that we support the principle of equal per capita shares of the capacity of the atmospheric sink, tied to the current projections of population growth per country for 2050.

Some will say that this is excessively harsh on industrialized nations, which will have to cut back the most on their output of greenhouse gases. Yet the one person, one share principle is more indulgent to the industrialized nations than some others, including the historical principle.

Allocating on the basis of equal per capita shares will be tremendously dislocating for the industrialized nations, and the mechanism of emissions trading can make this transition much easier. Emissions trading works on a simple economic principle: If you can buy something more cheaply than you can produce it yourself, you are better off buying it than making it. In this case, what you can buy will be a transferable quota to produce greenhouse gases, allocated on the basis of an equal per capita share.

Appropriate Scale

The ancient Greek iconoclast Diogenes, when asked what country he came from, is said to have replied: "I am a citizen of the world." Until recently, such thoughts have been the dreams of idealists. But now we are beginning to live in a global community. The impact of human activity on our atmosphere exemplifies the need for human beings to act globally. On this issue, as well as others, the planet should become the basic unit for our ethical thinking.

Reading the Genre

1. This essay is organized into five distinct sections. What does Singer do in each of them? How do the headings help readers follow his logic? (See "Creating a structure," p. 172, and Chapter 26, "Organization," p. 374.)

2. Where and how does Singer handle opposing viewpoints? Does he treat objections fairly? (See "Address counterpoints when necessary," p. 87, and Chapter 21, "Critical Thinking," p. 343.)

3. Notice Singer's use of personal pronouns—*we* and *they* especially—in this essay. How does the author's word choice influence the tone of his proposal? (See Chapter 32, "High, Middle, and Low Style," p. 400.)

4. How does this proposal incorporate research? How does Singer use hard evidence to support his claims about ethics and fairness? (See "Assemble your hard evidence," p. 83, and "Read sources to find evidence," p. 457.)

5. **WRITING:** Before he gets to his proposal, Singer reviews a series of alternative philosophies and acknowledges, "Each of these principles of fairness, or others, could be defended as the best one to take." Choose a principle other than the "equal per capita shares" approach that Singer advocates, and fashion a proposal around that idea of fairness. You might, for instance, support the "historical principle," defend George W. Bush's view, or argue for an approach that aggressively targets emission reduction rather than stabilization. (See "Examine prior solutions," p. 170.)

6. **MULTIMODALITY — PRESENTING DATA:** Choose one set of statistics discussed in this essay and present it in a visual format. (See Chapter 49, "Tables, Graphs, and Infographics," p. 550.)

68

Literary Analyses: Readings

GLORIA NAYLOR
From "The Meanings of a Word"

Beyond sexual misconduct and death, everything else was considered harmless for our young ears. And so among the anecdotes of the triumphs and disappointments in the various workings of their lives, the word *nigger* was used in my presence, but it was set within contexts and inflections that caused it to register in my mind as something else.

In the singular, the word was always applied to a man who had distinguished himself in some situation that brought their approval for his strength, intelligence, or drive:

"Did Johnny really do that?"

"I'm telling you, that nigger pulled in $6,000 of overtime last year. Said he got enough for a down payment on a house."

When used with a possessive adjective by a woman—"my nigger"—it became a term of endearment for her husband or boyfriend. But it could be more than just a term applied to a man. In their mouths it became the pure essence of manhood—a disembodied force that channeled their past history of struggle and present survival against the odds into a victorious statement of being: "Yeah, that old foreman found out quick enough—you don't mess with a nigger."

In the plural, it became a description of some group within the community that had overstepped the bounds of decency as my family defined it. Parents who neglected their children, a drunken couple who fought in public, people who simply refused to look for work, those with excessively dirty mouths or unkempt households were all "trifling niggers." This particular circle could forgive hard times, unemployment, the occasional bout of depression—they had gone through all of that themselves—but the unforgivable sin was a lack of self-respect.

A woman could never be a "nigger" in the singular, with its connotations of confirming worth. The noun *girl* was its closest equivalent in that sense, but only when used in direct address and regardless of the gender doing the addressing. *Girl* was a token of respect for a woman. The one-syllable word was drawn out to sound like three in recognition of the extra ounce of wit, nerve, or daring that the woman had shown in the situation under discussion. "G-i-r-l, stop. You mean you said that to his face?"

But if the word was used in a third-person reference or shortened so that it almost snapped out of the mouth, it always involved some element of communal disapproval. And age became an important factor in these exchanges. It was only between individuals of the same generation, or from any older person to a younger (but never the other way around), that girl would be considered a compliment.

Consider multiple meanings.

Though Gloria Naylor is not specifically analyzing a literary work in her famous essay, she is carefully analyzing language. Importantly, Naylor is considering the multiple meanings that single words can have, depending on how they are spoken, when, and by whom. Naylor examines the ways that the words *nigger* and *girl* come to mean different things depending on context. This sort of close attention is necessary to any analysis of language or literature; both readers and writers must be open to the ways that words can mean very different things to different audiences.

In your own literary analysis, or just in the notes you take as you read a work of literature, identify contentious or seemingly powerful words. These might be words that appear frequently—or rarely, but with great effect. Then investigate how these words might mean different things if spoken by different people, if spoken *to* different people, and if spoken in different times and places. Writers choose their language very deliberately, and deciphering the meaning of that language will help you gain a greater understanding of the work as a whole.

When you begin to organize your analysis, layer your interpretations of these important words within your writing, as Naylor does. That is, offer one reading of the meaning of the word, then offer an alternative reading, and then offer yet another possibility. This technique can be used in any literary or rhetorical analysis essay, either as a brainstorming strategy to uncover deeper questions or as an organizational strategy to bring together a broad analysis. Look for more than one way to interpret any literary or rhetorical text, considering not just what the words mean to you, but what they could mean to a variety of audiences, and what the words might mean if they were phrased just slightly differently. Building this kind of flexibility will allow you to see that, as Naylor suggests elsewhere in her essay, language "achieves its power in the dynamics of a fleeting moment."

FORMAL ANALYSIS   Adam Bradley teaches literature at the University of Colorado, Boulder. An expert scholar on both hip-hop poetics and the writer Ralph Ellison, he is the coeditor of the *Yale Anthology of Rap* (2010) and of Ellison's posthumously published (and unfinished) novel *Three Days Before the Shooting . . .* (2010). This essay comes from *Book of Rhymes* (2009), an in-depth analysis of rap as poetry.

ADAM BRADLEY

Rap Poetry 101

Prologue

This is hip hop. You are in a small club, standing room only. Maybe it's the Roots or Common or some underground group about to perform. Bodies press tightly against you. Blue wreaths of smoke hang just above your head. From the four-foot speakers at the front of the stage, you hear the DJ spinning hip-hop classics — A Tribe Called Quest, De La Soul, Rakim — charging the crowd as it waits, five minutes, ten minutes, longer, for the show to begin.

As the music fades to silence, a disembodied voice over the PA system announces the headliner. Lights grow warm, blue turns to yellow, then to red. The first beat hits hard, and the crowd roars as the MC — the rapper, hip hop's lyrical master of ceremonies — glides to the front of the stage. Hands reach for the sky. Heads bob to the beat. The crowd is a living thing, animated by the rhythm. It can go on like this for hours.

Now imagine this. It happens just as the performance reaches its peak. First the melody drops out, then the bass, and finally the drums. The stage is now silent and empty save for a lone MC, kicking rhymes a cappella. His voice fades from a shout to a whisper, then finally to nothing at all. As he turns to leave, you notice something stranger still: lyrics projected in bold print against the back of the stage. It's like you're looking directly into an MC's book of rhymes. The words scroll along in clear, neat lines against the wall. People stand amazed. Some begin to boo. Some start to leave.

But you remain, transfixed by the words. You notice new things in the familiar lyrics: word-play, metaphors and similes, rhymes upon rhymes, even within the lines. You notice structures and forms, sound and silence. You even start to hear a beat; it comes from the language itself, a rhythm the words produce in your mind. You're bobbing your head again. People around you, those who remain, are doing it too. There's a group of you, smaller than before but strong, rocking to an inaudible beat.

The change is subtle at first. Maybe it's a stage light flickering back to life. Maybe it's a snare hit punctuating that inaudible rhythm. But now the lights burn brighter, the beat hits harder than ever, the MC bounds back on stage, the crowd reaches a frenzy. It's the same song, just remixed.

Through the boom of the bass you can still somehow hear the low rhythm the words make. Lines of lyrics pass across your mind's eye while the sound from the speakers vibrates your ear-drums. For the first time you see how the two fit together—the sight and the sound. Rap hasn't changed, but you have. This is the poetry of hip hop.

Rap Poetry 101

I start to think and then I sink
into the paper like I was ink.
When I'm writing I'm trapped in between the lines,
I escape when I finish the rhyme . . .
— Eric B. & Rakim, "I Know You Got Soul"

A book of rhymes is where MCs write lyrics. It is the basic tool of the rapper's craft. Nas raps about "writin' in my book of rhymes, all the words pass the margin." Mos Def boasts about sketching "lyrics so visual / they rent my rhyme books at your nearest home video." They both know what Rakim knew before them, that the book of rhymes is where rap becomes poetry.

Every rap song is a poem waiting to be performed. Written or freestyled, rap has a poetic structure that can be reproduced, a deliberate form an MC creates for each rhyme that differentiates it, if only in small ways, from every other rhyme ever conceived. Like all poetry, rap is defined by the art of the line. Metrical poets choose the length of their lines to correspond to particular rhythms — they write in iambic pentameter or whatever other meter suits their desires. Free verse poets employ conscious line breaks to govern the reader's pace, to emphasize particular words, or to accomplish any one of a host of other poetic objectives. In a successful poem, line breaks are never casual or accidental. Rewrite a poem in prose and you'll see it deflate like a punctured lung, expelling life like so much air.

Line breaks are the skeletal system of lyric poetry. They give poems their shape and distinguish them from all other forms of literature. While prose writers usually break their lines wherever the page demands — when they reach the margin, when the computer drops their word to the next line — poets claim that power for themselves, ending lines in ways that underscore the specific design of their verse. Rap poets are no different.

Rap is poetry, but its popularity relies in part on people not recognizing it as such. After all, rap is for good times; we play it in our cars, hear it at parties and at clubs. By contrast, most people associate poetry with hard work; it is something to be studied in school or puzzled over for hidden insights. Poetry stands at an almost unfathomable distance from our daily lives, or at least so it seems given how infrequently we seek it out.

This hasn't always been the case; poetry once had a prized place in both public and private affairs. At births and deaths, weddings and funerals, festivals and family gatherings, people would recite poetry to give shape to their feelings. Its relative absence today says something about us — our culture's short attention span, perhaps, or the dominance of other forms of entertainment — but also about poetry itself. While the last century saw an explosion of poetic productivity, it also marked a decided shift toward abstraction. As the poet Adrian Mitchell observed, "Most people ignore poetry because most poetry ignores most people."

Rap never ignores its listeners. Quite the contrary, it aggressively asserts itself, often without invitation, upon our consciousness. Whether boomed out of a passing car, played at a sports stadium, or piped into a mall while we shop, rap is all around us. Most often, it expresses its meaning quite plainly. No expertise is required to listen. You don't need to take an introductory course or read a handbook; you don't need to watch an instructional video or follow an online tutorial. But, as with most things in life, the pleasure to be gained from rap increases exponentially with just a little studied attention.

Rap is public art, and rappers are perhaps our greatest public poets, extending a tradition of lyricism that spans continents and stretches back thousands of years. Thanks to the engines of global commerce, rap is now the most widely disseminated poetry in the history of the world. Of course, not all rap is great poetry, but collectively it has revolutionized the way our culture relates to the spoken word. Rappers at their best make the familiar unfamiliar through rhythm, rhyme, and wordplay. They refresh the language by fashioning patterned and heightened variations of everyday speech. They expand our understanding of human experience by telling stories we might not otherwise hear. The best MCs—like Rakim, Jay-Z, Tupac, and many others—deserve consideration alongside the giants of American poetry. We ignore them at our own expense.

Hip hop emerged out of urban poverty to become one of the most vital cultural forces of the past century. The South Bronx may seem an unlikely place to have birthed a new movement in poetry. But in defiance of inferior educational opportunities and poor housing standards, a generation of young people—mostly black and brown—conceived innovations in rhythm, rhyme, and wordplay that would change the English language itself. In *Can't Stop Won't Stop: A History of the Hip-Hop Generation*, Jeff Chang vividly describes how rap's rise from the 1970s through the early 1980s was accompanied by a host of social and economic forces that would seem to stifle creative expression under the weight of despair. "An enormous amount of creative energy was now ready to be released from the bottom of American society," he writes, "and the staggering implications of this moment eventually would echo around the world." As one of the South Bronx's own, rap legend KRS-One, explains, "Rap was the final conclusion of a generation of creative people oppressed with the reality of lack."

Hip hop's first generation fashioned an art form that draws not only from the legacy of Western verse, but from the folk idioms of the African diaspora; the musical legacy of jazz, blues, and funk; and the creative capacities conditioned by the often harsh realities of people's everyday surroundings. These artists commandeered the English language, the forms of William Shakespeare and Emily Dickinson, as well as those of Sonia Sanchez and Amiri Baraka, to serve their own expressive and imaginative purposes. Rap gave voice to a group hardly heard before by America at large, certainly never heard in their own often profane, always assertive words. Over time, the poetry and music they made would command the ears of their block, their borough, the nation, and eventually the world.

While rap may be new-school music, it is old-school poetry. Rather than resembling the dominant contemporary form of free verse — or even the free-form structure of its hip-hop cousin, spoken word, or slam poetry, rap bears a stronger affinity to some of poetry's oldest forms, such as the strong-stress meter of *Beowulf* and the ballad stanzas of the bardic past. As in metrical verse, the lengths of rap's lines are governed by established rhythms — in rap's case, the rhythm of the beat itself.

The beat in rap is poetic meter rendered audible. Rap follows a dual rhythmic relationship whereby the MC is liberated to pursue innovations of syncopation and stress that would sound chaotic without the regularity of the musical rhythm. The beat and the MC's flow, or cadence, work together to satisfy the audience's musical and poetic expectations: most notably, that rap establish and maintain rhythmic patterns while creatively disrupting those patterns, through syncopation and other pleasing forms of rhythmic surprise.

Simply put, a rap verse is the product of one type of rhythm (that of language) being fitted to another (that of music). Great pop lyricists, Irving Berlin or John

Lennon or Stevie Wonder, match their words not only to the rhythm of the music, but to melodies and harmonies as well. For the most part, MCs need concern themselves only with the beat. This fundamental difference means that MCs resemble literary poets in ways that most other songwriters do not. Like all poets, rappers write primarily with a beat in mind. Rap's reliance on spare, beat-driven accompaniment foregrounds the poetic identity of the language.

Divorced from most considerations of melody and harmony, rap lyrics are liberated to live their lives as pure expressions of poetic and musical rhythm. Even when rap employs rich melodies and harmonies—as is often the case, for instance, in the music of Kanye West—rhythm remains the central element of sound. This puts rap's dual rhythms in even closer proximity to one another than they might usually be in other musical genres. Skilled MCs underscore the rhythm of the track in the rhythm of their flows and the patterns of their rhymes. As a consequence, the lyrics rappers write are more readily separated from their specific musical contexts and presented in written form as poetry. The rhythm comes alive on the page because so much of it is embedded in the language itself.

Many of the reasonable arguments critics offer to distinguish musical lyrics from literary poetry do not apply to rap. One of the most common objections, voiced best by the critic Simon Frith, is that musical lyrics do not need to generate the highly sophisticated poetic effects that create the "music" of verse written for the page. Indeed, the argument goes, if a lyric is too poetically developed it will likely distract from the music itself. A good poem makes for a lousy lyric, and a great lyric for a second-rate poem. Rap defies such conventional wisdom. By unburdening itself from the requirements of musical form, rap is free to generate its own poetic textures independent of the music. Another objection is that popular lyric lacks much of the formal structure of literary verse. Rap challenges this objection as well by crafting intricate structures of sound and rhyme, creating some of the most scrupulously formal poetry composed today.

Rap's poetry can usefully be approached as literary verse while still recognizing its essential identity as music. There's no need to disparage one to respect the other. In fact, perhaps more than any other lyrical form, rap demands that we acknowledge its dual identity as word and song.

The fact that rap is music does not disqualify it as poetry; quite the contrary, it asserts rap's poetic identity all the more. The ancient Greeks called their lyrical poetry *ta mele*, which means "poems to be sung." For them and for later generations, poetry, in the words of Walter Pater, "aspires towards the condition of music." It has only been since the early twentieth century that music has taken a backseat to meaning in poetry. As the poet Edward Hirsch writes, "The lyric poem always walks the line between speaking and singing. . . . Poetry is not speech exactly—verbal art is deliberately different than the way that people actually talk—and yet it is always in relationship to speech, to the spoken word."

Like all poetry, rap is not speech exactly, nor is it precisely song, and yet it employs elements of both. Rap's earliest performers understood this. On "Adventures of Super Rhymes (Rap)" from 1980, just months after rap's emergence on mainstream radio, Jimmy Spicer attempted to define this new form:

> It's the new thing, makes you wanna swing
> While us MCs rap, doin' our thing
> It's not singin' like it used to be
> No, it's rappin' to the rhythm of the sure-shot beat
> It goes one for the money, two for the show
> You got my beat, now here I go

Rap is an oral poetry, so it naturally relies more heavily than literary poetry on devices of sound. The MC's poetic toolbox shares many of the same basic instruments as the literary poet's, but it also includes others specifically suited to the demands of oral expression. These include copious use of rhyme, both as a mnemonic device and as a form of rhythmic pleasure; as well as poetic tropes that rely upon sonic identity, like homonyms and puns. Add to this those elements the MC draws from music — tonal quality, vocal inflection, and so forth — and rap reveals itself as a poetry uniquely fitted to oral performance.

Earlier pop lyricists like Cole Porter or Lorenz Hart labored over their lyrics; they were not simply popular entertainers, they were poets. Great MCs represent a continuation and an amplification of this vital tradition of lyrical craft. The lyrics to Porter's "I Got You Under My Skin" are engaging when read on the page without their melodic accompaniment; the best rap lyrics are equally engrossing, even without the specific context of their performances. Rap has no sheet music because it doesn't need it — rapping itself rarely has harmonies and melodies to transcribe — but it *does* have a written form worth reconstructing, one that testifies to its value, both as music and as poetry. That form begins with a faithful transcription of lyrics.

Rap lyrics are routinely mistranscribed, not simply on the numerous Web sites offering lyrics to go, but even on an artist's own liner notes and in hip-hop books and periodicals. The same rhyme might be written dozens of different ways — different line breaks, different punctuation, even different words. The goal should be to transcribe rap verses in such a way that they represent on the page as closely as possible what we hear with our ears.

The standardized transcription method proposed here may differ from those used by MCs in their own rhyme books. Tupac, for instance, counted his bars by couplets. Rappers compose their verses in any number of ways; what they write need only make sense to them. But an audience requires a standardized form organized around objective principles rather than subjective habits. Serious readers need a common way of transcribing rap lyrics so that they can discuss rap's formal attributes with one another without confusion.

Transcribing rap lyrics is a small but essential skill, easily acquired. The only prerequisite is being able to count to four in time to the beat. Transcribing lyrics to the beat is an intuitive way of translating the lyricism that we hear into poetry that we can read, without sacrificing the specific relationship of words to music laid down by the MC's performance. By preserving the integrity of each line in relation to the beat, we give rap the respect it deserves as poetry. Sloppy transcriptions make it all but impossible to glean anything but the most basic insights into the verse. Careful ones, on the other hand, let us see into the inner workings of the MC's craft through the lyrical artifact of its creation.

The MC's most basic challenge is this: When given a beat, what do you do? The beat is rap's beginning. Whether it's the hiccups and burps of a Timbaland track, the percussive assault of a Just Blaze beat, knuckles knocking on a lunchroom table, a human beatbox, or simply the metronomic rhythm in an MC's head as he spits a cappella rhymes, the beat defines the limits of lyrical possibility. In transcribing rap lyrics, we must have a way of representing the beat on the page.

The vast majority of rap beats are in 4/4 time, which means that each musical measure (or bar) comprises four quarter-note beats. For the rapper, one beat in a bar is akin to the literary poet's metrical foot. Just as the fifth metrical foot marks the end of a pentameter line, the fourth beat of a given bar marks the end of the MC's line. One line, in other words, is what an MC can deliver in a single musical measure — one poetic line equals one musical bar. So when an MC spits sixteen bars, we should understand this as sixteen lines of rap verse.

To demonstrate this method of lyrical transcription, let's take a fairly straightforward example: Melle Mel's first verse on Grandmaster Flash and the Furious Five's classic "The Message."

One   TWO   Three   FOUR
Standing on the front stoop, hangin' out the window,
watching all the cars go by, roaring as the breezes blow.

Notice how the naturally emphasized words ("standing," "front," "hangin'," "window," etc.) fall on the strong beats. These are two fairly regular lines, hence the near uniformity of the pair and the strong-beat accents on particular words. The words are in lockstep with the beat. Mark the beginning of each poetic line on the one and the end of the line on the four.

Not all lines, however, are so easily transcribed; many complications can occur in the process of transcription. Consider the famous opening lines from this very same song:

One   TWO Three FOUR
Broken glass everywhere,
people pissin' on the stairs, you know they just don't care.

Looking at the two lines on the page, one might think that they had been incorrectly transcribed. The only thing that suggests they belong together is the end rhyme ("everywhere" and "care"). How can each of these lines—the first half as long as the second, and with fewer than half the total syllables—take up the same four-beat measure? The answer has everything to do with performance. Melle Mel delivers the first line with a combination of dramatic pause and exaggerated emphasis. He begins rhyming a little behind the beat, includes a caesura (a strong phrasal pause within the line) between "glass" and "everywhere," and then dramatically extenuates the pronunciation of "everywhere." Were it not for an accurate transcription, these poetic effects would be lost.

Sometimes rap poets devise intricate structures that give logical shape to their creations. Using patterns of rhyme, rhythm, and line, these structures reinforce an individual verse's fusion of form and meaning. While literary poetry often follows highly regularized forms—a sonnet, a villanelle, a ballad stanza—rap is rarely so formally explicit, favoring instead those structures drawn naturally from oral expression. Upon occasion, however, rap takes on more formal structures, either by happenstance or by conscious design. For instance, Long Beach's Crooked I begins the second verse of "What That Mean" by inserting an alternating quatrain, switching up the song's established pattern of rhyming consecutive lines.

Shorty saw him comin' in a glare
I pass by like a giant blur
What she really saw was Tim Duncan in the air
Wasn't nothin' but a Flyin' Spur

By rhyming two pairs of perfect rhymes *abab* ("glare" with "air" and "blur" with "spur"), Crooked I fashions a duality of sound that underscores the two perspectives he describes: that of the woman onlooker and that of the MC in his speeding car. By temporarily denying the listener's expectation of rhyme, he creates a sense of heightened anticipation and increased attention. Using this new rhyme pattern shines a spotlight on the playful metaphor at the center of the verse: What the woman saw was the San Antonio Spurs' MVP Tim Duncan in the air, otherwise known as a flying Spur, otherwise known as his luxury automobile, a Bentley Continental Flying Spur. The mental process of deciphering the metaphor, nearly instantaneous for those familiar with the reference and likely indecipherable for anyone else, is facilitated by the rhyming structure of the verse. Rhyme and wordplay work together to create a sense of poetic satisfaction.

Rap's poetry is best exemplified in these small moments that reveal conscious artistry at work in places we might least expect. It is this sense of craft that connects the best poetry of the past with the best rap of today. Consider the following two verses side by side: On the left is Langston Hughes's "Sylvester's Dying Bed," written in 1931; on the right is a transcription of Ice-T's "6 'N the Mornin'," released in 1987. Though distanced by time, these lyrics are joined by form.

Hughes's form relies upon splitting the conventional four-beat line in half, a pattern I have followed with Ice-T's verse for the purposes of comparison; I might just as easily have rewritten Hughes's lines as two sets of rhyming couplets. This adjustment aside, the two lyrics are nearly identical in form. Each employs a two-beat line (or a four-beat line cut in two) with an *abcb* rhyme pattern. They even share the same syntactical units, with *end stops* (a grammatical pause for punctuation at the end of a line of verse) on lines two, four, six, and eight. Both draw upon the rhythms of the vernacular, the language as actually spoken. This formal echo, reaching across more than a half century of black poetic expression, suggests a natural affinity of forms.

I woke up this mornin'	Six in the mornin'
'Bout half past three.	Police at my door.
All the womens in town	Fresh Adidas squeak
Was gathered round me.	Across my bathroom floor.
Sweet gals was a-moanin',	Out my back window,
"Sylvester's gonna die!"	I made my escape.
And a hundred pretty mamas	Don't even get a chance
Bowed their heads to cry.	To grab my old school tape.

Rap lyrics properly transcribed reveal themselves in ways not possible when listening to rap alone. Seeing rap on the page, we understand it for what it is: a small machine of words. We distinguish end rhymes from internal rhymes, end-stopped lines from enjambed ones, patterns from disruptions. Of course, nothing can replace the listening experience, whether in your headphones or at a show. Rather than replacing the music, reading rap as poetry heightens both enjoyment and understanding. Looking at rhymes on the page slows things down, allowing listeners — now readers — to discover familiar rhymes as if for the first time.

Walt Whitman once proclaimed that "great poets need great audiences." For over thirty years, rap has produced more than its share of great poets. Now it is our turn to become a great audience, repaying their efforts with the kind of close attention to language that rap's poetry deserves.

Reading the Genre

1. What is the thesis of this literary analysis? How does Bradley use both rap lyrics and other writers' analyses as evidence to support his claims? Are you persuaded by his argument? (See "Use texts for evidence," p. 186; "Find good sources," p. 197; and "Read sources to find evidence," p. 457.)

2. This essay opens with a scene in a club. How does Bradley's introduction set up and support his main idea? (See Chapter 30, "Introductions and Conclusions," p. 391.)

3. Bradley compares the genres of poetry and rap lyrics. What similarities does he find? How does the comparison support his argument that rap is a form of poetry? (See "Focus on genre," p. 196.)

4. **WRITING:** Pick your favorite hip-hop song or select one from *Billboard*'s list of recent hits (www.billboard.com/charts/r-b-hip-hop-songs#/charts/r-b-hip-hop-songs). Using the terminology that Bradley introduces and the method of transcription he describes, write a literary analysis essay of the song's lyrics.

5. **MULTIMODALITY — PERFORMANCE:** Bradley's analysis asks readers to imagine hip-hop songs without music to appreciate the lyrics as poetry. Try doing the opposite: Choose a traditional poem and perform it as a rap. Consider what the music video might look like for this poem.

TEXTUAL ANALYSIS   Zadie Smith wrote her first novel, *White Teeth* (2000), when she was a twenty-two-year-old student at Cambridge in the UK. Her most recent novel, *NW*, was published in 2012. She is also a very successful and influential cultural critic. This literary analysis comes from *Changing My Mind* (2010), a book of "occasional essays."

ZADIE SMITH

Their Eyes Were Watching God: What Does *Soulful* Mean?

When I was fourteen I was given *Their Eyes Were Watching God* by my mother. I was reluctant to read it. I knew what she meant by giving it to me, and I resented the inference. In the same spirit she had introduced me to *Wide Sargasso Sea* and *The Bluest Eye*, and I had not liked either of them (better to say, I had not *allowed* myself to like either of them). I preferred my own freely chosen, heterogeneous reading list. I flattered myself I ranged widely in my reading, never choosing books for genetic or sociocultural reasons. Spotting *Their Eyes Were Watching God* unopened on my bedside table, my mother persisted:

"But you'll like it."

"Why, because she's *black*?"

"No — because it's really good writing."

I had my own ideas of "good writing." It was a category that did not include aphoristic or overtly "lyrical" language, mythic imagery, accurately rendered "folk speech," or the love tribulations of women. My literary defenses were up in preparation for *Their Eyes Were Watching God*. Then I read the first page:

> Ships at a distance have every man's wish on board. For some they come in with the tide. For others they sail forever on the horizon, never out of sight, never landing

until the Watcher turns his eyes away in resignation, his dreams mocked to death by Time. That is the life of men.

Now, women forget all those things they don't want to remember, and remember everything they don't want to forget. The dream is the truth. Then they act and do things accordingly.

It was an aphorism, yet it had me pinned to the ground, unable to deny its strength. It capitalized *Time* (I was against the capitalization of abstract nouns), but still I found myself melancholy for these nameless men and their inevitable losses. The second part, about women, struck home. It remains as accurate a description of my mother and me as I have ever read: *Then they act and do things accordingly*. Well, all right then, I relaxed in my chair a little and laid down my pencil. I inhaled that book. Three hours later I was finished and crying a lot, for reasons that both were, and were not, to do with the tragic finale.

I lost many literary battles the day I read *Their Eyes Were Watching God*. I had to concede that occasionally aphorisms have their power. I had to give up the idea that Keats had a monopoly on the lyrical:

She was stretched on her back beneath the pear tree soaking in the alto chant of the visiting bees, the gold of the sun and the panting breath of the breeze when the inaudible voice of it all came to her. She saw a dust-nearing bee sink into the sanctum of a bloom; the thousand sister-calyxes arch to meet the love embrace and the ecstatic shiver of the tree from root to tiniest branch creaming in every blossom and frothing with delight. So this was a marriage! She had been summoned to behold a revelation. Then Janie felt a pain remorseless sweet that left her limp and languid.[1]

I had to admit that mythic language is startling when it's good:

Death, that strange being with the huge square toes who lived way in the West. The great one who lived in the straight house like a platform without sides to it, and without a roof. What need has Death for a cover, and what winds can blow against him?

My resistance to dialogue (encouraged by Nabokov, whom I idolized) struggled and then tumbled before Hurston's ear for black colloquial speech. In the mouths of unlettered people she finds the bliss of quotidian metaphor:

"If God don't think no mo' 'bout 'em than Ah do, they's a lost ball in de high grass."

Of wisdom lightly worn:

"To my thinkin' mourning oughtn't tuh last no longer'n grief."

Her conversations reveal individual personalities, accurately, swiftly, as if they had no author at all:

"Where y'all come from in sich uh big haste?" Lee Coker asked. "Middle Georgy," Starks answered briskly. "Joe Starks is mah name, from in and through Georgy."

"You and yo' daughter goin' tuh join wid us in fellowship?" the other reclining figure asked. "Mighty glad to have yuh. Hicks is the name. Guv'nor Amos Hicks from Buford, South Carolina. Free, single, disengaged."

"I god, Ah ain't nowhere near old enough to have no grown daughter. This here is mah wife."

Hicks sank back and lost interest at once.

"Where is de Mayor?" Starks persisted. "Ah wants tuh talk wid *him*."

"Youse uh mite too previous for dat," Coker told him. "Us ain't got none yit."

Above all, I had to let go of my objection to the love tribulations of women. The story of Janie's progress through three marriages confronts the reader with the significant idea that the choice one makes between partners, between one man and another (or one woman and another) stretches beyond romance. It is, in the end, the choice between values, possibilities, futures, hopes, arguments (shared concepts that fit the world as you experience it), languages (shared words that fit the world as you believe it to be), and lives. A world you share with Logan Killicks is evidently not the same world you would share with Vergible "Tea Cake" Woods. In these two discrete worlds, you will not even think the same way; a mind trapped with Logan is freed with Tea Cake. But who, in this context, dare speak of freedoms? In practical terms, a black woman in turn-of-the-century America, a woman like Janie, or like Hurston herself, had approximately the same civil liberties as a farm animal: "De nigger woman is de mule uh de world." So goes Janie's grandmother's famous line — it hurt my pride to read it. It hurts Janie, too; she rejects the realpolitik of her grandmother, embarking on an existential revenge that is of the imagination and impossible to restrict:

> She knew that God tore down the old world every evening and built a new one by sun-up. It was wonderful to see it take form with the sun and emerge from the gray dust of its making. The familiar people and things had failed her so she hung over the gate and looked up the road towards way off.

That part of Janie that is looking for someone (or something) that "spoke for far horizon" has its proud ancestors in Elizabeth Bennet, in Dorothea Brooke, in Jane Eyre, even — in a very debased form — in Emma Bovary. Since the beginning of fiction concerning the love tribulations of women (which is to say, since the beginning of fiction), the "romantic quest" aspect of these fictions has been too often casually ridiculed: Not long ago I sat down to dinner with an American woman who told me how disappointed she had been to finally read *Middlemarch* and find that it was "Just this long, whiny, trawling search for a man!" Those who read *Middlemarch* in that way will find little in *Their Eyes Were Watching God* to please them. It's about a girl who takes some time to find the man she really loves. It is about the discovery of self in and through another. It implies that even the dark and terrible banality of racism can recede to a vanishing point when you understand, and are understood by, another human being. Goddammit if it doesn't claim that love sets you free. These days "self-actualization" is the aim, and if you can't do it alone you are admitting a weakness. The potential rapture of human relationships to which Hurston gives unabashed expression, the profound "self-crushing love" that Janie feels for Tea Cake, may, I suppose, look like the dull finale of a "long, whiny, trawling search for a man." For Tea Cake and Janie, though, the choice of each other is experienced not as desperation, but as discovery, and the need felt on both sides causes them joy, not shame. That Tea Cake would not be *our* choice, that we disapprove of him often, and despair of him occasionally, only lends power to the portrait. He seems to act with freedom, and Janie to choose him freely. We have no power; we only watch. Despite the novel's fairy-tale structure (as far as husbands go, third time's the charm), it is not a novel of wish fulfillment, least of all the fulfillment of *our* wishes.[2] It is odd to diagnose weakness where lovers themselves do not feel it.

After that first reading of the novel, I wept, and not only for Tea Cake, and not simply for the perfection of the writing, nor even the real loss I felt upon leaving the world contained in its pages. It meant something more than all that to me, something I could not, or would not, articulate. Later, I took it to the dinner table, still holding on to it, as we do sometimes with books we are not quite ready to relinquish.

"So?" my mother asked.

I told her it was basically sound.

At fourteen, I did Zora Neale Hurston a critical disservice. I feared my "extraliterary" feelings for her. I wanted to be an objective aesthete and not a sentimental fool. I disliked the idea of "identifying" with the fiction I read: I wanted to like Hurston because she represented "good writing," not because she represented me. In the two decades since, Zora Neale Hurston has gone from being a well-kept, well-loved secret among black women of my mother's generation to an entire literary industry— biographies[3] and films and Oprah and African American literature departments all pay homage to her life[4] and work as avatars of black woman-ness. In the process, a different kind of critical disservice is being done to her, an overcompensation in the opposite direction. In *Their Eyes Were Watching God*, Janie is depressed by Joe Starks's determination to idolize her: He intends to put her on a lonely pedestal before the whole town and establish a symbol (the Mayor's Wife) in place of the woman she is. Something similar has been done to Hurston herself. She is like Janie, set on her porch-pedestal ("Ah done nearly languished tuh death up dere"), far from the people and things she really cared about, representing only the ideas and beliefs of her admirers, distorted by their gaze. In the space of one volume of collected essays, we find a critic arguing that the negative criticism of Hurston's work represents an "intellectual lynching" by black men, white men, and white women; a critic dismissing

Hurston's final work with the sentence "*Seraph on the Suwanee* is not even about black people, which is no crime, but *is* about white people who are bores, which is"; and another explaining the "one great flaw" in *Their Eyes Were Watching God*: Hurston's "curious insistence" on having her main character's tale told in the omniscient third person (instead of allowing Janie her "voice outright"). We are in a critical world of some banality here, one in which most of our nineteenth-century heroines would be judged oppressed creatures, cruelly deprived of the therapeutic first-person voice. It is also a world in which what is called the "Black Female Literary Tradition" is beyond reproach:

> Black women writers have consistently rejected the falsification of their Black female experience, thereby avoiding the negative stereotypes such falsification has often created in the white American female and Black male literary traditions. Unlike many of their Black male and white female peers, Black women writers have usually refused to dispense with whatever was clearly Black and/or female in their sensibilities in an effort to achieve the mythical "neutral" voice of universal art.[5]

Gratifying as it would be to agree that black women writers "have consistently rejected the falsification" of their experience, the honest reader knows that this is simply not the case. In place of negative falsification, we have nurtured, in the past thirty years, a new fetishization. Black female protagonists are now unerringly strong and soulful; they are sexually voracious and unafraid; they take the unreal forms of earth mothers, African queens, divas, spirits of history; they process grandly through novels thick with a breed of greeting-card lyricism. They have little of the complexity, the flaws and uncertainties, depth and beauty of Janie Crawford and the novel she springs from. They are pressed into service as role models to patch over our psychic wounds; they are perfect;[6] they overcompensate. The truth is, black women writers, while writing many wonderful things,[7] have been no more or less successful at avoiding the falsification of human experience than any other group of writers. It is not the Black Female Literary Tradition that makes Hurston great. It is Hurston herself. Zora Neale Hurston—capable of expressing human vulnerability as well as its strength, lyrical without sentiment, romantic and yet rigorous and one of the few truly eloquent writers of sex—is as exceptional among black women writers as Tolstoy is among white male writers.[8]

It is, however, true that Hurston rejected the "neutral universal" for her novels—she wrote unapologetically in the black-inflected dialect in which she was raised. It took bravery to do that: The result was hostility and disinterest. In 1937, black readers were embarrassed by the unlettered nature of the dialogue and white readers preferred the exoticism of her anthropological writings. Who wanted to read about the poor Negroes one saw on the corner every day? Hurston's biographers make clear that no matter what positive spin she put on it, her life was horribly difficult: She finished life working as a cleaner and died in obscurity. It is understandable that her reclaiming should be an emotive and personal journey for black readers and black critics. But still, one wants to make a neutral and solid case for her greatness, to say something more substantial than "She is my sister and I love her." As a reader, I want to claim fellowship with "good writing" without limits; to be able to say that Hurston is my sister and Baldwin is my brother, and so is Kafka my brother, and Nabokov, and Woolf my sister, and Eliot and Ozick. Like all readers, I want my limits to be drawn by my own sensibilities, not by my melanin count. These forms of criticism that make black women the privileged readers of a black woman writer go against Hurston's own grain. She saw things otherwise: "When I set my hat at a certain angle and saunter down Seventh Avenue . . . the cosmic Zora emerges. . . . How *can* anybody deny themselves the pleasure of my company? It's beyond me!" This is exactly right. No one should deny themselves the pleasure of Zora—of whatever color or background or gender. She's too delightful not be shared. We all deserve to savor her neologisms ("sankled," "monstropolous," "rawbony") or to read of the effects of a bad marriage, sketched with tragic accuracy:

> The years took all the fight out of Janie's face. For a while she thought it was gone from her soul. No matter what Jody did, she said nothing. She had learned how to talk some and leave some. She was a rut in the road. Plenty of life beneath the

surface but it was kept beaten down by the wheels. Sometimes she stuck out into the future, imagining her life different from what it was. But mostly she lived between her hat and her heels, with her emotional disturbances like shade patterns in the woods — come and gone with the sun. She got nothing from Jody except what money could buy, and she was giving away what she didn't value.

The visual imagination on display in *Their Eyes Were Watching God* shares its clarity and iconicity with Christian storytelling — many scenes in the novel put one in mind of the bold-stroke illustrations in a children's Bible: young Janie staring at a photograph, not understanding that the black girl in the crowd is her; Joe Starks atop a dead mule's distended belly, giving a speech; Tea Cake bitten high on his cheekbone by that rabid dog. I watched the TV footage of Hurricane Katrina with a strong sense of déjà vu, thinking of Hurston's flood rather than Noah's: "Not the dead of sick and ailing with friends at the pillow and the feet . . . [but] the sodden and the bloated; the sudden dead, their eyes flung wide open in judgment. . . ."

Above all, Hurston is essential universal reading because she is neither self-conscious nor restricted. She was raised in the real Eatonville, Florida, an all-black town; this unique experience went some way to making Hurston the writer she was. She grew up a fully human being, unaware that she was meant to consider herself a minority, an other, an exotic, or something depleted in rights, talents, desires, and expectations. As an adult, away from Eatonville, she found the world was determined to do its best to remind her of her supposed inferiority, but Hurston was already made, and the metaphysical confidence she claimed for her life ("I am not tragically colored") is present, with equal, refreshing force, in her fiction. She liked to yell "Culllaaaah Struck!" when she entered a fancy party — almost everybody was. But Hurston herself was not. "Blackness," as she understood it and wrote about it, is as natural and inevitable and complete to her as, say, "Frenchness" is to Flaubert. It is also as complicated, as full of blessings and curses. One can be no more removed from it than from one's arm, but it is no more the total measure of one's being than an arm is.

But still, after all that, there is something else to say—and the "neutral universal" of literary criticism pens me in and makes it difficult. To write critically in English is to aspire to neutrality, to the high style of, say, Lionel Trilling or Edmund Wilson. In the high style, one's loves never seem partial or personal, or even like "loves," because white novelists are not white novelists but simply "novelists," and white characters are not white characters but simply "human," and criticism of both is not partial or personal but a matter of aesthetics. Such critics will always sound like the neutral universal, and the black women who have championed *Their Eyes Were Watching God* in the past, and the one doing so now, will seem like black women talking about a black book. When I began this piece, it felt important to distance myself from that idea. By doing so, I misrepresent a vital aspect of my response to this book, one that is entirely personal, as any response to a novel shall be. Fact is, I *am* a black woman,[9] and a slither of this book goes straight into my soul, I suspect, for that reason. And though it is, to me, a mistake to say, "Unless you are a black woman, you will never fully comprehend this novel," it is also disingenuous to claim that many black women do not respond to this book in a particularly powerful manner that would seem "extraliterary." Those aspects of *Their Eyes Were Watching God* that plumb so profoundly the ancient buildup of cultural residue that is (for convenience's sake) called "Blackness"[10] are the parts that my own "Blackness," as far as it goes, cannot help but respond to personally. At fourteen I couldn't find words (or words I liked) for the marvelous feeling of recognition that came with these characters who had my hair, my eyes, my skin, even the ancestors of the rhythm of my speech.[11] These forms of identification are so natural to white readers—(Of course Rabbit Angstrom is like me! Of course Madame Bovary is like me!)—that they believe themselves above personal identification, or at least believe that they are identifying only at the highest, existential levels (His soul is like my soul. He is human; I am human). White readers often believe they are colorblind.[12] I always thought I was a colorblind reader—until I read this novel, and that ultimate cliché of black life that is inscribed in the word *soulful* took on new weight and sense for me. But what does *soulful* even mean?

The dictionary has it this way: "expressing or appearing to express deep and often sorrowful feeling." The culturally black meaning adds several more shades of color. First shade: *soulfulness* is sorrowful feeling transformed into something beautiful, creative and self-renewing, and—as it reaches a pitch—ecstatic. It is an alchemy of pain. In *Their Eyes Were Watching God*, when the townsfolk sing for the death of the mule, this is an example of *soulfulness*. Another shade: To be soulful is to follow and *fall in line* with a feeling, to go where it takes you and not to go against its grain.[13] When young Janie takes her lead from the blossoming tree and sits on her gatepost to kiss a passing boy, this is an example of *soulfulness* A final shade: The word *soulful*, like its Jewish cousin, *schmaltz*,[14] has its roots in the digestive tract. "Soul food" is simple, flavorsome, hearty, unfussy, with spice. When Janie puts on her overalls and joyfully goes to work in the muck with Tea Cake, this is an example of *soulfulness*.[15]

This is a beautiful novel about soulfulness. That it should be so is a tribute to Hurston's skill. She makes "culture"—that slow and particular[16] and artificial accretion of habit and circumstance—seem as natural and organic and beautiful as the sunrise. She allows me to indulge in what Philip Roth once called "the romance of oneself," a literary value I dislike and yet, confronted with this beguiling book, cannot resist. She makes "black woman-ness" appear a real, tangible quality, an essence I can almost believe I share, however improbably, with millions of complex individuals across centuries and continents and languages and religions. . . .

Almost—but not quite. Better to say, when I'm reading this book, I believe it, with my whole soul. It allows me to say things I wouldn't normally. Things like "*She is my sister and I love her.*"

1. But I still resist "limpid and languid."
2. Again, *Middlemarch* is an interesting comparison. Readers often prefer Lydgate and are disappointed at Dorothea's choice of Ladislaw.
3. The (very good) biography is *Wrapped in Rainbows: The Life of Zora Neale Hurston* by Valerie Boyd. Also very good is *Zora Neale Hurston: A Life in Letters*, collected and edited by Carla Kaplan.

4. *Dust Tracks on a Road* is Hurston's autobiography.

5. All the critical voices quoted above can be found in *Zora Neale Hurston's* Their Eyes Were Watching God: *Modern Critical Interpretations*, edited by Harold Bloom.

6. Hurston, by contrast, wanted her writing to demonstrate that "Negroes are no better nor no worse, and at times as boring as everybody else."

7. Not least of which is Alice Walker's original introduction to *Their Eyes Were Watching God*. By championing the book, she rescued Hurston from forty years of obscurity.

8. A footnote for the writers in the audience: *Their Eyes Were Watching God* was written in seven weeks.

9. I think this is the point my mother was trying to make.

10. As Kafka's *The Trial* plumbs that ancient buildup of cultural residue that is called "Jewishness."

11. Down on the muck, Janie and Tea Cake befriend the "Saws," workers from the Caribbean.

12. Until they read books featuring nonwhite characters. I once overheard a young white man at a book festival say to his friend, "Have you read the new Kureishi? Same old thing—loads of Indian people." To which you want to reply, "Have you read the new Franzen? Same old thing—loads of white people."

13. At its most common and banal: catching a beat, following a rhythm.

14. In the *Oxford English Dictionary*: "*Schmaltz* n. informal. excessive sentimentality, esp. in music or movies. ORIGIN 1930s: from Yiddish *schmaltz*, from German *Schmalz* 'dripping, lard.'"

15. Is there anything less soulful than attempting to define soulfulness?

16. In literary terms, we know that there is a tipping point at which the cultural particular—while becoming no less culturally particular—is accepted by readers as the neutral universal. The previously "Jewish fiction" of Philip Roth is now "fiction." We have moved from particular complaints of Portnoy to the universal claims of Everyman.

Reading the Genre

1. Smith identifies some key literary features in Zora Neale Hurston's writing: aphorisms; the lyrical, mythic language; colloquial dialogue. Find definitions for these literary terms and forms. Then find examples of other authors who use these techniques.

2. This is a literary analysis of a novel, but it is also an essay about the conventions of literary analysis itself. What rules does Smith set for her own critical analysis, and how does she come to break them? In academic writing, how are you expected to emulate the "high style" or "neutral universal" traditionally adopted by literary critics, and in what ways do you want to respond more personally in your own analytical writing? (See Chapter 32, "High, Middle, and Low Style," p. 400.)

3. What does *soulful* mean to you? If you don't identify with that term, find a word that encapsulates the kind of writing (or art, or expression) that makes you respond personally, and explain why you have chosen this word.

4. **WRITING:** Smith admits that part of the reason she was skeptical about *Their Eyes Were Watching God* was because her mother gave it to her. Write your own personal narrative about a book that someone shared with you. This could be a novel, or it could be a children's book you read when you were much younger. (To jog your memory, visit the children's section of your local library.) How did the experience of sharing this book shape your feelings about it?

5. **MULTIMODALITY — CHARACTER SKETCHES:** To attempt to capture colloquial language, as Hurston does in her novel, eavesdrop on some conversations around campus. Don't record entire conversations, but simply write down some of the most interesting phrases, sayings, and colloquialisms you hear. Don't identify any of the people you overhear, but if you find you can't do this, get permission from those you observe. Then discuss your findings as a class, focusing on how certain phrases seem to suggest certain types of characters or personalities. If it helps, you can try and sketch pictures of the types of people that the quotes and phrases make you visualize. The goal here is to recognize how language and dialogue also create powerful images, identifications, and associations.

TEXTUAL ANALYSIS   Camille Paglia is a culture critic and professor of humanities and media studies at the University of the Arts in Philadelphia. A founding contributor for *Salon.com*, she publishes articles in dozens of magazines and newspapers worldwide, and her most recent book is *Glittering Images: A Journey Through Art from Egypt to Star Wars* (2012). This essay on Joni Mitchell comes from her book, *Break, Blow, Burn: Camille Paglia Reads Forty-Three of the World's Best Poems* (2005). Mitchell is the only songwriter among this group of the world's best poets; Paglia defends her choice of the singer, and through her analysis of the song "Woodstock," reveals the complexity of Mitchell's writing. The song lyrics are reprinted before the essay.

JONI MITCHELL

Woodstock

I came upon a child of God
He was walking along the road
And I asked him, where are you going
And this he told me

I'm going on down to Yasgur's farm   5
I'm going to join in a rock 'n' roll band
I'm going to camp out on the land
And try and get my soul free

We are stardust
We are golden   10
And we've got to get ourselves
Back to the garden

Then can I walk beside you
I have come here to lose the smog
And I feel to be a cog   15
In something turning

Well, maybe it is just the time of year
Or maybe it's the time of man
I don't know who I am
But life is for learning   20

We are stardust
We are golden
And we've got to get ourselves
Back to the garden

By the time we got to Woodstock   25
We were half a million strong
And everywhere there was song
And celebration

And I dreamed I saw the bombers
Riding shotgun in the sky   30
And they were turning into butterflies
Above our nation

We are stardust
   million-year-old carbon
We are golden   35
   caught in the devil's bargain
And we've got to get ourselves
Back to the garden

CAMILLE PAGLIA

"Woodstock"

In the 1960s, young people who might once have become poets took up the guitar and turned troubadour. The best rock lyrics of that decade and the next were based on the ballad tradition, where anonymous songs with universal themes of love and strife had been refined over centuries by the shapely symmetry of the four-line stanza. But few lyrics, stripped of melody, make a successful transition to the printed page. Joni Mitchell's "Woodstock" is a rare exception. This is an important modern poem—possibly the most popular and influential poem composed in English since Sylvia Plath's "Daddy."

"Woodstock" is known worldwide as a lively, hard-driving hit single by Crosby, Stills, Nash, and Young (from their 1970 *Déjà Vu* album). This virtuoso rock band, which had actually performed at the Woodstock Music Festival in August 1969, treats Mitchell's lyric uncritically as a rousing anthem for the hippie counterculture. Their "Woodstock" is a stomping hoedown. But Joni Mitchell's interpretation of the song on her album *Ladies of the Canyon* (also 1970), where she accompanies herself on electric piano, is completely different. With its slow, jazz-inflected pacing, her "Woodstock" is a moody and at times heartbreakingly melancholy art song. It shows the heady visions of the sixties counterculture already receding and evaporating.

In the sleeve notes and other published sources, the verses of "Woodstock" are run together with few or no stanza breaks. Hence the song's wonderfully economical structure is insufficiently appreciated. My tentative transcription follows the sleeve in omitting punctuation but restores the ballad form by dividing lines where rhymes occur. "Woodstock" is organized in nesting triads: Its nine stanzas fall into three parts, each climaxing in a one-stanza refrain. In Mitchell's recording, the three refrains are signaled by the entrance of background scat singers—her own voice overdubbed. At the end, this eerie chorus contributes two off-rhymed lines that I insert in italics.

Mitchell the poet and artist has cast herself in the lyric as a wanderer on the road to Woodstock, beckoning as a promised land for those fleeing an oppressive society. She meets another traveler, whose story takes up the rest of part one (1–12). Hence "Woodstock" opens with precisely the same donnée as does Shelley's "Ozymandias" ("I met a traveller from an antique land / Who said . . ."). Responding with her own story, Mitchell's persona repeats her companion's hymnlike summation ("We are stardust / We are golden") to indicate her understanding and acceptance of its message (13–24). Now comrades, they arrive at Woodstock and merge with a community of astounding size. From that assembly rises a mystical dream of peace on earth and of mankind's reconnection to nature (25–38).

The song's treatment by a male supergroup automatically altered it. The four musicians, bellying up front and center, are buddies — the merry, nomadic "rock 'n' roll band" whom the lyric's young man yearns to join (6). But Mitchell's radical gender drama is missing. Presented in her voice, the lyric's protagonist is Everywoman. The wayfarers' chance encounter on the road to Woodstock is thus a reunion of Adam and Eve searching for Eden — the "garden" of the song's master metaphor (12). They long to recover their innocence, to restart human history. The song's utopian political project contains a call for reform of sexual relations. Following Walt Whitman or Jack Kerouac, the modern woman writer takes to the road, as cloistered Emily Dickinson could never do. She and her casual companion are peers on life's journey. Free love — "hooking up" in sixties slang — exalts spontaneity over the coercion of contract.

The rambler is "a child of God," like Jesus's disciples on the road to Emmaus, because he desires salvation — but not through organized religion (1). He has shed his old identity and abandoned family, friends, property, and career. Like her, he is a refugee. Indifferent to his social status, she honors him in the moment. And she asks no favors or deference as a woman. Her question — "where are you going" — implies: Where is this generation headed (3)? Is it progressing, or drifting? Does it aim to achieve, or merely to experience? And if the latter, how can raw sensation be bequeathed to posterity without the framing of intellect or art?

He's on his way to "Yasgur's farm"—the festival site on six hundred acres of rolling pastureland in upstate New York, a working dairy farm owned by the paternal Max Yasgur (5). It is nowhere near the real Woodstock, an art colony town seventy miles away. Most of those who flocked to the three-day Woodstock festival were the white, middle-class children of an affluent, industrialized nation cut off from its agrarian roots. In Mitchell's song, their goal, "Yasgur's farm," becomes a hippie reworking of Yahweh's garden. The young man planning "to camp out on the land" to free his soul is a survivalist searching for primal nature (7–8). Michael Wadleigh's epic documentary film *Woodstock* (1970) records the violent gale and torrents of rain on the second day that turned the field into a morass. The "rock 'n' roll band" coveted by the traveler is ultimately the festival audience itself, united in music—an adoptive family of brothers and sisters who were rocked by lightning and who rolled in the mud.

"We are stardust / We are golden": the refrain is a humanistic profession of faith in possibility (9–10). Mankind was created not by a stern overlord but by sacred nature itself. It's as if the earth were pollinated by meteor showers. To be golden means to be blessed by luck: Divinity is within. "We've got to get ourselves / Back to the garden": Woodstock pilgrims need no Good Shepherd or mediating priesthood (11–12). When perception is adjusted, the earth is paradise now. The woman wanderer is touched by the stranger's sense of mission: "Then can I walk beside you" (13)? Woman as equal partner rejects the burden of suspicion and guilt for man's Fall. She too is a truth seeker: She has "come here to lose the smog"—the smoke that gets in our eyes from romantic love and from the cult of competition and celebrity in our polluted metropolises (14). She feels egotistic preoccupations lifting as she becomes "a cog / In something turning"—the great wheel of karma or of astrological cycle (15–16). (Woodstock was initially called an "Aquarian Exposition" to mark the dawning of the harmonious Age of Aquarius.)

The impulse for migration to Woodstock could be "just the time of year," when summer juices surge and vacationers flock to mountains or sea (17). But if it's "the time of man" (a gender-neutral term), Woodstock's mass movement is an epochal transformation (18). The lyric's apocalyptic theme can be understood as a healing amelioration of the modernist pessimism of Yeats's "The Second Coming"—a poem that Mitchell would daringly rewrite for a 1991 album. Yeats's sinister beast slouching toward Bethlehem has become a generation embarked on a spiritual quest.

"I don't know who I am": The road to Woodstock leads to self-knowledge or self-deception (19). As a name, "Woodstock" is fortuitously organic, with associations of forest and stalk or lineage: Streaming toward their open-air sanctuary, the pilgrims are nature's stock, fleeing a synthetic culture of plastics and pesticides. (In her raffish hit song "Big Yellow Taxi," Mitchell says, "They paved paradise / And put up a parking lot / . . . Hey farmer farmer / Put away that DDT now.") The festival-goers believe, rightly or wrongly, that music is prophetic truth. "Life is for learning," for expansion of consciousness rather than accumulation of wealth or power, "the devil's bargain" (compare Wordsworth's "sordid boon"; 20, 36). The returning refrain hammers the point home: We own everything in nature's garden but are blinded by ambition and greed.

The lyric seems to take breath when the pair, with near ecstasy, realize their journey has been shared by so many others: "By the time we got to Woodstock / We were half a million strong" (25–26). The first "we" is two; the second, by heady alchemy, has become a vast multitude. It's as if Adam and Eve are seeing the future—the birth of Woodstock nation, forged of Romantic ideals of reverence for nature and the brotherhood of man. As the two melt into the half million, there is an exhilarating sense of personal grievances and traumas set aside for a common cause. The crowd is "strong" in its coalescence, however momentary. "Everywhere there was song / And celebration": Duty and the work ethic yield to the pleasure principle, as music breaks down barriers and inhibitions (27–28). The group triumphs, for good or ill.

The artist's "I" reemerges from the surging "we" of the Woodstock moment: "I dreamed I saw the bombers / Riding shotgun in the sky / And they were turning into butterflies / Above our nation" (29–32). Is this a shamanistic or psychedelic hallucination? Or is it a magic metamorphosis produced by the roaring engine of rock, with its droning amps and bone-shuddering vibration, eddying up from the earth? The bombers are the war machine then deployed in Vietnam. During her childhood, Joni Mitchell's father was a flight lieutenant in the Royal Canadian Air Force. Thus "Woodstock" aligns the modern military with mythic father figures and sky gods, as in William Blake's engraving *The Ancient of Days*, where Yahweh, crouched in a dark cloud, launches spears of sunlight from his rigidly out-thrust down-stretched hand.

"Riding shotgun" means guarding a stagecoach in the Wild West. Why are the bombers on alert—to smite foreign enemies, or to monitor domestic subversives? Rebel children are the nation's new frontier. The bombers, Pharaoh's pursuing chariots, can destroy but not create; they helplessly follow social change from a distance. Their alteration to butterflies "above our nation" suggests an erasure of borders, restoring the continental expanse of pre-Columbian North America. It's as if mistrust and aggression could be wished away and nationalistic rivalries purged around the world. The impossibility of this lovely dream does not negate its value. Perhaps the armored warplanes are chrysalises hatching evolved new men, the pilots floating down on parachutes to join the festival of peace. But we cannot live as flitting butterflies. Civilization requires internal and external protections and is far more complex and productive than the sixties credo of Flower Power ever comprehended.

In spatial design, "Woodstock" tracks along the wanderers' narrow path, then suddenly expands horizontally at its destination, where the half million have gathered. Buoyed by "song," the lyric now swells vertically to the sky, where it bewitches and exorcizes its harassers. Finally, it sweeps backward in time to take in geology: We are "million-year-old carbon" (34). Our Darwinian origins are a primeval swamp of lizards and plants, crushed to a fertile matrix. We are kin to rocks and minerals, the lowest of the low in Judeo-Christianity's great chain of being. What injects life into the song's stardust and carbon is not the Lord's breath but music. By affirming our shared genetic past, furthermore, Mitchell's metaphor conflates the races: We are carbon copies of one another. If at the cellular level we're all carbon black, then racial differences are trivial and superficial. And carbon under pressure transmutes to the visionary clarity of diamond.

The grandeur of Mitchell's lyric, with its vast expanse of space and time, is somewhat obscured in its carefree performance by Crosby, Stills, Nash, and Young, who are true believers in the revolutionary promise of Woodstock nation. By literally re-creating the "song and celebration," their bouncy, infectious rock rendition permits no alternative view of the festival, even though by the time their record was released, the disastrous Altamont concert had already occurred, exposing the fragility of Woodstock's aspirations. (*Gimme Shelter*, the Maysles brothers' 1970 documentary on the all-day festival at Altamont Speedway near San Francisco, captures the discord and violence leading to a murder in front of the stage.) CSN&Y's evangelical version of "Woodstock" was meant to convert its listeners to pacifism and solidarity. But six months after release of their single, the group had bitterly broken up. They themselves couldn't hold it together. And Mitchell's love affairs with two band members (Crosby and Nash) also ended.

In the hesitations and ravaged vibrato of her recording of "Woodstock," Joni Mitchell confides her doubts about her own splendid vision. Partly because she did not perform at Woodstock, her version has more distance and detachment. Her delivery makes lavish use of dynamics, so that we feel affirmation, then a fading of confidence and will. This "Woodstock" is a harrowing lament for hopes dashed and energies tragically wasted. It's an elegy for an entire generation, flamingly altruistic yet hedonistic and self-absorbed, bold yet naive, abundantly gifted yet plagued by self-destruction. These contradictions were on massive display at Woodstock, where the music was pitifully dependent on capitalist technology and where the noble experiment in pure democracy was sometimes indistinguishable from squalid regression to the primal horde.

An extended coda begins, as if the song doesn't want to end. The lyrics dissolve into pure music—Woodstock's essence. The coda, with its broken syllables, is a crooning lullaby that turns into a warning wail. Mitchell is skeptical about groups;

she longs to join but sees the traps. When her voice falls away, her reverberating piano goes on by stops and starts. The entire power of "Woodstock" is that what is imagined in it was *not* achieved. Woodstock the festival has become a haunting memory. Mitchell's final notes hang, quaver, and fade. Cold reality triumphs over art's beautiful dreams.

Reading the Genre

1. Paglia closely reads every line and word of the song "Woodstock." How does this reading allow her to suggest that the song is telling one particular story? Do you think there could be other meanings, or do you think Paglia got it right? (See "Examine the text closely," p. 195, and Chapter 20, "Smart Reading," p. 340.)

2. Is Paglia's reading shaped by the fact that a woman wrote this song? How important is it in literary analysis to consider a text's author? Explain your answer.

3. Paglia writes about the different recorded performances of the song. In what ways does the song's meaning change when the song is performed by different bands, with different instrumentation, or in different venues?

4. How does Paglia describe the social context in which the song was written? What might change if the song were written and performed today? (See "Focus on social connections," p. 197).

5. **WRITING:** Read lyrics written by one of your favorite artists (song lyrics are readily available online). Do a close, line-by-line and word-by-word analysis of the song. Using this close reading, what assertions can you make about the subject of the song? Support these claims by finding out more about who the author is, how and where the song has been performed, and what social context the song was written in. (See Chapter 38, "Finding Print and Online Sources," p. 442.)

6. **WRITING:** Watch some footage, on YouTube or DVD, of one of your favorite bands performing live, and write an analysis that focuses not on the lyrics or the music but on the performance itself. Consider, for example, the stage set, the lighting, the band members' movements, and their interaction with the crowd.

HISTORICAL ANALYSIS   A historian and cultural critic, Sara Buttsworth teaches at the University of Auckland in New Zealand. She has published books and academic essays on subjects ranging from World War II to *The Lord of the Rings* and *Buffy the Vampire Slayer*. In this essay, she applies her expertise in folklore to a fresh reading of Stephenie Meyer's popular *Twilight* series.

SARA BUTTSWORTH

CinderBella: *Twilight*, Fairy Tales, and the Twenty-First-Century American Dream

Forget Princess, I want to be a Vampire!
— T-shirt slogan, 2009

Preface

Once upon a time there was a dark forest of deep green where magical creatures simultaneously offered succor and peril, sanctuary and slaughter. At the edge of this forest lived a girl with skin as white as snow, a luscious blush to her cheeks, dark hair that rippled down her back, and a smell more tempting than ripe apples. The girl, whose name meant "beauty," lived in exile with her father, for whom she kept house, cleaning and cooking with good will. She liked to read and had feet that would not dance and a mind that was silent to the probing of others. Bella and her father were not poor exactly, but they had little to spare. Peerless as she was, she had no real friends among her own kind. Instead, she fell in love with an outsider—a prince who had the face of an angel, beastly appetites, and skin that reflected sunlight better than any glass slipper. Bella did not always heed warnings never to stray from paths in the forest and was therefore lucky to be befriended by the wolves living there—guardians of the forest and the "provincial town" of Forks. The wolves cared not that Bella wore no hood of red, only that her blood continued to pump through her veins, lending its color to her pale cheeks—and that she did not become the handsome prince's next meal.

The Dreams of Lambs and Lions

The novels (and film adaptations) of the *Twilight Saga* operate in the dreamlike realm of the fairy tale, where horror and romance coexist. Bella's quest for eternal youth and a literal happily-forever-after follows a tradition that has often governed the behavior of young women in different ways through the centuries. This tradition has its roots in the storytelling of peasants around their hearths. The stories began to be much more formally didactic for the emerging middle classes when Charles Perrault and his contemporaries transformed oral folktales into their literary *contes des fées* ("fairy tales") for the glittering salons of Paris society in the seventeenth and eighteenth centuries. Once fixed on paper, folktales were later recast and redefined by the morality of the Brothers Grimm in the nineteenth century and were later broadcast worldwide by Disney studios throughout the twentieth and into the twenty-first centuries.[1]

The personal details of young women like Bella Swan have changed over the centuries, along with the cultural contexts of the stories in which they appear, displaying various skills, virtues, and levels of intellect. Throughout the twentieth century, particularly with the standardized morality and global reach of Disney films, heroines—even the feisty ones of the latter part of the period—have continued to be rewarded for, but never rescued from, their patience, passivity, and pallid beauty.

Stephenie Meyer's stories are a gripping read from beginning to end partly because of their fairy-tale appeal, which, far from being "timeless," is very much of *this* time. References to heroines and romantic couples (both doomed and happy) outside the folkloric realm abound in the *Twilight* novels: The writings of Shakespeare, Emily Brontë, and Jane Austen are Bella's staple entertainment. But Bella's story, with its stance on premarital sex, fidelity, self-sacrifice for a prolife attitude, and the questions it begs about how young women in a "postfeminist" age are supposed to be able to "have it all," make Meyer's work very much a fairy tale of the twenty-first century.

The *Twilight* novels make use of a number of important factors that have remained constant in fairy-tale texts. Perhaps the most important fairy-tale factor Meyer has employed is the transformative power of "survival tale[s] with hope."[2] As characters within fairy tales survive the challenges they meet, they are transformed and attain their hearts' desires. Meyer's heroine is no exception to the personal transformation that is undergone by so many fairy-tale protagonists. And it is no great leap to see Bella's story as a "survival tale with hope." So, in considering the *Twilight Saga*, it is not the resemblance to fairy tales that poses a quandary. Rather, the problem lies in deciding which fairy tale it resembles the most. Fragments of *Snow White*,

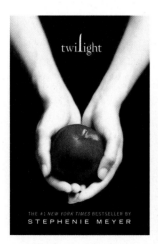

Cinderella, *Beauty and the Beast*, and *Little Red Riding Hood* are *all* discernible throughout Meyer's work, so which story is it that binds this romance together?

The answer to this question is a story within a story. The fairy tale most apparent in these books is actually the American Dream—another story of "survival with hope" that has been handed down through the generations and adapted to changing cultural ideals and socioeconomic contexts. Bella comes from a lower-middle-class background. Her father, Charlie, is a small-town chief of police, and her mother, Renée, has a nondescript occupation (other than being Charlie's, and then Phil's, wife) and level of education that, foreshadowing her own child's early marriage and motherhood, seems to have been cut short by early marriage and pregnancy. Renée did not marry up in the same way that Bella does, and her neglected offspring certainly climbs up an entire socioeconomic beanstalk in marrying into the extremely wealthy Cullen family.

Bella may not have worn rags at the beginning of her story, but by its end she certainly has unfettered access to riches both materially and in terms of opportunities. And throughout the *Twilight* series, the American conviction that the United States is unique among nations, following different rules and pursuing a destiny different from that of other cultures (that is, the "exceptionalism" of the United States on the world stage), an idea that has been at the center of the American Dream since the Puritans, is evident in its heroine, its vampires, and its werewolves, glittering as brightly as diamonds in the sun. What Bella's story illustrates above all else, however, is that the American Dream tradition for young women in the early twenty-first century remains a variant of *Cinderella*. With or without glass slippers, it is the right marriage that elevates one out of the dark cabin in the woods to the sunlit castle on the hill.

As surely as Old World stories tell of Jack's winning a king's ransom by way of a handful of magic beans, and Dick Whittington becoming lord mayor of London in reluctantly parting with his cat, the American Dream posits that upward mobility can be, and is, a reality. Anyone, according to this fairy tale, can grow up to be president—if he is a boy that is (and history suggests that those who have had any real hope of gaining access to this Dream have also been overwhelmingly white, the current U.S. president notwithstanding). What it means for a man to reach his goals has changed over time; Puritans tended to focus on community and being closer to God, for example, whereas by the mid-twentieth century the emphasis had shifted toward each person's freedom to develop an individual identity. The individual successes that have been the dream since the late nineteenth century have continued to dominate and tend to preclude any analysis of how class, race, or gender can be barriers to success.[3] But the possibility of transformation in a single person's life, rather than collective revolution, is the key to the fairy-tale kingdom of the American Dream. Many staple fairy tales of European origin feed into this utopian vision of individual, community, and national success — if the fool can marry the princess and become king, why not become president? The mythical success of the "everyman" is all around us.

But what if you are a girl: Can you become president or will you always just be someone else's queen? The Cinderella myth is alive and kicking up its glass slippers in a plethora of literary and cinematic texts produced in the late twentieth and early twenty-first centuries, to the extent that an entire "princess culture" has emerged.[4] The American Dream continues to be regularly invoked and reinvented, from popular fiction to popular film to the speeches and treatises of successive U.S. presidents, including Barack Obama (one of his books even has the American Dream in its title: *The Audacity of Hope: Thoughts on Reclaiming the American Dream*). Just how accessible is this goal for young women? The *Twilight* stories are very much a part of this nexus of myths as tales of upward mobility, standing at the crossroads between the Old World and the New. Peppered with direct and indirect fairy-tale references and a reverence for baseball, the ending that allows Bella to "have it all" consists of early marriage, dying young, and staying pretty.[5] Throughout Meyer's saga, Bella is in many ways as blank as her 1950 Walt Disney predecessor, and other than her delicious smell, it is that and her unselfishness (like Beauty's and Cinderella's before her) that attract Edward, her prince.

This essay explores the *Twilight* novels in the context of fairy-tale tradition, including the American Dream, and the ways in which this tradition can shed light on just how tight the glass slipper is. The analysis is divided into two parts, the first on the American Dream, and the second on Cinderella stories—although obviously teasing these apart completely is not entirely possible, and fairy-tale references abound in both. The characters of Carlisle and Edward best illustrate some of the changes in the tradition of American Dream stories. And just as the Cullen male leaders best exemplify this tradition, the Quileutes represent those who have been, and continue to be, consistently excluded from it. The Cullen coven and Bella illustrate the ongoing importance of American culture's vision of itself as "different" from other nations, not only in their "cross-species" relationships and "puritan" diet, but in relation to the European vampire aristocracy, the Volturi.

The second part of the analysis focuses more on the female characters, especially Bella, Esme, and Rosalie, who are all heiresses to the legacies left behind by their fairy-tale predecessors—for the most part the heroines of twentieth-century cinematic tales. Both sections demonstrate the ways in which the Cullen family (of which Bella is really a part right from the beginning, almost as if she was "born to be a vampire" of the Cullen ilk) represents the different ideals of individual morality for men and women, individual success, social mobility, and the unique aspects of American culture that are the dreams any American Cinderella's heart might harbor (*Breaking Dawn*, 524).

Creatures of the Night: Defenders of the Dream

The transformative power of the fairy tale, and of fairy-tale heroes, is often one of turning established hierarchies on their heads. This fantasy is as crucial for the American Dream, where an individual can attain wealth and power regardless of his origins or structural or social obstacles, as it is for its fairy-tale siblings. The fool can be king for a day, for a lifetime, or for several, but the fool does not want to get rid of the social order that oppresses him. He merely wants to be on top of it. The hierarchies of society remain intact in the traditional folktale, but he who was at the bottom manages through hard work, perseverance, and sometimes dumb luck, to end up in a far loftier position than the one from which he started out.[6]

The *Twilight Saga* can also be seen as upending literary hierarchies in some ways, since vampires are not necessarily villains. Rather than the transgression, excess, and sexual deviance that have traditionally been keys to vampire stories, the Cullens and their friends represent chastity, morality, and restraint.[7] Interestingly, while the Cullens represent such a break with literary vampire traditions, they do not seek to overturn the vampire order. In the same way, to be opposed to their own great material wealth would jeopardize their ability to move through both vampire and human worlds (and other than perhaps Carlisle, none of the Cullens would ever really dream of questioning their right to fabulous riches). While they live outside many human systems of operation, they do use them to their advantage. Much as the Puritans represented a break from the "evils" of the Old World they fled as they sought Utopia in the New, the Cullen family, headed by Carlisle, represents a break from the excesses and cruelties of Old World vampirism. The New World is still the place to make your fortune, however, and, through hard work, to gain access to a little piece of paradise in this world and the hereafter.

Long before Thomas Jefferson wrote "life, liberty, and the pursuit of happiness" into the Declaration of Independence in 1776, before Abraham Lincoln ascended from a log cabin to the White House, and before Horatio Alger penned his popular fictions of rags-to-riches glory for those who worked hard and cared for others in the late 1860s, the Puritans arrived in the New World with their Spartan ways and their hopes of attaining a better life in the now and in heaven. Cultural historian Jim Cullen (not to be confused with Meyer's Cullens), in his book *The American Dream: A Short History of an Idea That Shaped a Nation*, stresses free will and individual choice as the key to the freedoms Americans have always held dear; he also examines how the Declaration had its roots in the hopes and fears of the Puritans who arrived in North America more than a century before.[8] The story and character of

Carlisle, father of the Cullen coven, can be viewed alongside these ancestors of the Founding Fathers.

In describing Carlisle as having been born the son of a seventeenth-century Protestant preacher, Meyer invokes memories of the Puritans, the religious reform movement that inspired small groups to break away from the Anglican Church in Britain and seek freedom from persecution in the new colonies on the East Coast of North America. The characterization of Carlisle's father as a leader of witch hunts, which leads to the literal demonizing of his own son, roots the entire Cullen family history in a search for freedom from persecution as they pursue a different way of life. The Puritan nature of the Cullens, while not evident in the trappings of wealth with which they surround themselves, is instead expressed through something even more basic to their identities: how they sustain their bodies through diet. It is their diet and desire to treat humans as people rather than as "pets" or "snacks" that set them apart from the Old World vampires — the Volturi and most of their followers.

In refusing to drink human blood, Carlisle sets an example that baffles the "nighttime patrons of the arts," Aro, Caius, and Marcus, who attempted to "cure his aversion to 'his natural food source' as they called it" (*Twilight*, 297). It is unclear what these attempts entailed. However, the impressions of the Volturi created in *New Moon, Eclipse,* and *Breaking Dawn* convey the idea that had they stopped feeling so indulgent in Carlisle's direction, the Volturi would not have hesitated to use a number of forms of coercion and persecution to achieve conformity. So, feeling that there was no hope of continuing his "religion" of caring for others and not sucking the life out of them, Carlisle fled seventeenth-century Italy and began a lonely extended life that eventually found him transforming Edward on his deathbed three centuries later. Freedom from persecution, a "puritan" diet, and an ethic of caring that leads Carlisle to transform only those who are close to death (and who become a part of his "family" rather than followers in a retinue) are among the ways in which Meyer reflects the notion that Americans (even if they are vampires!) have a unique culture among the nations, which is crucial to the American Dream.[9] Through dint of hard work and self-sacrifice, Carlisle overcame his appetites to the extent that, rather than living apart from people, he could live among them and be a pillar of the various communities through which he moved. As he says while dealing with Bella's injured arm in the opening chapters of *New Moon*, "Like everything in life, I just had to decide what to do with what I was given" (*New Moon*, 35).

Hard work and a strong moral center led Carlisle to a life of which he is proud. His diet means he maintains the ethics of Puritanism, but his profession and long life mean he can still achieve the luxuries that only great wealth can afford. Political scientist Cal Jillson has claimed that like Puritans, for Quakers (a similar breakaway seventeenth-century sect), "[W]orking, saving, and investing led to prosperity and enhanced one's role in the community because thriving was taken to be a visible sign that one was living in the light of the Lord's grace." But it was the very material success that followed their Protestant work ethic that inevitably undermined the communitarian emphasis of the early Puritan and Quaker communities: As they became wealthier, they often ceased to live as simply as their founders had.[10] There appears to be no such conflict for the New World vampires of the Cullen coven. Excess, in the vampire world it seems, is largely related to food.

The subtle differences between the characterizations of Edward and Carlisle move *Twilight*'s American Dream into the twentieth century in terms of values and aspirations. While Carlisle does represent individual success, he is also the founder of a community and completely bound to it. Where Carlisle's commitment to his little coven has much to do with faith, Edward's is based on love and loyalty—and his affections can waver, depending on which sibling he interacts with and whether or not their behavior accords with his own code of conduct.[11] He is much more of a loner than Carlisle, and this very much makes Edward a twentieth-century man.

Edward becomes a vampire in 1918 as Spanish influenza wreaks its havoc worldwide and kills more people than died in combat during the whole four years of World War I. Edward's pre-vampire life is sketchy, but he appears to have been from a well-off upper-middle-class family. Prior to contracting influenza, Edward was about to join the army (although he would most likely have missed out on World War I action, as the war was nearly over by this stage). Following his "transformation," Edward discovers a talent for mind reading and, with a minor rebellious detour, does his best to live up to Carlisle's example. Here we see a dream become a legacy passed down from one generation to the next. In Edward's case, and the case of the other vampires who are friends and allies of the Cullens, while they ultimately come together as a community, it is their personal independence that is to be defended at all costs.

Edward's many gifts are stressed throughout the four novels, including his capacity to read minds, his musical abilities, his determination, and his intellect, which helps him to earn a number of degrees in medical science. What separates, and perhaps elevates, Edward above his brothers and sisters is how he uses all of his extra time. For example, in *Breaking Dawn*, when Charlie is first introduced to the newly transformed Bella, we see a family no longer as interested in maintaining the need for the human charade of winding down for the evening: Where Emmett and Rosalie are involved in constructing a massive house of cards, transient and trivial, Edward moves to the piano—a demonstration not only of skill but of talent. Edward is the only one of the Cullen children who demonstrates more than a fleeting interest in education and research, and his qualifications are far more worthy than the display of high school graduation caps in the *Twilight* film indicates. He does not need to sleep and therefore works on honing his particular skills and interests. It is this work ethic and the desire to use, rather than squander, the gifts he has that make him the perfect heir to Carlisle's legacies. It is not just his good looks that make him the prince of this American fairy tale: It is his morality, his intellect, and his unswerving commitment to his family's way of life that crown him in Bella's eyes.

Both Carlisle and Edward demonstrate through their chosen lifestyles the emphasis on a unique, individual destiny that is so important to the American Dream. However, other than diet, morality, and hard work, there is another element crucial to the national mythologies of the United States. To this end, I would like to make a slight detour here to discuss a minor character from *Breaking Dawn* who not only invokes the Founding Fathers and the spirit of the Wars of Independence, but who also exemplifies one of the ongoing themes of the twenty-first-century American Dream: individual freedoms. We meet Garrett as the Cullens begin to gather their friends and allies in preparation for the impending doom of a visit from the Volturi. One of the first things we hear him utter is, "The redcoats are coming, the redcoats are coming" (*Breaking Dawn*, 680). Garrett takes us back to Paul Revere's famous midnight ride, one of the most mythologized events of the American Revolutionary War. In what has become known as the original national conflict for autonomy and freedom from Old World dictatorship, the Revolutionary War is where and when Garrett became a vampire. And Garrett calls the Volturi out:

> "The Volturi care nothing for the death of the child. They seek the death of our free will. . . . So come, I say! Let's hear no more lying rationalizations. Be honest in your intents as we will be honest in ours. We will defend our freedom. You will or will not attack it. Choose now, and let these witnesses see the true issue debated here." [. . .]
>
> Aro smiled. "A very pretty speech, my revolutionary friend."
>
> Garrett remained poised for attack. "Revolutionary?" he growled. "Who am I revolting against, might I ask? Are you my king? Do you wish me to call you *master*, too, like your sycophantic guard?"
>
> "Peace Garrett," Aro said tolerantly. "I meant only to refer to your time of birth. Still a patriot, I see." (*Breaking Dawn*, 719)

Garrett seeks to expose not only the Volturi's aristocratic pretensions, but also the Machiavellian power games with which they seek to direct all talent to their will and whims. Once again Meyer invokes an event that has become integral to American historical mythology. And because vampires are almost unkillable, Garrett's response places freedom from autocracy (and aristocracy) at the forefront of the stories of her individual vampires. Here, too, we see the idea of a unique American destiny at work. It is not only differences in diet that separate the Cullens and some of their friends from their Old World counterparts, but the value they place on individual talent and individual free will. No one is forced to join the Cullens' stand against the Volturi, and talents are not turned on friends except for training purposes. This forms a sharp contrast to the "guard" of the Volturi, who do indeed call Aro, Caius, and Marcus *master*, and whose minds and talents are bent to their masters' will through the talents of vampires like Chelsea, who is able to alter how people feel about one another and weaken the bonds between them, and Jane, who can inflict excruciating pain from a distance with her mind.

In spite of different story arcs for female characters (see below), Meyer also puts distance between the Old and the New Worlds in their treatment of women. While there are females with active talents in the Volturi retinue, these "wives" are never mentioned by name and hover like prized yet useless possessions in the confrontation with the Cullens. The women of the Cullen family and friends all have their own names and their own talents — put to use in the defense of what they hold dear. So once again we see the New World vampires standing against those of the Old and demonstrating the power and value of free will and individual choice.

A unique nature and destiny is also demonstrated by the Quileute wolves — they are not the same as the Children of the Moon, whom Marcus hunted almost to extinction. Their alliance with the vampires of Forks is completely unprecedented. But Jacob Black and his pack, even in this fairy tale, operate outside the magical realm of the American Dream, much as Native Americans have sought their own sovereignty and been excluded from opportunities for educational and material success in colonial and postcolonial North America. The Founding Fathers' City on the Hill came into existence only because they conquered the indigenous populations.[12] Younger Native Americans continue to struggle with the poverty and social problems endemic on many reservations, which keeps them from the material, community, and individual successes promised by the American Dream. The alternative Native American dreams of their own nation and self-determination cannot coexist with the dominant and dominating hegemony of the United States.

The Quileutes in Meyer's story are bound *to* their roles as guardians — which are crucial — and *by* the boundaries of the reservation, their territory. While Jacob, who ditches school on "the Rez" and excels as a mechanic, is worthy, moral, and magical, he is never on equal footing with the wealthy, white, upper-class Edward. While Bella may flirt with Jacob, and momentarily toy with the idea that she and he should have been together, Jacob was never going to be the prince in her story. He is not white, unnaturally beautiful, or wealthy. He cannot, by virtue of his race, species as shape-shifter/wolf, and socioeconomic position help her to rise, socially or economically, nor can he even help her to "evolve" into a being like himself, as Edward can. The American Dream may allow Beauty to befriend the wolf, but in order to live (or die?) the dream that says she *can* have it all, she must marry the Beast/Prince and herself become transformed.

CinderBella and Her Sisters

Much like Hansel scattering breadcrumbs through the dark forest, Meyer has peppered her books with fairy-tale references. The very cover of *Twilight* tempts the reader, Snow White–like, with its rosy red apple.[13] Isabella Swan's own name is itself a fairy-tale signifier, her first name meaning "beauty" in its abbreviated form, and the surname reminiscent of many tales, from the "Swan Maidens" to "Six Swans" to the "Ugly Duckling" (the latter's transformative aspect is one that Bella by inference applies to herself, since in her own mind she does not fulfill the beautiful potential of her name until her "undead" life). But what of the American Dream for our fairy-tale heroine?

J. Emmett Winn points to a number of Cinderella stories, such as *Working Girl* (1988) and *Pretty Woman* (1990), which incidentally is also a Disney film, as examples of ongoing mythologies of the American Dream.[14] Beautiful, hardworking, and moral (in spite of Vivian's occupation as a prostitute in *Pretty Woman*), the female characters Winn discusses rise above their circumstances and enrich the lives of those around them. However, Winn does little to discuss the fact that Cinderella stories are the specifically *feminine* form of the American Dream. From drudgery and strong expressions of morality to sartorial transformation, these stories bear striking similarities. Even when the woman in question attains a desired career as a part of her new life, it is always through her relationship to a man. While for men the ways to achieve their dreams, and even the dreams themselves, have changed over time, for women landing the prince remains a constant in the climax to their stories. Carlisle and Edward are shining examples of masculinity and progress, whereas Bella is depicted as old for her years and is by implication an old-fashioned heroine.

The *Twilight Saga*'s female characters follow narrative arcs that color them as either worthy, and therefore accepting of their fates, or as shallow and selfish and therefore open to criticism and punishment of some sort. Bella's story and those of Esme and Rosalie echo the fairy-tale legacies of both pre- and post-Perrault stories. The clearest influences in these stories, however, largely seem to come from the twentieth-century productions of Disney studios. Meyer's grim tales are inflected by twenty-first-century sexual politics. With their focus on "morality" at the expense of education, or honesty about teenage sexuality, they are in some ways more conservative than their seventeenth-century predecessors.[15] While Bella may flirt with her wolf to gain information, and get into bed with him to get warm, she remains fully clothed at all times. She bears little resemblance to the pre-Perrault Little Red Riding Hood, who does a striptease for the wolf before escaping out the back door: Her attempts to help in the battle against Victoria's minions in *Eclipse* consist of self-sacrifice and self-harm, not cunning.[16] And while Edward climbs to her room every night, all activity between him and Bella remains charged yet chaste. Unlike the story of Rapunzel, there is no punishment for promiscuity and giving birth to illegitimate twins for our twenty-first-century heroine—she does not let down her hair until she is properly married.[17]

When Bella first meets Esme, she is reminded of an ingénue of the silent-film era. Moments later, Bella observes that "It was like meeting a fairy tale—Snow White in the flesh" (*Twilight*, 282). The reference to silent films and Snow White hearkens back to the original American celluloid Cinderella, Clara Bow in *It* (1927). This reference, despite the "waves of caramel colored hair," intersects neatly with Walt Disney's first feature-length animated film, *Snow White and the Seven Dwarfs*, released in 1937. Both Clara Bow's character, Betty Lou, and Snow White know "someday my prince will come," both have pale complexions, and both have heart-shaped faces framed by bobbed hair. But there are some differences worthy of examination. Clara Bow's It-girl is the classic flapper of the 1920s, a time of frivolity, flagrant displays of wealth, and unease about changes in the postwar sexual behavior and roles of women. The "It" factor refers to sexuality. As hemlines rose, women gained the vote, and more and more women entered the workplace, Clara Bow's portrayal of Betty Lou encompassed both the hedonism and the anxiety of the era.[18] Despite the monumental changes that were occurring, the ideal presented by Hollywood's dream factory was still marriage, even in a text such as *It*. However, the flighty, manipulative, and sexualized behavior of Betty Lou, in spite of the Cinderella ending that implies that she was a "good girl," suggests that ultimately Esme more nearly resembles Disney's *Snow White*.

Carlisle is Esme's prince, and his "kiss" saves her life following her suicide attempt after losing a child. Esme has hobbies in architecture and the restoration of furniture and buildings, but this is described as something in which she dabbles rather than the "calling" pursued by Carlisle. This interest in houses is an extension of Esme as "homemaker," much like Disney's Snow White, who whistles while she works and worries terribly that the dwarfs have no mother. And the cottage Esme constructs for Bella and Edward is also straight out of *Snow White* or 1959's *Sleeping Beauty*. Esme's mothering instincts and her capacity for love and devotion are what make her the ideal companion for Carlisle. She is devoted to her "children" in spite of the threat that having a human girl in their midst poses; she wouldn't care if Bella had "a third eye and webbed feet" if it made Edward happy (*Twilight*, 286). While Esme may be the (unbeating) heart of the Cullen family, however, it is Carlisle who is its head and the leader of their way of life.

At the end of the Great Depression, *Snow White*, whose princess Esme resembles so strikingly, marked the beginning of Walt Disney's dominance as the chief peddler of fairy tales and dreams — and not only to an American audience. Walt Disney is himself representative of the American Dream in the early twentieth century: Having pulled himself up by his bootstraps, he built his success in the 1930s, when destitution and despair were the lot of so many, and ended up the chief controller and dictator of the "happiest place on earth."[19] For many people growing up in the twentieth and twenty-first centuries, Disney *is* the chief source for fairy tales. This all-American studio and corporation have taken tales that originated in Europe and retold and repackaged them to the entire world in a kind of reverse colonization of the imagination. Often known as the "great sanitizer," "Disney's trademarked innocence operates on a systematic sanitization of violence, sexuality, and political struggle," purging these where they had been present in earlier versions of these fairy tales.[20] But as Naomi Wood pointed out, the "squeaky clean" feel of Disney texts was a part of the "American prurience that was so appealing and acceptable to his audiences."[21]

Certainly the "classic" Disney princesses in *Snow White*, *Cinderella*, and *Sleeping Beauty* represent beautiful heroines whose excellence in the domestic arts and beautiful bell-like singing voices are what commend them — much like the "feminine ideals" of the mid-twentieth century. Cinderella makes wishes on soap bubbles and passively receives the gifts of her fairy godmother. It is not she who seeks to find her own way to the ball, but her furry companions who go to work, making a dress fit for royalty. She is beautiful and blond — and blank. Her identity is defined first by her subordinate position in her family there among the cinders, and then as the "wife" of Prince Charming. Her dreams go no further than being on the arm of someone who can elevate her from being a servant in one household to presiding over another — neither of which belongs to her. The 1950 Disney *Cinderella* does not need to be named to be present in *Twilight*, but a direct reference does tie the two texts together. The spells of Cinderella's fairy godmother shimmer when Carlisle engages Jacob in a discussion of his DNA:

> "Your family's divergence from humanity is much more interesting. Magical almost."

"Bibbidi-Bobbidi-Boo," I mumbled. He was just like Bella with all the magic garbage. (*Breaking Dawn*, 237)

Jacob introduces another princess, Sleeping Beauty, overtly into Meyer's text in his less than cordial relationship with Rosalie: "The look on Rosalie's face made it clear that I wasn't welcome to one of them. It made me wonder what Sleepless Beauty needed a bed for anyway. Was she that possessive of her props?" (*Breaking Dawn*, 253).

Rosalie's long blond hair and breathtaking beauty, even among the Botticellian vampires, reinforce the connection to the 1959 animated feature. Rosalie herself has told her story as a fairy tale gone awry.

Renowned for her physical beauty, Rosalie was the daughter of an aspiring middle-class family in the 1930s, a family that never felt the effects of the Great Depression. While the Hales had wealth, their position in banking suggests that their material well-being was at the expense of others who lost everything during the hardships of the early 1930s. So while they fulfilled the upwardly mobile part of American mythology, they did not possess the other requirement of moral strength and a willingness to help others.[22] Dreams of wealth without the desire or the capacity to improve the lives of those around you are empty dreams. And in *Twilight* the princess of such dreams, Rosalie, was similarly without substance. Rosalie, in *Eclipse*, attempts to explain to Bella why she should hold on to being human. For Rosalie, being turned into a vampire was more a punishment than a reward: a punishment for a shallow existence premised on little more than her good looks and her sense of entitlement. The fairy tale that had been promised in life — "This was everything they'd dreamed of. And Royce seemed to be everything I'd dreamed of. The fairy tale prince, come to make me a princess. Everything I wanted, yet it was still no more than I expected. We were engaged before I'd known him for two months." — ended in gang rape (*Eclipse*, 157). Beauty is a potential trap in many fairy tales, and without the moral center of self-sacrificing devotion of a true fairy-tale heroine, Rosalie's unhappiness continues in her afterlife.

It would be wrong to imply that Disney heroines have not changed over time, even though, ultimately, the end result of fulfillment through marriage has been maintained. Ariel (*The Little Mermaid*, 1989) and Belle (*Beauty and the Beast*, 1991), the two princesses who essentially rebooted the appeal of Disney animated magic for a new generation, represented significant change from their sweet, mop-wielding, predecessors. Both heroines have been somewhat influenced by feminism in their intellectual curiosity and their possession of much more bravery and capacity for action than Cinderella. Ultimately they too marry to rise socially, above the sea and out of "this provincial life," and their dreams of new ideas and experiences fade with the closing kisses of these stories. The women in the *Twilight* novels also exhibit feminist traits, both historical and contemporary, or they would simply have no appeal to a twenty-first-century audience. But they too have their eyes on the prize of marital bliss.

For example, Rosalie's whole existence seems to revolve around just being beautiful—but there are tongue-in-cheek references to her skills as a mechanic in both the books and the *Twilight* movie. This is more than a jibe at the incongruity of a beautiful blond emerging from underneath a car. It resonates with skills Rosalie may well have acquired during World War II, when in a time of national emergency women were being told (by a woman also called Rosie), "We can do it!" and encouraged to take on the jobs and skills of men, before being encouraged back to the kitchen and the bedroom at war's end.[23] But technical skill is not required of these radiant women and is indulged because they will never need to use it as a profession, unlike Jacob, whose class and ethnic background in these depictions seem to necessitate knowledge of a "trade" rather than aspiration to a profession.

Bella is introduced to the reader as sacrificing the life she loved in the sun so that her irresponsible mother can pursue her own happiness. Renée's happiness itself revolves around remarriage to a minor league ballplayer, her own entrée to the American Dream through "the American pastime." Bella then moves into the dark and gothic atmosphere of the town where her father is the chief of police, but like so many fairy-tale fathers, he is benign but largely absent. Bella may not sing while she does housework, but she takes on the role of housewife for her father much like her 1950 predecessor. Bella's blankness of mind for Edward poses a mystery, and it is one of the things that attract him. Along with devotion, beauty, and self-sacrifice, this feminine silence is often present in many fairy tales and has over many centuries acted both as a punishment of young women and a feature that attracts male fairy-tale heroes.[24] Her silence of mind and her silence with regard to keeping the secret of the Cullens' existence both become gifts in the end, since Bella's blankness becomes the means of saving her entire family from the games of the Volturi.

Bella toys with the idea of college but mainly as a device for the only ambition she ever clearly expresses — maintaining her hold on Edward. Before her relationship with Edward solidifies, we hear of Bella working to supplement her meager college fund, and we later learn she has applied to a university in Alaska (mainly because she could use this as a ruse to disguise her own transformation into a vampire). However, we never know what it is she might like to study or what she might like to pursue in terms of a career. Much like Belle in *Beauty and the Beast*, Bella does not really fit into "provincial" Forks. Like Belle, her longings for more are not clearly articulated, and this "more" seems to be fulfilled by both Beauties' choice of Beasts.

Beauty and the Beast was first published in French in the first half of the eighteenth century (translated into English in 1759), and includes clear evidence of class struggle and the aspirations of the merchant class for the trappings and privileges of the aristocracy.[25] It is a part of what folklorists call the "Cinderella cycle" of tales, and follows a familiar trajectory of feminine self-sacrifice and devotion being ultimately rewarded through marriage. The Disney text subtracts the element of class conflict, despite the obvious socioeconomic differences between Belle and the Beast. In this way, and in dressing Belle in a way reminiscent of the cinematic version of the original American fairy tale *The Wizard of Oz*, we have a truly American fairy tale that fits with the "classless" society of American Dream mythology.

Pre-vamp Bella makes a great deal of not accepting expensive gifts — a part of her "morality" is her rejection of the trappings that highlight the inequalities between herself and Edward. Along with Bella's father's profession, other indicators of Bella's class difference from the Cullens are constant throughout the *Twilight* novels. Like any Cinderella, her premarriage wardrobe is scanty and occasionally supplemented by the good fairy Alice. Bella's father's profession and income mean that the house they live in is small and shabby, and she has access only to antiquated communications technologies. Bella's car is an ancient Chevy truck that, while safe, has none of the style or speed of any of the vehicles in the Cullens' garage. CinderBella never complains about her circumstances, and that is a part of her charm. But where she protests extravagance extended in her direction before her nuptials, she has no such qualms in accepting the benefits of the Cullens' wealth after marriage, especially when this can assist her transition from human to vampire.

Conclusion: What Price the Glass Slipper?

The *Twilight Saga* is very much a twenty-first-century morality tale with a fairy-story ending. It is also a "survival story with hope" that invokes and enacts the premises, and promises, of the American Dream in all of its forms, both masculine and feminine. The Cullens represent morality, wealth, and the unique qualities of the New World vampires from the seventeenth century to the present. They work hard at staying secret, staying together, and maintaining their "vegetarian" diet. Bella makes sacrifices to keep her family happy and never complains about her limited lot in life. Her selflessness and character as a good girl mark her as exceptional in portrayals of young women in contemporary popular culture. She is also an exceptional "newborn" vampire — even for her New World family. But the things that make Bella's narrative an extraordinary vampire story make her a rather ordinary Cinderella. Beyond being a Cullen, she has no ambition, and unlike Carlisle and Edward, she seems unlikely to carve out her own separate path. And while the ultimate battle may take place after Edward and Bella's wedding, and while Bella plays an active role in her family's defense, the curtains still close on a kiss to last forever after.

Edward laughs off what in Meyer's saga are merely myths about vampires. However, the "truths" communicated by the American fairy tale remain. Moral good little girls can marry princes and become more talented through that marriage, stay beautiful, and never need to worry about juggling work and child care—but only if they adhere to whatever society dictates as moral and good, and only if they accept marriage as the ultimate happy ending. Bella fulfills the self-sacrifice quotient required of a fairy-tale heroine in the numerous conflict scenarios where she offers herself up to fate in order to try to save those around her. She is often selfish and self-indulgent but always self-sacrificing when it comes to those she loves. Bella works hard, remains a virgin until marriage, and refuses an abortion even when her own life is at stake. And she is rewarded. In the ultimate wish fulfillment, Bella escapes the pains of aging in a society that purports to venerate knowledge but is really enamored of that most fleeting of shiny toys—youth. "Forget Princess, I want to be a Vampire" sums up an entire culture whose ideal of having it all conflicts with the realities of income differences and sexual inequality that still characterize American society. All happily-ever-afters come at a cost, and the price Bella pays is her life.

Notes

1. Fairy-tale theorists, such as Jack Zipes and Robert Darnton, argue that the roles for women in such tales were much more fluid in the oral storytelling cultures that predated Perrault. In fixing the tales in published literature (at a time when private and public spheres and a strict demarcation of gender roles were becoming more rigid for emerging middle classes) that had a strongly didactic function, the strictures on feminine behavior became much more apparent. Even in the literary traditions of the seventeenth, eighteenth, and nineteenth centuries, however, there is much variation according to changing behavioral norms and the socioeconomic, cultural, and religious backgrounds and genders of the

authors. There have, of course, been many more producers of fairy-tale texts than the three cited in this section, but these are the three most well-known examples in the progression from oral to literary to cinematic texts. See, for example, Jack Zipes, "Breaking the Disney Spell," in Elizabeth Bell, Linda Haas, and Laura Sells, eds., *From Mouse to Mermaid: The Politics of Film, Gender, and Culture* (Bloomington and Indianapolis: Indiana Univ. Press, 1995), 21–42; Jack Zipes, *Why Fairy Tales Stick: The Evolution and Relevance of a Genre* (New York: Routledge, 2006); and Robert Darnton, *The Great Cat Massacre and Other Episodes in French Cultural Theory* (New York: Basic Books, 1984), 9–74. There remains, as Zipes points out in a number of his works, great potential for subversion in the fairy tale even in the face of such monolithic dream factories as Disney studio.

2. Zipes, *Why Fairy Tales Stick*, 27.

3. See Cal Jillson, *Pursuing the American Dream: Opportunity and Exclusion over Four Centuries* (Lawrence: Univ. Press of Kansas, 2004). See also J. Emmett Winn, *The American Dream and Contemporary Hollywood Cinema* (New York: Continuum, 2007).

4. Peggy Orenstein, "What's Wrong with Cinderella?" *New York Times*, December 24, 2006, www.nytimes.com/2006/12/24/magazine/24princess.t.html.

5. I wish I could claim to have ownership of the "dying young, staying pretty" idea. I first heard it articulated in the season 2 episode of *Buffy the Vampire Slayer*, "Lie to Me," where a former friend of Buffy's, Billy Fordham, who has terminal brain cancer, articulates it as the ideal of every American teen. Fordham's quip may have origins in a famous quote supposedly attributable to 1950s teen idol James Dean: "Live fast, die young, and leave a beautiful corpse." There is also a 1979 song by punk band Blondie titled "Die Young, Stay Pretty."

6. Darnton, *The Great Cat Massacre*, 59.

7. In fact, Bella herself makes reference to some of these tales: "It seemed that most vampire myths centered around beautiful women as demons and children as victims; they also seemed like constructs created to explain away the

high mortality rates for young children and to give men an excuse for infidelity" (*Twilight*, 116). What she doesn't mention is the voluptuousness and inferred homosexuality of many male and female vampires in literary and cinematic texts, including Bram Stoker's *Dracula*, which was first published in 1897, and Joseph Sheridan Le Fanu's *Carmilla*, published in 1892, to all of their cinematic incarnations throughout the twentieth century. It is highly unlikely that any homosexual vampires exist in the Cullen-verse, and while the consumption of blood can incite a fury, its orgiastic quality seems to relate more to gluttony than to sex. For commentary on aspects of sexual transgression in *Dracula* see, for example, Christopher Craft, "Kiss Me with Those Red Lips: Gender and Inversion in Bram Stoker's *Dracula*," *Representations* 8 (Autumn 1984): 107–133.

8. Jim Cullen, *The American Dream: A Short History of an Idea That Shaped a Nation* (New York: Oxford Univ. Press, 2003), 10, 38.

9. "American exceptionalism" is a term originally coined by Alexis de Tocqueville, the famous French writer who was so enamored of the nascent democracy in the United States in the nineteenth century. Originally this was intended to convey a sense of difference through a nation made up of immigrants making a new life distinct from the old. A factor that encouraged this "difference" was life on the frontier. The term has come into much wider usage in the twentieth century, particularly after World War II, and has come to stand for the things that make America distinct and distinctly "virtuous" in contrast to the rest of the world. For an overview of the history of this idea, see Deborah Madsen, *American Exceptionalism* (Edinburgh: Edinburgh Univ. Press, 1998).

10. Jillson, *Pursuing the American Dream*, 29.

11. This is not to say that Carlisle's feelings are not those of love and loyalty, but he has a commitment to a bigger picture in his faith in God and God's will.

12. Jillson, *Pursuing the American Dream*, 58.

13. "What's with the Apple?" is an FAQ on Meyer's Web site, to which she responds with the following:

The apple on the cover of *Twilight* represents "forbidden fruit." I used the scripture from Genesis (located just after the table of contents) because I loved the phrase "the fruit of the knowledge of good and evil." Isn't this exactly what Bella ends up with? A working knowledge of what good is, and what evil is. The nice thing about the apple is it has so many symbolic roots. You've got the apple in Snow White, one bite and you're frozen forever in a state of not-quite death. Then you have Paris and the golden apple in Greek mythology—look how much trouble *that* started. Apples are quite the versatile fruit. In the end, I love the beautiful simplicity of the picture. To me it says: *choice*.

The Official Website of Stephenie Meyer, FAQ page, www.stepheniemeyer.com/twilight_faq.html.

14. J. Emmett Winn, *The American Dream and Contemporary Hollywood Cinema* (New York: Continuum Books, 2007).

15. Abstinence classes instead of sex education, in addition to abstinence pledges and leagues in high schools, have been a part of a growing politics of the religious right in the United States, which in spite of / because of these attempts to keep young people ignorant and/or chaste "leads the industrialized world in teen-pregnancy, abortion, and sexually transmitted disease rates." Susan Rose, "Going Too Far? Sex, Sin and Social Policy," *Social Forces* 84, no. 2 (December 2005): 1207.

16. For an involved and fascinating examination of all the incarnations of Little Red Riding Hood, see Jack Zipes, ed., *The Trials and Tribulations of Little Red Riding Hood* (New York: Routledge, 1993).

17. In the first edition of *Die Kinder und Hausmärchen der Brüder Grimm*, published in 1812, Rapunzel falls very obviously pregnant and reveals herself to the witch in asking: "Tell me Godmother, why my clothes are so tight and don't fit me any longer?" "Wicked Child," cried the Fairy. In the second edition, published in 1819, Rapunzel betrays herself thus: "Tell me, Godmother, why is it you are so much harder to pull up than the young prince?" Friedrich Panzer, ed., *Die Kinder und Hausmärchen der Brüder Grimm*, cited by Maria Tatar in *The Hard Facts of the Grimms' Fairy Tales* (Princeton, NJ: Princeton Univ. Press, 1987), 18.

18. See Cynthia Felando, "Clara Bow Is *It*," in *Film Stars: Hollywood and Beyond*, ed. Andy Willis (Manchester, Eng.: Manchester Univ. Press, 2004), 8–24.

19. Elizabeth Bell, Lynda Haas, and Laura Sells, "Introduction: Walt's in the Movies," in Bell, Haas, and Sells, *From Mouse to Mermaid*, 2–3.

20. Ibid., 7.

21. Naomi Wood, "Domesticating Dreams in Walt Disney's *Cinderella*," *The Lion and the Unicorn* 20, no. 1 (1996), muse.jhu.edu/journals/lion_and_the_unicorn/ v020/20.lwood.html.

22. See Jillson, *Pursuing the American Dream*, 71, where he uses *The Great Gatsby* (first published in 1925) as an example of the bankruptcy of the dream where only the pursuit of material wealth is present.

23. For an examination of the not-so-successful campaigns to mobilize American women during World War II, see D'Ann Campbell, *Women at War with America: Private Lives in a Patriotic Era* (Cambridge, MA: Harvard Univ. Press, 1984). "Rosie the Riveter" has become an icon for the mobilization of women and a recognition of women's skills. At the time, however, this was not enough to overcome much of the backlash against women who joined untraditional trades and professions in the war effort.

24. Successive chapters of Marina Warner's *From the Beast to the Blonde: Fairy Tales and Their Tellers* (London: Chatto and Windus, 1994) discuss the history and power of the myth of feminine silence.

25. Jerry Griswold, *The Meanings of Beauty and the Beast: A Handbook* (Toronto: Broadview Press, 2004), 27, 59.

Reading the Genre

1. Buttsworth's analysis focuses on similarities between the *Twilight* novels and traditional fairy tales. What, according to the author, are the major characteristics of fairy tales as a genre? How does she see those characteristics mirrored in Stephenie Meyer's vampire stories? (For more on genre, see the Introduction, p. xix.)

2. How does defining the *Twilight* series as fairy tale enable Buttsworth to critique cultural values? What set of values does she target, and what conclusions does she reach? (See "Focus on social connections," p. 197.)

3. **WRITING:** Choose another cultural text that shares conventions with the fairy-tale genre — possibilities include the *Hunger Games* trilogy by Suzanne Collins or the *Harry Potter* series by J. K. Rowling, the movies *Slumdog Millionaire* (2008) or *The Princess Bride* (1987), and reality television shows like *American Idol* or *The Bachelor* — and write a literary analysis of that text focusing on the ways that it does or does not conform to the conventions of the fairy-tale genre.

4. **WRITING:** Vampire stories have become tremendously popular in film, literature, and television. Choose three contemporary vampire texts and compare them in an essay. What themes seem consistent? What themes are unique to each text?

5. **MULTIMODALITY—COMPOSING VISUALLY:** Write and illustrate an original fairy tale. In your story, upend some of the conventions of the genre to create new possibilities for young female characters.

CULTURAL ANALYSIS   Gish Jen is a novelist, short story writer, and literary critic. Her books include *Who's Irish?* (1999), *Typical American* (1991), *Mona in the Promised Land* (1997), *The Love Wife* (2004), and *Tiger Writing: Art, Culture, and the Independent Self* (2013). She also contributes to the *New Yorker*, *The Atlantic*, the *New York Times*, *Ploughshares*, and the *New Republic*. This essay first appeared in *A New Literary History of America* (2009), edited by Greil Marcus and Werner Sollors.

GISH JEN

Holden Raises Hell

The Catcher in the Rye

Some critics don't like it. *Catholic World* notes its "formidably excessive use of amateur swearing and coarse language," and there seems to be some question as to whether an alienated, hard-drinking, chain-smoking flunky like its adolescent protagonist, Holden Caulfield, is going to prove a good influence on the young. Other critics, though, "chuckle and . . . even laugh aloud," and many compare Holden to Huck Finn. Sociologist David Riesman, who has just published *The Lonely Crowd* (1950), assigns *Catcher* to his Harvard undergrads as a case study. Still, the overall critical reception is within the normal bounds of book publishing; Harcourt Brace, which rejected the book, does not yet have much to live down. As for sales, well, the book has done fine in hardcover but, what with the recent invention of the perfect binding—a book binding using glue rather than stitching—there is now the paperback to consider. Doesn't *Catcher* seem like the sort of book that might do well in the new format?

And so it does, going on to sell over 60 million copies. Moreover, in 1956, some dam in critical interest seems to burst. Study after study is published; the 1950s are dubbed "the Decade of Salinger"; contemporaneous writers complain of neglect. Holden Caulfield is compared not only to Huck Finn but to Billy Budd, David Copperfield, Natty Bumppo, Quentin Compson, Ishmael, Peter Pan, Hamlet, Jesus

Christ, Adam, Stephen Dedalus, and Leopold Bloom put together. What critic George Steiner calls the "Salinger industry" swells fantastically, until it sits like a large, determined bird on a bunker-like egg.

Where did this start? In a 1940 letter to a friend, a twenty-one-year-old Salinger describes his novel in progress as "autobiographical"; decades later, too, in an interview with a high school reporter — the only interview he's ever given — Salinger says, "My boyhood was very much the same as that of the boy in the book." Of course, there are differences. Unlike Holden, Salinger is, among other things, a half-Jewish, half-Catholic brotherless World War II vet who attended a military academy. He did, though, like Holden, flunk out of prep school, and he was also, like Holden, manager of his high school fencing team, in which capacity he really did, according to his daughter, Margaret, once lose the team gear en route to a meet.

More important, Salinger seems to have shared Holden's disaffection. Numerous youthful acquaintances remember him as sardonic, rant-prone, a loner. Margaret Salinger likewise traces the alienation in the book to him, though it does not reflect for her either her father's innate temperament or difficult adolescence so much as his experiences of anti-Semitism and, as an adult, war. Where Salinger fought in some of the bloodiest and most senseless campaigns of World War II and apparently suffered a nervous breakdown toward its end, shortly after which — while still in Europe — he is known to have been working on *Catcher* — it is hardly surprising that Holden's reactions should evoke not only adolescent turmoil but also the awful seesaw of a vet's return to civilian life. Holden may be a rebel without a cause, but he is not a rebel without an explanation: It is easy to read the death of his brother as a stand-in for unspeakable trauma. And witness the notable vehemence with which Holden talks about the war — declaring, for instance, "I'm sort of glad they've got the atomic bomb invented. If there's ever another war, I'm going to sit right the hell on top of it. I'll volunteer for it, I swear to God I will."

But what of Margaret Salinger's theory regarding anti-Semitism? She characterizes Salinger as sensitive about his Jewishness, with good cause: A few years before her father's arrival at the military academy, the picture of a Jewish student who had graduated second in the class was printed on a perforated page in the yearbook, so it could be torn out. We note, too, in Ian Hamilton's unofficial biography, a letter from the father of a girl to whom Salinger once proposed, describing him as "an odd fellow. He didn't mingle much with the other guests [at their Daytona Beach hotel] . . . . He was — well, is he Jewish? I thought that might explain the way he acted. . . . I thought he had a chip on his shoulder."

Interestingly, Salinger's sister, in an interview, while supporting the anti-Semitism thesis, focuses on his in-betweenness as well. "It wasn't nice to be part-Jewish in those days," she says. "It was no asset to be Jewish either, but at least you belonged somewhere. This way you were neither fish nor fowl." Additionally complicating the picture is the fact that Salinger seems to have grown up revered by his Irish-Catholic mother but disparaged by his Jewish father, who wanted him to enter the family food-import business. Fish and fowl, adored and criticized, Salinger was remembered by some military academy classmates as a guy whose conversation "was laced with sarcasm," but by others as "a regular guy," and by teachers as "quiet, thoughtful, always anxious to please." Strikingly, this sometimes scathing student wrote a class song so convincingly straight ("Goodbyes are said, we march ahead / Success we go to find. / Our forms are gone from Valley Forge / Our hearts are left behind") it is still sung at graduation. He edited the yearbook, too, with what so completely passed as earnest conscientiousness that though it is tempting, given his active interest in acting, to view his activities as virtuoso performances of deep subterfuge, they might also be imagined to have been painfully disconcerting. Holden's description of himself as "the most terrific liar you ever saw" might well have applied to Salinger, and Salinger's own judgment of his divided nature, in this era before "situational selves," might well have involved the word that haunts his book, "phony."

A poignant part of Salinger's genius seems, in any case, to include the way that he transmutes — as he perhaps feels he must — his particular issues and injuries into a more enigmatic "autobiography" of alienation. And it can only be counted ironic that the result comes to exemplify American authenticity: like James Dean, Holden Caulfield is for many the very picture of the postwar rebel. Young, crude, misunderstood, he stands up to conformist pressures, is drawn to innocence, et cetera. Never mind that Holden is white, male, straight, sophisticated, rich, and a product of the 1940s; he personifies anguished resistance to '50s America—indeed, for many, America's truest self. Whether Salinger intended his creation to assume anything like this role—indeed, if he had any notion of the projection of a national identity as a desirable literary goal (as did his contemporary, John Updike, for example)—is unclear.

And is there not something if not phony, then at least a little wacky, about Holden's enshrinement in American culture? To some degree, academia took its cue from the culture; *Catcher*'s skyrocketing sales amid the mid-'50s "youthquake" fairly demanded explanation. Critics like George Steiner saw the book as all too fitting for the paperback market—short, easy to read, and flattering "the very ignorance and moral shallowness of his young readers." But others saw its success as a promising development, indicative of something enduringly young, defiant, and truth-loving in the American spirit. Drawing on the work of Donald Pease, critic Leerom Medovoi has described how a new cold war American canon arose around this time, in which American Renaissance works like *Moby-Dick* and *Adventures of Huckleberry Finn* were cast as a "coherent tradition that dramatized the emergence of American freedom as a literary ideal, somehow already waging its heroic struggle against a prefigured totalitarianism." He provocatively describes how *Catcher* came to join those works and how the lot of them, read as national allegories, located the very essence of American-ness in principled dissent, even as McCarthyism cast it as un-American.

No doubt other scholars, being scholars, disagree. Still, Medovoi's ideas may, in conjunction with the book's Mona Lisa–like ambiguity, help explain how *Catcher in the Rye* came to occupy what by other measures seems a strangely high place in American letters, for it strays notably from mainstream literary values. The novel is, to begin with, often precious and sentimental. What's more, while the critic Alfred Kazin is, I think, on the mark in ascribing the excitement of Salinger's stories to his "intense, his almost compulsive need to fill in each inch of his canvas, each moment of his scene," the writing in *Catcher* is nowhere near so alive with *moti mentali*. And the whole, too, is slight. Salinger, who has published only this one novel to date, once characterized himself as "a dash man and not a miler"; and indeed, though *Catcher*'s opening episodes explode with life, the whole reads like a novella that only just managed to shed its diminutive. It does not develop appreciatively through its middle, for example; Holden neither deepens nor comes to share the stage with other characters. Instead the book starts to feel narrow and maniacally one-note; reading, one wonders whether its real contribution lies in its anticipation of Christopher Lasch's *The Culture of Narcissism*. In contrast to, say, *The Great Gatsby*, this is manifestly not a book to be studied for insight into the novel form.

Unless, that is, one is interested in how a book can hit home with no evidence of its author's ever having read Henry James's "The Art of Fiction." *Catcher* demonstrates, among other things, how variously and mysteriously novels finally work, and how even sophisticated audiences tend to genuflect to art but yield to testimony. We are enthralled by voices that tell it like it is. Or, in the case of *Catcher*, that seem to. My sixteen-year-old son—who has, coincidentally, been reading *Catcher* for his tenth-grade English class even as I write—puts it this way: "You feel [with *Catcher*] like you're in on the real story," but in the end *Catcher* is a break from reality rather than a source of information about it. He likens Holden's appeal to that of Harry Potter: Just as Harry speaks to children because Harry is like them, only "special" and able to do magic, Holden interests my son because Holden rebels and "gets away with it" in a way my son guesses—rightly—he would never. In short, one part of *Catcher*'s appeal lies in its purveyance of fantasy. This can have value—helping an audience reflect on the real limits of its freedom, for example—but can support solipsism, too. Alfred Kazin takes the harsh view, characterizing Salinger's audience as "the vast number who have been released by our society to think of themselves as endlessly sensitive, spiritually alone, [and] gifted, and whose suffering lies in the narrowing of their consciousness to themselves"—ranks that would no doubt include

Mark David Chapman, who had a copy of *Catcher* in his pocket when he assassinated "phony" John Lennon, as well as John Hinckley, who, also under Holden's influence, attempted to assassinate Ronald Reagan.

Other explanations of the book's popularity, though, must include its outrageous humor and must-read status, as well as its author's celebrity. Aggressively reclusive, Salinger's discomfort with the commodification of his work and person leads him, first, to shun all publicity—no interviews, no author bios—and then, in 1966, to cease publication. Still, despite his reported contempt for hippies and his support of the Vietnam War, he becomes, for the '60s counterculture, the consummate dropout. And though in subsequent years he is repeatedly caught in an unflattering light, he retains an aura of martyred integrity, which the recurring censorship of *Catcher* only intensifies.

Academia, too, presses on. Critic Alan Nadel, noting that the cold war blossomed in the period between 1946—when, for unknown reasons, Salinger withdrew from publication a ninety-page version of the book—and 1951, when it was published, interestingly sees in Holden not so much heroic nonconformity as a reflection of McCarthyism. Many features of the narrative—the obsession with control in its rhetorical patterns, as well as its preoccupation with duplicity and the compulsion to "name names"—bespeak, for Nadel, a psychic imprisonment in which the performance of truth-telling can never yield truth. And indeed, the insistence of phrases such as "I really mean it" and "to tell the truth" do finally seem to signal quicksand more than terra firma. Holden at story's end is under interrogation—more isolated than independent, more defeated than defiant. "D. B. [Holden's brother] asked me what I thought about all this stuff I just finished telling you about. . . . If you want to know the truth, I don't know what I think about it," he says, touchingly. "I don't know what I think about it": Is this the author of the military-academy class hymn wondering about the act and value of writing? Has Holden, the avatar of American authenticity, become an avatar of American inauthenticity? Here Salinger's funhouse proves, once again, I think, ours.

Bibliography

Paul Alexander, *Salinger* (Los Angeles, 1999). Harold Bloom, ed., *Holden Caulfield: Modern Critical Views* (New York, 1990). Catherine Crawford, ed., *If You Really Want to Hear about It: Writers on Salinger and His Work* (New York, 2006). Warren French, *J. D. Salinger, Revisited* (Boston, 1988). Ian Hamilton, *In Search of J. D. Salinger* (New York, 1988). Joyce Maynard, *At Home in the World* (New York, 1998). Leerom Medovoi, *Rebels* (Durham, NC, 2005). Alan Nadel, *Containment Culture: American Narratives, Postmodernism, and the Atomic Age* (Durham, NC, 1995). Margaret A. Salinger, *Dream Catcher* (New York, 2000). J. D. Salinger, *The Catcher in the Rye* (1951; New York, 1989). Jack Salzman, ed., *New Essays on* The Catcher in the Rye (Cambridge, 1991). J. P. Steed, ed., The Catcher in the Rye: *New Essays* (New York, 2002).

Reading the Genre

1. *The Catcher in the Rye* has been widely read and widely discussed. How does Jen use other critics' assertions about the book to establish an overview and to support her own claims? (See "Draw on previous research," p. 186.)

2. What strategies does Jen use to integrate material from her research? What do these other voices add to her analysis? (See "Clearly identify the author and works you are analyzing," p. 192; "Follow the conventions of literary analysis," p. 203; and Chapter 44, "Incorporating Sources into Your Work," p. 466.)

3. Jen cites several flaws in J. D. Salinger's novel. What does she see as its weaknesses? How does she explain the book's enduring popularity with readers and scholars, even in spite of these problems?

4. Can you think of a fictional character who defines your generation the way Jen believes Holden Caulfield defined his? What makes this character representative of you and your peers?

5. **WRITING:** How would *Catcher in the Rye* be different if its main character used Twitter, Facebook, a blog, or Skype instead of a notebook to share his thoughts? (See Chapter 48, "Understanding Digital Media," p. 542.) Write a short analysis of the ways technology has changed how teenagers communicate — and how those changes diminish or enhance feelings of isolation.

6. **MULTIMODALITY—BOOK COVER:** Jen's discussion of *The Catcher in the Rye* should give you a good sense of the novel, even if you haven't read it yourself. Based on your impressions — from Jen's analysis or your own reading — design a cover for the book.

69

Rhetorical Analyses: Readings

GENRE MOVES Rhetorical Analysis

SUSAN SONTAG

From "Notes on 'Camp'"

Many things in the world have not been named; and many things, even if they have been named, have never been described. One of these is the sensibility—unmistakably modern, a variant of sophistication but hardly identical with it—that goes by the cult name of "Camp." . . .

1. To start very generally: Camp is a certain mode of aestheticism. It is one way of seeing the world as an aesthetic phenomenon. That way, the way of Camp, is not in terms of beauty, but in terms of the degree of artifice, of stylization.

2. To emphasize style is to slight content, or to introduce an attitude which is neutral with respect to content. It goes without saying that the Camp sensibility is disengaged, depoliticized—or at least apolitical.

3. Not only is there a Camp vision, a Camp way of looking at things. Camp is as well a quality discoverable in objects and the behavior of persons. There are "campy" movies, clothes, furniture, popular songs, novels, people, buildings. . . . This distinction is important. True, the Camp eye has the power to transform experience. But not everything can be seen as Camp. It's not all in the eye of the beholder.

4. Random examples of items which are part of the canon of Camp:

   Zuleika Dobson
   Tiffany lamps
   Scopitone films
   the Brown Derby restaurant on Sunset Boulevard in L.A.
   the *Enquirer*, headlines and stories
   Aubrey Beardsley drawings
   Swan Lake
   Bellini's operas

Visconti's direction of *Salome* and *'Tis Pity She's a Whore*

certain turn-of-the-century picture postcards

Schoedsack's *King Kong*

the Cuban pop singer La Lupe

Lynd Ward's novel in woodcuts, *Gods' Man*

the old *Flash Gordon* comics

women's clothes of the twenties (feather boas, fringed and beaded dresses, etc.)

the novels of Ronald Firbank and Ivy Compton-Burnett

Make your notes into an essay.

In this famous essay written in 1964, Susan Sontag actually lists fifty-eight "notes" about "camp" sensibility. She seems to create this long list because she simply has too much to say about "camp" to narrow her focus effectively. When assembled, though, Sontag's list of notes and "random examples" gives the reader a distinct impression of her topic and provides specifics that begin to support her generalizations about a slippery subject.

Likewise, some of the texts or performances or phenomena that you might want to analyze will feel as though they are too complicated and multifaceted for you to choose just one thesis, or even to choose just four to five supporting ideas. Or you may be the sort of writer who prefers to think in lists — and you would rather gather lots of different ideas than focus on just one to begin with.

In your own rhetorical analysis, you might create such a list as a form of prewriting. Consider simply creating a list of responses, ideas, evaluations, and arguments about the thing you are analyzing. For instance, if you are evaluating an advertisement, you'd want to watch it multiple times and record as many impressions and observations as you can about the ad. Then reorder your list to make it more organized. You might see ways that certain thoughts build on or respond to other thoughts. Then you can choose one major idea and seek some other ideas that work to support your larger thesis; the rest can probably be discarded. But you might also consider shaping your notes into an unconventional essay, as Sontag does so successfully here.

DISCOURSE ANALYSIS   Deborah Tannen is a professor in the linguistics department at Georgetown University, and her book *You Just Don't Understand: Women and Men in Conversation* (2001) was on best-seller lists for years. She has also written about the ways people talk at work, with friends and siblings, and in the press, politics, academics, and law. This rhetorical analysis, adapted from Tannen's book *You're Wearing That? Understanding Mothers and Daughters in Conversation* (2006), is also a sociolinguistic analysis, or discourse analysis — a study of the ways language is used and how conversation structures relationships. This adapted essay first appeared in the *Washington Post* in 2006.

Oh, Mom. Oh, Honey.: Why Do You Have to Say That?

Deborah Tannen

The five years I recently spent researching and writing a book about mothers and daughters also turned out to be the last years of my mother's life. In her late eighties and early nineties, she gradually weakened, and I spent more time with her, caring for her more intimately than I ever had before. This experience — together with her death before I finished writing — transformed my thinking about mother-daughter relationships and the book that ultimately emerged.

All along I had in mind the questions a journalist had asked during an interview about my research. "What is it about mothers and daughters?" she blurted out. "Why are our conversations so complicated, our relationships so fraught?" These questions became more urgent and more personal, as I asked myself: What had made my relationship with my mother so volatile? Why had I often ricocheted between extremes of love and anger? And what had made it possible for my love to swell and my anger to dissipate in the last years of her life?

Though much of what I discovered about mothers and daughters is also true of mothers and sons, fathers and daughters, and fathers and sons, there is a special intensity to the mother-daughter relationship because talk — particularly talk about personal topics — plays a larger and more complex role in girls' and women's social lives than in boys' and men's. For girls and women, talk is the glue that holds a relationship together — and the explosive that can blow it apart. That's why you can think you're having a perfectly amiable chat, then suddenly find yourself wounded by the shrapnel from an exploded conversation.

Daughters often object to remarks that would seem harmless to outsiders, like this one described by a student of mine, Kathryn Ann Harrison.

"Are you going to quarter those tomatoes?" her mother asked as Kathryn was preparing a salad. Stiffening, Kathryn replied, "Well, I was. Is that wrong?"

"No, no," her mother replied. "It's just that personally, I would slice them." Kathryn said tersely, "Fine." But as she sliced the tomatoes, she thought, can't I do anything without my mother letting me know she thinks I should do it some other way?

I'm willing to wager that Kathryn's mother thought she had merely asked a question about a tomato. But Kathryn bristled because she heard the implication, "You don't know what you're doing. I know better."

I'm a linguist. I study how people talk to each other, and how the ways we talk affect our relationships. My books are filled with examples of conversations that I record or recall or that others record for me or report to me. For each example, I begin by explaining the perspective that I understand immediately because I share it: in mother-daughter talk, the daughter's, because I'm a daughter but not a mother. Then I figure out the logic of the other's perspective. Writing this book forced me to look at conversations from my mother's point of view.

I interviewed dozens of women of varied geographic, racial, and cultural backgrounds, and I had informal conversations or e-mail exchanges with countless others. The complaint I heard most often from daughters was, "My mother is always criticizing me." The corresponding complaint from mothers was, "I can't open my mouth. She takes everything as criticism." Both are right, but each sees only her perspective.

One daughter said, for example, "My mother's eyesight is failing, but she can still spot a pimple from across the room." Her mother doesn't realize that her comments — and her scrutiny — make the pimple bigger.

Mothers subject their daughters to a level of scrutiny people usually reserve for themselves. A mother's gaze is like a magnifying glass held between the sun's rays and kindling. It concentrates the rays of imperfection on her daughter's yearning for approval. The result can be a conflagration — whoosh.

This I knew: Because a mother's opinion matters so much, she has enormous power. Her smallest comment — or no comment at all, just a look — can fill a daughter with hurt and consequently anger. But this I learned: Mothers, who have spent decades watching out for their children, often persist in commenting because they can't get their adult children to do what is (they believe) obviously right. Where the daughter sees power, the mother feels powerless. Daughters and mothers, I found, both overestimate the other's power — and underestimate their own.

The power that mothers and daughters hold over each other derives, in part, from their closeness. Every relationship requires a search for the right balance of closeness and distance, but the struggle is especially intense between mothers and daughters. Just about every woman I spoke to used the word *close*, as in "We're very close" or "We're not as close as I'd like (or she'd like) to be."

In addition to the closeness/distance yardstick — and inextricable from it — is a yardstick that measures sameness and difference. Mothers and daughters search for themselves in the other as if hunting for treasure, as if finding sameness affirms who they are. This can be pleasant: After her mother's death, one woman noticed that she wipes down the sink, cuts an onion, and holds a knife just as her mother used to do. She found this comforting because it meant her mother was still with her.

Sameness, however, can also make us cringe. One mother thought she was being particularly supportive when she assured her daughter, "I know what you mean," and described a matching experience of her own. But one day her daughter cut her off: "Stop saying you know because you've had the same experience. You don't know. This is my experience. The world is different now." She felt her mother was denying the uniqueness of her experience — offering too much sameness.

"I sound just like my mother" is usually said with distaste — as is the wry observation, "Mirror mirror on the wall, I am my mother after all."

When visiting my parents a few years ago, I was sitting across from my mother when she asked, "Do you like your hair long?"

I laughed, and she asked what was funny. I explained that in my research, I had come across many examples of mothers who criticize their daughters' hair. "I wasn't criticizing," she said, looking hurt. I let the matter drop. A little later, I asked, "Mom, what do you think of my hair?" Without hesitation, she said, "I think it's a little too long."

Hair is one of what I call the Big Three that mothers and daughters critique (the other two are clothing and weight). Many women I talked to, on hearing the topic of my book, immediately retrieved offending remarks that they had archived, such as, "I'm so glad you're not wearing your hair in that frumpy way anymore"; another had asked, "You did that to your hair on purpose?" Yet another told her daughter, after seeing her on television at an important presidential event, "You needed a haircut."

I would never walk up to a stranger and say, "I think you'd look better if you got your hair out of your eyes," but her mother might feel entitled, if not obligated, to say it, knowing that women are judged by appearance — and that mothers are judged by their daughters' appearance, because daughters represent their mothers to the world. Women must choose hairstyles, like styles of dress, from such a wide range of options, it's inevitable that others — mothers included — will think their choices could be improved. Ironically, mothers are more likely to notice and mention flaws, and their comments are more likely to wound.

But it works both ways. As one mother put it, "My daughters can turn my day black in a millisecond." For one thing, daughters often treat their mothers more callously than they would anyone else. For example, a daughter invited her mother to join a dinner party because a guest had bowed out. But when the guest's plans changed again at the last minute, her daughter simply uninvited her mother. To the daughter, her mother was both readily available and expendable.

There's another way that a mother can be a lightning rod in the storm of family emotions. Many mothers told me that they can sense and absorb their daughters' emotions instantly ("If she feels down, I feel down") and that their daughters can sense theirs. Most told me this to illustrate the closeness they cherish. But daughters sometimes resent the expectation that they have this sixth sense—and act on it.

For example, a woman was driving her mother to the airport following a visit, when her mother said petulantly, "I had to carry my own suitcase to the car." The daughter asked, "Why didn't you tell me your luggage was ready?" Her mother replied, "You knew I was getting ready." If closeness requires you to hear—and obey—something that wasn't even said, it's not surprising that a daughter might crave more distance.

Daughters want their mothers to see and value what they value in themselves; that's why a question that would be harmless in one context can be hurtful in another. For example, a woman said that she told her mother of a successful presentation she had made, and her mother asked, "What did you wear?" The woman exclaimed, in exasperation, "Who cares what I wore?!" In fact, the woman cared. She had given a lot of thought to selecting the right outfit. But her mother's focus on clothing—rather than the content of her talk—seemed to undercut her professional achievement.

Some mothers are ambivalent about their daughters' success because it creates distance: A daughter may take a path her mother can't follow. And mothers can envy daughters who have taken paths their mothers would have liked to take, if given the chance. On the other hand, a mother may seem to devalue her daughter's choices simply because she doesn't understand the life her daughter chose. I think that was the case with my mother and me.

My mother visited me shortly after I had taken a teaching position at Georgetown University, and I was eager to show her my new home and new life. She had disapproved of me during my rebellious youth, and had been distraught when my first marriage ended six years before. Now I was a professor; clearly I had turned out all right. I was sure she'd be proud of me—and she was. When I showed her my office with my name on the door and my publications on the shelf, she seemed pleased and approving.

Then she asked, "Do you think you would have accomplished all this if you had stayed married?" "Absolutely not," I said. "If I'd stayed married, I wouldn't have gone to grad school to get my PhD."

"Well," she replied, "if you'd stayed married you wouldn't have had to." Ouch. With her casual remark, my mother had reduced all I had accomplished to the consolation prize.

I have told this story many times, knowing I could count on listeners to gasp at this proof that my mother belittled my achievements. But now I think she was simply reflecting the world she had grown up in, where there was one and only one measure by which women were judged successful or pitiable: marriage. She probably didn't know what to make of my life, which was so different from any she could have imagined for herself. I don't think she intended to denigrate what I had done and become, but the lens through which she viewed the world could not encompass the one I had chosen. Reframing how I look at it takes the sting out of this memory.

Reframing is often key to dissipating anger. One woman found that this technique could transform holiday visits from painful to pleasurable. For example, while visiting, she showed her mother a new purchase: two pairs of socks, one black and one navy. The next day she wore one pair, and her mother asked, "Are you sure you're not wearing one of each color?" In the past, her mother's question would have set her off, as she wondered, "What kind of incompetent do you think I am?" This time she focused on the caring: Who else would worry about the color of her socks? Looked at this way, the question was touching.

If a daughter can recognize that seeming criticism truly expresses concern, a mother can acknowledge that concern truly implies criticism—and bite her tongue. A woman who told me that this worked for her gave me an example: One day her daughter announced, "I joined Weight Watchers and already lost two pounds." In the past, the mother would have said, "That's great" and added, "You have to keep it up." This time she replied, "That's great"—and stopped there.

Years ago, I was surprised when my mother told me, after I began a letter to her "Dearest Mom," that she had waited her whole life to hear me say that. I thought this peculiar to her until a young woman named Rachael sent me copies of e-mails she had received from her mother. In one, her mother responded to Rachael's effusive Mother's Day card: "Oh, Rachael!!!!! That was so WONDERFUL!!! It almost made me cry. I've waited 25 years, 3 months, and 7 days to hear something like that."

Helping to care for my mother toward the end of her life, and writing this book at the same time, I came to understand the emotion behind these parallel reactions. Caring about someone as much as you care about yourself, and the critical eye that comes with it, are two strands that cannot be separated. Both engender a passion that makes the mother-daughter relationship perilous—and precious.

Reading the Genre

1. In addition to rhetorical analysis, this essay offers a discourse analysis — a study of language use. How does Tannen present the evidence (the specific discourse) that she will analyze? How do you think she chose this evidence — these examples of discourse? (See Chapter 21, "Critical Thinking," p. 343, and Chapter 41, "Annotating Sources," p. 456.)

2. Think about Tannen's categories for analysis — such as "yardsticks," "technique," and topics like the "Big Three." How do these categories allow her to analyze what is said, how it is said, and how people deal with what is said? (See Chapter 25, "Strategies," p. 367.)

3. How does Tannen address the danger of stereotypes in this essay? How does this essay consider race, class, and gender differences? Identify parts of this essay where Tannen considers individuality. (See Chapter 33, "Inclusive and Culturally Sensitive Style," p. 408.)

4. This essay has many quotes. Closely review how Tannen handles these quotations. What kinds of signal words does she use to introduce and summarize quotes? How does her language add meaning to the quotes? (See Chapter 44, "Incorporating Sources into Your Work," p. 466.)

5. **WRITING:** Do some fieldwork. Sit at a busy table in a cafeteria, restaurant, or food court, and observe what is said and how. Take detailed notes, keeping your subjects anonymous or — if you're in doubt of your ability to do that — get permission from everyone you observe. Using your notes, make observations about how the people you observed interacted, based on what they said and how they said it. How do people talk about food? How do families interact? How do food workers relate to customers? (See Chapter 39, "Doing Field Research," p. 447.)

ANALYSIS OF AN ADVERTISEMENT   Renowned teacher and cultural critic Stanley Fish has written a number of books, most recently *How to Write a Sentence: And How to Read One* (2011). He has taught at many colleges and universities, and though famous as a literary theorist, he also teaches law. The following article first appeared in the *New York Times* blog *Opinionator* in 2008.

NYTimes.com

Posted: May 4, 2008, at 4:47 PM
From: Stanley Fish

The Other Car

Six years ago my wife and I traded in two cars for two new-used ones. Twice in a few weeks, one of us drove an old car up a ramp to the cavernous second floor of the dealership and just left it there. Well, not quite, for later we reported to each other the same experience. Each of us walked away, but then looked back, realizing that this familiar friend would be gone from our lives forever and, more poignantly, that we were abandoning a faithful, if increasingly troublesome, retainer.

These feelings were of course irrational. Inanimate objects do not have emotions (Stephen King's Christine and Arthur Clarke's HAL are cautionary exceptions), and it makes no sense to experience guilt at having mistreated them (can you in fact mistreat, except in a technical sense, a machine?), but I am sure that we were not unique in our self-reproaches and misgivings.

Avis Rent-a-Car certainly agrees with me, for that company is now running a series of commercials featuring older cars that are being neglected and fear being discarded in favor of the shiny new and with-it high-tech vehicles available, on demand, for around $45 a day. The genius of the commercials is that they foreground the sexuality that informs the relationship between the car owner and the object of his/her affection.

It is of course a commonplace to note that sex is a staple of automobile advertising, but in most ads the idea is that a car with the right curves will attract the girl with the right curves; the piece of machinery is instrumental to the effort to attain the object of desire. But in the Avis ads, the piece of machinery *is* the object of desire (there is a hint of the human-cyborg union promised at the end of the first *Star Trek* movie), and the very act of desiring it constitutes infidelity.

In three of these ads, infidelity is not a metaphor; it is literally what is going on; and the parallels between car-adultery and husband/wife adultery are delineated with such precision, point for point, that the experience of watching is uncomfortable for anyone who has been on either the giving or receiving end in this age-old scenario.

My favorite (and a favorite on the blogosphere) is entitled "Look Back." It features, in the starring and tragic role, a battered red Saab 900 (I own a black one). The scene opens on a sparsely populated airport parking lot. A well-dressed man is getting himself together in preparation for boarding. He puts some trash on the dashboard, gets out of the car, kicks the door shut (wince!), and puts a coffee cup on the roof.

While all this is happening, the car is speaking in a mournful male voice. It/he says, "So, he's going away with Avis, again. He'll get something with the GPS so that he can find his lattes and his driving range. If that's the way he wants it, fine." But this moment of bravado-dignity doesn't last. As the philandering driver walks away, he pauses and rummages in his pocket, concerned that he may have left something in the old clunker. Hope revives, and the Saab says, "Did he just look back? I think he looked back."

The last shot is of the parking lot, empty except for the forlorn automobile sitting there with an abandoned coffee cup, which it cannot see, on its abandoned "head." Another voice — here's where the traditional commercial kicks in — chimes in cheerfully, "One more reason why Avis should be your other car."

One viewer who rates the ad on the Internet likes it, but complains that "the gender of the voice of the vehicle should be the opposite gender of the owner." No, these ads are indifferent to gender. Lust is lust and betrayal is betrayal, whether the relationship is gay or straight.

In another ad ("Three Days"), the straying partner is a woman who has just returned from a three-day vacation. As she settles into the front seat, the car, a tired-looking, sickly green thing, spots the Avis receipt in her handbag, just as a wife or husband might spy a telltale matchbook from a restaurant in a town neither of them has ever visited. The car voice-over comes on, and it is sarcastic: "Who does she think she's kidding. You know what she's been doing in Miami. You sit here staring at a cement wall, alone, and she has the gall to just show up three days later and pretend that she doesn't smell like 'new car.'" (Another gender reversal: It's usually the woman who smells perfume on the man.) The ad ends with more sarcasm: "She was with a Prius hybrid. Oh, suddenly, she's an environmentalist?"

In the third ad, "Conference," the cuckolded vehicle is a Buick, sitting, iced-over, in a parking lot. A flier for a New Mexico resort is on the seat. The Buick speaks: "He said he had to go to Santa Fe for work. Big Conference. Right! You know what's happening. He's driving around with another car. He'll say he was with a client. He was probably with that red Cadillac CTS from Avis, again." Just before the word *again* (the equivalent in this series of Poe's "nevermore") is intoned, a piece of ice, obviously a tear, falls from the Buick's tail light.

When the hucksterish voice of the company spokesperson chirps, "With dozens of the hottest cars to choose from, there's a reason Avis is your other car," the effect is jarring because the dramatization has been so affecting. We care about these people — I mean cars — and the intrusion of the profit motive is unwelcome.

Strange to say, these are not good ads precisely because they are so good. The point of a commercial is to make the viewer fall in love with the product, in this case the hot cars Avis is pimping. But the viewers of these commercials are more likely to give their affections to the product's victims, for it is from their point of view that the narrative has been presented.

While Avis's intention is, no doubt, to advance its corporate fortunes through these commercials, the image the ads project is less than flattering. Avis comes across as the supplier of temptation, the enabler of seduction, a corporate madam. Its stable of "hot cars" lures men and women to default on their responsibilities, to throw away the tried and true, to surrender to the meretricious glitter of the new. But these wiles are defeated by the sympathy we are made to feel for those who have been harmed by them.

Who would have thought that in the early years of the twenty-first century, advertising would give us a morality tale of such power?

I still wonder whenever I see a car that looks like one of those I have discarded whether it is in fact mine. Forgive me.

1. What are the rhetorical appeals that Fish identifies in the advertisements? What is the dominant rhetorical appeal of the ads? How is this appeal made, and what is the desired effect? (See "Consider how well reasoned a piece is," p. 228.)

2. The online version of this article includes hypertext links to all three of the ads that Fish analyzes. What do these links add to the essay? Do we need to be able to see the advertisements ourselves to understand Fish's analysis? (See "Make the text accessible to readers," p. 231.)

3. **WRITING:** These ads give emotions, thoughts, and voice to inanimate objects. In this way, the advertisements' creators get to imagine an emotional world that doesn't exist — they write monologues for neglected cars. Write a similar monologue from the perspective of the rental car. How does it feel to be shiny and new? How does it feel to be used only temporarily, never committed to or owned? How might you create a monologue from the perspective of a new car that might be used, inversely, to sell used cars?

4. **MULTIMODALITY—AUDIO MONOLOGUE:** In groups, in pairs, or on your own, write an advertisement for a new product, using a monologue written from the perspective of the old product it will replace. What would the old product say that might make you desire the new product instead of it? Record this monologue and play it for your peers.

CULTURAL ANALYSIS   Laurie Fendrich is an artist, an art critic, and a professor of fine arts at Hofstra University. Her articles about both art and art education have been published in the *New York Times* and *ArtNews* magazine, and her drawings and paintings have been exhibited in museums and galleries in the United States and Canada. This article originally appeared in the *Chronicle of Higher Education* in 2008.

The Beauty of the Platitude

LAURIE FENDRICH

Platitudes—hackneyed declarative sentences that assert the truth—are maligned for a reason. Ordinarily found in speech (most people know enough to avoid them in writing), platitudes assert everything—and nothing—all at once. Because they've been uttered so many times previously, and in so many trivial conversations, they tend to arrive stillborn, no more than a clump of meaningless words. Their form, stiff and unbendable by nature, permits little if any wiggle room for play. Just as greetings like "Hello" are conversation-starters, platitudes like, "Life is a process of change," or the one that's most particularly grating to me as an artist—"Art is a form of communication"—are conversation-stoppers.

For the educated, who are on call 24/7 to be as clever and quick-witted as possible, to be caught uttering a platitude is as embarrassing as being caught making a grammatical error. Once it's slipped out of the mouth (by accident, of course), the only recourse is to quickly smother the mortifying moment by piling on a few sentences making it clear the platitude was meant ironically.

Sometimes platitudes are a way for the speaker to assert his or her power over others. For example, "Education is the key"—a particularly popular platitude in today's lexicon—frequently masks a hidden agenda. It doesn't mean, "Education will make you successful in life," as much as it means, "If only you'd come around to my position, you'd be right." To say, "Education is the key" is often no more than code for the command, "Think like I do."

Then there are the platitudes that, although clearly intended on takeoff to mean well, and to comfort the suffering, can accidentally land very roughly. One of my colleagues, a classicist who teaches courses in etymology, told me he can't stand it when people say, "Death is a part of life." Whenever he hears those words, he says, he always thinks, "No it's not. It's death. That's why it's got its own word." This little platitude is particularly fascinating because it easily can be turned on its head to become, "Life is a part of death." Since only a mortician could possibly take comfort from these words, however, this particular baby never got off the ground.

Not all platitudes are bad. Like WD-40, the handiest and most efficient grease for opening that pesky stuck drawer, some platitudes open stuck conversations. Moreover, they lend a human loveliness, if not a liveliness, to speech. They work beautifully when people can't find any way to end a bad conversation.

For example, a long tale of woe, coming from a nice but bothersome neighbor, can be abruptly and satisfactorily ended with the gentle platitude, "Well, you know, life is a process of growth and change." Repugnant and new-agey as it might seem to an intelligent soul to utter this sentence, it can be a powerful, yet delicate, deus ex machina when applied with care. The conversation instantaneously leaps from wallowing in muck to a happier plane where, not so surprisingly, it all works out for the best.

Reading the Genre

1. How many specific types of platitude does Fendrich identify? How does her identification of types of platitude lend an organization to this short essay? (See "Creating a structure," p. 230, and Chapter 34, "Vigorous, Clear, Economical Style," p. 412.)

2. Write a paragraph about education using as many platitudes as you can think of. Reread this paragraph and find one platitude that seems to say something important. What exactly does this platitude mean, and how does it help you to write about education?

3. Watch an athlete or entertainer being interviewed (online or on television), and identify the platitudes he or she uses. Why would athletes and entertainers use these platitudes? Underneath the platitudes, do you sense that the interviewee really wants to say something different? (See "Take words and images seriously," p. 220.)

4. **WRITING:** Building on question 3, rewrite an interview with a famous athlete or entertainer, replacing platitudes with the statements you believe this star would *really* like to make. Then develop a list of interview questions for this person that might lead the interviewee to give answers that aren't "conversation-stoppers."

FILM ANALYSIS   Daniel D'Addario is a staff writer for *Salon.com*. *The Lone Ranger* movie starring Johnny Depp cost $215 million to produce. The film grossed just $89 million in the United States and received a largely negative critical response.

Salon.com

Posted: Wednesday, July 3, 2013, at 1:15 PM EST
From: Daniel D'Addario

Johnny Depp's Tonto Misstep: Race and *The Lone Ranger*

The actor's turn as a Comanche character is another chapter in an ugly racial history, experts say.

Johnny Depp has tossed on a lot of outlandish costumes in his long career. In the *Pirates of the Caribbean* franchise, he plays a buccaneer; in *Dark Shadows*, a vampire; in *Charlie and the Chocolate Factory*, an androgynous confectioner.

And with today's new release *The Lone Ranger*, he's adding "American Indian" to the pile of personas he's tried on — and scholars of American Indian history are not pleased.

Depp, who has claimed in the past to have Indian heritage (a claim that Indian Country Today, a media network for the American Indian community, has contested), is playing Tonto, one of the longest-running Indian characters in American media. It's also an intensely problematic one. Depp, who was adopted into the Comanche Nation after signing on to *The Lone Ranger*, claims that his role is a "salute" to American Indians, and *Smoke Signals* director Chris Eyre, an American Indian, has said, "I completely respect Johnny Depp for making this movie happen and for him to try and rewrite Tonto for a new generation." Some critics, including *Salon*'s Andrew O'Hehir, have found bright spots in the film even while acknowledging the problems inherent in its casting. Depp has screened the film for the Comanche Nation —with many leaders of various tribes in attendance — and Disney donated proceeds from the Los Angeles premiere to the American Indian College Fund.

But for all the trappings of enlightened cooperation, the new Tonto may read as more of the same — and less a salute than an insult.

Tonto, the loyal sidekick of the Lone Ranger (played in the 2013 film by Armie Hammer), has evolved a great deal even prior to the current incarnation. "He may be the most pervasive American Indian character of the twentieth century," said Chadwick Allen, the coordinator for the American Indian studies program at Ohio State University and the author of a forthcoming book about Tonto. "And he's purely fictional, unlike Pocahontas, Sacajawea, Crazy Horse, Sitting Bull, or Geronimo. It's not surprising he keeps getting recycled. He's perfectly malleable for whatever the dominant fantasies are for native culture."

Those fantasies have included, said Allen, an "older, diminutive in stature, explicitly half-breed" version of Tonto, one who perpetually needed saving and didn't have his own horse, in the early *Lone Ranger* radio serials (on which Tonto was played by a white man). He was portrayed as bloodthirsty rather than concerned with justice, dovetailing with what Allen called "the savage stereotypes of the Indian."

But in 1936, as the Lone Ranger empire continued to blossom, "Tonto becomes full-blooded, taller, more robust, and around the same age as the Lone Ranger" — coinciding with the implementation of the Indian Reorganization Act, a law that allowed some self-government to American Indians along strictly proscribed lines that resembled American government. When Americans needed Tonto to be a

Peter Mountain/© Walt Disney Pictures/courtesy Everett Collection.

bumbling incompetent or a bloodthirsty savage, he could do that; after the Reorganization Act, effectively intended to help "Americanize" the tribes, he became slightly less than equal in the quest for justice. Harvey Markowitz, the coauthor of *Seeing Red: Hollywood's Pixeled Skins* and an assistant professor of sociology at Washington and Lee University, described the Tonto character as "justification for treating [American Indians] as children, putting them on reservations, and training them to be white people as you take away their land."

The best-known iteration of Tonto remains the one played by Jay Silverheels in *The Lone Ranger* TV series, which ran from 1949 to 1957, a time during which "Indian termination policy" saw Indians forcibly "integrated" into society and reservations' special status revoked. Allen described the TV Tonto as "skilled and robust and detached from any native loyalty." It was Silverheels who popularized a certain halting pidgin-speak and the term "Kemosabe," as well as a renewed loyalty to the Lone Ranger that felt like a white ruling class reassuring itself.

But it was his halting speech that made Tonto such a memorable character — a halting speech pattern that would seem to be only slightly dialed down in the trailer, in which Depp says, "A vision told me, great warrior would help me on my quest" and "You find treasure, you find the man who killed your brother." In both clauses, a definite article has been sucked into the vacuum produced by an ethnic stereotype. Silverheels's Tonto "didn't have power to articulate his point of view in a way that had any eloquence with the viewing public," said Joanna Hearne, a professor of English at the University of Missouri and the author of *Native Recognition: Indigenous Cinema and the Western*. "It didn't reflect the eloquence of indigenous people and it certainly didn't reflect the knowledge embedded in the language systems of indigenous people."

As for Silverheels himself, said Hearne: "He was typecast, but he did use his power to work behind the scenes for Indian actors in Hollywood. . . . He helped them with their professional careers, he helped them get on-screen. He helped politicize that work in a productive way." Depp, for all that he has been adopted by the Comanche tribe (after saying that Indians "have to think, somewhere along the line, I'm the product of some horrific rape. You just have that little sliver in your chemical makeup"), is in fact undoing Silverheels's advocacy by taking a role away from an Indian actor by playing Tonto.

"In some ways, [the so-called practice of 'redface'] has become less common," said Hearne, "but Native actors aren't always hired for lead roles. Think about the werewolves in *Twilight*. Most of the actors playing the wolf pack have Native ancestry. But the lead actor doesn't."

And stereotypical portrayals of American Indians are still very much with us: "Look at the products on the shelf at the grocery store," said LeAnne Howe, a professor of American Indian studies at the University of Illinois and Markowitz's coauthor. "Or the Jeep Cherokee. The Pontiac. Land O'Lakes butter. The Native American cigarettes [American Spirits]." The white idea of that which is Indian — leaving aside the vast number of differences between tribes, American Indians are generally seen as exotic, stoic, "connected with the land" — is among the most easily monetized tropes for anyone seeking the patina of American-ness. The Disney corporation is surely hoping Americans will spend their Independence Day holidays indulging the exoticism of Tonto.

"Other stereotypes, whether Asian, African-American, Mexican-American — have become muted," said Howe. I don't think that's the case with American Indians because we are fewer in numbers. People excuse it as saying they're honoring us by having representations of Native Americans on butter."

For some, perceptions of Tonto have changed with time. Howe initially found Tonto sympathetic: "I grew up in the '50s. I grew up watching Tonto on television. Jay Silverheels for me was heroic. He was the only American Indian I would ever see on television, ever. I look at that today with different eyes."

"It demeans and makes invisible modern American Indians today," continued Howe. "No one can take us seriously unless we have some crazy headdress on."

Every generation gets the Tonto it deserves, perhaps, and only the weekend box-office returns will tell if this one, as played by Depp, catches the imagination of the American public. But for an entertainment culture that evidently seems more concerned with rehashing old stories of itself than in telling a new story in which an American Indian has some agency beyond helping the white man's quest, Johnny Depp's the perfect actor; "American Indian" is just another costume he can throw on.

Reading the Genre

1. D'Addario looks to scholars in American Indian history for their opinions on the Tonto character. In this way, his rhetorical analysis is based on secondary research, and this helps him understand the history of this character. What is the effect of Depp and the film's creators' failure to look to these experts before they made the film? Given the availability of such information, why do you think they made that choice? (See "Pay attention to audience," p. 220.)

2. What would happen if D'Addario ended his essay by mentioning the few positive reviews of the movie, and Depp's efforts to gain the approval of the Comanche Nation, instead of beginning the essay with these details? (See Chapter 30, "Introductions and Conclusions," p. 391.)

3. **WRITING:** Look at the ways that other offensive characterizations of Native Americans have been challenged recently, including prominent sports team names and mascots. How are these characterizations defended? What rhetorical tricks are used to justify the use of images and stereotypes that many people find offensive? Study one specific example and write a rhetorical analysis essay — as D'Addario does, look for what American Indian scholars have to say about the issue as well. (See "Distinguish between primary and secondary sources," p. 438.)

4. **MULTIMODALITY — VISUAL ESSAY:** Create a short visual essay exploring an aspect of American Indian history. For example, a visual essay on the 1830 Indian Removal Act could include archival images and quotes as well as before-and-after maps and statistics. You can begin your research by digging into the scholarship of the experts cited in D'Addario's essay. As you will see, they have written about more than just Tonto.

ANALYSIS OF AN ADVERTISEMENT
Caroline Leader is a staff writer and senior columns editor for *FlowTV* (www.flowtv.org). In the following analysis, she scrutinizes the ways men are depicted in advertisements aimed at women.

FlowTV

Posted: June 18, 2010
From: Caroline Leader

Dudes Come Clean: Negotiating a Space for Men in Household Cleaner Commercials

A mother walks into her kitchen, surprised to find her husband and son busy at the dishwasher. The husband explains that he set a record for the most dishes cleaned in one load, 61 dishes and a garlic press, and that the son is trying to beat it. His wife insists that 61 dishes will overcrowd the dishwasher and some dishes will not get clean, to which the husband retorts, "Got clean when I broke the record!" He continues to hover over the son, sabotaging his efforts, as the wife looks on, disgruntled.

Commercial advertising persists as one of the most contentious sites of ideological discussion in mass media. Especially in TV commercials, where time constraints limit the range of complex narratives, advertisers must rely on what attracts their target audience. By relying on standard narrative forms, advertisers "reduce production costs, and conform to audience expectations."[1] Some industries, like household cleaning aids, rely on traditional selling points and representations to sell their products. Household cleaner commercials — dish washing aids, laundry detergents, surface cleaners, etc. — generally target women, especially mothers, and portray women in their advertisements. They are stewards in the domestic space, concerned with the cleanliness and health of the home.

Men or male figures do feature in household cleaner ads, but generally to reinforce the woman as the active cleaner. Husbands often appear in the periphery, either separate from the action or a cleaning novice who looks to the wife to find the solution. This tradition has been challenged over time, with commercials that feature men as cleaners (usually inadequate ones[2]). More recent campaigns by prominent brands — Tide and Cascade of Procter & Gamble, and also the emerging "green" company Seventh Generation — complicate the role of the father and husband as participants in the maintenance of the home.

The female homemaker is traditionally the protagonist and often the only character in a household cleaner advertisement. Even when children or husbands are present, it is typically the singular task of the mother to clean spills, wash clothes, and generally maintain the beautiful home. Other family members represent a kind of playful chaos, which only the mother's determination and work ethic can counteract. While the product may lighten her workload, it is still her responsibility to buy, use, and enjoy the products. It is also important that the woman finds contentment in the clean home. At the conclusion of a commercial, we will often see the triumphant and serene smile on the woman's face as she surveys her domestic landscape.

The recent Cascade campaign (2009–present) parodies the traditional household cleaning narrative, upsetting the "natural order" in the home, but does not overthrow the ideologies inherent in the more traditional narrative. The Cascade commercial referred to as "World Record" — noted in the introduction of this paper — follows a traditional narrative arc of a household cleaner commercial; the dishwasher is dirty, we hear about the cleaning power of Cascade and the dishes are cleaned.[3] It is instead the dynamics between the characters that deviate from the norm. Instead of ending in bliss, the ad leaves us with a sense of disorder in the home. First, the introduction of the husband as the cleaner is jarring. Although the wife holds the traditional knowledge — that a "too full" dishwasher will never properly clean the dishes — the husband has learned that the power of Cascade can overcome a full dishwasher. However, because the commercial is comedic, we excuse these abnormal occurrences; the masculine competition in a traditionally domestic site, and more importantly, that Dad is cleaning. Because of the unreliable nature of the family narrative in this commercial, we do not see the father as a steward of the home, and the tradition of the feminine domestic sphere is not challenged.

Another commercial, Tide's "Busted," takes the man's role as cleaner a little further. In the advertisement, the father stains his wife's tablecloth while eating a Sloppy Joe, but gets it out with Tide, thereby avoiding trouble. The wife/mother is absent during the entire process, and the father and sons clean Mom's tablecloth, which provides them with a sort of bonding and learning experience.[4] In the Tide ad, the woman is visually absent and therefore independent of the domestic scene, but we still acknowledge her as the maintainer of cleanliness. It is Mom's tablecloth and she is the one who will be upset to see it ruined. The father, on the other hand, enjoys a carefree, "plate-less" meal with his sons. He may be the one who cleans it up, but he is still representative of chaos and messiness. Just as in the Cascade ad, the husband takes over the role of cleaner, but does not challenge the wife's as the primary arbiter of cleanliness.

Men also tend to appear in household cleaner commercials that do not include the act of cleaning, thereby bypassing the danger of feminization. Many advertisers focus on their brand "story" as opposed to the efficacy of the product. Often referred to as the self-congruity theory, advertisers align the personality of their brands with the perceived personality of their consumers, hoping to establish brand loyalty.[5] My first example brings us back to the Tide brand, with a commercial called "Dad." Like the earlier Tide commercial in this paper, we see another man and his son. The primary shot zooms out from the baby's face, strategically catching the father's wedding ring and eventually widening to a touching scene of the two napping on a clean set of linens. The soft female vocals in the background express a (woman's) need to be with the family, the two we see napping in the shot. The ad may feature male characters, but the ultimate audience is the absent mother, similar to the other Tide ad, "Busted."

Seventh Generation, the eco-conscious household and hygienic care company, also approaches the household cleaner commercial as a chance to express their company mission over the efficiency of the products. Known as "Protect Planet Home," the campaign supports a sustainable, environmentally friendly world.[6] The aired TV commercial depicts slices of life from different characters' points of view. Some are men, some are women, but the important element to note is that no one is actively cleaning. The commercial focuses on the responsibility of consumers to buy "green" products and promotes a verdant, harmonious world. For Seventh Generation, the consumer may be male or female, but the duty of cleaning is not addressed and therefore does not place the woman, the man, or anyone, as the primary maintainer of the clean home.

Household cleaner commercials are no longer limited to the product comparison or cause-and-effect narratives that only feature women in the home. As we've seen, men have entered the domestic space as participants in maintaining a clean home. In addition, commercials have stepped outside the act of cleaning and focused more on the lifestyles of their consumer markets. Ultimately, the household cleaner commercial is about family and harmony in the home. As such, it behooves advertisers to maintain a traditional — or at least non-controversial — depiction of the family, focusing on women as the primary consumers and homemakers, and men as their helpers.

Notes

1. Fairclough, N. (2000). Critical analysis of media discourse. In P. Harris & S. Thornham (Eds.), *A media reader* (2nd ed.) (pp. 308–325). New York, NY: New York University Press.

2. Elliot, R. et al. (1993). Re-coding gender representations: Women, cleaning products, and advertising's "New Man." *Journal of Research in Marketing, 10,* 311–324.

3. This video is no longer live. Original content was on the Cascade site at http://www.cascadeclean.com/en_US/video.do#.

4. The race implications of Tide's ad campaign are out of scope for this paper.

5. Mulyanegara, R.C., Tsarenko, Y., & Anderson, A. (2009). The Big Five and brand personality: Investigating the impact of consumer personality on preferences towards particular brand personality. *Journal of Brand Management, 16*(4), 234–247.

6. This video is no longer available for public consumption. Original content was on the Seventh Generation site at http://www.seventhgeneration.com/protecting-planet-home.

Reading the Genre

1. The first paragraph of this essay is a blow-by-blow account of a single commercial. Why is this kind of description so vitally important in a rhetorical analysis? (See "Make the text accessible to readers," p. 231.)

2. What major rhetorical appeals are evident in the commercials Leader analyzes? (See "Consider how well reasoned a piece is," p. 228.)

3. How does Leader extend her analysis of advertisements for cleaning products into an argument about gender roles in popular culture? What is that argument? (See "Make a difference," p. 224.)

4. The purpose of a television advertisement is to sell something, not necessarily to be artistic — or intelligent. With this in mind, how is conducting a rhetorical analysis of a television commercial different from doing so with a political speech, a Web site, or an op-ed in the newspaper?

5. **WRITING:** While some television advertisements are worthy of deep analysis, others may not be. List ten commercials you have recently seen, and choose one that seems deserving of study. Describe it in detail, and then jot down any inferences your description lets you make about the commercial. If the commercial still seems worthy of close examination, write a rhetorical analysis. If not, choose another commercial and start over. Repeat the process until you find a commercial worth writing about. (See "Choose a text with handles," p. 224.)

Acknowledgments

Leigh Alexander. "Domino's, the Pizza That Never Sleeps." Copyright © 2013 The Atlantic Media Co., as first published in the *Atlantic Magazine,* June 6, 2013. All rights reserved. Distributed by Tribune Content Agency, LLC.

Natalie Angier. "Almost Before We Spoke, We Swore." Copyright © 2005 by Natalie Angier. Originally published in the *New York Times.* Reprinted by permission of the author.

Kamakshi Ayyar. "Cosmic Postcards: The Adventures of an Armchair Astronaut." Copyright © 2013 Project Wordsworth. Reprinted by permission of the author.

James Baldwin. Excerpt from "If Black English Isn't a Language, Then Tell Me, What Is?" Copyright © 1979 by James Baldwin. Originally published in the *New York Times.* Collected in *James Baldwin: Collected Essays,* published by The Library of America. Used by arrangement with the James Baldwin Estate.

Michael Barone. Excerpt from "The Beautiful People vs. the Dutiful People," *US News & World Report,* January 16, 2006. Copyright © 2006 US News & World Report. By permission of Michael Barone and Creators Syndicate, Inc.

Emily Bazelon. "Hitting Bottom: Why America Should Outlaw Spanking," from *Slate,* January 25, 2007. Copyright © 2007 The Slate Group. All rights reserved. Used by permission and protected by the Copyright Laws of the United States. The printing, copying, redistribution, or retransmission of this Content without express written permission is prohibited.

Sven Birkerts. Excerpt from "Reading in a Digital Age," *The American Scholar,* Spring 2010. Copyright © 2010.

Adam Bradley. Prologue and "Rap Poetry 101," from *Book of Rhymes: The Poetics of Hip Hop* by Adam Bradley. Copyright © 2009 by Adam Bradley. Reprinted by permission of Basic Civitas Books, a member of the Perseus Books Group.

Peter Bregman. Excerpt from "Diversity Training Doesn't Work," *Psychology Today* Magazine, March 12, 2012. Copyright © 2012 Sussex Publishers, LLC. Reprinted with permission.

David R. Brower. Excerpt from "Let the River Run Through It," *Sierra,* March/April 1997. Copyright © 1997.

Robert Bruegmann. Excerpt from "How Sprawl Got a Bad Name," from *American Enterprise,* Volume 17, issue 5, June 16, 2006. Copyright © 2006.

Sara Buttsworth. "CinderBella: *Twilight,* Fairy Tales, and the Twenty-First-Century American Dream," from *Twilight and History,* edited by Nancy Reagin. Copyright © 2010 by Nancy R. Reagin. Reprinted by permission of Turner Publishing. All rights reserved.

Nicholas Carr. Excerpt from "Does the Internet Make You Dumber?" *Wall Street Journal,* June 5, 2010. Reprinted with permission of the Wall Street Journal. Copyright © 2010 by Dow Jones & Company, Inc. All rights reserved worldwide. License number 3434970912672 and 3434971079436.

Rachel Carson. From "The Obligation to Endure" from *Silent Spring* by Rachel Carson. Copyright © 1962 by Rachel Carson, renewed © 1990 by Roger Christie. Used by permission of Houghton Mifflin Harcourt Publishing Company and by permission of Frances Collin, Trustee. All copying, including electronic, or redistribution of this text is expressly forbidden. All rights reserved.

Index